★

Leisure and Recreation Management

To
my wife, my family
and my friends

Leisure and Recreation Management

Second edition

★   ★   ★

GEORGE TORKILDSEN

LONDON   NEW YORK

E. & F. N. Spon

First published in 1983 by
E. & F.N. Spon Ltd
11 New Fetter Lane, London EC4P 4EE
Second edition 1986
Reprinted 1987

© 1986 George Torkildsen

Printed in Great Britain at the
University Press, Cambridge

ISBN 0 419 14060 3

British Library Cataloguing in Publication Data

Torkildsen, George
Leisure and recreation management—2nd ed
1. Recreation—Great Britain—Management
I. Title
790'.06'9   GV75

ISBN 0-419-14060-3

Contents

★

Part Two: Recreation philosophy

Contents

Part Four: Recreation planning

Part Five: Management

★

ILLUSTRATIONS

Chapter 1
Great Yarmouth Marina Centre – a local authority project financed, developed and managed in collaboration with the commercial sector. (Courtesy of the Borough of Great Yarmouth.)

Chapter 2
Variety Club Sunshine Coach. (Courtesy of the Variety Club of Great Britain.)

Chapter 3
Mecca Leisure Social Club, Harlow. (Courtesy of Len Toms, Harlow Gazette.)

Chapter 4
Symbols of National Agencies. (Courtesy of the Arts Council of Great Britain, The Central Council of Physical Recreation, the National Playing Fields Association and The Sports Council.)

Chapter 5
Active play – a need for all children. (Courtesy of John Sari Photographers and Harlow Development Corporation.)

Chapter 6
Forest horse-ride. (Courtesy of John McCann Photography and Harlow Development Corporation.)

Chapter 7
Bar at Bletchley Leisure Centre. (Courtesy of John Donat Photography and Faulkner-Brown, Hendy, Watkinson, Stonor (Architects).)

Chapter 8
Companionship – an important element in leisure for the aged. (Courtesy of G. Howald, Berne, Switzerland and the National Playing Fields Association.)

Chapter 9
A competitor in the Stoke Mandeville National Paraplegic Games, 1981. (Courtesy of Richard Gardner.)

Chapter 10
London Marathon, 1982. (Courtesy of John Gichigi, Allsport Photographic.)

Chapter 11
Morecambe Leisure Park. (Courtesy of Faulkner-Brown, Hendy, Watkinson, Stonor (Architects).)

Chapter 12
Rhyl Sun Centre. (Courtesy of Barry Wilkinson Photography and Gillinson, Barnett and Partners (Architects, Engineers, Planners and Designers).)

Chapter 13
A meeting of management staff at Harlow Sportcentre. (Courtesy of Len Toms, Harlow Gazette.)

Chapter 14
It's a knockout – programming for friendly rivalry between towns.

Chapter 16
Marketing Lancaster University's 'Come Alive' campaign. (Courtesy of Lancaster University.)

Chapter 17
Industrial Exhibition in the Sports Hall at Harlow Sportcentre. (Courtesy of Len Toms, Harlow Gazette.)

Preface

★

This book is written for all those people who are interested in exploring the fascinating world of 'leisure' and 'recreation' and its management. They may be top recreation and leisure executives, senior managers, middle managers, first-line managers, recreation officers at all levels, supervisory managers or trainee managers. They may be organizers and administrators, policy-makers, planners, researchers, or students and lecturers in a wide range of recreation management and leisure courses. In addition there are very important recreation 'fringe elements', including those people involved in architecture, planning and local government other than recreation, community workers, teachers, politicians and many others.

This is the first book of its kind written in the United Kingdom. The subject areas are relevant to the wide spectrum of recreation organizations and personnel, whether in the public, private or commercial sectors. Most of the subject areas also apply universally. People's needs are the same the whole world over. The expression of need through recreation is also much the same. The principles of management apply to all organizations, to all resources and facilities, to all programmes, and to all problems encountered.

The book seeks to answer some simple questions on a complex phenomenon: what is leisure and recreation? How is it planned, provided for, managed and controlled? How can greater opportunities be provided through improved management?

My motivation in writing the book stems from a preoccupation and overwhelming interest in recreation and its management. Having been involved for over twentyfive years as teacher, manager, director, lecturer and consultant and having been part of the movement towards the development of the community recreation centre and the emerging 'profession' of recreation management, I have felt destined to write about it. The Government Working Party on the Training for Recreation Management and its report indicates the considerable importance of the subject and its future in the United Kingdom. More pertinently, it acknowledges the need for well-trained managers of recreation, be they in government, in private or in commercial recreation.

This is a book that deals in the concepts of recreation, in the processes of planning for recreation and with its management. It is concerned also with approaches towards better management and in management performance itself. It is not, however, a technical textbook dealing with buildings, facilities, maintenance, catering, accounting, or with arts, sports, countryside recreation and social recreation in and of themselves. These aspects are covered by many other publications, by the Sports Councils, Arts Councils, Countryside Commission and national agencies.

A good deal has been written of late concerning the 'hardware' of recreation – recreation technology, buildings and design, and management courses have been devised to teach the aspects of accounting, economics, statistics, survey techniques, quantitative methods, research and the like. Little, however, has been written about the nature of the management of leisure opportunity or about recreation 'software', the quality of the management, the principles underlining recreation provision and the 'people' approach to recreation planning and programming. What does leisure mean to people? What does recreation do for people and why provide opportunities and management for it to occur? It is to these questions that the book directs itself and provides practical suggestions as to how good management can create better opportunities for recreation to occur for even more people, more often.

My hope is that you will find this publication both interesting and valuable.

George Torkildsen

Acknowledgements

★

I thank all who helped in any way in the production of this book through their work, support, information, advice or understanding.

I acknowledge the administrative and secretarial assistance of Rita Tomlin and Valerie Beadle and their assistant Gaynor Bond (with the first edition) and Jan Allen and Trixie Kurn with the second edition.

In the latter stage of editing and completing the manuscript invaluable assistance was given by Gwynne 'Grif' Griffiths, by Ian Barclay and Colin Sinclair, with the first edition and by John Chapman with the second edition.

I also wish to thank the following for their direct and indirect help by supplying information, critiques or ideas: Roy James, Peter Cullen, Tony Veal, Ted Blake, Professor Ray Maw, Jane Foulsham and Rosemary Wellings (with Chapter 11 in the first edition).

This book could not have been written without a background of knowledge accumulated over the years from individuals and institutions. These include: Polytechnic of North London department of Extension Studies and department of Management, Polytechnic of Central London Built Environment Research Group and School of Management, National Playing Fields Association, Sports Council, Association of Recreation Managers, Harlow and District Sports Trust with whom I have been associated for 25 years and the staff, past and present, at Harlow Sport-centre, with whom I gained much of my practical experience in management, my business colleagues and associates Ron Pickering, Dr Don Anthony, Bill Stonor and Gerry Perrin and all my colleagues and friends in recreation management including PNL DMS(R) students 1971–81 who, most of all, made me face the problem areas which this book tries to grapple with.

To all and many more, thank you.

Introduction

★

Leisure and recreation activity revolve around *policy, planning, resources, facilities, finance, services, programmes* and *management*. Through these means opportunities are offered or made available to people to indulge in recreation, whether passively or actively. I believe that recreation providers should be concerned, not just with the quantity of the facilities, but with the *quality* of the recreative experience for the individual. Provision for recreation is made by three main contributors – *private* individuals and groups, *commercial* operators and *public* authorities.

This book is concerned with the provision and management of 'leisure' and 'recreation'. But the first thing to be said about provision and management is that nature provides us, in the natural environment, with abundant resources for recreation, so much so that, one could argue, there is no need for expensive additional facilities, services, programmes and management. Nature has provided the grass and the fields, the trees and the woods, rivers, rain and sunshine. We have the challenge of the mountains, the seas and the sky. We have beauty to behold, solitude in the country and peace away from the crowds.

The second thing to be said about provision and management is that we, as individuals, or with families or among friends, are quite capable of providing for all our recreational needs and for our children or those unable to care for themselves, without additional facilities, services, programmes and management. Nature has provided us with the means to survive, to seek, to explore, to find, to grow and to multiply. It has certainly provided us, not only with the desire to play and to find recreations, but also with the *human capacity and resourcefulness* to do so.

Yet the demand for man-made additional resources for recreation for people is greater now than it has ever been. Opportunities are needed for some children just to learn how to play with other children, to play with water and sand and to explore their environment. Indeed the problem is so acute that it has needed government, institutional and voluntary agencies to promote the concept of the 'child's right to play'. The International Year of the Child focused attention on the plight of children in slums, in traffic-congested areas, in high-rise blocks and in bad homes and housing conditions.

The energies of young people, increasingly seen channelled frustratingly into needless violence, or acts of vandalism, evidence unsatisfied needs. Leisure opportunities for the adventure, the noise, the speed and the independence of youth can assist in meeting some of the needs. Opportunities are needed for adults, for families, for the loner, the lonely, the old, the handicapped and the delinquent to *experience* recreation, which may enhance their quality of life.

Hence, the cornerstone of recreation and its management must be concerned first, foremost and always with *people*, not just resources, buildings and facilities, but with the human rights, the dignity and the uniqueness of the *individual*. It is from this standpoint that recreation provision and management are debated and this thread, however tenuous, will link discussion on principles, planning, services and management and endeavour to forge a bridge between the philosophy of recreation and the practical services and management needed for it to occur for people more often.

The book is developed around three main themes: *philosophy*, *provision*, and *management* in the field of leisure and recreation. Put another way the concern is with *thinkers*, *enablers* and *doers*. At one extreme, some people believe that thinkers tell us what the problems are and offer no solutions, providers provide unnecessary facilities and then tell others to get on and use them, and organizers, in their muddled amateur fashion, tell others what to do and how to do it, because they cannot do it themselves. I take the view that management is concerned with thinking, enabling and doing and that the Recreation Manager should encapsulate the essential ingredients which span the fields of philosophy, provision and management in the context of recreation.

A Recreation Manager is not someone who comes out of a college with a certificate; there can be no instant Recreation Manager. Nor is he or she someone who, through years of experience, can operate an establishment efficiently but has no knowledge about the effectiveness of the operation, what the needs of the consumers are and how opportunities can be provided to meet those needs. Rather, a Recreation Manager is a person, younger or older, who has evolved with a mix of education, training inside and outside the job situation, and some experience, into a person with motivation, ability and sufficient understanding to create and manage opportunities for people at whatever level is satisfying for them. Hence the bland statement that 'any good manager can manage anything' is not supported unequivocally.

Many employers equate management with administration and thus appoint administrators. While the good manager should be able to administer, organize and learn, administration is only one of the many

functions of management. The emerging profession of recreation management is accumulating many good administrators. This book is written
in the hope that the 'profession' will accumulate many good managers.

The book is written in five main parts or stages of leisure and recreation
management.

Part One seeks answers to the question: who are the *providers* of
recreation services, resources and facilities? Those involved in recreation
policy, research and management must know about the world in which
they live – the recreation market place, the providers and their influence.
It is written in four chapters. Chapter 1 deals with the *public sector*,
Chapter 2 with the *voluntary sector* and Chapter 3 with the range of
commercial providers. The overlap and interrelationship between the
three is evident, though the three can be analysed as partially separate
sectors. Public recreation is enabled, controlled and guided to some
extent through a whole range of *national agencies* and these are very briefly
described in Chapter 4.

Having looked at the world of recreation provision and the nature of
the providers, *Part Two* asks the most important question: *what* is to be
managed? The first tenet of management is to know what it is you are
supposed to be managing. Most researchers have considerable difficulty
in answering the question: what is recreation and how can it be managed?
This simple question provides a multitude of answers to a complex
phenomenon. Despite the problems of overlap and interrelationship,
Chapters 5, 6 and 7 study the concepts of *play*, *recreation* and *leisure* as
distinct entities to discover what they are and what they mean to people.

In Chapter 8 an attempt is made to bring together the play/leisure/
recreation trilogy and to suggest a possible interlocking relationship
between them.

Part Three is concerned with the people, the individuals, who are to
benefit from leisure and recreation provision and management. Chapter 9
considers the *needs and motivation* of people towards leisure and recreation
activity and Chapter 10 focuses on the major factors which influence and
condition leisure and recreation choice.

Part Four is the *planning process* itself. Chapter 11 relates to the planning
approaches and suggests a greater people-orientation and involvement in
order to achieve the aims of recreation services. Chapter 12 is written in
two parts. The first is concerned with the birth and development of the
community recreation centre and the second considers the planning and
design aspects relevant to the management of facilities.

Part Five is the part which is traditionally accepted as 'management'. A
person is appointed to a position of, say, manager of a recreation centre
and is told to get on with the job and 'manage'. Many believe that
recreation management starts from there. This book takes a different view
from the outset. It is suggested that far from starting with the facility,

recreation management starts with the people it is intended to serve and their needs, an understanding of the recreation 'product', the market place, and the providers, and an involvement in the planning process. Management, it is contended, is a beginning-to-end process. The techniques of facility management, however, are an important and essential *part* of the process. In Chapter 13 the principles and approaches to *management, leadership* and *decision-making* are considered. Chapters 14, 15, 16 and 17 get down to the more 'nitty-gritty' of recreation facility management, i.e. *programming, staffing, marketing* and *event organization*.

Finally, in Chapter 18 the question of training for recreation management is considered: who manages recreation? Who do they represent? Who trains them? Is recreation management a profession? These questions are debated. Chapter 18 has been entirely re-written to take account of the rapid changes since the first edition, the publication of the 'Yates' Report, the formation of the Institute of Leisure and Amenity Management and the growth in the leisure industry.

★

PART ONE

The providers of leisure opportunity and recreation services

★

Public recreation is made possible by means of resources and management. A range of facilities is needed both indoor and outdoor, in and around the home, in the urban environment, in rural areas and in the countryside. A range of services and programmes is needed to meet the diverse needs and demands of individuals, families, groups, clubs and societies.

Many demands are met through resources and equipment in the home. Some demands are met, in part, through outdoor facilities such as gardens and open spaces, allotments, play areas and sports grounds. Other demands are met, in part, through a range of indoor facilities for entertainment, art, music, drama, literary activities, education, sport and physical recreation, hobbies and pastimes. This range of activity requires general and specialist facilities in the form of halls and meeting rooms, libraries, theatres, museums, sports and leisure centres, swimming pools, community centres, entertainment centres, pubs, clubs, cinemas, concert halls, craftrooms and workshops. Recreation in the countryside requires good roadway networks, maps and signposting, stopping-off points, scenic viewing points, picnic sites, car parking, camping and caravan sites, clean beaches and lakes, water recreation areas, walkways, footpaths, nature reserves and very many others.

Demands are met, however, not just by providing facilities but in attracting people to use them through services, management policy and management action. The range of facilities in urban areas and in the countryside is increasing, and becoming more sophisticated. With it come greater opportunities and greater problems – problems which recreation professionals must help solve through improved management.

The providers of services and facilities for recreation come mainly from within the *public, voluntary* and *commercial* sectors. The pressure on land and on financial capital in the United Kingdom has encouraged the main providers to give serious thought to combining their efforts, pooling resources and making the best use of existing resources. However, with some notable exceptions, habits die hard and changes come about slowly. The picture is one of entrenchment in many cases, in the face of logic and common sense, where organizations and authorities cling on to an undiluted autonomy. Even within the public sector, co-operative ventures between county councils and district councils have progressed little since the relative euphoria of the early 1970s.

It is recognized from the outset that there is considerable *overlap* between the sectors and that in many cases the three sectors will be involved in the same kinds of provision and services. They are also increasingly dependent on each other. However, there appear to be fundamental and distinct differences in philosophy, objectivity and approach, which need to be understood in order to provide appropriate recreation services.

Criticism is often levelled at one provider's service comparing it with an apparently more successful service, yet often the two providers are working to entirely different goals and have different constraints in their paths to success. This part of the book, therefore, helps recreationists to understand the essential characteristics of the three main sectors, to appraise the most useful and most harmful aspects of each and point in the direction of the right provision for the right people. It also aims to illustrate the range and diversity of national agencies concerned in an advisory and supportive capacity with the planning and provision of recreation facilities.

The objectives of Part One are therefore to describe and explain the role of the public, voluntary and commercial providers, to show their similarities and differences, to appreciate their collective importance and also to understand the nature and function of the national recreation organizations. Chapters 1, 2 and 3 deal with the public, voluntary and commercial sectors respectively and Chapter 4 considers the national agencies.

Chapter 1

Recreation provision in the public sector

★

1.1 INTRODUCTION

In the United Kingdom public services and facilities for recreation can be provided by a public authority or by legislation for the general use of the public, such as common lands or forests open to the public, parks and gardens, swimming pools and museums. Some facilities are provided by public funds for a restricted use such as educational establishments, facilities for Her Majesty's Services and restricted forestry areas. Commercial operators have naturally veered towards those facilities and activities that give a good return on their investment. The increasing costs of land and construction have left the local authorities the task of providing more of the land extensive facilities such as water recreation and parks, and more of the expensive buildings such as swimming pools, theatres, sports centres and concert halls.

Local authorities provide a wide range of facilities and services for recreation. They also provide for recreation, often indirectly through financial and other support, through planning decisions and generally by acting as an 'enabling authority'. Local authorities, thus, play a major role in the provision of facilities and opportunities for public recreation.

Government agencies, like new town corporations, regional water authorities and national park boards, also have major roles in recreation provision. All these bodies have powers or duties to assist in or to initiate provision.

Chapter 1 is written in the following manner. *First*, a brief overview is given to describe the range and scope of provision made by public sector providers. *Second*, the development of local authority leisure and recreation services is considered. Particular attention is paid to specific enabling Acts of Parliament, to local government reorganization and to the policy of shared use between education and recreation services. *Third*, local authority services are seen within the framework of central government controls. *Fourth*, the duties and responsibilities of local government departments, officers and members are looked at in relation to leisure and recreation services. *Fifth*, corporate management and comprehensive recreation departments are considered. *Finally*, the problems, constraints and opportunities for local government recreation provision and management are highlighted and summarized.

1.2 THE RANGE AND DIRECT PROVISION BY LOCAL AUTHORITIES

The scope of recreation and leisure services within local authorities is very wide. However, there are a number of identifiable elements and spheres of influence; different authorities will have some or all of these elements depending on the location and the size of the authority, its policies and its responsibilities. These spheres and elements are shown in Fig.1.1. They include sport and physical recreation, informal recreation, countryside recreation, children's play, arts and 'cultural' activities, entertainment and events, catering, museums, conservation areas, tourism, youth and community services, adult education, libraries, and community, voluntary and social services elements. Many of the elements are combined or overlap; no two authorities are exactly alike either in provision or management. There are general similarities but specific differences.

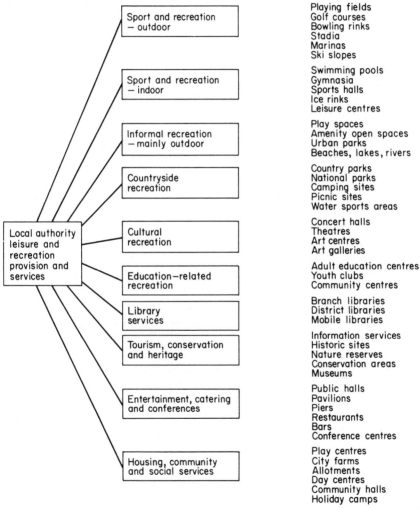

Fig. 1.1 Ten local authority leisure and recreation elements and spheres of influence.

The Centre for Urban and Regional Studies [1] estimated that in 1978 local authorities were the providers of 12 000 libraries, 500 art galleries and museums, 1300 community centres and halls, 600 indoor swimming pools, 400 indoor sports centres and 150 golf courses. The Sports Council estimated that municipal leisure responsibilities in England in 1980/81 included 600 sports halls, 700 swimming pools, 200 golf courses, 130 000 hectares of park and 49 000 hectares of playing fields [2]. The number of municipal facilities continues to grow. For example, the Sports Council's building programme for 1984 identifies 35 new sports halls, 6 indoor bowls halls, 2 ice rinks, 5 indoor pools and a range of outdoor facilities.

Local authorities provide their range of facilities in a variety of ways. The public has free access to a large number of facilities for which no direct payment is made, such as urban parks, playgrounds, libraries, picnic areas, nature trails, beaches and country parks. While the public does not pay directly for these amenities it does so indirectly through the rates. Local authorities also provide facilities such as swimming pools, playing fields, golf courses, marinas, arts centres, theatres and sports centres, where there is a direct payment by the user, albeit at a charge which is often highly subsidized.

Local authorities are important providers of leisure, education, arts and cultural activities, through schools and colleges, art galleries, museums, concert halls and libraries. They have statutory duties to provide public libraries, though there are widely varying standards of provision. Youth and community services are provided usually through education, but the totality of services is a mixture of local authority provision and services provided by voluntary bodies.

While local authorities often look to commercial and voluntary sectors to provide for social activity and entertainment, they, nevertheless, do provide for entertainment both directly and indirectly. Directly, they provide, for example, through village and community halls; community centres are particularly widespread in new town developments. Directly, they also provide through the provision of civic halls which are used for entertainment and urban parks with their bandstands and entertainment facilities. Many new leisure centres are also prime venues for public entertainment.

1.2.1 Expenditure and manpower

Local authorities spend a considerable amount of tax and rate-payers' money. It is estimated that the total net expenditure by local authorities in England and Wales in 1986/87 for leisure and recreation including indoor and outdoor recreation facilities, cultural facilities, tourism promotion and catering was £1113 million [3]. This expenditure has risen each year: £746 million in 1981/82, £836 million in 1982/83, £915 million in 1983/84, £987 million in 1984/85 and £988 million in 1985/86. Table 1.1 outlines the 1985/6 estimates.

In 1986/87 the average estimated expenditure per head of population was £22.78, with variations from £11 to £69 in the London boroughs, from £18 to £30 in the metropolitan areas and from £10 to £36 in the non-metropolitan districts. The widest variations are in the non-metropolitan districts. Within the districts expenditure per head of population ranged from as little as 87p in South Bucks to as much as £61 in Brighton, £55 in Leicester and £52 and £50 in the new towns of Harlow and Thamesdown respectively. While there are these wide variations in expenditure from area to area they must be seen as crude indicators of provision only and not of performance [3]. Statistics are subject to varying interpretations and do not give a complete picture of leisure and recreation facilities. In addition these figures do not include education-related provision such as libraries and youth and adult services, where such wide variations do not occur. Table 1.2 outlines the average non-educational leisure and recreation expenditures per head between Greater London, metropolitan areas and non-metropolitan areas.

Within the expenditure of £1113 million in 1986/87, £676 million was incurred on sport and recreation, £175 million on cultural facilities with roughly half the costs on art galleries and museums and the other half on theatres, entertainment and the like. The cost of swimming pools accounted for 14% of the sport and recreation budget, the cost of leisure centres with and without pools 22% and the cost of urban parks and open spaces some 47% of that budget. Table 1.3 shows the expenditure analysed by divisions of service.

Public expenditure in the library services in England and Wales was £404 million in 1985/6 and estimated to be £390.3 million in 1986/87 [4]. Taking into account sport and recreation, the arts, libraries, youth services and adult education, local authorities in England and Wales spend well over £1500 million on leisure services each year.

Public expenditure by central government *and* local government on arts, libraries and museums was estimated to have been £15.98 per head over the whole of England, Scotland and Wales in 1983/84. HM Treasury sources put the total public expenditure on arts, libraries and museums in Great Britain at £787 million in 1985/86 and £765 million in 1986/87 [5].

This brief analysis of local authority expenditure on leisure and recreation indicates that the vast majority of services, manpower and finance is used for the traditional, existing facilities. Despite the emergence of new facilities such as indoor recreation centres and country parks it is clear that it is the staffing and management of *existing* provision which predominate local authority recreation services. When education-related services and libraries are included in the comprehensive recreation coverage then the picture becomes even more evident with all the new areas of recreation expenditure taking up less than 10% of the total. In terms of expenditure on recreation, local authorities are dominated by two services – those relating to the libraries and urban parks.

Local authorities are major employers. However, in line with current

Table 1.1 Local authority leisure services expenditure

Data as returned by responding authorities 1986/87 estimates	London Boroughs £000	Metropolitan Districts £000	English Non-Met		Wales		Total		Total 1986–87 £000
			Counties £000	Districts £000	Counties £000	Districts £000	Counties £000	Districts £000	
Sports and recreation:									
Indoor:									
Swimming pools	22 424	28 511	56	41 339	132	4 748	188	97 022	97 210
Sports halls and leisure centres with pools	16 171	22 598	67	57 293	(17)	11 570	50	107 632	107 682
Sports halls and leisure centres without pools	5 133	11 253	545	21 844	205	4 003	750	42 233	42 983
Community centres, public halls	7 402	7 116	6	22 831	18	2 868	24	40 217	40 241
Outdoor:									
Sports facilities	3 214	4 895	376	15 324	6	3 863	382	27 296	27 678
Golf courses	(320)	518	0	1 012	0	27	0	1 237	1 237
Urban parks and open spaces	75 678	80 639	67	139 392	0	20 798	67	316 507	316 574
Country parks, amenity areas, picnic sites and nature reserves	547	4 418	9 409	5 476	1 073	1 233	10 482	11 674	22 156
Allotments	32	609	399	1 031	0	211	399	1 883	2 282
Grants and contributions	6 109	1 364	2 769	6 769	463	412	3 232	14 654	17 886
Total sports and recreation	**136 390**	**161 921**	**13 694**	**312 311**	**1 880**	**49 733**	**15 574**	**660 355**	**675 929**

Arts activities and facilities:									
Theatres, halls, arts centres and places of public entertainment	27 099	6 669	405	30 187	771	3 061	1 176	67 016	68 192
Art galleries and museums	3 874	15 841	8 786	21 834	526	1 483	9 312	43 032	52 344
Public libraries in 'cultural use'	7 812	9 769	4 144	8	171	1 055	4 315	18 644	22 959
Arts activities promoted by local authorities in other premises	2 219	708	573	2 340	4	144	577	5 411	5 988
Grants and contributions	6 497	5 363	4 611	8 212	461	359	5 072	20 431	25 503
Total arts activities and facilities	**47 501**	**38 350**	**18 519**	**62 581**	**1 933**	**6 102**	**20 452**	**154 534**	**174 985**
Other recreation and leisure:									
Promotion of tourism	145	2 606	1 916	13 897	70	1 511	1 986	18 159	20 144
Catering	(151)	(79)	(56)	(1 766)	0	(231)	(56)	(2 227)	(2 283)
Administration	30 070	31 261	6 806	82 533	420	9 695	7 226	153 559	160 785
Other miscellaneous activities and facilities	10 855	5 296	1 313	14 001	47	1 720	1 360	31 872	33 232
Grand total	**224 810**	**239 355**	**42 192**	**483 556**	**4 350**	**68 530**	**46 542**	**1 016 251**	**1 062 792**
No. of authorities included in total	31	34	38	290	8	35	46	390	436
Total no. of authorities	33	36	39	297	8	37	47	403	450
Estimated net expenditure all authorities 1986/87	**236 802**	**263 573**	**43 664**	**492 779**	**4 350**	**71 351**	**48 014**	**1 064 505**	**1 112 520**
1985/86	200 998	228 842	41 073	448 297	3 583	64 733	44 656	942 870	987 526
Change on previous year (%)	**+17.81**	**+15.18**	**+6.31**	**+9.92**	**+21.41**	**+10.22**	**+7.52**	**+12.90**	**+12.66**
Total population (000s)	**6 745 540**	**11 186 827**	**29 250 220**	**29 213 374**	**2 820 000**	**2 819 826**	**32 070 220**	**49 965 567**	**49 965 567**

Source: *Leisure and Recreation Statistics 1986/87 Estimates* [3].

Table 1.2   Leisure and recreation estimates England and Wales 1986/87 (1985/86)

	Net totals (£ million)	Expenditure per head of population (£)
London	237 (201)	36.50
Metropolitan	264 (229)	25.56
Non-metropolitan – England	536 (489)	18.37
Non-metropolitan – Wales	76 (68)	26.86
All authorities	1113 (988)	22.78

Source: *Leisure and Recreation Statistics 1986/87* [3].

Table 1.3   Net expenditure analysed by divisions of service (%)

Indoor swimming pools	9.2
Indoor sports halls and leisure centres with pools	10.1
Indoor sports halls and leisure centres without pools	4.0
Community centres	3.8
Indoor sports and recreation	**27.1**
Outdoor sports	2.6
Golf courses	0.1
Urban parks and open spaces	30.0
Country parks/nature reserves	2.1
Allotments	0.2
Grants and contributions	1.6
Outdoor sports and recreation	**36.6**
Theatres, halls, arts centres and places of public entertainment	6.4
Public libraries and other venues in 'cultural' use	2.8
Art galleries and museums	4.9
Grants and contributions	1.7
Cultural facilities	**15.8**
Promotion of tourism	1.9
Catering	CR 0.2
Administration	15.1
Other miscellaneous activities and facilities	3.1
Other Recreation and leisure	**25.9**
Total net expenditure in 1986/87: £1113 million=	**100%**

Source: *Leisure and Recreation Statistics 1986/87 Estimates* [3].

policies to contain public expenditure, the number of staff has fallen. The combined local authority manpower has recently regained its previous peak of March 1979. Approximately 3 million people were employed in local authority services in 1985 [6]. The public libraries and museums in Great Britain were staffed by 36 000 in 1979 and by 37 300 in 1985.

Recreation, parks and baths were staffed by 84 900 in 1979 and by 87 500 in 1985.

1.2.2 Support services

Local authorities are not simply providers of facilities. They have a support service to perform. They support organizations of all kinds – private institutions, voluntary organizations and even commercial bodies, when it is shown that greater service will be given to the public by so doing. The support given is basically of two kinds. The first is to make 'its own' facilities and equipment available for use, with or without charge. The second is to make financial grants.

The local education authorities are usually involved in support to youth and community services and organizations, for example, by making schools available for youth and adult classes, and by making capital and annual grants to community associations and other social groups. They may pay the salaries of wardens, leaders, teachers and managers of purpose-built community centres.

Local authorities have *discretionary powers* to assist in all manner of ways. They can assist trust bodies to provide theatres and sports centres, sports clubs to provide bowling greens and tennis courts and community groups to provide facilities for children's play, community arts or facilities which help the aged. The authorities also provide considerable support, indirectly, by sponsoring arts, sports and entertainment festivals and major events, by meeting deficits or by funding community events and activities.

The powers available to local authorities to support recreation services are very considerable. Often, small services or small grants given to organizations to help to provide for themselves can benefit the community enormously. The redistribution of local authority funds for recreation based on individual, group and social need could enhance particularly recreation opportunity for the disadvantaged in the community.

1.2.3 Planning

The local authority planning function is crucial to recreation. As planning authorities they can assist with the availability of land and resources. As housing authorities they can assist with leisure in and around the home, in gardens and walkways, in play areas associated with high-rise dwellings, in access to community provision.

Local authorities give planning consent. They make decisions on development proposals and give consent for recreational facilities provided by other agencies. Planning authorities have to consider proposals in the context of broad overall and long term policy. To consider recreation planning in local terms only would not take account of increased mobility, greater affluence and the movement across local authority boundaries. Countryside and regional facilities are particular areas of vulnerability for poor planning. Urban fringe recreation is gaining greater importance, not only because of higher expectations but also because of the cost of travel.

Another aspect of movement into recreational areas is holiday-making, tourism and sightseeing. Since local government reorganization many local authorities have taken up their greater powers relating to the enhancement of tourism.

1.2.4 The local authority as provider: an overview

This brief introduction is sufficient to show that local authorities are major providers of leisure and recreation opportunities through recreation *planning, facilities, services, budgets* and *support*. They have a *duty* to provide recreation opportunities through education and libraries. They have very wide *discretionary* powers in England and Wales to assist the arts, sports, informal recreation, countryside recreation, libraries, entertainment, conservation, tourism and youth and community services. In addition to these direct services, local authorities can assist recreation through many *indirect* ways such as planning and housing and through social services that help the disadvantaged, who may *need* recreation services more than most, but who may make the least demand.

1.3 GOVERNMENT AND RECREATION: THE DEVELOPMENT OF LOCAL AUTHORITY SERVICES

Recreation services and facilities are subject, like all other services, to the laws of the land; while there is no comprehensive leisure or recreation Act, recreation is made possible and is guided and constrained by a whole variety of acts, laws, statutes, government circulars and reports and regulations both national and local. In *The Recreation Management Handbook* (3rd Edn) [7] there are listed over sixty Acts of Parliament which enable and channel recreation provision and services. Of these, over half have become law since 1960, an era which has seen a major advance in the provision of facilities and growth of recreation participation. However, some laws still apply, which were introduced 100 years ago and which cannot meet the needs of a liberalized modern society.

Acts of Parliament impose duties or confer authority or powers to provide for recreation. Acts which have a great bearing on recreation provision cover such diverse areas as allotments, swimming pools, parks, catering, clubs and associations, betting and gaming, public entertainment, libraries, licensing, preservation, waterways, employment, local authorities, institutions, charities and companies.

What is immediately evident in studying the public provision for recreation is that it is *historical, traditional, institutional* and *facility orientated*. Progress must be made within and through the system; changes will come about slowly. Despite the surge of new facilities in the 1960s and 1970s, the bulk of local government expenditure on recreation is still reserved for parks, pitches and pools, which is clearly a result of what exists, what is tradition, what local government is geared up to handle and what is known and understood.

What follows in this section is a very brief history of government legislation in providing for rercreation services since the middle of the 19th century.

1.3.1 The origins of recreation services

The origins of local authority recreations services as we know them today go back to the 19th century. There were many earlier statutes and Acts but these were often enacted to restrict games and recreation. It was not until the latter part of the 19th century that physical training and games were encouraged but even then they were associated with military needs and later with moral welfare and public health. The idea of public 'recreation' was founded to combat the oppression and harmful effects caused to the working population by the Industrial Revolution. Recreation was also for physical, moral and cultural improvement. Baths and wash-houses, parks, libraries and museums began to be provided by philanthropists and some local authorities, particularly those in new industrial cities.

The *Baths and Wash-Houses Act* (1846) from which many of our present-day baths departments originated, was concerned primarily with personal cleansing and hygiene. However, swimming pools were built alongside them mainly for instructional purposes, but also for recreation. Today, the recreation role is paramount and the baths service in many cities embraces other indoor provision in the form of sports halls, squash courts and entertainment facilities.

Many parks departments also originated in the second half of the 19th century. Then, as now, urban open spaces and parks were laid out with flower beds and lawns, shrubberies, bandstands, ornamental gardens and water areas. Again the movement was partly philanthropic and partly local authority. Many bequests of land were received and many acquisitions made. Parks departments, like the baths departments, expanded their sphere of authority and took over areas for organized outdoor sports and facilities for tennis, athletics, golf, boating, bowls and the range of outdoor entertainments and festivals.

The *Public Health Act* (1875), an Act still in force in 1981, was the first major statutory provision enabling urban authorities to purchase, lease, lay out, plant, improve and maintain land for use as public walks or pleasure grounds. The Act was silent as to their use for the playing of games and later statutes had to be passed to empower local authorities to set aside parts of such lands for the playing of games. In the *Public Health Act* (1936) authority was given to provide public baths and wash-houses, swimming baths and bathing places, open or covered, and the right to close them to the public for use by school or club and to charge admission.

It was not until the passing of the *Physical Training and Recreation Act* (1937) that a radical change took place. There was unrest in Europe; nations were being forced to prepare themselves for war; the need for a strong, fit nation was paramount thinking behind the Act. The Act was thus very much a movement towards national fitness. Nevertheless, with the Act we get away from the Victorian idea of 'public walks and pleasure grounds' to playing fields, gymnasia, swimming baths, holiday camps and camping sites, and other buildings and premises for physical training.

Local authorities could acquire land for facilities and clubs, with or without charge for their use. Wardens, teachers and leaders could also be provided and authorities could contribute to expenses incurred by voluntary organizations. The 1937 Act was the first major Act to use the word 'recreation' but support from government had come, not because recreation was fun and enjoyable, but on the grounds of social and physical health and welfare, character training and improvement. Molyneux [8] has shown that a close study of that Bill 'leaves one in no doubt that the accent was much more on physical training than on recreation'.

1.3.2 Post-war improvements to recreation services

The recreation lobby continued promoting its arguments during and after the Second World War. Organizations such as the Central Council of Physical Recreation and the National Playing Fields Association played an effective persuasive role.

The *Town and Country Planning Act* (1947) made it possible for the development plans of local planning authorities to define the sites of proposed public buildings, parks, pleasure grounds, nature reserves and other open spaces or to allocate areas of land for such use. Powers were extended in the *Town and Country Planning Acts* (1971) (1974). The *National Parks and Access to the Countryside Act* (1949) gave local planning authorities, whose areas include a national park, opportunity to provide accommodation and camping sites and to provide for recreation. The scope of countryside recreation was greatly enhanced with the passing of the *Countryside Act* (1968). The Act *permits* local authorities to provide recreation facilities; the 1949 Act placed a *duty* to manage National Parks along with other permissive powers. The 1968 Act has encouraged new provision such as country parks, picnic sites, nature trails, bird sanctuaries and physical recreation – sailing, fishing, walking and camping. Considerable importance has been given to the debate relating to use and abuse of the countryside, the preservation of heritage and the needs of conservation.

Local authorities have considerable powers to provide for recreation through *education* facilities, personnel and services. The successive major *Education Acts* of 1918 and 1944, coming after two world wars, gave education authorities permissive powers (in 1918) to create facilities for social and physical training and then in 1944 made it *mandatory* on all education authorities to provide adequate facilities for 'recreation and social and physical training' for primary, secondary and further education. This resulted not only in the growth of the Youth Service, adult education and physical education (and hence sport) but also in the growth of facilities such as sports grounds, swimming pools, larger gymnasia and some sports halls. However, it was not until many years later that additional finance, through other local authority sources, made it possible to increase greatly the standards of provision. Only by joint planning and provision between different tiers of authorities or between different departments were the larger community-based facilities made possible.

Despite the progress throughout the 20th century up to this point, and despite the statutory and enabling Acts of Parliament, governments consistently viewed recreation as a beneficial means *towards some other ends*. The report of the Wolfenden Committee [9] published in 1960, led to the eventual recognition by Parliament of recreation in its own right.

1.4 THE TRANSITION: AN AWAKENING TO RECREATION

An acceptance of the benefits of recreation in its own right did not come until the 1960s. But the initiative did not come from the Government. The Wolfenden Committee was appointed in October 1957 by the Central Council of Physical Recreation (CCPR) and produced its report *Sport and the Community* in 1960 [9] to examine the factors affecting the development of games, sports and outdoor activities in the United Kingdom and to make recommendations to the Central Council of Physical Recreation as to any practical measures which should be taken by statutory or voluntary bodies in order that these activities may play their full part in promoting the general welfare of the community.

The special factors and problems examined by the committee were *the gap* (where they endorsed the Albemarle Committee's recommendations [10] about the place of physical recreation in the Youth Service), coaching, organization, administration and finance, amateurism, international sport, the press, television and radio and Sunday games. The committee recommended the establishment of a Sports Development Council and £5 million as the amount to be distributed in cash in any one year. A figure of £5 million was also recommended as an annual sum to be sanctioned over and above existing permissions for capital expenditure by statutory bodies. Although a Sports Council was to be formed many years later the recommendations were never implemented. The report, however, was a watershed in the eventual acceptance of recreation by Parliament.

The Wolfenden Report and the Albemarle Report both stressed the need for more and better facilities for indoor sport and recreation. Even before the Wolfenden Report was published the first community sports centre had been planned, had opened its first facilities and appointed its first manager. The centre was developed by a charitable trust – the Harlow and District Sports Trust. The Crystal Palace National Sports Centre was also under construction and was eventually opened in 1964. Again the spearhead was a voluntary organization, the Central Council of Physical Recreation in collaboration with statutory authorities and government.

During the 1960s, in addition to new proposals for sport and recreation and for youth and community services, the expansion of education services, library services and the arts was also proposed. The Plowden Report, *Children and their Primary Schools* (1967) [11] advocated the development of community schools to encourage interaction between home and school and proposed that a policy of 'positive discrimination' should favour schools in neighbourhoods of social and home disadvantage.

The Public Libraries and Museums Act (1964) repealed all other legislation, some going back to before the turn of the century. It placed a *duty* on every library authority to provide a comprehensive and efficient library service – to promote and improve the service. From April 1974 non-metropolitan counties, metropolitan districts and the London boroughs became library authorities. The Department of Education and Science Circular 5/73 *Local Government Reorganization and the Public Library Service* [12] stressed greater links between the major services for education, health and social services in encouraging activities for the whole community.

The arts have been the subject of numerous reports since the mid 1960s, for example, the 1965 White Paper, *Support for the Arts: the first steps* [13]. The 1976 Maud Report [14] sponsored by the Calouste Gulbenkian Foundation has been greatly influential. Redcliffe-Maud recommended that counties and districts should have a *duty* to ensure a 'reasonable range' of opportunity for arts enjoyment and that there should be a development plan for the arts with linkages to the education, libraries, museums and sport and recreation services.

1.4.1 Obstacles and progress to the new recreation philosophy

Despite the acceptance of recreation and the enabling Acts of Parliament, many of the major proposals for sport, the arts, and the youth and community service were never introduced. In addition, in practical terms, local authorities and other providers had still to operate through a maze of acts or sections of old statutes. They also had to operate through a proliferation of departments and, as Molyneux pointed out [8] the system allows and almost encourages separate policies, separate budgets and different attitudes and changing policies towards recreationists, particularly the clubs.

In 1968, with the establishment of a new county borough merging five former authorities, Tees-side County Borough established a major committee and matching department for the arts and recreation. The new department, headed by a chief officer, spanned former services covering the arts, libraries, museums and art galleries, entertainments, sport and physical recreation, baths, parks and catering. Similar restructuring followed in a number of other authorities and in London boroughs.

One of the major influences which led to these developments was the inquiry headed by the then John Redcliffe-Maud into the machinery of local government administration and this was reported in 1967 [15]. It recommended the streamlining of committees and departments. Recreation services were ready to begin to rationalize the total sphere of leisure and recreation.

1.4.2 The policy of shared use between education and recreation services

The 1960s and 1970s witnessed not only the advent of new purpose built facilities for recreation and the restructuring of local government administration but also the recognition that thousands of schools and education facilities throughout the country were in essence embryo community leisure and recreation centres. For example, the provision in schools of indoor facilities for physical education and recreation account for the majority of indoor spaces developed by the public sector for indoor sports.

Department of Education and Science and the Ministry of Housing Local Government Joint Circular 11/64:49/64, *Provision of Facilities for Sport* [16] advanced a new policy guideline:

'In assessing local needs and the resources to match them it is appropriate to consider how far facilities for sport and physical education already provided or in the course of provision at schools and other educational establishments can be shared with other users or can be economically expanded to meet those needs. Consultation with other authorities will

be necessary not only because facilities in one area may serve neighbouring areas, but also there will normally be more than one authority with
powers to provide them'.

The Ministry of Housing and Local Government Circular 31/66 *Public
Expenditure: Miscellaneous Schemes* [17] drew attention again to the savings
which could be achieved by joint provision and the need for consultation
with the new regional sports councils on new projects. The Department
of Education and Science Circular 2/70 *The Chance to Share* [18] gave more
control to local authorities over their own local expenditure, free of
government control, for locally determined schemes including almost all
sport and recreation schemes. Local authorities could now go ahead in
providing facilities, provided they stayed within their overall block
allocation of capital investment.

1.5 LOCAL GOVERNMENT REORGANIZATION AND ITS EFFECT ON RECREATION

A Royal Commission under Lord Redcliffe-Maud was established in 1966
to consider the structure of local government in England, outside Greater
London [19]. The commission proposed that the greater part of England
should be divided into 58 unitary authorities. Public reaction to the
unitary concept was, in general, unfavourable and three of the four local
authority associations preferred a two-tier system. A government White
Paper in 1970 [20] proposed a new structure based on 51 unitary areas and
five metropolitan areas. In 1971 the new Conservative Government's
alternative proposals emerged in two White Papers – one for England and
the other for Scotland – and a consultative document for Wales [21–23]. A
compromise solution of a two-tier structure and a radical reorganization
of boroughs and urban and rural districts was proposed.

The Local Government Act (1972) gave effect to the proposals contained in
the 1971 White Paper. The Act conferred no new powers but transferred
the previous powers to the new local authorities. *The Local Government
(Miscellaneous Provisions) Act* (1976) brought together the various powers
relating to the provision of leisure and recreation facilities. The Act
consolidated most of the powers for leisure services other than those
relating to 'cultural' and 'educational' services. The Act *permits* local
authorities to provide such recreational facilities as it thinks fit, unlike the
Libraries Act of 1964 which placed a *duty* on library authorities to provide
services.

In 1974, six new metropolitan county councils were established and the
1400 existing district councils were reduced to 333 (see Fig. 1.2). As far as
recreation services were concerned the greatest impact was felt in the 296
non-metropolitan district councils. These councils were now larger, more

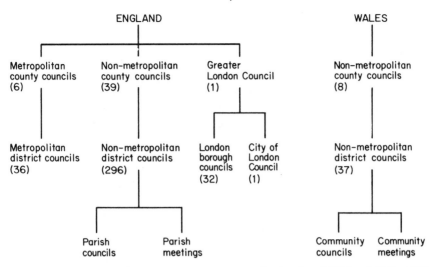

Fig. 1.2 Revised local government structure – England and Wales. NB In 1985 the government passed legislation to scrap the Metropolitan County Councils and the Greater London Council.

powerful and had in many cases inherited a range of facilities – parks, entertainment halls, swimming pools and sport and leisure centres. Reorganization also encouraged the creation of new facilities particularly indoor leisure centres *before* reorganization actually took place. Some district councils, for example, which were due to be amalgamated into new larger districts, were anxious to put their part of the new district firmly on the map and provide their area with good community facilities – a lasting reminder of their heritage. They forged ahead, often with expensive capital projects, leaving the new districts to pick up the tab, both in terms of paying back capital debts and in the on-going revenue deficits.

Prior to local government reorganization in 1974, most local authorities were structured on the basis of a number of departments operating under the control of committees. The committees competed for their share of the available financial resources. The Bains Report [24] placed emphasis on the *corporate approach to management*. It was felt that in this way an authority could formulate more realistically its long term objectives covering all services, and make forward planning projections.

With increased facilities, increased awareness towards community recreation and the emergence of new larger departments, jobs were created for managers within recreation services and rapid promotions and movements of staff were prevalent throughout the United Kingdom.

1.6 LOCAL AUTHORITY SERVICES: POWERS AND RESPONSIBILITIES

The framework for the powers and responsibilities of local authorities is derived from the *Local Government Act* (1972). Parliament authorizes local authorities to take specific actions. The Act provides the machinery but the Government retains the power to operate it. Local authorities are constrained in the way in which they act and exercise their considerable powers.

1.6.1 The framework under central control

Local authorities are independent administrative bodies created by Parliament. However, certain Ministers of State have power to direct them in the exercise of their duties. The Minister with prime responsibility for local government is the Secretary of State for the Environment. The 1972 Act prescribes the constitution of the principal councils. They are:

1. County councils
2. County district councils
3. Parishes and communities
4. Greater London Council
5. London borough councils
6. The City Corporation

Four district forms of central control of local authorities have been identified by Seeley [25] – *legislative, administrative, financial* and *judicial* – and the main reasons for central control include:

1. The need to ensure that local authority expenditure is consistent with the Government's general economic policy.
2. The high proportion of local authority income by way of government grant, and the need to control the spending of it.
3. The national importance of the work of local authorities and the recent tendency to require certain minimum standards of provision.
4. The need to protect rate-payers against possible financial mismanagement.
5. The desirability of protecting local authority staff against arbitrary dismissal and the need to provide suitable machinery for the settlement of disputes.

Local governments are required by law to conduct their business under the constraints and guidelines provided by Parliament. They must be and *must be seen to be* accountable to the public. The overall management hinges around three main structures: the *committee* structure, the *officer* structure and the *departmental* structure.

Local authorities have to provide certain services and, therefore, need certain departments. They have a duty to appoint certain officers and they have permissive powers to appoint others. Hence the structures in local government are made up with a mixture of '*have* to's' and '*may* do's'. This renders all local authorities *similar*; it also renders all local authorities *dissimilar*.

The work of a local authority cannot be undertaken without money and it is the financial considerations which loom largest at the end of the day. The local authority budget is the single most important function, the mainspring of its activities.

1.6.2 Finance

The local authority is a *business* organization. Finance is needed for recreation services and can be classified under two main headings: *capital* finance and *revenue* finance. Capital funding is accessible to local government from several sources though capital expenditure is principally financed through borrowing sanctioned by central government. Capital projects in the 'key sector' – 'those projects where national considerations and the need for maintenance of minimum standards weigh heavily' – are controlled through programmes agreed with the departments responsible [26]. However, most recreation and leisure projects fall into the 'non-key sector'. For these projects each authority or group of authorities is given a block allocation for each year to be spent as it so wishes. These 'locally determined schemes' are dependent on a fixed allocation from the government each year. This allocation has fallen sharply since the mid 1970s and recreation services have had to compete against many other even more pressing services. However, there are sources other than borrowing from which to finance capital expenditure. Some of the ways are outlined below along with the main sources of capital funding.

1. Direct grant from central government.
2. Loans from central government (key-sector/non-key sector/rate support grants).
3. Revenue contributions (though these would reduce the revenue programmes).
4. Capital receipts through the sale of other assets e.g. local authority land.
5. Capital internal funds e.g. Community Amenity Funds.
6. Loans from commercial concerns and a variety of joint arrangements with development companies and funding institutions.
7. User finances such as lotteries.
8. Rates.

Finance from these sources is used to develop and construct amenities for use by members of the public, whether through clubs and organizations or by direct local government management.

Revenue finance is needed to support the on-going running costs of the service and facilities. The finance is generated from:

1. Users – income from fees and charges and trading such as through admission fees, library fines, hire of facilities and catering.
2. Grant aid from central government – Urban Aid grants, Sports Council and Arts Council grants.
3. Rates – payable to the council by its citizens.
4. Rates – rate support grant from central government.

Like capital expenditure, revenue expenditure has also been strictly limited in recent years. Local authorities have powers, however, under Section 137 of the *Local Government Act* (1972), to levy and spend the product of a 2p rate for the benefit of its area.

1.6.3   Financial links with private and commercial sources

Restrictions in powers of borrowing *and* spending and the decrease in finance for locally determined schemes and in the rate support grants limit severely the expansion of local authority leisure and recreation services. As we have seen, local authority capital expenditure on recreation facilities normally falls within the locally determined schemes sector for borrowing purposes. In times of economic restraint it is the sector in which the most severe cuts are made. Other services receive greater priority. This state of affairs has prompted some local authorities to explore a variety of ways of funding new capital projects including capital sales, the formation of recreation trusts, joint schemes with commercial enterprise, lease and lease back schemes, deferred purchase methods, partnership projects and commercial development where a developer purchases, develops and manages leisure projects and the council benefits from 'planning gain'. Planning gain is a well established concept whereby a private developer will provide facilities deemed to be in the public good as a trade off for the provision of land and planning permission for commercial development which would provide a fair return on capital outlay.

One example of local authority control and commercial capital funding and management through joint action between a local authority and commercial developers is the sea front development in the borough of Great Yarmouth – a £5.7 million indoor leisure development [27]. A 25 year lease/lease back arrangement was agreed between the council and C.I.N. Industrial Investments Limited, a company wholly owned by the National Coal Board Superannuation and Pensions Schemes, in December 1978 in the sum of £4.5 million. A lease of plant and equipment was also arranged with Lloyds Industrial Leasing Limited at £870 000. Module 2 Limited drew up a 'Design and Constructional Management Contract' and a 21 year operational management contract was entered into with Trusthouse Forte Leisure Limited on a basis of a management and incentive fee. Opening in June 1981, the first nine months to end March 1982 recorded 829 000 attendances. Subsequent years, however, saw a drop in attendances from 838 000, 679 000 to 560 000 in March 1985. Further, the anticipated level of revenue surpluses were never realized and the early surpluses have now turned to small deficits. The council has budgeted for gross revenue expenditure of £998 000 for the year ending March 1986 and net operational expenditure of £47 000 but this is a fraction of the costs which would have applied under traditional local authority management.

Since the lease/lease back contract was signed, the *Local Government Planning and Land Act* (1980) has introduced an entirely different system of capital expenditure control. The control is now focused on capital *expenditure* rather than on borrowing. Hence, it would suggest that the lease/lease back arrangement described above would only be available within the financial scope of approved capital allocations and not additional to those allocations. Nevertheless, some councils are investigating a number of methods to provide new capital projects. As Davies and Halliwell [17] point out, 'new techniques continue to be developed to assist local authorities in the provision of facilities and a study of methods such as building under covenant, company and trust formation and the use of capital receipts all look particularly rewarding'.

1.7 MANAGEMENT IN LOCAL GOVERNMENT: THE POLICY MAKERS

Management of local authority recreation services is a highly complicated process. It revolves around the local authority structural framework and involves a very large number of people: elected members, voluntary committee members, departmental staff from several departments, facility managers and staff, and all the organizations and programmes through which recreation is made available to the public. Elected members, however, are of utmost importance to the management of recreation services. *They decide policy, they decide what is to be built and made available, they budget and they control.*

1.7.1 The role of the members

Councillors are citizens who devote part of their time to the service of local authorities. They are not salaried but can be paid allowances. The business of local authorities takes time, if often arduous and complex. A councillor is a representative of his or her area. He or she is essentially a man or woman of the people, and should represent the community and involve the community. A councillor should be seen as making decisions not just for the community but *with* the community.

A councillor may find himself or herself managing or at least taking decisions relating to parks, swimming pools, theatres, allotments, community associations, clubs, and deciding over hundreds of events from festivals, orchestral concerts, tournaments and bingo to mother and toddler groups. He or she is part of a decision-making process that deliberates over thousands of decisions during his period as a councillor. Each decision, whether it be the spending of millions of pounds on a new leisure centre or the granting of a few pounds to a little recreational league club, touches the lives of the people in his community. In terms of recreation, therefore, one of his functions is to see that the resources, facilities, leadership and programmes are available for the community. The councillor needs skill and political muscle.

The role of the elected representatives should be viewed in many contexts – the jobs they have to do, the decisions they have to make, the roles they have to play, the constraints under which they have to work, their time, their ability and their motivation. Councillors are motivated by a variety of factors. They enter public life perhaps as a form of self-expression, and self esteem, a hobby, an interest, by accident, as a means of influencing local affairs, or out of deep moral, social or political conviction. One can only speculate on the inner reasons; outwardly they stand because they wish to serve the community, in the way they see open to them. The Bains Study Group [24] suggested that they stand on five main grounds – an interest in policy, in welfare, in management, in community and/or in finance. Jones [28] suggested that they stand for three main reasons – as spokesman and watchdog (75%), as specialized policy-maker (20%) and one who establishes priorities (5%).

1.7.2   The constraints on members' actions

The adage that councillors make policy decision and officers carry them out is too simplistic. The policy-making process and its implementation are the function of both. The councillor is constrained in decision-making. First, he or she is one of a group, even if chairman. *Second*, work must be kept within strict cash limits. Councils can receive up to two-thirds of their expenditure from central government in the form of rate support grants (provided they do not overspend) the rest coming from local rates and income. Increases in expenditure may not receive rate support grants; councils are, therefore, wary of stepping over their cash limitations. *Third*, party politics now operate to a significant extent in local government; the party system is at its strongest in the larger urban areas and at its weakest in rural areas, according to Seeley [29]. There are arguments both for and against the party system in local government. *Fourth*, the councillor is constrained by the management system and town hall organizational strategy. Under corporate management, for example, there will exist a strong and perhaps formidable group of chief officers and an even stronger group of inner-circle councillors. A councillor will need the support of the management team. Here lies an important role for a councillor – that of appointing senior management staff. *Fifth*, the councillor is inundated with paperwork. He or she must have the ability to understand and digest. *Sixth*, councillors must give time: time for meetings, time for those they represent. A councillor must give of himself or herself.

1.7.3 The member's role in recreation services management

Councils often provide *facilities* as an answer to presumed recreation need. But community support, community service and leisure opportunity may be the greater need for many people. A councillor's job in the field of recreation provision, opportunity and management is, therefore, to use the local authority framework, departments and staff to determine needs and demands, establish policies, aims, priorities and objectives, make decisions, implement measures to achieve them, monitor progress and make evaluations. In providing for recreation demand and need, councillors must be working with and through officers, with recreation involved people in the community, and with the public – the users of the services being provided.

In order to undertake these responsibilities councillors need the ability, the opportunity and the motivation to achieve results. Their decisions are based on intuition, feel, experience and gut-reaction. Their decisions are based, too, on some knowledge and information acquired from their officers but rarely, if ever, from training. Councillors have the authority and the power. They are 'trained' on operational experience. Recreational professionals must, therefore, inform, educate and influence councillors in the execution of their important task in the field of recreation.

1.8 CORPORATE MANAGEMENT WITHIN LOCAL GOVERNMENT

Corporate management aims to provide a framework for local government business, whereby the needs of a community are viewed comprehensively; the activities of the local authority are planned and directed in a unified manner to satisfy those needs to the fullest extent possible within available resources. Corporate management requires a master plan combining policy making, corporate planning and collective management. The following main steps have been identified in the process of corporate management [30].

1. To identify and as far as is practicable analyse and quantify the needs and problems of the community.
2. To specify the objectives of the authority and to identify the alternative methods of achieving them.
3. To evaluate these methods and in the light of the resources needed and benefits to be secured decide on appropriate courses of action.
4. To examine the interrelationships of different departments.
5. To formulate action programmes to achieve agreed objectives for several years ahead.
6. To implement action programmes and undertake periodic systematic reviews of programmes and progress.
7. To monitor changing needs and modify action programmes, where necessary, and to evaluate performance.

Thus, according to Seeley [30] 'corporate management constitutes a total system of management embracing planning the activities, undertaking and controlling them, and monitoring and modifying them in the light of experience, all within a concerted or corporate framework'.

The committee structure envisaged in the Bains Report has been used as a guideline by many authorities but by no means all. The structure is outlined in Fig. 1.3. The management team envisaged in the Bains Report comprises the chief executive and a group of chief officers. The study

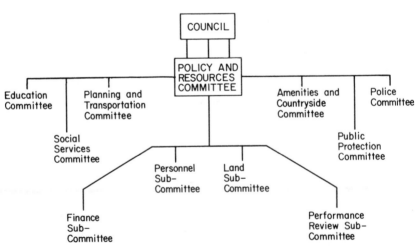

Fig. 1.3 Committee structure – non-metropolitan county (Bains Committee proposals).

group felt that the management team should number about six and that some of the chief officers in a larger authority might, therefore, not be members (see Fig. 1.4).

Corporate management under a smaller authority can take on various organizational structures. One could be considered under five main departments, as in the hypothetical example in Fig. 1.5.

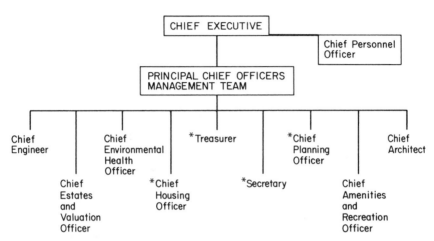

Fig. 1.4 Departmental structure – larger non-metropolitan district (Bains Committee proposals). * Members of management team. Local circumstances may justify additional members.

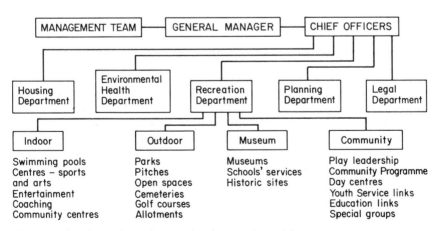

Fig. 1.5 One hypothetical example of recreation within corporate management including the chief officers of each department.

Community recreation services can be greatly enhanced where corporate management includes a chief recreation officer within the management team. However, just bringing together the main recreation departments or sections does not in itself guarantee a comprehensive approach, and comprehensive attitude to recreation planning and management. Policies may be set to achieve a balance of provision but biases towards one type of provision or another, depending on the views of the officers, may still be prevalent.

1.9   COMPREHENSIVE RECREATION AND LEISURE DEPARTMENTS

Comprehensive and composite recreation and leisure departments came about as a result of many factors which include:

1. Local government reorganization with authorities reforming and grouping into larger bodies with greater stocks of recreation resources.
2. The acceptance by many councils of the advantages of corporate management following the Bains recommendations.
3. The establishment of new government agencies like the Sports Council and the Countryside Commission.
4. Structure planning and corporate planning, which arose from the *Planning Act* (1971).
5. New types of facility such as leisure centres, art centres and country parks.
6. The emergence of a new 'breed' of recreation professionals with an emphasis on comprehensive recreation management.
7. Government reports and circulars encouraging links between major services e.g. Circular 5/73 on libraries.

The following arguments can be put forward for composite departments:

1. Much better use can be made of existing resources.
2. By bringing together separate, disparate departments – parks, baths, museums, entertainment – there can be more effective development, siting and administration of new facilities.
3. A stronger linkage can be forged between 'district' plans and 'education' plans for better dual use and joint provision of facilities.
4. More effective liasion is afforded with planning, education and social services committees and their departments.
5. The aims and objectives of recreation services can be thought out anew, particularly as recreation services under older systems had been established on other objectives.

6. A more effective link can be made between users of facilities, voluntary bodies and others.
7. More effective liaison can be forged with regional agencies like the regional sports and arts councils.
8. Better ways can be found to utilize commercial capital and expertise in the wider range of community recreation.
9. Recreation expectation is fast becoming more sophisticated and widening; comprehensive departments can look more effectively at *total community plans* and networks.

These and other factors all add to the trend towards larger and more comprehensive local authority recreation and leisure services and departments. Many of these factors are debated more fully by Veal and Travis [31] who also point out that, despite the recommendations for composite departments, these departments are by no means universal. Indeed in 1978 less than one-third of the districts overall had a single leisure services department, as is shown in Table 1.4. However, the first half of the eighties has seen an expansion in the trend towards separate leisure services departments.

It is clear that the pattern is far from uniform. In some authorities recreation services is a major directorate with principal officers, planners, researchers and managers. In some authorities recreation still remains a

Table 1.4   District councils: leisure services departments

	Non-Metropolitan districts	Metropolitan districts	London boroughs	Total
	Percentage of authorities			
Single leisure services departments	30	22	27	29
Single non-leisure services departments	47	0	0	39
2 leisure services departments	10	53	24	14
1 leisure, 1 non-leisure department	7	6	30	9
2 non-leisure departments	1	0	0	1
3 or more leisure departments	4	17	15	5
3 or more departments, 1 non-leisure	2	3	3	2

Source: *Municipal Year Book* – adapted by Veal and Travis [31].

fragmented service and is often splintered into several departmental responsibilities. In yet other authorities recreation is seen as a unit but is swallowed up within a general service department such as technical services or even within housing. In the larger authorities and the metropolitan districts, in particular, large departments exist but there is often a traditional split between 'sports' and 'arts' departments. Hence, recreation and leisure services are by no means standardized. Different areas have different needs and what is appropriate for one area may be inappropriate for another. However, better *general* rationalization and standardization will improve recreation management effectiveness.

1.10 THE COMPLEXITIES OF RECREATION MANAGEMENT IN LOCAL GOVERNMENT

Local authorities have a very important role to play in the provision and management of recreation. However, they are considerably constrained in what they can do and the way in which they can go about it. The problems are often complex and revolve around a number of separate and interrelated issues. Some of the problems are outlined below and taken cumulatively they show how difficult it is for authorities to provide what is needed, particularly in a society with growing expectations and widening freedom.

1.10.1 Recreation provision: a piecemeal inheritance

First, administration of recreation services at all governmental levels is complex, often confusing and peculiar to the British government, tradition and way of life. Some of the strengths and many of the weaknesses stem from the way in which the pattern of active recreation pursuiits developed. Organized recreation, for example, was originally a matter for private and voluntary effort. By the time 'statutory' provision began to supplement this, numerous agencies were already established and working in the field. They were uncoordinated and autonomous. Recreation provision and management is thus a patchwork quilt strategy, not just of shades and colours but of different materials, textures and threads. When we look at facilities alone even within the same authority, it appears that we have somehow managed to keep the left hand in ignorance of what the right hand is doing. Today it is now clear that for generations we have wasted many of our resources and facilities by keeping strict divisions between school, youth, community, young and old. Often the problem has been, not a shortage of facilities, but rather administrative weakness and an *inability to coordinate* functions of separate departments within different tiers of local government.

The lesson for Recreation Managers is that authorities must make the fullest use of existing resources. It would also appear that local authorities have in the past concentrated too much on facilities and not enough on services and opportunities. If local authorities are to serve all sections of the community, including those who are disadvantaged, then supplying facilities alone is not enough. Community developments, partnerships, 'outreach' programmes, neighbourhood schemes, community leaders and 'animateurs' must be encouraged. Groups of many kinds can benefit not just from cash sums but from support in a variety of guises, e.g. staff, leadership, offices, administration, free publicity and 'moral' support.

The advantages of a fully integrated approach can be beneficial to neighbourhood and communities. Residents of deprived urban neighbourhoods are almost entirely dependent on public recreation facilities, whereas residents of more affluent neighbourhoods will have a wider range of recreational alternatives. Future facilities must be planned more effectively. *This entails public participation, the involvement of recreation professionals throughout the planning stages, designing, siting and managing facilities effectively and developing community recreation programmes with which the community can identify.*

1.10.2 Government fragmented in approach to recreation

Second, recreation administration is fragmented. Different Acts of Parliament and regulations govern *separate* services such as social, health, community, education, tourism, the countryside, sport and outdoor recreation, and the arts. Tourism is a function of the Department of Trade; arts come within the Department of Education and Science; sport and outdoor recreation are the province of the Department of the Environment. Other departments too, such as the Home Office, the Department of Health and Social Security, the Ministry of Agriculture, Fisheries and Food and the Department of Transport are also involved in recreation provision. Many of the functions, however, are devolved to agencies such as the Tourist Boards, the Arts Council, Sports Council and Countryside Commission.

The multi-sector and multi-department approach of central government and the resulting complexity and overlap, constitutes inherent problems between the 'fit' between central government and local government. Furthermore, most local authority functions, for example libraries and adult education, have central government controls, guidance and sources for grant aid. However, this is not universally applied, for example children's play, entertainment, catering and urban parks fall into several sectors and no one department takes overall responsibility.

1.10.3   County council and district council overlaps

Third, not only is there a lack of 'fit' between central government and local government, there is a lack of 'fit' between levels of government within local authorities. *The Local Government Act* (1972) invests in all the county councils and district councils *equal powers* to provide recreation and leisure facilities for the community. Thus county councils and district councils have concurrent powers which lead to overlapping and duplication. The exceptions to this general provision are education, libraries and national parks. School, youth service and adult education recreation facilities are provided only by education authorities i.e. the metropolitan districts and the 'shire' counties. Libraries, in England, are also provided from these same councils. County councils tend to provide for recreation in the form of countryside recreation facilities, through grants to voluntary bodies and to specific jointly provided recreation establishments. District councils are more concerned with the close-at-hand facilities and in particular facilities for sports and the arts.

1.10.4   Permissive and mandatory powers

Fourth, in Scotland and Northern Ireland a *duty* has been laid on local authorities to provide recreation facilities but in England and Wales local authorities are under *no obligation* to provide for recreation other than through education, libraries, allotments and some national parks. The 'duty to provide' was specifically rejected by the Government in its 1975 White Paper *Sport and Recreation* [32]. Local authorities should thus have *permissive* powers.

Why should statutory obligations differ in different parts of the United Kingdom? Veal [33] considered the matter in this way:

'Whether more compulsion would make any difference to leisure provision by the local authorities is debatable. If governments wish to pressurize or direct local authorities to provide services they generally have to provide at least a proportion of the funds and also to set standards of provision. The evidence suggests that local authorities will generally adopt standards if they are soundly based and will make provision if resources are provided, without the need for compulsion. In times of economic stringency statutory services such as adult education and libraries seem to be as susceptible to cuts as non-statutory services.'

However, as we have seen, the variation in expenditure between authorities on non-statutory services is much greater than in the statutory services: in some areas expenditure is high as £45 per head of population while in other is it below £1.50 per head for sport, recreation and cultural provision.

1.10.5 Services combined or separated at local level

Fifth, at local level recreation services can be combined through corporate management and comprehensive departments, *or* partially combined *or* remain separated into autonomous departments – community services, libraries, parks, baths, entertainments. Even where comprehensive re-creation departments exist, they are known and have titles which vary from one authority to the next. For example, among the variety of titles are 'recreation and amenities', 'amenities and recreation', 'recreation services' and 'leisure services'; these appear to be the most popular. Veal [33] discovered that some sixty different titles are used to describe chief officers in this field.

1.10.6 Planning and management policy problems

Sixth, it is not surprising that given obligatory and permissive powers through different major government departments and a variety of local authority methods we have a patchwork development of services and problem of policy. Fundamentally the status of recreation is still prob-lematic and planning for recreation is *not* a main priority for local government and features only peripherally in many structure plans.

A second management policy problem is that local government depart-ments have often been unclear about their aims and objectives. Local authority recreation aims and goals are often all-embracing – 'to serve the whole community' – and can mean all things to all men. They are difficult to translate into operational objectives which can be measured to see whether they have been achieved. What are the needs? Why is provision made? Failure to understand such questions arises from the lack of understanding or consensus about provision and need.

A third fundamental problem in local authority recreation administra-tion is the inevitable bureaucracy which comes through public accounta-bility, public service, institutionalized systems and approaches which render the whole machinery a slow moving animal, one which cannot readily respond to the needs of a fast moving, changeable and flexible society.

1.10.7 Problems of working within the system

Seventh, several management problems exist at an officer-manager level, and these have an effect on the face-to-face work with the community. Five problems are identified.

1. Officer and staff behaviour is often controlled and guided by formal, organizational structures and by the 'purple book' [34]. This system of

'working to rules' can inculcate formal attitudes and responses to informal and flexible situations. It is opposite to the freedom spirit of leisure.

2. The formal approaches tend to make it difficult for local government to attract or to articulate with the socially disadvantaged who find little identification with the services. The Department of the Environment (DOE) Report *Recreation and Deprivation in Inner Urban Areas* [35] describes the problems which arise when simple approaches to providing recreation facilities 'for the whole community', without considering the special needs of particular groups, are adopted. A similar lesson is drawn from the report *Fair Play for All* [36] by Hillman and Whalley.

3. The 'apparent' constraints of public accountability, allied to local government 'standards' tend to make local authorities wary and uneasy concerning commercial investment. Greater cooperation may be essential in times of economic recession. But over and above the financial inducements there can be benefits for all concerned. For example, the DOE Report [35] has indicated that commercial outlets like pubs and clubs often do as much or more for the socially disadvantaged in the community as the local authority itself in terms of leisure participation.

4. Following local government reorganization, the speed with which new recreation departments came into existence meant that they were being founded on little that had been tried and tested. In addition many new recreation personnel were recruited, often without relevant experience and with little qualification in the field. To add to this situation an emerging 'profession' of recreation management was taking shallow root. Senior posts were being created and promotions made with rapid movement of personnel following. The situation has stabilized considerably but there is yet insufficient exchange of management information or management education and training *for those actually in the field*.

5. Complicating the whole recreation scene in local government is the confusing array of 'professional' bodies involved in the field of recreation. The Government Working Party on the Training for Recreation Management [37] has spent considerable time on studying these bodies and the roles they can play individually and collectively for recreation in the future. The disparate approaches to training, for example, lead to a lack of career structure and many other factors vital to recreation management.

1.11 SUMMARY: THE PROBLEMS AND OPPORTUNITIES FOR RECREATION AND LEISURE THROUGH THE PUBLIC SECTOR

In this chapter we have considered the scope of recreation provision within the public sector and the role of local government in particular.

Local authorities in England and Wales, despite not having to provide recreation facilities, do so as part of the service to the community. The impetus for improved facilities and management of recreation by local authorities is a cumulative result of a number of factors – the rise in the standard of living, more free time, greater mobility, higher education, plus the drive by leisure 'agencies' and the recognition of recreation by government as being important in its own right. In addition, local government reorganization, the introduction of corporate management, the acceptance by many authorities of the policy of dual use and joint provision and the birth of the community recreation movement, are all important features in the awakening and new enterprise to be found in many local authorities in the late 1960s and early 1970s.

1.11.1 The problems

The management of recreation at all levels is complicated by many inherent and some institutional constraints. In addition to the major constraining limitations on both borrowing and spending, ten key problem areas are highlighted below:

1. National and most local services are fragmented and there is often overlap between separate departments. While most local services have central government guidance or controls, some important services do not.
2. County councils and district councils have concurrent powers which lead to overlap and duplication and often result in political policy rifts.
3. Most powers relating to recreation are permissive and not mandatory in England and Wales, resulting in wide variations of provision and expenditure.
4. In overall planning terms recreation is still not regarded as a main priority; until it is, a comprehensive policy is unlikely to emerge.
5. In terms of management, many local authorities' aims are unclear and objectives are not measurable.
6. A number of styles and systems of management are adopted by local authorities, for example the same programmes can be free, highly subsidized, minimally subsidized or economic.
7. Corporate management has been recommended through government study groups but the practice still remains only partially im-

plemented across the country: recreation services have been enhanced where a chief officer is part of the management team.

8. New recreation departments, centres and facilities have been developed without, in many cases, the leadership of experienced and
trained recreation professionals.

9. The plethora of quasi-professional bodies, many with wide
operational experience, has reflected the split-image of recreation
management in the United Kingdom.

10. Local government, by its nature of public accountability and
bureaucratic systems, has been slow to adapt to changing demands;
the systems are inflexible compared with other systems of management.

Local authorities on the one hand are unsure of the role the commercial
sector can play in community recreation and find it hard to 'handle'
commercial enterprise; on the other hand they find it equally hard to
articulate with the socially disadvantaged through their recreation resources and formal programmes.

1.11.2   Recreation opportunities through local government

The problems relating to local government management of recreation
need to be balanced against the major recreation opportunities available
to and through local authorities.

Recreation and leisure services, while not subject to statutory direction,
is one of the areas in local government under *less* constraints from central
government. There is room to manoeuvre, flexible approaches are possible and the public is able to take a much greater share in the provision of
resources and opportunities to meet community demands and needs.

It has been shown that local authorities have considerable permissive
powers. They can act independently or in partnership; they can enable,
support and encourage self-help and initiative. Local authorities can
exercise such controls as they feel are appropriate to differing situations.
One of the local government's major 'powers' is the opportunity to help
people to help themselves and fashion part of their own destiny. They
equally have the power to help those who are unable to help themselves
and to provide various opportunities which would be denied the community without local authority assistance.

Hence, local authorities have many powers and opportunities to provide for community recreation. One role which local authorities can take
upon themselves is that of *coordination*. In all districts there are a whole
range of providers, with a wide range of services and facilities. There is a
need for coordination, support and enabling functions to be performed to
make the best possible use of the immense voluntary, commercial,

institutional and governmental services. This is the job for the local authorities in general and local councils in particular.

REFERENCES AND NOTES

1. Centre for Urban and Regional Studies (1981), *The Role of Central Government in relation to the provision of leisure services in England and Wales*, CURS Research Memorandum 86, prepared 1978, CURS, University of Birmingham.
2. Sports Council, *Annual Report 1980/81*, Sports Council, London.
3. Chartered Institute of Public Finance and Accountancy (1987), *Leisure and Recreation Statistics 1986/87 Estimates*, CIPFA, London.
4. Chartered Institute of Public Finance and Accountancy (1987), *Public Library Statistics 1986/87 Estimates*, CIPFA, London.
5. Central Statistical Office (1987), *Social Trends 1987*, Chapter 10, Leisure. HMSO, London.
6. Central Statistical Office (1987), *Social Trends 1987*, Chapter 4, Employment, HMSO, London.
7. Institute of Recreation Management (1981), *The Recreation Management Handbook*, 3rd edn. E. and F.N. Spon, London.
8. Molyneux, D.D. (1968), Working for Recreation, *Journal of Town Planning Institute*. Volume 54, No. 4 April, p.149–156.
9. The Report of the Wolfenden Committee on Sport (1960), *Sport and the Community*, Central Council of Physical Recreation, London.
10. Command 929, Ministry of Education (1960), *The Youth Service in England and Wales*: Report of the committee November 1958 (the Albemarle Report), HMSO, London. And read: Department of Education and Science (1969), *Youth and Community Work in the 70s*, HMSO, London.
11. Central Advisory Council for Education (England), (1967), *Children and their Primary Schools*, Volume 1: The Report, Volume 2: Research and Surveys, for Department of Education and Science, HMSO, London.
12. Department of Education and Science (1973), Circular 5/73: *Local Government Reorganization and the Public Library Service*, HMSO, London.
13. Command 2601, Department of Education and Science (1965), *Support for the Arts: the first steps*, HMSO, London.
14. Redcliffe-Maud, Lord (1977), *Local Authority Support for the Arts*, Gulbenkian Foundation, London.
15. Ministry of Housing and Local Government (1967), *Management of Local Government*: Volume I. Report of the Committee and Volume V; Local Government Administration in England and in Wales, HMSO, London.
16. Department of Education and Science and Ministry of Housing and Local Government (1964), Joint Circular 11/64 and 49/64 – *Provision of Facilities for Sport*, DES, London.
17. Ministry of Housing and Local Government (1966), Circular 31/66 – *Public Expenditure: Miscellaneous Schemes*, MHLG, London.
18. Department of Education and Science (1970), Circular 2/70 – *The Chance to Share*, DES, London.

19. *Report of the Royal Commission on Local Government in England 1966-1969: The Redcliffe-Maud Report* (1969), HMSO, London.
20. Command 4276 (1970), *Report of Local Government in England*, HMSO, London.
21. Command 4584 (1971), *Local Government in England: Government Proposals for Reorganisation*, HMSO, London.
22. Command 4583 (1971), *Report of Local Government in Scotland*, HMSO, London.
23. Welsh Office (1971), *The Reform of Local Government in Wales*, HMSO, London.
24. Study Group on Local Authority Management Structures (1972), *The New Local Authorities: Management and Structure – The Bains Report*, HMSO, London.
25. Seeley, I.H. (1978), *Local Government Explained*, Macmillan Press, London p. 153.
26. Ibid., p. 128.
27. Davies, H.M. and Halliwell, E. (1981), *Innovations in Leisure, a Sea Front Development*, Borough of Yarmouth.
28. Jones, G.W. (1973), The Functions and Organisation of Councillors, *Public Administration*, Volume 51.
29. Seeley, I.H. (1978), *Local Government Explained*, Macmillan Press, London.
30. Ibid., p. 67.
31. Veal, A.J. and Travis, A.S. (1979), *Local Government Studies*, **5,** No. 4, July/August.
32. Command 6200 (1975), *Sport and Recreation*, HMSO, London.
33. Veal, A.J. (1980), *Local Authorities and Leisure*, unpublished paper; University of Birmingham.
34. National Joint Council for Local Authorities, *Administrative, Professional, Technical and Clerical Services Handbook*, NJCLA, London.
35. Department of the Environment (1977), *Recreation and Deprivation in Inner Urban Areas*, HMSO, London.
36. Hillman, M. and Whalley, A. (1977), *Fair Play For All, A Study of Access to Sport and Informal Recreation*, Broadsheet No. 571, Political and Economic Planning, London.
37. Department of the Environment (1978), *Recreation Management Training Committee: Interim Report* (A Discussion Paper; Chairman Anne Yates), HMSO, London.

Chapter 2

Recreation provision and services in the voluntary sector

★

2.1 INTRODUCTION: VOLUNTARY PROVISION IN THE NON-PUBLIC SECTOR

Chapter 1 was concerned with the public sector. We now turn to aspects within the non-public sector.

The non-public sector is vast and complex and diversified. It exists in collaboration with the public sector and is often interlocked with it. Its history, evolution and influence on the British way of life is unique; its importance to the provision of opportunities for recreation is immense. In numerical terms, the non-public sector is dominated by *voluntary* bodies, which help to meet some of the needs of many millions of people.

This chapter is concerned with the voluntary sector. *First*, a brief sketch is made of the wide range and diversity of voluntary providers and their complex interrelationships. *Second*, the role of voluntary groups in society is considered and set against their historical background. *Third*, the importance of group and club belonging is shown because it has a crucial part to play in the management of groups of like-minded people in the recreation setting. *Fourth*, the different types of voluntary participation organizations and groups are shown which illustrate their individual and collective contributions to leisure opportunity.

Finally, two types of provider – charitable trusts and industrial sport and recreation clubs – are studied to understand their function and relevance to community recreation but, more important, to understand their approach to recreation management. It might appear incongruous to include industrial clubs in the voluntary sector. However, the clubs are invariably managed as private, non-profit making organizations, hence in terms of management they can be equated with the voluntary sector rather than with the commercial sector.

2.2 THE RANGE OF VOLUNTARY PROVIDERS

The resources, facilities and opportunities offered to people through the vast range of many thousands of voluntary bodies collectively represent a significant contribution to the field of recreation and leisure. Voluntary bodies vary greatly, from neighbourhood groups to national organizations. The voluntary sector is dominated by a vast array of leisure and recreation *clubs and associations*.

Sport is managed in large measure by local voluntary sporting clubs and associations, which are the backbone of sport in the United Kingdom. Governing bodies of sport are linked nationally by organizations such as the Central Council of Physical Recreation. The role of the Sports Council is to support sport and physical recreation groups at all levels, the vast majority being voluntary amateur groups.

Arts, community arts and cultural activities in their variety are largely catered for through local societies, associations and groups of many kinds. The regional arts associations themselves, while dependent on grant sources, are nevertheless voluntary bodies, supported by the Arts Council.

Informal outdoor recreation is encouraged through organizations such as the National Trust, Ramblers' Association, local walking and cycling and other clubs. Tourism is encouraged through voluntary organizations like the Youth Hostels Association.

General recreation and leisure are catered for by a large number of social, entertainment or multi-activity organizations. Consumer organizations protect interests particularly with leisure products. Women's Institutes, community associations, religious organizations, youth organizations and hundreds of others all go to make up the array of resources and opportunities for recreation and leisure participation. In nearly all cases, other than the conservation of buildings and lands, all these voluntary organizations are concerned with the interests of their members and users. They help to provide and manage leisure opportunity.

2.2.1 Private and institutional bodies

Private and institutional bodies such as landowners, employers, universities, schools, colleges and institutes make an important contribution to provision and services for recreation. Many firms provide social and sporting facilities. University extramural departments provide adult education classes. Many universities and colleges provide holiday residential courses, partly as a means of keeping residential accommodation and services open throughout the long vacations. The growth of the 'activity holiday' has been rapid in recent years. Private schools, like Millfield, have become famous for their 'schools of sport'. Private landowners also play a significant part in the provision for informal recreation. They own much of the rural land in the United Kingdom which is the setting for outdoor informal recreation. They also own and manage facilities for public recreation through historic houses, country parks and many of the great tourist attractions [1].

2.2.2 The overlap and interlock with other sectors

In many cases voluntary bodies are inextricably linked to public providers and public money. Charitable trusts are often partly sponsored by local authorities and, in some cases, wholly subsidized. Advisory and counselling services such as the Citizen's Advice Bureaux, while volunteer based, are funded almost entirely by local authorities. Local councils support and initiate many thousands of voluntary groups and projects and in many cases fund and staff them. The interlocking between many voluntary bodies and public authorities is part and parcel of the wide framework of public community services, including recreation.

Some voluntary organizations are also tied to commercial bodies. Many sporting institutions might perish without the financial backing and marketing skills of major commercial companies. At local level many clubs rely on the brewer's contribution or the room at the back of the pub.

Complicating the issue further is the problem of demarcation between what is commercial and what is private. Some private institutions and voluntary organizations adopt a style of management which in certain elements is wholly commercial. With some private landowners the earning of income is a major objective and therefore in terms of management they can be considered very similarly to commercial bodies. That situation is clear. However, in relation to voluntary clubs and public authorities the position is less clear.

The differences and similarities between commercially run public houses and some private members' clubs illustrate the point. In 1904 there were 90 000 public houses compared with only 6600 clubs licensed to sell alcohol to members. By 1946 there were 81 000 public houses and 17 000 clubs. In 1980 these figures were 73 000 and 30 000 respectively [2]. The method used by the Business Statistics Office to calculate members of pubs and clubs has changed since 1980, making more recent comparisons difficult. As the clubs are non-profit making, the 'profits' they do make can be directed towards additional services to members, including cheap beer. Some clubs also purchase beer from breweries at the lowest rates and are, therefore, able to achieve greater gross profit margins than some commercial operators. Furthermore, unlike pubs, clubs can house gaming machines yielding high jackpots, while pubs are restricted to relatively low winnings because by law they are primarily drinking establishments not entertainment and gambling establishments. Clubs may also pay lower rates for housing certain machines. Hence commercial management practice is not restricted to commercial business.

2.3 VOLUNTARY CLUBS AND ORGANIZATIONS IN HISTORICAL CONTEXT IN THE UNITED KINGDOM

Voluntary recreation and leisure groups have existed for centuries but not in the number and variety of relatively recently. In the 18th century the coffee-house was, for the 'gentlemen of leisure', a social group – a club in embryo. In 1708 there were 3000 coffee-houses, each with its 'habitual circle' [3]. They were in theory open to all, as many clubs are today, but often developed into clubs for specified groups, with restricted membership. In the United Kingdom today we find that many private and institutional bodies often confine the use of their facilities to certain types of activity and certain groups of people. They manage their affairs on a more *restricted* club basis. Most national governing bodies for sport were also formed from the creation of interest groups, of like-minded people. For example, the MCC (Marylebone Cricket Club), the founder of the game of cricket as it is played today, developed out of the White Conduit Club, which had been formed out of the earlier Star and Garter Club. Leisure interest groups like the Royal Horticultural Society date back to 1804 and animal societies such as the Royal Society for the Protection of Animals to 1824. The Cyclists' Touring Club was formed in 1878. Indeed 50% of the national voluntary leisure groups identified by the English Tourist Board have been in existence for over 50 years [4].

In early industrial Britain recreations were often communal affairs based on seasons, festivals and commemorative events. The sports, dances, processions and ceremonies were within the context of the whole community as they are in underdeveloped or simple societies today. It was the rationalization of work that led to a separate and identifiable sphere of social life [5]. Simultaneously, the first half of the 19th century saw the disappearance of 'old playgrounds' which were not replaced by anything new until the growth of clubs and provision for recreation by *voluntary* bodies later in the century. Unions, factories and schools established their own football clubs; YMCAs and the Sunday School movement created clubs for recreation. Clubs featured in the 18th and 19th centuries as important organizations in the recreative and social life of the community. The great expansion of clubs took place in the last quarter of the 19th century but this was not a long-term trend. According to Tomlinson [6], increased mass consumerism, delocalization of and amalgamation between organizations contributed to the levelling off of the development. For example, working mens' clubs developed through several stages from the last quarter of the 19th century. A stage of high patronage was followed by one of emancipation. 'In-house' entertainment and political life then ran hand in hand before social and economic aspects became dominant. But the most significant development has been the move towards professionally-based entertainment. The switch has produced a change in the membership participation from *producer to consumer* patterns. Despite these changes activities such as snooker and darts have continued and with television exposure have increased.

Many voluntary movements and associations arose out of the Depression as responses to social injustice. For example, the National Association of Women's Clubs arose in that way. Many were post Second World War outlets for wives of unemployed and for unemployed women themselves. With increasing unemployment in the 1980s one can only speculate as to whether 'free time' clubs and associations will be formed to meet newly 'created' needs.

2.4   LEISURE PARTICIPATION IN VOLUNTARY GROUPS

People go to extraordinary lengths and exhibit wide variations of behaviour in expressing their individual and collective needs in their leisure. People express themselves in all manner of participation groups, for example there are religious, community and welfare groups, men's, women's, old people's and young people's groups, advisory and counselling groups or para-medical and military groups. Some people join clubs and associations that are culturally uplifting or educational. Some join acting, ballroom, jazz, dancing, keep fit, slimming, singing, operatic or pop groups; others play sport in groups, sail the seas with yachting clubs and climb with mountaineering groups. Many groups identify themselves by wearing badges or special clothing; others have a uniform to create a new identity – a leisure identity.

2.4.1   The range of groupings

The range of groups is wide and diversified and no adequate classification has yet been made to cover all groups that exist. Several different types of grouping can, however, be identified. *Some* of them are listed in Table 2.1 but the overlaps are many, for example, many uniform groups are youth groups, many women's groups are welfare groups and so on. The list is by no means an attempt at a classification or taxonomy; it is simply a means of showing the range and diversity of voluntary leisure groupings.

The English Tourist Board [4] identified the membership of 211 national voluntary leisure groups with over 8 million members collectively of which 29% belong to youth groups, 27% to sports groups, 13% to conservation and heritage groups, 8% to touring groups, 7% to women's groups and 7% to animal or wildlife conservation groups. The National Trust is by far the biggest national organization with a membership of over 1 million – a rise of over 700% in 20 years. Well over 40% of the groups identified have memberships of over 5000. Over the long term (with exceptions such as some church, cycling, paramedical and women's groups) very few national groups have had a fall in membership. Even the British Cycle Federation and Cyclists' Touring Club have reversed the steep declines with increases of 45% and 68% respectively since 1970. The 1970s has seen a rise in the number of national leisure groups and many groups have doubled in membership. In addition to the national organizations there are many thousands of regional and local groups and societies, for example, 1000 local history societies.

Table 2.1 Range of voluntary organizations

Community organizations	Community associations, community councils
Community actions groups	National Council for Voluntary Organizations, Inner City Unit, Inter-Action Trust Limited, Gingerbread
Children's groups	Fair Play for All, Pre-School Playgroups Association, Toy Library Association
Youth organizations	Scout Association, Girl Guides' Association, National Council for YMCAs, National Association of Youth Clubs
Women's organizations	National Federation of Women's Institutes, National Union of Townswomen's Guilds, Mothers' Union, Women's Voluntary Service (WVS)
Men's groups	Working men's clubs, servicemen's clubs
Old people's groups	Darby and Joan Clubs, Senior Citizens
Disabled groups	Gardens for the Disabled, Disabled Drivers' Motor Club
Adventure organizations	Outward Bound Trust, Duke of Edinburgh's Award, National Caving Association
Outdoor activity organizations and touring groups	Camping Club of Great Britain and Ireland, Youth Hostels Association, Central Council of British Naturism, Ramblers' Association, British Caravanners' Club
Sport and physical recreation organizations	Keep Fit Association, British Octopush Association, National Skating Association of Great Britain, Cycle Speedway Council, GB Wheelchair Basketball League
'Cultural' and entertainment organizations	British Theatre Association, Museums Association, English Folk Dance and Song Society, British Federation of Music Festivals
Educational organizations	National Institute of Adult Education, Workers Educational Association, National Listening Library
Hobbies and interest groups	National Association of Flower Arranging Societies, Citizens Band Association, Antique Collectors Club, Handicrafts Advisory Association for the Disabled, British Beer Mat Collectors' Society
Animals and pet groups	Pony Club, Cats Protection League

Environmental, conservation and heritage groups	National Trust, Friends of the Earth, Royal Society for the Protection of Birds, Keep Britain Tidy Group, Save the Village Pond Campaign, Rare Breed Society
Consumer groups	Consumers' Association, Campaign for Real Ale (CAMRA)
Counselling organizations	British Association for Counselling, Citizens Advice Bureau, Alcoholics Anonymous, Marriage Guidance Councils, Samaritans Incorporated
Philanthropic groups	Rotary International in Great Britain and Ireland, Inner Wheel, Variety Club of Great Britain, Golddiggers
Paramedical organizations	British Red Cross Society, St. John Ambulance Brigade
Uniform groups	Voluntary Reserves, TA, Sea and Army Cadets, Air Training Corps
Religious groups	Methodist Church Division of Social Responsibility, Church Army, Church of England Children's Society
Political groups	Political parties, trade unions

2.4.2   National organizations for young people

National organizations for young people make a considerable contribution to the youth movement. Most of the national organizations are based on beliefs, faith or commitment to a cause. The YMCA/YWCAs, for example, offer philosophies of life as well as outlets for recreation and leisure pursuits. The nature of the belief or the cause is usually universal, such as 'the brotherhood of man', therefore, these organizations tend to be both national and international. The Scout and Guide Movement continues to have a large membership with 1.3 million members in the UK collectively [7]. Many youth groups are 'uniform groups' such as the Boys' Brigade but the non-uniform participation groups have grown in recent years. Compared with 1961 twice as many young people participate in the Duke of Edinburgh's Award Scheme – 159 000 in 1983. The Community Service Volunteers programme for deploying previously unemployed young people has extended rapidly with a rise in weeks of full-term service from 8100 in 1978, 22 700 in 1979, 34 200 in 1980 and 44 000 in 1983 [72].

Most youth organizations depend on adult volunteers. In 1983 the Scout Association had 90 000 adult uniformed leaders, and the Girl Guides Association over 78 000 leaders and helpers. The National Association of Youth Clubs had 28 000 voluntary workers and the Duke of Edinburgh's Award Scheme 43 000 organizers, leaders, instructors, assessors and helpers, the great majority in a voluntary capacity [7].

Leisure participation, therefore, is not just the participating in an activity but, in these cases, the giving of service. Indeed millions of people in Britain and all over the world participate in voluntary groups which give service to others.

2.4.3 National women's organizations

There are a very large number of women's groups. The two major national bodies are the National Association of Women's Clubs and the National Association of Women's Groups; their membership has been falling over many years. These bodies, however, are significant in terms of numbers when compared with the Women's Institute, the Townswomen's Guild and the Mother's Union. The National Federation of Women's Institutes claimed to have a membership of 385 000 in 1980 and 355 000 in 1983 compared with 440 000 in 1971. The National Union of Townswomen's Guilds had a membership of 180 000 in 1980 and 160 000 in 1983 compared with 216 000 in 1971 [7,8]. Even with these major associations there has been a slow, but long-term, decline in membership.

2.4.4 Sports groups and associations

To the layman a 'recreation' group is synonymous with a sports group – a sports club. The sports club and associations have been the means by which millions of people take part in leisure pursuits. Sport can no longer be considered as a minority activity in the United Kingdom. Martin and Mason [9] estimate that some 30 million people take part in sport of some kind fairly regularly. But sport is spread over a very large number of activities.

120 national sporting associations are listed in *The Recreation Management Handbook* (3rd edn) [10] which represents many thousands of clubs. In addition there are multi-sport clubs and associations, associations for sport for the disabled, sports medicine and sports science organizations and over 100 international associations connected with the sports 'scene' in Britain. The single-sport club still remains, however, the group to which the majority of organized sportsmen and women are affiliated. The sports club is the primary interest group. Because of the wide variety of sport most individual sports have well below one million participants.

The results of the *General Household Survey, 1983* [11] indicate that participants in sports do not represent a cross-section of the UK population. They are younger than average and a very high proportion are men.

Non-manual groups are generally the most active and the top income group is the most active in most of the sports. Many sports, however, differ from the general profile.

The numbers taking part in sport have been rising rapidly particularly over the past few years. Racket sports, keep fit and indoor sports, have risen the most. Excluding walking, the most popular activities in outdoor sports are: Swimming in the sea (3%), football (2.8%), golf (2.4%), athletics (1.9%) and angling (1.8%). All the rest involve less than 1.5% of the population. The most popular indoor sports are: billiards/snooker (8.0%), darts (7.2%), swimming (7.0%), keep fit/yoga (3.2%), squash/fives (2.4%) and badminton (2.0%).

Darts and billiards are largely pub games and both have recently come to be featured on television, which could explain some of their popularity. These sports are male dominated; if the figures are looked at by gender, then it is found that 15% of *men* play billiards/snooker. It should be borne in mind also that the figures represent people aged 16 years and over. It is generally accepted, for example, that as many as 75% of swimmers are under 16. There were only two sports activities in the list in the *General Household Survey, 1983* [11] in which women were more active than men, namely horse-riding and keep fit/yoga. Many activities could be described as mixed, but a large number were mostly or primarily male dominated.

Many of the most popular activities are *individual* rather than group orientated. However, with exceptions such as walking and swimming, increases in participation (such as angling) lead to more club members and more clubs and associations, i.e. the growth of clubs reflects the increase in numbers. Taking as an example outdoor informal and countryside recreation, we find that the Camping Club of Great Britain and Ireland increased from 110 000 members to 174 000 members between 1970 and 1984. Membership of the Royal Society for the Protection of Birds grew from 98 000 in 1971 to 470 000 in 1983 [12]. The *National Angling Survey 1980* estimated that there were 3.7 million anglers aged 12 and over in Great Britain and that two-thirds were aged under 35 [8].

2.4.5   Arts, community arts and cultural groups

Another area of voluntary groups in leisure is encompassed in the modest, all-embracing word 'art' and the misnomer 'cultural activities' as though everything else in the leisure field is uncultured! (The very image of something 'cultural' can act as a barrier to many groups in the community.) Voluntary groups within the field cover art, music, drama, amateur operatics, crafts, a whole host of creative outlets and all the activities which go under the title of 'community arts'. The British Theatre Association estimates the total number of amateur dramatic groups in

Britain at 20 000. Many groups within the category of 'arts' are capable of outstanding achievements in helping themselves, and some societies can assume great prominence within communities.

There has been some movement within community arts towards the encouragement of ethnic arts and some revivalism. Khan [13] has identified the needs and problems of many ethnic arts groups. Some revivalism is shown in the resurgence of folk clubs, morris dancing and similar heritage arts and there was a new festival spirit in the 1970s which produced over 100 major new festivals.

Community arts, it is claimed, can reaffirm the 'natural role of our culture in society', and can be used as 'social cement' to hold people together within communities [14]. Studies of community arts can show, however, just how little community response there very often is. Nonetheless, community arts can take on a much wider interpretation and many voluntary organizations involve some members of the community at the 'street' level, who may never have participated.

The comparison of participation with frequency rankings in the *General Household Survey, 1983* shows the effect of *regular commitment* to activities such as music, drama and adult classes, which, although practised by only small minorities, achieve much higher rankings on the frequency scale than on the participation scale. Amateur music and drama achieve the highest frequency rates compared with all other entertainment and cultural pursuits. The lesson for Recreation Managers is that some people wish to commit themselves to a leisure pursuit and take part in it both *frequently* and *regularly* and this should be borne in mind in programming plans.

2.4.6 Religious groups

One of the major 'leisure' time occupations for millions of people is concerned with religious observance, church-going and its associated activities. The church has been and still remains a foundation for a great number and variety of leisure time organizations. Although the church has tended to emphasize the work ethic, as an institution it has in large measure been related to the free time of the majority of church-going people. The strict observance of some religions such as Islam require participation which breaks into traditional work times; nonetheless, religious institutions are largely leisure time institutions.

In the Christian church the word holiday stems from the celebration of a holy day. Until the Reformation in England, peasants enjoyed eight weeks holiday as part of the church calendar of 'special' events. Today the Christian churches in the United Kingdom are giving far more attention to the uses and abuses of leisure particularly relating to the aspects of coping with involuntary free time. For example, the Methodist Church

Division of Social Responsibility has published its position on 'leisure and the Church' [15]. One of its ministers has also written extensively on the subject. In *Looking at Leisure*, David Bridge [16] expresses the church's dilemma:

'Despite the fact that the Church is a spare-time activity for almost everyone except its paid servants, the idea that the church should play a positive role in the world of leisure seems incongruous. Chaplains are appointed to industry and the move is greeted as enlightened and progressive. The chaplain to a football club, however, is greeted with amusement and the assumption that it is all part of a scheme to get a free season ticket. All the chaplain to a night club receives is a sly grin and a dig in the ribs'.

Altogether there were 51 000 Christian churches in the United Kingdom in 1980 – only slightly fewer than the number in 1975. The UK Christian Handbook [12] estimates that there will be some 7.3 million (mainly adult) church members from all Protestant, Roman Catholic and Orthodox churches in the United Kingdom by the end of 1985 but church membership (16% of the population) will continue to decline and church attendance will remain far lower than the membership figures suggest. However, there has been a substantial increase in the smaller denominations such as the Independent and African and West Indian Protestant churches. The significance of religious participation is possibly much stronger with many of the minority groups in the United Kingdom. The hundreds of temples, mosques and synagogues and the increase in, and wide variety of, new 'fringe' religions indicates how important beliefs and causes are to people's use of their leisure.

Hence, there is a wide variation in 'participation', from little parish church communities of a handful of people to congregations of hundreds and thousands. An example of the latter is in the USA. The Crystal Cathedral in California was built at a cost of £8 million. The cathedral is a 'drive-in sanctuary'. It is bigger than Notre Dame, 13 storeys high, heated by solar power and equipped with the latest in television and sound facilities. It holds 4000 people and the structure can be seen from outer space as a four-pointed star. Instead of saying 'amen', the congregation are encouraged to honk their horns! Such is the diversity within Christianity, let alone between the many religions and faiths which are practised. Religious observance remains a major outlet and influence on man and his leisure time.

2.4.7 Community, welfare and charitable groups

Voluntary organizations concerned with community welfare often create opportunities which would not otherwise have existed. They have been formed to meet particular social or other problems. Tenants associations and housing associations have been formed to meet social problems; parent/teacher associations have been formed to forge links between school, parent and community. Where gaps exist in the public institutional framework and *where people become isolated*, special groups are often formed. The pre-school play groups, for example, are concerned with children and their development. They group together and take voluntary actions which can result in play schemes, play buses, adventure playgrounds, social meeting places and opportunities for parents and workers as well as for the children. The mothers of the hundreds of thousands of pre-school children possibly get as much fulfilment from the organization as do the children themselves.

The General Household Survey, 1981 suggested that about 10% of the adult population participate in social and voluntary work. The National Council for Voluntary Organizations [17] estimates that at least six million people in the United Kingdom help the work of charities and voluntary organizations. The British Red Cross had 114 000 members in 1980 and 105 000 in 1983 and the St. John Ambulance Brigade 79 000 in 1980 and 77 000 in 1983. In contrast with the decline in paramedical groups, organizations like the National Association of Leagues of Hospital Friends were on the increase with 466 000 members in 1979 and 475 000 in 1980. The next three years, however, saw a reversal of this trend with membership standing at 450 000 at the end of 1983 [7].

Much voluntary work is carried out in connection with charities. Just under 4000 new charities were registered in 1983 and by the end of that year there were nearly 147 000 charities on the register, an increase of around 13 000 since 1979. Most major charities (those with income over £4 million in a year) are concerned with human social causes. According to the Charities Aid Foundation, the total income of the top 200 grant seeking charities in 1983/84 was nearly £820 million [7]. Dr Barnardo's, the Salvation Army and Oxfam raised £32.4 million, £31 million and £19.7 million respectively in 1983/84. Yet leisure charities also exist. Indeed, the National Trust raised and spent more than any other charity in 1983 – £48.1 million income and £40.6 million expenditure [7].

During the 1970s a network of advisory, counselling and consumer services grew up. There are over 1500 advice centres, including 973 Citizens' Advice Bureaux. Other counselling services such as Alcoholics Anonymous, Samaritans Incorporated and Marriage Guidance Councils have also increased, the former threefold in the past decade.

Hence, voluntary organizations and charities have had an important part to play in the life and leisure of people. They have a history of pioneering work in meeting people's needs. They enable thousands of people to *give service to others*. While government provides the benefits of a welfare state in the United Kingdom and commercial operators provide for leisure time enjoyment for millions of people, hundreds of charities provide many vital services in meeting some of the needs of many needy people and causes.

The National Council for Voluntary Organizations (NCVO) was founded in 1919 as the National Council of Social Service and on April 1 1980 became the NCVO. Its aims are 'to extend the involvement of voluntary organizations in responding to social issues, to be a resource centre for voluntary organizations and to protect the interests and independence of voluntary organizations'. [17] NCVO works with 143 local councils for voluntary service, 37 rural community councils, community associations and a wide range of other voluntary and community groups. In its 1984/ 85 Annual Report it lists a membership of 439 national voluntary organizations and many professional associations and public bodies including government departments and associations of district, country and metropolitan authorities. However, NCVOs membership is not fully representative of the range of the voluntary sector as it admits and is taking steps to remedy. What is of interest to recreation managers is that NCVO believes strongly that *all voluntary organizations need management skills if they are to be effective* and it has embarked on a series of management development and training courses.

The lesson for the Recreation Manager is that millions of people wish to give service to others in their leisure time. Opportunities should be provided for them to do so.

2.4.8 Community group action: adventure playgrounds

An example of community group action arising out of the felt needs of parents and community workers and national organizations is that of the development of adventure playgrounds. The adventure playground movement serves as an example of community action through a voluntary organization. Adventure playgrounds were first developed before the Second World War in Copenhagen. 'Adventure playground' is the term used to describe a playground – always with leadership – on which the free expression of children's development is encouraged by the provision, not so much of equipment, as of materials which can be used for a wide range of activities.

Such activities include building huts, walls, forts, tree climbing, digging, camping, team and group games, cultural and creative activities and voluntary service such as the cutting of firewood, decorating, shopping and housework for the elderly and disabled. The sphere of operations can be, and usually is, far wider than the boundary limits of the playground.

In their early days in Great Britain the idea of a playground which appeared an untidy mess, disorderly and noisy, with children using hammers, axes, nails, chisels and lighting fires was repellent to the minds of some local authorities whose elected representatives may have grown up in the tradition of orderly parks and open spaces and 'keep off the grass' and supervised team games. However, resourceful pioneers formed themselves into the Adventure Playgrounds Association, registered themselves as a charity, negotiated with local authorities over such matters as land acquisition and were able to appeal for funds. Today in London alone there are 40 adventure playgrounds, five specializing in adventure play for handicapped children.

The Recreation Manager has an important role in helping groups of people to negotiate with public bodies, planners, architects and other organizations. Supporting groups, by helping them to run their own projects, may be more important than providing projects 'on a plate'.

2.5 THE ROLE OF VOLUNTARY GROUPS IN SOCIETY

It is clear from the range and growing variety of leisure groups that such participative behaviour is important to people. What is the role of the voluntary group?

Life in modern Western civilization is more complex than life in underdeveloped or simple societies. Voluntary groups have, therefore, to play a far greater role in modern society [6]. In simple societies there can be no real voluntary association or club-life, whereas in advanced society there exist numerous small-scale associations catering for varying numbers of individuals. In modern society people can behave *both as individuals and collectively within groups*. Leisure has importance in that it has potential for both individual and group expression. Individuals can *choose* their group identity.

One of the motivations for corporate action in the recreation and leisure field is often that individuals and groups of people find themselves *isolated* and cut off from opportunity and support. This accounts for the growth in pre-school playgroups during the 1960s and 1970s according to the Voluntary Organisations Research Unit [18]. Voluntary groupings are initiated at a grass-roots level. They usually start with people's felt needs, demands, wishes or inclinations. They are *voluntary*. They might become involuntary, according to Tomlinson [6] in either of two ways – by becoming commercialized and turning into entrepreneurial bodies, or by turning inwards and becoming secret societies.

In terms of the management of community recreation the primary interest groups should feature strongly in any comprehensive community programme. People want to retain their individuality, yet many people want to *belong* to groups. The Recreation Manager has the dilemma in planning and programming the extent to which provision should be made for group interests. Understanding group belonging and group behaviour (covered in Chapter 13 on management) will assist the manager in coming to terms with the problem.

2.5.1   Similarities and differences between clubs and associations

At first glance clubs appear to be decidedly different. A ladies' darts club meeting in the local pub might appear very dissimilar to the ladies' choral club meeting in the church hall. Hutson]19] has shown, however, that there are many basic similarities between all forms of clubs and voluntary associations. There are similarities in patterns of activity and the ways in which clubs develop and decline. She has shown how organizers tend to form a distinct closely connected elite within a town or region. Social class, life cycle, physical mobility, kinship and sex roles affect both patterns of attendance and leadership. Voluntary associations tend to reflect 'the economic and social milieu' and tend to be dominated by a group of people of similar type. This leads to a proliferation of many small groups. Hutson claims that:

'. . . clubs and voluntary associations are a mark of "postcommunity" society which has a predominance of single interest relationships. They are felt to create a sense of community at a time when other ties between people living in the same area are weakening. The importance of clubs will also increase as leisure time in all phases of life expands'.

Researching in two communities in the Swansea district Hutson found that associations tended to be dominated by middle class *or* working class, newcomer *or* long term resident, young *or* old, 'chapel people' *or* others, people from the council estate *or* people from private houses. Like-minded people tended to gather together and form associations. Recruitment was normally along lines of friendship or kinship. Most clubs are social clubs whether the primary activity is social or not. People who are felt 'not to belong' to the predominant group were often kept out through formal procedures. Young people were kept out of many organizations because meetings were held in pubs or in public buildings where deeds or constitutions prohibited them. In the areas studied there were often internal political pressures and several examples of cliques leaving a club as another clique took over. These may be some of the reasons why newcomers, if they are in any numbers, tend to set up their own associations rather than join existing groups. Hutson found that while youth clubs were more socially mixed, and some associations *claimed* to draw members from all social categories, most clubs did not.

2.5.2   Group belonging and recreation management

Study of the differences and similarities of clubs and associations reveals four important factors for the Recreation Manager to consider:

1. All the clubs tend to be, at least, partially *exclusive*. Many clubs, theoretically open to all in principle, have been able to 'guarantee' their exclusiveness with membership systems, invitations by friends or family, subscription rates, conformity to rules and regulations and many other subtle social factors and social filters. (These factors are considered in a later chapter.)

2. Clubs are not static but changing organizations. Clubs are often small, autonomous groups, with close bonds, friendship ties and a strong sense of belonging to something which is theirs. Factions, cliques, committee disagreements, manoeuvring for positions, concern with self-interest and standing on 'principles' all go to make up the club scene. Disagreement with one committee may lead to the fall of the organization or the growth of a rival organization. The Wolfenden Committee Report (1978) on voluntary associations [20] found that, 'New organisations are formed to meet newly discerned needs, others die. Yet others change their emphasis or venture into fresh fields . . . There is nothing static about the scene'. The Recreation Manager should bear in mind, therefore, that new clubs, in particular, are likely to change in membership and will have different leadership patterns within the first few years. Shorter term initial bookings of facilities and flexible and supporting management roles may need to be given.

3. Clubs display similarities in behaviour: they are *social groupings*. Clubs vary in their activities, their apparent interests and in their *raison d'être* but whatever their objective, most associations function as a meeting place for like-minded people. Even single-interest groups, e.g. a dance club or netball club, run many events unconnected with their primary activity and these are usually *social* events such as dances and discos, children's parties, floats in carnivals, money raising events and so on. Sports clubs can be seen in some senses as less exclusive than some other clubs but just like other leisure groupings sport generates separate groups and activities for different social categories. The Queen's Lawn Tennis Club will attract a very different clientèle from the club affiliated to the local community sports centre or park. Recreation Managers must not, therefore, neglect the important social and meeting aspects of group leisure participation.

4. Clubs are dependent on support services such as premises. They meet in private houses, pubs, hotels, church halls, community halls or public buildings. Local authorities, commercial bodies and all the institutions who have premises and administrations can be important enablers in providing support services and premises. The local authority's *coordinating role* plays an important part in this respect.

2.5.3 New leisure identities

One of the characteristics of leisure time participation is that a considerable proportion of people take on new roles, new leisure roles. They are no longer factory worker, bank clerk or housewife. They become leader, coach, club chairman, golfer, sailor, official, youth worker, lay preacher or sergeant-major. In some cases the adoption of new identities is intensified by the wearing of the uniform. The uniform is the symbol of the organization; it gives identity, image – *it stands for something*, a belief in what we are doing.

The taking on of new roles in leisure time is an interesting phenomenon and may be significant. There is commitment, purposefulness and responsibility. Are these meaningful roles absent from other aspects of everyday life? What does it tell us about having clearly defined group norms and cultures?

2.6 SUMMARY: THE VOLUNTARY PROVIDERS OF LEISURE AND RECREATION OPPORTUNITIES

This part of the chapter has considered the vast range and scope of the voluntary providers of leisure and recreation. The range includes private and institutional bodies, landowners, associations, charities, clubs and all manner of groups. The overlap and interlock with both public and commercial organizations is substantial in some areas. In historical context, the voluntary provider has always been important to the recreation field, indeed the most important until recent decades. Voluntary groupings can be classified in a number of ways. We have considered groupings of young people, women, sports groups, arts groups, religious groups, community welfare groups and others. The role of the voluntary groups in advanced societies is increasingly important. People can behave as unique individuals but also may choose to belong to groups.

The range and diversity of voluntary leisure groupings, the motivations of people and the apparent need to belong and to participate with others, are significant factors in the management of leisure and recreation and as such should be studied by recreational professionals. Clubs offer individuals a group identity. Inter-club competition and rivalries reinforce the identity and sense of belonging. Membership can confer status, offer purposeful activity and a sense of importance. Do voluntary organizations hold one of the keys to personal self-fulfilment?

2.7 RECREATION TRUSTS: A VOLUNTARY/PUBLIC MANAGEMENT SYSTEM

At the start of this chapter reference was made to the interrelationships between local authorities and voluntary bodies. Local authorities can have an influence on the provision made by other organizations, for example, through planning powers, or through joint planning or through cooperating with other organizations in the provision of facilities. One such mechanism of cooperation is the *charitable trust*.

The recreation trust system of management is a hybrid. It is normally conceived as private, independent initiative, but it normally needs financial assistance from statutory sources in the form of grants and loans in order for it to survive and prosper, particularly in regard to community recreation. The trust is an administrative system for coordinating and managing facilities as a charity. Its formation involves legal formalities, bearing in mind that any such trust must be for the benefit of the public at large.

The establishment of a trust, whether by, or in association with, a local authority, has the advantage that the projects initiated by it become eligible for grant aid for capital expenditure from sources not normally open to a local authority. This not only lessens the burden on the rates, but also as a voluntary organization with charitable status a trust is entitled to 50% mandatory relief from rates and also to any discretionary relief which the rating authority might decide to allow. They can be linked to supporters' clubs, lotteries, fund raising and other schemes. It would, however, be a mistake to think that the link with the local authority will always be wholly advantageous. At times of financial stringency there could be withdrawal of official support, and as elected representatives change over the years, there is a risk that support may be reduced or even withdrawn altogether.

2.7.1 The trust and the communities

Apart from the financial benefits, there is the advantage that the local community helps to share the responsibility for the provision and management of its recreational facilities, instead of having them provided and managed solely by a local authority and financed entirely from rates. Many local authorities welcome joint committees, even when they (the local authorities) have provided all the finance. There is no reason why this should not be the case. The ideal trust should prove a flexible administrative instrument and one which might well command more support and interest from a local community than if it were purely a local authority responsibility. On the other hand the project should in the long run benefit from the stability, continuity and financial resources of the local authority.

In relating the trust system to the provision of facilities it must be realized that there are many ways of developing and managing facilities. Much will depend on the local circumstances, the underlying philosophy on which the scheme is based and on the objectives of the proposed project. It is not inferred that one method of management is better than another or that there is a best solution; each method may be the right management in the particular circumstances. However, the trust system works successfully in many artistic, historic and sporting projects. For example, the start of the community recreation centre movement began at Harlow in 1960 by means of a sports trust. It must, of course, be seen against a background of a rapidly developing town with immense resources of potential leadership from industry, education, local government and the professions. In addition, Harlow Sportcentre was a pioneering scheme started at a time when authorities had not seen the potential of the community recreation centre. The Harlow Arts Trust established some years later is controlled almost entirely by the local authority and a recent innovation – the Harlow Recreation Trust – was conceived and is managed by the council as a means of continuing the expansion of community recreation in times of recession.

2.7.2   Trust system advantages and disadvantages

The trust system has both advantages and disadvantages. In summary some of these are:

(a)   Advantages
1. Direct access by senior management officers to executive control, cutting down some levels of bureaucracy and streamlining decision-making.
2. The trust system is flexible. The governing body can be built up on a widely representative basis to include all appropriate authorities, industry, commerce and local community.
3. It represents partnership between statutory and voluntary organizations.
4. It is eligible for grant aid and savings on the rates.
5. As a voluntary enterprise it can encourage a strong spirit of community endeavour. As such it may have to raise substantial local funds for capital and maintenance. Members of *some* trusts feel in some way that it is their own, and they have partly to pay for it and look after it. Many paid staff too can feel a greater sense of personal commitment.
6. This spirit of voluntary enterprise can produce economies in operation.
7. Its great strength could be in its contribution to the future. Being flexible and free from too many ties with authorities, the system lends itself to experimentation, new ideas and pioneer projects. Many of the facilities built and ideas formulated as trust projects have been tried and built upon successfully elsewhere.

8. As a voluntary self-governing project, it encourages leaders in commerce, industry, the professions and the community to want to be associated with it.
9. Being a non-political body the trust can establish a system of key-member stability and can build upon the experience gained by executive members over years of development. Local authority projects may well suffer from changes of either personnel or party political representatives more often that is good for the project.

(b) Disadvantages

1. There are usually insufficient capital resources. Often many savings have to be made, particularly in ancillary accommodation, which some local authorities may not be able to make.
2. There are insufficient operational resources. If a comprehensive programme is to be given, the need may exist for guaranteed local authority financial assistance. This becomes even more imperative where, for example, swimming facilities or a theatre exist or where a social service is seen as the highest priority. A voluntary body, although it may be giving a much needed community service, can often be at the mercy of local and county councils, needing to approach them 'cap in hand' for assistance.
3. Trusts constantly need to raise large sums of money from their own resources.
4. Often there are too few staff, many giving service beyond the 'call of duty'. Without the immense backing of a large authority the work load is heavy on such staff.
5. Members of the public in many urban areas have become used to the idea of having good recreation facilities. Many may not care or even know that a theatre or sports centre is being run by a trust. To the public it is a public facility.
6. Trust executives of a small governing body carry a heavy burden of responsibility.

2.7.3 Summary and lessons for management: trust systems

Projects are often well managed where authority lies in a small, strong, high calibre, independent committee, with wide terms of reference and complete control of day-to-day management. This may be easier to achieve in the recreation trust but there is no reason why a local authority project should not be run in such a way. However, it is important that the committee is independent, has strong powers and is not constantly blown by the course of political persuasion.

A voluntary organization has considerable assets. It can forge ahead through its own enthusiasm and initiative. It is free to experiment; it encourages community and commercial support; it saves the ratepayers money *but* it needs support and encouragement from authorities in the way of subsidy, grants, technical advice and help towards capital development and running costs.

The day of community service having to beg for financial assistance should end and it can do so if local authorities and voluntary organizations collaborate from the beginning, and set a constitution and framework where both are partners. It is of interest to observe that in the 1980s with local authority cutbacks and constraints on both borrowing *and* spending local authorities themselves were setting up fund raising recreational trusts.

The trust system can be the bridge between voluntary bodies and statutory authorities; *it represents partnership*. There is precious little land, money or resources available for organizations and authorities to continue to pay and develop recreational facilities themselves without the widest consultation, cooperation and coordination.

2.8   INDUSTRIAL RECREATION PROVISION

The last area within the voluntary sector to be looked at is industrial recreation. It may seem incongruous to consider industrial provision within this sector and not within the commercial sector. However, industrial recreation by and large is the provision of private facilities, ostensibly not provided for commercial gain, but for the workforce as private individuals. It is conceded at the outset that a happy workforce may achieve greater efficiency and output and thereby greater profits, but in terms of management, industrial provision is more akin to the private members' club than to the commercial enterprise. This section, therefore, does not look into the sociological relationship between work and leisure but rather gives the background to industrial recreation and seeks answers to the role of industry as providers of community recreation and its management.

2.8.1   History and development of industrial sports and social clubs

The development of the industrial sports and social club in the latter part of the 19th century has often been attributed to the philanthropic motives of benevolent and paternalistic employers, influenced by religious and humanitarian ideals. However, underlying this, more practically-orientated motives may have been at work, and certainly the development of industrial recreation into and through the 20th century is unlikely to be attributable solely to the altruistic behaviour of the employer.

A number of factors have been put foward as being influential in, or motivating the decision by an employer to contribute large capital and recurrent expenditure towards the provision, maintenance and management of facilities for the recreational benefit of the employees. Six influencing factors can be identified:

Philanthropy This factor – the employer's basic concern for the welfare and quality of life of his workers – though unlikely to have been the pervasive influence throughout the development of industrial sports and social clubs, cannot be cynically dismissed, particularly with regard to their early development.

Fitness for work The need for a physically and psychologically fit workforce to maximize production, may be seen as justification for the provision of recreation facilities and opportunities for employees. British industry has not yet extended this concept to the degree that countries on the Continent have, where work sessions are interspersed with exercise sessions, labelled 'break-gymnastics' or 'work bench callisthenics', accompanied by some claims of up to 25% improvement in production [21].

Reduction in staff turnover The cost of training new staff can be high and consequently a return on investment in terms of employee stability and loyalty may be required. The provision of recreation facilities for the employee may encourage such loyalty and stability.

Company image By concerning itself with the welfare of its employees a company can promote a benevolent image which may (depending on the nature of the company) be beneficial to its trading function. It may also be influential in attracting quality workers into its ranks.

Company prestige To a large extent this is related to the company's image. There may be a need to emulate other companies which *have* made provision for their employees for both prestigious reasons and to compete on equal terms in the labour market.

Employee pressure Employee pressure may be brought to bear on an employer for the company to provide facilities for a newly formed social club or football club, particularly in a situation where the company is setting up in a new area, and its employees have an interest in organizing such activities.

The provision of company services and facilities is likely to have been influenced by a combination of these and other specific factors, not all of which will have been relevant at any one time.

Whatever the motivation, the beginnings of industrial recreation provision started in the 19th century, with the founding of Pilkington's Recreation Club in 1847. The growth of company clubs in the latter part of the 19th century and the early part of the 20th century was evident with the early days being dominated by such pioneers as Pilkington, Cadbury and Rowntree, the latter expanding beyond provision for purely physical recreation to include clubs for painting, dancing, drama and photography.

Following the 1914–18 war many industrial clubs sprang up, often associated with religious and welfare organizations. However, the Depression caused a decline in the number of clubs owing to the closure of companies and impetus was only once again regained after the Second World War. During the war British personnel gained first-hand experience of recreation provision in the USA, Canada, Australia, South Africa and other countries, and participated in a range of sports that were normally beyond their experience. On returning to civilian life this experience proved influential in expanding the range and scope of activities offered by industrial clubs.

However, both Cullen [21] and Parker [22] reported a decline in the movement in the 1960s with some of the smaller companies being unable to sustain an acceptable level of interest among their employees, and consequently selling or using the facility's land for building development, and this is still partially the case. But the picture is a far from clear one. Cullen's 1979/80 industrial recreation survey [23] revealed that twice as many clubs were formed in the 1970s as disbanded and these new clubs were 'by no means' connected solely with large companies (more than 1000 employees); few companies had disposed of recreation sites and relatively few clubs reported a decrease in interest. In Cullen's survey practically all respondents either wholly or partly agreed with the statement:

'Almost irrespective of the level of employee interest in company sports and social clubs, these clubs and their facilities are now looked upon by company employees as a normal 'fringe/welfare benefit' – a sort of background benefit which is always available to the employee, whether or not he or she actively uses the club and its facilities.'

From this survey there appears to be considerable confidence in industry and commerce that industrial recreation clubs will continue to make a significant contribution to the total provision for recreation in the next decades.

2.8.2 Industrial recreation today

It is impossible to make an accurate estimate of the number of industrial sports and social clubs in England and Wales, let alone guess the numbers in the United Kingdom, Europe and elsewhere. Even basic statistical data is sometimes contradictory. Cullen confirms this picture: 'in the past 15 years estimates made by various authoritative bodies concerning the number of industrial sports and social clubs in existence in England and Wales have ranged between 1000 and about 25 000!'[23] In addition, the types of clubs vary enormously, from industrial 'giants' to small local manufacturers; the programmes vary from a few activity sections to as many as 30 activity sections in a club and there are considerable differences in funding.

The *type and size* of the company appear to have a bearing on provision for with its greater financial and physical resources a firm with 2000/3000 or more employees can offer a wider range of activities and opportunities. Despite the suggested decline in provision among the majority of firms (those with less than 1000/2000 employees) it would seem that industrial recreation amongst the larger companies is still in a healthy state.

The Shell Lensbury Club, for example, has four sites – 40 acres in Teddington, a boathouse in Putney, facilities at Shell-Mex House and the Shell Centre in Waterloo. It employs 180 staff. The Shell Centre has squash courts, a theatre/cinema, rifle range, indoor swimming pool and large sports hall. With a captive membership of 13 200 the centre is managed as a very large private sports centre.

The goals of industrial clubs may vary, but in general clubs appear to aim at providing recreation opportunities for their company work-force. It is strange, therefore, bearing in mind the preponderance of working-class employees, particularly in manufacturing industries, that some of the finest facilities and programmes are clearly directed towards middle-class tastes, and that while more working class people join company clubs than other clubs nonetheless professional and semi-professional employees predominate [24]. It would also appear that in general the majority of industrial workers do not participate in company organized sport or recreation and often less than 10% of employees use company facilities [25]. However, the younger male unskilled or skilled manual worker appears overall to be well represented. Yet the pattern is variable; 'some clubs are predominantly "staff" rather than "works" clubs, "middle-aged" rather than "young" and so on' [23].

This raises the contentious issue of under-use of industrial reaction facilities, and the possibility of shared use with the community in order to maximize facility potential. Former Minister for Sports Dennis Howell [26] considers it:

'A great crime . . . when good sports facilities are just not being used by people at company sports clubs. When this happens then they should be offered for the use of the whole community. A terrible trend of today is to hear of many industrial clubs closing their doors. Some firms are even selling open ground for development, instead of using it for recreational purposes.'

However, many clubs hold that industrial sports facilities are for use by company workers alone. While not necessarily supporting such a premise Dale Best [27] states the industrial objective:

'Industrial organizations are in business to make a profit, they are not directly concerned with the community need for recreation provision. Company provision is made to ensure the health, happiness and satisfaction of the workers with a view to high productivity'.

In addition the employees themselves are reluctant to share their facilities. A Regional Sports Council survey [28] identified a willingness among the majority of industrial firms to make their sports facilities available to outsiders but because the majority of sports facilities are maintained with the help of weekly contributions from employees, they were jealously guarded by the company clubs themselves.

The practical problems of preservation of standards, employee safeguards, cost of additional use, bar and excise licences, security, staffing costs and legal and insurance problems are also put forward as reasons against involvement with the community, as is the problem of community clashing with company use, particularly in those industries where shift work is prevalent.

Another, perhaps major, but underestimated reason for 'keeping themselves to themselves' may be that the industrial sector provision offers recreational experiences which are *different* in kind from those offered in the public sector – 'identification', 'small units', 'belonging', 'minority groups e.g. aero modelling catered for', 'getting together with work colleagues' [23]

Cullen's survey indicates that practically all companies with their own leisure facilities provide access of some kind to individuals and groups other than their own employees, but this is 'usually carefully limited'. Families, retired employees, members' guests and associate members are the main beneficiaries and large companies make available high standard facilities for county matches, national sports coaching, sports festivals and the like.

Shared use, however, is the exception rather than the rule. Some companies do encourage dual use of their facilities, notably some of the national banks who allow school use of facilities, stage representative matches in a variety of sports, and in the case of the Midland Bank, organize their own annual inter-school sports tournaments. Inevitably the motives for this are again not purely altruistic, and the publicity received by the banks as a result of staging these events helps create a good public image and provides a means of recruitment of suitable employees. Despite these exceptions, it would appear that few clubs extend their use to the general public in spite of pressure to do so, and clubs usually limit outside membership.

2.8.3 The organization of industrial sports and social clubs

The problems of trying to generalize about the organization of industrial sports and social clubs are evident. No two clubs are alike; the kinds of industry and the facilities offered vary enormously; and each company has its own history, problems and idiosyncracies. This is true with the methods adopted for financing the clubs, although a joint responsibility can be identified with the company usually owning the facilities and being responsible for or contributing to their upkeep, either by donating pound for pound, making an annual block grant or paying off any deficit incurred. From the other side, the employees contribute via subscriptions, wages, sectional fees, fund raising, social activities, bar takings, bingo, fruit machines and in some cases lotteries.

The manager or 'sports and social secretary' of the larger clubs has wider responsibilities than his counterpart of the earlier years, who was usually not a recreation specialist and probably a senior employee who undertook the task for the last ten to fifteen years of his working life with the company. As well as a knowledge of management techniques, licensing laws and financial control the industrial Recreation Manager should also be providing a programme relevant to the needs of his company's workforce. The extent to which the manager simply performs a caretaker role, letting out the facilities to worker-organized clubs, or the extent to which he performs the role of enabler, actively promoting and encouraging participation through coaching schemes, special events and leagues, and for the unattached as well as the club user, is not clear, and again is likely to differ from organization to organization.

With exceptions most programmes revolve around the traditional games and social activities. This may reflect the limited provision in the smaller companies and the need for them (although the practicality may be more limiting) to expand their concept of recreation beyond the confines of sport in order to cater for a larger number of their workers. However, as pointed out earlier the range and diversity of industrial recreation programmes is so varied and often unique to the company that generalizations are wholly misleading.

2.8.4 Other industrial outlets

Industry is involved in sport and recreation in a number of ways other than making provision solely for its own workforce. Essentially this involvement can be split up into two areas – promotion and sponsorship and joint provision. Sponsorship is covered in Chapter 3.

Joint provision of recreation facilities by industry and local authorities for use by both employees and the community was advocated *over 60 years ago* by B. Seebohm Rowntree, when in *The Human Factor in Business* [29] he wrote:

'That adequate opportunity for wholesome recreation is desirable for all workers, especially in view of the shortening of the working week will not be disputed. The question is whether an employer has any responsibility in connection with the matter. I think the right answer is that if many of his workers live near the factory he should satisfy himself that adequate recreational facilities exist for them. He may do this in two ways: either he may provide adequate recreational facilities for his own employees only, or, by his influence and possibly also his financial help, he may assist communal effort to provide such facilities for the community as a whole. Strong arguments can be brought forward in favour of either course. In the case of a town where voluntary committees or local councils are seeking to provide playing fields, clubs and similar amenities for the general public, it is certainly a disadvantage if large employers refuse to cooperate in the public effort because they are concerned merely with their own employees'.

This view was more recently endorsed in *The Pilkington Report* [30] (the report of the study group appointed by the Sports Council to investigate industry and community recreation in St Helens) when they stated that:

'. . . the Study Group was firmly of the opinion that, in the logical development of sociological planning following all the improvements in the overall standard of living, it is no longer the function of private or public industry to provide recreational facilities for the exclusive use of their own work people but that they might well combine their resources with those of the local authorities in order to provide facilities which could be used and enjoyed by all.'

Examples of such joint provision are available from the early 1970s. In Prescot in Lancashire, British Insulated Callender's Cables Ltd provided a site valued at £50 000 for a new swimming pool complex, estimated to cost £224 000 – a joint venture between the Prescot Urban District Council and the Whiston Rural District Council. Dunlop Semtex in Monmouth gave up their sports ground to provide a site for a swimming pool and sports hall, to be provided on a school campus by three local authorities and the local education authority. In return the firm was allowed block bookings of the facilities for their employees. In Merthyr Tydfil a local authority outdoor pursuits centre has been built to which Hoover Ltd donated £20 000. In 1985 a new leisure complex opened in the Aldgate, London, called 'Summit'. It has been financed by a large insurance company and is open to use by both the company's employees and residents of the London Borough of Tower Hamlets. There are many similar examples but they remain the exception rather than the rule.

2.8.5 Industrial recreation abroad

Other countries have taken some leads in industrial welfare. In Sweden, for example, central government, local authorities and private firms combine to support recreation. The Swedish Inter-Company Athletics Association founded in 1945 with 333 inter-company clubs now has more than 12 000 clubs affiliated to the national association. The interest shown by families taking part in walks and other activities led to the association's FM clubs and *every* family in Sweden has been invited to join the national scheme. The international ski competition against their Norwegian counterparts in 1970 attracted more than 1 000 000 starters; 303 000 took part in skating, 180 000 in swimming. There are youth activities and holiday activities on a national scale. The magazine *KORP* is an all-important instrument in the movement with a circulation of over 42 000 per issue [31]. Another innovation is the association's link with the Swedish Gymnastics Federation for pensioners' gymnastics. Every year some 200 'monitors' are trained for this work.

In West Germany there are a number of medically controlled health centres which 'recondition'. Employees within the scheme, particularly those over forty, can stay at centres for a few weeks without loss of pay. Similar centres exist in many countries, for example in Russia and Soviet satellite countries, Switzerland, Austria, Holland and Israel. Industrial management in many European countries, notably Sweden, France, Holland, Belgium and the 'people's democracies' has begun an assault on the degenerative effects of modern work. Alongside the more traditional forms of sport carefully timed 'break gymnastics' or work bench callisthenics have been introduced and this kind of tension releasing activity has been well received. In the USSR these activities are described as 'production' gymnastics because of the apparent increases in productivity. In America the National Industrial Association has over 800 companies belonging to it, many with elaborate and extensive facilities and programmes. However, a variety of estimates suggest that up to another 50 000 companies have recreation programmes and facilities.

A Belgian study notes improvements in production of up to 25% [21]. Cullen described how in a productivity-conscious Japanese firm, two teams of girls complementarily work a four-hour shift. Each team spends two hours seated at ergonomically designed benches doing fine, fingertip precision work. After a break for orange juice they are given twenty minutes basketball or gymnastics, followed by one hour's packaging, which is deliberately non-automated in order to provide a certain minimum amount of exercise for the larger muscle groups [21].

Finland is the 'promised land' of organized activity and that is why there are many active sports organizations for industry like the Workers Sports Association and the Central Union of Workers Sport Association. In addition to the main Finnish Sports Federation, since the beginning of the century conditioning sports have been held in firms and factories. At the instigation of the Finnish Working Place Sports Committee, research work in depth covering 2200 of Finland's largest firms has been undertaken [32]. The seriousness when applied to sporting pastimes is unpalatable to the British sense of fun and freedom, but we must be aware of industrial consequences, and there is much to learn from the experience of others.

2.8.6   The way ahead

Can companies apply the same drive and imagination in discharging responsibilities to employees and the community as they do in meeting responsibilities to shareholders? If so there can be an even brighter future.

The promise of industrial recreation is complex and job demanding. Recreation leadership is essential; sound philosophy and training is needed. The Recreation Managers' Association has begun to lay the foundations for nationwide company sports regional development; the Sports Council has listed sport and industry within its scheme of priorities.

Industrial firms and companies provide a large share of the nation's sports facilities. If these facilities became widely available they would obviously contribute greatly to community recreation. Companies possessing good sports facilities, particularly those in areas where the recreational needs of a community have outstripped the resources available to cope with them, have a ready-made opportunity to demonstrate their goodwill. At the moment there are some impressive examples of the co-operative spirit in joint planning, use of land and facilities for dual purpose, day time use and extension of club membership to the general community, in which many of the employee's friends and acquaintances are to be found. These, however, remain the exceptions. The most recent survey of industrial reaction facilities confirms this [23]. With one exception all plans for additional facilities, indoor and outdoor, are purely company/club ventures.

2.9   SUMMARY: VOLUNTARY SECTOR PROVISION

This chapter has been concerned with recreation provision in the voluntary sector. The sector is vast and diversified and is linked with both the public and commercial sectors. The voluntary sector is dominated by clubs and associations. By its sheer volume of organizations and numbers of people, there are more people involved in the management of leisure and recreation in the voluntary sector than in the other sectors. Voluntary organizations give people both the chance to participate and the opportunity to become involved in all levels of organization and management. They also give the opportunity to serve. Part summaries of this chapter have already been given concerning voluntary groups in Section 2.6, management by trust in Section 2.7.3 and industrial club management in Section 2.8.6. In terms of community recreation in its widest sense, managers must be aware that the voluntary sector, more than other sectors, holds many of the keys to individual self-fulfilment – one of the main purposes of leisure and recreation management.

REFERENCES AND NOTES

1. This is discussed more fully in Institute for Family and Environmental Research and Dartington Amenity Research Trust (IFER/DART), *Leisure Provision and Human Need: Stage One Report* (for DOE) IFER/DART, London, item 4.68.
2. Central Statistical Office (1981), *Annual Abstract of Statistics 1981*, HMSO, London.
3. Stephen, L. (1910), quoted in Tomlinson, A. (1979), *Sports Council/Social Science Research Council Review: Leisure and the Role of Clubs and Voluntary Groups*, Sports Council/SSRC, London.
4. English Tourist Board. (1981), *Aspects of Leisure and Holiday Tourism*, ETB, London.
5. Thompson, E.P. (1967), quoted in Tomlinson, A. (1979), *Sports Council/Social Science Research Council Review: Leisure and the Role of Clubs and Voluntary Groups*, Sports Council/SSRC, London.
6. Tomlinson, A. (1979), *Sports Council/Social Science Research Council Review: Leisure and the Role of Clubs and Voluntary Groups*, Sports Council/SSRC, London.
7. Central Statistical Office (1985), *Social Trends* 1985, Chapter 11: Participation, HMSO, London.
8. Central Statistical Office (1985) *Social Trends*, 1985, HMSO, London.
9. Martin, W.H. and Mason, S. (1984). *The UK Sports Market*, Leisure Consultants, Sudbury, Suffolk.
10. Institute of Recreation Management (1981), *Recreation Management Handbook*, E. and F.N. Spon, London.
11. Central Statistical Office (1985), Information from GHS 1983 in *Social Trends 1985*, Chapter 10: Leisure, HMSO, London.
12. Central Statistical Office (1985), *Social Trends* 1985, Chapter 10; Leisure, HMSO, London.
13. Khan, N. (1976), *The Arts Britain Ignores*, Gulbenkian, London.
14. Arts Council (undated), *Community Arts Evaluation Working Group Report*, Arts Council, London.

15. The Methodist Church Division of Social Responsibility (1976) *Leisure and the Church*, The Methodist Church, London.
16. Bridge, D. (1978), *Looking at Leisure*, Epworth Press, London, p.9.
17. National Council for Voluntary Organisations, *Annual Report 1984/1985*.
18. Voluntary Organisations Research Unit (1979), unpublished data.
19. Hutson, S. (undated), *Sports Council, Social Science Research Council: A Review of the Role of Clubs and Voluntary Associations based on a Study of Two Areas in Swansea*, Sports Council/SSRC/, London.
20. Wolfenden Committee (1978), *The Future of Voluntary Organisations*, Croom Helm, London.
21. Cullen, P. (1966/7) Whither Industrial Recreation Now? *Sport and Recreation* Volume 7, 4 October 1966 and Volume 8, 1 January 1967, Cevtral Council of Physical Recreation, London.
22. Parker, S. (1971) *The Future of Work and Leisure*, MacGibbon and Kee, London.
23. Cullen, P. *Industrial Recreation Survey 1979/80*, unpublished data and notes on findings.
24. Ministry of Housing and Local Government Urban Planning Directorate (1967), *Provision of Playing Pitches in New Towns*, MHLG, London.
25. Sillitoe, K. K. (1969), Government Social Survey, *Planning for Leisure*, HMSO, London.
26. Dennis Howell in an interview reported in *Recreation Management*, March 1970.
27. Best, D. (1971), Polytechnic of North London, Diploma in Management Studies thesis, unpublished.
28. Greater London and South East Council for Sport and Recreation (1971), *Industry and Community Recreation: report on a working party*, GLSESR, London.
29. Seebohm Rowntree, B. (1921), *The Human Factor in Business*.
30. Sports Council Study Group (1968), *The Pilkington Report*, Sports Council, London.
31. *Swedish Association of Inter-Company Athletics Handbook*, Stockholm.
32. The Finnish Society for Research in Sports and Physical Education, *Physical Education and Sports in Finland*: Publication No. 14 (1972), Werner Södersttröm Osakeyhtiön kirjapaino, Porvoo, 1972.

Chapter 3

Commercial providers of recreational services, products and facilities

★

3.1 INTRODUCTION

In the previous two chapters attention was focused on the public and voluntary providers of recreation and leisure services and facilities and it was shown that there is a level of integration and overlap between them. This chapter is concerned with the commercial provider. While the motive for commercial recreation provision is very different from the other major sectors, there is still further overlap, inter-sectorial involvement and collaboration such that strict demarcation lines are not indelibly drawn. The promotion of a prestige sporting event indicates the relationship between the three sectors.

The Gillette London Marathon, now sponsored by Mars, was held for the first time in 1981. The event was initiated by an individual, organized by a *voluntary* board of governors, promoted in collaboration with the sport's governing body, supported by the *local authority* – the Greater London Council – and sponsored by a *commercial* company. The inter-sectorial relationship is typical of many major sporting events. Nevertheless, despite corporate approaches, there are discernible differences in the commercial approach to recreation provision.

The major difference between the commercial operator and the public or voluntary operator is the *raison d'être* of the business, the *primary* objective of the commercial operator being that of financial profit or adequate return on investment. Other sectors may make profits but are established and in being for other *primary* purposes.

This chapter is written in the following manner. *First*, a general overview of commercial recreation is given to set the scene. *Second*, the growth of the multinational companies is shown to be of major significance in the supply of leisure services and products to the public. *Third*, each of the main constituent elements making up the commercial 'package', relating to the home, social recreation, entertainment, sport, art, tourism and sponsorship are covered as distinct units, although their interrelationships cannot be overlooked.

3.2 THE COMMERCIAL PROVIDER

Commercial organizations do not have an intrinsic interest in recreation, in and of itself, but in recreation *as a source of profit*. This is not to say that many organizers and organizations are not deeply involved in recreation, nor is it to say that there is no altruism on the part of the providers. Indeed, patronage has long been an element in recreation provision, and commercial support has kept alive many activities which would not otherwise have survived. In addition, the mass media have been responsible for increasing interest and participation in a whole range of leisure pursuits, such as snooker, darts, bowls and golf. However, while there is a desire to increase the popularity of a number of recreative pursuits, commercial operations (outside the realm of patronage) will only maintain their interest if there is direct or indirect benefit to the organization.

In terms of numbers, millions of people buy sports equipment and cinema tickets, eat out socially, drink, smoke, gamble, watch television and are entertained in their leisure time, through services and products provided commercially.

The *General Household Survey 1983* (GHS) [1] looked at participation in selected social and cultural activities. Table 3.1 shows how important the commercial sector is in providing leisure facilities and services. It accounts for the first four ranked pursuits and the fifth, sixth and seventh rankings – visiting historic houses, going to the seaside and to the theatre – have substantial commercial components.

The objective of the commercial provider is to make money by serving the public. The public provider is also concerned with serving the public. Hence, *the enterprise, whether public or commercial, must attract the public or fail.*

However, does the commercial provider provide what the public needs? Are the products and services what the public actually needs or wants, or is the public persuaded to want them? Is the public obliged to

Table 3.1   Participation in selected social and cultural activities (annual averages)

Ranking of participation	Leisure pursuits	Participation as % of sample	
		Men	Women
1	Going out for a drink	64	46
2	Going out for a meal	41	40
3	Dancing	10	12
4	Visiting historic buildings	8	8
5=	Going to the cinema	7	8
5=	Seaside outings	7	8
7	Going to the theatre/opera/ballet	4	5
8	Park outings	3	4
9=	Country outings	3	3
9=	Amateur music and drama	3	3
9=	Going to museums/art galleries	3	3
12=	Going to fairs/amusement arcades	1	2
12=	Attending leisure classes	1	2

Source: *General Household Survey 1983* [1].

take what is on offer? Product choice is often limited in order to streamline production. For example, a few large breweries control the majority of Britain's public houses. Without voluntary consumer organizations such as CAMRA (Campaign for Real Ale) the specific wishes of people could become secondary to products and distribution efficiency. Catering outlets on motorways illustrate the point. They often give some of the worst service and most expensive fare and may serve to spoil a day's recreation outing. Customers have the choice of alternatives – take what is on offer or go without.

The commercial provider is, therefore, in essence, different from other providers – being literally, in it for the money. Yet many private businesses are not always 'commercial'; they do not make profits. 40% of USA commercial ventures apparently never make a profit but break even or go under and 50% of the rest of the companies make only marginal profits. In such a climate many private/commercial leisure organizations find it hard to stay in business and compared to public sector business competition is fierce and many companies and services go under.

Changing trends in leisure spending add to the uncertainty. Nevertheless there have been substantial areas of growth such as wine consumption, DIY, sports, video and home computers as shown in Table 3.2.

3.2.1 The range of commercial provision

Commercial organizations make a major contribution to many kinds of leisure and recreation provision. These are divided into six main areas for description and discussion in this chapter:

(a) Recreation in and around the home
Home making, gardening, keeping pets, do-it-yourself, hobbies, reading newspapers, magazines and books, playing records, tapes, games and musical instruments, watching television, listening to the radio, learning for pleasure and entertaining.

(b) Social recreation
Smoking, drinking in pubs, clubs and wine bars, eating in restaurants, gambling on the pools, bingo, lotteries and betting, dancing, driving for pleasure, window shopping, visiting beauty parlours and dating/ marriage bureaux.

(c) Entertainment, the arts and education
Going to the theatre, cinema, concerts, discotheques and social events, visiting libraries, art galleries, museums and historic houses and studying at private language and dancing schools.

Table 3.2 Trends in leisure spending in the United Kingdom 1980–84

	1980			1984	
	£ million	% of total consumer spending		£ million	% of total consumer spending
Eating out	5871	4.29	Eating out	8211	4.20
Beer	5320	3.89	Beer	7734	3.96
Holidays abroad	3510	2.57	Holidays abroad	5380	2.75
Foreign visitors	2961	2.16	Foreign visitors	4319	2.21
Spirits	2720	1.99	Spirits	3498	1.79
Holidays in UK	2420	1.77	Wine	3185	1.63
Wine	1914	1.40	Holidays in UK	2819	1.44
Television	1823	1.33	DIY	2398	1.23
DIY	1591	1.16	Sports	2214	1.13
Gambling	1574	1.15	Television	2206	1.13
Sports	1418	1.04	Gambling	2083	1.07
Newspapers	1088	0.80	Newspapers	1614	0.83
Audio equipment	1025	0.75	Video	1445	0.74
Pets	969	0.71	Pets	1233	0.63
Toys and games	566	0.41	Audio equipment	1128	0.58
Records and tapes	548	0.40	Gardening	817	0.42
Gardening	517	0.38	Records and tapes	692	0.35
Photography	476	0.35	Books	670	0.34
Books	451	0.33	Toys and games	667	0.34
Arts and Crafts	347	0.25	Photography	550	0.28
Magazines	317	0.23	Home computers	501	0.26
Video	200	0.15	Magazines	481	0.25
Cinema	147	0.11	Arts and crafts	450	0.23
Musical instruments	108	0.08	Musical instruments	229	0.12
Home computers	27	0.02	Cinema	124	0.06

Source: Adapted from *Leisure Futures* (Henley Centre for Forecasting Autumn 1985) [2].

(d) Sport and physical recreation
Keeping fit, jogging, playing squash, tenpin bowling, snooker, darts and golf, buying sports equipment, participating in riding schools, ice skating, yachting, saunas, health spas, joining sports and country clubs and attending sports events.

(e) Tourism, holidays and informal recreation
Staying at hotels, guest houses and caravan and camping sites, visiting safari and wildlife parks, zoos, historic sites, craft centres, garden centres, participating in pleasure touring and travel and taking part in adventure and activity holidays and weekend breaks.

(f) Sponsorship
Expanding the sports, arts and entertainment markets through commercial support.

Inevitably problems arise in trying to categorize the enormous field of leisure provision by the commercial sector. Overlaps are obvious: for instance, is driving for pleasure a social recreation or tourist recreation? Should a skiing holiday be classified under tourism or physical recreation? The classification above, therefore, is simply a convenient means of dividing areas up for descriptive purposes.

3.3 MAJOR COMMERCIAL COMPANIES

The commercial leisure industry is made up of many thousands of businesses, from the neighbourhood sports or hobbies shops to the giant multi-nationals. While the industry is widely diversified and contains many retailers with only a few full-time staff and Saturday part-timers, the large companies predominate. The commercial sector is dominant in the provision of cinemas, theatres, bowling alleys, ice skating, horse racing, greyhound and speedway tracks, bingo halls, restaurants, public houses, ballrooms and many others.

Wembley Stadium is the major example of the commercial outdoor and indoor sport and entertainment complex, which has developed to include not only the world-famous stadium but an indoor arena, the Wembley Conference Centre, squash centre, hotel and office block. The squash complex, formerly a tenpin bowling alley, comprises 15 courts, including a 'centre court' with 350 seats (provided in partnership), which is used as a court for national championships.

The Brighton Conference Centre and the Brighton Marina are examples of the expanding commercial leisure market. The marina was opened in 1979 and is said to be the largest in Europe enclosing 126 acres of water and land. There are over 1800 moorings. Within the marina there are a supermarket, restaurants and gift shops. However, financial problems meant that the second phase development could not take place. In 1985 the £55 million marina development was bought by the Brent Walker Group for £13 million. A major development comprising a superstore, hotel, aparthotel, health hydro, leisure centre and indoor water theme park is under construction and will operate alongside the existing working marina. Brighton's conference and exhibition business earned over £32 million in 1984 [3] with over 136 000 conference delegates. The Brighton centre alone earned for the town an estimated £9.4 million.

A number of companies have extended the range of leisure services into the development and building of country clubs, leisure centres, golf and leisure clubs, health clubs and squash complexes. One of the largest sports and leisure membership clubs is the Redwood Lodge Hotel and Country Club. The club had over 6000 members in 1985. A wide range of facilities include 6 outdoor tennis courts, indoor and outdoor swimming pools, 18 squash courts, 6 badminton courts, 16 snooker tables, a 200-seater cinema and a hotel with 72 bedrooms. Founded by an individual entrepreneur in the early 1950s the club has changed hands over the years and is now the enterprise of the Ashton Court Leisure Group.

However, despite many major developments by relatively large companies, these providers are dwarfed by the expanding leisure giants – the multinational companies.

3.3.1   The multi-national companies

The most significant change in the past two decades has been the increase in the size of the multinational companies through mergers, takeovers and diversification of interests. They dominate the commercial leisure industry. Three examples of multinational providers are described to illustrate the point briefly. They are: Grand Metropolitan Ltd (Grand Met.), The Rank Organization Ltd (Rank) and Trusthouse Forte Ltd (THF).

(a)   Grand Metropolitan Ltd

This company has wide leisure interests, including hotels and catering, brewing and retailing and wines and spirits [4]. The hotel and catering division includes 90 hotels and 280 UK Berni and Schooner Inns. The brewing and retailing division is a confederation of four companies: Watney Mann and Truman Breweries (5000 tenanted public houses); Chef and Brewer (1500 managed public houses); Watney Mann National Sales and Soft Drinks (handling Coca-Cola in Southern England).

The Consumer Services Division – comprising a mix of retail, leisure, holiday and contract service activities – falls into three units: 'Retailing' includes the Host Group with 1450 managed pubs, 240 Berni Inns, 12 Huckleberry's fast food outlets and Mecca Bookmakers (600 betting offices); 'Leisure and Holidays' takes in Mecca Leisure's official social clubs, night clubs, restaurants and sports centres, as well as several holiday businesses; 'Contract Services' embraces Grandmet Catering, providing catering services to some 1700 commercial and industrial clients. The Consumer Services Division achieved sales of £1054.5 million in 1983 with a trading profit of £73.6 million, an increase of about 9% compared with the previous year. In 1980 Mecca Leisure renovated Streatham Ice Rink and opened other centres including a bingo social club in Harlow and a squash/night club in Purley. In 1983 the new Rendevous

Casino opened at the Hilton Hotel to complement the group's established casinos – the Palm Beach, the Ritz, the Casanova, the Sportsman and the Golden Nugget. In 1985 the interests of Mecca Leisure were bought out by management from the parent company with a public flotation planned for autumn 1986.

Multinational companies are a major source of employment. The average number of persons employed in the UK by Grand Met. during 1983 was 136 297 including 42 728 part time staff. The company achieved trading sales of £4468.8 million in 1983 compared with £3848.5 million in 1982 with trading profits of £407.0 million in 1983 and £354.8 million in 1982.

(b)   The Rank Organisation Ltd

The leisure interests of this company include Odeon and Gaumont cinemas in the UK, and other cinemas elsewhere in the world, motorway service areas, discothèques, restaurants, marinas, hotels and Butlin's holiday centres [5]. The group manufactures or markets television sets, radios, ciné cameras, audio visual and stage equipment. The company had a turnover in 1983 of £704.7 million and a trading profit of £38.2 million compared with a trading profit of £33.2 million in 1982. In 1983 the company employed over 20 000 people.

Rank Leisure division had a turnover of £142 million and a trading profit of just over £11 million, an increase of over £4 million compared with 1982. This recent upturn in the financial returns comes largely as a result of the company's priority of the disposal of activities unable to achieve profitability targets. In 1983 the closure of holiday centres in the UK, the rationalization of restaurant and catering facilities and the sale of some technical operations contributed £25.4 million. However, despite a continuing period of consolidation, new leisure ventures are appraised by the company. A few years ago, the company introduced ice skating on a synthetic plastic surface in the Brighton Kingswest complex.

(c)   Trusthouse Forte Ltd

This is another multinational company with wide leisure interests in tourism, hotels, restaurants, theatres, motorway service areas and airport catering services for 75 airlines at 20 airports. THF operates 185 Little Chefs, 54 Kardomah restaurants, amusements parks, self-catering holiday villages and 24 sports centres among its many interests [6]. The company operates 810 hotels with 72 299 rooms (the largest hotel group in Britain), including 34 Post Houses. THF achieved trading receipts of £503.3 million in the half year to 30 April 1984 compared with £440.2 million in the corresponding period in 1983. Sales for the whole of 1983 totalled £1012.0 million producing a trading profit of £134.8 million. The Catering and Leisure division achieved trading receipts of £260.9 million in the first half of 1984 and a trading profit of £6.4 million.

One of THF's major subsidiaires is the catering company Gardner Merchant. The major leisure acquisition in 1980 was a substantial part of EMI, including the Blackpool Tower complex and three London theatres – the Prince Edward, the Prince of Wales and the Palace.

These three examples – Grand Met., Rank and THF – show that the consumption of leisure services and products by millions of people is made possible through the large multinational companies. In financial terms, the object of the commercial exercise, the large companies swallow up the majority of public spending on commercial leisure services.

Rising operating costs, the success of the multinationals and further mergers suggest that the large companies will become even larger. They are able to provide the range of products and services now demanded either at the level of sophistication to match demand or to create the kind of demand which can be translated into financial profits. The question of whether created demand will meet individual and group need is an issue which is considered in Chapter 9.

3.4 HOME-BASED LEISURE

Commercial providers have enormous influence in home leisure pursuits. The *General Household Survey 1983* (GHS) [7] shows that among 98 leisure activities participated in during the four week period prior to interview, the most frequent rates of leisure participation were in home-based activities. The British Broadcasting Corporation estimated that the average weekly time spent watching broadcast television in the United Kingdom in the first quarter of 1984 was 21¾ hours among men and 25½ hours among women. Listening to the radio accounted for an average of almost 9½ hours per week in the whole of 1983 [8], and a considerable 63% of the 1983 GHS survey sample listened to records and tapes during the four week period prior to interview.

In addition to passive pursuits, people were actively engaged at home. 44% undertook gardening, 56% read, 36% undertook do-it-yourself jobs and house repairs and 27% needlework. In comparison, only 11% went dancing and only 7% went to the cinema.

The nature of home-based leisure activities and their enjoyment will be affected by factors such as housing conditions, availability of gardens and standards of living. Leisure time use will vary according to the home itself, home improvements, family interests and hobbies, and material possessions of the household which may be leisure 'instruments' in themselves (television, video, radio) or may be time saving appliances (vacuum cleaners, washing machines) which release members of the household from various tasks and so create greater leisure time. Another often underrated factor pertaining to leisure at home, is the keeping of pets. There are estimated to be in the region of six million dogs and four million cats in Great Britain.

Three broad areas of home-based leisure have been artificially devised and separated, but only for descriptive purposes in this section. They are

1. The media in the home.
2. The home as an object of leisure.
3. The home as an area for recreation and social activity.

In reality the areas overlap or are interwoven. Moreover, many elements, such as reading newspapers, are bound up with going to work, as much as with leisure in the home.

3.4.1　The media in the home

The media have the most influential effect on leisure in terms of what people do with their time. Media in the home revolve around not only television viewing but also radio, records, tapes, hi-fi, newspapers, books and magazines.

(a)　Television viewing

The motivations for watching television are not identified in the *General Household Surveys*, but are likely to include a mixture of needs for entertainment, information, education, social cohesion (e.g. watching television may become a 'family activity') or simply because there is, either through lack of opportunity or apathy, nothing else to do. Viewing appears to be the most frequent amongst children and the elderly, although overall there has been an increase in the time spent watching television over the last fifteen years, with average viewing time per individual per week increasing from 16 hours in February 1967 to almost 24 hours in the first quarter of 1984 [8].

The commercial sectors' direct involvement with television revolves around the commercial stations which make the programmes and advertise products, and in the manufacture of the television sets themselves.

The Independent Broadcasting Authority (IBA) is responsible for both Independent Television (ITV) and Independent Local Radio (ILR) in the United Kingdom. The IBA was created by Parliament in 1954. Its responsibilities were extended to include local radio in 1972 and a new television service on Channel Four started transmission in autumn 1982. In addition a nationwide breakfast-time television service started early in 1983.

The IBA is completely self-supporting and no income is received from licence fees. It has four primary tasks:

1. The IBA selects and appoints the programme companies.
2. It supervises the programme planning.
3. It controls the advertising.
4. It transmits the programmes.

Over 100 hours of programmes are on average presented to viewers each week in each of the 15 networks. Independent television and radio services are paid for by the sale of spot advertising time. This advertising time is not sold by the IBA itself but by the programme companies. The IBA obtains its income from rentals paid by these independent companies. The frequency, amount and nature of the advertisements must be in accordance with the *IBA Acts*. The total income of the Independent Television companies collectively in 1981/82 was about £680 million, of which 98% came from advertising sales. 60% of the income was spent on the programmes themselves [9]. The manufacturer and retailer income from the sale of television sets totalled over £300 million in 1976. In 1970, there were over 15.5 million monochrome television broadcasting receiving licences issued and 274 000 colour licences. In 1978 there were just over 7 million monochrome and over 11 million colour licences issued [10]. By 1980 there were 5.1 million and 13.3 million respectively, i.e. 72% of homes had colour television licences: in 1983, there were over 3.4 million monochrome and over 15.1 million colour licences issued. According to the BBC [10] the average viewer watches television 2 hours 55 minutes per day and the percentage distribution of the audience averages 38% BBC 1, 11% BBC 2, 49% ITV and 2% Channel 4.

(b) The spin-offs from owning a television set
The commercial sector is also involved in a number of other ways with leisure provision via the television. The biggest influence is, of course, that of *advertising*. A second is the recent expansion of the *video recorder* market. A third is the use of the television for active participation, i.e. *video games*. A fourth growth area is the use of the television as an *information service*, for example, *Ceefax* and *Oracle*.

The market for video software was worth around £485 million in 1983 with around 30% of households owning video cassette equipment [2]. It will be interesting to see when the use of video-recorders becomes even more widespread, whether the greater flexibility it affords in terms of enabling the viewing of programmes when it is convenient rather than when they are transmitted, will lead to an increase in leisure participation away from home or conversely whether the growth in the home video film industry will produce the opposite effect with home-based leisure becoming more popular than ever.

Projections for the future use of television indicate that leisure behaviour could be markedly affected by technological advances. Many see mechanisms such as Ceefax as being the forerunners of more sophisticated systems where not only will information about leisure pursuits such as concerts, sporting events, theatre and entertainment, and even clubs and organizations specializing in particular activities or hobbies, be more readily accessible, but it may also be possible to book and pay for tickets, restaurants etc. via the same system. Only time will show whether such advances will be both universally accepted and used. Some have suggested that the growth of home-based leisure could be the embryo of an introverted society. In 1979 a Finnish social psychologist wrote 'The family is alive but not well!' [11].

(c)   Radio listening

Listening to the radio is another popular area primarily home-based media-related leisure activity. The BBC has 4 radio networks and 30 local radio stations, BBC research [8] estimates that the number of hours of radio listening per person per week in 1983 averaged 9 hours 23 minutes, although only 2 hours 9 minutes of this was to commercial and independent local radio. There were 48 local radio commercial stations in 1983 and the annual income of the ILR companies in 1983 was about £70.3 million, 38% of which was spent on the programmes and 25% on other services [12]. This revenue is steadily increasing as advertisers have come to recognize the value of the radio as a medium for advertisement. Between the BBC and IBA there are plans to reach the vast majority of the population through a network of 150 local radio stations, i.e. almost twice the number of stations on the air in 1983.

In relation to listening to the radio it is interesting to query how much time spent doing so is *purely* for leisure, and in fact how much is actually *home-based*. Often the radio is listened to in conjunction with the pursuit of markedly non-leisure activities such as doing the housework, cooking and driving to work and it would be interesting to see whether this accounted for the greater part of radio-listening time. In addition because of the portable nature of the radio it is not a solely home-based medium, providing entertainment and information when travelling (either in a car or on foot) and in conjunction with other leisure pursuits such as visiting the beach or sitting in the park. In fact the extent to which listening to the radio is a leisure pursuit in its own right is likely to be limited for the majority of people with its greatest use being in conjunction with other work or leisure activities.

(d)   Records and tapes

Listening to records and tapes is another booming home-based leisure pursuit. However, since 1979 the UK based record companies have suffered a slump in business which, in 1983, was only partially offset by the boom in sales of 12" singles. 'Singles' carry all the disadvantages of hit or miss and the fees demanded by artists continued to spiral. Some small independent labels in contrast have continued to increase in a modest way. The effects of the video disc and compact disc, in addition, are becoming significant.

Total revenue in 1983 of £287.1 million was barely sufficient to stay level in real terms with 1982 [13]. The low price of imports had an effect and the average price of an LP increased by a little under 6% during the year, marginally below the inflation rates. The price of prerecorded tapes actually showed a fall during the year and this contributed to a volume increase of 18% over the year and a peak of 27% during the third quarter. According to British Phonographic Industries (BPI) it has not been the prerecorded tape market which has suffered predominantly from the effects of home taping; this practice takes its toll primarily on discs. BPI estimates that domestic copying results in lost sales of a value in excess of £250 million at retail prices and that some 10% of all recordings made result in a lost sale.

(e) Reading

The written word is another source of home recreation although, as with the radio, it is not solely a home-based pursuit. Publication of newspapers, magazines and books is primarily the prerogative of commercial organizations although private, voluntary and government organizations publish technical and research material that could conceivably be read for pleasure. Direct commercial involvement can also be found with the organization of book clubs, while indirectly leisure behaviour may be influenced by the content of magazines, both in terms of their advertising and the values they promote.

The number of book titles reflects people's interest in reading. There were 68% more book titles issued in 1979 than in 1961 [14]. The highest increases were in political science, natural sciences and history. The United Kingdom is serviced by 5000 library service points and about 700 mobile libraries [15]. There are also 10 000 libraries in homes and hospitals. UK libraries have 137 million books and 3.6 million discs and tapes. [15A]

The extent of the popularity of the written word can be found in the National Readership Survey of 1983 [16]. This discovered that 76% of men and 70% of women aged 15 and over read at least one national daily newspaper and 78% of men and 74% of women read at least one Sunday newspaper. One third of those interviewed read an evening paper. Analysis of the three social class divisions A and B, C1 and C2 and D and E indicates that the *Daily Telegraph, Daily Mail* and *Daily Express* were the most popular newspapers among Class A and B while *The Sun* and *Daily Mirror* were the most popular among classes C1 and C, and D and E. Although many people read more than one national daily newspaper almost 30% in *each* social class do not read any. General magazines were read by 41% of the sample population and women's magazines were read by 29% of the adult population. The spiralling cost of television advertising prompted many media buyers to turn towards the profusion of women's magazines as an alternative.

3.4.2   The home as an area for recreation and social activity

As well as accommodating the various leisure media, the home can be used as a base for recreation and social activity, for the playing of indoor games, for informal gatherings, parties, hobbies and other activities. The commercial sector's involvement here is with the provision of the necessary accoutrements and equipment for the pursuit of such activities.

Alcohol is one such provision. The increasing popularity of home drinking is indicated by the increase in off-licence sales, and the rise in the number of off-licences in the ten years between 1969 and 1979 from 27 434 to 36 182 (an increase of 22%) [17].

The sale of tobacco might also be added to home-based social provision, although as with radios it is neither an exclusively home-based activity nor a purely leisure one. Its popularity, or rather that of cigarettes, has been waning with a drop in sales over the past decade due largely to greater public awareness of the potential health hazards and the restrictions imposed on advertising. However, there seems to have been a compensatory rise in sales of the 'safer' tobacco products such as cigars and pipe tobacco. While the actual expenditure on tobacco has risen the percentage of total consumer expenditure has been decreasing steadily since the early 1960s. The *General Household Survey* figures for 1982 show that the prevalence of cigarette smoking has continued to decline among men but not among women. In 1972 there were 52% of males over 16 who smoked. By 1982 this was 38%. In 1972 41% of women smoked and this reduced to only 33% by 1982, with an increase in heavy smoking (20 plus per day) over that period [1].

Home-based leisure in terms of playing indoor games and playing with toys has been a developing market. The sales of indoor games and toys increased from approximately £80 million in 1969, to £323 million in 1979 [17]. The developing 'technology' games, the insatiable demand for more updated board games such as 'Dallas', 'Risk' or 'Trivial Pursuits' and the innovation of world best-sellers like Rubik's Cube stimulate commercial investment and expenditure by the public.

3.4.3   The home as an object of leisure

The house and garden can in themselves offer opportunities for leisure activity, depending on whether home improvement and gardening are viewed by the individual as leisure or as an unwelcome commitment. Whatever the motivation there appears to be an increase in activity in this area. Home improvements together with normal house maintenance entail considerable expenditure on do-it-yourself tools and equipment. In 1983, householders spent an average of £2.35 per week on housing maintenance, repairs and improvements. As shown in Table 3.3, in 1983

Table 3.3 Participation in selected home-based leisure activities (annual averages)

Ranking	Leisure pursuits	Participation as % of sample	
		Men	Women
1	Listening to records/tapes	65	62
2	Reading books	50	61
3	Gardening	50	39
4	House repairs/DIY	51	24
5	Needlework/knitting	2	48

Source: *General Household Survey 1983* [1].

51% of men and 24% of women undertook house repairs and do-it-yourself. Martin and Mason [18] found that 40% of householders own a power drill and that there had been a 2.1% gain in do-it-yourself spending per annum at constant prices.

The *General Household Survey, 1983* also looked at participation in selected home-based activities. Table 3.3 shows that nearly all the activities require supplies and equipment provided by the commercial sector.

Gardening and the provision of gardening implements is the other area of 'home improvement' in which the commercial sector is involved. Martin and Mason found that 70% of all dwellings had a garden and the popularity of the garden (either as a place for cultivation or for other leisure activity) is reflected in Sillitoe's [19] finding that the item wanted most was a private garden, or one larger than that already possessed, and was backed up by Young and Willmott's [20] survey which showed that 44% of those who already had gardens wanted larger ones, 35% the same size, 18% smaller and 3% did not care.

3.5 SOCIAL RECREATION OUTSIDE THE HOME

Moving away from home as an area for and object of leisure activity, provision in terms of social recreation can be divided up in a number of ways, e.g. gambling, eating and drinking out, window shopping and many more.

3.5.1 The sale of alcohol

One institution which seems to perform a unique and distinctive function is the public house. As a focal point for social activity, the selling of alcohol, and often staging live music events, the pub would appear to cater for a variety of needs. Between 1969 and 1979 pubs and other on-licences in England and Wales rose from 76 834 to 88 846, an increase of 13.5% [17]. Alcohol consumption rose frm 17.5 million proof gallons to 40 million proof gallons during the same ten years, i.e. an increase of 128.5%! Yet between 1980 and 1982 the number of licenced outlets went into a slight decline although consumption continued to rise. As seen in Table 3.1 64% of men and 46% of women had 'gone out for a drink' in the 4 weeks prior to interview.

The alcohol industry is dominated by the few major breweries, although consumer demand, focused through consumer organizations, has led to the growth of some small, independent breweries and at least one major brewery has reversed its policy of standardization of its product – in this case beer.

The breweries not only cater directly for leisure activity via their own outlets, but also give financial aid to private clubs in the form of grants and loans for the improvement or expansion of premises, usually in return for use of their products. Sales of alcoholic drink associated with eating out are also high. The size of the catering industry can be indicated by the Department of Employment figures for 1983 [21]. In that year there were 962 000 employees in the catering and hotel industry in the United Kingdom including 185 000 employees in restaurants, cafés and snack bars and 234 000 employees in public houses. (See Chapter 18, item 18.10.1 for the 1983 figures for employees in the leisure 'industries'.)

3.5.2   Gambling

Another favourite area of social recreation is that of gambling. This includes amusement arcades, the pools, bingo, on- and off-course betting, casinos and lotteries. According to the Department of Employment there were 92 000 employees in the betting and gaming industry in 1979. The Home Office report *Gambling Statistics Great Britain 1968–78* [22] shows that the amount of money staked, apart from casinos, fell in real terms during the 1970s. 80% of off-course betting relates to horse racing and 20% to greyhound racing, whereas the money staked on on-course betting is equally divided between the two. Attendances at horse race meetings have also slumped since the legalization of off-course betting; attendances at greyhound racing have fallen too. However, the latest horse racing attendance figures from the Horse Racing Betting and Levy Board reveal a slight increase in horse racing attendances – the average daily attendance at meetings rose from 3931 in 1983 to 3980 in 1984.

In 1983 £3068 million was staked on off-course betting, £343 million on on-course betting, £468 million on football pools, £1218 million on casino gaming and £490 million on bingo, i.e. £5587 million on these activities alone.

It would appear from all the data available that four out of every five people in Great Britain gamble in one form or another, despite the drop in the number of betting shops and the drop in spectator attendances. In

1983 6% of all men and 1% of all women placed bets; 26% of men and 11% of women did the pools [1]. In 1979 there were 12 475 betting offices, a decrease of 13.7% since 1971, when there were 14 462. However, there has been an increase in the number of casino clubs and gambling machines over the same period. In 1971 there were 108 casinos; in 1979 there were 128 – an increase of 15.6%. In 1971 there were 159 700 gaming machines and by 1979 these had increased by 9.2% to 175 800 [22]. However, by 1983 there had been a reversal in the trend with only 119 casinos and 159 600 machines.

The number of bingo clubs increased in the first part of the decade but by 1979 had almost declined to 1971 levels. This decline is continuing in the eighties: the number of clubs stood at 1661 in 1980 and only 1436 in 1983. A Gaming Board survey [23] of bingo clubs in 1978 indicated that there were 5–6 million regular bingo players in Great Britain, over 80% of whom were women, 90% of whom were over 30. The *General Household Survey, 1983* shows a surprisingly higher participation rate among men [1]. In the four weeks prior to interview 5.5% of all men and 11% of all women played bingo.

The overlap with local authority provision is further seen in relation to gambling, normally regarded as a highly commercial activity. Since the *Lotteries and Amusements Act* (1976), which came into force in May 1977, the Gaming Board of Great Britain is responsible for all local authority and society lottery schemes. By April 1983, nearly 5031 lottery schemes had been registered. Lotteries have become a main area of gambling with £46.4 million staked in 1983. New government legislation came into force in spring 1986, allowing the sale and consumption of non-alcohol drinks and refreshments in betting shops.

3.6 ENTERTAINMENT AND THE ARTS

Commercial leisure provision for entertainment and the arts outside the home covers a number of areas, although these can be divided into two basic categories – that which encourages active participation (e.g. ballrooms, discos, dance schools and perhaps some other commercially provided education courses such as language learning) and that in which provision is generally geared towards audience and spectators. This section deals primarily with the latter, for active participation can easily fit into other categories of leisure.

Dancing is one of those activities which is difficult to categorize under one heading, probably being as comfortable under social recreation or active indoor physical recreation as it is under entertainment and the arts. Dancing, as revealed by the *General Household Survey, 1980* [1A] is the most popular entertainment activity, with 12% of males and 15% of females participating in the four-week period prior to the interview. It is most popular among the 16–19 year age groups with 25% of males and

42% of females taking part, but it remains the most popular activity even among 35–59 year olds with 13.5% participating.

3.6.1   Audience and spectator activities

Attending the cinema and theatre, going to popular and classical concerts, visiting art galleries or going to shows and cabarets are all part of the audience and spectator activities provided by the commercial sector.

Going to the cinema emerged as the second most popular entertainment activity in the GHS 1977 and GHS 1980, with 11% of males and 10% of females in the sample attending in the four weeks prior to the interview in both years. The *General Household Survey 1983* reveals a marked decline in cinema attendances in recent years – only attracting 7% of males and 8% of females in that year. Cinema attendance is most popular among young people; the 1980 GHS revealed that in the age group 16–19 33% of males and 33% of females visited a cinema in the four week period with two-thirds of all unmarried teenagers visiting the cinema at least once a week. Cinema attendances have, however, fallen dramatically from a peak of 1635 million in 1946 to 156.6 million in 1972 and then to 103.5 million in 1977. There was an upturn, however, in 1978 with attendances of over 126 million and a capacity of 22%, the highest capacity for many years. However, the increase in attendances did not continue into 1979 with attendances estimated at 112 million by one source [24] and 119 million 'admissions' by another [25]. Numbers were again falling in 1980 and by 1983 were down to an all time low of 63.1 million. The number of films submitted to the British Board of Film Censors dropped by 40% between 1974 and 1980 but has risen significantly over the last few years to 378 submissions in 1984. The trend in advertising in the cinema has grown steadily and was worth £17 million in 1979.

Production, distribution and exhibition of films and cinema ownership are in the hands of a few large companies such as Thorn EMI and Rank and there are only a few cinemas run by independent operators. Confronted with a drastically contracting market these commercial operators closed many cinemas from a mid 1950s peak of 4709 cinema sites to 1420 in 1971 and 978 in 1979. In 1983, the number of cinema complexes was down to 707. Along with a decline in actual cinema sites the number of screens has increased from 1428 in 1971 to 1564 in 1979 but by 1983 had also begun to fall, standing at 1293 screens.

The growth in the number of screens was brought about by the division of many of the existing cinemas into triple screen units, and these now account for 39% of all cinema admissions. Conversions have taken place at large single cinemas where capacity was too great for the numbers attending, and this has led to a greater choice of films on these sites consequently appealing at any one time to a wider audience. However, the decline in number of cinema sites has left many towns without cinemas and commercial organizations now consider 30 000 as the minimum population to support a cinema. This policy can cause problems when new towns are built with a population less than 30 000 but have a high proportion of young people.

The advent of multi-screen complexes with 6, 8 or even 12 screens, many at out of town sites, will add further to the accessibility factor and will cater for the mobile populations. The development of multiplex cinemas in the USA and certain European countries has contributed to maintaining and increasing admissions in those countries. Thorn EMI Screen Entertainment operates the largest chain of cinemas in the UK – 287 screens on 106 sites – is confident that this pattern can be repeated in the UK and is committed to a development programme of some 20 multi-screen cinemas during the latter half of the 1980s.

Going to the theatre would appear not to be as popular as going to the cinema, with the GHS 1983 showing that only 4% of males and 5% of females in the sample population had attended the theatre, opera or ballet in the previous four week period. The percentage of females had dropped to 5% in the GHS 1980 survey. There was an even distribution amongst all age groups, but theatre-goers were predominantly from higher socio-economic groups. It has been estimated [26] that there were 37 million theatre visits in Britain in 1981.

One half of the 140 professional theatres in Great Britain are owned or rented by commercial companies. Forty of these are found in London, but West End theatres are finding it difficult to make a profit owing to competition from subsidized national theatres and now civic surburban theatres, and there is a declining number of commercial theatres in the provinces to accommodate touring plays and musicals.

Slightly lower figures for visits to museums and art galleries are found in the GHS 1977 with 4% of males and 3% of females attending museums and art galleries in the four weeks prior to interview. Male attendances had dropped to 3% in the GHS 1980 and remained at this level in the 1983 survey.

There are 110 commercial art galleries in London, which all tend to be small and specialized, compared with ten in the public sector, which tend to be large and comprehensive.

3.7 SPORT AND PHYSICAL RECREATION

All the indications point to the conclusion that sport is an expanding market. More people are playing sport, more sports are being played and consumer spending on goods and services is likely to keep rising during the next five years. Commercial providers are concerned in sport and physical recreation in a number of key areas, for example, active sport participation, spectator sport, facilities, sports sponsorship and leisure and sports goods and equipment.

3.7.1   Active sport

The commercial sector is involved in the provision of facilities for partici-pants in only a limited number of sports. Of the outdoor sports only golf, tennis and water sports are provided in any great numbers by commercial concerns and in the case of golf and tennis these are usually provided as part of a leisure complex which also provides squash, table tennis, snooker and other ancillary facilities. Of the indoor sports only snooker, tenpin bowling, squash and ice skating are provided by commercial organizations.

Veal's study *Sport and Recreation in England and Wales: Adult Participation 1977* [27] reveals that golf and tennis are the two most popular outdoor sports which require capital investment for the provision of facilities. In the GHS 1977 participation levels for these sports were 3.3% and 2.9% for the four weeks prior to the interview representing between 1.5 million and 2 million participants for each sport. The 1983 GHS shows that golf has become increasingly popular with 4% of males and 1% of females now playing the game. Tennis participation has declined slightly with 1% of both males and females playing in the four weeks prior to interview. Participation in sport and physical recreation, whether in local authority, voluntary or commercial facilities usually requires an outlay for kit and equipment. The commercial sector is inevitably involved in the provision of such equipment and there appears to be an expanding market for these goods.

3.7.2   Spectator sports

Spectator sports in general are not run by commercial enterprise, coming instead under the auspices of their relevant governing bodies. However, commercial involvement is rarely far away, although the width and depth of its involvement varies from sport to sport. Sponsorship, for instance, has only become accepted relatively recently by the governing body of Rugby Union, whereas it has been commonplace in Association Football for many years.

Association Football is still the most popular spectator sport (here 'spectator sport' refers to actual attendance, rather than watching via the television set). In the GHS 1980, 8% of the male population and 1% of females interviewed had attended a match in the previous four weeks. However, at the time of the 1983 survey, the figures had dropped to 6% of males and 1% of females. Indeed, soccer spectatorship has declined since the post-war years, with a decrease from 41 million attendances in the

1948/49 season dropping to 24.6 million in 1978/80, 21.9 million in 1980/81 and down to 18.4 million by the end of the 1983/84 season in the English Football League matches. The decline in Scotland has not been so sharp until the 1980/81 season with a sharp decline from 3 million to 2.5 million attendances.

The decline is greyhound racing has been noted earlier although paid attendances for 1984 still totalled nearly 4.9 million. Indeed spectator sports are generally less lucrative in terms of receipts from attendance, although boxing and in particular wrestling still appear to be popular. Other popular indoor spectator sports are indoor tennis and indoor show-jumping and along with boxing and wrestling lend themselves to viewing by comparatively large audiences. There are, however, some indoor sports such as snooker, and more recently darts which cannot accommodate large audiences on site but which, nevertheless, have become popular spectator sports through the medium of television.

Hence, although there has been a decline in the traditional spectator sports, others have increased in following, many as a direct or indirect result of television coverage and commercial sponsorship. Tennis and golf are examples. The Golf Open Championship attendances illustrate the point. At Lytham in 1963, there were 24 585 attendances, and at the same course in the 1969 and 1979 championships there were 46 000 and 134 500 attendances respectively.

3.7.3 Leisure goods and equipment

A substantial industry to supply leisure goods, clothing and equipment has developed. The manufacture, distribution and retailing of a vast range of goods exists, from yachts, canoes, tents, bicycles and hang-gliders, to tracksuits and special footwear, to rackets, balls, snooker tables, dart boards, trampolines and goal-posts, to hi-fi, records, video, electronic devices and games of every kind, and to gardening implements and do-it-yourself tools. Spending on sport alone serves to illustrate this point.

Nearly £1500 million was spent in the UK on sports goods and services in 1983 of which roughly one third related to the hire of sports facilities and other sports services, according to Martin and Mason [28].

They calculated that £928 million was spent on sports goods: £460 million on equipment (31%), £273 million on leisure clothing (18%) and £195 million on sports footwear (13%) and they forecast an increase in volume of business of 10% per annum, with clothing and footwear the fastest growing sectors. They estimated that over the ten years 1973–83, spending on sports goods rose by 37% in real terms. The sports goods trade is an expanding one but imports are increasing; 59% of all sports equipment comes from abroad, compared with 44% four years ago and around one-quarter back in 1973.

In 1983 boating was by far the largest individual market (although affected by the economy) with £195 million, followed by golf £96 million and swimming £81 million. Considerable increases have occurred with keep fit and racket sports which are in vogue; leisure fashion clothing continues to be an expanding market. Martin and Mason forecast [28] that the big spenders on sports goods in 1987 will be boating (substantially in the lead), golf, swimming, lawn tennis and athletics. In terms of sports services they forecast the leading contenders as billiards and snooker, golf, squash and fives, horse riding and athletics.

3.8   TOURISM AND HOLIDAYS

The commercial sector is closely involved with the tourist industry. This industry might be seen, very broadly, as providing for three markets in the United Kingdom:

1. Foreign visitors to the UK.
2. Britons holidaying (including visiting tourist attractions, day trips etc.) in the UK.
3. Britons holidaying abroad.

Inevitably the provision for all three markets is interlinked with some facilities and services provided by the commercial sector used by both foreigners and Britons alike, and with British travel agents organizing holidays both at home and abroad. There is also a close interrelationship between the commercial sector and others – private, voluntary, local authorities and government funded bodies such as the British Tourist Authority (BTA) – who also provide for and influence tourist development.

The definition of a tourist according to the English Tourist Board is 'anyone staying away from home for more than 24 hours'. However, within that definition there are various forms, and closely linked to tourism are day visitors or 'day trippers' who return home within 24 hours.

There were substantial increases in both the volume and value of tourism to England in 1984. For Britain the value of tourism exceeded the £10 billion mark. The Chairman of the English Tourist Board states in the 1984/85 Annual Report that

'Tourism in England with an estimated turnover in 1984 of £8,575 million, provides employment for more than a million people in England and is creating new jobs at the rate of at least 40 000 a year. It is undoubtedly Britain's biggest growth industry. It is also a vital foreign currency earner and has the clear potential to become our largest industry of all by the turn of the century.' [29]

(a) Overseas visitors

Since 1974 the annual number of overseas visitors to the UK (on holiday, on business or visiting friends and relations) has grown from 8.5 million to 13.7 million, a growth of 60%. This growth in the number of visitors is reflected in the level of expenditure which has been rising steeply since 1982 (at constant prices).

Figures issued by the Department of Trade and Industry indicate that 13 712 000 overseas visitors arrived in Britain during 1984 which represents an increase of 9.7% on 1983, contributing a massive £4194 million to the national balance of payments. North American visitors accounted for a major proportion of this increase, the strength of the Dollar against Sterling producing a 17.4% increase for the year to a record level of 3 330 000 visitors.

(b) Home tourism

Domestic tourism (excluding day visits in this definition) has also grown significantly, from 114 million visits in 1974 to 140 million in 1984, though with some peaks and troughs. Again, recent growth has been particularly rapid. Earnings from domestic tourism grew over the same period from £1.8 billion in 1974 to nearly £6 billion in 1984, though at constant (1980) prices the trend is largely flat.

The demand for business and conference tourism in Britain is also increasing in both volume and value. 20 million trips, 50 million nights and £1150 million are attributed to this category of tourism.

(c) Day trips

Most definitions and calculations of tourism exclude day visits. In practice, of course, day visits are a major component of domestic tourism and leisure activities and represent an important potential source of revenue. Visitors to the castles, abbeys, forts and other monuments of England topped four million in 1984, the year in which their management was taken over by English Heritage. Overall, visitor numbers increased by 146 000 over 1983.

Tourism activity – and the potential for day visits – is also well illustrated by the dramatic growth over the last 20 years or so in the opening of new tourist attractions in England; from about 800 in 1960 to over 2000 in 1983. Indeed, half the tourist attractions open to the public in 1983 had opened for the first time in the previous 15 years.

3.8.1   Tourist accommodation

According to specialists Pannell Kerr Forster Associates, 1984 was an extremely successful year for the hotel industry in the UK, with many companies reporting considerable profit increases. The positive trends of 1983 and 1984 are continuing, particularly with regard to the London hotel market which is reaping the benefits of decreasing levels of tariff discounting.

Historically, London has been the premier destination within the UK attracting consistently high levels of visitors due to its position as the capital city, the seat of government, and the centre for business, culture and entertainment.

However, occupancy levels of provincial hotels showed a sharp increase in 1984 of 9.1% compared with the previous year to average 65.5% for the twelve month period.

The overflow in demand for London bedspace is likely to result in a shift to the provinces, particularly if exchange rates continue to favour tourism from Europe and North America. Tourism specialists believe that this will be beneficial to traditional tourist centres such as the south coast resorts, Stratford-upon-Avon, York and Edinburgh which could be combined into tours including several days in London.

Both foreign and British tourists require accommodation and this could involve any of a number of options, ranging from hotels to camping and caravanning sites and holiday homes. The types of accommodation may be simply a base from which to tour or visit the surrounding area or it may provide leisure activity in its own right such as holiday camps or hotels that provide sporting and entertainment facilities. At the Aviemore Centre in the beautiful Spey Valley leisure facilities include swimming, squash, ice skating and curling. A number of first class hotels are clustered around the Centre and caravan parks extend the variety of services and self service accommodation. Hotel groups such as THF and Crest are increasingly giving attention to linking leisure facilities to their hotels and a number already do so. Many prestige hotels, particularly in holiday resorts, have sporting facilities, swimming pools, squash courts and tennis courts within the hotel precinct. A good example is Brend Hotels, Saunton Sands Hotel in Braunton, North Devon. Country Club Hotels Redwood Lodge Hotel and Country Club in Bristol and South Marston Hotel and Country Club in Swindon are examples of substantial sports provision alongside hotels – more substantial than major public provision. Gleneagles Hotels hotel at the world famous golf course now has a superb indoor pool, saunas and spas, tennis and squash courts in addition to their bowls, shooting and fishing facilities. The £4.5 million Gleneagles Club was opened in 1985 at London's New Piccadilly Hotel with individual membership for the leisure club costing £900. The Skyline hotel near Heathrow is an early example of a hotel with an indoor pool set in an artificially-created tropical setting.

Gosforth Park Hotel is one of the luxury Thistle Hotels. Its leisure centre, called the 'Leisure Club' comprises high standard free-form pool, saunas, jaccuzies, sunbeds, lounges, fitness room, squash courts, cocktail bar and outdoor trim trail. Weekend hotel bookings have increased substantially and the spin-offs to bar, catering and room occupancy and special events are considerable.

The proportion of holidays taken in British hotels would appear to have dropped since 1961 with a fall from 40% of all holidays to 25%. A corresponding increase in the use of other forms of holiday accommodation is evenly spread between camping, caravanning, rented accommodation, holiday camps and staying with friends or relatives. Bargain weekend breaks and other marketing initiatives may well have halted this decline.

3.8.2 Holidays

The number of holidays taken by British holidaymakers has increased long term for both holidays in Great Britain and holidays abroad, an increase of 70% overall since 1961. As shown in Table 3.4 holidays in

Table 3.4 Holidays taken by British holidaymakers

	Numbers in millions						
	1971	*1973*	*1976*	*1979*	*1980*	*1982*	*1983*
Holidays in Great Britain	34	41	38	39	37	33	34
Holidays abroad	7	8	7	10	12	14	15
Total holidays by British residents	41	49	45	49	49	47	49

Source: British Tourist Authority, *Annual Report* [30].

Great Britain reached a peak in 1973 with 41 million holidaymakers. Holidays abroad reached a record level in 1983 with 15 million British residents going abroad. The Association of British Travel Agents (ABTA) estimate that approximately 4–5 million holidays were package tours sold by their members. Here, then, is another area of commercial involvement – that of organizing holidays at home and abroad. Generally this occurs commercially through travel agents and tour operators and in 1985 ABTA estimated its membership included 5632 travel agent offices and 632 tour operators.

3.8.3 Holiday attractions

As well as organizing tours the commercial sector is also involved with the provision and maintenance of tourist attractions such as historical buildings, zoos, wildlife and amusement parks.

The British Tourist Authority estimates that in 1980 Britain's major art galleries and museums and selected historical properties received 53.5 million visitors; historic houses, gardens and ancient monuments received 44 million visitors, 11% of whom were overseas visitors. In 1983, the Science Museum attracted 3.4 million visitors, the Tower of London approximately 2.2 million, the British Museum 2.8 million and Windsor Castle Precincts 0.7 million.

One area of provision which has only recently begun to be considered in the United Kingdom is that of the theme park. Theme parks have become very popular in the USA since Disneyland resurrected the amusement park industry in 1955. By 1975 there were 35 major theme parks in the USA attracting 64 million customers. Their philosophy has been one of excellence, cleanliness, courtesy and safety. These create an atmosphere of fantasy, glamour, escapism, prestige and excitement. These 'parks' have been successful in other countries such as Summerland in Tokyo and Tivoli in Copenhagen.

Britain's first theme park was Thorpe Water Park at Chertsey, the concept and development of Leisure Sport Ltd. The predominant theme is water with activities such as water skiing and tourist attractions such as 'Bluebird' and Viking Longships. Its development encouraged the provision of other 'theme' facilities elsewhere in the United Kingdom. However, many of the theme parks have not been resounding success stories. Britain's only world-rated theme park is Alton Towers in Staffordshire. It offers a combination of magnificent surroundings, historic heritage and fun and fantasy. John Broome, the Chairman and chief executive of Alton Towers Limited, has transformed the stately home and gardens into one of the finest leisure parks in the world, which attracted over 2 million visitors in 1985. Battersea Leisure Ltd, headed by John Broome, plan to convert Battersea power station into a £50 million leisure centre. Planning permission was granted by Wandsworth Council in spring 1986.

The English Tourist Board has a 'register' of 95 Leisure Parks which are establishments that can be enjoyed by all the family. The Board also publishes a list of activity and hobby holidays which in 1983 totalled 526 different holidays. In 1985 the total had risen by 82% to 954 which illustrates that this is a major holiday growth market [31].

3.8.4 Tourism and transport

This very brief sketch of tourism and the commercial provider's role would be incomplete without some reference to leisure transport. Travel and the mode of transport can be a leisure activity in itself, whether by car, coach, boat, barge, train or plane. The importance of the commercial sector and leisure travel is summed up by Roberts [31].

'Transport as a leisure activity in itself (pleasure motoring, from home, canal boat tours, sea cruises etc.) as a linkage between home and leisure destinations, or a means of enlarging their destination's attractions (coach tours, car trips, boat trips, fishing excursions etc.), forms a high proportion of leisure expenditure . . . The commercial sector is directly or indirectly involved in all leisure transport modes in addition to the private car. The sector owns and operates shipping lines, aircraft, coaches, some railways in Continental Europe, taxis, pleasure boats and others. It supplies cars and bicycles for hire; provides catering services; provides the boots for hikers, and the shoes for less ambitious walkers. The supply of equipment generally (for example bicycles) is the prerogative of the commercial sector. Finally, it provides marinas and often owns seaside piers which provide landing stages for shipping.'

The tourism and holiday market is a major commercial leisure industry. It is another expanding area in which the emerging profession of recreation management must consider the management of leisure opportunity for people. Two facts are worth noting. First there are a number of personal and social reasons for travel which may be as important as the destination itself. Second, travel is normally expensive and those who can afford it can go further and in greater comfort. Poorer people travel less. Even a journey across a large city with a young family could be formidable. More than most forms of leisure, travel is shaped by cost both direct and indirect.

3.9 SPONSORSHIP

Sponsorship has been defined as 'the provision of financial or material support for some independent activity which is not intrinsic to the furtherances of commercial aims, but from which the supporting company might reasonably hope to gain financial benefits' [33]. It differs from patronage where the financial, material or professional expertise is given by a commercial company to an activity for philanthropic reasons, without looking for any material reward or benefit.

Sponsorship can benefit the company in a number of ways:

1. By increasing publicity.
2. By helping to reinforce or change its corporate image.
3. By improving public relations, improving trade relations or providing a vehicle for the promotion of company products.

The scale of sponsorship can vary enormously, from contributions of thousands or millions of pounds from large conglomerates to promote national sports to the donation of a cup or prize from a small sports shop to a locally run competition.

3.9.1   Sports and the arts

Sports sponsorship began to develop in the United Kingdom in the early 1960s and dramatically expanded with the ban placed on television advertising of cigarettes. The cigarette companies had £6 million budgeted for television advertising, a large part of which was consequently redirected into sponsorship of sport since sport had a wide appeal, helped promote a 'healthy image', thus attempting to counteract anti-smoking propaganda, and probably – most importantly – lending itself to surrogate advertising through the press and television. However, in 1977 Denis Howell, then the Minister for Sport, placed a ceiling on the amount of sponsorship that cigarette companies could give to sport, and there has been a consequent withdrawal of some companies from this area of sponsorship.

Sponsorship has helped some sports to survive and others to flourish. Snooker and darts are cases in point but other, once minority spectator sports are now thriving. Basketball has turned from an insignificant spectator sport into an expanding one. The Carlsberg National League, formerly the George Wimpey National League now attracts 'star' international players. The Kellogs National Basketball Cup was once the Asda National Cup. All the top clubs are sponsored. Davenport brewery, Nissan and Walkers Crisps, for example, hope that their team will be successful and reach basketball cup and championship finals and so achieve televised matches. Ice Hockey has experienced a similar growth pattern. There are now two divisions of teams within a Heineken League.

The most heavily sponsored sport is motor racing, followed by horse racing, golf, tennis, show jumping, and cricket and these are thought to be so because of their wide television coverage. The international sports promotion market is claimed to be a $100 billion market, though estimates vary greatly [34]. It is believed that in the United Kingdom there are over 1000 companies spending between £50 million and £60 million on sponsorship annually backed by a further £50 million or so spent on marketing and promotions [35]. Spending on sports sponsorship events in the UK is much greater than that for the arts. There are, however, signs that some sponsors are shifting their ground in favour of the arts.

Until recent years, the arts were more the subject of commercial *patronage*. The latest estimate [34] is that business sponsorship now amounts to about £23.5 million a year and this is growing particularly from the major banking corporations and tobacco manufacturers. In 1983 BAT Industries (tobacco manufacturers) for example, undertook to give the London Philharmonia Orchestra £300 000 over three years. In the same year, Barclays Bank sponsored the Royal Shakespeare Company, National Westminster Bank the North and Scottish Operas, Midland Bank the Covent Garden Proms and Lloyds Bank the National Youth Orchestra. National Westminster and Barclays also have a history of sponsoring sport.

The building societies and insurance industry are also increasingly involved in sponsorship. Norwich Union are heavily committed and Cornhill has supported Test Cricket since 1978. Before Cornhill started sponsorship 2% of the population ranked Cornhill as one of the major companies. The company claim this has now risen to 16% – a direct result of Test Cricket sponsorship. The company after only seven Test matches with their name attached to each of the press, radio and television reports, was ranked the fourth best-known in Great Britain. However, sponsorship is not always a success story. There are some financial disasters, or companies do not achieve expected targets, or the company's name no longer has benefits in one or other direction. The brief history of sponsorship has shown it to be a rapidly changing and fluctuating industry. Among the problems are that the larger the sponsorship investment, the greater the harmful effects could be when money is withdrawn, particularly when there is not a successful takeover. With many sport and art events, or leagues or clubs the need for continuity is essential.

3.9.2 The major companies

It is apparent that although there are many hundreds of commercial companies sponsoring all manner of leisure pursuits and events, sport and art events gain the most from sponsorship. It is also clear that it is the major companies investing heavily in sponsorship that dominate the market financially.

As might be expected the major sports services and equipment companies have a considerable stake in sports sponsorship – Yonex Open Badminton Championships, Corals Greyhound Golden Hurdle, Speedo Swimming Internationals, the Dunlop over 50s cricket competition and hundreds of others. However, in cash terms the major sponsors tend to be the national banks, the oil companies, tobacco manufacturers and brewers. The Whitbread Round the World yacht race and the Virginia Slims Tennis Tournaments are typical.

Why do the 'big four' – *banks, oil, tobacco* and *alcohol* – need sponsorship? Although commercially powerful they are vulnerable to tarnished public images. Banking and oil are connected with huge profits, drinking is linked with alcoholism and crime, and smoking with lung cancer. *Sponsorship helps to buy respectability.* Respectability means a good public image. Good images create favourable impressions to buy products and services.

3.9.3   Sponsorship and television

The major sponsor's main motive is not to aid sport and the arts but to achieve maximum publicity. Maximum publicity means exposure on television. By far the greatest sponsorship of sport is seen on the two BBC television channels. The BBC's charter, however, explicitly forbids paid advertising. The BBC cannot advertise. Commercial television cannot sponsor, but the line between advertising and sponsorship is somewhat tenuous.

There appears to be a qualitative difference between the two. The publication of a company brand name constitutes advertising; the company's name does not. The company nevertheless can get *more* exposure per hour for its name than would be permissible on the independent television network. During two successive weekends taken at random – 6/7 April 1985 and 13/14 April 1985 – examination of the Radio Times revealed that at least 18 hours of BBC television coverage was given to sponsored sporting events. These included the Rugby League Silk Cut Challenge Cup, the Rugby Union Thorn EMI County Championship Final, the Ladbroke University Boat Race, the Hewlet-Packard Amateur Swimming Association National Short Course Championship, the Ice Hockey Heineken League and the 1985 Embassy World Snooker Championships with a record £300 000 in prize money. During the two weeks of the Championship snooker was covered on both BBC channels during prime viewing time.

It is not surprising to find, therefore, that the highest jump in sponsored television hours in the first half of 1984 was made by snooker – almost 27 hours. Soccer, the British national sport, lost an hour of sponsored coverage during the same period and now trails way behind snooker (by 76 hours). This is an indication of the influence of both television and commercial sponsorship. Sports sponsorship is big business. Detailed computer compilations costing several hundreds of pounds are available from *Sportscan* which give detailed information about who sponsors sport, for how much and why. Of the free 'advertising' of sport transmitted on television in 1984 the biggest spenders were the tobacco companies and the list of sponsors includes some 800 others, including over 90 new companies, with only 10 losses despite the recession. In 1975 there were 1200 hours of television sport. In just the first half of 1984 there were 1184 hours. With the increased popularity of sponsorship and the fourth television channel and breakfast television, UK sponsorship via the media is increasing still further.

1984 was a most significant year in the use of sports sponsorship as a communications medium. By January 1985 *Sportscan* had identified approximately 1400 companies involved in the sponsorship of sport. 28 different industries are now involved with sport, and 1984 saw a much wider spread of activity across not only events and new events, but in coaching, training, award schemes, youth, women's sports, facilities and equipment, as well as teams and individuals. [36]

From a recreation management viewpoint, whether companies are advertising or sponsoring events and projects, they are all marketing to draw customers to their services and products by creating favourable impressions so that people will buy what the company has to offer rather than a competitor's product.

3.10 COMMERCIAL PROVIDERS: SUMMARY

This chapter has been concerned with the commercial providers of leisure services, facilities and products. The magnitude and complexity of the commercial sector is evident and the overlap and involvement with both the voluntary and public sector further complicates the scene. What is clear is that commercial providers of facilities, services and products for leisure consumption, have by far the greatest influence on people's use of leisure time. This is seen particularly in leisure in and around the home, and in the media in particular. It is seen in social recreation where many millions of people gamble, eat and drink out, are entertained and make trips to the countryside. The holiday and tourist industry is an expanding commercial market and the continuing rise in active recreation has expanded the leisure and sports goods markets. Sponsorship has made it possible to promote many sports and arts events and has helped to bring major sporting attractions of the highest calibre into the homes of millions of people through television.

Despite the overlap between the three main sectors, the commercial sector is quite different from the other two. The commercial provider is in it for the money. In order to reap the best profits and returns on investment, management policies, approaches and techniques employed by commercial managers are often very different from those employed in the public sector. The Recreation Manager should be aware of the differences and learn which approaches and techniques are best applied to specific situations. Many general management principles will apply to all recreation whether in the public, private or commercial sectors. However, many specific differences will apply to different management situations. *Recreation management is thus both general and specific.*

Commercial leisure and recreation is a massive industry in terms of investment. It is limited, however, in what is likely to be provided through its market. Capital investment must produce an adequate return on investment and this therefore excludes many costly land based resources and social service elements. The need for co-ordination between the public, commercial and voluntary sectors is thus of immense importance.

REFERENCES AND NOTES

1. General Household Survey 1983 data in Central Statistical Office (1985) *Social Trends 1985*, HMSO, London; GHS 1980 data in Central Statistical Office (1982) *Social Trends No. 13, 1983*, HMSO, London.
2. Henley Centre for Forecasting (1985), *Leisure Futures, Autumn 1985*.
3. *Brighton Conference News*, April 1985.
4. Grand Metropolitan Ltd Annual Report 1983.
5. The Rank Organization Annual Report 1983.
6. Trusthouse Forte Ltd Annual Report 1983 and Half Year Statement 1984.
7. Office of Population Censuses and Surveys, Social Survey Division (1985), *Social Trends No. 15, 1985*, HMSO, London.
8. British Broadcasting Corporation surveys in Central Statistical Office (1985), *Social Trends 1985*, HMSO, London.
9. Independent Broadcasting Authority (1983) *TV and Radio 1983*, IBA, London.
10. British Broadcasting Corporation (1984), *BBC TV Facts and Figures 1984*, BBC, London.
11. Tolkki-Nikkonen, M. (1979), *Adult Education in Finland*, No. 3, 1979.
12. Indepedent Broadcasting Authority (1984), *Focus on Independent Broadcasting 1983*, IBA, London.
13. British Phonographic Industries (1984), *A statistical description of the British Record Industry*, BPI Yearbook.
14. *The Bookseller*, reported in Central Statistical Office (1980), *Social Trends 1981*, HMSO, London, Chapter 11.
15. Central Statistical Office (1980) *Social Trends 1981*, HMSO, London, Chapter 11.
15a *Social Trends 1984*, HMSO, London.
16. National Readership Survey 1983, reported in Central Statistical Office (1983), *Social Trends 1984*, HMSO, London.
17. Central Statistical Office (1981), *Annual Abstract of Statistics 1981*, HMSO, London.
18. Martin, W.H. and Mason, S. (1978) *Leisure Markets in Europe*, 3 volumes, Financial Times, London.
19. Sillitoe, K.K. (1969), *Planning for Leisure*, HMSO, London.
20. Young, M. and Willmott, P. (1973) *The Symmetrical Family*, Penguin Books, Harmondsworth.
21. Department of Employment statistics in Central Statistical Office (1985), *Annual Abstract of Statistics 1985*, HMSO, London.
22. Home Office (1979), *Gambling Statistics Great Britain 1968–78*, HMSO, London.
23. Home Office Survey report in Central Statistical Office (1980), *Social Trends 1981*, HMSO, London.
24. Department of Trade figures in Central Statistical Office (1980), *Social Trends 1981*, HMSO, London; (1985) *Social Trends 1985*, HMSO, London.
25. Wolk, S. (1980), *Marketing*, August 1980.
26. The Arts Council (1982) *Facts and Figures*.
27. Veal, A.J. (1979), *Sport and Recreation in England and Wales; Adult Participation 1977*, Centre for Urban and Regional Studies Research Memorandum 74, University of Birmingham.

28. Martin, W.H. and Mason, S. (1984) *The UK Sports Market*, Leisure Consultants, Sudbury, Suffolk.
29. English Tourist Board (1985) Annual Report 1984/85, ETB, London.
30. British Tourist Authority *Annual Report* 1981, and see Central Statistical Office, *Social Trends 1981, 1982, and 1985*, HMSO, London.
31. English Tourist Board (1980), *Activity and Special Interest Holidays in England 1982*, ETB, London.
32. Roberts, J. (TEST) (1979) *Sports Council/Social Science Research Council Review: The Commercial Sector in Leisure*, Sports Council/SSRC, London, p.12.
33. English Tourist Board (1978), *The Give and Take of Sponsorship*, ETB, London.
34. Promotion material for the 4th International Sport Summit, June/July 1981 in London.
35. *Sportscan*, (1985) Sports Sponsorship Computer Analysis July–December 1984, London.

Chapter 4

The national agencies

★

Arts Council
OF GREAT BRITAIN

Arts Council
OF GREAT BRITAIN

Arts Council
OF GREAT BRITAIN

Arts Council
OF GREAT BRITAIN

Arts Council
OF GREAT BRITAIN

4.1 INTRODUCTION

In Chapters 1, 2 and 3 we have seen that the providers for recreation come from the public and non-public sectors and that the whole picture is a complex one. Central government is not a single entity but a federation of separate departments, each with its own policy and ministers. The position with local government is more comprehensive though still fragmented. In providing for recreation central and local governments work with and through a number of quasi-statutory institutions and agencies. Some have been established by Royal Charter, some by legislation and others by ministerial direction. For example, the regional councils for sport and recreation were set up following a government White Paper and the Sports Council itself is almost entirely dependent on grant-in-aid. Central government, therefore, carries considerable weight and influence on national agencies.

There are a whole range of national, regional and local agencies which assist in providing for public recreation. This chapter is concerned with the national agencies. They are often hybrids of public and private providers and while their primary function is not to provide facilities some of them do, and all of them influence provision through grants, loans, technical advice or support of some kind. The major agencies such as the Sports Council, the Countryside Commission and tourist boards form a *regional* network of services.

In this chapter a brief look is taken at some of the major national agencies that have an influence on recreation and its management, namely the Arts Council, the Sports Council, the Central Council of Physical Recreation, the National Playing Fields Association, the Countryside Commission, the Forestry Commission, the Water Space Amenity Commission, the British Waterways Board and the newly formed Play Board – the Association for Children's Play and Recreation. The tourist industry has already featured in Chapter 3.

4.2 THE ARTS COUNCIL OF GREAT BRITAIN

4.2.1 History of the Council

The Arts Council of Great Britain was established by Royal Charter in 1946. The impetus for its creation was the success of the Council for the Encouragement of Music and Arts which had been established during the Second World War. The Arts Council's funds were made available from parliamentary grant-in-aid, with its first grant totalling less than £250 000.

The council established its own regional offices, but in the 1950s these were phased out and in their place sprang up the regional arts associations. These associations now work closely with the Arts Council but are nevertheless independent of it, being separate organizations funded from a variety of sources, including the Arts Council.

A working party was set up in 1978 at the request of the Arts Council to examine the council's functions. The report recommended a more efficient and economic organization structure, and the majority of its recommendations have by now been carried out with a reduction in the size and number of committees and delegation of more executive powers to the council officers.

Scotland and Wales have their own councils. The members of the Scottish Arts Council and of the Welsh Arts Council are appointed by the Arts Council of Great Britain with the approval of the appropriate Secretary of State. Both councils are run along similar lines to those described for the Arts Council, and both are funded from its grant-in-aid. Each produces its own annual report to show how such funds are allocated.

4.2.2 Aims and organization of the council

The Arts Council's aims are threefold:

1. To develop and improve the knowledge, understanding and practice of the arts.
2. To increase the accessibility of the arts to the public throughout Great Britain.
3. To cooperate with government departments, local authorities and other bodies to achieve these objects.

The council itself is a body of 20 individuals with wide experience in the arts and public life. They are appointed by the Minister responsible for the Arts after consultation with the Secretaries of State for Scotland and Wales. The council is advised by specialist panels and committees, composed of professionals and laymen from different fields. The present structure of these committees and panels is shown in Figs. 4.1 and 4.2.

The administration and implementation of policies and decisions is carried out by a permanent staff of officers divided into a number of departments controlled by a department director. Presiding over all departments and directors is the Secretary General.

4.2.3 Allocation of funds

Each year the council receives a grant-in-aid from the Government, on the vote of the Office of Arts and Libraries. For 1983/84 this was approximately

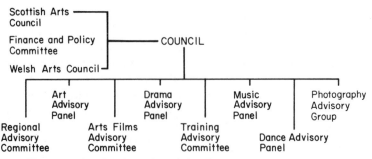

Note: Finance and Policy Committee is in effect a sub–committee of Council.

Fig. 4.1 Arts Council advisory panels and committees at 12 April 1985. Source: The Arts Council of Great Britain.

£93.5 million, £101 million in 1984/85 and £106 million in 1985/86. The Council publishes annual reports which give a detailed description of its work and the way in which the grant-in-aid has been spent. Table 4.1 shows its expenditure for 1984/85 and 1983/84 together with the percentage of this expenditure allocated to each category. A comparison showing the proportion of total expenditure allocated to these categories shows little difference between the proportions allocated each year, but what is of interest is that nearly one-third of the Council's total expenditure is consumed by the national companies, the same proportion as is shared between the Scottish and Welsh Arts Councils and all the regional arts associations. In 1985/6 £29.5 million was allocated to the four national companies – Royal Opera House, English National Opera, National Theatre and the Royal Shakespeare Company.

4.2.4 Regional arts associations

As mentioned earlier, the regional arts associations are independent organizations although they work closely with the Arts Council. They promote the development and expansion of the arts in their region with funds received from local authorities, local education authorities, industry, charitable trusts, private patrons and the Arts Council. Different associations place different emphasis on the various art forms and the manner in which they promote them, but the main services they provide are: grant-aiding, the promotion of events, publications and publicity, advice and research, planning and coordinations and help for artists. There are twelve associations in England, three in Wales and none in Scotland.

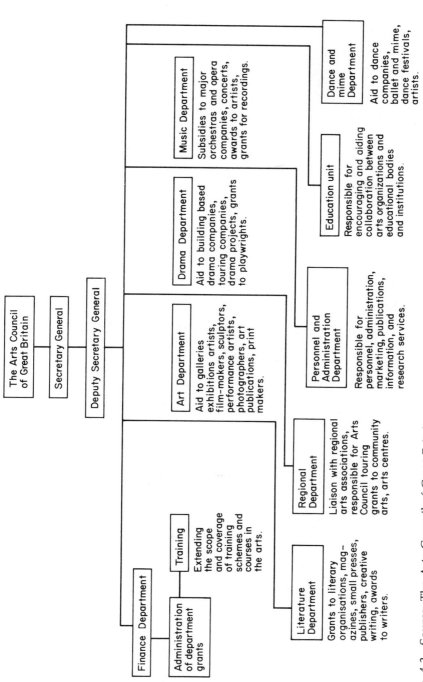

The Arts Council of Great Britain

Secretary General

Deputy Secretary General

Finance Department

Administration of department grants

Training
Extending the scope and coverage of training schemes and courses in the arts.

Literature Department
Grants to literary organisations, magazines, small presses, publishers, creative writing, awards to writers.

Regional Department
Liaison with regional arts associations, responsible for Arts Council touring grants to community arts, arts centres.

Art Department
Aid to galleries exhibitions artists, film-makers, sculptors, performance artists, photographers, art publications, print makers.

Personnel and Administration Department
Responsible for personnel, administration, marketing, publications, information, and research services.

Drama Department
Aid to building based drama companies, touring companies, drama projects, grants to playwrights.

Education unit
Responsible for encouraging and aiding collaboration between arts organizations and educational bodies and institutions.

Music Department
Subsidies to major orchestras and opera companies, concerts, awards to artists, grants for recordings.

Dance and mime Department
Aid to dance companies, ballet and mime, dance festivals, artists.

Fig. 4.2 Source: The Arts Council of Great Britain.

Table 4.1 The Arts Council expenditure and allocation of funds

	Expenditure 1984/85 (£)	Expenditure 1983/84 (£)	Total expenditure 1984/85 (%)	Total expenditure 1983/84 (%)
Scottish Arts Council	12 024 000	11 938 831	12.3	12.8
Welsh Arts Council	7 107 300	6 536 830	7.3	7.0
National Companies	30 597 011	29 102 935	31	31
Music	8,906,059	6 346 456	9.1	6.8
Dance	3 061 103	2 875 360	3.1	3
Drama	12 411 367	11 864 459	12.7	12.7
Touring	3 958 044	6 041 566	4	6.5
Art	3 555 314	3 529 074	3.6	3.9
Literature	786 942	837 168	0.8	0.9
Arts Centres and community projects	1 243 078	1 186 456	1.3	1.3
Training in the Arts	667 706	637 585	0.7	0.7
Regional arts associations	12 338 483	11 179 148	12.6	12
Miscellaneous donations, reports, surveys, publications	68 130	175 241	—	0.2
Housing the Arts	1 145 700	979 000	1	1
Total expenditure	97 870 237	93 230 109		

Source: Arts Council Annual Report 1984/85 [1].

4.3 THE SPORTS COUNCIL

4.3.1 The history of the Council

In 1935 the Central Council for Recreative Physical Training (CCRPT) was created. It was established as a voluntary organization by physical education specialists to coordinate the work of organizations concerned with physical training but soon broadened the scope of its activities to include consultation and coordination with the governing bodies of sport.

In 1937 the Government's *Physical Training and Recreation Act* gave rise to the National Fitness Council (NFC) together with a £2 million grant to provide for sport and physical recreation. The NFC was never established and the CCPRT seized the opportunity to take over both the NFC's responsibility and finance. After the Second World War the CCRPT became the Central Council of Physical Recreation (CCPR), receiving a grant through the Ministry of Education, opening its first national recreation centres and establishing a network of regional offices throughout the country.

The Wolfenden Report of 1960 [2], commissioned by the CCPR, identified the need for a Sports Development Council. In order to satisfy this need the Sports Council was eventually established in 1965. Originally it was simply an advisory body, closely linked to the Government through the Civil Service, with a government minister as its chairman. However, in 1972 it was granted independent status by Royal Charter, taking over both the staff and assets of the CCPR and assuming responsibility for the Technical Unit for Sport (TUS) which prior to this had come under the auspices of the Department of Education and Science.

The implementation of policies and decisions taken by the Sports Council is undertaken by a permanent staff of officers who work for various units which are ultimately presided over by the Director General. Of particular interest to the Recreation Manager are the Sports Development Unit, the Technical Unit for Sport which provides advice on the design and construction of facilities, the Press and Publicity Unit which produces the Council's bimonthly magazine, and all other Council publications, and the Information Centre which acts as a clearing house for national and international information and holds a collection of material for reference purposes.

The Sports Council has nine regional offices with the responsibility for implementing Sports Council policies with regard to the needs of the particular regions they serve. They provide technical and advisory services to local authorities, voluntary sports bodies and other organizations.

The Sports Council also administers six national residential sports centres with the primary object of meeting the top-level requirements of select sports. The centres are: Crystal Palace (athletics, swimming and other major sports), Holme Pierrepont (water sports), Lilleshall (soccer, gymnastics, cricket etc.), Bisham Abbey (tennis, hockey, rugby etc.), Plas y Brenin (mountaineering) and Cowes (sailing). In addition to the Sports Council there are three national councils. The Scottish Sports Council and the Sports Council for Wales were set up as independent executive organizations by Royal Charter in 1972. They receive annual grant-in-aid direct from central government and perform similar general functions to those of the Sports Council. The Sports Council for Northern Ireland was established by statute in 1974. It advises government on capital expenditure and financially assists Voluntary Sports Organizations in a number of ways. The members of all three councils are appointed by their respective Secretaries of State.

4.3.2   Aims and organization of the Council

The main aims of the Council are as follows:

1. To promote general understanding of the social importance and value of sport and physical recreation.
2. To increase the provision of new sports facilities and stimulate fuller use of existing facilities.
3. To encourage wider participation in sport and physical recreation as a means of enjoying leisure.
4. To raise the standards of performance.

The Sports Council itself at present consists of a chairman, two vice-chairmen and 24 members, appointed by the Secretary of State for the Environment. It is advised by four main committees: Policy and Resources, National Resources, Regional Resources and Publicity, Information and Research.

4.3.3   Allocation of funds

The Sports Council receives an annual grant from central government to spend as it sees fit providing there is no contravention of government policy. The Council publishes its accounts in its annual report and Table 4.2 shows a breakdown of its expenditure for 1984/85 and 1983/84.

The Sports Council's first grant-in-aid was £3.5 million in 1972. This had risen to £15.5 million by 1979 (£5.5 million at 1972 price levels according to the Council's Annual Report 1979/80). The grant was increased to £19.3 million in 1980/81, to £21 million in 1981/82 and had risen to £28.6 million by 1984/85 with additional grants for areas of special need

Table 4.2   Sports Council expenditure and allocation of funds

	Expenditure 1984/85 (£)	Expenditure 1983/84 (£)	Total expenditure 1984/85 (%)	Total expenditure 1983/84 (%)
Staff costs	3 452 030	3 268 231	10	10.5
National centres	6 537 037	5 869 280	19.6	18.9
Sports developments (grants to governing bodies etc.)	10 068 793	8 338 106	30.2	26.9
Regional and local facilities	6 824 223	8 965 676	20.4	28.9
Sports Council Trust	2 590 827	1 777 771	7.8	5.7
Other national facilities	584 345	149 649	1.8	0.5
Other administrative expenses	1 726 875	1 436 075	5.2	4.6
Training courses and conferences	136 525	245 514	0.5	0.8
Research, publicity and information	1 456 853	971 664	4.4	3.1
Depreciation	916	916	—	—
Total expenditure	33 378 424	31 022 882		

Source: Adapted from Sports Council Annual Report 1984/85 [3].

such as in inner cities and for young people. The work of the Sports Council has been rationalized in recent years into a ten year plan, beginning with a five year rolling programme of expenditure for 1983–88, which is revised annually. This is shown in Table 4.3. Read references [4] and [5] for more detail.

The Sports Council for Wales also published its ten year strategy 1986–1996 [6]. The Strategy and the ten year plans are discussed in Section 11.3.2.

The grant-in-aid allocation to the Scottish Sports Council in 1984/85 was £4.3 million of which 33% was allocated to national governing bodies and 35% to national sports training centres and national facilities. The Sports Council for Wales received grant-in-aid of £2.852 million in 1984/85. The Sports Council for Northern Ireland staff and budget are subject to the approval of the Northern Ireland Department of Education. Its 1984/85 approved deficit of £986 000 supported financially and otherwise 74 governing bodies of sport. The council's grant to voluntary organizations in 1984/85 was £383 200.

Table 4.3 Rolling programme 1983/88 (NB Figures for 1983/88 are expressed in 1981 prices)

	Approved budget (£000s)						
	1982/83	1983/84	1984/85	1985/86	1986/87	1987/88
Salaries, national insurance and superannuation (other than for National Centre staff)	3 070	3 250	3 600	3 800	3 650	3 650
Administrative expenses	1 175	1 150	1 240	1 270	1 260	1 250
Net running costs: National Centres	2 025	2 100	2 100	2 100	2 200	2 200
Grants to governing bodies for administration, coaching, competitions including internal events and other expenditure on sports development	7 430	10 420	11 870	12 570	10 770	10 270
Other non-capital expenditure	305	250	250	250	250	250
Research and information	980	1 000	1 060	1 080	940	950
Capital expenditure:						
Sports Council National Centres	1 565	2 600	1 700	1 000	800	900
Other National Centres	185	700	1 900	3 000	3 600	3 500
Regional and local facilities	6 092	8 700	19 800	21 950	22 950	23 000
Loans	590	740	1 020	1 450	1 800	2 050
	23 417	30 910	44 540	48 470	48 220	48 020
Receipts: repayment of loans	170	290	420	600	850	1 150
other	470	370	370	370	370	370
Totals	22 777	30 250	43 750	47 500	47 000	46 500

Source: The Sports Council (1983) A Forward Look: Rolling Programme 1983/88 [5].

4.3.4 The regional councils for sport and recreation

In 1976 nine regional councils for sport and recreation were set up by the Minister of State for Sport and Recreation to replace the regional sports councils. These councils supply a forum for consultation among local authorities, local sports councils, various regional bodies of sport and recreation and other interested parties. They are concerned with the planning of facilities and the promotion of opportunities for participation in organized sport and recreation, as well as with informal countryside recreation and the conservation problems inherent in its development. Following the DOE Circular 73/77 *Guidelines for Regional Recreational Strategies* July 1977 [7], the regional councils are also responsible for the production of strategy plans for the development of recreation within their regions.

The chairman of each council is appointed by the Minister of Sport, and the secretariat of the councils are provided by the staff of the regional offices of the Sports Council.

4.4 THE CENTRAL COUNCIL OF PHYSICAL RECREATION

4.4.1 The role of the Central Council of Physical Recreation (CCPR)

After the transference of the CCPR's staff and property assets to the Sports Council in 1972 the member bodies of the CCPR voted to retain the CCPR's independence as a forum for the national and governing bodies of sport and recreation. In addition the Royal Charter setting up the Sports Council specified the need for a 'consultative body' to the council, and CCPR has been accorded this role.

The CCPR is thus an independent voluntary body with the following objectives:

1. To constitute a standing forum where all national governing and representative bodies of sport and physical recreation may be represented and may collectively or through special groups, where appropriate, formulate and promote measures to improve and develop sport and physical recreation.
2. To support the work of specialist sports bodies and to bring them together with other interested organizations.
3. To act as a consultative body to the Sports Council and other representative or public bodies concerned with sport and physical recreation.

The CCPR has over 250 governing and other bodies of sport and recreation in membership, encompassing some 87 000 local sports clubs.

In order to facilitate the meeting of organizations with similar interests and problems, the CCPR has structured itself into six divisions:

1. Games and Sports Division.
2. Movement and Dance Division.
3. Outdoor Pursuits Division.
4. Water Recreation Division.
5. Division of interested organizations.
6. Major spectator sports Division.

The CCPR also provides a number of services to its member bodies including a press service, help with sponsorship, legal advice and assistance with fund raising.

The CCPR's income for 1983, which helps to fulfil its role, was £223 448, of which £179 194 was derived by contract from the Sports Council, the rest coming by way of subscriptions, gross interest and surplus on events.

4.5   THE NATIONAL PLAYING FIELDS ASSOCIATION

4.5.1   The role of the National Playing Fields Association (NPFA)

Prior to 1925 the supply of public recreational facilities was a local matter with provision being spasmodic and held back by the lack of central direction. The National Playing Fields Association, a voluntary body, was founded in 1925 to offer such direction by encouraging the provision of adequate playing fields and recreation facilities throughout the country. The association was incorporated by Royal Charter in 1933, and in 1963 was registered as a national charity.

The main aim of the association is to stimulate the provision of playing fields, playgrounds and recreation centres by publicity and technical and financial assistance. The work is for the benefit of the whole community, but the major emphasis lies with young people and the handicapped.

In order to carry out its aims the association has a Council of 15 composed of representatives and individuals from a wide range of recreation and educational spheres. From the members of this council an executive committee is elected to be responsible for the work of the subcommittees. At present there are two subcommittees: technical and appeals. A small full-time staff implements the policy and decisions of the Council in most counties in England and Wales. There are affiliated Playing Fields Associations and a branch association in Scotland. The NPFA provides a number of services for use by local authorities, sports clubs, voluntary organizations and others concerned with the aims it is trying to promote.

Like all charitable institutions a major preoccupation of the NPFA is concerned with fund raising. It derives its funds mainly from voluntary donations but also receives a small Sports Council grant towards administration costs (£35 765 in 1983) and a grant from the Voluntary Services Unit.

4.5.2 Advisory services

(a) Children's play

Until April 1984 the NPFA had a Children and Youth Department supported by seven regional play advisers, which gave practical advice on children's play, including adventure playgrounds, holiday play schemes, play leadership, equipped playgrounds and insurance. The department also ran a resource centre in Birmingham where waste materials from industry and commerce were gathered and stocked for use by adventure playgrounds, play centres and play schemes. In April 1984 responsibility for children's play passed to the Association for Children's Play and Recreation, now popularly known as Playboard.

(b) Technical advice

Advice is available on the provision, design, layout and construction of playing fields, athletics tracks, playgrounds and indoor recreation facilities as well as on technical problems such as playing field drainage.

(c) Grants and loans

Advice about the various sources of financial assistance for schemes and help with applications can be obtained from the county associations. The NPFA itself may also be able to provide grant aid or a low interest loan, although funds are limited.

(d) Publications and information

The association publishes a wide range of literature, and until 1984 housed in its London headquarters an information centre with a reference library and the facility for borrowing books, photographs and slides. Unfortunately, financial constraints necessitated the recent closure of this facility.

4.6 THE COUNTRYSIDE COMMISSION

4.6.1 Development and role of the Countryside Commission

The first government report concerned with the countryside was that of the Addison Committee in 1929. This recommended the setting up of national parks with the twin aims of conservation and recreation.

Twenty years and a number of reports later, the 1949 *National Parks and*

Access to the Countryside Act created the National Parks Commission and gave it the power to establish national parks. Ten of these parks were designated between 1950 and 1955 being, in order of creation, the Peak District, the Lake District, Snowdonia, Dartmoor, the Pembrokeshire Coast, the Yorkshire Dales, Exmoor, Northumberland and the Brecon Beacons. Areas of outstanding natural beauty (often smaller than the parks) were also established. Concern soon began to grow, however, about the conflicting claims of conservation and recreation within the national parks and a need was seen to ease the pressure on the parks by developing countryside recreation and conservation in general. To this end the 1968 *Countryside Act* abolished the National Parks Commission and set up the Countryside Commission with the purpose of keeping under review: 'matters relating to the conservation and enhancement of landscape beauty in England and Wales, and to the provision and improvement of facilities of the countryside for enjoyment, including the need to secure access for open-air recreation'. Independence from the Department of the Environment was granted by the *Wildlife and Country-side Act 1981*, when the Countryside Commission became a grant-in-aid body.

The role of the Commission in relation to the countryside is very similar to that of the Sports Council in relation to sport. It does not itself provide facilities but provides finance and expertise for providing bodies, particularly local authorities. It has the power to aid financially countryside projects such as picnic sites, country parks and the development of long-distance footpaths, to designate national parks, areas of outstanding natural beauty and heritage coasts, and to advise on countryside planning and management. It undertakes research into all aspects of countryside management and usage and produces educational and informative literature about the countryside in general, and specific areas such as national parks and long-distance footpaths.

The members of the Commission, numbering about twelve, are appointed by the Secretary of State for the Environment and the Secretary of State for Wales. In matters affecting Wales the Commission is assisted by a specially appointed committee. The Commission has fewer than 100 staff, who are all Public Servants. About half of the staff are placed in the Commission's eight regional offices. The Commission receives an annual grant from central government to cover its direct expenditure (estimated at approximately £12.6 million in 1983/84). Of this, 12% was to be spent on salaries and administration, 4% on research and experiments, 21% on information and publicity, and 65% in grants. The national parks, which since 1974 have been managed by their own committees (one for each park, comprising local authority and Countryside Commission members) receive their own grant from central government, totalling £7.9 million for 1985/86.

4.6.2 The Countryside Commission for Scotland

Scotland has a separate Countryside Commission, set up under the *Countryside (Scotland) Act 1967*. It is financed directly from central government and its members are appointed by the Secretary of State for Scotland.

4.7 THE FORESTRY COMMISSION

4.7.1 The development and role of the Forestry Commission

The Forestry Commission is the largest landowner in Britain, with 3 million acres. It was constituted in 1919 by an Act of Parliament, being charged with the responsibility for the interests of forestry. Its primary role is that of timber production.

In 1935 the Commission recognized the public's need for greater opportunities of access to its forests for recreational purposes and opened the first of its forest parks in Argyll. This was followed by a forest park in Snowdonia in 1937 and there are now seven forest parks in all.

The commission is responsible to the Ministry of Agriculture, Fisheries and Food, and to the Secretaries of State for Scotland and Wales. It is administered via its seven 'conservancy areas' and has a total staff of 8000.

4.7.2 The Commission and recreation

In 1970 the Commission set up a conservation and recreation branch at its headquarters and established eleven recreation planning officers in each of its conservancy regions. Recreation plans for each of these regions have been written.

In terms of recreation provision, the Commission provides viewpoints, forest walks, picnic sites, car parks, holiday cabins and camping and caravanning sites. It accommodates other activities including car rallying, orienteering, horse-riding, deer-stalking, fishing, hiking, rock-climbing, canoeing, swimming, boating, potholing, skiing and nature study.

In 1977, 24 million day visits were made to the commission-owned woodlands, the principal activities being walking and picnicking. The problems resulting from the primary forest needs, tree planting and felling and the secondary recreation requirements, need policy sensitivity and diplomatic management. In addition to the user problems, the commission must make a return on investment. The greater the provision for public recreation, the more difficult it becomes to show the level of profit required.

4.7.3 The Nature Conservancy Council

The Nature Conservancy Council, though not part of the Forestry Commission, is an agency that controls and manages large areas of national nature reserves with 100 wardens. Part of their job is to make the public aware of the countryside and nature and to enhance understanding and enjoyment. They are an important part of recreation services and management.

4.8 THE WATER SPACE AMENITY COMMISSION

The Water Space Amenity Commission was set up by the *Water Act 1973*, which was concerned with the re-organization of the water industry. The Commission was established to advise the ten newly appointed Regional Water Authorities in England on their functions relating to the recreational and amenity use of water. It was also to advise the Government on national policy with respect to this.

The Commission comprises the chairman of each of the regional authorities and ten members appointed by the Secretary of State in consultation with bodies such as the Sports Council, the Countryside Commission and the English Tourist Board.

The Commission is concerned with the waterside environment as well as with the recreational use of the water itself.

4.9 THE BRITISH WATERWAYS BOARD

The British Waterways Board was set up by the *Transport Act 1962*, and given responsibility for the majority of inland waterways and their associated reservoirs in the *Transport Act 1968*. In the same year an amenity division was set up within the Board to plan and develop the recreational use of the waterways, primarily in conjunction with local authorities and private enterprise. The division is responsible for the licensing of craft, recreation research and the running of two hire cruiser fleets. In 1983, 23 454 boat licences and registrations were issued.

The Board is responsible for 2000 miles of canals and rivers, approximately half of which are classified as cruising waterways and 93 reservoirs. Nearly 30% of its annual income is from grant-in-aid, which for 1983 was £30.7 million.

4.10 THE ASSOCIATION FOR CHILDREN'S PLAY AND RECREATION – PLAY BOARD

4.10.1 History of Play Board

The Association for Children's Play and Recreation Limited – Play Board – was established in 1983. This followed pressure over many years by voluntary organizations (especially the National Playing Fields Association) to increase public and political awareness of the importance of children's play.

As a result of lobbying and considerable parliamentary interest, the Department of the Environment was identified as the lead department for children's play and the Minister for Sport was given the responsibility for coordinating central government response.

For the first three years of its life the new agency – which was rapidly established as an independent voluntary organization – was allocated a grant of £700 000 per annum. A Board of Trustee Directors undertook the direction of the Association in its early days until an elective and appointed structure was set up. The current Board principally consists of:

1. Individuals elected from the National Play Advisory Committee who are themselves elected from Play Forum, the membership arm of Play Board.
2. Representatives from the local authority associations.
3. Some of the original Trustee Directors.

Play Board has a head office in Birmingham and area offices in Leeds and London. Work in Wales is funded by the Welsh Office and in Northern Ireland by the Northern Ireland Education Department. The position in Scotland is still under review.

4.10.2 Aims of Play Board

The principal aims of Play Board are fourfold:

1. To promote facilities for play, recreation and other leisure-time opportunities for all children.
2. To carry out, encourage, commission and publish research into children's play and recreation.
3. To provide an educational, advisory, information and promotional service to raise awareness of the importance of play.
4. To provide a coordination and development role with voluntary organizations concerned with children's play and recreation.

Within these broad aims, Play Board intends to:
1. Provide a 'good value for money' advisory service based on sound

information principally to local authorities and voluntary organizations who share its aims.
2. Establish the present state of play facilities as well as future requirements.
3. Identify the present and future support and training needs of parents, volunteers and paid adults who work with and for children.
4. Work with, and in support of, organizations who provide services directly for children and act as a focus in advising central government on children's play and recreation.
5. Work with the local authority association nationally to encourage all their members to recognize the importance of children's play and to use local resources as effectively as possible.
6. Work with voluntary organizations, commercial bodies and local authorities to improve the quantity and quality of opportunities for children in their free time.

Play Board's staffing currently consists of a Chief Executive, Organization Director, Research and Information staff, Play Forum staff, Regional Play Officers and Administrative staff. It is building up a substantial computer based information service.

4.11 NATIONAL AGENCIES AND RECREATION MANAGEMENT

Although they are not primarily providers of facilities, the national agencies have an important role to play in helping to provide resources, financial aid, technical support and management of facilities.

The Sports Council strategy *Sport in the Community . . . The Next Ten Years* [4] to increase mass participation and meet the needs of several target groups has been enhanced through its own schemes and partnership initiatives. These include the Ever Thought of Sport? and What's Your Sport? campaigns, the Indoor Tennis Initiative in collaboration with the All England Club and the LTA, the partnership National Demonstration Projects and the Action Sport programmes. These initiatives are referred to in Chapter 11 within a recreation planning context.

In countryside recreation alone thousands of staff manage and supervise a whole range of resources – country parks, water recreation, National Trust lands, national parks. Hence, national agencies are not just enablers and semi-government agents but employers of Recreation Managers. In addition, training for recreation management has been recognized and instigated by agencies such as the Sports Council. The council initiated the first working party on the training for recreation management and over the past years has run a highly successful management project: the Sports Centre of the Year Award (see Section 12.6.1). This scheme has made the single most important contribution to the effective management of purpose-built recreation facilities.

Study of the national agencies has revealed the important part that good management has to play at policy and practical levels. Countryside recreation, for example, is fraught with conflicts of interest and management. The services are fragmented; there is considerable overlap between the many different agencies. There are conflicts between planning, agriculture, forestry, tourism, water resources, sport, recreation and conservation. Recreation management has an important part to play in overcoming the problems and providing enhanced leisure opportunity.

REFERENCES AND NOTES

1. The Arts Council of Great Britain Annual Report 1983/84.
2. Wolfenden Committee (1960), *Sports and the Community*, Central Council of Physical Recreation, London.
3. The Sports Council Annual Report 1984/85.
4. The Sports Council (1982), *Sport in the Community . . . The Next Ten Years*, Sports Council, London.
5. The Sports Council (1983), *A Forward Look: Rolling Programme 1983–88*, Sports Council, London.
6. The Sports Council for Wales (1985), *National Strategy 1986/1996 Consultative Document*, Sports Council for Wales, Cardiff.
7. Department of the Environment (1977), Circular 73/77 – *Guidelines for Regional Recreational Strategies*, DOE, London.

NB Information about the national agencies has been gathered either from annual reports, promotion material or in direct discussion with officers.

   With the passing of legislation to disband the Metropolitan County Councils and the Greater London Council, the roles of agencies such as the Arts Council and Sports Council will be expanded to take on further responsibilities.

RECOMMENDED ADDITIONAL READING

Evans, J.H. (1974), *Service to Sport: the story of the CCPR, 1935–1972*, Sports Council London.

★

PART TWO

Recreation philosophy

★

The objective of Part Two is to describe and explain three
related recreation phenomena – 'play', 'recreation' and
'leisure'. Each concept is studied as a separate entity in
Chapters 5, 6 and 7 to try to understand its nature and to
identify what similarities and differences exist between the
three. An attempt is then made in Chapter 8 to interrelate
the three concepts to try to discover whether there is an
integrated base or logical conceptual framework from which
recreation planning and management should stem. The
implications are examined as they relate to leisure
opportunity and recreation services.

Chapter 5

Play

★

★

5.1   INTRODUCTION: WHY STUDY PLAY?

The objective of this section is not to produce a theory or to propound philosophies and beliefs. Rather it is to attempt to look at play conceptually, to draw out characteristics of play behaviour and to try to understand what it is and why people play. While this is impossible to do without reference to interrelated concepts such as recreation and leisure, the purpose in this part of the book is to focus on the phenomena, play, recreation and leisure as *separate* entities. The reasons for this are fivefold. *First*, there does not appear to be an acceptable all-inclusive definition or theory of play. *Second*, a great diversity of behaviours are labelled play – everything from games to gambling, from adventure to vandalism, from lazing to utter exhaustion. *Third*, we need to discover whether 'play', 'recreation' and 'leisure' differ and how they do. A weakness plagues the emerging profession of recreation management; it is the lack of attention given to relating the tangents of play, recreation and leisure into a *cohesive* and *usable* whole. It seems clear that the three concepts are used on the one hand to explain three distinct phenomena, each of which is an important primary element; yet on the other hand the terms are often used indiscriminately and frequently interchanged. As a consequence, understanding is limited, owing to the blurring of definitional lines and reliance placed on generalized assumptions which have no acceptable research background. [1]

Fourth, if recreation management is to blossom into a profession with a philosophy, an ethic and professional standing, it needs to establish itself as a discipline with a basic framework of terminology and understanding. At present, recreation theory, and consequently recreation planning, appear to be flowing in several diverse directions in search of this cohesive perspective. *Fifth*, if we can understand *what* it is and *why* people play we shall then have a fundamental basis upon which planning should be based [2]. If we know what motivates people to participate, conflicts over priorities and facilities would be quickly resolved. On the other hand, if we have no basic insights into why people play, then we cannot have any confidence either in the facilities we produce or the programmes we manage, for we will not know whether they are relevant or appropriate.

Although no single definition or meaning may be adequate for each term, by understanding the range of meanings more completely, recreation professionals can be in a better position for determining which services would qualify as play, as leisure and as recreation as separate or combined services.

In this first section relating to play, only one major assumption is made and that is that play is beneficial to people. Because it is, we should try to understand *what* it is and *how* we can present situations and opportunities for it to occur. It is hypothesized that such an understanding is a cornerstone of the emerging profession of recreation planning and management.

In this chapter 'play' is studied in the following manner. *First*, it is introduced to show that it is by no means a simple phenomenon but an extraordinarily complex one. *Second*, play is placed in historical perspective. *Third*, some of the theories of play – classical, recent and modern – are analysed and *finally*, play philosophy and theory are discussed in the light of their meanings and practical application as far as they relate to recreation planning, services and management.

5.2 PLAY: A COMPLEX PHENOMENON

People play. They appear to have done so from the dawn of man. Why do they? Is play the same phenomenon as recreation? Is it leisure? Is it a range of activities in which people indulge throughout their life span? If so, why does one person choose one activity, another choose something entirely different? To one, an activity may be play; to another the same activity could be drudgery. What determines one's attitude? What determines the choice? It is upbringing, ability, stature, education, employment, status, personality, the pressure of the social group or friends? Given the right ingredients can choices be determined, predictions made and demands gauged? If so, major planning problems can be tackled realistically.

Play is a mystery, an enigma. It is understood, yet misunderstood, known yet unknown, tangible yet so internal to the individual that it is untouchable. It is utterly individual, yet universal. The play of children is accepted but the play of adults has a stereotyped image of muddy footballers on muddy pitches. However, play is not confined to the games of children, the sport of young men, the family outing or the Christmas party. Play can pervade all aspects of life, not just physical play but the play of the mind, the play of words, the play of communications with people. To Sebastian de Grazia [3]:

'The world is divided into two classes. Not three or five or twenty. Just two. One is the great majority. The other is the leisure kind, not those of wealth or position or birth, but those who love ideas and the imagination. Of the great mass of mankind there are few persons who are blessed and tormented with this love. They may work, steal, flirt, fight, like all the others, but everything they do is touched with the play of thought'.

Play then can be evident in all walks of life, at home, at school, at work, in politics and unions, in religion, in business, in crime and vandalism, in international dealings and even in war. The film *Oh, What a Lovely War!* carried the caption 'the ever popular war game folks with songs, battles and a few jokes'. The problem with war is that for some it can be a game – it can be fun!

. One of the distinguishing signs of the play world is its strict adherence to invented rules, which suspend the ordinary rules of real life. The attitudes encompassed in play rules carry over from the play world into the 'real' world. While boxers play to Queensberry Rules, soldiers 'play' to the rules of the Geneva Convention and some criminals have a code of acceptable behaviour. Parliamentary and local government rules are cloaked in the playful seriousness of *obligatory procedures*, the 'Mr Chairmans', the 'points of order' and the adherence to the 'laws of the game'. Sometimes, as with children's games, it would appear that the procedures are more important than the business itself. Fair play is often play acceptable to the rules. In this context it is curious to find how much more lenient society is towards the cheat than it is towards the spoilsport. As Huizinga [4] points out, the spoilsport shatters the play world, robs it of its illusion (*in lusio*, 'in play'); the game ends. (If I can't bat, I'll take my bat and go home.) The cheat, on the other hand, pretends to be playing the game and, on the face of it, acknowledges the magic circle, the rules; the game continues.

Suffice it to say at this point that play, normally reserved for the playing field, is indelibly printed in the lives of men and women, boys and girls. It spans the frivolous to the utterly serious, the shallow to the deeply emotional. Play is in the very nature of man himself. As life is a mystery, so is play. What explanation is there for the mystery?

5.3   PLAY IN HISTORICAL PERSPECTIVE

5.3.1   The Greek heritage

The roots of play philosophy and theory reach back to ancient times. In many respects the classical era of Greece was one of the most enlightened. Although child labour was common, children had an important place in classical society. Play was given a valuable position in the life of children according to both Plato and Aristotle [5,6]. Play and leisure gave opportunity to develop. The primary force was education (*paideia*), educating man in his true form, inculcating qualities of responsibility, honour, loyalty, pride, beauty. The philosophic writings which remain indicate the dedication to state and culture, the highest value being productive citizenship. It is not surprising, therefore, to note that play (*paideia*, i.e. the same word as education) was considered an aspect of enculturation and cultural reinforcement. Plato says [7]:

'In order, then, that the soul of the child may not be habituated to feel joy and sorrow in a manner at variance with the law, and those who obey the law, but may rather follow the law and rejoice and sorrow at the same things as the aged – in order, I say, to produce this effect, chants appear to have been invented, which really enchant, and are designed to implant that harmony of which we speak. And, because the mind of the child is incapable of enduring serious training, they are called plays and songs, and are performed in play'.

Aristotle [8] believed that the child should spend the first seven years at home. Until the age of five he would impose no lessons and no tasks. It was a time of games and tales and stories, which should be 'foreshadowings of future knowledge'.

Hence, play to the Greeks appeared to be associated with childhood. Yet the citizenship of adult life and the appreciation of aesthetics, music, art, athletics, drama and poetry might be seen as the products of play. Today we tend to look at the opportunities for play as incorporating free choice, freedom from compulsion, often spontaneity. But the Greek citizen was bound to social commitment. There was a belief in universal personality/character which was held to be true of all noble persons. Hence, life's activities were structured to fulfil this ideal. Play then, was a means of integrating children into Greek culture. Aristotle supported happiness as an ultimate goal, through fulfilment of the individual, i.e. through the 'good life'.

The ancient Greeks laid a foundation of thought regarding play that has endured to influence recreation today. The perfectability of human nature through play, its usefulness in mental, physical and social well-being and the necessity of social control were of importance.

5.3.2 Post-Greek modifications

Later civilizations modified Greek attitudes towards play. The Roman culture exploited leisure and provoked a hedonistic philosophy which abandoned the concepts of moderation and balance in play behaviour. The ensuing over-reaction to play left its mark on the cultures to follow. The Church took strict moral control over play expression, using religious holidays, celebrations and projects to vilify and channel natural play inclinations. There emerged a suspicion of play as a social threat. The Church turned people from a concern with self in this world to a concern for self in the next world and preparation for it. The Middle Ages marked a period of lack of concept of childhood. Children were viewed simply as small adults but with low status. Obedience and passive acceptance of God's will characterized the ethos of these times. Play, the active seeking of new experience, retained little place in the ideals of this world. The body was thought to detract from more spiritual activities; thus every effort was made to curb its impulses. The Reformation acted to further restrict play among those following its creed. Work became all important. Play consequently became separated from work behaviour, and was considered morally dangerous.

Important contributions in the 18th and 19th centuries to counteract the decline in play philosophy came from Rousseau, Froebel and Schiller. Rousseau in his revolutionary text *Emile* espoused the idea of the natural child – the child of nature; mankind should return to a state of nature marked by simplicity and freedom. His philosophy was one of the cornerstones of the development of physical education in schools. Schiller [9] took a more aesthetic view of play, a new respect for play with a hint of Greek idealism.

'Man shall only play with Beauty, and he shall play only with Beauty . . . Man plays only when he is in the full sense of the word a man, and he is only wholly Man when he is playing.'

Froebel continues this philosophical direction [10]

'Play is the purest, most spiritual activity of man at this stage . . . A child that plays thoroughly, with self-active determination, perseveringly until physical fatigue forbids, will surely be a thorough, determined man, capable of self-sacrifice for the promotion of the welfare of himself and others'.

Froebel emphasized a belief in self-esteem, self-determination and self-discipline. The Froebel Kindergarten was fashioned not only on age-related growth needs but also on the need for opportunity for individual expression and spontaneity.

During the 19th century, the early education movement produced a new interest in play which culminated in a number of theoretical propositions attempting to explain and justify play. The ideas of Rousseau, the emergence of higher socio-economic strata and the reformist and revolutionary ideas forced society to accept two major changes – *a distinction between the child and the adult and the acceptance of play as an end in itself.*

5.4 PLAY THEORIES

Play theories can be classified in a number of different ways. This section is divided broadly into three categories – classical, recent and modern theories.

5.4.1 Classical theories

Many attempts have been made to explain the nature and function of play. The history of classical play theory has become relatively well known. Five of these theories are better known than the rest and survive in the literature today: the *surplus energy, instinct, preparation for life, recapitulation* and *relaxation* theories.

(a) Surplus energy

Schiller saw play as non-survival – important, aesthetic but essentially purposeless. Spencer [11] added two components: imitation and a physiological explanation. The surplus energy theory, sometimes referred to as the Schiller–Spencer theory, describes play as the expenditure of over-abundant energy which is unused in the normal processes of life sustenance. This theory assumes that energy is produced, is stored, must be used and its expenditure is made by behaviour which we call play. But it assumes too much and does not explain why children play when fatigued or to the point of fatigue. Further it is concerned only with the play of children. In addition, in terms of energy expenditure it does not stand up to scientific explanation.

(b) Instinct

The instinct theory suggests that play is caused by the inheritance of unlearned capacities to behave playfully. But this theory explains little, it ignores the fact that people learn new responses that we classify as play and the whole scientific basis for explaining certain behaviours as instinct is proving to be unscientific and unacceptable today. Ellis [9] describes the difficulty: 'Because there is play there must be a cause which we will call an instinct.'

(c) Preparation

Groos [12] proposed that play of children was practice for life. The preparation theory, based on Darwinian thinking states, that play is caused by the efforts of the player to prepare for later life. Play helps in the struggle for survival by enabling the practice and perfection of skills needed in later life. This is another type of instinct theory, and is sometimes referred to as the instinct–practice theory. However, play occurs most frequently in animals that live in rapidly changing circumstances. It takes no account that adults who have mastered life skills, also play. Moreover, the theory assumes that the players inherit the capacity to predict which responses will be critical later; they thus need information about the future.

(d) Recapitulation

Play is explained in the recapitulation theory as an outcome of biological inheritance. It is another Darwin-influenced theory. Children are a link in the evolutionary chain from animal to man, experiencing the history of the human race in play activities. Stanley-Hall [13] believed that play patterns were instinctive, generic expressions and re-enactments of early man's activities, i.e. a recapitulation of racial development seen in water play, digging in the sand, climbing trees and in tribal gangs. The theory has been generally discarded. There appears to be no linear progression in our play development that seems to mirror the development of a species. The theory does not explain activities dependent on our advanced technology.

(e) Relaxation
Urban life puts people under extreme strain. The relaxation theory propounded by Patrick in *The Psychology of Relaxation* [14] proposed that playful activity was caused by the need to find compensating outlets to allow relaxation and recuperation from the tension and stress of work. Man finds change of activity is refreshing and regenerates the human organism in preparation for the return to work. However, the theory does not explain children's play nor the strenuous activities of many play activities.

(f) Classical theories: summary
Most of the early theories were based on instinct as motivation of human play and these theories now only survive when they are incorporated in other theories of play behaviour. So today we find that play is considered to be *much more complex* than earlier theories suggested. All the older theories have some small merit, seeming to explain some aspects of behaviour, but they are over optimistic in their simplicity. Each is relevant to different sets of problems. They take no account of individual differences. 'Old soldiers never die' and they linger on in the literature as armchair theories [2]. They seem to explain, albeit curiously, some aspects of human behaviour, but they have logical shortcomings and are not substantiated by empirical findings.

5.4.2   Recent theories

In contrast to the classical theories, recent theories (after the turn of the 20th century) are concerned with the individual and his behaviour, attempting to explain the differences among the play of individuals. In his analysis of theories, Ellis [15] lists five major recent theories, namely, *generalization, compensation, catharsis, psychoanalytic development* and *learning*. Other theories view play as an all-embracing phenomenon: as an *end in itself*, as the *basis of civilization and culture*, as the roots of *social behaviour*, as a *reflection of society*.

(a) Generalization and compensation

Two of the theories – generalization and compensation – rely on the belief that people's play choices are a result of the nature of their work. People who perform work tasks well and are satisfied by them, will tend to behave similarly during their leisure time. The compensation theory suggests that adults select their leisure activities to compensate for the tendency of the work situation to deny satisfaction of their needs.

These are two inadequate theories. They explain some elements of some people's play behaviour but they assume on the one hand that aspects of work are rewarding and on the other that work is damaging or does not satisfy some needs. However, the theories are at least compatible since workers find satisfactions and frustrations in work and might make varied leisure selections that represent either generalization or compensation. These theories are over-simplistic, too general and take no account of pre-school play.

(b) Catharsis

The cathartic theories of play stem from classical Greece where dramatic tragedies and some music were believed to purge the audience of their emotions. The belief was that giving vent to feelings and emotions releases them. (This belief has been extended into justification for spectator sport, which allows the purging of aggression in a regulated and harmless way.) But it is questionable whether substitute acts reduce tension.

Feshbach [16] questions the validity of the theory that the expression of aggression in a socially approved form will reduce the amount of socially disapproved aggressive behaviour. Aggression researchers are finding that frustration leads to heightened aggressive feelings, but that subsequent aggressive behaviour does not reduce aggression. For example, verbal aggression towards a frustrator does not reduce aggression towards him but may actually *increase* it. Berkowitz and Green [17] indicate that 'aggression begets aggression'.

(c) Psychoanalytic

In the psychoanalytic theories of play concern for individual behaviour is clearly paramount. Interest stemmed from the observations of Freud [18] who observed that much play is motivated by pleasure. His ideas were later amended and formalized by Wälder [19] to show that play has multiple functions and cannot be explained by a single function. This work was expanded still further by Erikson [20]. Hence, the psychoanalytic theory goes beyond the pleasure principle to explain the play of children that is related to experiences that are not pleasant. Children have only a tenuous mastery of their environment which is confusing, complex and difficult. There are encounters that they cannot control which often are unpleasant. To Freud the opposite to play is not what is serious but what is real.

The three processes (according to Freudian theory) which influence behaviour are the *id, ego* and *superego*. The primitive pressures of the 'id' are opposite in polarity from the demands of our conscience –the super-ego. Between the two lies the 'ego', which balances the extremes. The balancing takes time; experience is accumulated and the 'superego' develops along with the 'ego'. The mechanisms for this balancing are acquired to some extent during play. Play is partially separated from reality and allows the 'ego' freedom to bend with the demands of the 'id' and 'superego'. An explanation is expounded by Ellis [21]: the child can try out new balance points and mechanisms; the ego can be exercised and in so doing work out conflicts between 'id' and 'superego'.

Psychoanalytic theory suggests that children consciously add actual elements from their environment to their fantasies, mixing reality and unreality into their play. Adults are seen as more constrained by society, emphasizing their grasp of reality, and hiding their tendency to deal with unreality in play. Thus adults are left with covert fantasies. Wälder suggests that 'fantasy woven about a real object is however nothing other than play.' [19].

The psychoanalytic methods of viewing the phenomenon of play led researchers like Melanie Klein to develop play therapy [22]. By playing out feelings a child can bring them to the surface, get them out into the open, face them, learn to control them or abandon them. When anxious a child will prefer to play with items which are salient to the anxiety e.g. hospitalized children prefer to play with toys relevant to the situation.

The psychoanalytic theory is yet another partial theory, explaining some aspects of play behaviour. It ignores play that is not presumed to be motivated by the need to eliminate the products of strongly unpleasant experiences.

(d) Developmental
Erikson [20] extended the ideas of infant development to stages of mastery and *life* development, taking into account effects of the environment. He identified play as a 'function of the ego, an attempt to synchronize the bodily and the social processes with the self. Play requires voluntary and non-compulsive participation, freedom from serious consequences and is non-productive. Play has a developmental progression in which a child adds new, more complex understandings about the world at each stage'. He identified three stages: 'autocosmic' play concerns bodily play, the 'micro sphere' is playing with toys and objects, and the 'macro sphere' develops sharing. For the child, Erikson feels that play may be used to work through and master reality. The child finds identity through play. Infant play between mother and child is all important; adult

behaviour and attitude are important. He relates this interplay to ritualization. The ritual expression combines the elements of play and social tradition, providing individual identity in a structured and/or communal fashion.

(e) Development and intelligence

A major contribution to the study of play stems from the research and writings of the Swiss child psychologist, Jean Piaget. In the main Piaget deals with play as an aspect of intellectual development. To Piaget [23] play interactions exactly parallel a development level of thought. The structure of intelligence is a function of two co-existing processes which operate together to produce adaptation to the environment. These processes he called *assimilation* and *accommodation*.

Assimilation is a process whereby the child imposes on reality his or her own knowledge and interpretations and thus often *alters reality* to fit what is known from previous experience. In contrast is the process of accommodation, whereby the child alters existing cognitive structures to meet with the demands of reality. Hence the child *modifies feelings and thoughts* when confronted with an object which appears novel: what he/she thinks is known must be altered to match what is encountered in the environment.

According to Piaget the balance between assimilation and accommodation constitutes the basis of intelligence and all behaviour is the 'acting out' of this cognitive interplay. Play is characterized by the assimilation of elements in the real world without the balancing constraints of accepting the problems of accommodating them, i.e. the behaviour that occurs when assimilation predominates can be described as playful and when accommodation predominates behaviour is viewed as imitative. Hence play is *manipulative*. Children alter and restructure environment to match experience and existing knowledge: reality is altered; the child creates an imaginary play world.

Piaget appears to say that play is *caused* by the growth of the child's intellect and is conditioned by it. But does play also reflect intellectual growth and contribute to it? A further question is, what happens to play if and when the intellect ceases to develop? Piaget believes that play eventually becomes a game played with rules and structure. Sutton-Smith [24] has raised many objections to this thesis. He believes that play remains important, does not become more realistic or rationalistic as intelligence develops, but remains symbolic, ritualistic, playful, even into adulthood. In essence, however, Piaget implies that play is the most effective aspect of early learning.

(f) Learning

Thorndike, Hull, Skinner and others view play as learned behaviour

'stimulus-response behaviour' [25]. A response has an increased probability of occurring if it is accompanied by a pleasant or reinforcing event.
Play is behaviour made in response to stimuli in the environment that is
not demonstrably critical for survival. Children's play responses are
learned as a result of their experiences. This theory assumes that children
act to increase the probability of pleasant events and decrease the probability of unpleasant events. If play behaviour is learned behaviour, then
the learning will occur as a result of a whole variety of 'reinforcers' and
reinforcing systems, for example, parents, other children and other
adults sharing the same cultural and environmental influences.

Empirical studies have been made by Roberts and Sutton-Smith [26], an
anthropologist and psychologist collaborating to study the role of games
in various societies. They have shown that individuals in different
cultures perceive games differently, depending on the values and attitudes prevalent, and that such games serve to relieve social conflict and
consequently enhance socialization. They put forward a theory of *conflict-
enculturation*. Conflicts induced by social learning, e.g. obedience,
achievement, responsibility training, lead to an involvement in 'expressive models' such as games, through which these conflicts are moderated,
lessened, assuaged. A learning process occurs which has cultural value
both to the players and to their societies. They tested the hypothesis by
studying the difference in rearing patterns and games played by the
children in three societies.

Games were defined as 'recreational activities characterized by organized play, competition, two or more sides, criteria for determining the
winner and agreed upon rules.' Games were divided into three classes:
games of *physical skill, strategy* and *chance*. The child rearing patterns were
categorized in terms of emphasis on *obedience, responsibility* or *achievement*.
Clear evidence was found for an association between the predominance
of one type of game and a particular emphasis in the rearing patterns.

Societies that reared their children for responsibility or routines with
little scope for individuality or creative problem-solving also seemed to
have a reverence for the intervention of divine gods. The rearing patterns
required the children not to reason but to do as they were told. Improvements in their circumstances were due to luck. In this atmosphere games
of chance predominated. In societies valuing achievement or performance, games of physical skill seemed to reflect this concern directly.
Children were consistently pressurized about performance. This anxiety
is apparently assuaged by the participation in games of skill. The third
relationship seemed to exist between games of strategy and emphasis of
the rearing patterns of obedience. Obedience training tended to require a
severity on the part of the rearers towards those in whom obedience is to
be inculcated. The child's own wishes and individuality are subverted.
Roberts and Sutton-Smith argue that these conflicts are displaced and

appear in games, where there are opportunities to control others.

Games of strategy were related to obedience training, high status groups and women. Games of chance were related to high routine responsibility training, such as punishment for display of initiative, and with lower status groups and were played by women more than by men. Games of physical skill put emphasis on achievement and were associated with higher status groups and were played by men more than by women.

As a result of the game activities, the children are seen as being better able to deal with the stresses imposed on them during their rearing, and thus more effectively enculturated.

This hypothesis was tested in a further setting. Roberts *et al.* [27] studied folk tales and games of complexity of societies. There seemed to be a clear increase in games of strategy as the society became more complex. Strategic games were indicative of cultural complexity, advanced industrial organization, high political integration, high social stratification, advanced agriculture and technology.

This theory of play and games states that the conflict induced by social learning are moderated through 'models' such as games. A learning process occurs which has cultural value both to the players and their societies. Girls who have higher obedience and responsibility training than boys tend to play games of strategy and chance; boys who have a higher achievement training than girls tend to play games of physical skill. It appears that the more types of game a culture has, the higher the achievement training in that culture. The conflict/enculturation hypothesis points to the interaction between the personality of the player and the demands of the rearing environment as the motive for the playing of games.

(g) An end in itself and the basis of civilization

Jan Huizinga, a Dutch historian, in his masterly book *Homo Ludens* presents the cultural approach to play. 'Play is older than culture, for culture, however adequately defined always presupposes human society, and animals have not waited for man to teach them their playing' [28]. Huizinga showed play to exist in every aspect of culture. He defines play as follows:

'Summing up the formal characteristics of play we might call it a free activity standing quite consciously outside 'ordinary' life as being 'not serious', but at the same time absorbing the player intensely and utterly. It is an activity connected with no material interest, and no profit can be gained by it. It proceeds within its own proper boundaries of time and space according to fixed rules and in an orderly manner. It promotes the formation of social groupings which tend to surround themselves with secrecy and to stress their difference from the common world by disguise or other means.'

To Huizinga, play is *self-justification*. It can be present in all aspects of life – work, business, leisure, sport, art, literature, music, religion and even in war. He believed most theories to be only partial theories, which justified play as a means to an end: play was seen to serve something which it is *not*, leaving the primary quality of play untouched. Moreover, civilization had compartmentalized play, had grown more serious, had put play into second place. For the full unfolding of civilization we cannot neglect the play element – 'genuine pure play is one of the main bases of civilization' [29]. Observation of the play rules were nowhere more important than in relations between nations. Once the rules were broken society would be in chaos.

Huizinga believed that to play we must play like a child. When, for example, the play spirit is lost from sport, sport becomes divorced from 'culture'. He gives no explanation as to why people play but he does describe play vividly. One can deduce from his description a number of interrelated characteristics:

1. Play is free, voluntary activity. There is more freedom in the play world than in the real world. We cannot play to order; if the player is forced, it changes its nature, it is no longer play. (Is some adult contempt for games the result of the extinction of the play element in early years?)
2. Play is indulged in for its own sake. It is unproductive and non-utilitarian.
3. Play is not 'ordinary' or 'real'. The player steps outside real life into a temporary sphere. Play is an interlude but real life may reassert itself at any time. The player knows it is only pretending, yet it is often utterly serious. Play is make-believe. There appears to be here a consciousness of the inferiority of play compared with the 'serious-ness' of life (e.g. hunger, homelessness).
4. Play has boundaries of space and time. It has its own course and meaning.
5. Play is creative. Once played it endures as a new found creation. It is repeated, alternated, transmitted; it becomes tradition.
6. Play is orderly, creates order. Into an imperfect world and confusion of life, it brings a temporary, limited perfection.
7. Play is regulated. It has rules and conventions. They determine what 'holds' in the temporary world. The new legislation counts; deviation spoils the play.
8. Play is 'uncertain'. The end result cannot be determined. When the result is a foregone conclusion then the tension and excitement is lost.
9. Play is social. Play communities tend to become permanent social

grouping even after the game is over (clubs, brotherhoods, gangs). Groups are often esoteric or secret – 'It is for us, not for others.' Inside the magic circle there are the laws and customs which suspend the ordinary rules of life.

10. Play is then symbolic.

Huizinga's theory is a philosophical one. Play exists, has always existed. It is its own justification. But self-justification is something that cannot be measured. It gives insights but not explanations.

(h) A reflection of society

The French sociologist, Roger Caillois, in *Man, Play and Games* has presented a socio-culturally based theory of play building upon the theory of Huizinga. Huizinga's theory had contained distinct elements – freedom, not 'ordinary', not 'serious', absorbing, non-material, bordered, ruled, orderly, social and secret. Caillois critically analysed the definition and redefined play as *activity which is free, separate, uncertain, unproductive, governed by rules or make-believe* [30].

Caillois developed a unique typology of the characteristic games of a society. Games are a culture clue, helping to reveal the character, pattern and values of a society. The basic themes of a culture should be deducible from the study of play and games no less than from the study of economic, political, religious or family institutions. He claimed that the destinies of cultures can be read in their choice of games. 'Tell me what you play and I will tell you who you are.'

Caillois identified four general classifications of games. The choice of games will reflect the society.

Agon (competition)	The desire to win by merit in regulated competition.
Alea (chance)	The submission of one's will to the luck of the draw.
Mimicry (simulation)	Assuming a strange personality.
Ilinx (vertigo)	The confusion that giddiness provokes.

1. The *agon* presupposes concentration, training, effort, the will to win and the vindication of personal merit. Formulation of rules makes it equal for everybody. The mainspring is the desire to excel and win recognition for ability.
2. *Alea* (the Latin for dice) are outcomes external to the player, over which he has no control (Bingo, lotteries etc.). Fate is the sole agent of victory; the luckier player becomes the winner. *Alea* negates work, patience, skill, it is a mockery of merit. It is the resignation of the will, a surrender to destiny.
3. *Mimicry* is the free suspension of the real. The player plays at believing, at pretending; he or she passes for another, hides behind a mask.

Every 'game' presupposes a temporary acceptance, if not an illusion (*in lusio* – entry into play) of an almost fictitious universe.

4. *Ilinx* comes from the Greek for whirlpool. Here the player seeks out the confusion that giddiness provokes – the whirling dervishes, big-dipper, the merry-go-round, the 'white knuckle rides' – that bring out the screams, terror, panic.

Games in each of the four categories were put on to a continuum representing an evolution from childlike play (*paidia*) to adult play (*ludus*). The first encompasses the spontaneous, frivolous, exuberant play, the frolic and the romping. The second is more concerned with man the thinker; the pleasure is in resolving difficulties. It represents those elements in play whose cultural importance seems to be the most striking. Rules are inseparable from play once play acquires an institutional existence.

According to Caillois, while the games reflect the functioning of a society, if corrupted, they indicate the weakness and potential dissolution of the culture. Furthermore, societies tend to prefer one theme or a combined theme, and this specialization contributes to the eventual disorganization of the society. Caillois asserts that these impulses are basic to human behaviour, and if they are not permitted expression in play, or if the play is contaminated by reality, then corruption occurs (See Table 5.1). Although not completely explanatory, and often weak in accurate identifications of social expressions, Caillois's theory does illuminate another perspective for analysis of play.

5.4.3 Modern theories

There are few modern theories of play. Play is increasingly seen as a mixture of different elements. Two theories are considered – play as a stimulus-seeking behaviour and play interpreted as playfulness.

(a) Play as stimulus-seeking behaviour

Michael Ellis' book *Why People Play* [2] is one of the most comprehensive and thorough studies of play in modern times. Ellis believes that there is no way of reaching any 'pure' definition and that the most satisfying explanation of play involves an integration of three theories: *play as arousal-seeking behaviour, play as learning and the developmentalist view of play*. There is considerable evidence to support the view that play enhances learning and development. The third aspect – the drive for optimal arousal – is advanced by Ellis.

Ellis shows that evidence is accumulating to explain some behaviour in terms of a drive to maintain optimal arousal. He defines play in this context as 'that behaviour that is motivated by the need to elevate the

Table 5.1 Corruption of games according to Caillois

	Cultural forms found at the margin of the social order	Institutional forms integrated into social life	Corruption
Agon (competition)	Sports	Economic competition Competitive examinations	Violence Will to power Trickery
Alea (chance)	Lotteries Casinos *Pari-mutuels*	Speculation on stock market	Superstition Astrology
Mimicry (simulation)	Carnival Theatre Cinema Hero-worship	Uniforms Ceremonial etiquette	Alienation Split personality
Ilinx (vertigo)	Mountain climbing Skiing Tightrope walking Speed	High-rise construction work	Alcoholism Drugs

Source: *Man, Play and Games* [30].

level of arousal towards the optimal' [31]. Put another way, play is *stimulus-seeking activity* that can occur only when external consequences are eliminated. 'When primary drives are satisfied the animal continues to emit stimulus-seeking behaviour in response to the sensoristatic drive. The animal learns to maintain an optimal level of arousal' [32].

Researchers in arousal theory find that it is the stimuli that are *complex, incongruous* or *novel* that lead to arousal. In addition the stimuli must have the ability to *reduce uncertainty* or *carry information* to the individual. Too much uncertainty and too much novelty will not be optimally arousing. Some intermediate level of information flow is optimally arousing. When situations are too complex they have no arousal potential and at the other end of the scale when the outcome is highly predictable there is little uncertainty and the arousal potential diminishes. For example, the *Times* crossword will have no arousal potential for the easy-crossword dabbler; the gifted player will not be stimulated by the novice opponent.

This stimulus-seeking model is very amenable to testing and can apply to animals and people young and old. The play 'spirit' for many adults is often the play of mind. Reading a thriller, following the fortunes of a favourite team in the newspaper, reading the stock exchange news, doing crosswords, playing *Trivial Pursuits*, problem-solving or just day-dreaming are all activities actively sought after by adults in particular, who by virtue of their age have a richer store of experiences. However, stimulus-seeking behaviour means more than merely seeking exposure to any stimuli. *The stimuli must have arousal potential.* Knowledge seeking, for example, results in the reduction of conflicts, mismatches and uncertainties. Laughter, humour and smiling are created by situations such as novelty, surprise, incongruity, ambiguity, complexity – all of which possess arousal potential. Fun has arousal potential.

Play, then, to Ellis is stimulus-seeking behaviour but not all stimulus seeking is play. The behaviour that seems to be clearly *non-utilitarian* is play. This may appear to lead to an artificial divide between work and play but clearly such stimulus-seeking behaviour can be found in both work *and* play. The theory appears to handle the question of work and play equally well. Indeed, it questions the validity of separating work from play.

Thus Ellis provides an explanation for both special and individual motivation towards play, and also describes a researchable, physiological base for play. In terms of its value to people and society play fosters individuality; it provides 'learnings' that reflect individual, unique requirements; it prepares for the unknown. *Play will not occur when the essential conditions necessary for play behaviour are absent.* One of the most important aspects coming out of this work is the realization that *people play when the control of the content of their behaviour is largely under their control.* Players should, therefore, transcend the immediate constraints of the reality of the situation when playing.

(b) Playfulness

The psychologist, J. Nina Lieberman [33], has studied a concept which she identified as *playfulness* and has observed and measured it in infants, adolescents, and adults. It is her thesis that playfulness is related to divergent thinking or creativity and that it has an important bearing on how we approach leisure. The three major components of playfulness are *spontaneity, manifest joy,* and *sense of humour.* Spontaneity shows itself in physical, social and learning dimensions and is a unitary trait in the young child. In the adolescent and adult, two separate clusters emerged in her studies which were labelled academic playfulness and social emotional playfulness, respectively. The traits characterizing academic playfulness were alert, bright, enthusiastic, imaginative, inquiring and knowledgeable. The outstanding characteristics of social emotional playfulness were entertaining, extroverted, joking, light-hearted, witty, making fun of himself/herself. The latter was also given the overall label of 'bubbling effervescence'.

At the infant level, Lieberman found that the more playful child was also the more creative boy or girl. This was expressed in fluency, flexibility, and originality of thinking. In terms of intelligence we know that two-thirds of the population fall within the middle range of intelligence quotients; in the case of creativity the evidence appears to suggest different degrees of endowment and in different areas, for example, in specific talents such as science, music, writing and painting. Playfulness can, therefore, be part of *any* individual's make-up. Moreover, because of its importance in a person's general approach to work and play, playfulness should, in Lieberman's submission, be encouraged and developed throughout the lifespan of people.

Assuming this to be the case we have to ask ourselves how playfulness can be developed.

1. *To develop spontaneity* Lieberman believes that there needs to be emphasis on gathering and storing facts beginning as early as the pre-school level. Only if the child has a storehouse of knowledge is there a basis for parents and teachers to encourage playing with various permutations. The 'finding out' at the elementary school level has the additional benefit of building up a foundation for adolescent spontaneity.
2. *Manifest joy* is the ability of showing pleasure, exuberance, friendliness and generally positive attitudes in everyday life. The joy that the adult shows at the child's growing competence will lead to the child's own sense of pleasure in his or her activities. There is an obvious link here in the reservoir of knowledge and *savoir faire* that leads to manifest joy. There is also the carryover into adult life and contribution to enjoyment of work and play.
3. 'The ability of engaging in good-natured ribbing, gentle wit, creative punning, as well as poking fun at yourselves and others', Lieberman includes in the category *sense of humour*. To develop this a climate needs to be created which encourages 'psychological distancing'. Evidence was found that the cognitively more mature children preferred less hurtful expressions of humour. In a helping and cooperating atmosphere and an awareness of 'prosocial' behaviour, a climate could be fashioned which inculcates the gentle type of humour rather than the biting, sarcastic kind. Humour is dependent on mastery of the situation; mastery can then lead to fun in learning.

Following Lieberman's argument, as we continue to learn throughout our lifespan, we therefore need to practice the psychological distancing which allows us to take the task at hand seriously but not ourselves; we need to free ourselves from being preoccupied with ourselves and with our own problems. This positive outlook is echoed in many parts of this book in order to cope, to be resourceful and for leisure to function as one of the means towards what Maslow terms 'self-actualization'.]34] Maslow stressed the need for individuals to develop to their fullest degree of independence and creative potential.

The next logical step to ask is how playfulness can help in our approach to leisure. It seems self-evident that any individual whose approach to everyday living embraces spontaneity, manifest joy and sense of humour, would be able to deal in a creative way with free time. It is apparent though that many individuals have these traits and are not aware of them or realize the benefits of applying them to leisure. Other people will need to actively practice them in order to make them part of their everyday repertoire. To what extent we can discover ourselves, our skills and aptitudes and acquire the ability of stepping back and laughing at ourselves, is a question we must follow up later in this book in terms of leisure management and leisure opportunity.

5.5 PLAY: SUMMARY

Play is important to the lives of people. It has personal meaning for each individual. Play behaviour appears to be possible in almost any life situation. It can be readily observed, particularly in children, but there is little agreement as to a definition or explanation of why people play.

There have been many theories of play. Classical theories may appear to have some 'common sense' wisdom but for the most part they are archaic and not very helpful theories with many logical shortcomings. Among the recent theories the learning, developmental and psychoanalytic theories show that play contributes to the development of intelligence and a healthy personality. Children gain pleasure, overcome unpleasant experiences and develop mastery of their physical and social environment.

Why play? There is no precise answer. Some claim that play is justification in and of itself without further rationalization but animals play as well as humans and this seems to indicate that it performs some survival function. In addition play does seem to be arousal-seeking behaviour, a seeking out of novelty, a preparation for the unknown and children, especially, learn and develop through play.

The descriptions and explanations of play have been in the past too simplistic and obtuse. They have been obscure because of our failure to recognize that play cannot be conceived as a simple concept. Play is a complex set of behaviours – 'a million permutations of human behaviour'. As play is utterly individual and play activity can be seen at any time and in all life situations, it follows, therefore, that almost any situation or activity can function for someone as a play activity, if undertaken in the spirit of play.

There appear to be several accepted characteristics of play in the absence of an exact definition. Play is *activity* – mental, passive or active. Play is undertaken freely and usually spontaneously. It is fun, purposeless, self-initiated and often extremely serious. Play is indulged in for its own sake; it has intrinsic value; there is innate satisfaction in the doing.

Play transports the player, as it were, to a world outside his or her normal world. It can heighten arousal. It can be vivid, colourful, creative and innovative. Because the player shrugs off inhibitions and is lost in the play, it seems to be much harder for adults, with social and personal inhibitions to really play. Play most often refers to the activities of children or to the 'childlike' behaviour in grown-ups. In this chapter we have seen that all – young and old – can play but as Millar suggests: 'Adults sometimes just play but children just play far more'. [35]

REFERENCES AND NOTES

1. Moore, V.L. (1976), *A Conceptual Model for Contemporary Recreation Theory and Service*, unpublished dissertation, University of Southern California.
2. Ellis, M.J. (1973), *Why People Play*, Prentice-Hall, Englewood Cliffs, New Jersey.
3. de Grazia, S. (1962), *Of Time, Work and Leisure*, Doubleday, New York, p. 359.
4. Huizinga, J. (1955), *Homo Ludens*, Beacon Press, Boston.
5. Aristotle (1926), *The Politics of Aristotle* (translated by Ernest Barker), Clarendon Press, Oxford.
6. Plato (1900), *The Republic of Plato* (translated by John Davis and David Vaughan), A.L. Burt, New York.
7. Plato (1952), *Complete Works*, Encyclopaedia Britannica, Chicago.
8. Aristotle (1952) *Aristotle 2: Great Books of the Western World*, Encyclopaedia Britannica, Chicago.
9. Schiller, F. (1965), *On the Aesthetic Education of Man*, Frederick Ungar, New York.
10. Harris, W.T. (1887), *The Education of Man*, (ed. F. Froebel) D. Appleton, New York. See editor's preface.
11. See Lehman, H.S. and Witty, P.A. (1927), *The Psychology of Play*, A.S. Barnes, New York.
12. Groos, K. (1901), *The Play of Man*, Appleton, New York.
13. Stanley-Hall, G. (1920), *Youth*, Appleton-Century, New York.
14. Patrick, G.T.W. (1916), *The Psychology of Relaxation*, Houghton-Mifflin, Boston.
15. Ellis, M.J. (1973), uses the classification of 'classical', and 'recent' theories put forward in Gilmore, J.B. Play: a Special Behaviour in R.N. Haber (ed), (1966), *Current Research in Motivation*, Holt, Rinehart and Winston, New York. p. 343–355.
16. Feshbach, S. (1956), *Journal of Personality*, 24, 449–62.
17. Berkowitz, L.A. and Green, J.A. (1962), *Journal of Abnormal and Social Psychology*, 64, 293–301.
18. Freud, S. (1974), *The Complete Works of Sigmund Freud*, Hogarth Press, London.
19. Wälder, R. (1933), The Psychoanalytic Theory of Play, *Psychoanalytic Quarterly*, 2, p. 208–24.
20. Erikson, E.H. (1950), *Childhood and Society*, Norton, New York.
21. Ellis, M.J. (1973), *Why People Play*, Prentice-Hall, Englewood Cliffs, New Jersey p. 58.

22. Klein, M. (1955), *American Journal of Orthopsychiatry*, 25, 223–37.
23. Piaget, J. (1962), *Play, Dreams and Imitation in Childhood* (translated by G. Gattengno and F.M. Hodgson), Norton, New York.
24. Sutton-Smith, B. (1966), *Psychological Review*, 73, 104–10.
25. Ellis, M.J. (1973), *Why People Play*, Englewood Cliffs, New Jersey, p. 70–76.
26. Roberts, J.M. and Sutton-Smith, B. (1962), Game training and game involvement. *Ethnology*, 1, 166–85.
27. Roberts, J.M., Sutton-Smith, B. and Kendon, A. (1963), *Journal of Social Psychology*, 61, 185–99.
28. Huizinga, J. (1955), *Homo Ludens*, Beacon Press, Boston, p. 13; see also Chapter 1: The nature and significance of play.
29. Ibid., p. 5; see also Chapter 7: The play-element in contemporary civilization.
30. Caillois, R. (1961), *Man, Play and Games*, Free Press of Glencoe, New York.
31. Ellis, M.J. (1973), *Why People Play*, Prentice-Hall, Englewood Cliffs, New Jersey, p. 110.
32. Ibid., p. 94.
33. Lieberman, J.N. (1977), *Playfulness: Its Relationship to Imagination and Creativity*, Academic Press, New York.
34. Maslow, A. (1968), *Toward a Psychology of Being*, 2nd edn, D. Van Nostrand, New York.
35. Millar, S. (1968), *The Psychology of Play*, Penguin Books, Baltimore, p. 256.

Chapter 6

Recreation

★

★

6.1 INTRODUCTION

In this chapter 'recreation' is studied in the following manner. *First*, the concept is introduced to show that recreation, like play, is a far from simple phenomenon and that confusion is evident in definition and understanding of it. *Second*, the range of ideas and theories of recreation is explored. *Third*, a discussion and synthesis of ideas is attempted which differentiates between recreation experience, activity, process and structure. *Finally*, a summary of findings and issues relevant to community recreation planning, services and management is presented.

6.2 RECREATION: AN OVERVIEW

The history of the organized recreation movement in the United Kingdom and in the USA is well documented, showing the early developments in the late 19th century and early 20th century [1]. There has been a close association with the recreation movement and the development of industrial society. The early 'childhood movement' shows similarities in the foundation of education and recreation but they developed along different paths to meet different needs of an industrialized society. Educated people would be better able to cope with the new industrial age; education has become, in part, an employment preparation institution; recreation became a contrast to work.

Many recreation theories view the concepts of play and recreation as one and the same thing. Others take the position that they are different entities. Play for example, is concerned with expression of energy; recreation is for relaxation and recuperation. However, from the initial years of recreation theory the view that recreation is adult activity and play is child's activity has been the predominant one.

The word 'recreation'; stems from the Latin word *recreatio*, which means 'to restore to health'. Hence the term, traditionally, has been thought of as a process that restores or recreates the individual. The historic approach in defining recreation has been to consider it as an activity that renews people for work. This approach to understanding recreation has obvious limitations; most people do not view recreation as a factor related to work or used to enhance job performance and a large proportion of the public does not undertake paid employment.

While some definitions refer to recreation as restoration, most focus on it as a form of activity. Others, while corroborating the activity approach, apply the condition to it of social acceptance. Most view the activity as unobligated. For example the *Dictionary of Sociology* defined recreation as: 'any activity pursued during leisure, either individual or collective, that is free and pleasureful, having its own immediate appeal, not impelled by a delayed reward beyond itself' [2]. Hutchinson [3] supports the social acceptance theory; recreation is 'a worthwhile, socially acceptable leisure experience providing immediate, inherent satisfaction to the individual who voluntarily participates in activity'.

Some authors look to recreation as being morally 'sound' and 'mentally and physically upbuilding'. Romney believed that recreation was not a matter of motions, but rather *emotions*. 'It is a personal response, a psychological reaction, an attitude, an approach, a way of life' [4].

Many recent definitions, however, do not regard recreation as being opposite to work, or being morally sound or even being activity at all; Avedon [5], and Gray and Greben [6], for example, look at recreation as providing personal well-being.

It is evident that there is considerable confusion in both a definition of recreation and an understanding of it. While it would be easy to say 'it is whatever you think it is', that is hardly a means of explanation. The confusion that does exist was portrayed aptly in an editorial in *Parks and Recreation* [7] which listed approximately 200 words or phrases describing what recreation is.

Accomplishment
Achievement
Acquired use of the senses
Aesthetic experience
Alienating boredom
Anticipation
Appreciating needs of others
Appreciation of new values
Awareness of spiritual, physical, and cultural aspects of the human sphere
Belief in a future for society
Better citizen participation
Better idea of where to go from here
Better perspective of life
Body achievement
Body awareness
Breakdown of minority and racial barriers
Bringing all people together
Broadened social feelings
Challenge
Challenging one's habitual patterns of mental and physical action to new experiences
Changes in self-esteem
Community working together
Community spirit
Concept of what kind of city (environment) I want to live in
Confidence
Coming down from an emotional or physical peak
Competing, struggling, overcoming challenges
Creative experience
Creative expression
Cultural sharing
Dangerous challenges
Developing ability to be innovative
Developing ability to lose
Developing ability to win
Developing avocations
Developing new skills
Developing personal expressiveness
Developing teamwork values
Developing unique personal identity
Development of friendship
Development of 'skills of living' in a pluralistic society
Diversity and pleasurable experience for all
Energizing the entire being
Enhanced communication
Enjoyment
Entertainment
Excitement
Exercise
Exhaustion
Expanded awareness
Expanded awareness of life

Expanded perspectives or views
Expanded understanding of people
Exhilaration
Exploring relationships
Exposure to new items
Family unity
Feeling at home with my environment
Feeling better about one's self
Feeling of belonging
Feeling of security in inner resources for one's life-style
Feeling of self-worth
Finding new talents
Friends
Frustration
Fun
Growth
Growth of interpersonal skills
Happiness
Health
Healthy relationship with mind and emotions
Helping others
Improved capacity of people to affect quality of their lives
Improved capacity to relate to children and young people
Improved community
Improved confidence in government and public service
Improved perception of own rationality
Improved self-confidence
Improved self-image
Improved sense of 'community'
Improved skills
Improvement of mental health
Improving my city and neighbourhood as a place to live
Increased imagination
Increased self-worth
Intensified skills
Interpersonal relations
Involvement
Injury
Inner peace
Joy
Knowledge
Learning
Learning about environment
Learning about one's self
Less destruction to our facilities

Lessening tensions
Making a contribution
Making friends
Management or risk
Mastery
Mental achievement
Mental exhaustion
Mental health
Mental stimulation
More joy in personal and family life
Motivation
Muscle tone and coordination
Mutual trust
New adventure
New experience
New friendships
Oneness of body and mind
Opportunity for interaction
Opportunity to identify enjoyable activities by trial and error
Outlet of emotions
Participation with others toward common goals
Peer group relationships
Physical fitness
Pleasure from beautiful and well-kept surroundings
Positive feedback
Positive relationships
Promoting feeling of belonging
Providing channels for creative self-expression
Providing interrelationships to improve racial skills
Providing socially approved models
Recreated mind, body, and spirit
Re-creating
Recreation leadership which provides bridge between peoples' good ideas and actual achievement of ideas
Reducing tension by venting emotional drives
Refined cultural horizons
Reflection
Refreshed spirit
Rehabilitation
Rejuvenation
Relaxation
Release valve against pressure of living in poverty, ignorance
Relief and tension

Relief from the anxiety of fighting for self-image
Risk
Sanity
Satisfaction
Seeking and finding challenges and excitement
Self-actualizing
Self-confidence
Self-discovery
Self-esteem
Self-expression
Self-fulfilment
Self-image
Self-satisfaction
Self-testing
Self-worth
Sense of achievement
Sense of control of one's destiny
Sense of human fellowship
Sense of reward
Separation from the mass
Service to people
Shared experiences

Simplicity in a complex/crowded urban life
Skills development
Skills in personal relationships
Socialization
State of mind
Status
Stimulating interests
Stimulating occupational goals
Stimulation of educational goals and objectives
Social skills
Strengthened personal competency
Success
Teamwork
Testing of body capabilities
Thrills
Understanding how I can help others
Understanding of other human beings
Understanding of potential to success
Use of time in interesting ways
Wider range of vision and comprehension of life

6.3 RECREATION THEORIES

It is clear that recreation is a far from simple concept to grasp and to understand. Indeed, hundreds of writers have attempted to do so and the literature is filled with a plethora of theories, a fact which cannot be escaped and cannot be ignored. There follows a brief summary of some of the definitions, which represent the range of ideas. More important, however, is the possibility that each description has some element of truth, which can aid our appreciation of what it is we are dealing with.

Hundreds of theories of recreation exist. They do not fall into any clear or logical categories. Most of them embrace a large number of interrelating elements, such as need-serving, satisfying, associated with activity, of value to society and so on. Most theories too appear to overstress values, outcomes and 'wholesomeness'. The research is so confused and overlapping that an attempt is made simply to highlight some of the main approaches to an understanding.

6.3.1 Recreation as needs-serving

Slavson [8] describes recreation as a 'need-serving experience'. Whatever the choice of recreation, each individual seeks to satisfy some inner need. Recreation is a response to pleasure cravings. But such a description concerns what recreation does, not what it is. Jacks [9] defines recreation as the 're-creation of something that gets damaged in human beings . . . the repair of human damage where it is repairable, and the prevention of it in the rising generation'. This is an inadequate definition also in that it mixes biological need with social need.

Nash also sees recreation as a means for satisfying the human need to express inner urges and drives. Recreation is the positive expression of leisure needs. He evaluates activity in terms of the degree of creative social contribution. Recreation, therefore, serves both individual and society. As can be seen from Nash's 'Participation model', the recreative life-style is active participative experience. He equates recreations with happiness.

'The happy man paints a picture, sings a song, models in clay, dances to a call, studies the stars, seeks a rare stamp, builds a cabin, raises pigeons, digs in the desert, romps with his grandchild, reads the Koran, dreams of rushing rivers and snow-capped peaks . . . he has a hundred things yet to do when the last call comes' [10].

Nash sees play as the childhood preparation for recreation in adult life and also a practice for work.

6.3.2   Recreation as leisure-time activity

By far the most widespread definitions and the ones most acceptable to providers of recreation services are that recreation is simply *those activities in which people participate during their leisure.*

The problem with this traditional view of recreation as activity is that it is heavily slanted in certain preconceived directions. Indeed, so much so, that to many people, recreation is synonymous with physical recreation and sport. In addition, providers tend to provide for activities and feel they are providing for recreation without knowing whether activities are the most appropriate and they are meeting the needs of people. Moreover, as we will find in the next chapter, there is no universally accepted definition of what constitutes people's leisure.

The Sports Council report, *Professional Training for Recreation Management*, describes recreation as 'the purposeful use of leisure time' [12]. Other official documents refer to it as 'the wholesome use of leisure time.' A Countryside Recreation Research Advisory Group report defined recreation as 'any pursuit engaged upon in leisure time, other than pursuits to which people are normally "highly committed" ' [13].

The Neumeyers [14] define recreation as any activity, either individual or collective, pursued during one's leisure time. Play is children's recreation, which is relatively spontaneous and pleasurable and is immediately satisfying. To the Neumeyers recreation has four basic elements: be-

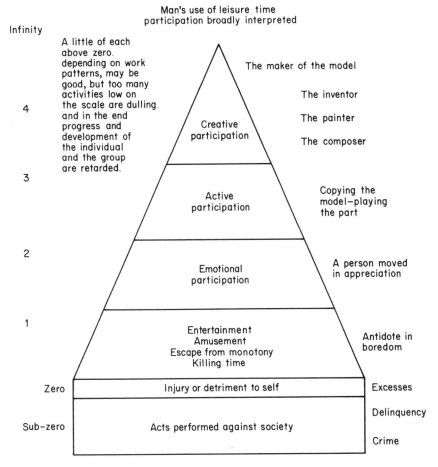

Fig. 6.1 Nash's conceptualization of man's use of leisure time. Source: Nash, *Philosophy of Recreation and Leisure* [11].

havioural expression during leisure, intrinsically valuable, motivated by rewards found within the activity and socio-culturally conditioned.

6.3.3 Recreation as value to individual and society

Recreation has been dogged by having to live up to a standard of high moral and social value for the 'good' of the individual and society. The moral connotations are held strongly by many writers, such as Miller and Robinson [15] Meyer and Brightbill [16], Butler [17] and many others.

Miller and Robinson see recreation as the process of participation in leisure from a specific perspective of leisure *values*. Play is free, happy, expressive behaviour that contributes to childhood development.

Recreation does not necessarily contain play but must *always* have a particular value framework related to appropriate and satisfying use of leisure. 'The leisure age makes possible for all a more vital family life, a more democratic community of equals a greater share in a civilization that is refined, humane, cultured and filled with beauty; and a synthesis of recreation and leisure to provide a new media for the search for truth, excellence, art, creativity and, ultimately man's self realization' [18].

Meyer and Brightbill propose that recreation contains the following characteristics and these contribute to fulfilling human needs – action, variety of form, motivation towards enjoyment, engagement during leisure, voluntary participation, universality, purposefulness, flexibility, creation of by-products. Recreation is also an attitude of mind regarding leisure behaviour and has a direct influence on those factors which create personality. It can produce feelings of well-being, satisfactions pertaining to positive identity, growth, creativeness, balanced competition, character, mental capacity, dignity of individual, physical conditioning, socialization and a coping attitude!

Not surprisingly Meyer and Brightbill view recreation as a social force. But such value-orientations placed on recreation are questionable. Such descriptions may well overstress presumed recreational benefits, and resulting services based on such presumptions might repel people rather than attract. However, there is no shortage of protagonists for such an orientation. Butler takes a similar view.

To Butler recreation is any activity which is not consciously performed for the sake of any reward beyond itself. It is usually experienced during an individual's leisure but it can result from his or her participation in any activity at any time. The activity becomes recreation because it elicits satisfactions. Butler sees recreation not so much as something concrete but as a *force* influencing people's lives, and as a system of services which provide 'wholesome' experience, to counteract disruptive social trends that tend to prevent individually self-selected, pleasurable expression.

It is logical to perceive that from this value orientation that 'wholesome' individual recreation will lead to recreation as an influence for a social 'good'. Miller and Robinson identify recreation as a social institution and Meyer and Brightbill see it both as a social force and structurally as a social institution. From their viewpoint community recreation is a means for improving and maintaining societal cohesion and the quality of life; its development is dependent on social participation. Hence community recreation is a system of services for wholesome, positively sanctioned activities.

6.3.4   Recreation as a re-creation

Most theorists have concentrated on the value of recreation and the outcomes of recreation. They have not addressed themselves to the recreation *experience* itself. Shivers [19] in *Principles and Practices of Recreational Services* focuses attention on 're-creation' although he treats play and recreation as virtually synonymous. Building on a theme of homeostasis (the process by which the body continues to produce the chemical balance necessary to maintain life, the process by which equilibrium is maintained), Shivers builds up to a definition of recreation based on the construct 'psychological homeostasis' – the satisfying of psychological needs, the process of mental balance. If homeostasis is the condition that motivates behaviour it must also serve as the motivational stimulus for recreation. When there is imbalance we move towards re-balance, in which harmony and accord between self and the environment are found. Shivers claims that this balance may be restored through recreation. Recreation 'is any consummatory experience, non-debilitating in character' [20]. It produces unity and harmony within the individual. *The unity of mind and body (psyche and soma) brought about at the time of 'consummation' is recreation.* The distinguishing feature is its consuming and absorbing quality. It has the power to seize and hold one's attention to such an extent that the very meaning of subjective time and environment disappears from view. In this respect it fulfils the need for psychological homeostasis. Hence, the individual experiences a balance or temporary harmony at the point of complete fulfilment from which stems a feeling of *re-creation* or re-birth. This realization of totality, i.e. complete integration by the individual *within* himself, is the recreational focus.

The basic difference between recreational value and recreation is in time rather than degree. Recreational value will be noted *after* the consuming experience has occurred, whereas recreation occurs *at the time of the experience.* This unity of mind and body Shivers describes as the 'unity concept' of recreation.

This theory has value in that it focuses our attention on what actually happens. However, there are a number of problems, for example, such complete absorption is rarely achieved and the theory begs the question whether every satisfying experience is recreation. However, if recreation is essentially an *experience*, it is central to the provision of recreation services. Yet very little is known about the 'experience', what it is and what it does for people. We have come far in the development of recreation facilities and programmes and services with so little understanding of the result we are trying to produce.

There have been some investigations into people's perceptions of recreation and what experiences they encounter but there has been no scientific validity of the findings and further studies are needed. One piece of research elicited from college students via self-reporting techniques the most significant and memorable recreation experiences they had ever had. The results were reported by Gray [21]. An extract of some of the findings is outlined in Table 6.1. It is shown that reactions to personal 'recreation experiences' indicate that recreation is a highly significant component of total *life* experience. It also suggests that activities that do not generate some of these kinds of feelings may fail to produce a recreational result.

Table 6.1 'What is this thing called recreation?'

Heightened or reduced sensitivity to temperature, colour and smell. The experience may be so intense it distorts normal sensory processes. A person may be oblivious to conditions of heat or cold.

Time distortion. 'Time stood still', 'An hour seemed like a minute'. Time distortion appears to be a product of unusual concentration where one's attention is fixed to the recreation experience to the exclusion of the usual sense of time.

Anticipation and expectation.

Reflection and a pleasant memory.

Escape. 'Getting away from it all.'

Novelty. The sense of 'for the first time' brings feelings of freshness and uniqueness.

Relaxation. Not just in the sense of relaxing but including release from social convention, retreat, change of pace, reduction in human encounter, fewer personal demands.

Self-testing; challenge; achievement. The challenge may be internal competition to meet personal goals and standards. Achievement, competence and *self-worth* were frequent components of the recreation experience.

Improved self-image. 'In the end we all experience only ourselves.'

Self-discovery.

Feeling a part of nature; beauty and awe. Heightened appreciation; unusual perceptive abilities.

Culmination: a turning point; reward for extended preparation; a watershed life event. Most people can recall a life event which was so important, so intense, so significant, and so memorable that it altered forever the course of their lives.

Heightened insight; perspective clarity; illuminating experience. Flashes of insight are important and often powerful events.

Order; regularity; clear and precise limits; rules.

Introspection; sorting out of life experience; release from sensory overload; contemplation; and communication with oneself.

Communion; love; friendship and identification with a group. Perhaps the strongest single motivation for many recreation activities is the wish for social response, and social response is their greatest reward.

Personal development; learning; extension of ability.

Refreshment; personal renewal; recovery of powers.

Common experience; shared hardships; teamwork.

Risk; apprehension; fear. Reported over and over again is the element of fear. It suggests the quality of being frightened is a part of the extraordinary experience.

Unity of mind and body; grace; coordination.

Feelings of excitement, freedom, control, power, creativity, inner peace, harmony, reward, competence. Recreation experiences are a power stimulus to emotional response.

A selection and adaptation from *Parks and Recreation* [21]

6.4 RECREATION: ANY KIND OF SATISFYING EXPERIENCE?

In broad terms recreation can be considered as activity and/or experience. But is recreation *any* kind of satisfying experience? If so recreation becomes all life's satisfying experiences. While philosophically this might be supported, in practical terms the scope could make it far too wide and all-embracing to present and manage recreation. Taking Shivers' belief that recreation is any consuming non-harmful experience could be interpreted as everything and nothing as far as recreation management is concerned.

Gray and Pelegrino [22] have adopted a similar definition which is psychological in nature. Recreation is defined in terms of a person's experiences:

'Recreation is an emotional condition within an individual human being that flows from a feeling of well-being and satisfaction. It is characterized by feelings of mastery, achievement, exhilaration, acceptance, success, personal worth and pleasure. It reinforces a positive self-image. Recreation is a response to aesthetic experience, achievement of person's goals, or positive feedback from others. It is independent of activity, leisure or social acceptance.'

It is what happens *within* a person that determines whether or not recreation occurs. The unity within oneself, the mood and the situational elements themselves all go to make up the recreational experience. Hence participating in an activity does not in and of itself provide recreation. The psychological response of the individual is what determines what is recreation for him or her.

There is an apparent drawback to the school of thought that defines recreation as any experience: it loses any connection to either leisure or activity. Graham and Klar sum up the practical difficulties [23]:

'Should all positive feelings be categorized as recreation? Is the scientist's moment of discovery recreation? Or the student's feeling of satisfaction with a term paper well done? If we assume that recreation is independent of either leisure or activity, virtually all satisfying experiences become labelled recreation which seems too far reaching and presents barriers to communication since that is not the context in which most people view recreation. Practically speaking, this definition will not be easily applied as it now stands since it incorporates so many types of experience. The psychological focus provided by Gray, however, is important and should be uppermost in the minds of leisure service practitioners'.

In its interim report, the Recreation Management Training Committee stated as their reference point: 'We take recreation to mean any life-enhancing experience which is the outcome of freely chosen activity' [24]. Here experience is allied to activity. Graham and Klar take the matter closer to 'recreation' activity. It is imperative, they believe, to put the 'experience' into a *recreation setting* to achieve understanding: recreation experience occurs as a direct result of involvement in a recreation activity. It is an emotional condition providing inner satisfactions and feelings of well-being. They define a recreation experience as:

'. . . positive emotional response to participation in a recreation activity, defined as such by the individual or by a sponsoring agency or organization. Responses associated with the recreation experience include feeling good about self and others, experiencing a sense of inner calm or personal satisfaction, or feeling an enriched sense of self-worth which results from motivators of either an intrinsic or extrinsic nature. There is a clear absence of stress and tension which produce anxiety; the joy of re-creative experience is achieved. The essence of the classical view of leisure is achieved' [25].

The principal difference between such a definition and that of Gray, is that it is not independent of recreation activity. *It is related to both leisure and activity*. It, therefore, avoids the broadness of Gray's definition which puts all positive experiences as recreation, which is extremely difficult to put into any operational context. Graham and Klar perceive recreation in narrower terms but retain the psychological component.

6.5 RECREATION: AN INSTITUTION AND A PROCESS?

Confusion exists in our understanding of how we can translate *individual* recreation into community sanctioned activity. We have seen that recreation can be viewed as an activity and as an experience. Extrapolating the recreation activity focus, recreation is to do with promoting activities, providing facilities, programmes and opportunities. As such recreation can be perceived as a structure – an institution. Following the experience focus, recreation is viewed as something which is personally motivated. In this sense it can be perceived as a *process* of what happens to an individual. Thus on one hand recreation can be perceived as a directing social force, on the other hand an inner directed experience.

As we have seen some authors propose the need for social control of recreation to protect dominant value systems and ensure the 'wholesome' use of leisure time, community well-being and to enhance quality of life. As a community force, therefore, recreation is perceived as a vehicle for preventing social disorganization and maintaining societal stability. Structurally, recreation is related to leisure time expression in contrast to work roles.

6.5.1 Recreation as a social process

Recreation experience according to Murphy [26] is a process whereby the human organism strives to reach optimal arousal levels, the primary ingredients of which are exploration, investigation, manipulation and learning behaviour. (Such a theory of recreation is akin to the play theory put forward by Ellis, see Section 5.4.3.)

Murphy, like several writers before him, lists an impressive array of physical, psychological, social and educational values as the potential outcomes of recreation. He views recreation, for example as a process towards self-realization, fostering interaction, novelty, challenge, diversity, adventure, identity and other qualities. It would appear that many of these needs are not being met through recreation programmes and he believes that a shift of emphasis towards an enabler–community catalyst role, will come about as a reflection of changing social demands. He puts forward a humanistic perspective for recreation services and believes that basic needs can and should be satisfied through recreation participation. In these terms recreation should be viewed from a process orientation, in order to see its role in the dynamics of change. Thus, to Murphy, recreation and leisure services are *processes*.

The process perspective includes aspects of psychological response rather similar to play – pleasure, self-actualization, fulfilment, satisfaction in the doing. Recreation requires freedom and activity and seems to absorb the participant to the point of complete involvement. A related element appears to be creativity both in process and outcome and recreation may well culminate in peak experience.

6.5.2   Recreation as a social institution

Kraus takes some important and differing views from many of the foregoing authors [27]. Recreation is more than a conceptual framework, a kind of activity, or a condition of existence. Instead, it refers to all the social institutions which have been formed to meet the leisure needs of people. It includes activities and organizations which are sponsored by government on various levels, schools, churches, industries, voluntary agencies and the business world – all of which provide varied recreational opportunities [28].

Kraus challenges many of the theories put forward: voluntary participation is dependent on available choices; immediate gratification does not necessarily occur with many activities that take time to master before they become fully satisfying; participating without extrinsic motivation is questioned – people engage in activities *often with goals in mind* and are motivated by external reasons. Community-based recreation is concerned with reinforcing the prevalent value system and must, therefore, provide a structured and manageable service which often precludes such aspects as voluntary, immediately satisfying and intrinsically-based participation.

Avedon [29] supports the social institution argument. He points out that as in the case of other social institutions 'recreation has form, structure, traditions, patterns of operation and association, systems of communication, and a number of other fixed aspects'. Kraus, in the second edition of *Recreation and Leisure in Modern Society* concludes that recreation has emerged as a 'significant' social institution: 'Once chiefly the responsibility of the family, the church or other local social bodies, it has now become the responsibility of a number of major agencies in our modern industrial society' [30].

The 1964 *Dictionary of Social Sciences* defines an institution as 'an aspect of social life in which distinctive value-orientations and interests, centering upon large and important social concerns, generate or are accompanied by distinctive modes of interaction.' The term institution is, therefore, different from the term association. An association is essentially composed of people, while an institution is essentially composed of interactions and interrelationships. They are social patterns that have distinctive value orientations, direct the order behaviour of human beings and characteristically tend to be permanent and to resist change. They exist because they have been reasonably successful in meeting the societal needs. Recreation in a collective social setting can thus be perceived as a social institution.

Trying to see what integration there is between these two elements of structure and progress, recreation may be seen according to Moore [31] as a social mechanism or institution which has evolved to meet leisure 'problems' that stem from post-industrial society. Inherently there is a belief in the right of the individual to self-expression, the expanding of experiences and horizons, *but* within society's social ethic. Recreation facilities, programmes and personnel have been provided to serve community-based leisure preferences.

6.6 RECREATION: SUMMARY

Recreation, like any other word, is an abstract symbol, having many meanings, depending on the context in which it is used. It has a ring of condescending moral, Puritan authority: whether you like it or not, take it; it does you good. In this context physical recreation is close to the outmoded concept of muscular Christianity. The word recreation suggests leisure activities, recuperation, relaxation, pleasure, satisfaction – but this does not reveal its nature. It is traditionally seen as an action performed. Its outward manifestation is that, but it contains a more inclusive meaning as well. Recreation for the individual can be a matter of emotions rather than motions.

Recreation as a concept of activity is understood. Recreation as an inner personal experience is yet to be understood, but it is from an *individual* as well as collective orientation that community recreation planning, programming and management should rebuild if people's needs are to be met.

The term recreation can be used in a variety of ways. One way looks at it in its traditional, institutional framework of activities, programmes, facilities and in the context of 'man the player'. Recreation can be an activity performed, a set or cluster of activities or leisure-time expressions. It has also been defined as a social institution and as a professional service. This stance is understood and generally accepted by society. However, what the experience of recreation is, and what it does for people is of the essence to purposeful planning and management of recreation.

From its re-creative centre, recreation can be seen as the 'new' man feeling, the 'aahh' feeling, the job well done, success, the top of the mountain – 'Eureka'. The experience is the moment itself; recreation value is post experience. A game of squash (under this definition) where the player feels let down with a poor performance or poor attitude, would not be recreation. A mother who normally is reinvigorated after a weekly relaxing sauna but has had to cut short her visit because the children are to be home early from school, may lose the completeness of the recreative experience.

Why recreation? There is no accepted scientific explanation as to why man needs recreation. It is generally accepted that while man needs to maintain a state of biological equilibrium, psychologically too one needs to restore a mental balance. It has been suggested, though not proved, that recreation can function as one of the means of achieving such a balance. However, man also seeks some degree of stress or activity that provides meaning to existence. The stress of effort helps to provide a form of biological and psychological 'tone' analogous to muscle tone. Effort, however, must be recognized by the individual as worthwhile, whether 'work' or 'leisure'.

In terms of recreation management, recreation is not only individual but also collective and deeply entrenched into a system of recreation providers and into the ways of life of people. In addition recreation as behaviour and institution cuts across several disciplines such as education, sociology, anthropology, psychology, physical education, planning and management. All these problems, the complexity and the interrelationships make it almost impossible to construct a unified theory. One definition which meets many of the points put forward in this chapter relating to the multi-faceted phenomenon of recreation and which comes close to an all round description is proposed by Kraus [30].

'Recreation consists of activities or experiences carried on within leisure, usually chosen voluntarily by the participant – either because of satisfaction, pleasure or creative enrichment derived, or because he perceives certain personal or social values to be gained from them. It may also be perceived as the process of participation, or as the emotional state derived from involvement.

When carried on as part of organized community or voluntary agency programmes, recreation must be designed to meet constructive and socially acceptable goals of the individual participant, the group and society at large. Finally, recreation must be recognized as a social institution with its own values and traditions, structures and organizations, and professional groups and skilled practitioners.'

Hence recreation can be viewed as personal experience (what it does to a person), as activities (the forms it takes) or as an institution (the structure in which it is made available to the community). Taken yet another way recreation can be viewed as a process (what happens to an individual) and as a structure (the framework in which recreation is practised). Its relationship to play and leisure is discussed in Chapter 8.

REFERENCES AND NOTES

1. One recent overview is presented by Kraus, R. (1978), *Recreation and Leisure in Modern Society*, 2nd Edn, Goodyear, Santa Monica, California.

2. Fairchild, H. (ed.) (1944), *Dictionary of Sociology*, Philosophical Library, New York, pp. 251–2.
3. Hutchinson, J.L. (1949), *Principles of Recreation*, A.S. Barnes, New York, p. 17.
4. Romney, G.O. (1945), *Off the Job Living*, A.S. Barnes, New York, p. 14.
5. Avedon, E. (1974), *Therapeutic Recreation Service*, Prentice Hall, Englewood Cliffs, New Jersey.
6. Gray, D.E. and Greben, S. (1974), *Parks and Recreation*, July 1974, p. 49.
7. Gray, D.E. and Greben, S. (1979), *Parks and Recreation*, 9, No. 3, March 1979, p. 23.
8. Slavson, S.R. (1948), *Recreation and Total Personality*, Association Press, New York.
9. Jacks, L.P. (1932), *Education Through Recreation*, Harper and Row, New York.
10. Nash, J.B. (1953), *Philosophy of Recreation and Leisure*, C.V. Mosby, St Louis.
11. Nash, J.B. (1960), *Philosophy of Recreation and Leisure*, William Brown, Dubuque, Iowa, p. 89.
12. Sports Council (1969), *Professional Training for Recreation Management* (Chairman D.D. Molyneux), Sports Council, London, p. 5.
13. Countryside Commission Recreation Research Advisory Group.
14. Neumeyer, M. and Neumeyer, E. (1958), *Leisure and Recreation*, Ronald Press, New York.
15. Miller, N.P. and Robinson, D.M. (1963), *Leisure Age: Its Challenge to Recreation*, Wadsworth, Belmont, California.
16. Meyer, H.D. and Brightbill, C.K. (1964), *Community Recreation*, Prentice-Hall, Englewood Cliffs, N.J.
17. Butler, G. (1968), *Introduction to Community Recreation*, McGraw-Hill, New York.
18. Miller, N.P and Robinson, D.M. (1963) *Leisure Age: Its Challenge to Recreation*, Wadsworth, Belmont, California, p. 164.
19. Shivers, J.S. (1967), *Principles and Practices of Recreational Service*, Macmillan, New York.
20. Ibid. p. 90.
21. Gray, D.E. (1980), *Parks and Recreation*, March 1980, 62–4 and 94.
22. Gray, D. and Pelegrino, D. (1973), *Reflections on the Recreation and Park Movement*, William C. Brown, Dubuque, Iowa, p. 6.
23. Graham, P.J. and Klar, L.R. Jr (1979), *Planning and Delivering Leisure Services*, William C. Brown, Dubuque, Iowa, p. 7.
24. Department of the Environment (1978), *Recreation Management Training Committee: Interim Report (A Discussion Paper) (Chairman Anne Yates)*, HMSO, London, p. 5.
25. Graham, P.J. and Klar, L.R. Jr (1979), *Planning and Delivering Leisure Services*, William C. Brown, Dubuque, Iowa, p. 8.
26. Murphy, J. (1975), *Recreation and Leisure Service*, William C. Brown, Dubuque, Iowa.
27. Kraus, R. (1971), *Recreation and Leisure in Modern Society*, 1st edn, Goodyear, Santa Monica, California.
28. Ibid., p. 263.
29. Avedon, E. (1974), *Therapeutic Recreation Service*, Prentice-Hall, Englewood Cliffs, New Jersey, p. 47.

30. Kraus, R. (1978), *Recreation and Leisure in Modern Society*, 2nd edn, Goodyear, Santa Monica, California; (1971), 1st edn, p. 37.
31. Moore, V.L. (1976), *A Conceptual Model for Contemporary Recreation Theory and Service*, unpublished dissertation, University of Southern California.

Chapter 7

Leisure

*To be able to fill leisure intelligently
is the last product of civilisation*

Bertrand Russell

★

7.1 INTRODUCTION

The third part of the play/recreation/leisure trilogy is studied in this chapter. So vast are the reaches of 'leisure' that it appears to bestride the Western world like a colossus. At one pole it is seen as a gigantic movement for great good in enhancing the qualify of life for the mass of people and at the other pole it is seen as a major 20th century problem, in which the great mass of people are seen as being incapable of coping with leisure.

This chapter is written in the following sequence. *First*, leisure is seen very briefly in its historical setting, from the millennia before Christ to its setting in modern times. *Second*, the variety of approaches to an understanding of leisure and descriptions and definitions of leisure are described and analysed. *Third*, the development of mass leisure and the ensuing assets and problems associated with this modern phenomenon are briefly considered. *Fourth*, leisure is studied in the light of its relationship and juxtaposition to the concepts and meaning of 'work'.

7.2 LEISURE: HISTORICAL PERSPECTIVE

That is the principal point, with what kind of activity is man to occupy his leisure

Aristotle

The first thing to be said about leisure is that it is not new. Leisure is an ancient idea. It has been identified with élitism and class privilege, particularly since the early Greek and Roman civilizations. However, it is probable that leisure began with primitive cultures when the pressures for sustenance, security and basic needs were removed, or in celebration after a 'kill' or during inclement weather.

In simpler societies the line between work and leisure is not indelibly drawn. In times past and even in many parts of the world today there are still people who work so hard and long to sustain themselves and their families that their lives are devoid of what we might term 'leisure'. Peasant life is often working to survive, and playing when opportunity permits. Opportunity for leisure came with the obligations towards festivals, celebrations, feasts, weddings and special days. Godbey [1] points out that there was no *deliberate* leisure, nothing that was the result of the exercise of individual choice. In such societies leisure is structured around the life cycle of necessary daily tasks; it is integrated into the daily or seasonal life pattern rather than being separate from it.

Cutter [2] states

'It was from these days or hours of primitive leisure, when crude but very real beginnings were made, that the arts, the sciences, the games and all the products of civilisation date. In fact, civilisations were the products of leisure and yet they have not always admitted their origin'.

Early advanced cultures, with clearly differentiated work roles, developed élite classes and leisure became associated with high culture, social standing and political status. For example, the Egyptian civilization (prominent from about 5000 BC until well into the Roman era) and the Assyrian and Babylonian cultures included many 'leisure' activities but these were primarily activities of the upper strata in society – the nobility, the military and religious leaders. Their activities included horse racing, wrestling, boxing, archery, arts, dance, music, drama, hunting, warfare and lavish entertainment. Drinking and gambling were common. In ancient Assyria and Babylon there were royal estates and parks, zoological and botanical gardens and large formal gardens of geometric designs. The terraced Hanging Gardens of Babylon became one of the seven wonders of the world.

7.2.1 Leisure and the Greeks

The early Greek civilization appears to have influenced current leisure thinking to an appreciable extent, and this is primarily as a result of the writings of Plato and Aristotle [3, 4]. At the height of Greek civilization (around 500 BC) the growing professionalization of sport, public entertainment and competitions, saw in contrast the birth of the 'leisure ethic' – the intelligent use of free time was the purpose of life.

Plato expressed a low regard for manual labour and a high regard for well-employed leisure, with the capable citizen performing music, drama, sport, citizenship and education during leisure time. In fact the early Greek word *skole* denoted both schooling and leisure. It led to the Latin *scola* and English *school* and *scholar*. Aristotle in Book 1 of the *Politics* defines leisure as time free from the necessity to work. Leisure is different from work (*ascholia*) and from children's play (*paidia*). Leisure leads to aesthetic, spiritual, or intellectual enlightenment through a search for understanding. Manual workers were believed to be incapable of leisure. This was not simply a case of discriminating against those earning a living by the sweat of their brows; it was rather a recognition that kinds of work performed in manual occupations made workers unfit for the duties of citizenship. Development of the concept of the natural slave was a solution to the problem of getting the necessary work done so that the rest of the city could be free for the more worthwhile pursuits. For 20th century leisure two aspects of that Greek civilization endure – the work–leisure distinction and the Greek leisure ethic.

(a) The work–leisure distinction

The work–leisure distinction may well have begun with the Greek philosophers. Work was associated with the toil of manual labour and with
providing the necessities of life, while leisure was valued as those
moments of life in which one contemplated the eternal truths, and
participated in music and drama. Aristotle placed business and war on
one side and leisure and peace on the other; this view held that no
occupation could be regarded as leisure, nor could leisure be anything
related to an occupation. 'We are unleisurely in order to have leisure', he
claimed, 'facts, as well as arguments, prove that the legislator should
direct all his military and other measures to the provision of leisure and
the establishment of peace.'

Plato did not share this understanding of work–leisure. In the *Republic*,
Plato employs the word *skole* with different meanings – as spare time, as
freedom from other activities and as self-possession or freedom. There is
a further concept of leisure as idleness. When Plato referred to this he
used the word *agria* – a degenerate condition and not to be thought of as
leisure. Hence leisure becomes the *quality* of the activity.

(b) The Greek leisure myth

The Greek conception of leisure was central to a much wider view of the
life and nature of a free man. However, the range of activities that
qualified as leisure was severely restricted. To Plato, music, poetry and
philosophy lead to beauty and eternal truths. To Aristotle, only music
and contemplation were worthy of the name leisure. Moreover, as
Godbey [1] points out, the style of life and leisure regarded as appropriate
to free men was in fact that of the privileged élite. Thus the Greek ideal,
even if it existed in the purest terms as set out in the writings, was for a
very small proportion of the population.

The Greek ideal is, therefore, something of a myth. Indeed, it is not
consistent with what actually occurred in ancient Greece in practice. The
early Olympic Games, the stadia, gymnasia, extensive gardens and the
open air amphitheatres for festivals all illustrate the range of leisure
pursuits and the range of public provision of facilities. In addition, while
in the early days all citizens were encouraged to participate and compete,
this spirit of amateurism gave way to specialist performers, commer-
cialization and mass spectatorship and led from the amateur to the
professional.

Although founded on slave labour and élitism, the Greek leisure ethic
shows that leisure can be an essential opportunity for the development of
man and the unity of body and mind. Moreover, whether myth of fact,
the *spirit* of the Greek ideal is still a goal which many prescribe to and seek
to emulate and there exist, even today, small enclaves of esoteric minority
pursuits devoted to the enlightenment of mankind.

7.2.2 The Romans

The empire of the ancient Romans established in 27 BC continued until AD 395 when it divided into Eastern and Western empires. The Roman culture spread across the known world. In ancient Rome military success and conquests led to affluence, a powerful nation and a move from agricultural democracy to urban populations with a class structure. Masses of the new urban population had very considerable free time and as many as 200 holidays a year by the year AD 354. Leisure was important for the Romans, but its importance was different from that of the Greek leisure ethic. To the Romans leisure was important for fitness for work. Sports were practised for maintaining physical fitness and for war. Leisure was utilitarian rather than aesthetic. Baths, amphitheatres and arenas were constructed for the benefit of the mass of the population. In Rome itself there were over 800 public baths at little or no cost to the public.

Free time, however, became a problem. Emperors attempted to keep people content by providing free food and entertainment – 'bread and circuses'. Slaves not only toiled but were also used for entertainment, which at first included music, drama and sports, but later included contests, simulated battles, chariot races and exhibitions of violence. Violent spectacles included animals and then humans; professional gladiators fought to the death. The Colosseum became the hub of life in Rome and large arenas, gymnasia, parks and baths were built in most large towns. The Circus Maximus could hold 385 000 spectators.

As Rome became more decadent it declined. Historians have suggested that the inability to cope with leisure was one cause for the fall of the empire [5]. Economically, and perhaps in other ways, the spectacles contributed to the financial ruin of the empire, as the aristocracy competed to outdo each other often to the point of bankruptcy.

Ancient Rome shows that mass leisure is no new phenomenon. It illustrates leisure in a social context of urbanization and the political use of leisure to quieten the masses. It also shows the massive investment in public recreation facilities and services and above all the growth of leisure *consumption* rather than participation. Later cultures used the example of Rome to show the consequences of uncontrolled misuse of leisure.

7.2.3 The Middle Ages

The fall of the Roman Empire and the spread of Christianity had profound and lasting effects on leisure and recreation. The Catholic church taught that the purpose of life was to prepare for the next life. The early part of the Middle Ages from about AD 400 to AD 1000 is often called the Dark Ages. The monasteries expanded, preaching hard labour, good works and self-deprivation. As a reaction to the extremes and debased activities of the Romans, the church prohibited most kinds of leisure activity except those relating to worship and religious observance. Work was glorified. Idleness was evil. However, while music and morality plays flourished, social drinking, gambling and secular music were practised by the public often on 'holy' day celebrations, and the aristocracy continued their leisure activities of hunting, falconry and in tournaments. But life in the Dark Ages was harsh to the common man.

During the late Middle Ages up to approximately AD 1500 there were some relaxations from the strictures of the Dark Ages, but life for the masses remained much the same with religious festivals, cock fighting and other activities coming as breaks in the round of toil. However, throughout the Middle Ages leisure élitism, a modified Greek ideal for the landed gentry and political leaders, continued. Leisure activities included hunting, hawking, music and dance. Sports and jousting were a means of entertainment, but were primarily preparation for feuding noblemen and for war.

7.2.4 Renaissance and reformation

The two movements, one a cultural revolution and the other a moral work-ethic way of life, developed in historical parallel. Over the centuries the power of the Catholic church declined permitting a reawakening in humanity and the arts. The 15th century marks the transition from the mediaeval world to modern Western civilization. This period of rebirth, developing in Italy and spreading across France and England is known as the *Renaissance*. It was not until then that leisure ideals became more generalized and more opportunities became available to the masses. The populace continued to enjoy both religious and secular festivals, but the development of printing in this period enabled literature to become available to a wider public since it had previously only been available to those who had studied in monasteries, universities and aristocratic homes.

Music, drama and dance were professionally performed in theatres and education became more readily available. Later, educators such as Rousseau and Locke espoused the benefits of play in the education of children. During these times the nobility became the patrons of the arts and the works of many of the great artists of that time hang in galleries all over the world today.

During the Renaissance, the Protestant *Reformation* took hold in many parts of Europe and later moved to America. The liberalism brought about by the Renaissance had also encouraged a pleasure-seeking aristocracy, a public more prone to drinking, gambling and practising cruel sports and a worldy and often corrupt church. These and other factors led to the

Reformation. Martin Luther began a revolt against the established church in Germany. Calvin and Knox began similar reformed churches. A time of austerity followed with emphasis on religious matters and a diminishing of many leisure activities. In some communities even children's play was discouraged as it was said to encourage idleness.

To counteract the growing religious opposition to active leisure pursuits, James I of England issued the *Book of Sports* in 1618, making it legal for working people to play certain games outside church hours. Although heavily suppressed by the Reformation, the cultural revolution of the Renaissance continued. In the 17th and 18th centuries parks and gardens were developed for the nobility who went hunting and fishing and enjoyed the beauty of the gardens. Commons and plazas were developed for the public. Holidays were declared by the Kings and Lords. The Tuileries and the Versailles gardens in Paris, the Tiergarten in Berlin and the Kensington Gardens in London were gradually opened to the public.

Although the Renaissance brought about more freedom for leisure for the common man, the Reformation has been shown to have had an even greater effect on Western attitudes. The Reformation was a period which idealized work and distrusted the evils of leisure – a work-ethic which has persisted throughout the 20th century. The Protestant ethic sought to condition leisure to behaviour fitting man for devotion and work. The humanism of the Renaissance sought the creativity and development of man through education and greater freedom in leisure. Regrettably, yet another revolution was to suppress still further the leisure development for the mass of the people.

7.2.5   Effect of the Industrial Revolution

The Industrial Revolution of the 18th and 19th centuries brought about profound changes. Factories brought about the growth of cities. Populations were uprooted from the land and from small towns and villages to the cities. The consequent rise in urban population overcrowding, poor housing, poverty, crime and the increase in working hours and child labour all militated against leisure. British industrial history records examples of the hardship caused by the Industrial Revolution and the exploitation of the workers, poor wages and conditions of the miners, the cotton mill workers and many others.

From the villages where people lived next to nature, where children could play in the fields and families could walk in the countryside, came cramped conditions with little room to play and little time to enjoy leisure. Recreation areas were not planned and life for the common man had reached a low ebb.

It was in response to this situation that the organized recreation movement began. At the turn of the century an interest in leisure, as it relates to industrial society, was awakened. It was during this period also that several of the writings and theories of play and recreation began to emerge. In America, Veblen [6] endeavoured to identify weaknesses in the industrial system. He criticized the 'leisure class' and its 'conspicuous consumption'. The institution of the leisure class is the 'outgrowth of an early discrimination between employments, according to which some employments are worthy and others unworthy'. With industrialism, the arbitrary division of labour and class continues to exist and to perpetuate itself. Status becomes symbolized by purchasing power and accumulation of wealth. To Veblen, writing at the turn of the century, leisure perpetuated leisure for the leisure classes.

It was out of times of hardship and social injustice that social pioneers influenced governments to act. In Britain public health and physical recreation, baths and parks and open spaces were gradually made available to the public. But leisure was never the right of the masses until it was won as a *separate* part of life from the excessively long working hours. The Saturday half-day was a significant turning point in Britain towards an acceptance of leisure for the mass of the people.

7.2.6   Leisure history: summary

Leisure as we know it today in Western civilization is a relatively new concept, historically. It is only in the 20th century that leisure and work for the mass of people have been split into separate areas of life where leisure activity is chosen on an individual basis.

This brief history of leisure has shown that it has been difficult to hang on to the elevated concept of the Greeks. Wars, religious stringencies and intellectual bias have stood in its path. Christians put the stamp of ascetic teaching on labour and leisure. Leisure (idleness) was condemned. When leisure did become accepted it was accepted conditionally, not as value in itself, but as a means of renewing for the work ahead. The word 'recreation' epitomizes the attitude of conditional joy; man works, wearies, takes recreation that he may work again. Take some free time but not too much! Too much leisure is unearned time. In 1982 even with approaching four million people unemployed in the United Kingdom, many people still regard social security payments as 'handouts' and as pandering to the idle. The Puritan work ethic is still very much part of attitudes towards work and leisure.

7.3   LEISURE: A VARIETY OF APPROACHES, DESCRIPTIONS AND DEFINITIONS

The English word 'leisure' appears to be derived from the Latin *licere*, 'to be permitted' or 'to be free'. Hence, the French word *loisir*, meaning free time and the English words *licence* and *liberty*. Thus, the word 'leisure' is associated with a complexity of meanings in our language. Generally it is defined in terms of 'freedom from constraint', 'opportunity to choose', 'time left over after work' or as 'free time after obligatory social duties have been met'. However, according to the Parrys leisure as a social phenomenon itself 'involves social constraint and social obligation and can best be thought of as being embodied in a whole way of life. Such an idea immediately invokes the concept of culture' [7].

The concept of leisure has widely varying responses to it. Leisure is commonly thought of as the opposite of work, but one man's work can be another man's leisure and several activities combine both leisure and work characteristics. Freedom from obligation is often regarded as a key attraction of leisure, but many non-work activities – domestic, social, voluntary, community – involve considerable obligation. Some regard leisure as being an opportunity for relaxation and pleasure but often people spend their leisure time in dedicated service, study, personal development, hard training, discipline and stress. *The problems of definition and understanding are considerable.*

Most theories have been developed in the 20th century or at the turn of the century. Many arose out of the troubles of the Industrial Revolution. Hundreds of writings, theories and descriptions of leisure have been written from then until this time. From the mass of literature, four discernible major approaches are evident:

1. Leisure as *time*.
2. Leisure as *activity*.
3. Leisure as a *state of being;* and most recently.
4. Leisure as an all pervading *'holistic'* concept.

Each of these areas is considered briefly below.

7.3.1 Leisure as time

Within the broad framework of leisure defined as time there are many interpretations. Some make a very broad distinction, defining leisure as the time when someone is not working primarily for money. Soule [8] made the distinction between sold time and unsold time: what a person does in sold time is 'the job'; time which is not sold is one's 'own time', one's 'free time'. This free time is thought of as leisure no matter what a person does with it. Hunter [9] too regards leisure as everything except time spend in paid employment. With such a definition, however, we are left with a large proportion of people's time which is filled in a multitude of ways. Such a definition of leisure is far too broad to be of use and is only perceived in the context of doing 'work'.

The *Dictionary of Sociology* [10] describes leisure as 'free time after the practical necessities of life have been attended to'. This gives 'surplus time' to do with as we please. Several other writers refer to leisure as free time or unoccupied time. To Weiss [11] 'leisure time is that portion of the day not used for the exigencies of existence'. The problem in viewing leisure as free time is that it is difficult to draw a line between necessities and spare time.

Parker [12] indicates that there is a distinct contrast between 'residual' definitions of leisure and other definitions. Residual time is the time left after taking out of total time everything that is not regarded as leisure. A widely quoted definition accepted by a number of government agencies was put forward by the Countryside Recreation Research Advisory Group in 1970. It defined leisure as 'the time available to the individual when the disciplines of work, sleep and other needs have been met'.

To Brightbill [13] and others, while leisure is concerned with time, it is only leisure if it falls into 'discretionary' time, i.e. time beyond existence and subsistence, 'the time to be used according to our own judgement or choice'. Hence, three time-slots are identified: existence, subsistence and discretionary. Yet the matter is complicated further: What is necessary for some will be discretionary for others and many necessary activities, for example, eating and sleeping may be chosen as discretionary activities. Although the distinction is made between the three segments it is clear that each segment is highly flexible, and each may be increased or decreased depending on individual circumstances. Brightbill's concern is with the uses of discretionary time. He sees leisure as an opportunity. There can be 'no choice, no judgement, no attitude and hence no freedom without opportunity. Nor can there be opportunity without time, which to me is the overriding component of leisure' [14]. He uses in his description of leisure the terms 'true leisure' and 'enforced leisure'. Enforced leisure describes the leisure time people do not seek such as through illness, unemployment or unwanted retirement.

In general it appears that the word leisure is correlated with positive or constructive behaviour. Free time appears to have some negatively charged characteristics. This aspect of leisure as time appears to establish leisure in a *positive relationship* to time.

7.3.2 Leisure as activity

Leisure is often perceived as the activities participated in during the time people have available to spend as they wish. A classical understanding of leisure was that it was made up of activities which enlightened and educated free men. Leisure was, therefore, made up of activities. Today we hear leisure described as a 'cluster of activities'.

The Neumeyers [15] define leisure as, 'an opportunity to engage in some kind of activity, whether vigorous or relatively passive, which is not required by daily necessities'. Kaplan [16], in describing leisure as activity saw it as an end, distinct from work which was a means to an end. A definition of leisure by the International Group of the Social Sciences of Leisure states that:

'Leisure consists of a number of occupations in which the individual may indulge of his own free will whether to rest, amuse himself, to add to his knowledge, or improve his skills disinterestedly or to increase his voluntary participation in the life of the community after discharging his professional, family and social duties' [17].

Nash viewed the use of leisure for specific activities on four levels: passive, emotional, active and creative involvement. His leisure model (see Section 6.3.1) illustrates use of leisure time with a progression of leisure activities in similar vein to Maslow's need hierarchy. Nash attaches a value to each level. Those at the apex of the pyramid are values to be regarded as worthy and those at the base are negative in value and undesirable.

Many look at leisure as activities freely chosen. Dumazedier considered leisure as activity apart from work, family and society obligations, to which we turn at will for either relaxation, diversion or broadening of our knowledge. However, in reality absolute freedom is rarely achieved. Dumazedier [18] coined the term 'semi-leisure' to describe those activities which one was obliged to do but that brought about satisfactions in the doing. Such activities as domestic, do-it-yourself, family obligations and the like could be pleasurable or diversionary and could function as 'semi-leisure'.

7.3.3 Leisure as an end in itself, a state of being

The complexity of definition is illustrated by Kaplan [19]. He describes several traditional concepts of leisure which he believes are basic to an understanding: the humanistic model, the therapeutic model, the quantitative model, the institutional model, the epistomologic concept and the sociologic concept. From the sociologic view, 'nothing is definable as leisure *per se* and almost anything is definable as leisure, given a synthesis of elements.'

What is described as the 'humanistic' model views leisure as an end in itself, a state of being. Pieper [20] stressed this idea: 'Leisure it must be understood, is a mental and spiritual attitude – it is not simply the result of external factors, it is not the inevitable result of spare time, a holiday, a weekend or a vacation. It is, in the first place, an attitude of the mind, a condition of the soul'. Leisure, to Pieper, was not a means to an end but rather an end in itself. (This is a concept similar to Huizinga's understanding of play.) Brightbill [14] also described leisure as 'a state of quiet contemplative dignity.' Larrabee and Meyersohn [21] saw it as a 'mood of contemplation'. To de Grazia [22] leisure is a state of being free of everyday necessity. He denounces as a popular misconception the notion that free time is leisure.

'Anybody can have free time. Free time is a realizable idea of democracy. Leisure is not fully realizable and hence an ideal not alone an idea. Free time refers to a special way of calculating a special kind of time. Leisure refers to a state of being, a condition of man, which few desire and fewer achieve' [23].

To de Grazia the mentality of clock watching prevents the contemplation of the Greek philosophy. It produces synchronization, impersonal tempo, conformity, unthoughtful action. The free time produced by industrialization is typified by passivity, an uncritical spirit, and craving for fun. We have not developed 'true' leisure for the masses. It may well be 'beyond the capacity of most people'. In de Grazia's opinion, leisure perfects man and holds the key to the future. It needs to break the grip of the machine and release human energy for free expression and exploration of truth, beauty and knowledge. He casts doubt on whether there is indeed any freedom in the quantitative framework called 'free time'. Marcuse [24], however, takes a totally opposing view, defining leisure as free time and questioning the freedom of leisure.

Parker enlarges on the argument, setting the semantic problems aside. If free time and leisure are different conceptually, they cannot be measured by the same criteria. The distinction is not confined to the area of non-work: it applies also in the work sphere.

'*Some* working time is "paid" time, but you do not have to be an employee in order to do work, and in that sense "anyone can have working time." Yet work as a certain kind of activity, a productive relationship between man and his environment may, like leisure, be something which few desire and fewer achieve. The two worlds of time and activity are thus not the domains of work and leisure respectively, but are both *dimensions* of work *and leisure*' [25].

Nakhooda suggested that the meaning of leisure to the layman could be defined as that part of the individual's daily life 'in which he finds himself free from the demands of his regular calling and able to enter upon any line of activity he may choose within his own interests – whether it be work or play or meditation' [26].

7.3.4 Leisure: an all embracing concept/an 'holistic' concept or leisure as meaning

While many authors define leisure as time, activity and state of being, most of them incorporate all three aspects, giving greater weight in one direction. Indeed, many of the prominent writers such as Kaplan, Brightbill, Dumazedier and de Grazia use *different definitions at different times depending on the point which is being made at the time*. This can be seen in several of the all-embracing descriptions of leisure. An umbrella approach, for example, is taken by Kaplan, Dumazedier and Murphy.

Kaplan [27] believes that one can take the stance and say that leisure is what people say it is, or what it means to them, or alternatively seek 'an ideal construct'. Hence, leisure can be classified as a bulk of time, freedom, an end in itself, a minimum of obligation, re-creation, self-improvement, social control, social symbols, sets of attitudes or motivations, physiological or emotional necessity. It can be:

1. An antithesis to economic 'work'.
2. A pleasant expectation.
3. A minimum of involuntary social role obligations.
4. A psychological perception of freedom.
5. A close relation to values of the culture.
6. The inclusion of an entire range from inconsequence and insignificance to weightiness and importance.
7. Often but not necessarily, an activity characterized by the element of play.

Leisure is none of these by itself but all together in one emphasis or another.
Dumazedier [28] also put forward a number of classifications of leisure:

1. A style of behaviour, and attitude at work, study or play.
2. Non-work.
3. The socio-spiritual and socio-psychologic obligations that influence individual people.

However, his preferred definition of leisure is that it is orientated towards a person's 'self-fulfilment as an ultimate end'. The three primary functions of leisure, according to Dumazedier are: *relaxation, entertainment* and *personal development*.

Within these three aspects people find recovery from fatigue, deliverance from bordeom and liberation from daily automatism. In relation to work, leisure has become a compensatory and escapist mechanism to counteract alienation from the job. A new leisure is emerging as a new force. 'Leisure is the expression of a whole collection of man's aspirations on a search for a new happiness, related to a new duty, a new ethic, a new policy and a new culture. A humanistic mutation is beginning.' While the new leisure is on the horizon it has not had the time to adjust to the challenge of overcoming the restrictive and traditional taboos within the inherited leisure.

Murphy [29] believes that leisure is increasingly recognized as the time available to be used at an individual's discretion – 'a self deterministic condition'. There has been erosion of the effectiveness of work to serve self-identity needs. In contrast there has been an increase in the value of leisure in establishing one's status and personal identity. He sees this as a major factor in the trend towards the fusion of work and leisure. The holistic view of leisure is seen in the context of the *wholeness* of the individual. A full range of possible forms of self-expression may occur during work *or* leisure. To Murphy [30], 'this perspective eliminates the dichotomy drawn between work and leisure, which has been a formidable barrier in the path to enjoyment of leisure opportunities for many people. According to the holistic concept . . . the meaning of work and leisure are inextricably related to each other.'

However, as we will see later in this chapter, work and leisure may not be as interrelated as Murphy suggests particularly in times of physical and psychological depression when people do not have the means to enjoy leisure, nor the attitude towards it, nor the perception of what it might mean in terms of life satisfaction.

The more important questions are: what does leisure do for people, how do they perceive leisure and what does it *mean* to them? Neulinger [31], a psychologist, takes an attitudinal approach. Leisure is concerned with people's attitudes. If it is concerned with attitudes then it is concerned with the perceptions of people. Leisure has three dimensions in his paradigm: it includes perceived freedom, it is intrinsic and it is non-instrumental. Leisure is the perception of free choice for the sake of doing or experiencing. Neulinger and Crandall [32] point out that we are no longer satisifed to just *name* the activities that people engage in; we now want to find out what they *mean* to people.

7.3.5   Leisure definitions: summary

Hence, leisure means many things depending on the way people see leisure functioning for them, on different interpretations and on the orientation we have towards it. An understanding of the basic orientations gives individuals the opportunity to sort through these and accept, reject or modify them.

As we have seen, there appear to be four main orientations to leisure, each having a variety of factors which colour and modify the basic approach. The first views leisure as blocks of time (e.g. existence, subsistence, discretionary and leisure). Leisure as a quantity of time is simple and measurable but very misleading. What time is actually leisure? We need to know what the time spent meant to the individual. The second views leisure as activities. Again, this is simple and convenient but no list includes all leisure; the list would have to include almost all life activities! The third looks at the effect that leisure has on an individual – what it does for him or her. Here leisure is viewed as a state of mind condition. But this renders leisure almost anything, anywhere, at any time. The fourth is a combination of the first three orientations. It is perceived in a *'holistic'* sense – the whole person approach. As Parker points out, while the first three meanings – time, activities and state of mind – often overlap, the classification is useful in determining which aspect of the word has the greater *emphasis* within particular contexts.

7.4 LEISURE TODAY: POTENTIAL AND PROBLEMS

Not only are there different descriptions and classifications of leisure, but also many theorists take differing views of leisure in relation to its importance, its assets and its problems in society. Is leisure a social problem? What are its mass benefits and problems? Two aspects of leisure – mass leisure and popular culture – illustrate the divergent opinions.

7.4.1 Leisure: a social problem?

Industrial societies have created leisure as we know it today. Godbey [33] refers to the creation of 'leisure potential'. He has put forward seven main factors which have contributed to the situation:

1. Increased production of material goods through the application of technology.
2. Creation of labour saving devices for household and other essential duties.
3. Decline of the influence of social institutions such as the church and the family in establishing pre-determined roles for individuals.
4. Differences in attitudes towards pleasure.
5. Substantial increase in the education levels.
6. Lack of physical fatigue associated with many forms of employment.
7. Increase in discretionary income.

Further, the increased potential for leisure has also created factors that have negated the *meaning* of leisure in our society. They include: limitless materialism, increasing societal complexity and change, increasing demands of labour and carryover of 'work values' into leisure. Thus while our potential for leisure has increased, we are nowhere near the society of leisure about which so much has been written. What has increased according to Godbey [34] is antileisure, i.e. activity which is undertaken compulsively, as a means to an end, from a perception of necessity, with a high degree of externally imposed constraints, with considerable anxiety, time consciousness, minimum personal autonomy and which avoids self-actualization. 'In regard to romance, the practice of taking a mistress has largely died out because it is too time consuming. It has been replaced by the "one nighter" '. In the same vein, Linder in *The Harried Leisure Class* [35] believes that sexual promiscuity today is primarily due to the desire to speed up the courtship process and achieve what intimacy can be achieved in a very short period of time! 'Time deepening' is the term some American theorists have given to the ability to do several things simultaneously and the tendency to cram as many activities as possible into the 24-hour day [33].

Linder, a Swedish economist, believes that life has become so demanding in time that consumption eliminates, for all practical purposes, the time necessary for leisure. This consumption production creates a 'leisure deficit'. Industrial society has set its face towards increasing economic growth by all possible means. Working hours have reached a plateau, rather than continuing their downward trend. He forecasts increases in the hectic tempo of living, decline in the usefulness of income and an increase in hardship on those who need human services the most. Linder has concern for the absence of a classical attitude to leisure. Affluent nations tend to devalue idleness and leisure, thereby reducing the potential for non-destructive development of human and natural resources.

From a sociological standpoint, Berger [36] identifies the primary differences between classical and Puritan attitudes. The Industrial Revolution produced an alteration in concepts of leisure and work which brought segmentation and separation. Leisure is no longer part of the way of the people but has become a relief from work, a reward and even rehabilitation. Berger asserts that there has been an alienation from work and loss of opportunities for personal achievement, identity and expression of prowess in work. The appeal to people by government and community to make wholesome use of leisure time, and to participate in community recreation programmes, he feels is ineffective because they fail to take credence of the social needs of leisure and the need to counteract work alienation. *People will reject participation when it is beyond their means or when activities express values they do not recognize.*

Hence, many writers view leisure as a social problem. Cutten [37] saw aspects of the problem in restlessness and the need for excitement, the inability to be alone, lack of self-discipline, boredom, fatigue and lack of play experience. The heart of the leisure threat according to those who see it as such is its unwise use; this in part can be attributed to a Puritan concern to avoid the debased consumption of leisure as seen in ancient Rome; an aspect of the problem is mass availability.

7.4.2 Mass leisure

In earlier Western societies full leisure opportunity was in the hands of a social élite who appeared to know what was expected of them and who had the means and the upbringing to deal with leisure. However, the 20th century has brought time for leisure not only for the few but also for the many. Leaders of the world governments in the last years of the 20th century have to ask the same question posed by Aristotle: with what activity is man to occupy his time for leisure? To Aristotle, people must be capable of handling leisure: 'The provision of an external opportunity for leisure is not enough; it can only be fruitful if the man himself is capable of leisure, and can, as we say, occupy his leisure or work his leisure (as the Greeks say)'.

de Grazia believes that even today there are many who are incapable of leisure: anyone can have free time, not everyone can have leisure. Others take a very different viewpoint. The emergence of mass leisure has reduced, if not eliminated, many of the previous social and class differences in leisure behaviour. Authors such as Roberts [38] consider that leisure is now the great equalizer. He indicates that there are typical leisure time occupations of people of all classes. Others, however, see the picture in another perspective. Despite the increases in time, affluence, travel and mass consumerism, there are differences between the classes particularly at both poles of the social spectrum. Dumazedier wrote about the cultural under-development of large segments of the French population. Kraus [39] believes that inequalities in leisure remain deep in modern society, particularly in the spheres of recreation, cultural taste and social contacts. Zuzanek [40] reported on a study of urban family expenditures in Canada. Respondents from the lowest family income quintile were spending five times less money on recreation than respondents from the highest quintile. Yet, in view of those who advocate an 'holistic' approach to leisure, emphasizing self-development and fulfilment through freely chosen *meaningful* activities, leisure participation will be particularly valuable for those people in society who are disadvantaged.

7.4.3 Popular culture

Within the framework of mass leisure has emerged the concept of 'popular culture'. It is important because it continually reaffirms common cultural values and *identity* of people in that culture. It also appears to embody or express the social and cultural change brought about in large measure through 'the new leisure'. Lewis [41] states:

'Popular culture, then is all culture not considered élite culture or serious art, or exclusively defined as the property of a minority subculture, and that is usually, but not necessarily, disseminated through some form of the mass media. It is culture consumed nearly entirely during the leisure time of the majority of members of a social system. Thus, my definition includes popular music, films, sports events, comic books, and even fast food dispensers such as McDonald's or Kentucky Fried Chicken'.

Put simply, Gans [42] points out, some culture is popular because people want it. It encompasses the kinds of pursuits and behaviour that most people do in their leisure and the marketing and communications market makes the ideas of popular culture available. We have already seen in Chapter 3 that commercial leisure is in large measure a vehicle for dispensing popular culture and we will see in Chapter 16 how it is marketed.

However, there is more to popular culture than just its popularity. It is popular not just because of its availability but because it represents and is part of social development. The growth of a youth culture with its fashion, tastes, music and ways of life is *symbolic of its identity*. If culture is the way of life of a people, then popular culture is part of *developing* of new types and new styles of culture – a new or different culture in the making. Some popular movements, however, will come and go – 'the mods', 'the rockers', the 'flower people'. There will be changes as are seen in the worlds of popular music and entertainment. Some things will be important at different times. Some new cultures will reject traditional cultures and mores and some people may well experience little of their traditional culture and heritage. There will also be counter-culture movements, such as between a more liberalized and a less liberalized society. Counter culture movements have been traced by Kando in *Leisure and Popular Culture in Transition* [43].

Lewis fears there is a real danger of 'cultural unemployment' as well as destruction of tradition. Kato's studies in Thailand show that the popular heroes are mostly Japanese television stars rather than local heroes [44]. Thai children see and hear very little about their 'national' popular heroes in the culture they consume. The fastest growing restaurant chain in Hong Kong in the early 1980s was McDonald's!

Most industrialized popular culture is targeted for a middle class, affluent urban audience, probably American, Japanese, British or French. 'As this material is beamed across the world, millions outside that target audience are exposed to it. To the extent they begin using it as a baseline against which to judge their own lives, one can predict an increase in feelings of dissatisfaction in such populations.' [41]. The impact of television is illustrated dramatically in the showing of the series *Roots* on American television. In 1978 there were believed to have been 130 million viewers in just 8 days; like many other successful *and* unsuccessful programmes they find their way across many parts of the world.

Lewis sees a threefold outcome of popular Western culture beamed across the world: firstly, it will bring out feelings of personal inadequacy, secondly, a turning outward to forms of political unrest and dissensions, and thirdly, developing countries will accept such popular culture as the goal towards which they should strive, at exactly the same point in history when the major economically developed countries are beginning to realize that the world does not have the energy nor the resources to support such life styles of leisure.

Popular culture, however, has brought to the mass of people television, radio, popular music, fashion, sport and new life horizons. Mass leisure and popular culture are part and parcel of Western civilization and must be fashioned to improve the quality of life for the great mass of people but at the same time preventing the destruction of a nation's culture and heritage.

7.5 LEISURE: ITS RELATIONSHIP TO WORK

The relationship between the concepts of 'work' and 'leisure' has been well debated and documented, though there are no satisfactory universally accepted theses. We have noted that some societies, both ancient and modern, have made a clear distinction between work and leisure.

7.5.1 Work: a heritage of slavery, a tradition of paid employment

History has shown that the life of leisure could only be pursued by those who had sufficient free time and means to free themselves from the 'curse' of work. The blessing of leisure for some meant intensive work for many. The Greek aristocracy could not have pursued their leisure without widespread slavery; the English aristocracy could not have been the epitome of the cultured stock without suppression of the poor.

Russell [45], in *In Praise of Idleness*, asserted that harm was caused by the belief that work was virtuous; the morality of work was the morality of slaves. Work was indeed slavery to the suppressed. The boys and girls who slaved in the coal mines and textile mills in England just over a century ago had neither the time nor the energy to enjoy leisure.

The word 'work' covers a multitude of things. It is often used synonymously with words such as 'labour', 'occupation', 'employment', 'effort', 'production'. Work may also be a time for personal development, creativity and other personal satisfactions. Marx's [46] ideal model of work was 'a process in which man and Nature participate, and which man of his own accord starts, regulates, and controls the material recreations between himself and Nature'. However, modern work tends to contradict this ideal. Specialization, fragmentation, isolation, rigid time structuring, repetitiveness and depersonalization contributes to anonymity, a sense of helplessness and alienation.

To the public at large the question 'What is work?' is so obvious that definitions and understanding seem to be totally inappropriate. Work is paid employment. It is concerned with earning a wage, the money on which to live. In addition work has been traditionally valued. It has been a means of self-identification. Traditionally, work is what adults, particularly adult males have to do. Leisure is something you don't have to do; traditionally it is conceived as freedom from commitment. Yet for those involved, many leisure activities require considerable commitment. It is clear to see that these two realms of 'work' and 'leisure' need to be considered not as dichotomized entities but in far more fluid and complex dimensions.

7.5.2 The work–leisure dichotomy

In modern Western civilization different approaches to the work–leisure dichotomy are evident. As Parker [47] outlined:

'One (clearly declining) is that work is the serious business of life and leisure is subsidiary or even non-existent. The second is that leisure is the aim and purpose of life and work merely a means to that end. The third is a more integrated approach: work and leisure as reconcilable parts of a whole life, such as that of the craftsman or artist.

An important clue to the relative importance attached to work and leisure is the choice that people make between having more income or more leisure. In non-industrial societies people tend not to seek additional work after they have achieved a comfortable margin of income over what they consider to be necessary. But among the economically advanced nations more people prefer additional work (overtime or a second job) to more leisure'.

Moonlighting has become a familiar term. It was used in Parliament during the 1979 Budget debate which was denounced as a 'moonlighter's charter'. Although moonlighting does not appear to be a major problem to employers, it could grow to significant proportions. The move away from standard hours for some, flexi-hours for others and the tendency to trade leisure for extra income, could become an issue in years to come.

Some of the relevant factors in appreciating the juxtaposition of work to leisure in modern times are as follows:

1. Working hours determine how much time is available for leisure.
2. Work may determine the energies, enthusiasm and motivations left over for leisure.
3. Some work affords leisure opportunity during work hours or as part of work itself.
4. Some jobs are more akin to certain types of leisure occupation.

There are several arguments to suggest a fusion of work and leisure:

1. More people use free time for work purposes both for employment

and for effort towards obligatory or non-obligatory actions.

2. Some work decisions are made with leisure in mind as one of the perks of the job.

3. Many leisure pursuits have become employment for some and extremely hard work for others.

Others, however, take the view that work and leisure are becoming more polarized. There is more free time available but not nearly as much as is popularly believed, perhaps no more than a few hours a week.

Two contrasting functions of leisure in relation to work have been put foward by Wilensky [48]: spillover and compensatory. People's work spills over into leisure, or is a continuation of work, or there is a continuation of work experiences and attitudes. On a compensatory level, leisure makes up for the dissatisfaction which is the outcome of work. Roberts believes that leisure gives more meaning to a person's life than work but the job usually influences leisure behaviour more than vice versa.

Three types of work have been suggested by Wilensky and by Berger [49]; work that is 'fulfilling', 'oppressive' or 'boring'. Parker [50] provided three types of work scenario: 'extension', 'opposition' and 'neutrality'. Bacon [51] found that there was little evidence to support the view that alienating work is associated with certain types of leisure behaviour. The things that people choose to do in their free time are unrelated to the nature of their employment.

In relation to work Kelly [52] suggested three types of leisure activity: 'unconditional leisure' is independent of work and freely chosen, 'coordinated leisure' is similar to work such as undertaking a hobby, and 'complementary leisure' which is independent of work in form and content but the need to take part is influenced by one's work such as being obliged to participate when it is expected of you.

Blauner [53] concludes that work remains the single most important activity for most people in terms of time and energy. Argyris [54] illustrates the difficulties of making leisure compensate for work: if people experience dependence, submission, frustration and conflict at work, and if they adapt to these conditions by psychological withdrawal, apathy and indifference, then these adaptive features will guide their leisure behaviour outside the workplace.

A case can be formulated to show work and leisure as opposites. However, this is a far from adequate formulation. Concepts such as play, recreation and leisure are relative terms. One man's play is another man's work: one man's leisure is another man's drudgery. In addition, the seriousness of work is seen in play and the play element in work.

7.5.3 Work, leisure and unemployment

Work has been traditionally *valued*. It has been a means of *self-identification*. A person's leisure appears to relate not only to individuality but to whether one is working, how satisfying the work is, whether one is unemployed and the extent of dissatisfaction with the situation, whether there is an overall feeling of being involved with society or alienated from it. The extent to which job dissatisfaction and unemployment fosters feelings of alienation is an important issue for leisure managers. *Can opportunities for recreation and re-creation counter life dissatisfactions?*

The *General Household Survey, 1977* [55] found that the unemployed are surprisingly active in sports but despite the wide range of active leisure pursuits, retired people and full-time housewives are markedly inactive. Many pursuits involve costs; many do not. The unemployed may be excluded from leisure activities which involve financial costs. Although they have free time, the constraints affecting the use of it, compounded by the apathy and disinterest that can affect some people who are desperately looking for work, can become a disabling preoccupation. Those people who are made to retire early, made redundant or who simply do not want to retire, can also find themselves feeling alienated, isolated and robbed of the purposefulness of life.

We are moving into a period of major unemployment and fewer jobs. The dependence on paid work as a means for organizing one's life and that of one's family is declining. The situation makes it a misnomer to consider 'leisure' as 'time' free from work when one is free to choose what to do. Also it is becoming less appropriate to consider 'work' only as a job for which one is paid. Over half the population – dependent children, houseworkers, the retired, the unemployed, students, the handicapped – are not in paid employment and, therefore, are not included in the present conceptual boundaries of such a definition of leisure.

7.6 LEISURE: SUMMARY

Leisure is an historic idea. During its evolution it has been considered in varying degrees from a quality of life reflecting the highest ideals of man to being the worst evil – the devil incarnate. Leisure has been perceived as blocks of time when we are freest to be ourselves, as activities, as a state of being, as an all-embracing attitude to life merging the three dimensions of time, activity and state of mind and as perceived freedom to choose.

Leisure has become the right of most people in Western civilization in the 20th century but time for leisure can be seen as both a blessing and a curse [56]. Time without the means, the motivation and the opportunity, or free time forced on to people, is not regarded as leisure. To function as leisure there appears to be a need for positive approaches to life and the activity. The idea of leisure potential stresses the need to offer opportunities for individuals to express themselves in ways of benefit to themselves and to society.

Leisure was thought to be totally opposite to work but increasingly leisure and work are considered to be on a continuum. Effort (work) is expended both at work and in many leisure activities. With high unemployment, early retirement, longer life and greater leisure potential, an understanding of the relationship between work and leisure is more important than ever before. Hence, work and leisure are not opposites; effort and application is needed in both. But neither are they fused as appears to be proposed in the 'holistic' ideas. Perhaps they might more accurately be described as working in parallel, having interlocking relationships. They may both have intrinsic social satisfactions but one is for most people a social necessity, the other for its own sake. Man is both *homo ludens*, man the player, and *homo faber*, man the worker. Worthwhile productive labour (effort) appears to be as essential to human self-fulfilment as positive, productive leisure. Both can lead to human satisfactions. It is leisure, however, free from compulsion and necessity which gives greater potential for human self-fulfilment.

The study of leisure has revealed that while ideas such as pleasure, freedom, contemplation, activity, self-expression and creativity are predominant, considerable stress is being put on leisure not only as an opportunity framework but also leisure as an *attitudinal* framework as well. How do people perceive leisure? What does it mean to them? How does leisure relate to play and recreation? These aspects are taken up in the next chapter. What are people's needs in the context of leisure? How do attitudes to choice and participation come about? These further questions are taken up in Chapters 9 and 10.

REFERENCES AND NOTES

1. Godbey G. (1978), *Recreation, Park and Leisure Services*, W.B. Saunders, Philadephia, p. 8.
2. Cutten, G.B. (1929), *The Threat of Leisure*, Yale University Press, New Haven, p. 2.
3. Plato (1952), *Complete Works*, Encyclopaedia Britannica, Chicago.
4. Aristotle (1952), *Aristotle 2: Great Books of the Western World*, Encyclopaedia Britannica, Chicago.
5. Miller, N.P. and Robinson D.M. (1963), *Leisure Age: Its Challenge to Recreation*, Wadsworth, Belmont, California.
6. Veblen, T. (1953), *Theory of the Leisure Class*, Mentor, New York.
7. Parry, N. and Parry, J. (1977), *Theories of Culture and Leisure*, paper presented at Leisure Studies Association Conference, University of Manchester, September 1977.

8. Soule, G. (1957), The economics of leisure, *Annals of the American Academy of Political and Social Science*, September 1957.
9. Hunter, G. (1961), *Works and Leisure*, Central Committee of Study Groups, London, p. 16.
10. Fairchild, H. (ed.) (1944), *Dictionary of Sociology*, Philosophical Library, New York.
11. Weiss, P. (1965), *Quest*, 5 December 1965, p. 1.
12. Parker, S. (1971), *The Future of Work and Leisure*, MacGibbon and Kee, London, p. 20.
13. Brightbill, C.K. (1963), *The Challenge of Leisure*, Prentice-Hall, New York, p. 4.
14. Brightbill, C.K. (1964), *Recreation*, 57, January 1964, p. 10.
15. Neumeyer, M. and Neumeyer, E. (1958), *Leisure and Recreation*, Ronald Press, New York, p. 17.
16. Kaplan, M. (1960), *Leisure in America*, John Wiley, New York, pp. 21–22.
17. Dumazedier, J. (1960), *International Social Science Journal*, 1, Winter 1960, p. 526.
18. Dumazedier, J. (1967), *Toward A Society of Leisure*, W.W. Norton, New York.
19. Kaplan, M. (1975), *Leisure Theory and Policy*, John Wiley, New York, Chapter 1 and p. 19.
20. Pieper, J. (1952), *Leisure the Basis of Culture*, New American Library, New York, p. 40.
21. Larrabee, E. and Meyersohn, R. (eds) (1958), *Mass Leisure*, The Free Press, Glencoe, pp. 2 and 252.
22. de Grazia, S. (1962), *Of Time, Work and Leisure*, Doubleday, New York.
23. Ibid., pp. 7–8.
24. Marcuse, H. (1964), *One-Dimensional Man*, Routledge, London, p. 49.
25. Parker, S. (1971), *The Future of Work and Leisure*, MacGibbon and Kee, London, pp. 24–25.
26. Nakhooda, J. (1961), *Leisure and Recreation in Society*, Kitab Mahal, Allahabad, India, p. 14.
27. Kaplan, M. (1960), *Leisure in America*, John Wiley, New York, p. 22.
28. Dumazedier, J. (1967), *Toward a Society of Leisure*, W.W. Norton, New York, see pp. 16–17, 37, 236–237.
29. Murphy, J. (1975), *Recreation and Leisure Service*, William C. Brown, Dubuque, Iowa, see pp. 6, 11, 15.
30. Murphy, J.F. (1973), The Future of Time, Work and Leisure, *Parks and Recreation*, November 1973, p. 26.
31. Neulinger, J. (1974), *The Psychology of Leisure*, Charles, C. Thomas, Springfield, Illinois.
32. Neulinger, J. and Crandall, R., The Psychology of Leisure, *Journal of Leisure Research*, 3, August, 1976, pp. 181–4.
33. Godbey, G. (1978), *Recreation, Park and Leisure Services*, W.B. Saunders, Philadelphia, pp. 10–12.
34. Godbey, G. (1975), Anti-leisure and public recreation policy, *Sport and Leisure in Contemporary Society*, (eds S. Parker *et al.*), Polytechnic of Central London, London.
35. Linder, S. (1970), *The Harried Leisure Class*, Columbia University Press, New York.

36. Berger, B. (1963), Sociology of Leisure, in *Work and Leisure: A Contemporary Social Problem* (ed. E.D. Smigel), College and University Press, New Haven.
37. Cutten, G.B. (1929), *The Threat of Leisure*, Yale University Press, New Haven.
38. Roberts, K. (1970), *Leisure*, Longman, London and Roberts, K. (1977), Leisure and life styles under welfare capitalism in *Leisure and Urban Society*, (ed. M.A. Smith), Leisure Studies Association, London.
39. Kraus, R. (1978), *Recreation and Leisure in Modern Society*, 2nd edn, Goodyear, Santa Monica, California.
40. Zuzanek, J. (1977), Leisure trends and the economics of the arts in *Leisure and Urban Society*, (ed. M.A. Smith), Leisure Studies Association, London.
41. Lewis, G.H. (1978), Popular culture and leisure. *Leisure Today*, (Journal of Physical Education and Recreation), October 1978, pp. 3–5.
42. Gans, H.J. (1974), *Popular Culture and High Culture*, Basic Books, New York.
43. Kando, H. (1975), *Leisure and Popular Culture in Transition*, C.V. Mosby, St Louis.
44. Kato, H. (1975), cited in Lewis G.H. (1978), Popular culture and leisure. *Leisure Today*, (JOPER) October 1978.
45. Russell, B. (1935), *In Praise of Idleness*, George Allen and Unwin, London.
46. Marx, K. (1952), *Manifesto of the Communist Party*, Encyclopaedia Britannica, Chicago.
47. Parker, S. (1971), *The Future of Work and Leisure*, MacGibbon and Kee, London.
48. Wilensky, H. (1960), Work, careers and social integration. *International Social Science Journal*, No. 4, 1960.
49. Berger, P.L. *The Human Shape of Work*, Macmillan, New York, pp. 218–19.
50. Parker, S. (1971), *The Future of Work and Leisure*, MacGibbon and Kee, London, pp. 101–102.
51. Bacon, A.W. (1972), The embarrassed self. *Society and Leisure*, 4, 1972.
52. Kelly, J.R. (1972), Work and Leisure: A Simplified Paradigm, *Journal of Leisure Research*, 4, 1972, pp. 50–62.
53. Blauner, R. (1964), *Alienation and Freedom: The Factory Worker and His Industry*, University of Chicago Press, Chicago.
54. Argyris, C. (1973), Personality and organisation theory revisited. *Administrative Science Quarterly*, 18, pp. 141–67.
55. Office of Population Censuses and Surveys, Social Surveys Division (1979), *General Household Survey 1977*, HMSO, London.
56. Read, for example, Glasser, R. (1970), *Leisure: Penalty or Prize?*, Macmillan, London.

RECOMMENDED ADDITIONAL READING

Haworth, J.T. and Smith, M.A. (eds) (1975), *Work and Leisure*, Lepus Books, London.
Chubb, M. and Chubb, H.R. (1981), *One Third of Our Time*, John Wiley, Chichester.
Kelly, J.R. (1982), *Leisure*, Prentice-Hall, Englewood Cliffs, New Jersey.

Chapter 8

Play/recreation/leisure: an integration?

★

★

8.1 INTRODUCTION

Part 2 has been concerned with three concepts – *play, recreation* and *leisure*. Each has been considered separately in Chapters 5, 6 and 7 as a discrete entity in order to understand its nature and composition. It has been shown that while each possesses unique characteristics, there is overlapping between the three and there is confusion in our understanding. Furthermore, the three words are often used interchangeably and this vagueness and ambiguity hinders understanding. Recreation professionals should, therefore, agree what they mean by the terms. This will avoid talking at cross purposes, will assist in communication and short-cut philosophical circular arguments.

The practical politician and the practising manager, however, may well ask the question: why should we start from theory? Surely our experience and practical knowledge is sufficient on which to plan? The answer to this is given by Ellis [1]. If we have an acceptable theory, if we know what motivates people to recreation, then we are better able to plan and manage effectively. If we have no basic insights and explanations into why people play and find recreation, we cannot be confident that the resources and programmes we provide are either relevant or appropriate. Recreation thinkers must, therefore, untangle the play/recreation/leisure web to understand something about its individual components, then put them together to present a 'whole', a basis from which the cause of recreation can be justified to policy makers, economists, planners and the public and a base constructed on which to rebuild.

The value of a theory is the degree to which it explains and predicts. Alas, no theory or explanation has been put forward which explains recreation satisfactorily. This, however, makes it possible for recreation philosophers to consider new ways of looking at 'recreation'. The best and latest thinking can be drawn together in a new theoretical framework. The output from the theorist should then be the input for the practitioner – the practising manager. However, one problem with the recreation industry is that it is a divided one. *There is a gulf between academic theorists and practical managers.* Recreation managers can help bridge this gap by becoming theory–practice orientated, i.e. putting into practice good theory. Recreation managers of such calibre will be able to serve the cause of recreation with far more enlightenment than ever before.

This chapter looks at the possibility and the problems of trying to achieve a linkage between the three concepts to form an *integrated* base from which recreation planning and management should stem and at the implications that arise from such an approach. *First*, play, recreation and leisure are analysed separately and summarily in their unique form. *Second*, the elements common to all and the overlaps are discussed and the possibility of an integration is considered. *Third*, the barriers and limitations to an integrated approach are highlighted and the assumptions listed. *Finally*, a re-orientation of community recreation services is suggested, giving emphasis to a more people-directed human service. Working from a change of philosophical direction, changes to the institutional base for recreation services are suggested.

8.2 PLAY AND ITS IMPLICATIONS FOR RECREATION SERVICES

'The concept of the uniqueness and worth of each individual is the cornerstone of our culture . . . Ideologically a human is most human when at play, as defined by our culture' [1]. Play is *activity*, freely chosen and indulged in for its own sake. It has intrinsic value; it is important and has personal meaning for each individual. Play is life vividly expressed – a speeded up version of life. The motives and feelings of ordinary life are lived through quickly, in abstract, but without their every day contingencies of anxiety and fear. The major outcome of play is a feeling of regeneration. One is revived. As Sutton-Smith puts it: 'The "vive" leads to revival. One judges he has had fun' [2].

The implications of play for recreation services could be profound, yet play does not appear to have a central place in the institution of recreation services other than children's play. If people's lives are enriched by play – physically, intellectually, spiritually – and if play raises the tone of life and brings colour into people's lives, then it is indispensable to the well-being of individual people and so to society. Therefore, *recreation professionals should create situations and promote factors that give opportunity for play to occur and limit those factors which militate against it.*

Can Recreation Managers 'organize' leisure to produce optimal arousing situations, offer opportunities for innovative experience where individuals control the content of their behaviour? Can we implant into recreation programmes the necessary ingredients such as exploration, investigation, manipulation, creativity and learning? For example, graded levels of instruction lead to complexity and creative problem-solving, clubs of like-minded people act upon each other to provide necessary complexity, and well-presented events produce the drama for heightened arousal and awareness.

Society is in need of many more innovative, vital people. Yet *extending playfulness contributes to non-conformity*, and some communities may well wish to severely limit its extensiveness. The playfulness of young people – growing up, mixing, noisy, rebellious, experimenting, testing the limits of the system – is difficult for parents, schools and society in general to cope with. Recreation opportunities can give some of the necessary adventurous behaviour patterns room to unfold, without the inhibiting everyday constraints.

Play in common usage is clearly understood. Activities are seen as playful, non-productive, not instrumental in the process of survival. Just play. In societies with a strong streak of puritanism, play, by virtue of being unrelated to survival and production of profit, stands outside and inferior to the processes of work.

Play is often assumed to be free and the player not motivated by the end product of the behaviour. By this argument, play cannot be controlled, planned, forced and remain play. However, man in modern society can never be totally free; we are always controlled to some extent by our environment. In addition there are many examples of play being motivated by the end product.

We refer to sport as being played by players. The study of play causes us to ask the question: how much do players in sport really play? The importance of the outcome, the external rewards (points, trophies, titles, press photographs, status) may make it all too serious to play, particularly when, for example, going through a losing streak in the competitive league. *External pressures may then sap the playfulness out of play*. It is easy to overstate the case – the spirit of play still abounds at all levels – nevertheless, it seems clear that the *product-orientation* of winning, rather than the *process-orientation* of playing well, plus the imposition of structures not of one's own making, can change the nature of the play experience. For games to remain in the domain of play, players should become part of the process of setting up structures, rules and controls. Indeed, administrators and officials of sports and arts are players themselves and can be playing as much as the participants themselves; in spectator sports play elements may well be seen as much on the terraces as on the court.

The study of play teaches managers that the important thing, whether it be with children or adults, is to invest considerable decision-making power in the hands of the participants. This is why some people like to belong to small autonomous groups, where they can feel creative and identified, where they can be masters of their own destiny, even for a short period of their week. Recreation programmers would be foolhardy to omit autonomous groups, clubs and associations from their recreation programmes.

Another lesson from the study of play is to resist the temptation of controlling, administering and providing 'on a plate'. The process of controlling the content of our behaviour is important for the play element to flourish.

8.3 RECREATION AND ITS IMPLICATIONS FOR COMMUNITY RECREATION SERVICES

Recreation can be described and defined in a number of ways. Two main ways of perceiving recreation are from an *activity* focus and from an *experience* focus. From an activity base, recreation is seen to be an activity related to sports, games, art and other leisure time pursuits. In this respect recreation is *product-orientated* and concerned with facilities and programmes. The activity focus presents recreation as a structure, a framework and as a *social institution* in society.

The experience focus is *process-orientated* and the concern is on what an activity *does* for a person. It has concern with self-fulfilment. A recreation experience can occur in varying degrees depending on the level of satisfaction experienced, much the same as other feelings, which may be of stronger or weaker intensity. This is consistent with the theory of self-actualization advanced by Abraham Maslow. Hence, recreation can be regarded as a *means* to an end or as an *end* in itself.

Looking at recreation experience it follows that whatever activity or situation renews, revises, refreshes and recreates for the individual, is a recreation for him or her at that time. This has far reaching implications for recreation services. *Any* activity implies no right or wrong, no good or bad, no moral issues at stake. But society will not allow *any* activity. Even while many liberal views are held in Western society, individuals are still constrained in what is and what is not acceptable behaviour.

Throughout its history, recreation has kept its moral tag and this has been part of its *non-appeal* to many people. Modern society, with its wide interpretation of what is moral and what is socially acceptable, casts doubt as to the value of interpreting recreation with high ideals of morally sanctioned behaviour. In recent times greater attention is being given to the debate as to whether recreation is primarily determined by the *nature of the activity*, the *attitude of the player towards the activity*, or the *player's psychological state during the activity*. Inherently there is a belief in the right of the individual to self-expression, the expanding of experiences and horizons, but within society's social ethic.

8.3.1 Recreation: practical considerations

The recreation professional has to live in a world of recreation traditions, systems, institutions, facilities, vociferous demands, employers, budgets and politicians. He cannot, therefore, present a complex picture of what recreation is. The problem in viewing recreation solely as experience is that it is almost impossible to define operationally, and it is difficult to communicate with understanding. We therefore need to find tangible criteria on which to base planning, management and programmes. For the recreation professional to communicate with policy-makers and public alike, it may be appropriate and beneficial to talk in terms of recreation experience arising out of recreation activity.

The recreation product appears to be a mixture of attitude, activity and satisfying experience. By using the terms *recreation activity*, which takes place during relatively free time, and *recreation experience*, which denotes positive feelings experienced by participants, involved in recreation activities, the manager is able to communicate the specific nature of programmes, while maintaining a consciousness of the *quality* of the activities from the point of view of the participant's feelings.

The implications of recreation theory are profound. Although recreation can occur at any time and almost any situation can function for it to occur, it is during leisure that recreation is more likely to come about. Furthermore, recreation *experience* is more likely to be 'felt' if the following factors are incorporated into recreation programmes and activities:

1. Recreation is personal, therefore activities should be concerned with individual satisfactions.
2. Recreation is concerned with freedom, therefore programmes should offer a satisfactory choice.
3. Recreation is refreshing, therefore activities should have immediate value, be novel and stimulating.
4. Recreation can be found in any activity – physical, social, intellectual, spiritual – therefore programmes must be concerned with the whole person.
5. Recreation is creative, therefore programmes should have concern for the indirect benefits and creations which arise from the activities.
6. Recreation will often arise through play, therefore opportunities for participation in the spirit of play with the players in control need to be encouraged.
7. The fullest recreation experience is found in oneness and unity, therefore activities should be sought which give opportunity for peak experiences.

8.3.2 The recreation institution

Regardless of the theorist's belief of what is recreation or what is not recreation, society has come to accept perceptions of recreation which are considerably clearer than that of the philosopher. Society's understanding is relatively consistent. Most people find no difficulty in identifying informal games of soccer, volleyball or netball as recreational, or in perceiving swimming, cycling, climbing and arts and crafts as recreation activities. These are the activities that have been offered by recreation administrators, clubs and organizations. *Recreation has become institutional-*

ized insomuch that we have a common understanding of the services, activities and events offered as part of the recreation service.

The institution of recreation appears to set limitations in the interest of society, interpreting leisure in a morally acceptable framework and placing play in a childhood context. Recreation seems to reinforce the elements of organization, competition, awards, achievement, progress and production. Only a small portion of public recreation programmes is for spontaneous and unstructured activities.

It may not be appropriate, therefore, to view recreation apart from *activity*, nor apart from *leisure*. However, what has become clear is the fact that although society views recreation in terms of activity, provided for people during their free time, this in itself does *not* provide the recreation professional with the principles and foundation on which to build a service and maximize its effectiveness.

What happens to the individual, what he or she *feels* about it and what it *means* to him or her are the most important considerations. Whatever the philosophical orientation or definition of recreation and leisure, the focus is on people. Recreation services must, above all, be human services.

8.4 LEISURE AND ITS IMPLICATIONS FOR COMMUNITY RECREATION SERVICES

Leisure can be perceived in a variety of ways as *time*, as *activities*, as a *state of being*, as *experience*, as *meaning* or as a framework of *opportunity*.

In order to measure it more easily, leisure has been thought of by many recreation professionals, sociologists, planners and by many individuals themselves, as a quantifiable period of time. However, even narrowing the concept down to a measure of time, there are still complex anomalies.

If leisure is a period of time, then *any activity* performed in that time can become a basis for an individual's leisure. This has far-reaching consequences for planners, policy makers and Recreation Managers. How do people use that time? Should Recreation Managers influence choices? In reality leisure time does not come up in sufficient blocks of time. There is often insufficient money, resources and facilities or poor mobility. Home based leisure may be partly a result of insufficient time-blocks and the fact that home leisure is cheapest. For example, television viewing is cheap, convenient and satisfying. Leisure in reality comes about through a conglomeration of activities: television, hobbies, drink, sex, gambling, roaming, lazing, reading, do-it-yourself, gardening, families, holidays, social visiting, church-going, service-giving, social contacts, physical recreation, arts and crafts.

But, as we have seen, leisure is not just time or activities but is also concerned with the experience during the time and during the activities. What do the activities mean to people? Lately, theorists are thinking not so much in terms of activities in given times but linking recreation and leisure into satisfying or life-enhancing experiences. *How do people perceive leisure and what does it mean to them?* If leisure is to fulfil its potential to meet the needs of people, then we must know as much about people and about the nature of leisure, as we do about the activities we so often refer to as leisure. If leisure is a human phenomenon – more than time, activity or experience – it has to perform a function for people. It has to provide opportunity. Managers must help to provide and enable people to take advantage of that opportunity.

8.4.1 Leisure opportunities

Opportunities afforded through leisure have awakened for many a spirit of self development, adventure and creativity. Economists and sociologists may tell us that we have not reached the age of leisure but it is clear to see that many people are in search of new leisure identities. The first London Marathon in 1981 attracted over 20 000 entries but for safety and organization only 7500 were allowed to run. In 1986 a massive 85 000 entries were received and 19 261 permitted runners was considered to be the maximum that the course could accommodate. In the UK in 1986 approximately 100 marathons were scheduled. The increasing army of joggers, orienteers, climbers, hang-gliders, cavers, skin-divers, parachute jumpers, surfers, sailors, dancers, amateur historians and archaeologists, painters, writers, actors, fitness fanatics and mediators show that people are looking for new, innovative activities and experiences. What are all these people searching for while sometimes risking their lives, money and wives and husbands? Maslow described it as peak experiences brought about by 'affirmation of our identity and confirmation of our existence.' In addition to peak experiences people are looking for self-fulfilment to be or become 'somebody' – all they are capable of becoming.

The search for identity is important in understanding leisure behaviour. It is a search for the *whole* person, not a split person. This idea is exemplified in the growth of spiritual and meditative movements. The Eastern disciplines and philosophies, for example, emphasize a unification of the body, mind and spirit, through movement, meditation and deep relaxation. These Eastern cults which promise a unity with oneself and with the universe have captured the imagination of the Western world perhaps because of the vacuum created by our artificial splitting of the body from the mind and spirit.

Some people, young people in particular, are now freer to try to discover themselves. Who am I? What am I here for? They are looking for ultimate experiences. Where does leisure management come into the search for identity? What is the Recreation Manager's role in this 'revolution of rising expectations'?

8.4.2 Leisure problems

While time for leisure can be used to enrich the lives of many people, to others it is a curse. The inability to relax, even for a moment, is a common complaint and evidence of neurotic disturbance; even holidays are taken at a work-rate pace. Some find it hard to take holidays, suffer from after-work irritability and the 'Sunday neurosis'. Most suicides occur during weekends, holidays and vacations. The attraction of 'moonlighting' – the second job – is not *just* for money. It indicates the relative importance given to work compared with leisure. It was reported that 4–8 million Americans need psychiatric assistance every year, 125 000 are treated in hospital for depression and 50 000 commit suicide! [3].

Leisure growth is historical – long term. Patterns change very slowly. Changes are subtle. Furthermore, time for leisure is being taken up by work-like activities, so that the potential for recreation for many people may be eroded. While leisure opportunity contains a time element leisure behaviour must not be time conscious, if people are to play and find satisfying preoccupations, interests and consuming recreation experiences.

8.5 INTERRELATING PLAY, RECREATION AND LEISURE

Our investigation into play, recreation and leisure has revealed some pertinent findings concerning their relationship.

First, each phenomenon is *distinct* in that it has features, characteristics and functions which give it a total make up or profile which distinguishes it from the others. We could have taken the view (like some theorists) that they are one and the same thing. This simplifies the issue but it would have been a false and dangerous assumption. There exists as we have seen sufficient evidence to state that play, recreation and leisure are *different* entities. These differences are summarized later in this chapter.

Second, within each profile, however, there exist very similar and sometimes many of the *same* features and components as are found in the other two. For example they all express degrees of freedom, self expression and satisfaction. Hence, play, recreation and leisure are *similar* to each other.

Third, possibly due to different starting points, the same phenomenon has been described with almost opposing descriptions. Play is seen as frivolous, spontaneous activity and yet also one of the foundations of civilization. Recreation is described as an inner-consuming experience and also as a structured social institution. Leisure is taken to be a measurable amount of discretionary time but also as the psychological perception of freedom to do and to experience leisure. Further, recreation has been considered as activity undertaken in leisure and as activity without regard to leisure.

This *overlap* and apparent confusion illustrates that play, recreation and leisure are multifaceted concepts, each possessing some of the facets that exist in either or both of the other two. In addition, collectively they are *multidimensional*.

Fourth, the similarities and the divergent dimensions flexibly *link* play, recreation and leisure together in such a way that they can each act, as it were, independently, jointly or in complete harmony. Take this situation: a friend attends a music and movement class for a variety of reasons which she may not be able to explain. Do we describe this as the period of time, the place, the activity, her attitude towards the activity, the spirit in which it is undertaken, the psychological state during the activity, the physical effort expended, the aches and pains, the experience of 'feeling great', the fun, the social experience or simply the joy of movement? What the activity does for her and what she feels about it are of the essence. The point is that there exist many activities and situations in which play, recreation and leisure function in bonded relationships. They are *interrelated*.

Play, recreation and leisure are, therefore, *different, similar, overlapping, multidimensional* and *interrelated*! To understand more about this relationship we need to consider the similarities, the differences, and discover how dependent they are on each other and the extent to which they can operate independently. First the similarities.

8.5.1 Similarities

Several words, ideas or themes are used frequently in describing play, recreation and leisure, namely the following.

Freedom   The free expression of play; the free choice of recreation; the freedom of choice in leisure.

Self expression   Each emphasizes individual self-expression.

Satisfaction   Play is characterized by satisfaction in the doing, manifest joy; recreation and leisure are both satisfying to various degrees.

Quality   The quality of experiencing is important to all.

Self-initiated   Play is usually self-initiated, though influenced by the situation and leisure also appears to be so in large measure; recreation too is self-initiated but can also be other-directed.

Absence of necessity   Play avoids external pressure, it cannot be forced and remain play; leisure has the same connotations; in recreation too there is an absence of necessity, but a level of obligation may be attached to recreation in its institutional setting.

Playfulness   Play, though often serious and intense, is abundant in playfulness, in fun; recreation is often playful but many elements are so product-orientated that they cease to be playful (competitive sport or music competitions may be more akin to work than to recreation or leisure); leisure is freer and 'looser' than recreation and therefore exhibits more playfulness.

Any activity   In its purest terms almost any activity can function as a play, recreation or leisure activity for someone; this is most evident in play activity; the same can be said of recreation and leisure from an 'experience' focus; recreation, however, is more socially constrained in its institutional setting.

Experiencing   Again in its purest terms, each has an inner dimension; play is totally absorbing in the doing ('lost in play'); re-creation is an inner-consuming experience of oneness; leisure can be the perception of freedom for the sake of doing or experiencing.

There are in addition many other features which pertain in different degrees of all three concepts. For example, play is characterized by *active behaviour*; leisure and recreation can be both active and passive behaviour with the word leisure extending to the condition of being leisurely or even just day-dreaming. Further, play is *intrinsic* behaviour – for its own sake. Most recreation and leisure is also for its own sake but a good deal is goal-directed and undertaken for a reason.

8.5.2 Differences

The differences between play, recreation and leisure are of two varieties. There are some *components* which do not apply to all and therefore differences are more evident. There are also, however, more subtle differences, not differences necessarily of characteristics but differences in *emphasis*, differences in strengths, styles and texture and difference in the degree to which the feature is important in the particular setting. There are also differences in *function*, for example, for learning or for refreshing or for just being at one with yourself and with the world. *Play, recreation and leisure have their own idiosyncrasies.*

Play   Play has far stronger emphasis given to the following characteristics: childlike (to play you must 'play like a child'); spontaneity; purposelessness; unreality ('only play'); stepping outside into a temporary world all of its own; nonconformity; sense of fun. It arouses the senses; is self-fulfilling behaviour. It is action packed; chooses its own activity. Play functions as a means of learning, mastery, discovery of oneself and the world; it is creative. Play is concerned with the whole person – a 'holistic' phenomenon. It has justification in and of itself; it is not justified through an association with recreation and leisure. It has many components and features but all these are encapsulated in the wholeness of play: its totality is within its own circumference.

Recreation   Unlike play, is a dual phenomenon or more accurately is made up of two separate and quite distinct phenomena which should go by different names.

The first dimension is *recreation activity* which is more understandable than its other dimension because it is known, it is seen and it can be measured. It is different from play and leisure; unlike play it is seen as adult leisure time activities. It is amenable to programming, organization and structure. It is conceived as the 'wholesome' use of leisure time, beneficial with personal and social end results – it does you good. As such it is value-orientated. Unlike play it appears to have to be justified. It carries far greater social responsibilities than leisure. It has concern with community well-being, for example, 'therapeutic recreation', 'industrial recreation', 'recreation counselling'. There is greater stress on its function

Play is

Free, active, arousal-seeking behaviour. It is justified in and of itself for the sake of doing or experiencing

Fig. 8.1   An all-embracing concept.

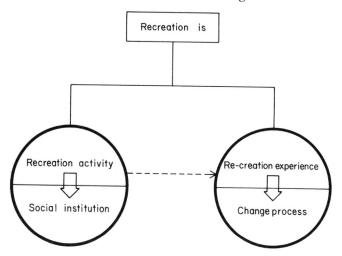

Fig. 8.2   A two-unit or two-dimensional concept.

for the good of society; there exists within its aspects of social control. Recreation in these respects can be considered as a *social institution*, a structure for recreation organizations, services and activities.

The second dimension is *recreation experience*. While conceptually re-creative experiences can occur out of almost any of life's activities, it is advisable for the recreation manager to view recreation experience arising out of recreation activity. The experiencing in its purest sense is characterized by an inner-consuming experience of oneness that leads to revival, akin in many ways to play; it is immediately satisfying and brings unity within. It is re-creative. Like all feelings it will have different strengths. At its highest it can be a 'peak experience'. Recreation experience renews, recovers energy, restores to wholeness and recharges the batteries. As such it is a *process* of recreating. Hence, whatever recreation activity refreshes, revitalizes, restores, recharges and recreates for the individual is a recreation for him or her at that time. (The same activity may not necessarily be recreative at another time.) Recreation can thus be considered as a *two-dimensional* concept.

Leisure can be perceived, like recreation, as containing the elements of play but it gives play the wider scope and interpretation that it deserves, bringing its application into the adult world as well as in childhood.

Leisure can also encompass the activities of recreation with fewer constraints and thereby also function as a means for experiencing recreation. Unlike play with its harmonious one all-embracing dimension and unlike recreation with its two separated dimensions, leisure has many dimensions. Unlike its relations, leisure has a *time* dimension – residual,

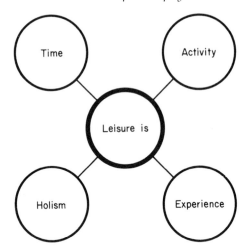

Fig. 8.3   A multidimensional concept.

discretionary or choosing time. Free time has connotations of both freedom and social problem, (a problem which the recreation institution has to grapple with). Leisure, like recreation, has an *activity* dimension but with stronger emphasis on freedom and width of choice stretching the bounds of 'acceptable' activities. Leisure also has an *experience* dimension, a 'state of being' existence. Leisure like play, has a '*holistic*' dimension, concerned with life satisfactions. Leisure runs parallel with work, each contributing to life's pattern. Hence leisure is multifaceted, expansive, multidimensional. It encompasses and widens the scope for play and recreation activity. It also functions as the psychological perception of freedom to choose to do and to experience. Some might argue that like play all these facets can be encompassed in leisure's 'holistic' conception. But the time and institution dimensions are different phenomena and are not conceptual. Therefore, to envisage an interrelationship between play, recreation and leisure we should think in terms of leisure being a *multi-dimensional phenomenon*.

8.5.3   Interrelationships

Recreation management is in reality a mixture and interrelationship of play, recreation and leisure. However, until we find *one* word that embraces the concept we must take one of the words we now have and use it as the main *pivot* around which the phenomenon revolves.

   Arguments can be presented for each concept as the main pivot: play as the unitary and basic entity for all people, recreation as the known and

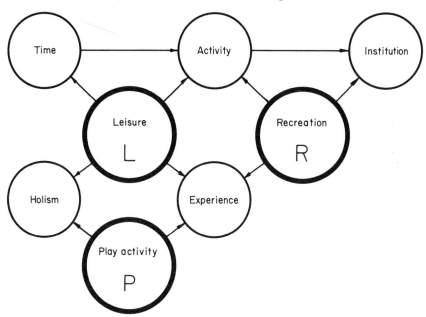

Fig. 8.4 A simple PLR molecule.

historical institution for public services and leisure having the widest characteristics and dimensions.

However, play by its association with spontaneity, playfulness and its childlike image would cause problems of credibility and adults would not accept 'play management and services' except in a children's context. Also play, philosophically, does not have to be justified by an association with recreation and leisure. Further, it will not encompass the institution of recreation.

Recreation has limitations also. Its re-creative experience dimension is yet to be understood. Its socially and morally acceptable activities image does not encompass the scope of leisure. In addition, its institutional framework does not cover the field adequately, particularly the voluntary and commercial sectors. Further, its two main units or dimensions are not flexible enough conceptually, at this point in history, to accommodate the many dimensions of the more liberalized entity of leisure.

Using *leisure* as both the pivot and the framework appears to make more management common sense a play–leisure–recreation concept (PLR). The many dimensions of leisure can, conceptually embrace the freedom of play, the recreation process and the recreation institution. Leisure can be presented as the *opportunity* and the means for play and recreation to occur.

Leisure has a time dimension which the others do not have. Time gives opportunity. Opportunity presents activities and these can lead to fulfilling interests. Leisure embraces both play and recreation. Like play it lays stress on freedom and human perfection. While recreation experience may be found in situations outside leisure, these are probably limited for the majority of people and as such come as a bonus for most people. Leisure gives a more complete picture of 'man the player' and 'man the worker' within its holistic dimension. As a multidimensional frame of reference leisure can also encompass recreation as a social institution. Over and above this its scope is wider and less conforming than recreation, 'looser' in organization and interpretation; it can cover those aspects at present outside the institution.

The book is not concerned with defining play, recreation and leisure or in producing a model or a paradigm. Its concern is with understanding, describing, opening new doors and building bridges between philosophy, provision and management of leisure and recreation. We have arrived at a point in this search for an understanding: leisure can be regarded as an individual and societal framework which offers the time, the situations, the activities and the psychological perception to be free to experience play, recreation and leisure; leisure presents opportunity for these things to occur. Until the English language constructs another word, 'leisure' can encapsulate the concept of PLR (L the pivot for PLR) and provide opportunity for it to be meaningful to people. The job of the recreation manager is to help people take advantage of that leisure opportunity. That opportunity can be seen as a favourable or advantageous combination of circumstances. It can be a suitable activity, occasion or time, an opening, a chance, a break. It allows the time and access to do and to behave in ways that we want to – to play, to rest, to enjoy, to contemplate, to re-create, to work, to be ourselves.

In summary, play, recreation and leisure are separate phenomena but they are inextricably linked to each other as in a molecular chain; action in one affects the others to varying degrees depending on the person and the situational elements.

8.6 BARRIERS TO INTEGRATION

Children at play do not compartmentalize themselves into physical, mental and spiritual beings. They play in a 'whole-person' way. This holds true for adults at play. One only has to observe an old people's talent contest to see the similarities. In adult life, play may provide the best opportunity for people to regain the unity of body, mind and spirit. However, there are a number of individual, societal and institutional barriers to providing integrated recreation services based on the needs of people. The reasons are complex and combined.

Individual people are limited in their response to recreation services and programmes and some of the factors responsible for this situation are:

1. People have physical, mental and social limitations.
2. Their environments limit choice, e.g. family, peer group, culture, resources.
3. Leisure for some is being eroded through many obligations or through insufficient blocks of time or through enforced free time, without the means or motivation to use it.
4. The choice of activities is limited to those that are socially acceptable.
5. The play spirit is eroding as play activities become work-like and highly structured.
6. Opportunity for peak experiences, excitement and adventure are limited for most.

Thus, people are not free agents; *activities are not the result of totally free choice and this militates against a 'whole person' approach to recreation services.*

It is suggested that recreation professionals do not adequately consider people's needs in formulating programmes. Are people given sufficient opportunity to seek personal fulfilment in their leisure? Does a rationale exist to justify public and private expenditure to support an institution for recreation services? Traditionally, public recreation departments have not been orientated towards a 'holistic' people-directed approach; they have directed their efforts towards the provision of facilities, activities and programmes without involving people in the plans. A more *qualitative* approach – what it does for the whole person – will reorientate professional values. This will, in turn, affect the principles and the aims of recreation services and programmes. This will, in turn, affect objectives, programmes and activities. There is some evidence of this multifaceted approach, particularly in areas of social disadvantage. Senior citizens' programmes can include not only recreational activities, but also health, nutrition, medical care and voluntary employment, making *use* of skills and talents. This *multiservice* approach also has benefits in assisting young people, who may be out of a job, who feel they have lost their identity and their *usefulness*. People need to expend energy and effort in useful ways, in something which is meaningful to themselves and others. Providing the skills, means and opportunities through leisure is one approach to meeting needs.

It is apparent that there are not only personal and social barriers to integrated services, there also exist strong organizational and institutional barriers. Commercial organizations are concerned with financial profits, therefore, monetary results are the ultimate aim. Many voluntary organizations and institutes are concerned with their own organizations, their own autonomy and their own programmes, in isolation to the needs of the larger community. Public authorities provide fragmented services between authorities, between tiers in the same authority and sometimes within the same department; there exists departmental autonomy and lack of evaluation and accountability. Fragmentation of services can lead to lack of continuity and duplication. This will lead to a poorer service. It is not uncommon to find people going from one local authority department to the next to find a satisfactory solution to a problem. *Organizations, professions, voluntary bodies and public departments all have a tendency to isolate themselves and operate independently.* They may not collaborate for fear of not receiving proper credit. Most organizations are prestige-orientated. Even public departments compete among themselves for a larger slice of the cake. The lack of integration and waste of energy and resources deprives the participant, whose needs may go unheeded. In people-services, such as recreation, there is often lack of accountability, through lack of evaluation. Services flow on and departments remain very busy but do they accomplish what they are supposed to do? Participant needs may go unmet, even though the *intent* is to fulfil them.

Hence, while an integrated approach to recreation service is desirable, there are personal limitations and traditional, organizational and institutional barriers in the way of such an approach. To provide appropriate services, principles must be founded on the best theoretical framework, the obstacles and limitations should be recognized and assumptions made on which services and programmes can be developed.

8.7   ASSUMPTIONS ON WHICH TO BUILD SERVICES AND PROGRAMMES

In order to provide public integrated services based on the needs of people, leisure authorities must make a number of assumptions on which to base principles, aims and objectives:

1. That the services are intended to meet individual needs so that a person can play and find recreation and fulfil needs in the way he or she chooses.
2. That programmes have concern with the whole person – a holistic approach.
3. That services help to redress the balance of lost time, lost opportunity, lack of awareness and lack of know-how.
4. That services are open to all citizens.
5. That priorities should be balanced to serve the greatest number and those in greatest need, recognizing that those in greatest need may well be in the minority.
6. That services should be comprehensive and not separate pockets of competing interests.

Superimposed on these factors is the overriding assumption that recreation needs management and, furthermore, that recreation can be managed. Leisure and play with their emphasis on freedom cannot be 'managed'. The question is: *can recreation be organized, planned and managed*? The institution of recreation *can* be managed; recreation activity is amenable to programming. Recreation experience however cannot possibly be guaranteed. However:

1. Leisure Managers can create an environment where recreation is more likely to occur.
2. Leisure Managers can extend the range of activities to offer a wide and varied choice.
3. Groups can be enabled to participate through supportive services.
4. Other groups can be encouraged to fashion their own destiny.
5. Work conditions can be improved to give people greater chance of self-expression, recreation activity and recuperation.
6. Education can be extended to inculcate leisure skills (physical, social, cultural and intellectual) which can help people to realize their potential.

In these and other ways management can help to extend opportunities. The assumptions provide principles on which to force a reorientation towards a people-approach to recreation services. The reorientation stems from the belief that each individual has worth and has need to express himself and herself and that society will benefit from citizens who have the ability, adaptibility and resourcefulness to cope, create and find fulfilment.

Freud was preoccupied with the mental state of neurosis. The recent 'reality therapists' like psychiatrist William Glasser, Victor Frankl and the late Abraham Maslow are concerned, not with childhood miseries, but with 'plans for the future', 'purpose' and 'attitude'. Maslow decided to concentrate on healthy people not sick people; 'Healthy people are people in whom *the will* is healthy.' Ninety-five per cent of Maslow's healthy subjects had frequent experiences of sudden overwhelming joy, a kind of bubbling over of sheer delight – 'peak experiences'.

Leisure time, without the opportunity, means and abilities to cope, can be a two-edged sword. Along with a marked increase in leisure participation there has been a marked increase in antisocial behaviour, particularly in those areas where leisure opportunity is low. Free time has not solved social problems – loneliness, poverty, job satisfaction. Leisure *time* may have exacerbated the problems. Can leisure *opportunity* help to solve some of them? The opportunity for leisure is of no value to people however, unless advantage is taken of it. This is where the Recreation Manager has a special role to play – that of enabling people to take up the opportunities.

The study of leisure shows how important it is to deal with men and women as complete, whole persons. In addition, it is important to look at leisure and work not as two discrete, mutually exclusive components of life. Work and leisure lie on a continuum or work in parallel. The interrelationships and the overlapping between the two are evident. 'Man was not born to work. Rather man was born with an innate capacity for effort, which can be dissipated in any activity be it sailing, cooking, sex, chess, Frisbee or art' [4].

Leisure, as a PLR concept, is a major sphere of life that brings innate satisfaction to people. It is not just a series of activities, not just uncommitted time, nor just experiencing satisfactions, nor just meaning or perception of freedom. Rather it is a personal and social opportunity to experience, behave and act in ways which are personally satisfying. To be able to grasp leisure opportunity people must develop interests which can be expressed through recreation activities. These activities need resources, organization, planning and management.

REFERENCES AND NOTES

1. Ellis, M.J. (1973), *Why People Play*, Prentice-Hall, Englewood Cliffs, New Jersey, p. 1.
2. Sutton-Smith, B. in the Education and Leisure Conference, Liverpool University, 1974, and can be found in a Columbia University paper, *An Ideology for Play*.
3. Godbey, G. (1978), *Recreation, Park and Leisure Services*, W.B. Saunders, Philadelphia, p. 13.
4. Levy, J. (1977), A recreation renaissance, *Parks and Recreation*, December 1977, p. 18.

★

PART THREE

Needs and influences on leisure participation

★

In Part One, the providers of recreation services in the public, voluntary and commercial sectors were studied. In Part Two, the recreation 'product' as a mix of play, recreation and leisure was considered. They were found to be separate entities but inextricably linked to each other.

The objective of Part Three is to consider the needs and motivations of the people who are to benefit from recreation services. What factors attract people to participate in recreation activity and what factors militate against participation? Chapter 9 deals with some perspectives of people's needs and leisure. Chapter 10 considers some of the main features which appear to influence and condition recreation activity choice. It is suggested that management policy and management operation can have strong influences on people, either to attract or inhibit participation.

Chapter 9

Leisure and people's needs

★

★

9.1 INTRODUCTION

We have seen in Part 2 just how important it is to understand something of the nature of leisure because leisure has meaning for individual people. What it does for people and what it means to people are important. How can leisure meet people's needs? In order to know this we must know as much about the needs of people as we do about leisure.

Community leisure and recreation services are said to be based on the needs of people. Yet, recreation policy-makers, researchers, planners and managers have insufficient insights into people's needs. Some commercial leisure, however, is marketed on considerable research into human motivations. The understanding of needs is fraught with great difficulties, different interpretations and different psychologic approaches. The complex picture is described in the Institute of Family and Environmental Research and Dartington Amenity Research Trust (IFER/DART) first-stage report on its study of leisure and human needs [1].

'There is no simple list of human needs, no single theory to explain them, no clear consensus about the principles underlying human motivation. Moreover, many writers on motivation have developed full-scale motivational theories without even referring to the concept of need; and amongst those who do hold needs to be both real and important phenomena, there are many significant differences of opinion as to what "needs" actually are. The range of this difference is perhaps illustrated best by Madsen, who examined some twenty major theories of motivation (1959): he then felt compelled to bring these up to date with a further volume examining another twenty or so more recent theories abut human motivation (1974). Even after completing this monumental task, he felt bound to admit that he had not done full justice to the range of theories in this field.'

Clearly, the satisfying of people's needs through leisure opportunity is one of the principles behind providing recreation services. What motivates people to recreation? This chapter considers the matter in three stages. *First,* a few pertinent theories of human motivation are briefly described. *Second,* consideration is given to the social needs of people. *Third,* needs are contrasted to demands and viewed in the context of recreation services.

9.2 THEORIES OF HUMAN MOTIVATION

9.2.1 Deficit, drive and equilibrium

One simple view is that human need is something that is missing, *a deficit*. It has been defined as 'any lack or deficit within the individual either acquired or physiological' [2]. Needs here are distinguished from drives and are seen as preceding them; they are the cause of motivation, rather than the motivation itself. Others equate the need with the motivating force [3].

McDougal [4] attempted to explain behaviour by reducing it to a series of innate, but modifiable *instincts*. Instinct theory has now been generally discarded, but McDougal's theory was in many ways a watershed in motivational theory. It led to the further efforts of behaviour scientists to discover why we behave as we do. It also led many psychologists to look for more widely extended and diffusive concepts which explain human motivation. One of the central ideas to be salvaged from McDougal's theory was that of the purposeful, *goal-directed* characteristic of the greater part of human behaviour.

Drive is goal-directed. It releases energy. It is generally considered to be the motivating factor within human personality. There appear to be different sorts of drives such as the drive for food, the drive for sex, the exploratory drive and so on. Summarizing the concept, Young [5] says: 'Drive is an organic motivation rather than something environmental. Drive is a persisting motivation rather than brief stimulation. Drive is an activating energizing process'.

Many psychologists who see the motivational aspect of human needs as drives, do so in conjunction with the idea of *homeostasis*. People have a fundamental need to maintain a state of relative internal stability, therefore needs can be perceived in terms of the elements that disturb homeostasis; drives are the forces which impel the individual to regain the equilibrium that has been lost.

Homeostasis is easiest to understand in terms of physiological needs, for example, the relief of cold or hunger. Needs which are social in nature – such as the needs for achievement, self-fulfilment, and acceptance are less easily accounted for in terms of homeostasis. However, as indicated in the discussion on recreation, the principle of 'psychological homeostasis' was used by Shivers as *the* basis of 're-creation' (see 6.3.4).

9.2.2 Psychoanalytic and psychosocial theory

All human behaviour is motivated according to Freudian theory. Nothing happens by chance, not even behaviour which appears to be 'accidental'. Everyday errors, accidents and slips of the tongue, far from being just accidental', are *caused* by underlying and unconscious wishes or intentions. In analysing dreams Freud found the same unconscious process at work. He traced the meaning of dreams and dream sequences which on a conscious level had no apparent meaning to the dreamer. On this hypothesis of 'psychic determinism', Freud built his theory of psychic structure and functioning [6].

In terms of motivation Freud saw two fundamental driving forces in man, the *sexual* and the *aggressive*. The sexual instinct or 'libido' is not simply the desire for sexual intercourse but gives rise to the whole range of erotic drives. Similarly, the aggressive instinct is not simply physical aggressions, but the whole component of mental activity that is destructive in nature. The basic drives which motivate all behaviour operate unconsciously at a basic level of the psyche known as the *id*. They are not fixed patterns of behaviour but function through 'external' demands and constraints, i.e. the 'realities' of the outside world. The two psychic structures which channel and modify the basic drives are the *ego* and *superego*. They direct the basic drives into socially acceptable channels.

Freud placed great emphasis on the developmental stages of early childhood, but little on the later life-cycle stages. Erikson [7], however, viewed development as a process which continues throughout the life-cycle in response to both 'internal' functional changes within the individual and external changes in the environment itself. Erikson's theory of development demonstrates that *needs themselves are developmental*. Each individual goes through a sequence of developmental phases, each terminated by a 'phase-specific crisis'. Each crisis embodies a radical change in some area of the individual's life. Erikson shows that the transition from one phase to another brings into play a *new set of needs* in the life of the person and correspondingly a new set of demands on the people around him. Thus, another main factor in understanding human need is the *relationship of the individual to other people and the environment*.

IFER/DART conclude: 'In theories of motivation need is seen as a state or force within the individual. This can be either a deficit state leading to a search for satisfaction, or else a state of psychological incompleteness leading to a movement towards completeness' [8]. In either case *need is a motivational concept referring to the processes, conscious or unconscious involved in goal-orientated behaviour*.

9.2.3 A hierarchy of needs

In management and leisure discussion the most often cited theory pertaining to needs is that of Maslow [9,10]. Maslow has suggested that *needs are hierarchically ordered*. At the base of the hierarchy are the primary physiologic needs of the human (e.g. food, sleep, sex, shelter) and at the apex of the hierarchy are those needs which are related to the psychologic

Fig. 9.1 Maslow's hierarchy of needs.

factors of self-actualization such as creativity and sense of achievement. According to Maslow, the lower needs must be satisfied *before* any of the higher needs come into play.

McLelland, however, says that the hierarchical nature of these needs is not self-evident [11]. He points out that each one of the needs has itself been selected by one writer or another as being the most important human need. McLelland himself emphasized the 'achievement' motive as one of the most basic motivational forces.

There are a number of problems in the application of Maslow's hierarchy, for example, needs are not necessarily hierarchically ordered, nor divided into sectors, but are often *overlapping* and occur *simultaneously*. However, the theory emphasizes the *developmental* needs of the individual. Need is no longer seen by Maslow as the reduction of some state of tension or the return to homeostatic equilibrium. Instead, man is seen as striving towards the fulfilment of more positive growth. Many others with a humanistic approach to psychology also emphasize the human need for self-actualization and growth [12]. Maslow's hierarchy is also a useful way of identifying and categorizing the different *types* of need that individuals have.

In Part Two we saw how play and leisure give opportunity for self-fulfilment and self-actualization. Maslow's theory also appears to embrace the idea of *re*-creation. To Maslow self-actualization means experiencing fully, vividly, selflessly, with full concentration and total absorption. Out of this deeper self comes the ability to play, to enjoy, to fantasize, to laugh, to loaf, to be spontaneous and to be creative. Thus play and creativity demand freedom from inner fears.

Tillman [13], building on this theme, examined needs and identified ten which are important in determining the 'leisure needs' of people, namely:

1. New experiences like adventure.
2. Relaxation, escape and fantasy.
3. Recognition and identity.
4. Security – being free from thirst, food or pain.
5. Dominance – to direct others or control one's environment.
6. Response and social interaction, to relate and react to others.
7. Mental activity, to perceive and understand.
8. Creativity.
9. Service to others – the need to be needed.
10. Physical activity and fitness.

However, the concept of 'leisure needs' is misleading. People have needs, which can be satisfied in a variety of ways. One way of meeting some of them may be through leisure opportunity. *Leisure needs as such may not exist.*

9.3 SOCIAL NEEDS

Bradshaw's conceptualization of needs is concerned with the problems that arise in identifying different types of *social* needs [14]. He suggests that social needs be classified into four categories: *normative, felt, expressed* and *comparative*. He explores a system by which the overlapping considerations of the four approaches to 'need' can be utilized to form a model to assist in making objective assessments of 'real' need.

Mercer [15] and, later, McAvoy [16] and Godbey [17] have applied Bradshaw's concepts to recreation. Godbey and others have expanded the number of classifications in the social needs model by adding additional categories: *created* needs, *changing* needs and *false needs*.

9.3.1 Normative needs and leisure

Normative needs represent value judgements that are made by professionals in the recreation and leisure field (such as criteria for open-space standards). These normative needs, stated as standards, are usually expressed in quantitative terms.

The use of normative needs as the major determinant of leisure provision can be challenged on a number of points. The development of standards is usually based on small group value orientations, often arbitrary and biased. They cannot be valid to the population as a whole. Another problem arises from the notion that services ought to be distributed equally throughout every community. Different communities may require different quantities and qualities of recreation and leisure services; the application of a universal set of standards can create problems. Seeley [18] notes that it is impracticable to lay down rigid standards and try to apply them to all urban areas, since requirements are inevitably influenced by a variety of factors that will vary in different areas. Normative, by definition, refers to the standards that reflect the needs of the majority of the population. However, such a perspective may not reflect or cater to the needs of certain types of minority populations, such as the physically disabled. Standards of provision can thus only be a guide at best.

9.3.2 Felt needs and leisure

The problem in determining felt needs is that people find difficulty in articulating their needs, which are influenced by one's aspirations and cultural environment. Felt needs can be defined as the desires that an individual has but has not yet expressed actively; they are based on what a person *thinks* he or she wants to do.

According to Mercer [19], felt needs are largely learned patterns; we generally want what we have become used to having. They are often a reflection of the normative needs that have been defined by social agencies (e.g. governmental, recreation and leisure service organizations.) Therefore, in many cases *felt needs are limited by the individual's knowledge and perception of available recreation and leisure service opportunities.* However, mass communication has expanded the individual's potential for knowledge and experiences ordinarily outside his or her realm of existence. Thus felt needs, on the one hand, are limited by an individual's perception of opportunities but, on the other hand, can be based on what a person *imagines* he or she would like to do.

The concept of felt needs can be of use to the recreation and leisure service for two reasons. First, it enables people to express desires of what they would like to do. Second, individuals are likely to be happier participating in what they perceive they want to do during their leisure, than they will be if their leisure options are dictated to them.

From the standpoint of an idealist, recreation services should function in a way which pleases everyone. However, organizational problems and the availability of physical and manpower resources limit achieving such an ideal. Public recreation organizations, in trying to give the greatest service to the greatest number, are concerned with collective welfare and collective opportunity, as distinct from an emphasis on individual need. Furthermore, the evaluation of felt needs is fraught with difficulty since what individuals 'think' they require may be quite different from what they actually require and ultimately do. The uses of questionnaires and personal interviews have the probability of this inaccuracy already built in and, therefore, the data from such research can only be a guide to recreational planning.

9.3.3　Expressed needs and leisure

Those activities which individuals actually participate in are known as expressed needs. They provide the manager with knowledge about current leisure preferences, tastes and interest. Expressed needs are felt needs 'put into action'. If leisure resources, programmes and services are based solely on expressed needs (what people are doing), the practitioner may preclude the initiation of new services and programmes. In addition, participants' behaviour is limited by the specific programmes that are available. This presents a circular dilemma: the participants' behaviour is limited by the specific programmes that are available. The participants use the services available and the practitioner limits the services to the participants' behaviour; thus the participants continue to have their behaviour defined and moulded by the current services offered.

On the other hand, by providing established activities, managers can accurately predict the outcomes and programming requirements. Consequently, the organization can be *efficient* with no waste of resources (though perhaps not effective). Expressed need can be quantified and utilized by the planner and manager in terms of activities undertaken, numbers involved and under-provision or over-provision in recreational areas. However, expressed need itself does not give a total picture of involvement *potential*. Factors of cost, access, weather and fashion may induce number fluctuations. New and novel provision may create its own demand, where none existed previously. Programming based on expressed needs may tend to favour those who shout loudest.

9.3.4　Comparative needs and leisure

Often an individual or organization will compare itself with another individual or organization. This may be done purely out of interest, or it may serve to help to identify deficiencies. The comparative needs approach can be applied to *services, facilities, resources* and *programmes*. For example, there may be differences in the services provided for special groups (such as the disabled, the elderly, the mentally retarded, and ethnic and racial minorities) and those provided for the rest of the population.

Care must be practised when utilizing the comparative needs method in needs assessment and programme planning. One cannot assume that what works well in one situation will automatically be effective in another. The intensity of the service needed may vary greatly between populations and groups within communities. Furthermore, each community may not have the necessary resources to pursue the fulfilment of equal services. Comparative needs are essentially concerned with social trends and the requirement of maintaining an equality of opportunity in recreational provision, when compared with other areas. Although this is an impractical ideal in some respects, it does have the effect of creating an awareness in the continuing developments of recreational provision. Perhaps the most important aspect of comparative need is illustrated in the particular areas of under-development and under-provision of urban communities.

9.3.5   Created needs and leisure

Godbey [20] has expanded on Bradshaw's taxonomy of social needs by adding a fifth need – *created needs*. The concept implies that policy-makers and professionals can create leisure interests and values *independent* of what people do or what they want to do. Created needs refer to those recreation activities which organizations have 'introduced to individuals and in which they will subsequently participate at the expense of some activity in which they previously participated' [20]. In other words, created needs refers to those programmes, services and activities solely determined by the organization and accepted by the participant without question, desire, or prior knowledge.

According to Edginton *et al.*, [21] the created needs approach can be useful to the participant and to the organization as a method of defining needs.

'Many individuals are grateful to organizations for helping them identify an area of interest that previously they had not considered. In a sense, the approach is a form of leisure education that is an important component of the philosophy of recreation and leisure service organizations. The organization also benefits by serving as an agency that creates opportunities for stimulation and enrichment. As a result, individuals may look to the organization as a vehicle for providing innovative experiences' [21].

Four problems, however, are apparent. First, implicit in the created needs approach is the notion that the professional's knowledge is sacrosanct, but it is wrong to assume that the professional is the only person with problem-solving capabilities. Second, it is important to recognize that the participant also has the ability to diagnose his or her felt, expressed and comparative needs. Third, as with the other approaches, the created needs method should be used in conjunction with all the available tools for defining and interpreting needs. Fourth, created needs may create needs which are inessential – which are *false* needs.

9.3.6   False needs and leisure

Young [22] points to the distinctions between what an individual is aware of needing, and what others may think is needed. This raises the issue of the value which is placed on need by the individual and by outsiders. These values may differ.

Marcuse [23] developed the concept that society encourages the individual to develop certain sorts of 'needs', which are not in any sense essential, but which serve the interests of society as a whole. Thus people acquire the 'need' for cars, radios or hi-fis which is in the general interest of society to promote. Such needs he calls false needs for the reason that they are not strictly essential. In fact, they are hard to prove different from other sorts of need, but, for Marcuse, they represent undesirable values.

9.3.7   Changing needs in leisure

Rhona and Robert Rapoport in *Leisure and the Family Life Cycle* [24] claim that although every person has needs, these needs *change* as one progresses from one phase of life to another. This theory appears to follow on directly from Erikson's 'phase-specific' crisis and 'decisive encounters' concepts (see Section 9.2.2). The key concepts which reflect the developmental nature of the changes in the life-cycle are, preoccupations – 'mental absorptions', interests and activities.

Preoccupations arise at a deep level of motivation. Some preoccupations might be present throughout the life cycle but tend to become particularly salient at a given phase. The preoccupations attributed to each stage in the life-cycle are worth considering, since they are of fundamental importance if local authorities are to make the most appropriate provision for different segments of the population. The major stages reported in Kew and Rapoport [25] are outlined below:

(a)   Stage one – youth (school years)
1. Emergent personal identity.
2. Tendency to fight against authority.
3. Exploration – experimentation and sexual, physical, mental and emotional stimulation.

(b)   Stage two – young adult (school-leaving to settling down)
1. Development of a social identity.
2. More intimate and committed relationships.
3. Tendency to re-integrate with family previously rejected.

(c)   Stage three – establishment (extended middle age)
1. Commitments to life investments of work and family.
2. Importance to productivity and performance.
3. Later tendency to question ideals and commitments – perhaps leading to disillusionment and depression.

(d)   Stage four – final phase (between end of work and of life)
1. Emphasis on achieving social and personal integration.
2. Attempts to achieve harmony with surroundings.
3. Major reorganizations of attitudes and demands.
4. Great variety of interests, dependent on very many factors.

The Rapoports believe that recreational activities arise out of interests and interests arise out of preoccupations. There is no one-to-one relationship between preoccupations and interests and particular interests can be satisfied through different activities. However, it appears that specific 'clusters' of interests are clearly related to each major life-cycle phase. The Rapoports' thesis is that all people have a quest for personal identity. At the root of their search, people have fundamental preoccupations. Specific preoccupations can be experienced through a variety of interests, and expression of interests may be facilitated through specific activities.

Complementing the work of Parker [26] on class-determined patterns and that of Young and Willmott [27] who have added a social change dimension, Rapoport and Rapoport suggest that *people's needs must be understood in the context of their personal development. This perspective cuts across and underlies class and sub-cultural patterns.* Each person is seen as having a 'career' consisting of separate but interrelated strands. Three major strands were identified and these relate to *family, work* and *leisure.* Each life strand, therefore, produces changes in preoccupations, interests and activities at life crises such as at marriage and at the birth of children.

9.4   NEEDS, DEMANDS AND RECREATION SERVICES

Recreation policy-makers, researchers, planners and managers often equate 'needs' with 'demands'. But there is a very real difference between the two. Lowry and Curtis [28] believe that a common error of regarding demand and need as synonymous, should be avoided. They see 'need' as the more fundamental concept and 'demand' generated perhaps by need.

Like the IFER/DART researchers they acknowledge the extreme difficulty in assessing need.

9.4.1   Needs and leisure demands

Researchers have generally been concerned with establishing recreation demand, rather than understanding people's need. Large scale surveys in Great Britain, for example, have identified certain demands but have not discovered what motivates people to recreation, why people participate and what the most important influences on participation are. 'Whereas a "need" appears to be conceptually "woolly" and operationally elusive, "demand" appears tangible, measurable, even predictable' [29].

Kew and Rapoport [25] in advocating that recreational provision be based on qualitative investigation into human needs, and particularly those changing needs associated with progression through stages of the life cycle, point out some shortcomings of recreational policies based on quantitative assessments of demand:

'Vociferous demands for specific sports facilities appear superficially to indicate the areas of greatest need, but palpable demand can be highly deceptive. Many groups of people in need, whose interests are not being fulfilled by existing provision – for example the handicapped, the elderly, the housebound mother – may express little or no demand at all'.

In recent years, however, there has been a growing dissatisfaction with macro-social demand studies and a feeling that if researchers are to provide information of real value to policy-makers and planners, they must look for approaches that are also of relevance to the people being researched. Knetsch [30] calls into question the concept of demand: 'The myth persists that somehow we are able to multiply population figures by recreation activity participation rates obtained from population surveys and call it demand'.

The Rapoports argue that in making decisions about 'demand' for leisure facilities, providers base their plans and actions partly on the 'feasible' extension of what already exists and is known to be workable and partly on reading people's 'needs' and social trends. Social research, it is claimed, which looks beyond palpable mass demand and begins from the people's side of the equation is more likely to lead to better informed decisions.

9.4.2   Needs and the recreation service

Effectiveness and efficiency are not one and the same thing. An *effective* recreation service could be described as one that ensures that the right opportunities are provided, at the right time, in the right place, based on the needs of the people it is intended to serve. This is, of course, impossible to achieve in the sense that any collective service cannot be all things to every person. Yet the *approach* which encourages ways for people to attain self-fulfilment can be stressed. If not, efficient services may not be *effective*. Providers may provide a service and ensure its smooth running and may make adequate use of its resources but the service could be *ineffective*. 'Of the two, the provision of an effective service is the more important, as it is better to provide a service that meets needs, however inefficiently, than to provide a super efficient service that meets nobody's needs' [31].

Although little direct research has been undertaken on the 'social' need of the individual being a prime motivating factor, Crandall [32] has reviewed relevant existing research. He concludes that the success of many recreation services may depend more on their ability of *bringing compatible people together* than on their programmes and facilities.'

'. . . social interaction may be as important in the enjoyment of many leisure activities as the facilities or activities themselves . . . One applied implication of these results is that in many settings, leisure programmes which facilitate social contact during leisure, should be more successful than those which focus only on the activities themselves'.

Although Maslow's concept has been criticized on the grounds that the self-actualizing needs are largely culturally determined, it is generally accepted that man has a need for psychological growth and that a social need is a basic survival need. Maslow's basic survival needs, physiological, safety and social needs, correspond with the hygiene factors of Herzberg [33], who regards them as preventative, in that they do no more than prevent unhappiness, while the higher needs of Maslow may be equated to some extent with the motivator factors of Herzberg. Hence both Maslow and Herzberg see man's ultimate need as being that of self-actualization and Farina [34] sees this need as the 'goal of leisure'.

Needs assessment attempts understanding of individual and group behaviour as it relates to recreation and leisure. It accomplishes several things. Through such assessment recreation planners and managers can become aware of people's underlying motivation, interests, opinions, habits, desires and knowledge regarding recreation and leisure. Practical ways of gathering such data include demographic characteristics, time use, leisure behaviour and opinions and attitudes. It has become abundantly clear, however, that methods must include *both* quantitative and qualitative assessments.

9.5 SUMMARY: LEISURE AND PEOPLE'S NEEDS

No single theory and no clear consensus exist relating to people's needs. In theories of motivation, need is seen as a force within the individual to gain satisfactions and completeness. There appear to be many levels and types of need, including the important needs of self-actualization and psychological growth. *'Leisure needs' as such may not exist*, rather there are human needs which might find satisfaction through leisure opportunity.

The concept of social need incorporating normative, felt, expressed and comparative needs has been enlarged to include created, false and changing needs. Needs appear to change in relation to one's life stage and one's preoccupations, interests and activities at that stage. It has been hypothesized that needs can be created but in so doing can result in some 'false' needs being brought about with both positive and negative results for the individual and society.

Needs assessment should allow for a broad base of public involvement. It is suggested that such an approach will:

1. Provide an increase in individual and community input and involvement in planning and decision-making.
2. Provide the planner with a better understanding of the community and individuals in it.
3. Provide information as to the activities in which people are involved, the activities in which they would like to be involved, and how these can be planned and provided for within an overall leisure delivery system.
4. Provide supportive facts and ideas on which to base decisions in the planning process.

Two very important factors have emerged, which argue against current recreation planning policies of standards of provision. First, people have *diverse* needs. Second, these needs *change* or take on greater or lesser degrees of importance according to one's stage in the life cycle. The individual chooses on the basis of certain personal and social elements current in his or her life. In terms of need, man is a three-dimensional person. He or she is like *everybody* else, requiring the basic needs of security, belonging and shelter; he or she is like some other people sharing the same wants, the same groups, the same interests. He or she is like *no other person* – a unique individual, the only one. *Leisure opportunity may enable a person to become a three-phase man or woman: to become all he or she thinks he or she is capable of becoming.*

REFERENCES AND NOTES

1. Institute of Family and Environmental Research and Dartington Amenity

Research Trust (IFER/DART) (1976), *Leisure Provision and Human Need: Stage 1 Report* (for DOE), IFER/DART, London, Item 2.5.

2. Morgan, C. and King, R. (1966), *Introduction to Psychology*, McGraw-Hill, New York, p.776.
3. Murray, H. (1938), referred to in Institute of Family and Environmental Research and Dartington Amenity Research Trust (IFER/DART) (1976), *Leisure Provision and Human Need: Stage 1 Report* (for DOE), IFER/DART, London, Item 2.8.
4. McDougal, W. discussed in Institute of Family and Environmental Research and Dartington Amenity Research Trust (IFER/DART) (1976), *Leisure Provision and Human Need: Stage 1 Report* (for DOE), IFER/DART, London, Items 2.10 and 2.11.
5. Young, P.T. (1961), *Motivation and Emotion*, John Wiley, New York.
6. Freud, S. (1974), *The Complete Works of Sigmund Freud*, Hogarth Press, London.
7. Erikson, E.H. (1959), Identity and the life cycle, *Psychological Issues*, 1, No. 1.
8. Institute of Family and Environmental Research and Dartington Amenity Research Trust (IFER/DART) (1976), *Leisure Provision and Human Need: Stage 1 Report* (for DOE), IFER/DART, London, Item 2.46.
9. Maslow, A. (1954), *Motivation and Personality*, Harper and Brothers, New York.
10. Maslow, A. (1968), *Towards a Psychology of Being*, D. Van Nostrand, New York.
11. McLelland, D. (1965), Achievement Motivation can be Developed, *Harvard Business Review*, November–December 1965.
12. For example, Carl Rogers (1961), referred to in Institute of Family and Environmental Research and Dartington Amenity Research Trust (IFER/DART) (1976), *Leisure Provision and Human Need: Stage 1 Report* (for DOE), IFER/DART, London, Item 2.22.
13. Tillman, A. (1974), *The Program Book for Recreation Professionals*, National Press Books, Palo Alto, California pp. 57–58.
14. Bradshaw, J. (1972), The concept of social need. *New Society*, 30, No.3, pp.640–43.
15. Mercer, D. (1973), The concept of recreational need. *Journal of Leisure Research*, 5, No.1.
16. McAvoy, L.H. (1977), Needs and the elderly: an overview. *Parks and Recreation*, 12, No.3, pp.31–34, 35.
17. Godbey, G. (1976), *Recreation and Park Planning: The Exercise of Values*, University of Waterloo, Ontario, January 1976, p.2.
18. Seeley, I.H. (1973), *Outdoor Recreation in Urban Areas*, Macmillan Press, London.
19. Mercer, D. (1973), The concept of recreational need. *Journal of Leisure Research*, 5, No.1, p.39.
20. Godbey, G. (1976), *Recreation and Park Planning: The Exercise of Values*, Unversity of Waterloo, Ontario, January 1976, p.13.
21. Edginton, C.R., Crompton, D.M. and Hanson, C.J. (1980), *Recreation and Leisure Programming*, Saunders College, Philadelphia, p.91.
22. Young, P.T. (1961), *Motivation and Emotion*, John Wiley, New York.
23. Marcuse, H. (1964), *One Dimensional Man*, Sphere Books, London.

24. Rapoport, R. and Rapoport, R.N. (1975), *Leisure and the Family Life Cycle*, Routledge and Kegan Paul, London.

25. Kew, S and Rapoport, R. (1975), *Beyond palpable mass demand, leisure provision and human needs – the life cycle approach*, Paper to the Planning and Transport Research and Computation (International) Co. Ltd. Summer Annual Meeting.

26. Parker, S. (1975), Work and Leisure Theory and Fact, in *Work and Leisure* (eds J. Haworth and M.A. Smith), Lepus Books, London.

27. Young, M. and Willmott, P. (1973), *The Symmetrical Family*, Routledge and Kegan Paul, London.

28. Lowry, G. and Curtis, J. (1973), Satisfying leisure needs, in *Managing Municipal Leisure Services* (ed. S.G. Lutzin), Institute of Training in Municipal Administration (ITMA), International City Management Association.

29. Institute of Family and Environmental Research and Dartington Amenity Research Trust (IFER/DART) (1976) *Leisure Provision and Human Need: Stage 1 Report* (for DOE), IFER/DART, London Item 3.14

30. Knetsch, J.L. (1969), Assessing the demand for outdoor recreation. *Journal of Leisure Research*, 1, No.2 p.85.

31. College, S. (1977), Recreation Research in Local Authorities: A Practitioner's View, in *Recreation Research in Local Authorities* (ed. A.J. Veal), CURS, University of Birmingham.

32. Grandall, R. (1977), *Social Interaction, Effect and Leisure*, Institute of Behavioural Research, Texas Christian University, unpublished.

33. Herzberg, F. (1968), *Work and the Nature of Man*, Staples Press, London.

34. Farina, J. (1974), Toward a Philosophy of Leisure, in J.F. Murphy, *Concepts of Leisure Philosophical Implications*, Prentice-Hall, New Jersey.

ADDITIONAL ESSENTIAL READING AND FOLLOW-UP TO IFER/DART REFERENCES

Institute of Family and Environmental Research and Dartington Amenity Research Trust (1981), *Leisure Provision and People's Needs*, (for DOE), HMSO, London.

Chapter 10

Leisure:
factors which influence participation

★

10.1 INTRODUCTION

Leisure patterns are not fixed or predetermined for either individuals or groups. Not only are there a multitude of factors which influence choice and participation, but also there is a complex relationship between them. In analysing people's needs in leisure, we have seen how misleading it can be to rely on only those factors which are easily quantifiable. For example, the 1980 and 1983 *General Household Surveys* [1,2] show that demand for leisure activities is influenced by a variety of interrelationships between age, gender, marital status, education, economic status, occupational group, hours worked, income, car ownership, type of household and other factors. Hence, there are both *individual* and *social* influences.

Rodgers [3] believes that such factors as age, sex, social class, upbringing and income will determine the overall probability of a person taking part in leisure activities and these factors change very slowly. However, at an individual level the decision to take up an activity is determined by such factors as cost, lack of time, absence or lack of awareness of facilities, lack of transport and domestic responsibilities. These situational factors are supplemented by less tangible factors such as motivation, social contacts and the social class connotation of some activities.

Because of the links and relationships between various influences, it is difficult to classify or group the factors with any accuracy. For the purpose of this chapter, three very broad but loose groupings are suggested: *personal* factors, *social and circumstantial* factors and *opportunity* factors. The first group of factors relate to the *individual*: his or her stage in life, needs, interests, attitudes, abilities, upbringing and personality. The second group relates to the circumstances and *situations* in which individuals find themselves, the social setting of which they are a part, the time at their disposal, their job and their income. The third group relates to the *opportunities* and support services available to the individual: resources facilities, programmes, activities, their quality and attractiveness and the management of them. Sensitive management, for example, can be a crucial factor in helping people to overcome seemingly insuperable obstacles.

Recreation policy and planning are by no means simple. There is a complex mixture and interaction when thinking about the factors which affect participation. Outlined in Table 10.1 are some of the discernible factors which individually or jointly or collectively affect participation. This listing is not comprehensive nor is it a classification but an illustration of the complexity and variety of influences which bear on an individual. In addition to all this, even if people have identical circumst-

Table 10.1 Influences on leisure participation

Personal	Social and circumstantial	Opportunity factors
Age	Occupation	Resources available
Stage in life-cycle	Income	Facilities – type and
Gender	Disposable income	quality
Marital status	Material wealth and	Awareness
Dependants and ages	goods	Perception of
Will and purpose in life	Car ownership and	opportunities
Personal obligations	mobility	Recreation services
Resourcefulness	Time available	Distribution of facilities
Leisure perceptions	Duties and obligations	Access and location
Attitudes and motivation	Home and social	Choice of activities
Interests and	environment	Transport
preoccupations	Friends and peer groups	Costs: before, during
Skill and ability – physical,	Social roles and contacts	after
social and intellectual	Environment factors	Management: policy and
Personality and	Mass leisure factors	support
confidence	Education and attainment	Marketing
Culture born into	Population factors	Programming
Upbringing and	Cultural factors	Organization and
background		leadership
		Social accessibility
		Political policies

ances and opportunities, still one person may choose one activity, another choose something entirely different. Nevertheless, by understanding some of the correlations between personal circumstances and participation, Recreation Managers can foresee some of the constraints and difficulties encountered by some people and management attitudes can be modified accordingly.

This chapter is concerned with some of these factors, though it is recognized that *of themselves*, they do not necessarily guarantee either participation or non-participation. Moreover, the factors themselves change, can be 'manipulated' and are often unpredictable. For example, in terms of provision, changing population structures can be recognized to some extent, but the impact and extent of the recent oil crisis and economic problems could not have been predicted accurately and the effect of these on leisure activities is still not completely known. Furthermore, 'leisure man' is different from 'working man' – he is less predictable and his decisions can be influenced by both good *and* poor management.

This chapter is written in three main groupings. *First*, the personal, family and educational influences are discussed. *Second*, the social, occupational, environmental and situational circumstances are debated. *Third*, leisure opportunities made available through such factors as programmes, management and accessibility are discussed and shown to have an important bearing on leisure participation.

10.2 INDIVIDUAL, PERSONAL AND FAMILY INFLUENCES ON LEISURE PARTICIPATION

The personality of an individual, his or her needs, interests, physical and social ability, the culture into which one is born, a person's will and purpose in life and a whole range of personal factors could influence choice and participation. Three factors are considered further below: age and stage in family life cycle, gender and education.

10.2.1 Age and stage in the family life cycle

Age has an important influence on leisure participation but its effect will vary depending on the person and the type of activity. For children there is a rapid change in the space of a few years from toddler to pre-school to junior to teenager, each calling for very different kinds of provision. Even for adults, there is a marked change with age, with participation in most active leisure pursuits declining sharply as people grow older.

The availability of time also has an influence on recreational participation and the greatest amount of free time appears to be concentrated at the extreme ends of the age continuum with the *adolescent* and the *retired* having considerably more time at their disposal than the middle age group who live under a greater degree of time pressure. Further, with the increased purchasing power of teenagers and the popularity of commercial entertainment amongst this age group there is a greater age segmentation in leisure choice. The sharpest fall with age occurs, for example, in cinema-going, which is predominantly a young person's leisure pursuit.

The *General Household Survey, 1983* [2] emphasized the general decline in leisure participation with increasing age but also revealed that some home-based activities such as gardening and do-it-yourself are most popular with the middle-aged. Some activities are relatively 'inelastic' to the change of age. These are generally regarded as home-based activities such as television watching and reading, while other activities such as playing cards and being members of voluntary organizations have a curvilinear trend with a slight increase in participation rates in one's late pre-retirement and early post-retirement phase.

Age should not be considered in isolation, however. Age may be *less restrictive than life cycle changes*, such as getting married and having children, while for some, participation may increase with age as a result of the children leaving home or a person retiring from work. Although age may influence the level of fitness and energy, a reduction in family and work responsibilities may more than compensate for this. The type of leisure activity is also likely to be influenced by the stage in the family life cycle. For example, single people may be more likely to go to a dance or club, while a married man with a family may be more likely to visit the seaside.

The importance of the life cycle has been discussed in Chapter 9. Sillitoe's study [4] stressed the importance of three critical events – marriage, parenthood and retirement, and the strong influence of both age *and* the stage in the life cycle was shown in the study *Leisure in the North West* [5].

10.2.2 Gender and leisure participation

The leisure patterns of males and females show similarities and differences. However, two major obstacles have faced women: family commitments, particularly looking after children, prevent many women from participating outside the home, and for many older women an upbringing that did not include pursuits such as physical recreation within their compass. For example, in the study *Leisure in the North West* it was found that gender makes little difference in participation rates for either full day or half-day trips and excursions but that there is a marked contrast to the impact of gender on sport and physical recreation. The ratio of men to women was 61:39, even though women outnumbered men by 54:46 in the sample. This finding is consistent with both Sillitoe [6] and the *General Household Surveys*. The GHS 1983 showed that of all the sporting activities only keep fit/yoga had a higher participation rate among females.

Max Hanna [7], however, found that while gender has been of fundamental importance in differentiating leisure activities, the two sexes appeared increasingly to share activities as more opportunities for women are opened up. Extending Hanna's thesis would suggest that many of the social filters, which can operate against female participation, will diminish and disappear. On the other hand, policies of provision appear in some cases to discriminate against women (e.g. male-dominated activity programmes). This being the case, it could lead to even greater dissatisfaction at the current patterns of supply and correspondingly high levels of demand. The problem is further compounded in that many other life factors militate against leisure equality. For example, when a women goes out to work as well as maintaining a house and family, the extent of her leisure time is eroded as the responsibilities for domestic work within the home are not normally abdicated.

Considerable evidence is accumulating relating to participation rates at leisure facilities such as libraries, theatres and recreation centres. The influence of gender with regard to participation in the use of the library service is unclear. Groombridge [8] found that in London 37% of the male community were members of the library service, whereas only 28% of women belonged to the libraries. A similar pattern was revealed at Runcorn with 55% of the visitors to the library being male, but with regard to the composition of the users of the mobile library the situation was reversed with the female users outnumbering the men three to one [9]. This seems to suggest that the permanent library site was inaccessible to many females, especially the housebound housewives with young children.

Within the 'cultural' field women are the predominant user. Mann [10] found that for all theatre audiences in Leeds, the highest proportion were women; at the ballet they comprised 73%, drama had a female audience of 69% and opera 59%. This is supported by Davey [11] at Hornchurch and by the Mass Observation Study in Birmingham [12].

Women are often more carless than men and in view of the dependence of sports participants on the car this is probably one of the factors that inhibits female participation. Studies at Sobell Sports Centre in London and a dual use centre at Reading showed the percentage of female users as 39% and 34% respectively [13,14]. However, a recent study at Harlow Sportcentre shows female use of the indoor facilities at 45% and at the Abingdon Leisure Centre female usage is said to be in the region of 2 females to every male. These reversals of the national picture are primarily due to programming activities which are more appropriate to female usage and providing back up services [15].

One of the misleading factors in looking at similarities and differences stems from the fact that most surveys have studied traditional recreation activities – sport, day trips, theatre – and organized activities like classes, clubs, team games and committed activities. Once a wider view of leisure is taken, encompassing the whole range of activities in and around the home, holidays, socializing, entertainment, excursions or walks in the park, a totally different picture begins to emerge.

Looking at the broader spectrum it would appear that overall participation rates do not differ substantially between men and women; women take a greater part in 'cultural' activities, men take part substantially more than women in active sport and sports spectatorship. When taking all leisure pursuits into account then the *similarities* in leisure participation between the sexes are more striking than the differences. Zuzanek's research appears to confirm this generalization [16].

10.2.3 Education and educational attainment and leisure

The *type* of education, the *length* of education and the educational *attainment* of people are closely related to upbringing, class, occupation, income and other factors. In terms of leisure participation, the better qualified tend to be male, young, in non-manual occupations and enjoying higher incomes. 'All these factors are reflected in higher participation rates for those with qualifications than for those without and, in general, the higher the qualification the greater the degree of participation' [17]. Why should this be the case? Four partial reasons are suggested: first, different social class subcultures have different patterns of socialization that appear to be transmitted to the next generation. These patterns have an influence on educational attainment. This process is known as 'social class learning'. Second, child rearing practices differ between the middle and working classes. Newsom, Davis and Spinley [18–20] found that the middle class teacher and the working class child may have a fundamentally different basic personality structure, which will affect communication between them. Third, according to Bernstein, Douglas and Martin [21–23] social class learning not only develops a higher proportion of middle class with high IQ than the working class, but middle class children have a more favourable attitude towards the whole school situation and hence are proportionally over-represented in higher education. Fourth, it is in school that attitudes, values and activities (music, drama, sport, crafts) are inculcated. Through this experience and home support the basis for subsequent demand is laid. 'In adult life the various "taste publics" are clearly the result of educational among other influences' [24]. Education influences the *type* of leisure choice to some degree.

Considerable evidence is available to support this view, from national surveys such as the *General Household Survey* and from specific research into leisure facilities such as libraries, theatres and recreation centres. For example, there is a sharp differential between members and non-members of the public library when related to educational institution and *level* of educational attainment. Possibly the biggest influence is within the arts. Mann [10] in Leeds, found that 57% of the whole drama audiences, 42% of opera audiences and 33% of ballet audiences were now at or had been at university or college of education. At Birmingham, the Mass Observation Study found that the influence of education attainment was of greater significance than social class [12].

With the exception of the pantomime all audiences had higher proportions of people who had completed their full-time education at 19 years of age and over. With sports and recreation centres the bias is still significant although not to the same extent. The studies of the Built Environment Research Group (BERG) [13,14] and Knapp *et al.* [25] reveal that of the users of the centres at Reading, Islington and Rugby, 26%, 33% and 21.5% respectively were in full-time education at the age of 19 years or more. 37% of the squash players did not leave full-time education until the age of 19 or over. *Leisure in the North West* [5] made a clear statement to support these findings: '. . . better and longer education stimulates sports participation: this is likely to be a powerful factor in the future growth of demand'.

The Rapoports [26] widened the educational emphasis to one of *resourcefulness*, which they perceive as the individual's capacity for developing interests and finding satisfying means of expression for them. The resourceful person could overcome many of the obstacles and constraints encountered. This aspect of leisure and education raises the question of whether people can be educated to make better use of their leisure time and thereby derive greater satisfactions. Some feel that such an approach smacks of paternalism – others take the more philosophical view: the beneficial use of leisure depends on an inner capacity; this capacity can be learned. Haworth [27] supports such a view. His plea is for education for living, a more 'holistic' view: the education of the 'whole' man, body, mind and spirit. In this respect education shares the same goal as recreation.

10.3 SOCIAL AND SITUATIONAL CIRCUMSTANCES AND LEISURE PARTICIPATION

The whole range of social and situational circumstances as they affect leisure participation include the home, school, work environment, income, mobility, time, social class, social roles and group belonging. In this brief section these aspects are considered further under three headings, income, social class and social climate.

10.3.1 Income and leisure participation

The *General Household Survey 1977* [17] examined *household* income. It was found that 'income levels were closely linked to participation rates, and for almost all the leisure activities examined the proportion participating rose with income'.

In only three activities (bingo, needlework and going to clubs) did participation not increase with income. Even where little or no financial outlay is incurred, such as walking, participation rates were also higher. Middle income groups, however, were more prominent in fishing, billiards, darts, bingo. With betting, bingo and doing the pools, participation rates fell among those with an income of over £100 per week.

Over an average working life white-collar workers earn appreciably more than blue-collar workers and often attract hidden benefits (perks, pension, less unemployment) which all add to one's lifestyle. Zuzanek [16] claims that 'the distribution of money spent for leisure and recreation follows traditional class lines most closely and points to rather significant social inequalities in modern industrial societies'. It is perhaps not surprising that since income correlates with both education and social class the higher income group has the higher participation rates in many recreational activities. Even with facilities and activities provided by the local authority such as for arts and sports, more people with higher incomes are attracted.

If lower income groups are to be attracted in larger numbers to community recreation then greater social service approaches would need to be applied, for example through differential subsidies, cheaper admissions, positive discrimination towards those who are disadvantaged, outreach programmes, the loaning of equipment free of charge, taster courses at minimal costs, community programming application, community bus services to facilities, improved marketing such as 'passports for leisure', incentives and above all sensitive and appropriate management.

The choice of activities and the amount of money that people can spend on entrance fees, equipment, travel etc. is the extent of people's *disposable* income. Those on unemployment benefits or state pensions may have little or no disposable income. Families with highest incomes tend to spend a smaller *proportion* of their income on essentials such as food and clothing and a greater proportion on non-essentials such as recreation. Manual workers when presented with a choice between more income and more leisure generally choose the former and consequently have to undertake overtime which in turn diminishes the disposable time available for recreational participation.

Personal property has much to do with leisure. However, what were once luxuries and leisure items are now considered almost as necessities. 'Necessities' such as alcohol, tobacco and cars are relatively insensitive to financial changes; large, discrete items like holidays (and house improvements) are vulnerable. People who earn or have more money have greater personal property and the 'wherewithal' to permit a wider choice of leisure pursuits. To own a large house with a garden and to drive a car immediately opens the door to leisure activities which will be denied to those living in a high-rise flat, without personal transport and with a low income.

10.3.2 Social class and leisure participation

The nature and meaning of social class is generally regarded as being problematic. 'Social class' can be regarded as 'a grouping of people into categories on the basis of occupation' [28]. Because of the interrelationship between social class and income, education and mobility, it is generally considered that social class, as determined by occupation, is the most influential factor in determining recreational participation. Occupation is not, therefore, an independent characteristic but closely associated with other factors.

In the *General Household Survey, 1983*, it was found that, generally, 'it was professional workers who tended to have the highest participation rates in leisure activities and unskilled workers who had the lowest rates. Particularly striking are the differences in participation levels for outdoor sports (over half of professional workers, falling to under 20% for unskilled workers)' [29]. Even playing and watching football were more popular among professional and skilled manual workers and the pattern is not confined to sport and the arts. Outings, sightseeing, entertainment, gardening and do-it-yourself showed similar bias. Even knitting and needlework were more popular among female professional workers. According to the GHS 1983 only two activities are more popular among manual workers – betting/doing the pools and playing bingo.

A number of other studies have been undertaken that give pointers to the importance or otherwise of social class and participant leisure activities. Libraries, the theatre, arts, sport, countryside recreation, clubs and adult education have been covered. There is considerable evidence to show that in general such leisure pursuits are followed far more by non-manual workers but some argue that the biasing is not as great as many claim. Groombridge [8] believes that this is the case with the library services, although his own study shows that professional men and women appear more frequently as library members. Half of those who have never been members belong to the three least skilled occupational groups. O'Kelly [30], assessing the present situation within the public library service, states 'It is widely recognized that public libraries in Britain today have lost their original function as aids in the self-education of the working classes and are now almost exclusively patronized by the well educated white middle class.' Furthermore, library staff and the literature itself appear to reflect this. In the theatres, many of which exist on grants from the Arts Council of Great Britain and subsidies from local authorities, the social class composition of audiences, though dependent on the type of performance offered, is nevertheless similarly biased. Drama, ballet and opera, for example, draw the great bulk of their audiences from the middle classes.

A study was undertaken by the Arts Council [31] at three Arts Centres – the Gardner Centre in Sussex, South Hill Park at Bracknell and the Chapter Workshops and Centre in Cardiff. The majority of users at the Gardner Centre are from the professional and managerial groups, since it is located on a university campus, but at the other two centres, where the range of activities is quite diverse, the same pattern exists but not to the same extent.

Studies of sport and recreation centres show similar participation patterns [13]. And at some centres follow-up studies some years later have shown that while the number of manual workers had increased, the *proportional* level of their use had declined [32]. Centres in new towns, inner city areas and at school campuses indicate similar patterns. Dual use recreation facilities, provided jointly by the school and local community, have considerable relevance to the 'spread' of participants. Many neighbourhood school/community centres report a cross-section of the public but close examination, for example, at a dual use centre in Reading [14], indicates that the social profiles of users are not markedly different from those using recreation centres provided wholly by a district council.

Hanna [7] claims that class divisions are strongly represented in sport, both in type of sport played, and in the type of facility used, even seemingly classless sports. Collins and Logue [33] in their study of public, private and commercial bowls facilities confirmed the predominance of non-manual occupations amongst bowlers (average of 69%) not dissimilar to previous sports centre findings. Even swimming, regarded as the most popular physical recreational activity, shows increased participation as one progresses up the social ladder, with the most significant social class differences found at the modern 'leisure' pools. Leisure pools in three different catchment areas were surveyed and shown to have an 'upscale' profile [34].

As with other activities, participation in informal outdoor recreation activities is dependent on availability and location of facilities. Hence in high density residential areas that are predominantly working class, such as the London Borough of Islington, which has the least amount of open space of any London borough, it is highly likely that its residents will use open spaces to a lesser degree than those residents in the outer London boroughs.

Sillitoe [4] in his national survey found that 'there is a tendency, in all areas, for overall club membership rates, especially amongst women, to be higher in the non-manual occupational groups.' Boothby and Tungatt [35], investigating a range of different clubs in Cleveland, support the findings claiming that the socio-economic status of members was heavily biased towards non-manual workers, with the exception of football clubs, but even these show a considerable under-representation with the unskilled manual section.

Hutchinson [36] found that adult education students were more likely to be from the higher socio-economic groups, with the exception of those who attend the Workers' Educational Association, where they tend to have a greater percentage of manual workers amongst their registered students, though this was by no means representative of the population. Hutchinson claims that 'half the adult population is inhibited in involvement in adult education by attitudes that are probably deeply rooted in social circumstances and earlier education'.

10.3.3   Social 'climate' and leisure participation

The IFER/DART researchers [37] refer to the concept of 'social climate', a complex of factors in addition to those which relate to age, gender, income, occupation and education. The attitudes and values of people in their social setting are seen as enabling or inhibiting factors concerned with leisure choice. Isobel Emmet's study in 1970 [38] is pertinent to an understanding of social climate. She argues, for example, that providers act both consciously and unconsciously as *social filters*, controlling who uses particular facilities and affecting the behaviour of those people. The social filters let through and channel different groups to different facilities. There appear to be both formal and informal social filters. The filters are influential in people adopting attitudes and behaviour appropriate to the situation. Behaviour patterns become habits. As Leigh [39] points out, 'The habits of leisure are habits of mind as well as habits of behaviour'.

Hanna [7] believes that there are inherent differences between the working and middle classes with rewards through luck and chance being more important value systems of the working class. 'Working class collectivism and preference for rewards deriving from luck rather than skill remains as strong as ever, which can be seen in the massive expansion of bingo and other forms of gambling, working men's clubs and holiday camps.' This view takes an opposing stand to the one that suggests that class is now of less importance than it was as a determinant of leisure choice. In this connection Caillois' games typology and his claim that the types and values of a culture can be understood from its play activities as much as from social and economic factors has relevance (see Section 5.4.2(h)).

Manual workers' preference for rewards deriving from luck rather than skill remains as strong as ever. Despite the cheapness of such activities as rambling, climbing, tennis and camping, these activities remain relatively middle class. Free museums and subsidized theatre lack working class patronage, as do evening institute classes. More manual workers may be playing golf but this is mainly on public golf courses and some private clubs are becoming more expensive and more exclusive. Also, the professional classes are finding an increasing number of esoteric and expensive ways of occupying their leisure time. Leisure between the classes differs not only in kind but also in quantity. The GHS 1983 [2] concludes that the 'middle' classes are not only more active culturally, socially and intellectually, but they also play more sport and travel more widely.

10.4   OPPORTUNITY AND LEISURE PARTICIPATION

It is no good providing opportunity unless good advantage is taken of it. Opportunity – making it possible for a person to participate or be involved

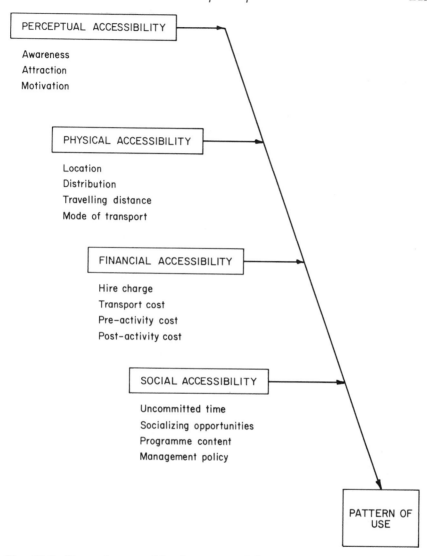

Fig. 10.1 Recreation participation: accessibility model. Source: Griffiths, *Recreation Provision for Whom?* [40].

– can be, in many instances, even more important to community participation than personal, social and circumstantial influences, despite current studies which show the strongest correlation between participation factors already discussed. Opportunity can come in a variety of forms: available resources and services, political policies, management styles and systems, community leadership and support, accessibility and so on. It is most likely that opportunity will entail various *interrelated* components.

From his study in Greenwich, Griffiths [40] arrives at the conclusion that the key factor that influences recreation participation is *accessibility* in its various forms. By accessibility Griffiths does not just refer to access and mobility; rather accessibility is defined as the 'ability to participate' where the constraints to participation have been eliminated. He divides accessibility into four main divisions – perceptual accessibility, physical accessibility, financial accessibility, and social accessibility. Each division contains various subdivisions. His 'Accessibility Model' is illustrated in Fig. 10.1. In this section four major opportunity factors are discussed briefly, namely, *perception, access and mobility, awareness* and *management*.

10.4.1 Perception and leisure participation

Perception refers to the world as it is experienced – as seen, heard, felt, smelt and tasted. Consequently the way an individual perceives the world will largely determine his or her behaviour. The way people *perceive* leisure provision (facilities, activities etc.) may influence their participation, more than the actual form of provision. Leisure provision is concerned with providing satisfying 'experiences' for people; facilities, programmes and activities are a means to achieving this. People who cannot feel identified, or who feel ill-at-ease, or uneasy with the style of management and organization, or with others using the facilities, will be deterred; indeed, preconceived ideas about leisure provision will influence a person's decision to even make an initial use of it.

Perception is increasingly being used in recreational planning, especially in the field of countryside recreation. Burton [41] in her studies relating to perceptual capacity found that one's perception of crowding in the countryside was related to one's level of educational attainment. Individuals of high educational attainment were more sensitive to crowding and thought of it as unpleasant; others actually preferred high levels of use. Like the countryside, people have varied perceptions about the city. 'Some people see the city as a place for having fun, for going out on the town; others feel oppressed by the tightly packed nature of its dwellings, excited by the hustle and bustle of city life or overwhelmed by its pressures' [42].

Perceptual capacity as such appeared to have little effect on recreational participation within a study undertaken in Greenwich by Griffiths [40] but the perception of one's actual neighbourhood appeared to have a significant effect in inhibiting recreational participation. The vast majority of those interviewed perceived their neighbourhood as being violent and the elderly were fearful of emerging out of the house at night. Even the close proximity of the police station to the library and the adult education institutes had little influence in encouraging the use of facilities at night.

The establishment of large recreational facilities has been claimed by some to have more merits than small facilities. Veal [43] states that a large building 'is more likely to be noticed' and 'more effective in inducing "civic pride" both in the public at large and in local politics'. Hudson [44], however, is of a different opinion and considers such buildings to be intimidating to potential working class users.

Consequently how the public perceive their neighbourhood and the facilities can either influence or inhibit recreational participation. As with attitudes, where a negative aspect is perceived, its modification may be most difficult to eradicate. *Positive* perception of recreation opportunity will enhance the desire and motivation to participate, will attract people and make them more aware of opportunities available.

10.4.2 Access and supply and leisure participation

Recreation participation undertaken outside the home involves some travel – walking, cycling, bus, taxi, car, train or plane. The method of travel can affect the level of satisfaction: one method will take more time; it can determine distance and destination; apart from walking all other means of travel incur financial cost; the method of transportation will lessen or heighten the experience, for example, travelling to a recreation centre, during rush hour, by public transport for a prepaid 5.30 p.m. court booking, could be harrowing.

The *Fair Play for All* study [45] would appear to confirm this: 'though low mobility can act as a deterrent, higher mobility is not necessarily a pre-requisite of greater participation: rather it can reduce some of the inconvenience associated with travel'. It is a well-accepted generalization, however, that greater mobility vastly increases participation in recreational activities outside the home. Families with cars have reported greater participation over almost the whole spectrum of activities than carless families. The mobility conferred by the ownership of a car has revolutionized people's use of leisure time. According to the *General Household Survey, 1983, 60%* of households in Great Britain had use of a car. For almost every activity, with the striking exception of bingo, the chances of participating in leisure activities was increased for car users by between 50 and 100%. One can only speculate as to whether the increased price of petrol, coupled with the economic recession will affect participation to any significant extent.

Concerning travel patterns to recreation facilities two major observations are made by *Fair Play for All*. First, given the present level of car ownership, which is well below the forecast trend, access to the use of cars is due to their use for work journeys; only two-thirds of women with licences in car-owning families had even optional use of the family car;

second, there is a mistaken belief in, or exception of, widespread car ownership and use; this is contrary to reality; much of the population has *low mobility* – and this may be the cause of much suppressed demand. The importance of the car for recreational participation is confirmed by Willmott:

'to be without a car – which is of course strongly correlated with low income and with old age – is to be handicapped. The motor car has brought many benefits. But in an already inegalitarian society, it has created a new kind of poverty and a new deprived class. The carless are increasingly cut off from the main stream of society, in the sense that many of the opportunities open to the growing majority with cars are denied to them. To the extent that public transport becomes more expensive and offers a poorer service than in the past, they are – and will be – worse off in absolute terms as well' [46].

An analysis of user surveys reveals the extent of the participant's dependence on the use of the private car. The users of sports centres are amongst the most dependent. At Harlow, Bracknell, Rugby and Sobell in the mid 1970s, the car as a mode of transport represented 77%, 89%, 78% and 42% of its users respectively [13,14]. The Sobell centre's comparatively low figure was largely due to its heavy school programme with 31% coming by coach with another 10% by bus. A similar pattern existed at dual use centres. Since then carborne users have increased substantially – 84% at Harlow Sportcentre [15].

Accessibility to recreation provision is influenced, however, by other important factors apart from transportation. The actual *location* of a facility is of the utmost importance and will affect use; the rate of use of the facility falls progressively as one moves further away from the facility. Veal [47] found with regard to post-war swimming pool users, that people living within 1 km of the swimming pool were four times more likely to use it than those who live between 1 km and 2 km away, and sixteen times more likely than those living between 3 km and 4 km away from the pool. *Distance decay*, whereby usage falls as the distance grows between the user's home and the facility, shows up in many examples – the use of national museums, the use of urban parks, the use of water resources. Maw's study of swimming pools showed not merely the effect of distance but also the significance of public transport as a means of access, particularly for the young. Those who lived near to the main bus or tube routes to Swiss Cottage came to the baths there more frequently than those (within the same distance) who did not [48].

Studies of six low cost sports centres were commissioned by the Sports Council and carried out over a six-month period from July to December 1977 [49]. Are the facilities *neighbourhood* facilities? Veal concludes that generally they are not – 60% of users of the centres live more than two miles from the centres. However, the reasons for this differ; some centres, although low cost, offer a wide variety of facilities. Some are well served by public transport. Some are widely used by clubs, and others attract users from a wider area due to the lack of other facilities. Only one facility has predominantly local use and this has a far more *social*, informal character than the other sports centres.

In terms of *travelling time*, the catchment area of even the largest recreational facility is comparatively small. Understandably the catchment area of community centres and libraries, especially in the urban areas, is very local. However, it is surprising to discover that so many of their users travel by car. Nevertheless, the level of distribution is an important element in the facility's accessibility to the community. Where local provision does not exist, facilities need to be located on bus routes, preferably at a nodal point of a bus network. Griffiths' study illustrates the point:

'the location of the bus stop immediately outside the library is indeed an asset and the proximity of the zebra crossing also aids the accessibility especially for the children and the elderly, but unfortunately the bus services are not geared up for recreational use as their service deteriorates in the evenings and at weekends, when most people have their greater leisure time' [40].

Hence access and mobility are crucial elements relating to leisure opportunity. It is a sobering thought to consider that, according to *Fair Play for All*, three quarters of non-car-owning households in the country are among the poorer 50% of households. In terms of facilities provided with public money, policies should exist which ensure the location of facilities on main transportation routes or within easy reach of the greatest number in the community. Where there is easy physical access and where local residents can walk to a facility, the recreational disadvantaged – elderly, carless, lower income groups, women with small children – could have far greater potential use.

10.4.3 Awareness and leisure participation

One accessibility factor that is frequently ignored in considering the linkage of demand for and supply of leisure activities is *awareness*. If people do not know that something exists they will obviously not go to visit it or see it. Because individual leisure facilities are not sought in the same way as a shopping centre or place of work, knowledge about them, particularly in urban areas, derives indirectly from seeing them, hearing about them, or reading about them. It has been shown that people passing a leisure facility *en route* to work or shop will be more likely to use that facility than a comparable one nearer home: they have become more aware of it. This factor has obvious implications with regard to the location of activities, as well as advertising and other marketing methods.

Generally the level of awareness of long-established recreational facilities is high. For example, Griffiths [40] sites Groombridge [8] who found that 79% of the community knew of the location of the nearest library. The extent of the services offered within such facilities, however, showed substantial gaps in public knowledge with over 70% of those interviewed being unaware that the library provided a record lending library, a study area and lectures.

The marketing of public sector facilities is generally regarded as being poor. In view of the cost and scale of provision of many local authorities it is surprising that this important aspect of management has received so little attention. Hence it is apparent that in most cases awareness of the recreational opportunities available to the general public has been largely achieved through indirect means such as passing the facility or by word of mouth via different social networks. More awareness can be encouraged by direct management policies, marketing and promotion to a wider public.

10.4.4 Management and leisure participation

People's use of leisure facilities is determined, as we have seen, by a number of discrete and interrelated factors. The management aspects of facility provision and leisure opportunity are no less important. Indeed, management viewed as a beginning-to-end process, becomes the key to greater or lesser use, the quality of resources and the key to enabling more people to find satisfying recreation experiences.

It has been abundantly clear that the presence or absence of facilities and opportunities, their accessibility, quality, pricing structures and policies, could have substantial influences on leisure participation. For example, the pricing, administrative and booking structures at a leisure centre could consciously or unconsciously establish a type of social filter.

Planning and management policy determines in the first place what facilities are to be provided. In the study *Leisure in the North West* of the four constraints of lack of opportunity, facilities, finance and time, lack of facilities was on the whole the second most important inhibitor behind lack of time. Secondly, the *quality* of facilities is an encouraging or constraining influence. Local authorities in the United Kingdom over this century have provided outdoor playing pitches for the traditional games of soccer, hockey, cricket and tennis. Marked dissatisfactions have been shown in the quality of the playing surfaces, the changing rooms, floodlighting, the entertaining of visiting teams, the opening hours and the general lack of consideration given to many clubs. The recreation satisfaction for people involved is likely to be lessened. Much of the

Sports Council's initial work and appraisals were undertaken to measure the degree to which governing bodies were dissatisfied with the state of their specialist sport facilities [50]. In the North West study in answer to the question, 'What changes and improvements would you like to see made at the sports facilities you usually visit?' 23% said that new buildings or equipment were needed. Among the ancillary facilities, changing rooms were in most urgent need of improvement. For many sportsmen and women, the convenience of parking, changing, entry to buildings, social atmosphere, friendly reception and 'welcoming' may be as important as the game itself. The *attitude* of the providers is therefore of crucial importance. The way a facility is managed can have a profound effect on whether or not it is used, to what extent it is used and by whom it is used. *Not only is management attitude and policy shown in atmosphere, image and pricing policy but also in the skill of programming for the people the facility is to serve.* Programmes geared towards males are likely to result in male dominated programmes. In recreation centres, for example, the number of young people, or males or females could alter depending on management attitude and programming, perhaps not significantly initially, but over time it could prove decisive.

This conclusion is reinforced by two studies. IFER/DART [51] reports on one survey on male and female levels of satisfaction with local sports facilities suggest that there are significantly more 'very satisfied' men and 'very dissatisfied' women. At Harlow Sportcentre and the Abingdon Leisure Centre [32,15] where positive discrimination was made in favour of mothers with young children through 'ladies activities', crèche and social facilities, the proportion of mothers with children attending the centre was far above the national 'average' reported by Sillitoe. This experience has been echoed by hundreds of managers of leisure centres. The need to socialize with others is a major motivating factor in influencing one's leisure choice. The activity itself may well be of quite secondary importance compared to getting out of the house, having the children looked after for an hour, and meeting and talking with people in the coffee bar. Management needs to be aware of these motivating factors in deciding management policy, programming and in providing an atmosphere of social warmth and welcome.

Relating to use of public recreation facilities Griffiths claims that:

'the mixture of policies that has emerged in most parts of the country, by conscious choice or innocent omission, has produced a stereotype pattern of usage. They have effectively restricted the access of the working class, females and particular sections of the community such as the elderly to public sector recreational facilities . . . the commonly observed disproportionate use by the middle class and by men is not some phenomenon, but a consequence of prevailing policies. Different policies can produce different patterns of use and thus the policy issue that arises is: what pattern of use do we want in publicly provided recreation facilities?'

It is abundantly clear that management policy, attitude and operation can attract *or* deter potential customers.

10.5 SUMMARY: FACTORS WHICH INFLUENCE AND CONDITION PEOPLE'S PARTICIPATION IN LEISURE

Many discrete, many complex and often interrelated factors condition people's choice and participation in leisure activities. Furthermore, there are the strongest links between leisure and other elements of life.

A person's age and stage in the family life cycle, such as marriage, parenthood and retirement affect opportunity and participation. Taking the widest view of leisure, the similarities in participation rates between men and women are more striking than the differences, though there are many specific differences and inequalities both within and between the sexes. The type and level of education people have undertaken has a profound effect on leisure participation. Education and recreation share the same concern for the development of the 'whole' man, body, mind and spirit, through different approaches. The amount of income and property a person has influences leisure participation. Since income correlates with education and social class, higher income groups have the higher participation rates in most active recreation activities.

Participation is closely and positively related to social status and prestige of one's occupation. The 'middle classes' not only are more active culturally and intellectually but also travel more and play more sport, compared with the 'working classes'. The way people perceive leisure provision influences participation. Preconceived ideas too, can have important positive or negative effects.

Car ownership has revolutionized people's leisure opportunity. The accessibility to facilities, their location and an awareness of opportunities are important considerations. People's use of facilities and services is affected to a considerable degree by management policy and management activity. Facilities must be both accessible *and* acceptable. The *attitudes* of providers, managers and the *quality of management* will help more people to find satisfying experiences through leisure and recreation opportunity.

While there are many constraints to leisure choices (and in practice few people are free agents to choose whatever they will) leisure can offer significant opportunity for individual action and for personal decision, should opportunity permit *and* the individual wish to exercise such choice. As choice has to do with the individual then two factors have to be stressed. First, there is a strong link between leisure and other elements of life and second, because it 'matters' to the individual, the quality of the experience is of paramount importance.

Finally, from observation and working experience of people's use of leisure, it is clear that a great many people overcome the limitations of a poor education, family obligations and personal handicaps and even overcome the obstacles of low income, insufficient facilities and resources, to find themselves preoccupying satisfying interests, self-fulfilling experiences and 'mountains to climb'. *Leisure and recreation management has much to offer in the way of enabling people to discover themselves – to reach beyond their grasp.*

REFERENCES AND NOTES

1. Office of Population Censuses and Surveys, Social Survey Division (1982), *General Household Survey 1980*, HMSO, London.
2. Office of Population Censuses and Surveys, Social Survey Division (1985) *General Household Survey 1983*, HMSO, London.
3. Rodgers, H.B. (1977), *Rationalising Sports Policies, Sport in its Social Context: International Comparisons*, Council of Europe Committee on Sport, Strasbourg.
4. Sillitoe, K.K. (1969), *Planning for Leisure*, HMSO London.
5. Patmore, J.A. and Rodgers, H.B. (eds) (1972), *Leisure in the North West*, North West Sports Council, Salford.
6. Sillitoe, K.K. (1969), *Planning for Leisure*, HMSO, London, p. 39.
7. Hanna, M. (1975), *Leisure*, IPC Sociological Monograph No. 12. See Institute of Family and Environmental Research and Dartington Amenity Research Trust (IFER/DART) (1976), *Leisure Provision and Human Need: Stage 1 Report* (for DOE), IFER/DART, London, Item 628 for fuller evaluation.
8. Groombridge, B. (1964), *The Londoner and his Library*, Research Institute for Consumer Affairs.
9. Cheshire Libraries and Museums (1978), *Runcorn District Library Market Research Study*, Cheshire County Council.
10. Mann, P.H. (1969), *The Provincial Audience for Drama, Ballet and Opera*, Survey in Leeds, University of Sheffield.
11. Davey, J. (1976), *Promoting a Regional Theatre: Queens Theatre, Hornchurch*, Polytechnic of North London, Diploma in Management Studies (R), unpublished.
12. Mass Observation (UK) Ltd (1974), *The Potential for the Arts In Birmingham*, Peter Cox Associates, Leamington Spa.
13. Built Environment Research Group (BERG) (1978), *Sports Council Study 15, Sport for All in the Inner City: Sobell Sports Centre*, Sports Council, London.
14. Built Environment Research Group (BERG) (1978), *Sports Council Study 14, Sport in a Jointly Provided Centre: Medway Sports Centre, Reading*, Sports Council, London.
15. Torkildsen, G. (for Harlow and District Sports Trust), Survey of Harlow Sportcentre 1984, unpublished, and interview with manager of Abingdon Leisure Centre, *Leisure Management*, April 1985.

16. Zuzanek, J. (1977), Leisure trends and the economics of the arts in *Leisure and Urban Society* (ed. M.A. Smith), Leisure Studies Association, London.
17. Office of Population Censuses and Surveys, Social Survey Division (1979), *General Household Survey 1977*, HMSO, London, p 130.
18. Newsom, J. and Newsom, E. (1963), *Patterns of Infant Care in an Urban Community*, Allen and Unwin, London.
19. Davis, A. (1948), *Social Class Influence on Learning*. Harvard Ingliss Lectures.
20. Spinley, B.M. (1953), *The Deprived and the Privileged Personality Development in English Society*, Routledge and Kegan Paul, London.
21. Bernstein, B. (1969), Social class and Linguistic development: a theory of social learning, in Halsey A.H., Floud, J. and Anderson, C.A. *Education, Economy and Society*, The Free Press, New York.
22. Douglas, J.W.B. (1964), *The Home and the School*, MacGibbon and Kee, London.
23. Martin, F.M. (1954), Some subjective aspects of social stratification, in Glass, D.V. *Social Mobility in Britian*, Routledge and Kegan Paul, London.
24. Parker, S. (1976), *The Sociology of Leisure*, George Allen and Unwin, London.
25. Knapp, B., Jenkins, C. and Bonser, K. (1976), *Long Term Study of the Influence of Rugby Sports Centre on the Sporting Life of the Town*, Centre for Urban and Regional Studies (CURS), University of Birmingham.
26. Rapoports referred to in Institute of Family and Environmental Research and Dartington Amenity Research Trust (IFER/DART) (1976), *Leisure Provision and Human Need: Stage 1 Report* (for DOE), IFER/DART, London, Item 6.50.
27. Haworth, J.T. (1975), Leisure and the individual, in *Sport and Leisure in Contemporary Society* (eds S.R. Parker *et al.*), Polytechnic of Central London.
28. Reid, I. (1977), *Social Class Differences in Britain: A Source Book*, Open Books, London.
29. GHS 1983 in Central Statistical Office (1985), *Social Trends 1985*, HMSO, London.
30. O'Kelly, J., The Political Role of Public Libraries, discussed in Griffiths, G.T. *Recreation Provision for Whom?* Unpublished dissertation, Cranfield Institute of Technology. N.B. References 18–23 are also debated by Griffiths.
31. Hutchison, R. (1977), *Three Arts Centres*, Arts Council of Great Britain, London.
32. Built Environment Research Group (BERG) (1977), *Sports Council Study 13: The Changing Indoor Sports Centre, Harlow 1968, 1973*, Sports Council, London.
33. Collins, M.F. and Logue, C.S. (1976), *Sports Council Study No. 10: The Organisation and Use and Management of Indoor Bowls Centres*, Sports Council, London.
34. Public Attitude Surveys Ltd (1979), *Sports Council Study No. 19: Leisure Pools, Bletchley, Whitley Bay and Rotherham*, Sports Council, London.
35. Boothby, J. and Tungatt, M. (1977), *North-East Area Study Working Paper 46, Clubs for Sports and Arts: Results of a Survey of facilities, members and activities in Cleveland County*, University of Durham.
36. Hutchinson, E. (1970), Adequacy of provision. *Adult Education*, March 1970.
37. Institute of Family and Environmental Research and Dartington Amenity Research Trust (IFER/DART) (1976), *Leisure Provision and Human Need: Stage 1 Report* (for DOE), IFER/DART, London, Item 6.20.

38. Emmet, I. (1971), The social filter in the leisure field. *Recreation News Supplement*, No. 4, pp. 7–8.
39. Leigh, J. (1971), *Young People and Leisure*, Routledge and Kegan Paul, London, p. 124.
40. Griffiths, G.T. (1981), *Recreation Provision for Whom?* Unpublished dissertation, Cranfield Institute of Technology.
41. Burton, R.C.J. (1973), A new approach to perceptual capacity: Cannock Chase research project. *Recreation News Supplement*, No. 10, December 1973, pp. 31–7.
42. Rapoport, R. (1977), Leisure and urban society in *Leisure and Urban Society* (ed. M.A. Smith), Leisure Studies Association, London.
43. Veal, A.J. (1973), *A Discussion of the Role of the Environmental Perception*, Centre for Urban and Regional Studies (CURS), University of Birmingham.
44. Hudson, S. (1974), *Recreation as a Social Service*, Paper presented at the Recreation Management Conference, Harrogate, 1974.
45. Hillman, M. and Whalley, A. (1977), *Fair Play for All, A Study of Access to Sport and Informal Recreation.* 43, Broadsheet No. 571, Political and Economic Planning (PEP), London.
46. Willmott, P. (1973), Car ownership in the London Metropolitan Region, *GLC Intelligence Unit Quarterly Bulletin*, No. 23, June 1973, pp. 5–19.
47. Veal, A.J. (1973), *Ashton-under-Lyne Swimming Pool Study: First Interim Report*, Centre for Urban and Regional Studies, University of Birmingham. Also read Veal A.J. (1979), *Sports Council Study 18: New Swimming Pool for Old*, Sports Council, London.
48. Maw, R. and Cosgrove, D. (1972), Working paper 2/72, *Assessment of Demand for Recreation – A Modelling Approach*, Polytechnic of Central London, London.
49. Veal, A.J. (1979), *Sports Council Study 20: Six Examples of Low Cost Sports Facilities*, Sports Council, London.
50. For example, Sports Council (1973), *Provision for Sport: Vol. 2, Specialist Facilities*, Sports Council, London.
51. See Institute of Family and Environmental Research and Dartington Amenity Research Trust (IFER/DART) (1976), *Leisure Provision and Human Need: Stage 1 Report* (for DOE), IFER/DART, London, Item 6.19.

★

PART FOUR

Recreation planning

★

The objectives of Part Four are threefold. In Chapter 11 some aspects of the recreation planning process and some of the approaches to planning are described and evaluated. A greater people-orientated approach is suggested. As the impetus for improved recreation management has arisen from the development of the community, indoor recreation centre, the history of this recent 'movement' and the types of recreation and leisure centres that exist in the United Kingdom are described in Chapter 12 and trends and influences are noted. Finally, the relationship between planning, design and management is considered by following a planning sequence in designing a hypothetical community recreation facility. Part Four is not a planner's guide for recreation planners. Rather it is a recreation manager's view − a layman's view − of the practitioner's potential and essential involvement in the planning processes.

Chapter 11

Recreation planning

★

$\bigstar$

11.1 INTRODUCTION

Planning has always been concerned – albeit often peripherally – with the provision of facilities for recreation. The evolution of the planning movement was closely associated with the 19th century fight for the retention of open spaces and commons which were threatened by unplanned urban development. The movement has evolved from a concern for public health, education and moral standards to problems of inner cities and countryside recreation and conservation. Since the *Public Health Act 1875* made provision for public walks and pleasure grounds, successive Acts of Parliament such as the *Physical Training and Recreation Act 1937*, the *National Parks and Access to the Countryside Act 1949*, and the *Countryside Act 1968* were formulated to meet changing demands. In this evolution the planner's role has been strengthened by the profession's wide powers over the control of land use.

The planner's dream is to provide the right facilities, in the best location, at the right time, for the people who need them and at an acceptable cost. Dreams, however, seldom become reality. Planning is not a static process but is a *dynamic* and changing one. Planners should work with all the disciplines involved in creating amenities and opportunities for people in neighbourhoods, villages, towns, cities and in the countryside. Planners themselves are only part of the planning process. They do not directly acquire and manage land and amenities. They identify locations for facilities according to acceptable planning principles. They seek to minimize conflicts of interests, traffic, noise, pollution and congestion. Planners help to make towns functional, attractive and healthy places; they also help to conserve, yet foster good use of the countryside.

Leisure planning, however, is often a neglected area despite the considerable advances made in recent years. Veal [1] states the problem:

'The problem with planning for leisure is that, generally speaking, the planning profession knows very little about leisure while the leisure professions know very little about planning. With some honourable exceptions, planners have tended to ignore leisure because they have had more pressing issues such as transport, housing or shopping to deal with. The leisure professions have ignored planning because they have been primarily concerned with *management* – the day to day operation of facilities and services. And yet the need for firmly based planning in the area of leisure is as great if not greater than in some other areas of public society. Leisure plans not only have to present politicians with proposals concerning the desirable quantity, types and distribution of facilities and services, they also very often have to present the case for any provision at all.'

The word 'management' is used in this quotation only in an operational context. This book takes the position that top level management should be concerned with policy, planning *and* operational management. Bereft of an input into policy, planning, outcomes and evaluation of services, the manager is rendered at best an efficient administrator, organizer, and controller of users and personnel. The Recreation Manager should be involved in planning because an involvement at the earliest stage can ensure elimination of factors incompatible with good management process and practice. An essential part of the planning process is to identify the needs of people and to provide products and services in response to those needs so that individual self-fulfilment can be achieved. How can planning assist in meeting need, in providing leisure opportunity and in maximizing participation?

This chapter is concerned with the planning process as it applies to recreation provision and management. It is not concerned with the actual techniques and methodology of planning. Rather the author's preoccupation is with the planning principles and processes as they relate to recreation and the Recreation Manager's influence in the planning process. *First*, approaches and methods at present employed in planning are considered. *Second*, more recent theoretical approaches are looked into in the light of the current systems. *Third*, government and national agencies and regional recreation planning are briefly summarized. *Fourth*, the place of recreation is viewed within structure and local plans. *Fifth*, three recent practical approaches initiated by government are debated and *finally* a needs-based recreation planning approach is suggested and guidelines are given which indicate how the Recreation Manager can be involved in the planning process.

11.2 APPROACHES AND METHODS AT PRESENT EMPLOYED IN RECREATION PLANNING

While the provision of recreation facilities and services has been spread among a number of providers, the planning aspects in terms of national, regional and local plans has been almost entirely a function of the public sector. Historically, a *paternalistic* concern for the health and welfare of the community was the major influence on recreation planning. The standard response was the provision of facilities such as parks, playing fields and swimming pools and these remain today as primary areas for local authority provision and finance. Planning policies today appear to be based on a number of combining factors or influences.

A common policy for the allocation of resources by local government is that of *equity* in the distribution of services. However, equity is by no means synonymous with equality – equal distribution of facilities does not necessarily provide either equal opportunity or equal participation. As we have seen from the previous two chapters, social inequalities exist and these help to fashion the patterns of leisure activity. The dubious use of standards to achieve equity is discussed later in this chapter. Other approaches are planning based on *demand* and on *social control*.

11.2.1   Recreation demand

Planning policies based on *demand* are attractive to local government decision-makers. If there is a demand for a particular type of facility and it is used to the optimum, then councils are more likely to say 'we have provided what was demanded – we have, therefore, met community wishes'. Supply and demand studies have also produced the norms and standards to which councils will turn to verify their decisions. If they appear to have the right quantity within a given population catchment then the job is being done. Planning based on demand is sanctioned by governmental agencies who produce guidelines and standards, it is clear cut, it is measurable, it is comparable to that of other authorities of similar size, it fits neatly into administrative packages and into formulae for grant aiding. However, planning based on apparent demand can be misleading.

First, the methods employed to measure demand have often been too simplistic and 'rule of thumb'. Each method is useful in part but not as sole indicator. One traditional method is a simple mapping approach, comparing the hierarchy in the provision of various types of leisure facility with the pattern of population characteristics and local accessibility. Another method is through the comparison of existing provision with norms and standards for various types of facility. A useful supplementary method is to make use of local knowledge in identifying the demand for new facilites, e.g.

1. Activities that are gaining or losing popularity.
2. Comparison with national trends.
3. Discussions with participants, managers and clubs.
4. Surveys of user attitudes and preferences.
5. Market research studies.
6. Consultations about suggested schemes.

Such methods are being actively encouraged, for example, through the Hertfordshires Association of Leisure Officers (HALO). However, despite the many exceptions and advances, crude demand assessments have been the rule, rather than the exception. Moreover, the majority have been solely quantitative, leaving any qualitative aspects to hunches, opinions and subjective judgements.

Second, demand studies have concentrated on counting the number of facilities and the number of heads. They have lacked the techniques to measure the quality of the recreational experience. However, assessment of demand should be related not only to the current level of participation but also to deferred and potential demand. Level of demand is also, to a large extent, dependent on existing facilities and existing perceptions.

Third, assessment of demand based on membership and participation rates as an index of growth in demand is also an inaccurate system. Membership of an organization does not necessarily reflect the level of active participation and can only be used as a broad guideline.

Fourth, the application of user surveys to specific facilities is also suspect if other recreational facilities and opportunities, not necessarily of the same type, are not taken into consideration. Household surveys too can be misleading if the size of the sample is too small to gauge minority activities which might be overlooked altogether.

The public participation movement, which varies from local bodies set up to fight for more children's play space to organizations such as the Council for the Preservation of Rural England, has had an effect on the comprehensive planning of leisure and recreation facilities. However, the better educated, more articulate and those already with more resources may make most demand, while those in most need are unlikely to be heard – and here the advocacy of recreation leaders becomes essential.

11.2.2 Social control

There is a strong and instinctive belief that provision for recreation will alleviate antisocial behaviour and many ills of the world. This belief is well established in the minds of both researchers and officers in local government. A study of delinquency amongst boys in Liverpool [2] suggested that one of the causes was the lack of recreational facilities. Another study [3] compared the extensive provision of recreational facilities at Torfaen with the dearth of facilities in Liverpool and concluded that the lack of recreational opportunity was the main cause for Liverpool's vandalism bill of millions of pounds each year.

Munn claims that Torfaen achieved a drop of 15% in reported levels of criminal damage over two years compared with other authorities, with very limited 'community opportunity'. Increases in criminal damage in such authorities varied from 40 to 60%. 'Where sound management and philosophies have been applied to recreational facilities, clearly boredom does not dominate the scene beyond the home, and a vital neighbourhood stability can be achieved.' [4] Other researchers, looking at the effect of participation in recreational activity, purport to show, for example, that sport has a positive moral influence and that athletes were less delinquent than non-athletes [5]. Others point out that there is no indication, however, whether sport attracts those persons who are, or are likely to become, delinquents [6]. Some go further to maintain that the professional middle classes who dominate the agencies impose their own value system on communities with different values and different needs [7].

To be fair to planners, however, they are under considerable constraints. In addition the specialist social planner has a particular contribution to make to recreational planning. *First,* he or she can show the special relevance of recreation to planning as a whole. *Second,* the techniques of social analysis to any assessment of urban and rural provision can be applied. *Third,* the planner can use the same techniques to monitor the effectiveness of any provision with a view to continual revision and adaptation of standards. *Fourth,* he or she can show how a long-standing concern for recreation might now be widened into planning for leisure as a whole.

Planning is a process of providing people with the best possible environments, opportunities and facilities bearing in mind the constraints within which decisions have to be made. Planning, therefore, is a form of corporate social action, and as such entails the restriction of certain rights for the common good. This can, however, have the simultaneous benefit of greatly expanding the scope of activities open to everybody.

11.3 STANDARDS OF PROVISION

It is more difficult to provide strategies for recreation planning than for other services since recreation provision in many cases is not mandatory. Local authorities do not *have* to provide. More fundamentally, recreation behaviour is by no means predictable in that it is a matter of personal choice. Provision should not, therefore, be based upon a simple set of measurements, criteria or rules. Surprisingly one of the most developed and widely accepted approaches to the 'equitable' distribution of recreational services is the usage of scales of provision, standards and norms (see Table 11.1). Many standards are not based on any empirical research but on long accepted assumptions of what is 'needed'. In addition equal distribution does not mean equal opportunity. In order to have the same opportunities for all sections of the community, it may well be necessary to have a policy of positive discrimination in favour of disadvantaged groups.

For some unexplained reason standards have a fascination for planners and politicians. They have an almost hypnotic effect of drawing attention to themselves as to a magnet. Veal [1] captures this paradox of leisure standards.

'Leisure planners love standards. This is one of the great paradoxes of our

Table 11.1 Standards of provision. Hundreds of local, regional and national 'standards' exist in the United Kingdom which relate to the provision of facilities for leisure and recreation. This table outlines some of the 'standards' or 'targets' frequently used by local authorities *c.* 1981, even though some of the authorities now no longer quote standards.

Category/facility	Standard	Recommended by
All public 'open' space	7 acres (2.82 ha) per 1000 population	National Playing Fields Association (NPFA)
All public 'playing' space	6 acres (2.42 ha) per 1000 population	NPFA
All pitches, courts and greens	4 acres (1.62 ha) per 1000 population	NPFA
Equipped playgrounds	0.5 acres (0.2 ha) per 1000 population	NPFA
Casual play within housing areas	1.0 acres (0.4 ha) per 1000 population	NPFA
Athletics and miscellaneous	0.5 acres (0.2 ha) per 1000 population	NPFA
Amenity open space	1.0 acres (0.4 ha) per 1000 population	NPFA
Allotments	0.5 acres (0.2 ha) per 1000 population	Thorpe Committee
Golf courses	1 9-hole course per 18 000 population	Sports Council
Metropolitan parks	150 acres (61 ha) within 2 miles (3.2 km) of population	Greater London Development Plan (GLDP)
District Parks	50 acres (20 ha) within 0.75 mile (1200 m) of population	GLDP
Local Parks	5 acres (2 ha) within 0.25 mile walking distance (400 m)	GLDP
District indoor sports centres	1 per 40 000–90 000 population plus 1 for each additional 50 000 population ($17 m^2$ per 1000 population)	Sports Council
Indoor swimming pools	1 25 m pool and 1 learner pool per 40 000–45 000 population ($5 m^2$ per 1000 population)	Sports Council
Squash courts	1 court per 6000 population	Squash Rackets Association
Indoor Bowling rinks	4, 6, and 8 rink centres to serve populations of up to 30 000, 44 000 and 59 000 respectively	Sports Council

Table 11.1 Continued

Category/facility	Standard	Recommended by
Ice Skating rinks	1 in conurbation of 250 000 within a 5 mile radius	National Skating Association of Great Britain
Community centres	1 per 10 000 population	National Federation of Community Centres
Libraries	1 per 15 000 within 1 mile walking distance of all	Bourdillion Report
District libraries	1 per 12 000 population, 60 hours opening per week	Library Advisory Council
Branch libraries	1 per 4 000 population, 30 hours opening per week	Library Advisory Council

time. When government Ministers try to tell local authorities how to organize their affairs they rise up as one and complain of threats to local democracy. And yet in the area of leisure provision, the one area where local authorities are virtually completely free from government interference, they frequently look nervously over their shoulders to ensure that *they* are sanctioning their activities.'

Standards, however, are necessary, important and useful when they have been drawn up with sound methodology and are used with flexibility, local knowledge and wisdom. Tempered with wise judgement they have considerable advantages. They give yardsticks against which to measure existing provision, they are easy to understand and communicate and they cover many of the facilities provided by local authorities. Veal [1] listed the advantages of standards: simplicity, efficiency, equity, in that they can lead to the same level of provision from area to area, authority in that they act as an external authoritative source, and measurability where progress can be monitored and assessed.

In giving targets, standards may at least get some things done. Criticism has been levelled at the standards of the National Playing Fields Association and those of the Sports Council as being drawn up on inadequate information, yet they have been a means of cajoling councils into action, have been a means of getting some things done and providing essential services which might not otherwise have developed. However, standards have built-in problems.

11.3.1 The problems of standards

Gold and Mercer [8,9] criticize standards for not being supported by empirical research; beliefs or myths have become accepted and with time have become institutionalized. They believe that the people who develop the standards differ in their social background from the majority of the population and by implication impose their own standards upon the population. They also argue that standards across the board do not take into account areas of deprivation, factors of accessibility, socio-economic or demographic differences. Hence, while standards have some advantages they have many disadvantages. *First*, they become *institutionalized* – written on tablets of stone. Once entrenched they become authoritative, unmoveable and are given far greater strength and importance than they merit.

The best known and most frequently applied recreation standards in Britain are those of the National Playing Fields Association (NPFA). Founded in 1925, the NPFA first established its 6 acres per 1000 playing space target in 1937. Reviews were undertaken in 1955 and 1971 to account for changing conditions. The target has been in use as the basis for *playing* space provision for 45 years. Briefly broken down the 6 acres includes 4 acres for pitches, 0.5 acres for playgrounds, 1 acre for casual play and 0.5 for athletics and other playing areas. The standard has been 'institutionalized' by other agencies lately into 7 acres of *open space* per 1000 population (a different measure to playing fields).

However, it is not just the long established standards that become authoritative. The Sports Council's first basis for estimating community indoor recreation provision, as an *approach* to planning, based on only five sport centres, became *the* standard for authorities and planners all over Great Britain throughout the 1970s.

Second, standards *vary*. Different authorities have different standards for the same leisure pursuit. Most major pursuits requiring public recreation facilities have standards – pitches, pools, indoor sports centres, libraries and so on. But all have a variety of standards. For example, there are four standards for allotments. One 'official' standard is given in Table 11.1 as 0.5 acres per 1000 population. However, the National Allotments and Gardens Society has a standard of 2.0 acres per 1000, i.e. four times as great as the 'official' standard. This promotes the questions; Whose standards? Who should make the standards? Should it be central government, local government, national agencies, governing bodies or the local community? At present, in many areas of recreation provision, nobody has a mandate to dictate what the standards should be.

The variation in standards is nowhere greater than in the assessment of outdoor playing space. While the NPFA open space standard calls for 7 acres per 1000 population, there is a very wide range of differing standards.

The *County of London Plan 1944* recommended a figure of 4 acres per 1000 for the London County Council. Winterbottom [10] suggested 3.5 acres and more recently in 1976 Evans [11] suggested 2.5 acres per 1000 population. These differences illustrate the problem: how can uniform standards be applied when they are often exceeded in small towns compared with severe shortages in inner-city areas? Islington, for example, has only 0.3 acres of playing space per 1000 and is unlikely ever to get anywhere near to any 'average'.

The inclination to try to apply standards across the board had been tempered by the time the *Greater London Development Plan* was published in 1969. Greater attention was being given to specific user groups. Variables of time, mobility and demand led, for example, to a proposed fourfold hierarchy of parks, from small local parks to metropolitan parks. It is necessary to take into account the size and function of open space. The distances of facilities to user populations is a problem which became evident with an across the board use of standards.

Third, as Veal [1] rightly points out it is the problem of *validity* that is the greatest problem with standards. The way they are derived is open to question and none more so than many of the major physical recreation standards of playing fields, swimming pools and indoor sports centres. Playing space standards, for example, are based on participation rates but participation is largely dependent on the level of supply. The number of swimmers will depend on the number of pools, their location and accessibility, whether they are all open to the general public, the strength of swimming in the area, the quality of provision, the type of pool, the marketing and quality of provision, whether instruction is good and cheap, and whether the water is warm. Political policies and the sensitivity of management to the needs of the community are so often underrated. Do policies exist, for example, to aim at making every member of the community into a swimmer?

To make assumptions that only so many people will play sports and so many people will swim is not only misleading, it perpetuates the traditional system of planning based on artificial standards. The jogging movement, the fun runs and the growth of squash all show how misleading *fixed* standards can be. The squash standards have rightly been revised as more people take up the game. Indoor sport centres have naturally increased the levels of indoor sports use quite dramatically within a few years. Hence standards of just a decade ago are no longer valid or appropriate. Alas, however, even those minimum standards have in most cases still to be met.

Fourth, while standards are usually fairly easy to understand they can be *misinterpreted* and used as a justification for taking no further action. Some authorities have been known to interpret standards to suit their own purposes, not those of the community. They do not wish to be seen as not providing. For example, some authorities may show that they have more than adequate indoor playing space but analysis might reveal that most of the total space is made up of small units quite unsuitable for activities in demand. Total leisure amenities might also include all the substandard facilities which are inadequate, vandalized or restricted to certain types of use. Hence, total space may be of little value. The *quality* and *capacity* of space is important. A study of standards in a West German city revealed enormously high swimming provision per head of population. Analysis revealed that it included many of the huge city lakes in the assessment!

Fifth, standards are inanimate, inhuman. They assume a 'need' for a facility rather than a need which might be fulfilled in a variety of ways. They are concerned with quantitative and not qualitative aspects of provision. They take no account of the leisure potential of the specific areas – local needs, local priorities, local differences and local environments and conditions. *Sixth*, while many leisure pursuits are amenable to standards of provision, many are not. Water recreation, tourism, heritage, entertainment and arts have no comprehensive basis for evaluation.

In Chapter 9 we saw that different people have different needs and that needs change during their life cycle. Different communities and different sections within those communities will need different approaches to planning depending on the level and types of provision that are needed. It is clear that we have expected too much of *the* standards in the past. Standards are but one criterion in planning for leisure and recreation.

11.3.2 Sports Council approach to standards

One of the major tasks given to the Sports Council when it was established, was that of undertaking surveys to assess the country's needs in sports and recreational facilities. Such a directive immediately led the Sports Council into the trap of providing approaches to planning – often using other agencies' estimates based on traditional demand-related quantitative methods – which inevitably became standards. In 1972 the Council published *Provision for Sport, Volume 1: Pools, Indoor Sports Centres, Golf Courses* [12], which assessed the needs and deficiencies of facilities for major sports in England and Wales. The requirement by 1981 was calculated as 447 new indoor poools, 970 golf courses and 815 indoor sports centres.

The assessment of future requirements for indoor sports centres established 'spheres of influence' related to travel time and then their populations projected to 1981. 'The requirement within each sphere of influence allows a first indoor sports centre for a population of between 40 000 and 90 000 and an additional centre for every 50 000 population above 90 000.' The calculation of golf course deficiencies was based on regional participation rates and players per thousand population to the 1981 projected population for the sphere of influence. The method of assessing the 1981 potential deficit for indoor swimming pools was a four-stage process including projected attendance, summer attendance numbers, estimation of minimum water area to accommodate peak hours and the selection of one of five categories of pool size of defined water area.

Volume 2 of *Provision for Sport: Specialist Facilities* [13] was concerned with standards for competition and training for individual sports. This was followed up in 1975 with *Sports Halls: A New Approach to their Dimensions and Use* [14]. In 1978 *Provision for Swimming* [15] produced a far more comprehensive approach to planning. Factors mentioned which should be taken into consideration are:

1. Access factors, e.g. travel distance, travel time, location of alternatives and cost.
2. Catchment factors, e.g. population size and age structure, transport and location.
3. Pool factors, e.g. water area, pool environment, hierarchy of provision and management.

Where a planning exercise proves to be impossible to mount, *minimum* standards of provision are suggested. Hence the Sports Council recognizes that different pool sizes and types are needed to serve different areas. Their hierarchy of provision is suggested as:

1. Neighbourhood/small community pool.
2. The district pool.
3. Sub-regional pools.
4. Regional pools.
5. National facilities.

Compared with most European standards the United Kingdom is under-provided for (in terms of public recreation facilities). The magnitude of the West German *Golden Plan*, France's *Mille Piscine* project, and the provision per head of population in Scandinavia, indicate that Britain has much to achieve beyond the 1981 targets, which receded with recession. Aware of this, the Sports Council launched its Ten-Year Plan, *Sport in the Community – The Next Ten Years 1983–1993* [16], an exciting strategy to increase participation and resources substantially.

The Sports Council concludes that sport must be understood and planned for against wider changes in society. There are three major themes in the strategy – mass participation, better facilities and international sports success.

Although the strategy covers a decade, specific targets were set for the five years 1983–87 as shown in Table 11.2. These are broadly fourfold:

1. Encouraging 1.8 million more women and 0.5 million more men to play sport regularly, including special target groups 13–24 and 45–59 year olds. The 'Ever Thought of Sport?' and the 'Over 50s' campaigns in recent times reflect that policy.
2. Raising standards of coaching and administration in 20 selected sports.
3. Promoting and encouraging the building of 800 new indoor sports halls (150 in areas of special social need), 50 new swimming pools, 3000 new or improved outdoor pitches or courts (600 in areas of special need). The Sports Council's SASH projects (Standardized Approach to Sports Halls) is one major promotion to increase provision in areas of need.
4. Promoting the establishment of national facilities: a new national indoor arena, a national outdoor stadium and national training centres for 11 different sports.

The Sports Council describes its 'standards' of provision, rightly, as minimum standards and furthermore, the Council has moved away from the notion of standards and, wisely, talks about strategies and specific targets.

'The country needs sport as never before. Sport is part of the fabric of society and invests the lives of ordinary people with a quality and a flavour unrivalled by virtually any other activity. If we are to help it to knit

Table 11.2 Targets for the 5 year programme

	Existing 1983	*Target for 1987*
Mass participation		
Indoor sport		
Women	3 100 000	4 100 000
Men	5 800 000	6 000 000
Outdoor sport		
Women	4 800 000	5 700 000
Men	6 800 000	7 100 000
Facilities		
Sports centres*	500	800 (150 in areas of special need)
Swimming pools	900	200 refurbished; 50 new
Playing pitches	35 000	3000 new or refurbished (600 in areas of special need)
National centres		7 new

* Two or more large indoor playing spaces and ancillary facilities.
Source: The Sports Council (1982) [16].

together our diverse society, we need to plan wisely and to execute those plans boldly.

That's why this strategy is not a shopping list of luxuries; it is a basic diet, and a vital part of a Life Support system for the coming decade.'

Evidence of this new approach to planning is illustrated in *Sports Council Study 24: Identifying the Market* [17] which highlights the problems of assessing catchment areas of sport centres and swimming pools. More factual information and much more sophisticated techniques are needed to provide a more sound base for policy decisions. The researchers confirm that facilities do have definable catchment areas and zones of transition where catchments 'fade away' but conclude:

'Each individual pool or centre has a unique catchment which cannot be reflected in general terms. Simplistic statements in relation to average distances travelled or population provision targets are of little value and may in fact serve only to confuse.'

The most recent initiative comes from the Sports Council for Wales. In 1985 the Council published its national strategy for the ten years 1986/ 1996. [18] The aims of the Council remain the basis for its work: to increase participation, to improve facilities, to raise standards and to provide a research and information centre. The recurring theme in the Strategy is the emphasis that it is a co-operative exercise – many agencies are involved in providing for sport and recreation in the community.

The Strategy identifies the role of sport and recreation in alleviating social problems, identifies the extent and location of facility requirements, quantifies the financial and resource implications, reaffirms the need for optimum use of existing resources and highlights the need for investment.

The calculation of demand is complex and is based on a 'supply-demand model'. This was constructed working on research undertaken by the Scottish Sports Council in conjunction with Planning Data Management Services of Edinburgh University. The model consists of three principal components: demand, supply and catchment areas. The model has basic assumptions which reduce its effectiveness in reality: all participants within a catchment have equal accessibility, all facilities exert similar attractions and the current pricing policies will remain unchanged. Yet it remains a valuable aid to planners in establishing priorities and identifying areas of deficiency.

In applying the model to Wales, the Strategy reveals a level of 'unsatisfied demand' in five areas of sports facility provision within the principality:

Indoor sports halls	75.3%
Indoor swimming pools	18.5%

Squash courts	28.7%
Golf courses	7.7%
Tennis courts	33.9%

The potential for meeting a proportion of this demand through bringing existing facilities into full comunity use is heavily stressed. If this were achieved, the model foresees a reduction in unsatisfied demand for indoor halls and pools to 46.1% and 15.2% respectively.

11.3.3 Standards: summary

It is clear that standards of provision, whether local, regional or national can be a very crude assessment of demand. As they are based on national information, they often bear little relationship to local circumstances; they deal in quantities, thereby ignoring the quality of provision, aspects of distribution, use and management. *The ready acceptance of artificial standards prevents planners from considering the unique qualities and possibilities of each situation.* Ready acceptance may preclude more dynamic, flexible and responsive approaches to planning.

As pointed out by Hertfordshire Association of Leisure Officers [19], national standards of provision can be used as a starting point by providing a useful bench-mark for measuring the adequacy of facilities in an area and for identifying sub-areas that may be under or overprovided, while recognizing that most standards indicate minimum levels of provision. From this initial assessment the need for further provision can be identified and more detailed standards of *locally formulated criteria* can then be used to test the feasibility of particular schemes.

11.4 THEORETICAL APPROACHES TO RECREATION PLANNING

Until recently the main planning research method has been the quantitative survey, based on the measurement of certain activities and behaviour patterns of a sample that used to predict demand, for example, the *Pilot National Recreation Survey Reports 1 and 2* [20], *Planning for Leisure* [21], *Leisure in the North West* [22], *and Indoor Sports Centres* [23]. From these surveys and the *General Household Surveys* considerable information has been gained concerning the use of facilities in terms of travel, time, age, sex, socio-economic status etc. Is this approach suitable? Roberts [24] feels that the holistic quality of individuals' lifestyles is neglected in this approach; people do not engage in random miscellaneous activities, they engage in wider systems of interdependent recreation elements related to the individual's total lifestyle.

Justification for the quantitative survey method is partially based on the assumption that usage of facilities is an indicator of needs. But usage is dependent on a number of influences and constraints. Shuttleworth [25] claims that quantitative analysis is based on the assumption that the relationship between personal characteristics and recreational patterns is constant. This assumption, he contends 'is fallacious'. It has been argued by Leonard [26] that in-depth case studies and participant observation are more valid and reliable than the more commonly used sampling survey techniques.

In the *Economics of Leisure and Recreation* [27], Vickerman develops a number of demand modelling and forecasting techniques for leisure travel based on concepts used in the economic appraisal of projects. Perry [28] in '*Models in recreation planning*' has used techniques such as regression analysis and gravity models from the world of transportation studies. Maw [29] reported in *Leisure Research and Policy* on a further approach to demand modelling. Previously time budget data had been used in isolation. Maw's 'leisure model' has greater emphasis on the concepts of preference, choice, substitution and awareness of facilities and has the potential to bridge the gap between the two approaches of mass demand studies and small grass roots studies.

Recreation Planning and Management [30] is a comprehensive textbook giving information about the planning and provision of outdoor recreation services. Although the American Outdoor Recreation Resources Review Commission stimulated interest in recreation research in the 1960s, no coordinated national research was undertaken until 1979 in the USA in the form of the *National Agenda for Recreation Research*.

Recreation Planning and Management, through a number of authors, addresses itself to many of the issues and tasks set out in the National Agenda – the value of public outdoor recreation, demand forecasting methods, identifying recreation preferences and the roles of people involved in the provision and management of outdoor recreation. Survey methods, the Delphi technique (qualitative forecasting relying on expert opinion), trend exploration, structure forecasting, Dynamics forecasting (an analytic approach to the study of systems), Search technique (identifying the values of a community) and other forecasting methods are reviewed.

Countryside and outdoor recreation planning research has developed ahead of other recreation planning. However, the contrasting viewpoints of policy makers, educators and planners still makes outdoor recreation planning an area in which Recreation Managers can play an important role – with inputs, assisting integration and with operational management.

11.4.1 A people-approach to recreation planning

Unfortunately, the quantitative approach has tended to insulate and isolate recreation research from other relevant fields. As pointed out in the discussion on people's needs and leisure, what is needed is greater explanation of what leisure means to people and the role it plays in their lives. Some recent approaches have in fact given greater emphasis to a people-orientation, where qualitative aspects assume greater importance and where recreation is considered not as something apart but rather a factor of everyday living. The major study for the Department of the Environment by IFER/DART [31] in the London Borough of Brent incorporated a whole range of methods of investigation including depth case studies over several years, systematic observation, depth interviews, quantitative studies and qualitative probing of people within the community, and the voluntary, commercial and public providers.

In *Leisure and the Family Life Cycle* [32], R. and R.N. Rapoport and Strelitz look beneath the surface of leisure planning and reveal underlying predispositions towards leisure: planning for people's leisure should not be undertaken simply by 'feasible' extensions of what already exists and is known to be workable and on hunches about what people's needs are; social research must look beyond mass demand and begin from the 'people's side of the equation'. By building up knowledge and information about people in leisure, by learning about their motivations, preoccupations, interests and activities and injecting this knowledge into the planning process of large scale fact finding, small scale local findings and community projects, decision-makers will have a broader platform on which to plan policies.

Shuttleworth [25] has put forward a 'recreation systems research strategy' for recreation planning. 'The most appropriate strategy to abstract recreation patterns and needs is one in which educational, sociological, planning and community development theories precede empirical investigation into the relationship of recreation systems with the matrix of social relationships in their milieu.' In the strategy, the underlying processes linking 'predictor variables' are identified. The overriding necessity is to perceive how recreation interrelates with other aspects of social life. Recreation has to be seen as an 'autonomous system' embracing the total network of social relationships in which the individual is involved. These relationships are located within such primary groups as the family, peers, school, work and neighbourhood units. These groups account for the majority of an individual's recreation time. Recreation activities appear to be selected from a range that will support systems or social relationships associated with the community's component groups. *Undue emphasis on the activity itself ignores the fact that the majority of recreation takes place in the 'social matrix's groups'.*

The importance of voluntary groupings, club belonging and social contacts was shown in the study of voluntary groups in Chapter 2. This is reinforced by Shuttleworth's 'network of relationships' and by Jackson [33] who claims that the recreation clubs system is the key to social solidarity as it has helped to transform kinship and work groups into neighbourhood units, thereby fulfilling innumerable needs. In his study, the most significant institution was found to be the working men's recreation club, which, through its close interrelationships with the community social network, integrates the individual into the community and reinforces social solidarity. Jackson claims that mutual interest groups and communities are of greater importance than the traditional 'place' community (spatial units). However, others [34] only partially support this and in the 'quality of life experiments' (see Section 11.7.1) it was found that *both* social entities and spatial units were of importance.

The Rapoports believe that community recreation institutes ancillary to the home should be created to 'articulate' with the life cycle of family, kin, friendship, occupational and educational interests. Stewart [35] has suggested the introduction of community councils composed of private individuals, as an adjunct to local government agencies. Friendship groupings manifest themselves in leisure in the form of recreation clubs. Local authorities can assist clubs with material resources, grants, expertise and support. One of the major ways of enhancing community recreation is via the educational system. Many believe that it is in the education system that the greatest potential lies, for schools, colleges and other educational institutions are, in embryo, community recreation centres.

11.4.2   Client–provider problems

Recreation services exist to meet citizen needs – they are the clients. However, the relationship between providers and clients, particularly between the local authority and the community is often strained and difficult as pointed out in the conclusions of Chapter 1. Bacon [36] claims that there has been the 'thoughtless imposition' of certain concepts regarding patterns of recreation by bureaucrats into communities, regardless of their needs. Ball and Ball [37] contend that planners have constructed 'large formal secondary institutions of recreation activity' which they have called 'hypermarkets of corporate activity', which tend to siphon off participation from the network of spontaneous informal ancillary facilities – home, church, pub or private club. Shuttleworth points to the considerable problems of communication together with the client–professional conflicts during the process of planning for community recreation: 'It is this inherent dissonance between the professional service to the client group and the administrative procedures, which constitutes the major problem in service organisations'[38].

The more community orientated approaches to recreation planning, therefore, suggest that it is essential to involve the community in policy formulation and provision and programme planning in order to reinforce concepts of solidarity and the network of community linkages. Further, planners must take into account the wider lifestyles of people and build on the primary interest groups such as the recreation club. It is clear that the role of the Recreation Manager in discovering community needs and supporting and enabling people to 'articulate' with the providers will help to ease the friction between people and 'the system'. The community approach to recreation planning and programming is taken up in Chapter 14.

11.4.3 The need for pragmatism

Planning policies and theoretical approaches and debate must however end in pragmatic decision-making and the effective use of resources to maximize public participation in what is being planned and provided. Practical techniques and sound methodology must apply at the end of the day. We are a long way from achieving a satisfactory methodology of planning for leisure. Veal [1] confirms this view. In his paper *Planning for Leisure: Three Approaches* he analyses the traditional approach – that of using standards and puts forward two further approaches – the 'Grid Approach' and the 'Organic Approach'.

The Grid Approach is a method of studying the current situation with regard to leisure in any community. 'It is a means of examining the impact of currently available facilities and services – the interactions between facilities and people', The Grid has two dimensions: one is the range of *groups* comprising the community (pre-school children, the disabled, the unemployed, the elderly/retired etc.) and the second is the range of leisure *facilities and services* available for the community. The essence of the approach is that it provides a framework for the overall assessment of leisure services. The Organic Approach is based on the principle that the case for additional facilities should be based on the levels and patterns of use within the community's existing leisure and recreation facilities. The method starts by examining the level of use of existing facilities. 'This seems an obvious step and yet is so rarely part of the formal planning procedure'. Are existing, facilities as fully used as possible? Can management improve this? Is there evidence of unmet demand at existing facilities? What are the alternative means of meeting demand? These and other questions are considered by means of a type of flow chart which culminates in identifying the facilities and services needed in a given community. These two systems and many other untried systems show that theoretically it is possible to combine approaches to leisure planning which could lead to greater effectiveness. Information collected through an organic approach and through the kinds of approaches already discussed could be fed into a grid system. Cognisance can be taken of existing resources, community needs and initiatives and target standards. In these ways a number of practical approaches could lead to more appropriate community recreation services.

11.5 GOVERNMENT, NATIONAL AGENCIES AND REGIONAL RECREATION PLANNING

While local authority powers for recreation are largely permissive in England and Wales, nevertheless, governmental 'guidelines' have considerable influence on provision. The idea of recreation provision as a social service has gained a measure of acceptance.

To summarize information already given in Chapter 1, in England three major government departments have particular responsibilities for leisure:

1. The Department of Education and Science (adult education, community schools, physical education, youth service, arts, museums, libraries and Arts Council).
2. The Department of the Environment (physical planning, local government, inner city partnerships, Countryside Commission, Sports Council and other agencies).
3. The Department of Trade (tourism).

In addition other departments of central government which have an interest in leisure include the Department of Employment, the Ministry of Agriculture, Fisheries and Food, the Ministry of Transport, the Department of Industry, the Home Office, which administers policy for licensing and broadcasting and is responsible for the allocation of urban aid; and the Department of Health and Social Security, which is responsible for schemes that include recreational opportunities for the disabled and handicapped.

The national agencies in England which have direct responsibilities for leisure include:

1. The Sports Council.
2. The Countryside Commission.
3. The English Tourist Board.
4. The Arts Council.

In terms of recreation planning all these national agencies have adopted a *regional structure* through which decisions on planning, management and investment are filtered. Of particular significance is the establishment of regional councils for sports and recreation, under the aegis of the Sports

Council and Countryside Commission, which are responsible for the preparation of *regional planning strategies* for sport and recreation. Other national agencies provide recreational opportunities, for example the Nature Conservancy Council and Forestry Commission. The water industry also makes a significant contribution to recreation in respect of both the water and the land. The National Water Council and the Water Space Amenity Commission (concerned with leisure use) no longer exist. A new 1983 organization – The Water Authorities Association – was formed by the Regional Water Authorities as a forum for development and coordination. The British Waterways Board similarly encourages the development of the amenity and recreational use of British inland waterways.

It is clear that *there exists no integrating, structural framework in Britain for recreational planning*. Major elements of recreation such as sport and physical recreation and the arts, are administered from different government departments. The *ad hoc* national agencies have no linkages. Even the 1975 Government White Paper [39], the nearest approach to a leisure policy, was limited to sport and physical recreation.

11.5.1 Government reports

Two important government reports attempted to bring greater cohesion and effectiveness into national and local recreation planning. They were:

1. The Select Committee of the House of Lords Report on *Sport and Recreation – 2nd Report* [40].
2. The government White Paper *Sport and Recreation* [39].

Among the Lords' Report's 62 recommendations covering activities, facilities, finance, water recreation, outdoor recreation, sport and dual use, the report called for fundamental policy changes. The whole concept of 'Sport for all' needed to be changed 'more appropriately' to 'Recreation for all'. A *statutory duty* (instead of the permissive powers) to provide adequate facilities for recreation reinforced by government grants and coordinated by a Minister of Recreation was suggested. Within the detailed recommendations the report called for better provision, better access, better regional and local strategies and improved coordination at central and local levels, management training and better use based on the twin criteria of maximum opportunity and choice, and for the wider sharing of financial, manpower and land resources. Sports clubs should enjoy rate relief, the Sports Council's grant-in-aid should be doubled, regional water authorities should receive aid and the committee recommended the creation of recreation priority areas, eligible for special aid.

The White Paper of 1975, following up on the Select Committee report applied to the United Kingdom excluding Scotland. The recommendation of statutory duties falling on local authorities was not taken up. There were three broad headings to the report's proposed 'programme of action', namely: resources, priorities and organization and coordination.

Under the heading 'resources' consideration was given to the joint provision of new facilities and to the wider dual use of existing facilities. Five key issues were identified as 'priorities': the under-provided inner urban areas, wider community use of major voluntary facilities, the importance of the youth sports programmes, recreation for the disabled and gifted participants in sport. In the context 'organization and coordination' the Government created new regional councils for sport and recreation in 1976 as successors to the former regional sports councils. They had widened responsibilities for all forms of outdoor recreation and were asked to prepare long term proposals for the planned provision of sport and recreation in a regional recreation strategy. An example of one of the subsequent regional councils' 'issues' reports is outlined below.

11.5.2 Regional recreation strategies

To give an example of government direction translated into action, the *Regional Recreation Strategy Issues Report* of the Greater London and South East Council for Sport and Recreation was published in 1979 [41]. The report identified several key issues. In summary they include the need to:

1. Develop policies for sport and recreation, in all countryside areas, that respect wider conservation and agricultural interests.
2. Encourage the development of sport and recreation to help improve the quality of life of people in deprived areas.
3. Secure effective implementation of the regional council's policies.
4. Identify deficiencies in provision and determine priorities.
5. Encourage more people to take part in sport and all forms of recreation.
6. Increase awareness and understanding of the environment.
7. Raise standards of performance in competitive sport.
8. Make the best use of every existing resource (the need for effective management is a major principle within this key issue).
9. Secure an increase in total resources.

The council states that the issues report is the beginning of a continuing process. Public discussion is encouraged and comments and contributions sought. (N.B. The Regional Recreation Study itself was published in January 1982.)

Elson [42] contends that the setting up of regional councils has been unfortunate in terms of the planning system as most metropolitan counties were well advanced with their policy work: the more organizations involved in policy formulation, the greater the procrastination. Collins

[43] considers that with such large regions many of the issues considered are in such broad terms that they are almost interchangeable between regions. Another weakness highlighted in the Sports Council/Social Science Research Council report *The Leisure Planning Process* [44] is that regional strategies generally omit the relationships between local and central government on the one hand and voluntary bodies on the other. The report also indicates that existing provision for leisure could be better used and that small scale initiatives may be more cost-effective than large. People, rather than facilities should be given greater emphasis, particularly in socially deprived areas.

Lord Selsdon's foreword to the Issues Report of the Greater London and South-East Council for Sport and Recreation captures the same kind of concern.

'We have already identified priorities which require action by Government, local authorities and other bodies. I am particularly concerned lest worthwhile proposals and recommendations be stifled by too much bureaucracy and lack of cooperation between the different organizations involved . . . We have many resources that are sadly under-utilized and at the same time we lack adequate facilities in many areas where there is proven need. We are confronted above all with the difficulty of encouraging cooperation between Central Government, local authorities and various sectional interests: at the same time we must recognize above all else our responsibility to the individual and to the family'.

The regional council's strategies have been further criticized because they are only advisory documents and so are not binding on any other body. Guidelines for the councils state that 'the main purpose of the strategies is to help improve the range of opportunities for participation in sport and recreation', but how this should be done is left unclear. Furthermore the councils have no direct control over finance.

11.6 STRUCTURE PLANS AND LOCAL PLANS

Structure plans for counties in England and Wales are written statements illustrated by diagrams which are produced by local planning authorities. They set out the broad parameters of land-use developments within a conceptual framework designed to guide change within the area for a 15-year period. They are concerned only with those elements in recreation and leisure provision that are of *strategic importance*.

The Department of the Environment (Circulars 98/74 and 4/79) [45,46] suggest that concentration is given to *key issues*. Much depends therefore, on whether an authority considers recreational provision to be a key issue. In reality, recreation and tourism have assumed a relatively minor role in comparison with issues such as housing and employment, though by 1985 tourism was seen to be the major growth industry in the UK.

Structure plans are designed to state the policies of the planning authority; they show developers which areas to be looking to and they show other local authority departments how their policies combine in spatial terms and in due course the whole country will be covered by approved structure plans.

Local plans are also being formulated by planning authorities for the development and other use of the land, and these can take three forms:

1. *District* plans are drawn up to cover whole areas such as a town.
2. *Action area* plans are designed where large scale social change is likely to start within ten years such as a town centre.
3. *Subject* plans set out local authorities policy in relation to specific

Advice from central government suggests that recreation is of secondary importance here too. 'Despite the opportunity offered by local plans for a comprehensive assessment of the various components associated with leisure, it appears that this opportunity may have been lost as local plans are now well advanced in many parts of Great Britain' [47].

The conventional methods used in local plans are those of standards and of the assessment of deficiencies, particularly in public open space.

'This is particularly regrettable for not only would it be possible to examine *needs* more sensitively at the local level, but the requirements for public consultation in local plans suggest that they could be a useful vehicle for identifying recreational issues which would not normally be uncovered by the traditional form of survey or by the identification of key issues. A comprehensive evaluation of *leisure* within development plans is therefore desirable since it is a peripheral subject within planning and comprehensive advice and guidance appear to be needed' [46].

A survey of local authorities carried out in 1979 [48] reveals how unsatisfactory is the current situation. Of the respondents, 33% had carried out no review of leisure facilities at all, 45% had achieved a recreation plan of some kind, while 20% had only looked at a limited aspect of leisure. A partial examination of the reports further revealed weaknesses in methodology, lack of comprehensive coverage, superficiality and the application of outdated and inappropriate standards. Only three plans were highlighted as exceptions – in Telford and Warrington, where the availability of funds from the new town development corporations was an important motivating factor, and in Southampton where the leisure services department has a separate research and development section, indicative of a commitment to this field of social planning.

11.7 PRACTICAL APPROACHES IN RECREATION PLANNING

In this brief appraisal of some aspects of recreation planning it has become evident that a more integrated approach between central government agencies, regional councils, local authorities, local organizations and local people themselves would assist in the goal of planning for people. Central initiatives to integrate recreation planning include: the 'Quality of Life' experiments, the Inner City Partnership Programmes and the Scottish Tourism and Recreation Planning Studies. These projects have received critical review by the Sports Council/Social Science Research Council researchers [34].

11.7.1 Quality of Life experiments

A government-sponsored community approach to recreation planning was carried out in the mid 1970s. Experiments to foster such an approach were attempted in parts of Clwyd, Stoke-on-Trent, Sunderland and West Dunbartonshire over a two-year period. The areas selected were poor in terms of facility provision. The experiments were sponsored by the Department of the Environment, the Department of Education and Science, the Welsh Office and the Scottish Education Department in association with the Arts Councils and the Sports Council. The aim was to secure 'integrated planning of recreational activities – cultural, educational and sporting' [49]. The object was to carry out "action research" to provide insights into the effect of the quality of life of people. Improving the quality of life was seen as 'helping to bring new experiences, develop latent interest and help along self-development'. The total public expenditure from central and local government was just over £1 million, divided equally between the four areas. The size, cost and scope of the experiments varied greatly, from small items for a youth theatre, costing a few pounds, to the cost of establishing a mobile theatre for over £30 000.

In each area there was an attempt to balance arts, sport and general community projects and the action programmes were classified as information services, transport, mobile leisure facilities, community theatre, community festivals, equipment pools, projects for young people and projects for the disadvantaged. The first experiments started in 1973 and the last ended in 1976. Joint circulars and reports were published and a film was produced. Many lessons were learned both for and against the way in which the projects were conceived and conducted. The ten main lessons covered in the Sports Council/SSRC leisure planning report [50] summarized briefly were:

1. The potential for self-help within the community. This potential required good leadership and the willingness and ability to create and systematically sustain a voluntary organization.

2. Local authorities can contribute in a variety of ways.
3. People who took part were already active in leisure and community pursuits.
4. Little emerged to support the need for new coordinating organizations.
5. Demand could be created for more innovatory forms of well-established entertainment. Non-traditional art did not find support.
6. Local sports associations appeared to be effective.
7. Regional sports and arts associations sometimes gave an impression of remoteness.
8. For 'everyday' leisure activities, the widening of the opportunity could be met by a localized network of buildings and activities.
9. Clear division of responsibility and the establishment of sound lines of communication proved important to effectively operate an action programme.
10. The system of evaluation proved practical, cheap and effective and provided the discipline of having to clarify ideas, define aims and keep progress under review.

The objective of the experiments was to inculcate and support communal self-help. With good leadership and good voluntary organizations there was considerable self-help and initiative within communities. However, some believe that local government and other public agencies saw the experiments as contributing more to social order and to economy than to individual well-being or quality of life. Lawless took an even more cynical view: 'The Quality of Life Experiment has strong claims to be the most irrelevant initiative ever devised by central government in the long search to eradicate urban deprivation on the cheap' [51].

Despite shortcomings the studies affirm the important role to be played by local authorities in *enabling* the community to help itself, for example through grants, paid leadership, use of schools for community recreation. The studies appear to confirm that communities are spatial units as well as social entities and that planning can, therefore, be in terms of areas and distances, that people are prepared to travel different distances to different types of facility and that facilities require given population catchments to support them. 'The major contribution of the Quality of Life experiments to leisure planning may be in the relative failure of an externally-induced impetus to bring about significant change in leisure patterns and their exposure of the significance of the community in sustaining a leisure system' [52].

11.7.2 Inner city recreation partnership projects

The 1975 White Paper placed priority on projects designed to meet the needs of deprived groups in large inner city areas. One of the major concerns was to get recreation services to the people who need them most. Many surveys of use of city leisure centres show that while they are well used, they are not used sufficiently by those they were primarily intended to serve.

The reports *Recreation and Deprivation in Inner Urban Areas* [53] and *Fair Play for All* [54] both highlight the complex variety of factors which militate against the disadvantaged making use of public services and facilities to the full. The reports pose incisive questions about the approach to leisure opportunities for the deprived. 'Policies for community provision in local urban areas have not been given as much attention as other policies for sport and recreation, in part due to the difficulties which public bodies seem to have in meeting the requirements at the community level' [55]. The problems for the disadvantaged in housing estates, parks and schools are highlighted, in addition to the disadvantaged groups themselves; youth, elderly, disabled and handicapped, women, ethnic minorities and teenagers in the inner city.

The White Paper *Policy for the Inner Cities* [56] is the Government's response to a range of inner city studies. 'Inner area programmes' (*not to* be confused with the recreation partnership projects) are given explicit priority in social and economic policy. Although no direct reference in the main body of the White Paper is given to recreation, a brief reference is made in the Annex to small scale sports and recreation facilities for young people and places for children to play.

In contrast the inner city partnership projects in England represent a corporate planning initiative of which recreation is a part. Particular groups within the population such as young people, the elderly and ethnic minorities have been identified. The inner city is seen as being deficient in recreation facilities and public open space. While such major factors as long term unemployment and poor housing are fundamental roots of social and economic malaise, nevertheless opportunities for constructive use of leisure are recognized as being important. The emphasis given to positive discrimination in favour of the disadvantaged has provided funds for projects in those areas defined as 'pinheads' of deprivation.

Hall states, however, that the overwhelming impression gained from the initial three-year action programme 'is one of a list of projects that have long been on departmental and committee shopping lists and which can now be developed through the partnership programme' [57]. However, one of the most important contributions of the inner city partnership projects is the recognition that recreation and leisure are valid forms of provision in deprived areas; there is a preparedness to support recreation financially both in terms of capital and revenue. This has policy implications for future general and recreation planning and can be an important lever towards sensitive social planning. The riots in Toxteth, Liverpool and in Brixton, London during 1981 brought added impetus and injections of government finance to help alleviate problems of social and economic stress. For example, the Sports Council's grants were enlarged through additional aid for inner city assistance. This, however, is but a drop in the ocean and while assisting in a small way will not meet deeply rooted social and economic problems. The integration of leisure opportunity into the whole fabric of community and economic life must be considered at the very highest levels of policy and planning.

In Scotland (where a *duty* to provide for recreation exists), there has been an attempt towards cooperative planning. *The Scottish Tourism and Recreation Planning Studies (STARPS)* [58,59] was designed to assist in the evolution of outline strategies for sport, outdoor recreation and tourism.

None of the approaches to recreation corporate planning, initiated by government, have been fully successful. However, they represent an attempt to take a more comprehensive look at recreation in the planning process. Control by large institutional bodies like central and large local governments and their national agencies, appear to be no long term answer to recreation planning. These experiments indicate the need for a community-based approach.

11.7.3 Recent Practical Sports Council Initiatives

Sport in the Community . . . The Next Ten Years (Sports Council, 1982) placed a strong emphasis on the need to promote mass participation. The Council recognized that to do this it required partners. For example, a series of Demonstration Projects was mounted where sports leaders combined with existing municipal, voluntary and commercial agencies to start new programmes and make best use of existing resources. Partners include, for example, the Women's Institute in Cambridgeshire, the British Sports Association for the Disabled, the Hampshire Probation Service and the College of St Paul and St Mary in Cheltenham.

The Ever Thought of Sport? campaign was the Council's Sport for All promotion aimed at 13–24 year-olds. The 1987 campaign 'What's Your Sport?, sponsored by the Milk Marketing Board, is the latest initiative to increase mass participation. The objective of the campaign is to provide a national information network, in collaboration with local providers of sport.

Action Sport is a partnership between the Sports Council and local organizations (often the local Council) and works through paid staff funded under the Manpower Services Commission's Community Programme. Its three-phase process will cover 70 areas of England by 1988. The opportunities include 'activity' programmes designed to meet the needs of the community, particularly the unemployed, ethnic minorities, the 50+ age group, women's groups and the disabled. Support comes from local authorities and community organizations. The sports leaders are local people trained to help, lead and organize activity programmes.

the opportunity to look at their existing tennis programmes and to plan for the future with backing from the Lawn Tennis Association, the All England Club and the Sports Council. The primary objective is to provide covered court facilities and in so doing, introduce more people to the sport and establish a local development programme based on the principle of year-round play.

11.8 PLANNING FOR PEOPLE; A NEEDS-BASED RECREATION PLANNING APPROACH

The recreation planning process has evolved during the past 100 years. Aspects of recreation planning have become a concern of government as a social service. National agencies have been established to promote leisure. Local government, the principal provider of facilities, has a direct stake in leisure services. There has also been increasing recognition of leisure as an entity and policies have emerged designed to use recreation and leisure planning to help a variety of social problems.

Local initiatives in recreation planning, such as the Hertfordshire officers' study, recognize the importance of recreation in local terms 'not just as an end in itself but as a means to improve the quality of individual and community life' [18]. But as Blackie *et al.* point out, despite these developements the organization of recreation planning 'is not a coherent process in either national or local government, and only fragmentary aspects exist at regional level' [60]. In addition, local government slowness, administration channels, departmentalism and lack of good communication networks militate against imaginative planning for community recreation.

A number of tentative conclusions can be drawn from the recent approaches to recreation planning. This concluding section deals with some of the lessons which have been learned and the elements that need to be included in the recreation planning process. It has been shown that human factors, such as individual satisfactions and primary group belonging, must be considered and that if planning is to develop policies based on needs, then people must be involved in the planning process and in decision-making. *Planning for people means putting people into the plans*. Administrators might suggest that this will hold up progress. However, rather than holding up progress there are considerable advantages in participatory planning.

In addition to the human factors, there are a number of factors relating to the *planning process* itself and to the role of government at all levels. To plan for people's needs, via recreation, there must be a plan and a logical framework in which to work. *Realism* is essential and facilities and programmes must be achievable within a reasonable time-scale.

A process of planning which enables people to play and find recreations of their choice, to use leisure in ways satisfying to them and without detriment to their own well-being or that of others is the goal which recreation planners and managers should constantly seek.

priority, a number of aspects which should be considered within the recreation planning process. The lists are designed with the Recreation Manager in mind and with those elements with which he or she should become familiar, so that the recreation management input into the planning process is both useful and meaningful.

List A gives ten factors which bear upon leisure planning and help or hinder participation. List B gives ten advantages of participatory planning. List C provides ten ways of improving the planning process and list D shows ten examples of how to get things done – the job of the Recreation Manager.

A. Ten individual leisure opportunity factors

1. *Leisure meanings* Single meanings cannot be ascribed to leisure activities such as competition, recreation, social, artistic. Any activity may have different meanings for different participants and may have several meanings for the same participant.

2. *Change* Leisure satisfactions are not constant but change throughout a person's lifetime depending on their stage in the life cycle. The life 'careers' of education, employment, marriage and family shape the satisfactions and expectations of leisure.

3. *Unequal opportunities* The supply of leisure opportunities is fragmented geographically and institutionally, so that resources and access to opportunities vary across the population. Opportunities to gain leisure enjoyment, therefore, are unequal.

4. *Adaptation* People adapt their leisure patterns to the opportunities and limitations of their environments; they also adapt their environments to their perceived needs and demands.

5. *Politics* Political and economic decisions help to fashion or compound many inequalities. These inequalities have shaped the leisure participation patterns of those subjected to deprivations.

6. *Mobility* Personal mobility, particularly for those without transport, or sufficient means for transport must be considered.

7. *Focal points* Leisure consumption is largely in and around the home. Hence, for planning purposes the neighbourhood, local schools, churches, community associations, pub etc. must be considered as focal points.

8. *Opportunity limitations* Much planning is based on collective demand studies. Low participation due to inadequate resources will tend to lead to continued meagre provision of the necessary resources for the activity. Thus inequalities caused by opportunity limitations are perpetuated.

9. *Facility orientation* Recreation planning has been largely what institutional bodies and planners have thought was needed. Demand

studies have led towards facility orientation. Recent town and country planning legislation has put a duty on local planning authorities to involve the public in the preparation of plans. However, if local plans put recreation as a non-priority, local people will not be involved in local recreation planning.

10. *Improving the software* Improving the software of recreation provision – communication throughout the community network, flexibility rather than bureaucracy, understanding recreation problems, groups and clubs – more than the *hardware* of land, facilities and builders is one of the keys to increased leisure satisfactions for many people in the community.

B. Ten advantages of participatory planning

1. *Common goals* Elected members, officers, institutions, voluntary organizations and people in the community work together for the development of common goals.
2. *Cooperation* People work in cooperation rather than in isolation. Vested interests are limited. Better understanding and commitment is achieved.
3. *Communication* Improved communication is achieved between groups and the community.
4. *Understanding needs* Increased understanding of the needs and wishes of the community is made possible.
5. *Understanding authorities* Increased understanding of the public institutions, and local authorities by the community is made possible.
6. *On-going process* Planning is seen as a beginning-to-end-process in which there is public participation.
7. *Decision-making* There is input into decision-making rather than reaction to decisions made.
8. *Information* All available information is used to its maximum benefit instead of isolated groups working on the same information.
9. *Duplication is minimized* The possibility of overlap of services, programmes and facilities is limited; overlap between public, voluntary and commercial sectors is limited. One inefficient use of resources is that councils rarely take into account the facilities and services in other areas outside their boundaries. The cooperation between adjoining authorities could benefit both communities.
10. *Optimum use* The best use is made of community resources, including funding sources, for example greater flexibility of budgets is afforded.

C. Ten ways of improving the process

1. *Coordinate planning* Recreation planning must be *integral* to all

planning and must coordinate provision between public, voluntary and commercial sectors.

2. *Continuing process*   Planning should be perceived as a *dynamic* process, not simply as the production of a plan.

3. *Limit fragmentation*   At central government there exists a fragmentation of recreation services, involving several major departments. This fragmentation should be limited, not increased at a local level.

4. *Integration*   Local government reorganization has made it possible, in theory, to integrate services but the 'lack of fit' between central and local government leads to lack of coordination. This situation must be improved.

5. *Corporate management*   New composite departments of recreation, where a chief officer is on the management team, has improved the position of recreation in the overall planning system.

6. *Qualitative surveys*   Standards of provision, quantitative surveys and demand modelling are all a short-fall in meeting needs. They provide superficial data; they lack insights. Concepts such as social solidarity, community networks and primary group belonging appear to be of greater importance.

7. *Policy direction*   The lack of direction from central government leads to a wide variety of interpretation of local powers. A duty to provide has not been imposed on authorities in England and Wales. Free from statutory obligations, an authority can provide what it considers necessary for its citizens; equally it can neglect to provide what is necessary.

8. *Rationalization*   The existence of *concurrent powers* over recreation which are split between tiers of local government, poses a major constraint to effective planning. Powers should be rationalized. Tier-coordination must be improved.

9. *Common goals*   In addition to a variety of interpretations there appears to be a lack of appreciation and understanding by those making criticial decisions. There is a lack of common goals. There are two few recreation planners. Recreation planning is a 'Cinderella', subject to the whims and fancies of elected members, committees, lobby groups and commercial profiteers. Recreation, thus, poses a complex planning, financial and management problem which Recreation Managers can help to solve.

10. *Corporate planning*   It would appear that recreation planning is still seen as a peripheral issue in overall planning. The central government fragmentation and local government overlapping of interest, suggests that the place of recreation and leisure in the corporate planning process must become integral to long term strategy.

D. Ten ways to get things done

1. *Identify areas of need* Recognize the interplay of social, political, economic and technical factors and the *complexity* of planning issues. Appreciate the relationship with social policy, for example education, community health, housing and the areas of greatest need such as 'vulnerable' disadvantaged groups.

2. *Advise planners* Make planners aware of the needs of recreation management in order to deliver services and opportunities for people in the most effective manner.

3. *Assist planners* Recognize the scarcity of recreation planners and the shortage of funding for recreation planning, research and training. The input from Recreation Managers, therefore, is even more important.

4. *Use existing resources* Recognize the scarcity of physical and other resources for recreation. Therefore, make full use of existing resources from all quarters.

5. *Site for optimum use* Understand that major costs in the life of facilities are not capital costs but revenue costs. In addition, costs are rising, not just for construction and revenue but also for recreation travel and equipment. Site for optimal use and build in *revenue viability* where possible.

6. *Plan to gain for communities* In addition to the financial advantages of *partnership planning* and joint provision strategies, partnership planning can involve various sectors of the community in the decision-making process. With commercial planners the aspect of planning gain to the community should be vigorously pursued.

7. *Provide for flexibility* All participating in the planning process must be made aware of the *dubious reliability of forecasting*. Facilities built and resources provided should, therefore, have some built-in flexibility to assist with expansion and change. Recreation habits are not static but change as opportunities present themselves.

8. *Set standards in context* Planning is not a product or a set of rules but a process through which conducive environments result. However, all should recognize that standards are important if taken in context. In addition, achieving some form of hierarchy of provision, adjusted to community situations, or tailor-made to meet particular circumstances is necessary for providing some format or structure.

9. *Inter-discipline team planning* All planning for communities should be with a team-based, inter-disciplined approach. Recreation chief officers or delegates should be involved in the overall planning for communities; planning officers should be part of, or give expert advice on, all the recreation department planning processes.

10. *Role of the Recreation Manager* The input from a recreation manager

can be crucially important to recreation planning. He or she can assist in many ways: have input into policy, help determine needs, monitor, evaluate options, interpret community feedback, set objectives, use action-based approaches and be the link person between community, authority and planner.

REFERENCES AND NOTES

1. Veal, A.J. (1981), *Planning for Leisure: Three Approaches*, Papers in Leisure Studies, No. 5, Polytechnic of North London.
2. Mays, J.B. (1954), *Growing up in the City: A Study of Juvenile Delinquency in an Urban Neighbourhood*, Liverpool University Press.
3. Campbell, B. (1977), The have-nots: Liverpool lock-out the haves. South Wales schools rule OK: *The Sunday Times*, 29 May, 1977.
4. Munn, J.M. (1976), Neighbourhood opportunity. An equation with vandalism, delinquency and the quality of life. Torfaen District Council. Leisure provision and the community. *District Councils Review*.
5. Schafer, W.E. (1968), *Interscholastic Athletes and Juvenile Delinquency*, at Symposium on Sociology of Sport, Madison, Wisconsin.
6. Debated by Griffiths, G.T. (1981), *Recreation Provision for Whom?* Unpublished dissertation, Institution of Technology, Cranfield. The point is also acknowledged by Schafer in a later publication in 1972.
7. Debated by Shuttleworth, J.J. (1979), The implications for urban community recreation planning and administration of recent research into community relations. *Society and Leisure*, 11, No. 2, pp. 483–99.
8. Gold, S.M. (1973), *Urban Recreation Planning*, Lea and Febiger, Philadelphia.
9. Mercer, D. (1973), The concept of recreational need, *Journal of Leisure Research*, 5, Winter 1973.
10. Winterbottom, D.M. (1967), How much open space do we need? *Journal of the Town Planning Institute*, 54: 4, pp. 144–7.
11. Evans, A.Q. (1974), The economics of the urban recreation system. *Studies in Social Science and Planning* (ed. J. Forbes) Scottish Academic Press, Edinburgh.
12. Sports Council (1972), *Provision for Sport, Volume 1: Indoor Swimming Pools, Indoor Sports Centres, Golf Courses*, Sports Council, London.
13. Sports Council (1973), *Provision for Sport, Volume 2: Specialist Facilities*, Sports Council, London.
14. Sports Council (1975), *Sports Halls: A New Approach to their Dimensions and Use*, Sports Council, London.
15. Sports Council (1978), *Provision for Swimming: A Guide to Swimming Pool Planning*, Sports Council, London.
16. Sports Council (1982), *Sport in the Community – The Next Ten Years*, Sports Council, London.
17. Cowling, D., Fitzjohn, M. and Tungatt, M. (1982), Sports Council (1983) *Study 24: Identifying the Market – Catchment Areas of Sports Centres and Swimming Pools*, Sports Council, London.
18. The Sports Council for Wales (1985), *National Strategy 1986/1996 Consultative Document*, Sports Council for Wales, Cardiff.

19. Hertfordshire Association of Leisure Officers (1978), *Leisure Planning: An Advisory Brief for District Leisure Appraisals.* HALO, Herts.
20. British Travel Association and the University of Keele (1967), *Pilot National Recreation Survey: Report No. 1*, BTA/University of Keele.
21. Sillitoe, K.K. (1969), *Planning for Leisure*, HMSO, London.
22. Patmore, J.A. and Rodgers, H.B. (eds) (1972), *Leisure in the North West*, North West Sports Council, Salford.
23. Birch, John G. (1971), *Sports Council Study 1: Indoor Sports Centres.* HMSO, London.
24. Roberts, K. (1974), *The Society of Leisure: Myth and Reality.* Paper presented to the Conference on Education and Leisure, University of Liverpool.
25. Shuttleworth, J.J. (1979), The implications for urban community recreation planning and administration of recent research into community relations. *Society and Leisure*, **11**, No. 2.
26. Leonard, L. (1974), Alternative methods of data collection for recreational site survey. *Recreational News Supplement*.
27. Vickerman, R.W. (1975), *Economics of Leisure and Recreation*, Macmillan, London.
28 Perry, N. (1973), Models in recreation planning. *Recreation News Supplement*, March 1973, pp. 2–9.
29. Maw, R. (1974), Assessment of demand for recreation. A modelling approach. *Leisure Research and Policy* (ed. I. Appleton), Scottish Academic Press, Edinburgh.
30. Lieber, S.R. and Fesenmaier, D.R. (eds) (1983), *Recreation Planning and Management*, E. and F.N. Spon, London.
31. Institute of Family and Environmental Research and Dartington Amenity Research Trust (IFER/DART) (1976), *Leisure Provision and Human Need: Stage I Report* (for DOE), IFER/DART, London.
32. Rapoport, R. and Rapoport, R.N. (1975), *Leisure and the Family Life Cycle.* Routledge and Kegan Paul, London.
33. Jackson, B. (1972), *Working Class Community*, Pelican Books, London.
34. Blackie, J.A., Coppock, J.C. and Duffield, B.S. (1979), *Sports Council/SSRC Review: The Leisure Planning Process*, Sports Council/Social Science Research Council, London.
35. Stewart, J.D. (1973), Area committees – a new dimension. *Local Government Chronicle*, June, 1973.
36. Bacon, A.W. (1975), *Social Caretaking and Leisure Provision: The Role of the Professional Middle Class in Planning and Servicing Leisure Facilities in a New Town.* Paper presented to the Symposium on Leisure, Polytechnic of Central London.
37. Ball, C. and Ball, M. (1973), *Education for a Change*, Penguin Books, Harmondsworth.
38. Shuttleworth, J.J. (1979), The implications for urban community recreation planning and administration of recent research into community relations. *Society and Leisure*, **11**, No. 2.
39. Command 6200 (1975), *Sport and Recreation*, HMSO, London.
40. Select Committee of the House of Lords (1973), *Report on Sport and Leisure – 2nd Report*, HMSO, London.

41. Greater London and South East Council for Sport and Recreation (1979). *Regional Recreation Strategy Issues Report*, GLSESR, *London.*

42. Elson, M. (1979), The urban fringe. *Open Land Policies and Programmes in the Metropolitan Counties.* Countryside Commission Working Paper 14, p. 70.

43. Collins, M. (1978), Preface, Roberts, J.A. *Review of Studies of Sport and Recreation in the Inner City.* Sports Council Study 17, p. 4.

44. Blackie, J.A., Coppock, J.C. and Duffield, B.S. (1979), *Sports Council/SSRC Review: The Leisure Planning Process*, Sports Council/Social Science Research Council, London, p. 25.

45. Department of the Environment (1974), Circular 98/74–Structure Plans DOE, London.

46. Department of the Environment (1979), Circular 4/79 – Memorandum on Structure and Local Plans DOE, London.

47. Blackie, J.A., Coppock, J.C. and Duffield, B.S. (1979), *Sports Council/SSRC Review: The Leisure Planning Process*, Sports Council/Social Science Research Council, London, p. 19.

48. Henry, I.P.D. (1980), Approaches to recreation planning and research in the district authorities of England and Wales. *Leisure Studies Association Quarterly*, May 1980.

49. Department of the Environment (1977), *Leisure and the Quality of Life: A Report on Four Local Experiments* (2 volumes), HMSO, London.

50. Blackie, J.A., Coppock, J.C. and Duffield, B.S. (1979), *Sports Council/Social Science Research Council, Review: The Leisure Planning Process*, Sports Council/Social Science Research Council, London, p. 20.

51. Lawless, P. (1978), *Urban Deprivation and Government Initiative*, Faber and Faber, London.

52. Blackie, J.A., Coppock, J.C. and Duffield, B.S. (1979), *Sports Council/SSRC Review: The Leisure Planning Process*, Sports Council/Social Science Research Council, London, p. 21.

53. Department of the Environment (1977), *Recreation and Deprivation in Inner Urban Areas*, HMSO, London.

54. Hillman, M. and Whalley, A. (1977), *Fair Play for All. A Study of Access to Sport and Informal Recreation*, 43, Broadsheet No. 571, Political and Economic Planning, London.

55. Department of the Environment (1977), *Recreation and Deprivation in Inner Urban Areas.* HMSO, London, p. 2.

56. Command 6845 (1977), *Policy for the Inner Cities*, HMSO, London.

57. Hall, P. (1978), Spending priorities in the inner city. *New Society*, 21–28 Dec. 1978.

58. Countryside Commission for Scotland, Forestry Commission, Scottish Sports Council and Scottish Tourist Board (1978), *Scottish Tourism and Recreation Planning Studies (STARPS).*

59. Coppock, J.C. (1979), Review of STARPS. *Recreation News*, March/April/May 1979, p. 5.

60. Blackie, J.A., Coppock, J.C. and Duffield, B.S. (1979), *Sports Council/SSRC Review: The Leisure Planning Process*, Sports Council/Social Science Research Council, London, p. 38.

RECOMMENDED ADDITIONAL READING

Dower, M., Rapoport, R., Strelitz, Z., and Kew, S., (1981), *Leisure Provision and People's Needs*, for the Institute of Family and Environmental Research/ Dartington Amenity Research Trust, HMSO, London.

Chapter 12

Recreation centres

★

12.1   INTRODUCTION

The community recreation centre as known today in the United Kingdom is a relatively new phenomenon but it has had a profound effect on recreation management. Not only have new facilities been created, but also the importance of good management has been brought to light. New types of provision, different ways of providing and different styles of management have been tried out within a short space of time. It is important, therefore, to study its influence, and learn from its rapid development so that the planning, design and management of future centres can be further improved.

The previous chapter dealt with the recreation planning process and later chapters deal with management. This chapter concerns the development of facilities and it is written in two parts. The first part traces the recreation centre movement and developments over its first two decades and highlights important landmarks and trends. The second part takes a brief look at the processes and ways of going about the planning of a new community recreation centre. It shows the interrelationships between planning, design and management.

12.2   THE HISTORY AND BIRTH OF THE RECREATION AND LEISURE CENTRE

The word 'history' when used in the context of just 25 years may seem to be a contradiction or misuse of the word; however, within this short space of time we have seen the birth and development of the modern leisure centre in the United Kingdom. Looking back over 25 years from 1960 to 1985 changes are reflected not just in political, economic and industrial matters, but in the ways of life of people. Changes in culture and lifestyles are nowhere more apparent than in the greater freedoms of expression displayed in our use of leisure time. As we have seen from the previous chapter leisure planning is changing slowly from the traditional approach of 'Here are the facilities – use them' to 'What are the recreational needs of the community and how can these be satisfied?'

Twenty-five years ago public leisure provision was largely centred around parks, pitches, and pools, with limited use of school gymnasia. Commercial provision was directed towards eating and drinking, cinema-going, gambling and entertainment. Industrial recreation was on the wane, and the backbone of British sport – the sports clubs – was in need of far greater facility and financial assistance, a situation which still exists today.

1960 saw the advent of the first community sports centre at Harlow, with the first community sports hall built there in 1964. The national sports centre at Crystal Palace also opened in 1964. Within one decade from that time 350 centres were constructed; today approx. 1000 exist in the UK. Harlow and others that followed like Basingstoke Sports Centre and the Forum at Billingham, were developed by charitable trusts. It is from this humble beginning of a sports trust at Harlow that the *community leisure centre movement took root: initiatives by voluntary organizations provided the impetus for public authority action.*

The early centres were designed primarily for sports. Through management enterprise the halls were utilized for dances, choral and orchestral concerts, exhibitions, banquets, fashion shows and entertainment of all kinds – but the centres were not designed with such use in mind.

12.2.1 Developmental signposts

There are several signposts depicting the journey from the early centres to more comprehensive centres such as the Crowtree Leisure Centre in Sunderland, the Magnum Centre in Scotland and the Sun Centre in Rhyl. The development is characterized not only by the number of new facilities but by the variety and type of provision. Names like 'Recreation Centre', 'Leisure Centre', 'Forum', Community Campus', 'Oasis', 'Magnum', 'Concordia' and 'Sun Centre' reflect this development.

Changes in provision and management have come about as a result of many factors; for example, central government directives such as joint planning initiatives, local government reorganization, Sports Council support, leisure architecture and management enterprise.

The Forum at Billingham (opened in 1967) with its theatre, ice rink, pool and hall showed that the *facilities* themselves dictated the type of use and user. In this case architecture and facilities met known demands and created new demands. At Bracknell, local government initiative adapted a sports centre into (probably) the first local authority leisure centre. Through management enterprise leisure activities such as roller skating, dances, circuses, and spectaculars of all kinds became part and parcel of the regular programme. In this instance *management* played a key part in dictating the programme.

At the Bletchley Leisure Centre (opened in 1973) a sophistication and quality hitherto only seen in the best hotels was incorporated into the design. The social, meeting and informal aspects were of major importance; bar and catering facilities became focal points. This centre led the way for new 'glossies', with carpets, lounge furniture, hi-fi, solarium sunshine, Caribbean beaches with waves and palm trees. Since then architects have taken the social and fun aspects as being as important as the functional participation aspects within leisure centres. Leisure pools at Rotherham, Whitley Bay, Swindon, Cramlington, South Shields,

Chester, Swansea, Sunderland, Broxbourne, Rhyl, Great Yarmouth, Romford, Fulham, Kingston-upon-Thames, Spennymoor and many others followed in its wake.

The scope and size of leisure centres have varied greatly from small centres, little more than a sports hall, to some leisure 'giants'. The Magnum Leisure Centre, an update of the Forum at Billingham, is an example of the latter. It is situated at the Harbourside of Irvine and Scotland's western seaboard and is surrounded by 150 acres of beach park.

The recreation centre, whether of traditional design or open plan can cater for large numbers of people. For example, Wyndley Leisure Centre, a separated 'wet and dry' recreation campus, has yearly attendances of approximately one million, over 10 000 members, over 400 coaching courses and over 600 special events each year. Sunderland's £6 million Crowtree Leisure Centre (opened in 1977/8) with leisure pool, ice rink, sports hall and major social and function suite, attracted over 4 million attendances in its first three years. A television advertising campaign and the development of the building's basement to provide further facilities resulted in an attendance of almost 1.5 million in 1984/85. It has gross annual expenditure of almost £2.2 million and income of over £0.9 million. 152 full time equivalent staff are needed to operate the centre at a staffing cost approaching £1.2 million in 1984/85.

The North Wales holiday resort of Rhyl opened a £4.25 million 'Sun Centre' in June 1980: an indoor leisure centre on the beach. The architects claim that it is the 20th century answer to the old seaside piers. With the coming of the railways Rhyl became a leading holiday resort at the turn of the century. In the 1940s its pier was washed away. In 1973 its famous 1000-seater theatre was demolished. The need was to bring life back into the town. The centre is the first phase of a leisure and entertainment complex designed to satisfy holidaymakers and daytrippers when inclement weather mars the day on the beach. At the Sun Centre the Merseyside sun seekers can enjoy subtropical temperatures and three leisure pools, one of which is the first indoor surfing pool in Europe. The centre includes an island cafe, licensed night club, refreshment and souvenir kiosks, radio-controlled car circuits, porthole windows looking out to sea, palm trees, children's splash pool with an octopus and elephant slide and a 200 metre monorail; an aquaslide was added in 1984.

12.3 JOINT PLANNING: THE SCHOOL AND THE COMMUNITY

In the 1920s Henry Morris advocated and developed 'village colleges' in Cambridgeshire where he was chief education officer. These institutions were combined school, adult education and social facilities, built with the positive aim of integrating school and local community. However, it was not until the late 1960s that the new school and community leisure centre movement began with four pioneer centres in Nottinghamshire at Bingham, Carlton, Worksop and Sutton in Ashfield following the Cumberland initiative. Today there are in the region of 250 jointly provided centres or centres at educational establishments.

The Joint Circular 11/64, *Provision of Facilities for Sport* [1], drew attention to the possibilities of obtaining better value for money by combining educational funds with other local authority or voluntary sources to provide sports facilities for use by both pupils and the general public. A later publication, Department of Education and Science Circular 2/70, entitled *The Chance to Share* [2], gave further impetus to the development of joint schemes. The concept was also encouraged in the House of Lords Report [3], the 1975 White Paper [4], and in a joint report, *Towards a Wider Use* [5].

The school is in essence a community leisure centre in embryo. There is basically nothing new about adult use of schools. However, the modification and extension of schools to provide for full adult public use, *plus* capital from other sources, *plus* a community management structure, collectively add up to a very new development. In such developments the community can make use of school premises for recreation, sport, social and cultural leisure pursuits on a casual basis and with clubs and associations. Community use can be made of schools during school hours, after school and during weekends and holidays. The difference is not just in the facilities and programmes alone but in the sharing of capital and revenue costs between the authorities in partnership. As a result, joint schemes are more financially viable than single authority schemes (see Table 12.4). Also, by adopting a partnership approach to planning, authorities can provide several centres on a jointly planned neighbourhood basis. In addition to economic advantages, there can be social advantages for both the school and the community where the development of a *community* centre can help to meet the needs from toddler to pensioner.

One of the major factors in helping to meet needs via the neighbourhood/school recreation complex is sound management. This will mean meeting the demands of casual community use, club demand, family recreation, school demand, entertainment and social recreation. Professional recreation management is entirely different from that traditionally associated with the supervision of education facilities beyond school requirements. It is claimed that where managerial staff of the right calibre have been employed, domestic, catering and vandal problems associated with casual public use of schools in their standard form have disappeared [6]. Whether this is as a direct result of management policy or better supervision and control is not clear though it is assumed that a combination of the two is likely. Jimmy Munn and his colleagues in

Torfean and in Nottinghamshire, where the first 'modern' school/community leisure centres were built, have been recreation management pioneers in this field.

A five centres study by Prescott-Clarke and Grimshaw [7] showed that school leavers are encouraged to continue participation in activities by the wider range of programmes at schools with community leisure centres. However, it is surprising how few school leavers actually do participate at the centres after leaving school, at some centres as little as 10%. Whaley's study in Torfean [8] shows that the very high participation rates by the Torfean community is largely due to the fact that 83% of the population is within 2 miles of a leisure centre and that 25–46% of users walk to the centres. Furthermore, Torfean's combination of high provision, local accessibility, low prices, marketing and sensitive management accounts for its high proportion of manual worker customers at its centres compared with other centres elsewhere.

The joint approach to planning appears to make social, recreation and economic common sense. It is *one* form of community recreation provision. On a national scale, should all the new schools and school extensions be developed and programmed with social *and* community in mind, the benefits to community recreation would be greatly enhanced. Tragically, for the community at large (including those pupils attending schools) many schools in the traditional standard form, devoid of community planning, are still being built in many areas of Great Britain.

12.4 JOINT PLANNING PARTNERSHIPS

The growth in the variety of recreation centres reflects a growing awareness that leisure is a concept of *multiple* activity. Several multiple leisure complexes have been developed in partnership between many authorities and agencies, for example in Manchester's Abraham Moss Centre, at Sutton in Ashfield, the Communicare (Community House) centre in Killingworth, the Cresset in Peterborough, the Spectrum in Warrington and at the Stantonbury Campus in the new city of Milton Keynes.

The Stantonbury Campus is a housing, education and leisure campus – a community 'village'. It comprises three schools, a major leisure centre, a main resource centre, a theatre and a community activities centre. The Abraham Moss Leisure Centre is part of a community school run in conjunction with a comprehensive school, College of Further Education and the Youth and Community Service. The site includes a library, recreation centre and social and community centres.

Sutton in Ashfield, with a population of 40 000, is a town in a declining coalmining area, designated 'grey' (semi-depressed) by the government.

Life was being slowly drained from the town. There was a need to attract industry and to inject life back into the community. The district council, therefore, planned to build a civic centre and a new pedestrian shopping centre; the education authority was planning to build a comprehensive school. The two authorities resolved to work in partnership.

Today in Sutton the school, adjacent to the shopping precinct, shares its building with an ice rink, bowls centre, a theatre and a sports hall. A day centre for old-age pensioners and handicapped people, the youth employment and probation offices, a youth centre and crèche are all in the same building as the school. Nearby are the public library and health centre. Adults have joined children in the language laboratory and remedial reading classes. Some mothers are taking the 'school' leaving examinations; others are using the craft areas and workshops. Such examples, however, at this and many other integrated centres, are few and progress is often held up by poor cooperation between authorities, departments, agencies, head teachers, managers and support staff.

The Cresset (originally the flame from which light and fire were rekindled) attempts to rekindle community endeavour through partnership. Those originally joined in partnership included the development corporation, the county council, the district council, the National Association of Youth Clubs, YMCAs, boys' clubs, the Spastics Society, Handicapped Housing Association and the Church. The facilities which revolve around an indoor 'market place' include halls, squash courts, play areas, toy library for physically and mentally handicapped children and meeting places. In addition, there are offices, housing, community services, a daycentre for old people, an ecumenical centre, an arts and crafts centre and motor car and cycle repair yard. The Spectrum Centre in Warrington, constructed in 1981, attempted the same kind of partnership between statutory, voluntary and commercial bodies but the commercial elements loomed much larger and the centre is being sold to private enterprise. However, it would be fair to say that none of these partnerships have worked entirely in the way they had hoped at the outset.

The new London Docklands Arena – a major part of the current regeneration of London's Docklands, providing for both community leisure and international sports competition – is a result of a unique marriage of the public and private sectors. The London Docklands Development Corporation, Department of the Environment, Sports Council, Amateur Athletic Association and the London Borough of Tower Hamlets have combined their public sector backing and funds with those of Bovis, GEC and Mecca in a unique joint enterprise which exemplifies the spirit of partnership essential to the regeneration of the Docklands and of inner urban areas generally. But this project, too, in its planning stages is fraught with problems, particularly in terms of viability.

12.4.1   Problems with partnership planning

While joint planning and community partnerships make economic and
social common sense, they are only advantageous *if they work*. Examination of a large number of partnership projects reveals a whole range of
problems, incompatibilities and jealousies between authorities which go
to militate against the achievement of aims and objectives. There appears
to be an inability in some cases for policy-makers, organizations and
managers to handle the complex relationships between education, community and social services, recreation, voluntary organizations, and
between the structured statutory requirements and the unstructured
requirements needed in recreation services. Integrated projects can produce problems of cooperation and management resulting in splendid
objectives not being realized through poor management performance.
For example, facilities adjacent to each other, and planned to run in
conjunction with each other are sometimes managed as independent,
isolated units, sharing little but the same car park.

In addition to the human problems, the problems of legalities, political
and financial sharing and organizational autonomy cause difficulties. For
example, an administrative and political dialogue between district and
county levels, or between councils and new town corporations, or with
central government can often be damaging to progress and vastly time
consuming. The 'promise' of grant aid, or financial support from foundations or commercial bodies may not materialize. All these factors and very
many more call for top level management of the highest calibre. The
Recreation Manager as *one* member of the team needs to be capable of
playing his or her important role.

12.5   ADAPTING THE OLD AND BUILDING THE NEW

In addition to purpose-built recreation and leisure centres and the joint
planning of leisure and community complexes, this era has seen adapta-
tions to existing buildings [9], the construction of low cost buildings [10]
and the location of centres within shopping precincts, and commercial
involvement in the leisure centre movement.

More capital has been invested in buildings for physical recreation than
for the arts but the community arts movement has been steadily growing.
There are some 150 arts centres which have been developed over recent
years and some experiments of buiding theatres alongside sports halls
and pools. These experiments have been only partially successful –
theatre audiences and tracksuited players make uneasy bedfellows.
However, where the design and management takes into account (as at the
Stevenage Leisure Centre) the different specific requirements for sport
and theatre, then greater success is achieved.

Very few purpose-built community arts buildings have been constructed. The Midlands Arts Centre for Young People in Birmingham is an exception. It was designed 'to cut across all the present divisions between education and culture' [11]. The centre, in the park by the lakeside, comprises indoor and outdoor theatres, craft rooms, workshops, studios, cinema, rehearsal rooms, puppet workshop and sports facilities such as a climbing wall and squash courts.

Despite the lack of purpose-designed facilities, architectural enterprise has been shown to advantage in the conversion of old buildings: Victorian mansions, factories, town halls, maltings, stations, a gas holder, an aircraft hangar, corn exchanges and many churches. There are still well over 100 redundant churches suitable and available for concerts, plays, exhibitions and community activities. Even an old gaol has been converted into a community recreation and arts centre. At Abingdon the old stone gaol beside the Thames dates back to 1812. Today it has a small theatre, music centre, exhibition room, cinema, swimming pool, sports hall and bars and cafeteria. The architectural problems were immense: columns were precisely fixed; all rooms required fire exits and there were structural problems with old masonry and timbers. Yet a successful adaptation was undertaken.

Another notable conversion is at St Helier in Jersey where an old military fort and barracks have been converted into a leisure centre which includes exhibition halls, sports, arts, entertainment, shops, walkways and tourist attractions. A major facelift in 1986 has given Fort Regent a number of new features, including a Swingboat, Rock-O-Plane, a Cine 180, a Haunted Swing, Ghost Train, a revamped Dodgem Cars area and an Astro Glide.

An unusual conversion is 'Cannons', a prestigious commercial leisure centre which is situated beneath the platforms of Cannon Street Station on the north bank of the Thames in London. The centre comprises 10 squash courts, multi-purpose halls, swimming and spa pools, a gymnasium, a health suite, 5 snooker tables, 2 bars and a silver service restaurant. Now in its sixth year of operation, membership stands at approximately 4000 with a further 400 names on a waiting list. The company are currently building extensive sports clubs in Melbourne and Singapore.

Perhaps the most exciting and farsighted current conversion scheme is that of Olsen Shed No. 2 at Millwall docks in the London Docklands Arena (see 12.4) – an ambitious project that will on completion be a venue for national and international indoor sporting events, athletics training, community sports, concerts and other forms of entertainment in a building that was previously a three acre disused shed in the centre of Docklands on the Isle of Dogs.

12.5.1 Recreation centre and shopping and business centres

Should a centre be located at the town centre or in the neighbourhoods? A strong case can be made for both and in reality the situation is not an either/or one. Neighbourhood shopping areas can be developed into 'round the corner' recreation centres so that in neighbourhood clusters we can find shops, pubs, churches, community arts and sports facilities, play areas and libraries. Centrally located facilities on a larger scale are also important to a recreation strategy plan for towns and cities.

There are many major leisure complexes, as we have already seen, in the town centres. The Eldon Square Recreation Centre is an example. The centre sits at the top of the building looking down into the mall of the new shopping precinct in the centre of Newcastle upon Tyne. The Merrion Centre in Leeds has 100 shops, a bowling centre, offices, dance hall, three night-clubs, a cinema and a hotel. A pedestrian walk system provides covered exhibition facilities and a sunken courtyard with connection to a new subway system. Vandal problems, however, in opening up the precinct at night, have caused the closure of the cinema at this complex and reduced the opening hours of town centre facilities in other parts of the country.

If shopping centres are to become the leisure centres of tomorrow then the user and management implications must be thoroughly appreciated. Often the financing of schemes, their location and their physical features take on far greater importance than the management of them. The linkages, visual control aspects and the use of such complexes when the shops are closed have important long term implications.

In the business and commercial sector, social recreation, gambling, entertainment, sport and conference business have been combined into commercial leisure complexes. Commercial centres include squash and country clubs, health farms, bingo halls, dance halls and major national and international centres such as those at the Wembley Conference Centre, the Brighton Centre and the Barbican Arts and Conference Centre.

The Barbican Centre, though not a commercial centre, has a major business function. Conferences and allied trade exhibitions provided £2.2 million of the centre's income in 1983–84 [12]. The centre can accommodate up to 2400 at conferences; the main concert hall seats 2000 and the small conference hall seats up to 400. The large hall is shared with the London Symphony Orchestra so the acoustics and interior design are of a very high standard. The arts centre also comprises a 1250 seat theatre and the Guildhall School of Music and Drama with its own 400-seat theatre. Close to the arts centre are the new premises of the Museum of London, combining the collection of the London Museum and the Guildhall Museum.

Hotel leisure facilities are increasingly being built to offer direct and indirect benefits to the owners and their customers, such as the take-up of spare accommodation during weekends, to offer holiday packages and extend hotel amenities for business clients. (see Section 3.8.1). In addition hotels are developing purpose-built country clubs, squash and health centres to provide for public recreation at a profit. The possible links between commercial and local authority provision and management are demonstrated in the leisure project in Great Yarmouth. (See Section 1.6.3 and read Chapter 3 on commercial provision.)

12.6   THE USE OF SPORT AND LEISURE CENTRES

In a period of only 20 years from the mid 1960s the number of indoor sports centres or sports hall has risen from a mere handful to approximately 875 in England and over 1100 in the United Kingdom. In the region of at least 500 of these have been provided jointly by county councils and district councils under joint management partnerships or in conjunction with education facilities. What has been the effect of this movement? Is the country getting value for its investment?

A great deal has been learnt from the use and management of the centres though any long term trends will have to wait for more research. Throughout the 1970s a whole range of studies and surveys were undertaken and the Sports Council has been collating many of these and evaluating the results [13]. The first major study surveyed five of the initial group of sports centres in different parts of England and Wales: Harlow, Lightfoot in Newcastle, Stockton, Bracknell and Afan Lido [14]. The fieldwork was undertaken in the late 1960s and the report published in 1971. Follow-up studies were undertaken in Bracknell and in Harlow, the latter published by the Sports Council under the title, *The Changing Indoor Sports Centre* [15] where it was found that attendances and membership and overall use had increased, a greater proportion of participants were involved as individuals, the use of the sports hall by all ages over 25 years had increased and the number of women over 25 years showed a marked increase; between 1968 and 1973 the age profile of users was five years older on average. A further comprehensive survey was undertaken at the Harlow Sportcentre by the author in 1984, which revealed amongst the many findings, that the ageing trend whilst continuing amongst women participants is not being sustained in the case of male users. Indeed, the only age group that has experienced significant growth in male participation rates at Harlow is the young adult group (i.e. 20–24 years). More follow-up studies of a number of centres are needed to indicate trends and changes.

Several studies were published in the mid 1970s. The Built Environment Research Group (BERG) in *Sport for All in the Inner City* [16] put the case of the Michael Sobell Sports Centre in Islington. In *Sport in a Jointly Provided Centre* [17] BERG studied the Meadway Sports Centre in Reading. *Six Examples of Low Cost Sports Facilities* was a study by Veal [10] of centres at Rochford, Bolton, London, Nottingham and Steyning. Leisure swimming pools were surveyed at Bletchley, Whitley Bay and Rotherham [18]. Atkinson and Collins [19] studied the impact of neighbouring centres, Arrowsmith [20] considered sports usage and membership at the Billingham Forum and Jenkins *et al* [21] looked at the impact of the Rugby Sports Centre. The Scottish Sports Council [22] completed a major, two-volume, study of sports centres and swimming pools in Scotland during the late 1970s.

Studies were also undertaken in Northern Ireland and Wales, the Sports Council for Wales undertaking a comparative study of sports centre users in Llangefni, Pembroke and Pontypool [23]. Since 1980 the Sports Council has commissioned two major studies into patterns of sports activity and usage of facilities. The first, Study 22, entitled *A Sporting Chance* (1981) [28] examines family, school and environmental influences on taking part in sport, whilst the second, *Identifying the Market* (Study 24, 1983) [29] provides detailed analysis of the catchment area of sports centres and swimming pools.

A discussion of the results of the studies and surveys is not undertaken in this book. A review of sports and leisure centre studies undertaken by Veal [13] is being prepared for publication by the Sports Council. In addition, evidence from the studies and examples are given in many parts of this book: in part 2 in relation to the influences upon leisure participation and in part 5 in relation to management and programming of community recreation. However, some of the findings are listed and readers are encouraged to study the main sources.

First, it is clear that new indoor centres increase participation substantially. In the 1970s there was an increase of nearly 50% in outdoor sport and recreation and over 200% in indoor activities (Fig. 12.1). A trebling of provision of sports halls and a 70% increase in swimming pool area were accompanied by a doubling of participation amongst men and women, from 10% to 23% of men and from 5% to 10% of women [24]. Between 1977 and 1980 participation in outdoor sport and recreation increased slightly more than participation indoors (Fig. 12.1). This change in the pattern of usage may, in part, be attributable to the slowing of the indoor sport centre building programme during the late seventies coupled with the rise in the provision of outdoor all-weather synthetic pitches and courts. The 1983 GHS figures show only minor changes to the general picture of participation since 1980.

Second, at present levels of indoor sports provision, it would appear that new 'dry' centres scarcely affect the use of existing facilities [21].

Third, the centres are used by a far higher proportion of young people in virtually all centres and the overall picture of the 'youngness' of the participants is illustrated in Fig 12.2.

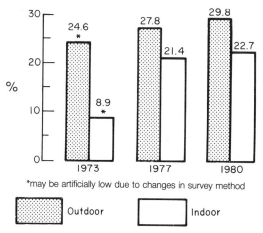

Fig. 12.1 Annual participation in sport 1973–80 (Great Britain). Source: GHS 1973/77/80 in *Sport in the community: The Next Ten Years* [30].

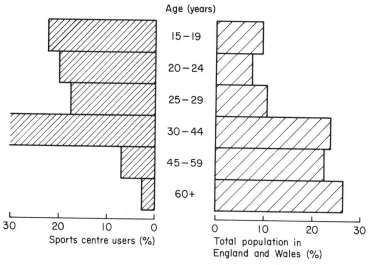

Fig. 12.2 Age profile of sports centre users. Source: Office of Population, Censuses and Surveys, and Veal [13].

Fourth, sport centre users generally have higher proportions of participants from the professional, non-manual and skilled groups than from the semi-skilled and manual groups as is shown in Fig. 12.3. As Collins [24] comments:

'we have done better amongst the car owners, the higher status

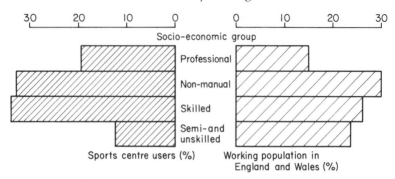

Fig.12.3 Sports centre users and the general population. Source: Office of
Population, Censuses and Surveys, and Veal [13].

professional and industrial job holders, the better educated, younger
men and worse amongst older people, poorer people, the more poorly
educated and poorly paid people and housewives. Total participation has
increased, but the gap between high and low participation groups
remains. Is that Sport for All?'

However, as pointed out earlier, neighbourhood centres and those
within walking distance and which have sensitive management and
marketing policies are able to change the profile of participants to a far
more balanced level.

Fifth, at present levels of distribution, the bulk of users of centres
continue to come from within 4 miles [24] although a recent survey
undertaken for the Sports Council (Study 24 – *Identifying the Market*)
reveals that within this generalization there is an enormous amount of
variation from centre to centre. Moreover, different activities have smaller
or larger catchment areas depending on the nature of the activity and the
'profile' of the community near to the centre. At the Sobell Sports Centre,
for example, skaters come from closer at hand compared with the
participants in racket sports, the needs of local young people in particular
being met through skating rather than squash and badminton. However,
as BERG points out: 'unless a centre is located close to good public
transport services, use by those who do not live within walking distance
will be almost entirely restricted to car owners'. [16].

Sixth, jointly provided centres appear to be more cost-effective than
separate provision, especially in 'dry' centres and especially in large *or*
small centres rather than medium sized centres. The work of Coopers and
Lybrand [25] illustrated in Fig.12.4 appears to indicate that in terms of
value for money we should be thinking of joint planning rather than
separate planning (a), smaller rather than larger facilities (b) and 'dry'
rather than 'wet' facilities (c).

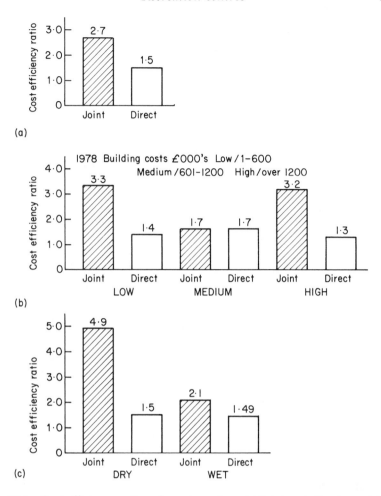

Fig. 12.4 Cost-efficiency ratios of sports centres. (a) Joint and direct provision. The cost-efficiency ratio is the usage of a centre divided by the operating costs, i.e. the number of admissions that can be provided per £ of operating costs. Joint centres tend to have higher cost-efficiency ratios than do separate provision centres – both wet and dry facilities. (b) Effect of size. Joint provision centres tend to be smaller than separate provision centres. This explains some of the variation in cost efficiency because smaller centres tend to be more cost effective. (c) Wet and dry facilities. For separate provision centres, there is little difference between the cost efficiency of wet and dry centres, contrary to the widely held view that swimming facilities are far less cost effective. Source: Coopers and Lybrand, adapted by Collins [24, 25].

Seventh, concerning the range of activities at centres, Veal's review [13] shows that while the possible range of activities is large (more than 30 activities), the bulk of space and time is taken up by a handful of activities.

These include badminton, five-a-side football and squash.

Eighth, sport and leisure centres continue to be heavily subsidized as we have already seen earlier in this chapter. The Scottish Sports Council study [22] showed that not only were the playing facilities subsidized but the use of social areas and cafeterias were also financially supported. What is further surprising is that substantial subsidy was needed even for squash (this is probably due to lower pricing policies compared with commercial organizations). Far greater attention is now being given at centres to revenue finance and greater economic viability.

This brief analysis of use of centres shows one undeniable fact: the impact of the recreation centre movement in the United Kingdom has been considerable in terms of indoor active leisure participation. Running parallel with this physical recreation movement has been the community art centres movement with the region of 200 art centres in Great Britain.

12.7 PROGRESS AND PROBLEMS OVER 20 YEARS

Recreation centre progress was swift over the late 1960s and early 1970s but a tailing-off of developments, caused by financial restrictions, meant that the target set by the Sports Council [26] of 800 centres by 1981 was not realized. However, today there are more facilities, more centres, more activities, more people participating and *more recreation management jobs* than ever before in the United Kingdom. There exists a much wider interpretation of leisure and a wider use of resources. The swing to local government provision has brought far greater public use, mass use and multi-use.

There have been considerable advances in technology – free form pools, wave machines, flumes, automatic entry systems, improved equipment and improved administration and accounting systems, but compared with facilities in many parts of the world the technology has not improved as much as one could have hoped for.

12.7.1 Trends and influences

Four major influences have had an important bearing on the recreation movement. The *first* is the fact that voluntary enterprise and initiative set the course for public authority action. The *second* feature has been the rapid swing from voluntary projects to local government provision. Today over 90% of the community recreation centres are local authority controlled. As Collins suggests 'the municipal leisure sector came of age' [24]. The *third* influence was the recognition by central government of the need, not only for improved provision, but also for better use of all resources through good management. For example, just *one* powerful decision – to give loan sanction priority to joint provision schemes – has resulted in over one third of the present day centres being provided under the joint provision umbrella. The *fourth* major influence has been the support of the Sports Council in two main directions:

1. Facility advice and small grants to providers.
2. Actions directed towards improved management performance.

This support is developing steadily and has in recent years been rationalized into a ten year plan [30] beginning with a five year rolling programme of expenditure for 1983–88 [31] which is reviewed annually.

The Sports Council Working Party on Professional Training for Recreation Management led to the diploma course in recreation management and one of the most influential factors in improved management of recreation centres has been the Sports Council Management Award, conceived by Ted Blake, initiated by the Facilities Unit of the Sports Council and enabled through sponsorship in its first five years by Nissen International (Sports Equipment) Ltd, and more recently by Vendepac.

In terms of management, the early managers were pioneers. They were intuitive, original, highly motivated and committed to what they were doing. They were successful because they made up for their lack of management training and business skill through time, effort and learning through doing. It became apparent, however, particularly with the moves of many of the original managers to posts of seniority in recreation services, that enthusiasm was not enough. Many of the programmes lacked objectivity. Of the first 70 centres that competed in the management award well over two thirds of them had no written centre objective and no guidelines, other than budget estimates, to measure their performance. The skills needed for good management and the need for training are debated in Chapter 18.

Running parallel with the recreation centre movement several participation trends can be recognized:

1. A growth in participation in physical recreation.
2. Substantial growth in indoor recreation participation.
3. Greater participation in individual pursuits.
4. A growth in social recreation.
5. Progress in the field of community arts.
6. The importance placed on the growth in outdoor pursuits allied to blocks of time spent away from the home and in holidays including activity holidays.

The recreation centre movement itself has developed rapidly along a number of different lines and not in a linear form. Four separate movements can be identified.

1. From a sports movement to a social movement.

2. From singular planning to joint planning.
3. From traditional facilities to experimental projects.
4. From centres to more comprehensive 'complexes' and to 'leisure environments' incorporating provision for education, recreation, sport, art, entertainment, social and welfare services, shopping, business and other commercial enterprises.

It has been shown that there needs to be a harmonious relationship between various providers and agencies and an interrelationship between policy, design and management. What lessons can be learned so that new leisure centres can be better planned? What influence does the Recreation Manager have on the planning and provision of a recreation centre? It is to this area that we now turn.

12.8   MANAGEMENT IMPLICATIONS FOR DESIGN OF AN INDOOR PUBLIC RECREATION CENTRE

Some recreation facilities have been planned, designed and built with insufficient consideration as to who and what the facility has been designed for (other than being broadly designated as a 'recreation centre', 'leisure centre' etc) and often only with cursory consideration of the management implications of the design. Facilties have been built and then management has had to organize the programming and staffing, produce income, limit expenditure and create management systems around the limitations of the design rather than the facility and its design being tailor-made to suit the requirements of the management and users. Since the capital cost of a facility may run into millions of pounds, with substantial recurrent running costs being borne by the tax and rate-payer each year, it is curious that this should still happen and that the decision to spend such sums has been based at times on political determination, the demands of pressure groups or simply envy of a neighbouring district or borough's facilities.

Good planning and design does not have to cost more than poor design. The question is whether management can perform its function effectively and efficiently. 'Poor design inhibits management expertise in terms of the use of facilities which may adversely affect income. Poorly designed buildings can depress staff which is often reflected in attitudes towards customers which, in turn, leads to poor public relations and again has a depressing effect upon income' [27].

Central government has been concerned with controlling capital expenditure, yet major recurring costs such as manpower and energy costs will far outstrip capital costs in the first stages of the life of the facility. *A planning equation of capital cost, revenue cost, user satisfaction and management function is called for.*

This section proposes that the facility should be the product of community and management needs and should be designed to meet these needs. The process which the Recreation Manager might follow in order to achieve this end is described in the following paragraphs. This process is basically concerned with the Recreation Manager's influence. Those who must ultimately use and manage the centre should be involved in the deliberations from inception to completion. The benefit of advice from a Recreation Manager or a recreation management consultant can be invaluable. The final cost of a project is committed in varying proportions through its life and decisions taken during the preliminary planning, feasibility and schematic design stages are more significant than any during the later stages.

The first stage of planning, design and management process in providing a community recreation facility could be conceived as follows:

10-Stage plan

1. Prepare a *strategy plan* if one does not already exist.
2. Appoint a multi-discipline *project team*.
3. Commission a *feasibility study*.
4. Approve or prepare a *schematic layout* and type of accommodation.
5. Consider *location and siting*.
6. Consider *financial cost limits* for both capital and revenue.
7. Make *decision*, define guidelines, constraints and outline brief.
8. Appoint *manager*.
9. Write *detailed brief* and *schedule of accommodation*.
10. Appoint *architect*.

This plan simplifies a complex pattern. It is not a linear model. For example, the site may already be available, the strategy plan may need modification in the light of the feasibility study, the project proposal may be altered in the light of costs, 'in-house' architects may already be on hand. However, the plan puts forward elements which must all be considered.

12.8.1 The strategy plan

The decision to build a recreation facility may *eventually* stand or fall on financial or political considerations. The reasons why a facility should be built, where it should be built and what type of facility it should be, do not. The need for a particular facility (or rather the needs that such a facility can help satisfy) does not go away because the money has. The money is only a means to an end, but the Recreation Manager needs to know what that end is, if financial resources are to be used wisely as and when they become available.

The starting point for the design of any recreation facility is, therefore, the organization's aims and objectives – its statement of purpose. Once the Recreation Manager knows what the objective is a detailed analysis and plan aimed at fulfilling this purpose can be produced. In the case of a local authority recreation department with the object of satisfying the recreational needs and the recreational deficiencies within the borough and/or district it serves, this would entail the production of a strategy plan. This plan would identify the recreational needs and the recreational deficiencies within the borough and put forward suggestions as to how these needs can be met and the deficiencies overcome. Among the suggestions for meeting the needs of a particular area may be the setting up of a recreation facility. The nature of the facility will be determined by the needs of the people and the area it is intended to serve.

To summarize, the organization states its purposes and objectives. A strategy plan is produced showing how it is going to achieve its objectives and establishing priorities for doing so. Within the strategy plan is a recommendation that a recreational facility should be built. The recommendation will state *why* it should be built, *where* is should be built, and *what type* of facility it should be. *When* it should be built will be dependent on its priority ranking and the funds available. *How* it should be built is the subject of the rest of this section. It will start with the project team and feasibility study.

12.8.2 The project team

A project team will have to be established, responsible for the management of the project during the feasibility study, design and construction stages. The members of the team should have the necessary expertise and experience to carry out these functions but the exact composition of the team would depend on the nature of the project. A local authority project team could involve the engineer, architect/planner, recreation officer, recreation management consultant or Sports Council regional officer, treasurer and the manager of the centre when appointed. A project leader will need to be appointed and should have the appropriate degree of authority with clear lines of responsibility and communication being agreed by all concerned. The team should produce a programme covering all stages of the project showing key dates when decisions and action are required.

12.8.3 The feasibility study

The purpose of the feasibility study is to produce a detailed outline of the facility required, together with estimates of capital and recurrent expenditure. To do this it must consider needs, establish demands and prepare and evaluate options, considering community, social, political, financial and other constraints. The production of the feasibility study could fall either to the recreation department, the Recreation Manager or to an outside consultant. If the study falls to the Recreation Manager his or her thoughts should progress through the feasibility study in something like the following sequence. We are designing for a purpose. Needs have been identified in the strategy plan and they have to be met. Therefore, what are our facility's objectives? What sort of programme will achieve these objectives? What will be our staffing requirements in order to carry through this programme? *Then* what is the best way to design this facility in order to meet our objectives and satisfy our staffing and programming needs? From all these factors a rough estimate of the financial implications of the project can be made.

Thus the feasibility study will need to include:

1. The objectives.
2. The broad programme.
3. The staffing ratios and organization.
4. A broad schematic layout.
5. Costings both capital and recurrent.
6. The use and management implications on design.
7. Forecasts relating to use and demand.

12.8.4 The schematic layout

This preliminary design stage can either be part of the facility study or may arise from the study. The schematic design should give the broad performance specifications, the general layout, the type of accommodation, plant and services. The question the Recreation Manager must consider is what facilities are needed and how they should relate to one another in order to meet the programming, staffing, management and user requirements. Staff and user flows, problems associated with the influx of large groups, potential user conflicts such as noise, danger, age differences and different levels or standards of play will affect the layout. The broad mechanical, heating, lighting, ventilation, structural and other relevant technical specifications will also be required and again must be carefully considered in view of the variety of user and management requirements. Hence the project team must have knowledgeable officers who can assist in or guide those involved in carrying out the work.

12.8.5 The site

Before producing a brief for the architect, a decision on the siting of the facility has to be made. Ideally the site should be chosen to meet the requirements of the facility rather than vice versa, but this will depend on the availability of sites and the options they offer. In practice if only one site is available it may have some influence on the design of the centre, although as with the availability of finance the ramifications of any changes should be carefully considered. An awareness of the possible sites in the area, where the centre is to be built should, therefore, occur prior to the feasibility study although it should not affect the outcome of the study at this stage since a knowledge of what *should* be built is necessary for the full implications of any changes in design to be apparent.

Location and siting is all-important. Conrad Hilton is reputed to have said that there were three factors that constitute a successful hotel which were, 'location, location, location'. A local authority leisure centre is a civic building supreme – a building for people, if ever there was one.

Factors that may be taken into consideration when choosing a site in the area required are: the preferred site area and shape – its accessibility to the community it is intended to serve, in terms of roads, footpaths, public transport etc. – its accessibility to contractors – the availability of services e.g. water, power, telephone lines, sewers – environmental factors – housing and amenities for staff – planning restrictions – restrictive covenants – ground conditions – and above all the awareness factors that will attract people to visit the facility, such as being in the eye of people going to work, to school or to the shops.

12.8.6 Financial considerations

Having ascertained the approximate size, scale and nature of the centre and its facilities, the staffing levels and shift patterns, and the estimated throughput and utilization, it should be possible to make a rough estimate of:

1. The *capital expenditure* and an estimate of equipment costs.
2. *Recurrent expenditure* – the staffing, heating, lighting, cleaning, maintenance, loan charges, and other costs per annum.
3. *Income* – again this can only be calculated roughly, but a knowledge of the probable programme and usage should be adequate for an estimate.

12.8.7 Decision to go ahead

With local authority recreation facilities, decisions whether to go ahead or not inevitably revolve around political and financial decisions. If the money can be found within the term of office of the majority party that has proposed the development, then the decision will be a financial one.

Problems arise if sufficient funds are *not* available to build the facility that is required to satisfy the community's recreation needs (an investigation into the possible *additional* sources of funds, e.g. Sports Council, Arts Council, inner city partnership, Urban Aid etc. should have been undertaken prior to this). In this situation there are a number of possibilities.

1. To *reduce the scale* of the centre perhaps eliminating certain facilities. The problem here is to what extent any reduction will affect the needs of the community. There will be a need to amend the centre's objectives, programming and staffing and the new design will have to be adapted to suit these. In other words any cutbacks should ideally start with the objectives and programming, with the centre being redesigned accordingly. If there are substantial cuts than it will be necessary also to return to the strategy plan and amend it accordingly, noting the recreational deficiencies that still exist owing to the limitations of the centre.

2. To *design in phases* with future extensions in mind. The design, however, should incorporate all the stages so that when the centre has finally been completed it will operate as an efficient and effective single unit. Inevitably changes in objectives, programming and staffing will have to take place, but should always be done with the final structure in mind.

3. To *shelve the project* until sufficient funds are available. There may come a point where the limitations on capital expenditure are so restrictive that the nature of the centre will have to be radically altered in order to come within these limits. In such a case it must be seriously considered whether or not to go ahead with the project since the final product may bear little resemblance to that which is actually required by the community. It may be considered prudent to reallocate the funds to other projects and wait until the necessary finance does become available.

Finally there may be financial restrictions imposed on the revenue budget – a centre may be required to make a profit, break even, or make a limited loss. The implications of such financial objectives on the centre's objectives, programme, staffing and consequently design, must be considered in the same way as those on capital expenditure.

12.8.8 The appointment of the manager

The date the facility manager is appointed will depend at which stage it is decided to go ahead with the project and this may depend ultimately on the feasibility study. In any case it should be no later than this stage (i.e. the go-ahead) and certainly prior to the preparation of the detailed schedule of accommodation towards which the manager will contribute both knowledge and experience.

12.8.9 The architect's brief, including schedule of accommodation

The brief is not just a schedule of accommodation. Nor is a brief a static, inflexible list. A brief needs to be developed from the aims and objectives of the facility to the user, management and operational needs. The manager's contribution is invaluable. The more client information that is available for the architect the better. The brief to the architect should include both the feasibility study and the schedule of accommodation. The brief should include the following aspects: project objectives – project description – operating information – design policy – site factors – space needs – service needs – preferences in structure, finishes, components – specifications and standards – programme requirement – statutory requirements – contractual requirements – and the schedule of accommodation.

(a) Schedule of accommodation

The schedule needs to be considered in detail in order that the final design actually 'works'. Small omissions or mistakes in design can cause big management headaches when they are transformed into bricks and mortar. In addition, with a good design brief the architect's first set of plans should be as close as possible to the design and management requirements.

The schedule of accommodation should detail the facilities required, their relationship to one another, their size, their service requirements (heating, lighting, power points, sanitation, ventilation etc.), the type of finishes required (for flooring, walls, toilet cubicles, changing cubicles, reception desk etc.), the number of people to be accommodated in each facility or area, and so on.

Consideration must be given to every aspect of design that will affect the management operation, and achievement of objectives of the centre. One way to cover some of these points is for the Recreation Manager to imagine the position of the various people who will have dealings with the centre. For instance, he or she can consider the position of a centre *user* and then ask the following questions. If I come by car where do I park? How do I get from my car to the centre entrance? Where do I pay? How do I get from the reception area to the changing rooms? Where do I put my valuables? Where are the toilets? If I am playing squash how do I get to the courts? If I finish at the same time as other people will there be enough showers? If I want a drink how do I get from the changing room to the bar? How do I get from the bar to the way out?

These types of question can be asked for users of the various facilities, for groups and families, for the two sexes, for people coming to entertainment events or spectator events, for people coming on foot or by bike.

The same sorts of question can be asked for the *staff*, for instance, for the receptionist: Where do I park? Where do I put my coat? How well can I control the entrance and exit to the centre? Can I reach the telephone, booking sheets, equipment for hire, typewriter and money till without inconvenience or leaving anything unsupervised? Where do I have my cup of tea? How do I contact the duty manager or make an announcement? What happens in an emergency?

Again this can be done for the other members of staff, the cleaners (How easy is the centre to clean? What sort of equipment will I need? Is the store big enough for this equipment? Are there enough power points? Where do I put the rubbish?), the supervisors, the delivery men, the ambulance men in an emergency, the disabled, the last person to lock up (Is there a light switch near the door?) and so on.

Consideration should also be taken of legislative and licensing requirements e.g. for the bar, for entertainments, fire regulations, the *Health and Safety at Work Act*.

(b) Manager and architect

If possible, the final brief should include the operational experience of the manager *and* the design experience of the architect. These twin experience elements should be harnessed. The building is a tool for management; the manager must take over the driving wheel. Experience will teach that the leisure centre must be robust. It will attract millions of attendances over the first few years, let alone a lifetime. It must be designed to take in long-term flexibility so that it can be expanded and changed, if necessary, in years to come – the design must have extendability. As we have seen the manager's input can include his or her knowledge relating to circulation, staffing, maintenance, administration, finishes, specialist equipment (such as tracking for dividing screens), good visual controls, storage, changing, programme requirements and a host of important operational details. Architects with experience will appreciate that while their leisure centre may be designed on open-plan lines, with the atmosphere and ambience for leisure enjoyment and with good contact between participants and spectators, that separate entities must work independently without interference with each other but each drawing from communal essential services. Hence, *both manager and architect input, before completion of the detailed brief, are essential*.

The cost of leisure building in the early 1960s was in the region of £20 per square metre. In 1985 it can cost £750 per square metre for a high standard leisure building. Good planning design and management based on sound recreation principles will ensure that money is well spent and that good lasting standards are achieved.

12.8.10 Appointment of the architect

Designing a leisure centre is a specialized job and should be handled by architectural teams that have the capability *and* a proven record so that they can design on the lessons of experience. When considering which architects to use, (even if in-house architects are available) it would be wise to obtain a shortlist of firms from the Royal Institute of British Architects (RIBA)/Sports Council or Arts Council and to visit the architectural practices and the centres they have designed. It will be important also to take references and learn from those who have to live with their designs. In this way architects can be chosen on merit *and* on their standards.

12.9 THE RECREATION CENTRE: SUMMARY

This chapter has traced the recreation centre movement over the past 25 years. The movement developed rapidly over the late 1960s and early 1970s. A number of changes in provision, in design and management have been shown. In particular the movements from singular to joint planning, from sports centres to leisure centres and from structured physical recreation to greater social recreation have occurred. However, there has been little coordination in the field and a whole series of 'one-off'' projects have been built and many of the recreation centres have not been thoroughly planned. The economic recession and the spiralling costs of energy, manpower and building means that every attempt must be made to get the best value for money in meeting the needs of the community via recreation facilities and programmes.

The recreation centre movement has given policy-makers and planners greater opportunity to meet community needs. It has given architects the chance to make new responses to community problems. It has given managers the opportunity to offer a wide and varied choice of activity and programme. Recreation facilities can be further improved by recognizing the interrelationship between policy, planning, design and management.

REFERENCES AND NOTES

1. Department of Education and Science and Ministry of Housing and Local Government (1964), Joint Circular 11/64 – *Provision of Facilities for Sport*, Department of Education and Science, London.
2. Department of Education and Science (1970), Circular 2/70 *The Chance to Share*, Department of Education and Science, London.
3. Select Committee of the House of Lords (1973), *Report on Sport and Leisure 2nd Report*, HMSO, London.
4. Command 6200 (1975), *Sport and Recreation*, HMSO, London.

5. Association of County Councils, Association of District Councils and Association of Metropolitan Authorities (1976), *Towards a Wider Use*, The Associations, London.

6. Munn, J. in several presentations during the late 1970s on behalf of the Borough of Torfean.

7. Prescott-Clarke, P. and Grimshaw, P. (1977), *Sport, School and the Community*, Research Working Paper No. 9, Sports Council, London.

8. Whaley, B. (1980), *Sports Centre Planning and Provision in England and Wales*, dissertation, University of Birmingham.

9. Sports Council (1975), (1978), *Sport for All in Converted Buildings*: Volumes 1 and 2, Sports Council, London.

10. Veal, A.J. (1979), Sports Council Study 20: *Six examples of Low Cost Sports Facilities*, Sports Council, London.

11. Quoted by John English, the first Director of Midland Arts Centre for Young People, in presentations to visitors during the late 1960s.

12. The Press Office, Barbican Arts Centre, July 1985.

13. Veal, A.J. (1981), *Sports Centres in Britain – A Review of User Studies*, draft report to the Sports Council.

14. Birch, J.G. (1971), *Sports Council Study 1: Indoor Sports Centres*, for the Department of the Environment, HMSO, London.

15. Built Environmental Research Group, Polytechnic of Central London (1977), *The Changing Indoor Sports Centre. Sports Council Study 13*, Sports Council, London.

16. Built Environment Research Group, Polytechnic of Central London (1978), *Sports Council Study 15: Sport for All in the Inner City*, Sports Council, London.

17. Built Environment Research Group, Polytechnic of Central London (1978), *Sports Council Study 14: Sport in a Jointly Provided Centre*, Sports Council, London.

18. Public Attitude Surveys Ltd, (1979), *Sports Council Study 19: Leisure Pools*, Sports Council, London.

19. Atkinson, J. and Collins, M.F. (1980), *The Impact of Neighbouring Sports and Leisure Centres*, Sports Council, London.

20. Arrowsmith, G. (1980), Research Working Paper 17: *Sports Usage and Membership at a Large Urban Complex: Billingham Forum*, Sports Council, London.

21. Jenkins, C., Bonser, K., Knapp, B., and Collins, M.F. (1981), *Sports Council Study 23: The Impact of Rugby Sports Centre*, Sports Council.

22. Scottish Sports Council, (1980), *A Question of Balance*, Volumes 1 and 2, Scottish Sports Council, Edinburgh.

23. Sports Council for Wales (1978), *Sports Centre Users: A Comparative Study*, Sports Council for Wales, Cardiff.

24. Collins, M.F. (1981), *What business are we in?*, paper presented at the Association of Recreation Managers Seminar, November 1981, Lytham.

25. Coopers and Lybrand Associates (1981), *Sharing does work: Sports Council Study 21*, Sports Council, London.

26. The Sports Council (1971), *Sport in the Seventies – Making Good the Deficiencies*, Sports Council, London.

27. Eastern Council for Sport and Recreation (1979), *Sports Centre Design with Management in Mind*, (Chairman: Margaret Hutton), written in conjunction

with the Association of Recreation Managers (Eastern Region) and the Eastern Council for Sport and Recreation, Bedford.

28. Boothby, J., Tungatt, M., Townsend, A.R. and Collins M.F. (1981), *A Sporting Chance: Sports Council Study 22*, Sports Council, London.

29. Cowling, D., Fitzjohn, M. and Tungatt, M. (1982), *Identifying the Market: Sports Council Study 24*, Sports Council, London.

30. The Sports Council (1982) *Sport in the Community – The Next Ten years*, Sports Council, London.

31. The Sports Council (1983) *A Forward Look. Rolling Programme 1983–88*, Sports Council, London.

★

PART FIVE

Management

★

The objectives of Part Five are to describe the principles of
management and their relationship to recreation, to consider
some general management factors which apply to all
managers, such as leadership and decision-making and to
look at specific management tasks in the recreation setting.
Chapter 13 deals with management principles and functions
and how recreation management can benefit from these.
Chapters 14, 15, 16 and 17 consider four important
recreation management functions, namely programming,
staffing, marketing and the organization of events. Practical
examples are taken from recreation situations particularly
those from purpose-built facilities like recreation centres.

Two main principles appear to be predominant: the
need for objectivity − planning, controlling and evaluating −
and the need to be people orientated − to have the ability
to motivate and handle staff and customers.

Finally in Chapter 18 a broad view of the recreation
management training scene is taken. The need for direction
and coordination and the formulation of appropriate
training schemes and a career structure are evident.

Chapter 13

Management

★

*If you are not contributing
to the solution of the problem
then you are part
of the problem yourself*

Chinese proverb

★

13.1 INTRODUCTION

Good management of recreation is concerned with setting goals and meeting objectives and targets, achieving optimal use of resources, achieving financial objectives, meeting priority needs and offering the most attractive services to meet recreational demands. In order to manage recreational resources, services and purpose built facilities managers need to understand the concept of management and the skills and techniques of management to achieve goals and objectives.

The quality of management determines to a large extent the type of use and viability of recreation resources and facilities. It is a key component whether facilities are large or small, whether they are run publicly, commercially or privately, whether they are run by a management committee, board of directors or an owner–manager.

Many recreation facilities in the United Kingdom, which have been poorly designed or have been adapted or converted to recreational use have become hubs of enterprising community programmes. This has been achieved through good management. In contrast some well-designed facilities with poor management have become lack-lustre community facilities with programme, staffing and viability problems.

Management is usually considered in terms of economic efficiency. Drucker [1] claims that it can only justify its existence by the economic results it produces. There may be greater non-economic results such as the contribution to community welfare but management has failed, according to Drucker, if it fails to produce economic results. It must supply goods and services which the public wants, at a price the consumer is willing to pay.

However, 'people service' programmes, such as many aspects of recreation management, differ in some fundamental respects from a commercial profit-orientated company. In human service programmes 'profit' needs to be defined in terms, not just of money, but in terms of a whole range of other additional criteria, for example, the physical, social and psychological benefits offered by the programme, the range of users attracted, meeting targets for, say, the socially deprived or the handicapped, improving performance, the numbers attracted from the locality it serves, and so on. Here targets are varied and *include* the level of viability aimed for. Extending this idea, some have tried to place an actual financial value on recreation participation.

David Gray is quoted [2] as saying:

'We desperately need a method of planning that permits social cost–benefit analysis. Lacking such a system we are turning control of our social enterprises over to the accounting mind. The accounting mind reaches decisions by a method in which short-range fiscal consequences are the only criterion of value . . . Recreation and park services will not survive in that kind of environment. Most of the great social problems that disfigure our national life cannot be addressed in a climate dominated by that kind of value system'.

Similarly Robert Wilder [3] states: 'The modern day name of the game seems to be quantification, justification, competition and cost-benefit analysis'. In search of a management tool by which to measure recreational benefits in terms of 'profit', Wilder has presented his 'Economic Equivalency Index' (EEI) which attempts to quantify recreation value in financial terms.

Management, therefore, can be considered to consist of general as well as specialist actions and processes, e.g. being 'profit' orientated. This chapter is concerned with some of these main general aspects of management, *First*, the management process is described. *Second*, traditional principles and functions of management are considered. *Third*, the job of managing people and the need for appropriate styles of management to meet different situations are taken into account. *Fourth*, two of the primary functions of management – leadership and decision-making – are studied. *Fifth*, the value of good communication within and between groups is discussed. *Finally*, the functions of management in the recreation setting are briefly introduced in anticipation of the chapters to follow on the programming and staffing aspects of recreation management.

13.2 THE MANAGEMENT PROCESS

Management is both an *active human occupation* and a *process* by which people and organizations achieve results.

Management is a distinct type of work. The ability to do a job is not enough. The good physical education teacher, swimming coach, librarian or sports administrator does not automatically make the good manager. While technical 'know-how' is important, management is more – it concerns the work of people, it concerns effectiveness and accountability for end results [4].

What is the distinct type of work which relates to the manager? Management is *not* a science, with precise laws and predictable behaviour. No foolproof rules exist which can replace the need for judgement, common sense and related experience. Management is *not* an art, if by that we imply intuition and individual judgement only, on the thesis that 'managers are born and not made'. Management is *not* a profession with a code of ethics, standards and ideals. Management appears to be a bit of each. 'It is the sum of art and science that makes a manager.'

While management is fundamentally concerned with human

behaviour, behaviour is not constant. Management situations vary. Management is concerned with change; it is continually flowing and interacting. Drucker emphasized this aspect of management:

'The job of management is never to be concerned with restoring or maintaining normality because normality is the condition of yesterday. The major concern of management, if they are to make their business effective, must be in the direction of systematically trying to understand the condition of the future so that they can decide on the changes that can take their business from today into tomorrow.'

Management is, therefore, a *continuous process*. It is both human behaviour and a continual process. It is both flexible and changeable. It needs a framework, core elements, basic functions and logic to achieve its results, for management is a *means* towards *ends*.

Management can operate directly, by the application of effort to secure the desired result, or indirectly, by creating those conditions conducive to producing the required results. In order to manage organizations, services and programmes effectively there must, then, be a clear understanding of the management process and aims by all those within the organization. This is especially relevant in organizations giving services, which call for high levels of motivation, work entailing much of the 'voluntary' spirit and duties often spreading into unsocial hours. Recreation services are a case in point. In addition, understanding something of the essence of the management process renders many of the management concepts and functions less obscure and lifeless. Management is often a matter of adjusting to change and changing conditions, and so gives few opportunities for precise measurement and experiments which provide the basis of scientific evidence. Nevertheless, scientific techniques are now indispensable to many enterprises. Scientific method is *objective*, it weighs evidence; it tests conclusions.

13.2.1 Management of changing situations

Management has been defined in a whole variety of ways; some explain its purpose at great length, others more directly. Drucker [5], for example, states that management is 'a multi-purpose organ that manages a business *and* manages managers *and* manages workers and work'. If *one* of these is omitted we would not have management or a business enterprise, according to Drucker. Here management is seen as a structure with functions. Later we will see management described more in terms of a process. Discussions on management often start with a search for the best definition of the word. A cursory look at dictionary definitions illustrates the problem. The verb 'to manage' can mean 'to direct', 'to handle', 'to influence', 'to exert control', 'to make submissive', 'to contrive', 'to use economically and with forethought, 'to cope with'. One can 'manage to make a muddle', 'succeed in one's aim', 'make proper use of' and 'manage on one's own'. Managing, therefore, has diverse meanings and differing interpretations. It also has varied interpreters. Its functions are changing, fluid and subtle.

Management, thus, depends on a variety of factors, for example, the situation, the information available, the people involved, the organization *and* the people doing the managing. In some significant measure, management depends on the person or persons doing the managing – management relates to people's behaviour. This conditions any definition of management. The qualities found in the good manager are, therefore, important in any definition of management.

What appears to be abundantly clear is that there is no *one* way, no one instant brew for instant management, no one management principle right every time. Management is malleable, amenable to change, flexible in organization. It has many functions. The manager is not just a creator, but also a planner and forecaster; setting objectives, motivating, leading, deciding, checking and monitoring performance. Management – in the simple idiom of today – is *getting things done with and through people*. As such management is a social process.

13.3 THE PRINCIPLES OF MANAGEMENT IN HISTORICAL PERSPECTIVE

Contemporary management practices have been influenced by many schools of management thought. The management 'movement' has progressed from the 'scientific movement' instigated by Frederick Taylor [6] and others at the turn of the century, through the 'human relations movement' influenced by Elton Mayo [7] and the now legendary Hawthorne studies, through the 'classical movement' stressing organization and administration and influenced by Henri Fayol [8] and Max Weber [9] to the behaviourist view of management put forward by Douglas McGregor [10] and Frederick Herzberg [11] who built on the inspiration of Abraham Maslow [12,13].

13.3.1 The 'scientific movement'

There is no unified theory of management. There is a diversity of management ideas. Frederick Taylor dominated the beginning of what has become to be known as the 'scientific movement' from the turn of the century until the 1920s. Many of Taylor's ideas are management foundation stones for many organizations and enterprises that sprang up in the first decades of this century. Time study was the basis for Taylor's system and the term 'time and motion study' emanates from his system. His was a system of reward: a fair day's work for a fair day's pay; the higher the productivity the higher the pay. The belief was born that optimum work environments would enhance productivity. However, one movement in particular – the 'human relations movement' – was to challenge some of the foundations of the scientific movement.

13.3.2 The 'human relations movement'

In the 1920s and early 1930s experiments were conducted at the Western Electric Company in Hawthorne, Illinois on the effects of lighting conditions and employee productivity. An experimental group of women worked in one room; a control group of women worked in another room. Lighting conditions were varied in the experimental group. It was discovered that not only did improved illumination result in improved productivity, but that *all* changes to illumination resulted in improvements, including levels of illumination which were highly unfavourable. In addition, it was discovered that as well as increased production in the experimental group the same improvements occurred in the control group. Researchers from Harvard led by Elton Mayo were called in to continue the studies [7]. After the illumination experiments other variables were also manipulated. For example, the experimental group were given scheduled work breaks, shorter working weeks and other benefits. Again productivity increased both in the experimental group *and* the control. Mayo's researchers then removed all the benefits from the experimental group. Yet again production increased in *both* groups.

What were the reasons for these effects? With the power of the trade unions today and the need for fair treatment for all employees we might not expect to find such results. Why had attitudes to work changed in this situation? Mayo's methodology was to spend considerable time in interviewing both the experimental group *and* the control group. Employees were made to feel that the company *genuinely cared* for them, cared about their problems and their feelings. Management were seen to be concerned about employees as people. The improved *social* conditions appeared to be more important than improved physical and environmental conditions. Hence came the dawn of the 'human relations movement' and the discovery that *the informal* organization and the *quality* of supervision had a highly significant effect on morale and productivity. This realization was one of the pivots in the human relations school of management – inter-personal relationships are important; management is a people-orientated business.

The paternalistic concern of management seen in Chapter 2 in relation to industrial recreation may well be one of the products of this management movement. Many businesses look to providing a good working environment, offer fringe benefits, social benefits and appear to show genuine concern for workers at work and away from work. Recreation services are people-orientated businesses with considerable face-to-face work and should benefit from such approaches to management.

The human relations movement has, however, had its critics. How widespread were the experiments? Are all satisfied employees the most productive? Mayo's concern for style of supervision, human relationships and employee welfare had challenged the doctrine of the scientific movement; in turn this people-centred movement was challenged by what has come to be known as the 'classical movement'.

13.3.3 'Classical' management theory

Classical management theory is concerned with the efficient design and structure of organizations – the administration of the business. Building on Taylor's theories, the Frenchman Henri Fayol had an important influence on management thinking. He emphasized five management processes which were applicable to any field of endeavour which required management:

1. *Planning* – examining the future and drawing up a plan of action.
2. *Organizing* – building up the structure of both people and material resources.
3. *Commanding* – instilling initiative, motivating, leading.
4. *Coordination* – unifying and harmonizing activity and effort.
5. *Controlling* – conforming to the plan and established principles.

To assist managers Fayol added 14 functions as management guidelines, which included concepts such as 'discipline', 'unity of command' and the 'scalar chair' (chain of command): these will be discussed in Chapter 15 in relation to staffing. Fayol's 'principles', which he saw as guidelines, were interpreted as the 'laws of the game'; suffering the same fate as the planning approaches (discussed in Chapter 11), being treated as fixed standards.

Weber's ideal organization was the bureaucratic administrative structure. As Wren [9] points out: 'Bureaucracy was conceived as a blueprint for efficiency which would emphasize rules rather than men'.

Classical theory is thus concerned with structures and hierarchy. Its fundamental principles have had profound effects on government and industry. Local government and hence public recreation services conform to formal structures, organizational charts, hierarchical structures. Considerable support is given to these structures: people know exactly where they stand and what is expected of them; they know their station, their role and their influence; their jobs are defined.

Classical management structuring appears to neglect a people-orientation. It is mechanistic. It is bureaucratic and hence red taped.

Formal structures have an effect on workers in that work tends to be put into its tight categories; departments tend to be subdivided into units; labour is divided in specialisms; inflexibility is encouraged and top to bottom chains of control become sacrosanct. In public recreation services we find that so-called comprehensive departments may well be a series of tightly closed administrative boxes and specialisms e.g. administration, finance, programming, catering and maintenance without lateral linking, or they are divided into parks, baths, youth, aged, able, handicapped – all acting out separate roles in separate units.

13.3.4 The 'behaviourist' view of management

One of the latest management movements is that towards a 'behaviourist' approach which has been in vogue since the early 1950s. It arose, in part, in opposition to the rigid structuring and organizational character of classical methods. It was felt that organization structures should be tempered with flexibility and a greater concern for employee involvement. The inherent possibilities for closed systems and discord needed to be eliminated; harmony would lead to improved work and work relationships. McGregor [10] Herzberg [11] Argyris [14] Likert [15] and others have enlarged management thinking within the behavioural approach, inspired by the work of psychologists such as Erich Fromm and Abraham Maslow and the human relations work of Elton Mayo. Maslow's concern that man should be 'self-actualized' whether at work or play led to the kind of thinking which stressed working patterns which encouraged people to express themselves in work and in leisure.

In an affluent society most physical and safety needs have been consistently satisfied; consequently it is the social and ego needs which are dominant. *Recreation Managers, like most other people, want to be recognized as individuals, to have some measure of control over the decisions in their working environment and their own jobs, to accomplish something worthwhile – to see themselves in something that is successful and meaningful.* The value system of managers has changed and is changing constantly.

McGregor adding support to the work of Maslow and influenced by the Hawthorne studies makes two basic approaches to management based on two main assumptions about human behaviour in his theory of motivation. The traditional value system of managers he labelled 'Theory X', which he believes is no longer applicable in today's management of people. He proposed his 'Theory Y' as the most appropriate alternative. The theory Y manager sees work as a natural part of life.

Theory X   This is the traditional view of direction and control. People are said to be lazy and have an inherent dislike of work. Most people have to be coerced, controlled, directed and even threatened before effort is made towards the achievement of organizational objectives. The theory also suggests that people prefer to be directed, respond when disciplined, wish to avoid responsibility, have relatively little ambition and want security above all else. In essence, theory X is the 'stick-and-carrot' approach, the carrot being money or reward and the stick being the threat of financial insecurity. McGregor believes that this must be replaced in modern management by theory Y.

Theory Y   This, in contrast, is the theory of the integration of individual and organizational goals. Effort in work is as natural as play or rest. External controls are not the only means for bringing about effort towards objectives. People can exercise self-direction and self-control when commitment is high. They respond to honest praise and resent punishment. Moreover, people learn, under proper conditions, not only to accept but also to seek responsibility; the capacity to exercise a relatively high degree of imagination, ingenuity and creativity in the solution of organizational problems is widely, not narrowly, distributed in the population, as the old style management of 'leaders' and 'followers' suggests.

Theory X managers will tend to *push* people to achieve a task.
Theory Y managers will tend to *lead* people to achieve a task.

It is clear that X and Y represent polarities which no managers can exclusively operate under. However, McGregor claimed that those managers operating predominantly towards the principles of theory Y were generally more successful in the following ways: their departments had higher outputs, staff showed greater motivation, there were fewer labour problems, lower labour turnovers, less waste and greater profits.

While X and Y share some of the same management goals, theory Y includes: 'The essential task of management is to arrange organizational conditions and methods of operation so that people can achieve their own goals *best* by directing *their own* efforts towards organizational objectives' [10].

McGregor's work has been enlarged by Likert [15], whose concepts are presented in four management systems: *system 1* 'exploitative – authoritative', *system 2* 'benevolent – authoritative', *system 3* 'consultative' and *system 4* 'participative'. Theory X is implicit in the autocratic first system; theory Y has the essential elements for the participative fourth system.

Likert shows that the nearer the management system is to system 4, the more productive the organization. It produces lower costs, higher earning, better union relations, more positive worker attitudes and higher morale. Conversely, the nearer the management is to system 1, the more it results in lower productivity, higher costs, poorer union relations and resulting lower morale.

The findings of McGregor and Likert confirm that more effective results can be obtained in industry by a people-orientated approach to management. That being the case then the implications for recreation service management could be considerable. If humanistic approaches to management can prove more effective in product-orientated industries, they should produce *more effective results* in service-orientated organizations such as those found in the public recreation 'industry', particularly as people are far more likely to express views and to exhibit wider forms of behaviour patterns.

Herzberg's theory of motivation relates to two main job satisfaction parameters: *hygiene factors* and *motivators* [11]. Hygiene factors are not part of the actual job but relate to the work environment in its many forms – policies, conditions, relationships, fringe benefits and so on. These factors may affect job performance but are not part of the job itself. Motivators on the other hand are concerned with the job. Is the job challenging? Does it carry responsibility, recognition for achievement, give prestige and esteem? Herzberg is concerned with job enrichment but his theory is limited by being preoccupied with just two strands of employment conditions.

Argyris [14] building on Maslow's self-actualization theme believes that job enrichment will increase employee initiatives and self direction. There would appear to be much in common between Maslow's theory, the ideas of Argyris, McGregor's theory Y and Likert's system 4. They are all concerned with job enlargement, job enrichment and self-fulfilment. But what becomes of these ideals in the practical world of budgets, cut-backs, redundancies, cuts in public expenditure, reductions in manpower in the recreation field and greater costs for less services? In the harsh world of recession the cry from industry is for greater output at less cost. Can the tenets of the 'behaviourist' management school, concerned with life satisfactions, still hold true for recreation services? The Recreation Manager has an even greater role to play in harder times.

13.4 MANAGEMENT FUNCTIONS AND PRACTICES

Most businesses and public recreation services appear to be based on classicial management theory. Many writers have revised Fayol's original model but generally the framework and logic have remained intact. For example, the essential first level functions of management were summarized by Fordham [4] as:

1. Planning (forecasting, setting objectives, establishing policies).
2. Execution (implementation of policies in an agreed manner).
3. Control (monitoring of performance and continued response to change).

The functions of management are seen as important because they are the *constituents* of every management job. The emphasis they receive, however, will vary according to the type of job, the level of the manager, the nature of the environment and many other factors.

It would appear that the classical principles of management theory adapted and modified to meet the needs of different organizations can be used as a basic framework for the management of recreation services, facilities and programmes. The processes of:

1. conceptualizing,
2. establishing objectives,
3. carrying out the plan and obtaining results through people,
4. seeking improvements and appraising results,
5. assisting subordinates and inspiring and motivating them,

would seem to have considerable relevance to management in the leisure and recreation field.

13.4.1 Management: a continuous and circular function

A model presented by MacKenzie [16] as 'The Management Process in 3-D' in *Harvard Business Review* illustrates a well-accepted traditional process of management. In the model, management is conceived as a *core* of three fundamental elements, namely: 'ideas', 'things' and 'people'. These core elements each have *main tasks, continuous functions* and *sequential functions*. The management process is conceived as a continuous and circular function: (Fig. 13.1).

1. Radiating from the core segment of *ideas*, the main task is that of conceptual thinking and formulating notions. The continuous management function is that of analysing problems, gathering facts, ascertaining causes, developing alternative solutions. The sequential function is planning. This leads to predetermining a course of action, forecasting, setting objectives, budgets, programming, procedures, allocating resources and standardizing methods.
2. Radiating from the core segments of *things* the main task is administration and executive affairs. The continuous management functions are making decisions, arriving at conclusions and judgements. The sequential function is organizing. This leads to arranging work to accomplish objectives, establishing structures, creating positions and defining responsibilities and authority.
3. Radiating from the core segment of *people* the major task is leadership. The continuous management function is influencing people to accomplish the desired goals, communicating with people and ensuring an understanding. The sequential functions are staffing, directing and controlling. The staffing category includes recruitment, selection, training and developing skills. The directing category includes

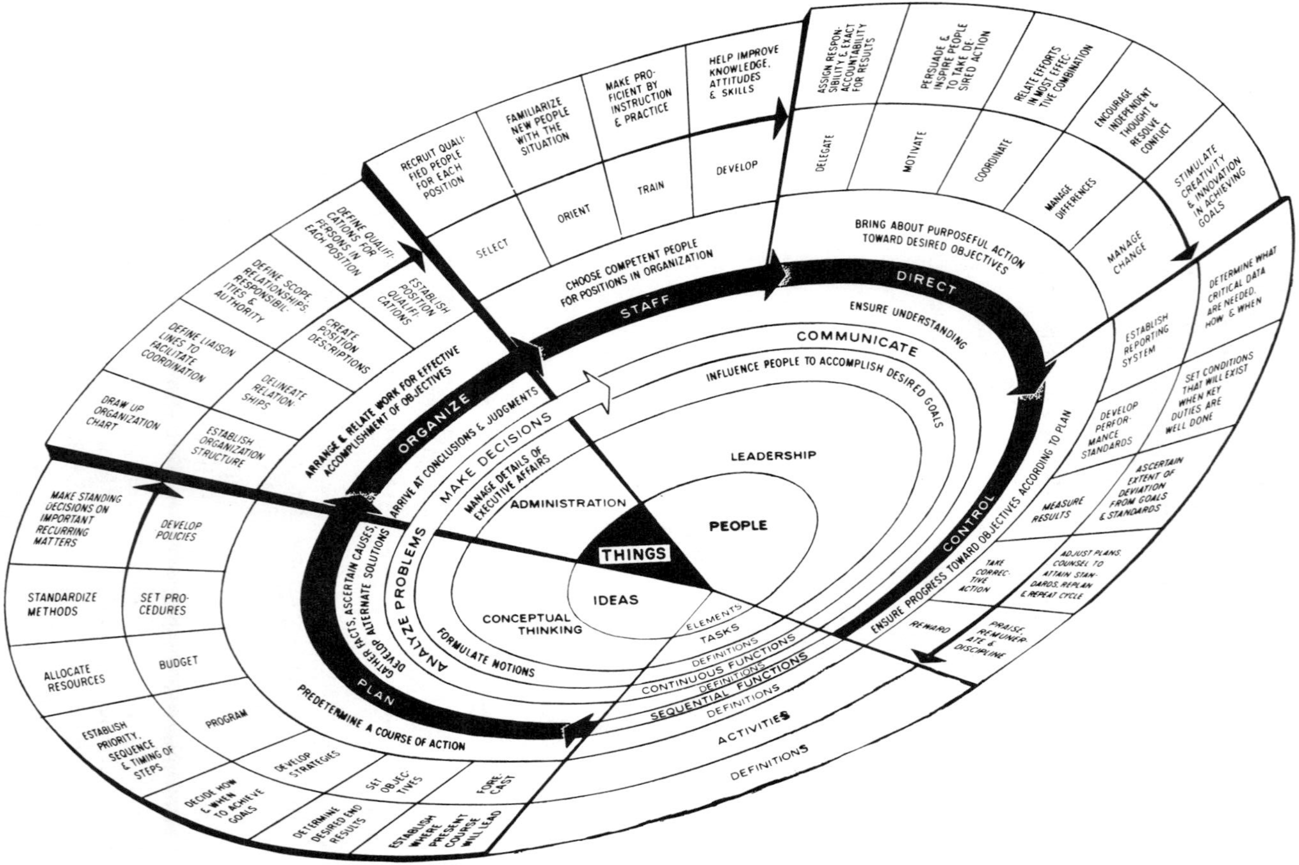

Fig. 12.1. The management process, in 2-D. Source: R. Mackenzie, Harvard Business Review [10]

delegating, motivating, coordinating and resolving conflicts. The control factors include establishing a reporting system, performance standards, measuring results, correcting and rewarding.

The study of traditional management theory, principles and functions reveals that there is a core of knowledge and skills that is needed for management at all levels. These core management tasks are basically of three types: conceptual, human and technical. In identifying these three areas Robert Katz confirms that individual management styles vary according to the management position one holds. This is illustrated in Fig. 13.2.

The Leisure Service Manager

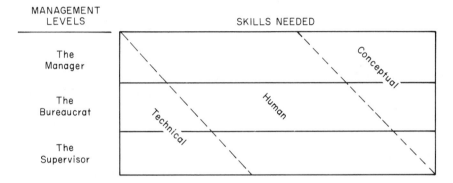

Fig. 13.2 Management skills. Adapted from Hershey, P. and Blanchard, K.H. *Management of organizational behaviour: utilizing human resources*, 2nd edn, p.9 (Edginton and Williams [27]).

The *conceptual* skills are developed on an understanding of the overall situations, the nature of the problems and complexities, and the ability to think clearly, analyse problems and plan carefully. These skills in formulating ideas and concepts determine the policies, orientation and objectivity of the organization, enterprise or programme being developed.

The *human* skills are concerned with people. They include the ability to select, develop, motivate, lead, decide, control and monitor performance. Managers must have good judgement and be able to work with and through people to meet objectives.

The *technical* skills are needed to incorporate experience and knowledge of the subject area, a sympathy with and understanding of the management environment and the methods and techniques which are needed to perform the tasks.

However, of critical importance is the appreciation that while management is concerned with planning, execution and control and is also with ideas, people and things, *management – in and of itself – is nothing*. It needs a situation, a context. *Management, therefore, is situational* – it needs something to manage. In this context, that 'something' is recreation, which needs both general and specialist management.

13.4.2   Management systems

While much management practice appears to be based on the classical movement, many additional management systems and techniques have been added to it or have been introduced in recent years and many have been influenced by the behavioural scientists.

Management by Objectives (MBO) has become a popular management system over the past two decades. So well-known has the term MBO become that there are a range of definitions of what it actually is. In addition several systems have been built upon the MBO technique of setting and achieving objectives. Some look to the system being a philosophy of management. Others take a more pragmatic view. George Odiorne [17], thought to be one of the founding fathers of the movement, defined MBO as: 'a process whereby the superior and subordinate managers of an organization jointly identify its common goals, define each individual's major areas of responsibility in terms of the results expected of him, and use these measures as guides for operating the unit and assessing the contribution of each of its members'. Whatever the differences of definition two main strands of MBO are linked as the cornerstones of the system: the setting of *objectives* and the *participation* by managers from all levels in an organization.

PPBS (Planning-Programming-Budgeting-Systems) is a specific method of applying systems theory, developed in the early 1960s by the US Department of Defence. Another method, *PERT (Programme Evaluation Review Technique)*, is a system of planning and control that uses mathematical concepts to identify key activities needed to accomplish a given project successfully. PERT incorporates a system known as *CPM (Critical Path Method)* which arranges activities in a flow sequence. These 'network' methods are more technically specific than *MBO* systems which involves the careful calculation of goals, methods of achieving them and evaluation of performance. (MBO is developed further in the next chapter in terms of programming by objectives).

13.5   MANAGEMENT STYLES

Management is a flexible commodity and must adapt to be appropriate to different situations. In addition different managers have different styles of management. The same manager may also have a number of different styles depending on the different situations. What is becoming clear is

Table 13.1 Adapted from *Situational Management*, by J. A. D'Arcy Cartwright [18].

The *Deserter* is a manager who lacks interest in both the task and relationships and often shows it. He or she is ineffective, not only because of the lack of interest but also because the effect of this on morale. Deserters shirk their own responsibilities and hinder the performance of others through intervention or by witholding information.

The *Bureaucrat* shows only tacit interest in the task and relationships. However, this manager is partially effective in that he or she follows the rules, maintains an air of interest and gets less personally involved in problems. The Bureaucrat goes through the right channels and is a stickler for detail. His or her orientation is to the rules of the game; statutes are dogma.

The *Missionary* is the kindly soul who puts happy relationships above all other considerations. Because of a low commitment to the task, a lack of responsibility in facing disagreements and an attitude to conflict which leads to poor management and low output, this manager is ineffective.

The *Developer* is one who places implicit trust in people. He or she is the 'effective cousin of the Missionary'. The difference between them is that the developer works with and motivates people in a given situation and develops the talents of others.

The *Autocrat* is one who puts the task above all other considerations, has no concern for relationships, he has no confidence in other people and is therefore ineffective. People fear and dislike the Autocrat, working only when pressured. The Autocrat has a powerful effect on the organization and does not know it. He or she helps to produce cliques, trouble-makers and deserters. 'At best he gets blind obedience, at worst he gets desertion.'

The *Benevolent Autocrat* places implicit trust in his or her own sound procedures. This is an effective manager whose main skill is getting other people to do what he or she wants them to do without resentment. Although like the task-orientated Autocrat, the approach is 'smoother'. Knows the job and the people and by and large gets the job done.

The *Compromiser* is both task and relationships orientated in situations where only one or the other is appropriate. Ambivalence and compromise appear to be his trademark. All that perpetuates mediocrity perpetuates the Compromiser's style.

The *Executive style* is reflected in the behaviour of the manager who sees the job as effectively maximizing the effort of others in both the short and long run task. He or she sets high standards for production and performance but recognizes that because of individual differences it is necessary to treat everyone a little differently. The Executive is effective in that commitment to both task and relationship is evident to all, and this acts as a powerful motivation. His or her effectiveness in obtaining results in both these dimensions also leads naturally to high production.

'Executive' management is often *team* management. The manager encourages participation and obtains commitment. He or she handles disagreement and conflicts as natural phenomena and through these situations achieves commitment and results. All the team feels intimately involved in both failures and successes.

---

that *a manager armed with only one style of management may be ill-equipped for the variety of different tasks and people to be handled.*

The Recreation Manager has different levels of staff. Many staff work long unsocial hours and undertake various types of work. The customers managers have to handle vary from individuals to groups, organized clubs, committees, governing bodies, councils and associations.

D'Arcy Cartwright [18] has made a colourful description of eight managerial styles: the 'Deserter', the 'Bureaucrat', the 'Missionary', the 'Developer', the 'Autocrat', the 'Benevolent Autocrat', the 'Compromiser' and the 'Executive', and these are described in Table 13.1. He preaches the style of the 'Executive'. It is task-objective, yet people-orientated in its approach to achieving the task. In this respect it is more closely linked to McGregor's theory Y and Likert's systems 3 and 4.

Is this also the style best suited to the Recreation Manager? It would seem that the exclusively task-centred, out-and-out *autocrat* may achieve some targets but he has many weaknesses. Within his staff there will be a high degree of scapegoating, little pride of ownership or personal commitment, and an unpleasant ethos. Staff will tend to refer to projects as 'mine' or 'theirs', not *'ours'*. There will be rigid lines of demarcation, lack of sensitivity and little flexibility.

The altogether *permissive* manager is even worse than the autocrat: Lacking interest; avoiding conflict; output is minimum; this manager is ineffective.

The *bureaucrat* is another poor manager but somewhat more effective, in that the objectives are at least recognized. But he or she lacks soul, flair and imagination. The bureaucrat knows the rules; there is *only* one, inflexible, channel. This is the kind of civil servant that saps managers' vitality in the myriad of red tape. Like some sports conventions, the rules and procedures appear more important than the game itself.

The *democratic* manager with the *executive style* is the most likely manager to succeed in the recreation business. He or she sees the job as effectively maximizing the efforts of others. He or she sets high standards for production and performance but recognizes that because of individual differences everyone must be treated a little differently but with the same fairness. This manager's commitment to both task and relationships is evident to all. He or she is not afraid of conflicts and recognizes them as important in understanding the task and the people; such behaviour is seen as normal and sometimes appropriate. Such managers often work with a *team*; they are concerned with participation and involvement; ideas can come from any quarter; the greater number of possibilities explored, the better the understanding of the problem. They still have to lead: the team cannot be hidden behind; they still have the ultimate decision but both manager and staff feel involved in the failures and successes. This style of management is an 'objective' art gained with experience and learning, allied to personal flair. Other styles of management will be far easier but it is this quality of management which is essential to the recreation service.

13.6 MANAGING PEOPLE:LEADERSHIP

To lead the people, walk behind them.

Lao-Tzu

This book is written for the people who work in recreation and leisure services at all levels of operation – top level directors and executives, senior managers, middle-managers and first-line managers, and those in the firing line who have the greatest face-to-face contact with the users and consumers.

The understanding of people and their motivations and the handling of people – staff and users – is probably the most important ingredient in the complex matrix that is good management. Thus, of the three core areas of skill the managers need – conceptual, human and technical – this chapter deals primarily with the human element. The conceptual ideas have been touched on in earlier parts of the book and will be drawn together in the next chapter in programme planning. The technical aspects are also considered in the chapters to follow.

13.6.1 Satisfying needs

In Chapters 9 and 10 it was shown how important it is for Recreation Managers to understand something of the needs of people and what motivates them to recreation. It was also shown how difficult it is to identify actual needs, which can be satisfied through recreation programmes and management. Yet management must begin with an attempt at understanding people.

Human behaviour depends on motivating factors, human needs and the factors affecting the individual's reactions to these needs. In Maslow's hierarchical needs model it was stated that the five levels in ascending order were physiological needs, safety needs, social needs such as belonging and acceptance, ego needs such as self-esteem and reputation and, at the apex of the model, the needs for self-actualization. In general it appeared that satisfied needs no longer motivate, but in practice complete satisfaction is rarely attained. Individuals are, however, more likely to do their work well when their basic needs are reasonably satisfied. Despite the problems associated with the theory, most researchers see the needs for self-esteem, self-fulfilment or *'self-actualization'*, and the social needs as being those that may find satisfaction through involvement in leisure and recreation.

The behavioural consequences of unsatisfied needs are complex and only partially understood. *Frustration* is a result of needs being unsatisfied. This in turn, if the frustration is fairly severe, can lead, it is widely thought (though it has not been conclusively proved) to a deterioration in work performance. Even more serious for the individual, prolonged frustration through creating inner conflict and anxiety can lead to real physical and mental illness, e.g. ulcers, neurosis.

There are four main characteristic outcomes of frustration: aggression, regression, fixation, and apathy or resignation. *Aggression* is a commonly encountered form of behaviour. The aggression can either be levelled directly against the source of the frustration or displaced against a substitute. If, because all external outlets are barred, or the source of the frustration is also admired, or the individual has been brought up to believe that any form of aggressiveness is wrong, then the aggression may turn inwards causing anxiety, low self-esteem and depression. This process is called introjection. *Regression* takes the form of primitive and childish behaviour. *Fixation* is the overwhelming compulsion to continue repeating a useless action or habit. It can be caused through excessive punishment. *Apathy or resignation* occurs after prolonged frustration and can affect the individual's whole attitude to life. People will give up the struggle and simply cease to care any more.

One of the main causes of frustration at work is bad leadership. Others, many of which result from poor leadership, include being prevented from completing a task, feeling a sense of failure and distrust of one's abilities, having one's drives towards self-expression and self-assertion curbed, inability to solve a task, and having no opportunity to use one's abilities freely.

13.6.2 Leadership

Management cannot be separated from leadership, though management is not leadership *per se*. Leadership has been described as a mixture of art, craft and humanity.

Management today is a complex phenomenon as we have seen. Leadership too is multi-faceted. In earlier decades there appeared to be a clear demarcation between 'leaders' and 'followers' based on traditions, class and upbringing, which divided 'boss' and 'workers'. In business management the leader was portrayed as a person, normally male, who was endowed with intelligence, initiative and the authority to lead men.

The task of managers in business industry and local authorities today calls for different styles of leadership. Take these statements for example: 'I'm paid to lead so I shall call the shots'; 'I delegate all departmental problems to departmental heads'; 'Consulting others wastes valuable time'; 'I always talk things over with my subordinates'. Each statement may be good leadership in particular situations.

Different styles of leadership will be appropriate to different situations. How can the modern manager be 'democratic' in dealings with subordinates and yet maintain the necessary authority and control in the organization to which he or she is responsible?

Over the past few decades has emerged the concept of 'group dynamics'. Social scientists revealed the importance of employee involvement and participation in decision-making. Democratic leadership began to be thought of as solutions coming from the ground floor and autocratic leadership attributed to the boss who makes most decisions himself. Generalizations, lacking research evidence, spoke in simplistic terms of leadership being either 'democratic' or 'autocratic' and even more misleading, these terms became, for some, synonymous with 'right' and 'wrong' styles of leadership and for others 'strong' leadership and 'permissive' leadership.

In answer to the question: 'What is leadership?' there appear to be three main schools of thought. First, leadership is a matter of *personal traits* (such as initiative, courage, intelligence). These traits must be possessed by individuals and then they are able to lead in most if not all situations. Second, who becomes the leader of a group and what the leadership characteristics are in the given case are a function of the specific situation. But *one person emerges* as the leader. Third, leadership is a *function*. Any or all of the members of the group may perform at various times specific leadership acts or functions which are necessary if the group's objectives are to be obtained. These functions include initiating, regulating, informing, decision-making and maintenance behaviour.

This third view of leadership appears to be currently accepted by most management educators as realistic and appropriate to a successful group in terms of achieving targets. However, all three views are relevant in given situations. Leadership, as well as being a function of management, is essentially human behaviour. The modern manager has to ask: 'what is the most appropriate leadership in this situation?' This brings us to leadership behaviour.

13.6.3 A leadership behaviour model

Robert Tannenbaum and Warren H. Schmidt [19] studied the range of behaviour adopted by leaders and presented the continuum or range of possible leadership behaviour available to a manager. In their model (see Fig. 13.3) each type of action is related to the degree of authority used by the boss and to the amount of freedom available to the subordinates in reaching decisions. Actions on the extreme left characterize the manager who maintains a high degree of control while those on the extreme right characterize the manager who releases a high degree of control.

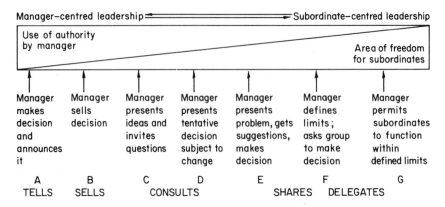

Manager–centred leadership ⇌ Subordinate–centred leadership

Manager makes decision and announces it	Manager sells decision	Manager presents ideas and invites questions	Manager presents tentative decision subject to change	Manager presents problem, gets suggestions, makes decision	Manager defines limits; asks group to make decision	Manager permits subordinates to function within defined limits
A	B	C	D	E	F	G
TELLS	SELLS	CONSULTS		SHARES	DELEGATES	

Fig. 13.3 Continuum of leadership behaviour. NB. Under F and G although the manager delegates he or she must still accept *full* responsibility. Adapted from Tannenbaum and Schmidt, *How to choose a Leadership Pattern* [19].

Within the continuum, Tannenbaum and Schmidt describe seven 'behaviour points':

1. *The manager makes the decision and announces it.* The manager identifies a problem, considers solutions, chooses one and reports the decision. No opportunity is given for subordinates to participate.
2. *The manager 'sells' the decision.* He or she identifies a problem and arrives at a decision. Instead of simply announcing it the manager tries to persuade the subordinates to accept it. Here he or she recognizes the possibility of some resistance and seeks to reduce it.
3. *The manager presents ideas and invites questions.* Subordinates are given opportunity for fuller explanations. The 'give and take' enables both manager and subordinates to explore more fully the implications of the decision.
4. *The manager presents a tentative decision subject to change.* Subordinates are able to exert some influence. Here the manager asks for frank reactions to a proposal, but reserves the right to make the final decision.
5. *The manager presents the problem, gets suggestions, and then makes a decision.* Up to this point the manager has come before the group with a solution of his or her own. Here staff have the opportunity to make suggestions as to the solutions. (For example: 'We are faced with long queues at reception and overcrowding in the changing rooms. Customers are complaining. What is wrong here? How do you think we can come to grips with the problem'?) The function of the group of staff becomes one of increasing the manager's range of possible solutions

and he will gain from the knowledge and first-hand experience of the staff in the 'firing line'. The manager then selects the solution.

6. *The manager defines the limits and requests the group to make a decision.* The manager passes to the group (possibly including himself or herself as a member) the right to make decisions. He or she defines the problem to be solved and the boundaries within which solutions can be found. (For example: 'The Arts Centre car park holds spaces for only 40 cars. Most of the space is being used by staff and helpers. We may be losing customers. We have space for a further 40 cars but only £1000 in the budget. Within the limits we can work out whatever solution makes the most sense to us. The trustees have agreed to back our decision.') In this situation the manager had decided that the problem should be worked out by the people involved. The problem is shared by the group and the decision is made by them.

7. *The manager permits the group to make a decision within prescribed limits.* This is the extreme degree of group freedom seldom encountered in business organizations and never encountered in, say, a local authority situation. In such a situation subordinates identify the problems, diagnose them and develop alternative strategies. Some might term this behaviour 'point' – abdication!

The continuum is important in several ways and in particular three main ways. First, it demonstrates that there are a *number of ways* in which a manager can relate to the group. At one end of the scale the emphasis is on the manager but as we move along the scale the focus is increasingly on the subordinates. In any situation, however, the manager must expect to be held responsible for the quality of the decisions made, even though operationally they may have been made on a group basis. The manager must accept and take the risk which is involved. *Delegation is not a way of 'passing the buck'*.

Second, it is important for the group to *recognize what kind of leadership is being adopted*. For example, if the manager has already decided what to do and wishes to inform them, it is absolutely right that this is done. To adopt a facade of involving the group in the decision-making process would be misleading and lead to considerable antagonism and frustration. The manager must be honest and clear in describing what authority he or she is keeping and what role the subordinates are being asked to assume.

Third, the democratic manager is not one who gives his or her subordinates the most decisions to make. That may be entirely inappropriate. There may be other more important priorities for them. The *quality* of involvement and decision-making is important. Low level decisions only, may simply prove to be patronizing.

13.6.4 Deciding how to lead

What factors should a manager consider in deciding how to lead? Much will depend on the circumstances. In emergencies, authoritative, autocratic leadership is eminently suitable. However, in longer-term organizational situations where leadership is an ongoing 'craft' and where the manager is working with and through other staff then there are four major factors which help to determine the style of leadership which is most appropriate: the personality, make-up and ability of *the manager*, the characteristics and ability of the *subordinates*, the characteristics of the *organization* and the nature of the *problem*.

(a) The manager

The manager's behaviour is a result of his or her personality, background, knowledge and experience. Among the significant internal forces are the manager's value system and the trust and confidence shown in the subordinates. For example, much will depend on the manager's strength of convictions, the importance attached to the personal, professional growth of the staff, the profits of the company or the service given to those who need most help.

(b) The subordinates

Assistant staff will have expectations of the manager. Each member of staff has his or her own personality and ability factors. The better the manager understands these forces within the group, the better his or her own part in achieving the best for subordinates and the organization can be determined.

Generally speaking, under the leadership continuum, the manager can permit subordinates greater freedom if the following conditions exist:

1. Assistant staff have high needs for independence.
2. There is a readiness to assume responsibility.
3. They have a high tolerance for ambiguity, preferring a wide area of freedom rather than all clear cut directives.
4. They have considerable interest in the problem and feel it is of importance.
5. They appreciate the goals of the organization.
6. They have sufficient knowledge.
7. They have been 'educated' to expect to share in decision-making; there is a climate of mutual confidence and respect.

(c) The Organization

In addition to the manager, the subordinates and their abilities to handle problems, management situations vary enormously. Much will depend on the organization itself, its aims and objectives and the efficiency of the group in given situations.

Organizations, such as a district council, will have traditional kinds of behaviour which are approved of and other kinds which are not. There may be a hierarchical structure where certain specialists, such as a greenkeeper or museum curator, are not part of the decision-making group. A commercially-orientated snooker and squash club may have appointed a manager who is, above all else, dynamic, decisive and persuasive. Leisure services departments within large authorities will have dispersed departments and sites which may preclude effective participatory decision-making. The organization and the efficiency of the group are then important considerations.

(d) The problem
The most important consideration is *the problem itself*. The nature of the problem will determine what degree of authority will be used – and the pressure of time. The problem itself may need specialist information or be of a complex nature involving many disciplines. The manager will need to be sure all the necessary knowledge is acquired within a given time. The pressure of time is often said to be the biggest headache, even though such pressures are sometimes self-imposed. With 'crisis' decisions a high degree of authority is likely. When time pressure is less intense, it becomes easier to bring others into a situation where group dynamics, skilfully handled, will become one of the tools to good management.

The forces of the manager, the subordinates and the situation, tend to determine the tactical behaviour of the effective manager, in relation to subordinates. *His or her behaviour, ideally, will be that which makes possible the most effective attainment of immediate objectives within the constraints faced.*

Day-to-day problems in the recreation field such as the upkeep and maintenance of the buildings and grounds, the staff systems, the programme, the handling of stock and the accounting for cash, will be more routine and administrative. A leadership pattern has been set and leadership choices are limited; changes are inappropriate.

However, long term decisions, strategies and solutions to new long range problems give opportunity to involve others in achieving goals more effectively. For example, a leisure centre's programme and system has been fixed for the coming 12 months, but a survey has indicated that only 25% utilization is being made by females and that the daytime use by shift workers, the unemployed and the retired is negligible. The manager is anxious to increase the proportions of these customers to meet the aims of the organization. He or she confers with the assistant managers, initially, and discusses with them the scope of the problem, the constraints to time and money and the need to acquaint the staff/user group with the problem.

Fig. 13.4 A leadership guideline and checklist to further illustrate the leadership task is shown in Table 13.2.

It is in the strategy and the tactics of handling the problem that the manager's leadership skills are put to the test. Can he or she raise the level of employee motivation? Can staff and key user groups be persuaded to accept change readily? Can the quality and effectiveness of managerial decisions be improved? Can teamwork and morale be developed? Can the manager both improve individual development and enhance the quality of the organization, and improve the satisfactions of the customers?

13.6.5   Many recreation personnel are leaders

All successful managers must be leaders. Many leaders, however, while doing a managing job are not termed 'managers'. Often they are community leaders, leisure centre supervisors, and the like. In addition to the managers, the supervisors also need leadership training. Indeed, it is they who undertake the majority of the face-to-face work.

The supervisor/leader or community leader is usually employed to get a job accomplished working through the group of people he or she has control over. The leader has three main interrelated areas in which to work:

1. The *task* to be done.
2. The *individuals* to work through.
3. The *team*.

Table 13.2 Leadership checklist

Key functions	Task	Team	Individual
Communication			
Define objectives	Identify task and constraints	Involve team Share commitment	Clarify aims Gain acceptance
Plan Organize	Establish priorities Check resources Decide	Consult Agree standards Structure	Assess skills Set targets Delegate
Inform Confirm	Brief group and check understanding	Answer questions Obtain feedback Encourage ideas/actions	Advise Listen Enthuse
Support Monitor	Report progress Maintain standards Discipline	Coordinate Reconcile conflict Develop suggestions	Assist/Reassure Recognize effort Counsel
Evaluate	Summarize progress Review objectives Replan if necessary	Recognize success Learn from failure	Assess performance Appraise Guide and train

Source: *Action Centre Leadership*, Industrial Society [20].

To achieve the task the leader must be aware that the team needs to work together in harmony and team spirit and that the individual in the team has personal needs which must also be met. He or she must, therefore, develop the individual and maintain the team. A breakdown in one area will affect the others, will hamper progress and prevent the effective accomplishment of the task. Figure 13.4 illustrates the overlapping between the three jobs of work involved in achieving the task.

13.6.6 Leadership: summary

The manager must be a successful leader in order to be effective. The manager must understand himself or herself and the individuals and groups being worked with. The manager recognizes that a high degree of subordinate-centred behaviour in helping to run an organization raises employee teamwork and morale and leads to effective togetherism. But this does *not* mean that a manager leaves all decisions to the staff. Situations vary and staff vary. Staff readiness and ability are important. The successful leader will behave appropriately in the light of his or her perceptions of the people and the situations, and cannot then be categorized as 'strong' or 'permissive'. He or she must have the insight and ability to act appropriately, remaining firm on cardinal principles, yet being flexible to permit degrees of freedom to the greatest advantage. In addition to leading personally, the manager must recognize that many subordinates fill important leadership roles themselves. They too need training in the 'art' of effective leadership. Leadership may result in the successful completion of a task but *effective* leadership occurs when the team of staff not only complete the task but do so willingly and find its accomplishment rewarding.

13.7 DECISION- MAKING

All decisions should be made as low as possible in the organization. The Charge of the Light Brigade was ordered by an officer who wasn't there looking at the territory.

Robert Townsend.

One of the leadership functions or acts is decision-making. How decisions are made is of importance. Hence the *process* of decision-making as well as the content of the decision is important for success. The manager and his or her group or groups should have an awareness of alternative decision-making procedures and processes.

Management has moved and continues to move from an intuitive 'art' with its 'rule-of-thumb' approach, to decision-making on a more scientific basis. Science, however, is not solely the science of economics, physics or mathematics but the sciences of people – the psychological processes which affect decision-making.

13.7.1 Types of decision

There are three main types of decision: Emergency decisions, Routine decisions and Debatable decisions [21].

1. *Emergency decisions* are needed under crisis. They require clear, quick and precise decisions, for example, to prevent destruction of the sports hall by a bomb, the possible drowning in the swimming pool, the fight at the discothèque dance or to make the call for ambulance, fire service or police.
2. The running of an organization and the ticking over of the service, revolve around *routine decisions*. Changes to the duty supervisor rota, the change of menu, or giving the blessing for additional staff for the forthcoming major events, are all within an organization's policy framework. Many of these routine decisions simply require a yes/no to maintain the status quo.
3. *Debatable decisions* are debatable because they change the status quo. They mean changes for people and their work. They are debatable because the chances are that they will be improved through consultations, given effective leadership. They are debatable because there may be a number of different ways of handling the particular situation.

It is these debatable decisions which tend to occupy a manager's time more than others. It is these decisions which generally lead to harmony or disharmony. It is these decisions with which this section is concerned.

13.7.2 The decision-making process

The decision-making technique has been suggested as having five phases: Phase 1 *Causes*: the reasons for being concerned with the problem; Phase 2 *Possible decisions*; Phase 3 *Consequences* and their probability; Phase 4 *Evaluation*: the importance placed on consequences; and Phase 5 *Choice*: the most appropriate, positive solution. The technique helps managers or groups to highlight the need for information and factual data and the relevance of it to the problem. It helps to analyse logically and so assist in effective decision-making.

Decision-making is, therefore, a *process* which can be divided into a number of stages. A variety of texts suggest a different number of stages [21,22] though much the same logic is apparent. For the purposes of this chapter ten simple stages are identified.

1. Defining the problem.

2. Gathering and examining information.
3. Consulting with people and considering their views.
4. Considering choices or alternatives.
5. Making the decision and deciding a course of action.
6. Communicating the decision.
7. Implementing the decision and following up.
8. Evaluation.
9. Feedback.
10. Modification.

Defining the problem   The process is dependent on *first* defining the problem. It is so obvious that it is often overlooked! It can be one of the hardest things to do (as many students writing theses will vouch for) but having defined the specific problem we are a long way forward in defining the answer. We have to be clear: what is *really* the matter? What is the decision supposed to achieve?

Gathering and examining information   What facts and information are needed? When are they needed by? What are the constraints and limiting factors? Are there cash limits, time pressures, staff shortages? Only use valid and useful information.

Consulting with people and considering their views   Others may think of ideas which you have not thought of. People need to be identified in the decisions that are reached. The Manager needs to identify who will be affected by the decision, to discuss with the group the facts and their implications, must involve the group and consider the opinions and views expressed.

Consider choices or alternatives   Consider all possible courses of action. We often stumble on to important ways of achieving results by keeping minds open to all the possibilities.

Make the decision and decide a course of action

Communicate the decision   In communicating the decision, the manager must be prepared to persuade people of its 'rightness'. This is made all the easier if staff have been involved in the decision-making or if the decision has been made by the representative group. Communicating decisions must be undertaken *sensitively*. For example receptionists at leisure centres, often working part-time, are rarely part of the centre decision-making team (and wrongly so in this author's opinion); they may learn about forthcoming events from the local newspapers.

Communicating the decision needs care, timing, sensitivity and above all the reasons *why* the decision has been made. Some Recreation

Managers are careful to inform the staff of the reasons but *fail to tell the customers why*. How often have we seen 'Sports Shop Closed', 'Keep off', 'No entry', 'Cafeteria Closed'. People tend to be more understanding and cooperative when they know *why*, and more so when they have been consulted. In communicating decisions enthusiasm is important. You only generate enthusiasm in others if you give decisions and reasons with conviction. *How* it is done is important. When briefing the staff team it is often best to undertake it collectively in order to show an open and frank situation and avoid the grapevine, the contrived gossip and the subsequent miscommunications and misunderstandings.

Recreation Managers often hide behind the memo in communicating decisions. They feel, in this way, that everybody knows, because the written word is clear. However, the written word is sometimes very unclear. It is conceived differently by different people; hidden messages might be imagined; there can be an air of mistrust. Communication is a two-way process – 'no one can ask questions of the memo'. '*You* must brief your decisions' [21]. When preparing the brief – spoken first, then written – the manager needs to envisage how people or he would *feel* on the receiving end of the decision. Managers have to place themselves in the position of the receiver, into the shoes of the other person.

Implementing and following up the decision   Implementing the decision then is a question of communicating the decision, briefing people together, whenever possible, being ready and willing to sell the decision with enthusiasm and belief and then confirming the decision in writing. Many 'debatable' decisions need a framework on which an evaluation can be made such as timing, targets and implementation. It is important that the manager follows up and monitors progress and sees that areas implementing changes and which create new problems, are smoothed over, particularly where people's *feelings* are concerned.

Evaluation, feedback and modification   Most debatable decisions need time to see whether they have been successful or unsuccessful and to what extent. Even the best preparation may result in the wrong decision being made. Once proof of its 'wrongness' is substantiated managers need the courage to admit the fact and try again.

13.8   COMMUNICATION

He that complies against his will
Is of his own opinion still.

Samuel Butler 1612–80

As we have seen, communicating is far more important then just transmitting a message. The way it is done can affect the attitudes and performance of staff. The purpose of communication is to ensure that whoever receives the message understands what is in the mind of the sender. This is not easy; what is obvious to the sender may be obscure to the receiver. *One-way* communication is fraught with difficulties. 'A' does not *know* if he is getting through to 'B'.

Many problems in management, in industry and in recreation services stem from the misunderstanding, misconceptions, mistrust and underlying *feelings* of not being put clearly in the picture, which arise from one-way communications.

If the goals of communication are to understand others, to get clear reception or perception, to get understanding, to get acceptance in order to get effective action, then *two-way* communication is essential.

13.8.1 Two-way communications

To communicate we must understand others. Each one of us is different from everyone else. We are different psychologically and physiologically. We vary in intelligence, education, religious beliefs, social background and experience.

These experiences create different frames of reference with the result that each person looks at the world around him in a particular and unique way. Our physical and mental make-up and our environment have a direct effect on our perception and judgement. All too often, when interpreting information we see or hear what we are taught 'ought' to be there and/or what we want to see or hear.

Thus there are barriers to communication in ourselves and these barriers also exist in our subordinates, our peers and our bosses.

The argument for two-way communication is not only a moral one – that of giving people the opportunity to fulfil their creative needs, to use their intelligence and imagination – it is also a practical one because the manager will become more effective by encouraging the group members to make full use of their abilities.

Peter Drucker in a public address put the argument against the purely persuasive approach to communication in the following way:

'In many cases human relations has been used to manipulate, to adjust people to what the boss thinks is reality; to make them conform to a pattern that seems logical from the top down, to make them accept unquestionably what we tell them. Frankly, sometimes, I think it is better not to tell employees anything rather than to say "We tell them everything, but they must accept it, and it is our job to make them accept it" '.

In this instance Drucker highlights the problems of forcing one-way communications on to people without their understanding and without understanding them.

The advantages of two-way communications are considerable. In small groups, such as those which apply in recreation settings (community arts centres, sports centres, recreation offices or community associations) the advantages can be summarized as follows:

1. Although one-way communication is faster, two-way communication is more accurate, particularly in complex situations.
2. Two-way communication will help both the sender and the listener to measure their standard of achievement and when they both see that they are making progress their joint commitment to the task will be greater.
3. The sender may feel under attack as the listener will pick up any mistakes and mention them. This is helpful rather than dangerous because a frank interchange of views will lead to a higher level of understanding and acceptance.

13.8.2   Communication networks

Communication networks have been the subject of much debate in recent years. Kent [23] identified the three most commonly used networks or patterns on which experimental work has been undertaken: the 'Circle', the 'Chain' and the 'Wheel'.

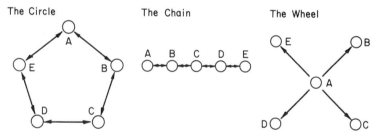

Given simple tasks the wheel was a consistently quicker and more accurate means of communication than the other two; the chain was the slowest and least effective. However, in terms of job satisfaction the circle was more effective than the other two. The circle was also more adaptable in complicated and ambiguous tasks. The wheel with its central 'gatekeeper' inhibited adaptability to changing situations.

Kent concludes that people never transmit information as well as they believe they do. He outlined commonly identified problems which restrict communication, for example, perceptual bias by the receiver, the distortion of information by the sender, the lack of trust on the part of both sender and receiver, too much information and power used to secrete rather than share information. The answer is to use more than one communication network. The formal and informal systems of communication Kent groups under four headings: 'hierarchal', 'expert', 'status' and 'friendship'. Further it is important to encourage the two-way flow of communications and to improve the coordination within organizations. 'A lateral rather than a vertical direction of communications in an organization will avoid the problem of one person becoming the "gatekeeper" of all information, a gatekeeper being a person who can withold or pass on information as he sees fit.'

In both public and commercial recreation management, a substantial level of communication is of the one-way kind. Orders come down from head office, sometimes by word of mouth through the chain of command and often via the written memo – a system subject to all the misunderstandings and misinterpretations imaginable. Managers and staff should be trained to handle work through greater levels of two-way communications for more effective achievement of the task and greater harmony within the team.

13.9 GROUP BEHAVIOUR

In business, including the management of recreation programmes and services, it is likely that the important decisions are taken in consultation with others. *Managers must, therefore, develop skills in understanding the behaviour processes at work when people are involved in the group decision-making process. It is clear that some behaviour assists in this work and some behaviour hinders progress.*

We have seen that two main management parameters are the *task* and the *relationships*. The task is the job that has to be done and the targets that have to be achieved. If these are achieved, as most important ones are, through people, then the relationships, the gel of people working together, becomes very important. The relationship aspects are referred to by management researchers as 'maintenance'.

What types of behaviour are relevant to the group's fulfilment of its task? What types of behaviour are relevant to the group's cohesion, working together and making the best use of the group's collective resources and strengths? What types of behaviour detract from group cohesion and are self-orientated rather than group/task-orientated?

Our study of management has revealed the importance, not only of the manager, but also the importance of the subordinates. Within recreation services the users and clients of all kinds also have considerable inputs into the services and can greatly enhance decision-making, if handled properly. Committees, forums, governing bodies, club offices, sports councils, arts councils, user committees, community groups and the like may all be represented in some form within recreation management.

The understanding, therefore, not only of managers and their staff but also of the whole gamut of individuals either singly, in groups or through formal committees is extremely important.

There are different types of group. Two main types can be classified as *'primary'* groups and *'secondary'* groups. Primary groups are made up of a relatively small number of people in a common task. Secondary groups are made up of a larger number and no one member has a clear picture of all the others. These groups can be further classified by their development, i.e. *formal* groups (those deliberately created) and *informal* groups (created by accident). In this section on group behaviour we are concerned with the primary groups.

13.9.1 Primary groups

Primary groups are made up of a small number of individuals engaged on a common task who have regular face-to-face contact with each other – the family, the play group, the mother and toddler group, the work group, the club, the church, the youth group. The primary group is an instrument of society through which individuals acquire many of their attitudes, opinions and ideals and one of the sources of control and discipline. The primary group can be one of the main satisfiers of an individual's need for status and emotional security. In the recreation context, the club leader, the society secretary and the sports coach fulfil status and emotional needs.

Primary groups tend to 'appoint' or have a natural leader. Generally speaking, *the more harmonious the group becomes the more efficient will be its performance in most respects.* The force of team spirit, belonging and sharing defeats and successes are extremely strong bonds. Disharmonious groups tend to be less effective. Primary groups appear to exhibit the following behavioural patterns:

1. Initial suspicion toward the newcomer.
2. Set standards of behaviour; non-conformity is often punished by the alienation of the individual from the group; acceptance of standards is rewarded by respect, emotional security and status.
3. Casting their members into roles which they are expected to maintain.
4. Indulgence in ceremonies and rituals; these strengthen the group bonding and emphasize the privilege of belonging. In recreation, we have, for example, initiation rites (Masonic, Rotary, Ancient Order of Foresters), intensification rites (annual dinners, stag nights, hen parties, presenting medals and trophies) and departure rites (parties, gifts and farewell speech-making.)
5. Groups, even undirected, set themselves tasks; if the task is not to its liking it will try to avoid it by splintering off, creating an 'enemy' to fight or run away from or letting someone else get on with it (this aspect was noted in Chapter 2 on voluntary bodies).

6. In group discussions individuals show behavioural patterns which are primarily directed towards the task and/or directed towards improving relations between members of the group and/or primarily concerned with self-interest or satisfying personal needs without regard to the group's problems.

Recreation Managers dealing with groups need to understand primary group behaviour and respect its standards, ceremonies and its collective and individual needs. Harmonious groups working together, helping the newcomer, and maintaining good relationships, are the groups likely to aid not inhibit, the fulfilment of managerial goals.

13.9.2   Modes of behaviour within a group

The modes of behaviour within groups have been termed:

1. Task-orientated.
2. Maintenance-orientated.
3. Self-orientated.

Table 13.3 illustrates the functional behaviours of groups primarily concerned with *task* orientation, the functional behaviours of groups which include additional concern for *group* maintenance and the dysfunctional behaviours of *self-orientated* individuals and groups. Both 'task' and 'maintenance' are important in varying situtations depending on the needs of both management and staff.

As can be seen from the table the behaviour within self-orientated groups hinders or obstructs the achievement of common goals. This behaviour can arise because the individual is faced with certain problems in the group, problems of identity, personal goals and needs versus the group goals and needs, problems of control and problems of intimacy within the group. These undercurrents cannot be ignored. They should be recognized and attempts made to integrate these individual needs with the group's goals.

The criterion of an *effective* decision is, therefore, the extent to which it has been carried through as decided. The more *commitment* to a decision which is gained in the group the higher the likelihood that the group will act in accordance with what has been decided. The process, the procedure, the *way* in which a decision is taken will affect the effectiveness of the decision.

As a guide Argyris and others [25,26] have put forward ten criteria, based on empirical research that they see as necessary for group competence and effectiveness. They are:

1. Contributions made with the group are additive.

2. The group moves forward as a unit, is team spirited, and there is high involvement.
3. Decisions are mainly made by consensus.
4. Commitment to a decision is strong.
5. The group continually evaluates itself.
6. The group is clear about goals.
7. It generates alternative ways of thinking about things.
8. It brings conflict into the open and deals with it.
9. It deals openly with feelings.
10. Leadership tends to go (or move) to the person most qualified.

13.9.3 Inter-group behaviour: conflict and cooperation

Individuals, because they have differing goals, needs and ways of looking at the world often find themselves in conflict with others. If an individual can only gain his goals at the expense of others, more conflict is likely.

Conflict, however, is not in itself undesirable; only through expression of differences can good problem-solving take place. For everyone to agree is as unrealistic as expecting that no agreement is possible. But conflict so severe as to disable the participants – prevent the continuation of problem-solving – is undesirable.

Some light can be shed on conflict and cooperation between individuals by looking at the problems of conflict and cooperation between *groups* [24]. There appear to be strong forces to keep members *in* the group.

What happens when two (or more) groups are faced with a problem of some kind involving their interest? The problem may be 'solved' by maintaining isolation between the groups, by enforcing unification of the two groups, or by allowing one group to destroy the other. By assuming that a real solution is wanted which satisfies both groups, then some kind of joint problem-solving process must take place.

Since group membership is such an important part of man's life it follows that inter-group conflict is likely to be especially acute. We cannot direct our hostile feelings within our own groups very strongly – to do so would invite rejection. Thus any inter-group problem-solving situation is likely to contain hostility, along with genuine attempts at cooperation. The more the inter-group situation is defined as *win/lose*, the more likely we are to see certain effects leading to confrontation. The more it is defined as *problem-solving*, the less likely the adverse effects. But the effects, however, never wholly disappear.

When inter-group exercises have been run in training laboratories it has been found that *within the group*, the group pulls in close; it sees only the best in itself and the worst in the other groups; it feels that it must guard certain territory; it demands more conformity from its members, the

Table 13.3 Group behaviour

Task-orientated groups	Maintenance-orientated groups	Self-orientated groups
Types of behaviour relevant to a group's fulfilment of its *task*:	Types of behaviour relevant to a group's remaining in good working order, having a good climate for task work, and good relationships which permit maximum use of member resources, i.e. *group maintenance*:	Types of behaviour which are not directed to helping the group work, but which actually interfere with effective group functioning, i.e. *Self-orientated behaviour*:
Initiating: suggesting procedure, defining problem, proposing tasks or goals, contributing ideas		*Dominating*: trying to assert authority or superiority in manipulating the group or certain members of it
Giving information or opinions: offering facts, providing relevant information, stating opinions or belief, giving suggestions and ideas	*Harmonizing*: attempting to reconcile disagreements, reducing tension, getting people to explore their differences	*Aggressing and blocking*: attacking group members or ideas and suggestions, pouring cold water on all different ideas, stubbornness beyond 'reason'
Seeking information or opinions: seeking facts, seeking relevant information, asking for opinions, seeking suggestions and ideas	*Gate keeping*: helping to keep communication channels open, facilitating participation of others, suggesting procedures which permit sharing remarks	*Seeking attention or sympathy*: drawing attention to oneself in various ways, attempting to call forth sympathy response through expressions of insecurity and personal confusion, deprecating oneself beyond reasonable limits
Keeping discussion focuses: concern with relevance and appropriateness	*Encouraging*: being friendly, warm and responsive, indicating by facial expression or remark acceptance of others'	
Clarifying and elaboration: interpreting ideas or suggestions, clearing up		

confusion, defining terms, indicating alternatives and issues

Summarizing: pulling together related ideas, restating suggestions after the group has discussed them, offering a conclusion for the group to accept or reject

Seeking decision: testing for readiness to make decision; seeking decision-making procedure

Obtaining commitment to decision: stating group's feelings in terms of a group decision, ensuring positive support for decision

Taking decision: putting into action the decision-making procedure.

contributions, obtaining commitment, helping others to participate

Compromising: modifying in the interests of group cohesion or growth, yielding status in conflict situations

Standard setting: expressing or suggesting standards for the group to attempt to achieve

Standard testing: attempting to evaluate the quality of the decision-making process in the group, testing whether the group is satisfied with its procedures

Pairing up: seeking out one or two supporters and forming a kind of emotional subgroup in which the members protect and support each other

Special interest pleading: speaking for particular interests (e.g. 'parks', 'baths', 'supervisors', vested activity interests) as a cover for prejudice or stereotypes which best fit the individual's needs and desires

Withdrawing: trying to remove the sources of uncomfortable feelings by psychologically leaving the group.

Sources: from work by Argyris and others and adapted from management courses [24–26].
NB *Both 'task' and 'maintenance' behaviour are important to effective managemet*

leadership changes with more control being accepted by group members and each group becomes structured, sometimes resulting in cleavages between subgroups. The interaction *between groups* reveals a tendency for members of one group to become hostile towards the other group, there is a reduction in communication between the groups, and a lack of willingness on behalf of the group to listen to the views of the other; there is a mistrust by one group of the other. On the 'resolution' of the conflict the *winning group* tends to retain its cohesion or become more cohesive. It becomes complacent, 'fat and happy', and there is a release of tension with a reduction in fighting spirit and greater playfulness. There is a high element of cooperation but little work is actually done. On the other hand, the *losing group* splinters, fights and reorganizes. There is an increase in tension, the group becomes 'lean and hungry'; and seeks scapegoats among its leaders and organization. If it sees future 'wins' as impossible it becomes introspective, self-blaming and depressed. *But*, the group can learn a lot about itself.

Effects like those described above are familiar enough in recreation services, political parties, committees, clubs, departmental sections and are exhibited in interdepartmental problems. How can these negative effects be reduced, so that good problem-solving can be maintained at a desirable level of conflict? The answer is to find an *overriding goal* – one which both (or all) groups accept as essential to reach and which *both can reach* – thus *'win/lose'* changes to *'win/win'* and both groups can be satisfied with their achievement.

13.10 MANAGEMENT IN THE RECREATION SETTING

Industry, commerce and local government in the UK and Europe have in the past seldom looked at recreation personnel as managers. It was not until the development of the community recreation centre that senior staff were readily called managers and doubts still exist in many quarters as to whether they are. For example, titles range from 'director', 'manager', 'amenities officer', 'supervisor' and 'recreation officer'. The director of one of the largest sports centres in Great Britain was in 1981 replaced by an 'administrator'. Names give images, impressions and status. Many managers of swimming pool complexes, with expensive plant and machinery, high levels of staff and attracting over 300 000 customers a year, have titles of 'superintendent'.

The question is raised, therefore, whether the Recreation Manager is different from other managers. The recreation setting can be very different from an industrial setting but *in essence* the Recreation Manager is no different from other kinds of manager. He or she must define the products or service. His or her function, whether in the public, private or community sector is to provide settings and opportunities for people's recreational experiences. The manager must define objectives, develop skills for the job and adapt to the situational demands. The manager in the recreation setting must have multi-skill qualities. He or she needs to be a planner, organizer, administrator, director, salesman, leader, negotiator, publicist and advertiser, caterer, barman, economist, public relations person, entrepreneur, diplomat, employer, chairman, committee member, writer, talker and, at many establishments, a teacher, coach, player, actor or performer. No manager can hope to be an expert in all these things but must be able to communicate, to talk the language, to know about sports or arts or about financial viability and needs to be able to read a set of accounts, know how to apply safety regulations and above all have an empathy with the users of his facilities. The manager must be a man or woman for all situations.

Recreation as a comparatively new comprehensive range of services, as an emerging profession and as a diversified mixture of organizations, could benefit greatly from proven simplistic management guidelines as a base plus new approaches in order to manage recreation services more effectively than ever before. We cannot start afresh. Public recreation is conditioned by history, institutionalism, known and workable administrative structures and traditional systems. They need change. Good management is needed now and for the future. However, to face the situation with a totally new management ideology is not practicable. People, organizations and attitudes change slowly – there must be understanding and acceptance in order to bring about satisfactory changes. Basic and simplistic methods help both understanding and progress, in such a situation. Advanced and more sophisticated theories could well hinder progress, if they are not understood or accepted. There is much to be said for practical, commonsense approaches to management.

Furthermore, there has been a rapid growing awareness that local authority operations have something to learn from their commercial counterparts despite the fact that the commercial sector chooses profitable activities. It has been shown that areas of non-profitability can be more cost-effective. In the commercial sector all efforts go towards producing financial profits.

The multiplier effects of attracting people and satisfying social needs lead to consumption of leisure products. Different management methods apply: opening times for maximum numbers, minimum staffing, staff incentives, vigorous marketing, quicker decision-making, greater degrees of autonomy, greater risk taking (after careful research), immediate stoppage or change of course in the event of failure and less conformity to regulations. The Recreation Manager should be aware of the different approaches and learn which techniques are best applied to specific situations.

13.10.1 Successful recreation management – the result of good managers

Good management is concerned with meeting aims, objectives and targets, achieving optimal use of resources, achieving throughput and financial objectives, meeting priority needs and offering the most attractive services to meet recreational demands. The quality of management determines to a large extent the type of use and viability of recreation facilities. Good management is largely the result of good managers – individuals who are responsible for providing direction to the organization and have the ability to move it towards its goals. Managers are directly responsible for much of the success or failure of an organization.

A recreation organization is a unit whose functions, primary or secondary, include the creation and distribution of services, programmes and activities that are used by individuals and groups during their leisure [27].

Management is the key factor in whether facilities are large or small, whether they are run publicly, commercially or voluntarily, whether they are run by a management committee, a board of directors or an owner-manager. Management must be appropriate to different situation and the manager must adapt his or her style to changing situations.

The job of the manager is to manage effectively and in doing so meet the goals of the organization and the needs of people. Effectiveness is measured by the degree to which an organization achieves its goals and objectives. This applies to all organizations whether in commerce or leisure. Two key elements are (a) the interaction between the organization and those who use the services, i.e. it is a people-orientated business, and (b) managers are involved in the achievement of its goals. Implicit within these elements – within community recreation – is the desire to meet the needs of people through leisure opportunity. To provide real leisure opportunity for people there must be effective management concerned with what is below the surface as much as what is above it. Measures of effectiveness must therefore include not only throughput, income and expenditure but also the range of people, the scope of the activities and the quality of the experience. Managers must ask themselves: 'to what extent have we met the needs of the people we are here to serve?'

Leisure and recreation management is therefore the process whereby a manager works with resources – especially human – to achieve goals and objectives. Good community recreation management must include qualitative as well as quantitative objectives. Understanding the process of management and the principles behind recreation services gives the essential foundation for good recreation management. Interpreting or setting policies for leisure and recreation organizations and the operational management processes including programming, staffing and marketing follow in the next three chapters.

13.11 MANAGEMENT: SUMMARY

In this chapter we have looked at the management processes, leadership, decision-making, communications and group behaviour. Management must be appropriate to different situations and the manager must adapt his or her style of management to be appropriate to changing situations. A manager needs to understand the processes involved in the way people behave within and between groups. It is suggested that the principles of good management apply to any field of collective human endeavour and recreation is no exception. The management principles and process apply whether in the public, the private or the commercial sector.

There are many differences between the three sectors but the similarities are fundamental. *Managers in all sectors are managing people and situations in such a way as to provide opportunities for people's recreation.* The management of facilities and the technicalities of specific management tasks are quite secondary to the management of people to achieve results and meet objectives and targets.

The study of management has shown that there are two main management parameters – the task (the job) and relationships (the people). There needs to be a balance between the two. Other areas of this book deal with aspects of task. This chapter has concentrated on the manager's need to understand people and the relationships between them, whether as individuals or within groups. Without this understanding, without the ability to communicate, motivate and lead, the manager's chance of successfully and effectively undertaking a task or meeting the needs of his or her users, is considerably reduced.

REFERENCES AND NOTES

1. Drucker, P.F. (1955), *The Practice of Management*, Pan Books, London p.19.
2. Gray, D.E. quoted in R.L. Wilder (1977), EEI: a survival tool. *Parks and Recreation*, August 1977, p.23.
3. Wilder, R.L. (1977), EEI: a survival tool. *Parks and Recreation*, August 1977, p.23.
4. Fordham, M. (1969/70), The recreation manager, *Recreation Manager*, December 1969, pp.19–20; January 1970, pp.6–7, 24–28.
5. Drucker, P.F. (1955), *The Practice of Management*, Pan Books, London, p.30.
6. The work of Taylor is fully considered in Wren, D. (1972), *The Evolution of Management Thought*, Ronald Press, New York.
7. Mayo, E. (1933), *The Human Problems of an Industrial Civilisation*, Macmillan, New York.
8. Fayol, H. (1930), Administration Industrielle et Générale (trans.

J.A. Coubrough), *Industrial and General Administration*, International Management Institute, Geneva, pp.40–107.

9. The work of Weber is fully considered in Wren, D. (1972), *The Evolution of Management Thought*, Ronald Press, New York.

10. McGregor, D. (1966), *The Human Side of Enterprise*, McGraw-Hill, New York.

11. Herzberg, F., Mausner, B. and Synderman, B. (1959), *The Motivation to Work*, John Wiley, New York.

12. Maslow, A.H. (1954), *Motivation and Personality*, Harper and Row, New York.

13. Maslow, A.H. (1968), *Towards a Psychology of Being*, D. Van Nostrand, New York.

14. Argyris, C. (1957), *Personality and Organisation*, Harper and Row, New York.

15. Likert, R. (1967), *The Human Organisation: Its Management and Value*, McGraw-Hill, New York.

16. MacKenzie, R. (1969), The management process in 3-D, *Harvard Business Review*, November – December 69.

17. Odiorne, G. (1965), *Management by Objectives: A System of Managerial Leadership*, Pitman, New York, p.55.

18. D'Arcy Cartwright, J.A. (1968), *Situational Management*, W.J. Reddin, Fredericton, NB, Canada.

19. Tannenbaum, R. and Schmidt, W.H. (1958), How to choose a leadership pattern. *Harvard Business Review*, March – April, pp.95–101.

20. From Association of Recreation Managers (Eastern Region) Seminars 1981, unpublished.

21. Video Arts Booklet, *Decisions, Decisions* to accompany the film *Decisions, Decisions*.

22. Welsh, A.N. (1980), *The Skills of Management*, Gower Press, Farnborough, Hants.

23. Kent, S. (1981), Good Communications, *Parks and Recreation*, September, 27–30.

24. Sheppard, Moscow Associates (1970), Management Seminars, Easbourne, January – February, unpublished.

25. Argyris, C. (1976), *Increasing Leadership Effectiveness*, John Wiley, New York.

26. Argyris, C. (1966), Interpersonal barriers to decision making. *Harvard Business Review*, 44:2. pp.84–97.

27. Edginton, C.R. and Williams, J.G. (1978), *Productive Management of Leisure Service Organizations: A Behavioural Approach*, John Wiley, New York, pp.3–6.

RECOMMENDED ADDITIONAL READING

Howard, D.R. and Crompton, J.L. (1980), *Financing Managing and Marketing Recreation and Park Resources*, William C. Brown, Dubuque, Iowa.

Chapter 14

Community recreation programming

★

14.1 INTRODUCTION

Preceding chapters have shown that the Recreation Manager must have sufficient knowledge to assist policy-makers in establishing guidelines for effective community recreation. In addition, the Recreation Manager must have sufficient knowledge of programming strategies, approaches and methods in order to direct staff in achieving the aims and objectives of the organization. Programming is important. It is a highly underrated factor in the promotion of community recreation. It is a complex process requiring excellent management. Programming must achieve optimal use of exisiting resources – facilities, manpower and finance – to meet community need and demand.

This chapter is written in several main sections. *First*, the questions are raised: what is programming, which agencies undertake recreation programming and what is a programme? *Second*, two main directional strategies – authority directed and community development – are debated. *Third*, a number of specific programming approaches and methods which fall within the two main strategies are briefly summarized. *Fourth*, the problems of community recreation programming and the lessons to be learned from current practices are noted and the suggestion of a comprehensive objective approach is put forward as a solution to many of the problems. *Fifth*, the chapter swings direction to the recreation facility programme planning process in which aims, market assessment, objective setting, choosing activities, taking action and evaluating are logically assigned to a continuous recreation programming sequence. *Finally*, a guideline programming model is put forward as an *aide-mémoire*.

The leisure field is so vast, varied and complex that in giving practical examples to support ideas, there has been a need for selection. Greater emphasis has been given to public community recreation services and leisure centre programmes and less attention to equally important issues such as arts, countryside recreation and education-related leisure pursuits.

14.2 WHAT IS COMMUNITY RECREATION PROGRAMMING?

Community recreation programming consists of planning, scheduling, time-tabling and implementing action which uses resources, facilities and staff to offer a wide range of services and activities – passive, active, routine, guided, graded, varied and special – within the reach of the community to be served.

Programming is a *process* of planning to meet the diverse needs of people. The programme is the essence of recreation services; it is their *raison d'être*. Yet it is important to remember that it is people and their needs which are the reasons for a recreation organization's existence and, therefore, people's *needs* must be the focal point of recreation services. Programmes are the tools of the Recreation Manager, the vehicles through which recreation opportunity is made available to the community.

The programme is *the single most important function* of a recreation organization. Everything that a department is concerned with – facilities, supplies, personnel, budgets, marketing, public relations, activities, timetabling, administration – is solely to ensure that opportunities exist for people to enjoy or experience recreation. This opportunity is made available through the programme.

One of the hallmarks of good programming is the extent to which individual satisfaction, individual welfare and the values of the participant are important aspects of the programme. *While numbers are important, the individual rather than the aggregate must be the core of the service*. Programmes are often judged on how many attended; qualitative aspects are rarely brought into any evaluation. In order to programme for people we should bring people into programme planning. It is important not just to dictate but to work towards participant planning.

14.2.1 Which agencies undertake recreation programming?

There are many sponsoring agencies involved in recreation programming: for example, education authorities, local government, commercial organizations, industry, HM Forces, religious organizations and private institutions, associations and clubs.

In terms of community recreation, however, local government should be the *coordinator* of services. Why? *Whether by statutory duty or not it is the only agency with a primary responsibility for provision and promotion of community-wide recreation using rates and taxes to do so*. Therefore, the local government agency needs to plan, prepare, create opportunities and a coordination network to handle community-wide recreation. It must first put its own house in order to ascertain whether it has the resources, knowledge and capability of undertaking this enormously complex task.

Local government has three main functions in the recreation programming process:

1. The *provision* of resources, facilities and activities.
2. The *coordination* of resources in the community and assistance to other providers and enablers.
3. *Management* and leadership.

14.2.2 What is a recreation programme?

What constitutes a programme? Does it have to be a class, a timetable of
bookings, a league, a list of events? Or can it be the availability of a
playground, a park, a school or venture trail? Or can it exist through the
distribution of services such as a recreation and leisure information
service which collates all that is going on? A programme is all these things
and a good deal more. It can take almost any form in the framework of
one's definition of what constitutes a recreation experience. However, in
terms of practicality programmes revolve around three basic elements:
activities, *facilities* and *services*.

1. *Activities* can range from the completely spontaneous variety to the
   highly structured and all stages in between. Informal activities can be
   anticipated within a community programme by creating opportunities, encouraging spontaneity, having resources available such as
   space, time and equipment – a ball to kick about, a wall to scribble on or
   deck chairs to sunbathe on. Structured activities, for programming
   purposes, fall into several major categories such as: *arts, crafts, dance,
   drama, entertainment, games, sport and physical recreation, hobbies, music,
   nature, social recreation, travel and tourism* and *voluntary service to the
   community.*
2. *Facilities* cover all areas, buildings, supplies and equipment within
   recreation. These can be designed and constructed for special purposes such as public swimming pools, designed for self-directed or
   spontaneous activity like a park, or just natural resources available to
   the public such as riverside walks, forests, beaches.
3. *Services* cover all methods and means through which people are
   enabled to enjoy recreation, for example, lending libraries, transport,
   community services and information services.

The recreation programme, however, is not a series of individual
activities strung together. It is a *carefully integrated and planned combination
of many activities* selected on the basis of individual and group interest,
related ideas, and themes organized to achieve particular aims. Among
these are the realization of personal fulfilment, satisfaction, enjoyment,
physical and mental health and the development of positive social
relationships. Essentially, programming is the balanced correlation of
leadership, required space, facility equipment, activity, and a participant
at an appropriate time and place.

14.2.3 Programme classification

How a programme is classified is not of major importance. However, the
type of programme needs to be known in order to communicate with the

public and avoid preconceived misconceptions. Programmes can be classified in a number of ways, for example by *function, facilities, people* and *outcomes*. By far the most usual classification is functional, i.e. by a listing of the activities offered. Often the functional classification is linked to special groups of people: children, youth, handicapped, aged, beginners, advanced and so on. Sometimes it may be important to classify the clientèle likely to use community recreation programmes.

Sociologists and psychologists tend to group people for classification into life stages. In Chapter 9 changes in the life cycle and their importance on recreation was discussed. Erikson [1] identified eight stages, six stages up to young adulthood and two stages beyond. Meyer [2] presented four adult stages. Farrell and Lundegren [3] identified a range of activities through eleven life cycle changes: pre-school, early childhood, late elementary, youth, teenage, young adults, early adulthood, maturity, later middle age, old age and senescence. However, these can be merged for many programmes, e.g. youth, teenage and young adults can be grouped together, or, the groups can be further broken down, e.g. pre-school into toddlers, infants and pre-school. Further classification can be made regarding the activities themselves: passive/active, structured/unstructured, planned/self-directed, high risk/low risk etc.

In summary, the community recreation programme is both the end product *and* the means of attaining the aims and objectives of an agency or organization. It has been defined as '. . the total experiences of individuals and groups resulting from community action in providing areas, facilities, leadership and funds. These experiences represent a wide range of activities, planned and spontaneous, organized and informal, supervised and undirected' [4]. An essential element that influences the success or failure of the programme to meet its stated objectives is *management*. This is the one ingredient, without which public recreation services lose much impact.

14.3 DIRECTIONAL PLANNING STRATEGIES TO COMMUNITY RECREATION PROGRAMMING

Two major directions for the planning of community recreation programmes, put simplistically are:

1. Planned programmes directed professionally by officers or authorities.
2. Programmes which emanate from the community itself.

They could be termed 'other directed' and 'community initiated'. Recreation texts describe the directions as *social planning* and *community development* [5].

The social planning approach is the most common. The basic

assumption underlying this process is that use of professional expertise and knowledge is the most effective way of meeting needs and solving community problems. Community development, on the other hand, is a method of organization in which the role of the professional is one of assisting individuals in the programming process, rather than intervening with services to bring about the desired changes. The locus of control is the important factor. Change occurs as a result of community intervention and involvement and not as a result of the diagnosis of a professional or the authority. *The process itself and the participation is part of the experiencing;* participants assume initiatives for their own development.

The social planning method is *participant dependent* and professional and authority controlled. The community development approach fosters participant *independence*. The distinction of the differing approaches is put cogently by Edginton *et al* [6]:

'It is important to draw a distinction between the work of a *community developer* and the work of a *social planner*. Perhaps the most important difference concerns the view that each has of the participant. The social planner views the participant as a consumer of his services. The role is to isolate individuals with needs and then intervene directly with services. The community developer, on the other hand, views participants as citizens with whom he or she engages in an interactive process of problem solving. The social planner is primarily involved in fact gathering in an effort to determine the needs of the individuals being served. Once the appropriate information has been gathered, it is used in the decision making process to develop a rational plan for the distribution of available or acquired resources. The community developer, however, maintains a basic strategy of change in which the role is to help individuals identify and bring about change through their collaborative efforts. The community developer works with individuals and small groups, whereas the work of the social planner is primarily carried out in large bureaucratic organizations. The skills needed by the social planner are primarily those of management and administration; the community developer's skills should be particularly strong in the areas of communications and small group behaviour'.

The adoption of a community development approach needs capable, trained men and women 'out in the field'. Community developers have become known by many names: encourager, enabler, catalyst, friend, adviser, activator. The French use the words 'animateur' or 'animateur sociale'. *Animateurs* are well trained, capable and sensitive people who work towards stimulating individuals to think about their own development and also the development of other people in the community, through community programming. They work to develop the leadership capabilities of others. They assist by supplying information about methods and procedures; they *enable* others to act for themselves.

14.3.1 Twin-directional strategies

Looking across the broad spectrum of recreation programming, it seems clear that to adopt one direction to the exclusion of the other would be inappropriate. Both strategies have merit. *A blend of the two is not only possible but also essential*. In addition to the directional mixture, the actual specific approaches and methods can be selected to meet particular sectors of the programme or to suit particular requirements. To achieve a blend and balance of direction and of approach calls for high skills of management and for programme planning objectivity.

14.4 SPECIFIC METHODS AND APPROACHES TO COMMUNITY RECREATION PROGRAMMING

Within the broad framework of the two main directional strategies lies a range of specific approaches and methods of programming. Farrell and Lundegren [3] present five approaches: programming by objectives, by desires of participants, by perceived needs, through a cafeteria style and by external requirements. Kraus and Curtis [8] consider five main approaches, four of which differ from Farrell and Lundegren's. Edginton *et al.* present 17 different methods [7]. From nearly 30 approaches which have been identified this section groups some of these together into twelve main specific approaches or methods. Providing for community recreation is so diverse and complex that there is no one approach, system or method which is suitable for all organizations, all situations or all people. The different methods are known by a variety of names; most of them have no agreed formal titles. Most methods appear to *evolve* as a result of the nature and the aims of the organizations themselves. The approaches covered within this section include: 'traditional', 'current trends', 'expressed desires', 'authoritarian', 'political–social', 'action– investigation–creation plan', 'external requirements', 'cafeteria style', 'demand', 'community-orientation' and 'community leadership' – des- criptions given by the various authors cited below.

This section needs to be read in conjunction with Chapter 9 and, in particular, Section 9.3 where the social needs of people were considered under seven headings: normative, felt, expressed, comparative, created, changing and false.

14.4.1 The traditional approach

This has been described as a 'rehash of the same old thing'. Such a description implies obsolescence. The approach, however, suggests that what has gone on in the past and is generally successful is likely to be repeated. It relies on the same format for future programme planning. It is not based on needs or even wishes or demands, but on what has worked before. The environment and the community are not considered or reconsidered. As a single approach it is ineffective. It can be a far more useful approach by learning from the past and making modifications for the future.

14.4.2 The current trends approach

This approach relies on identifying recent trends or activities in vogue and programming around them. This has benefits in meeting some new demands. However, needs are not identified. The approach is totally experimental. It is likely to serve only a segment of the market and what may work in one area may be a total failure in others. Fads such as skateboarding and BMX are important to provide for but must be seen in context.

14.4.3 The expressed desires approach

By asking people and through questionnaires and surveys, it is assumed that desires are ascertained. Therefore, by programming for people's wishes they are given what they apparently want. But will this result in actual participation? And which activities will meet which desires? Such an approach is extremely difficult to administer but is a valuable tool for the programme planner: it gives information about people's attitudes and behaviour. The limitations of the approach are that people are limited by their past experiences. By widening choices and horizons and creating opportunities new interests can become new recreation habits.

14.4.4 The authoritarian approach

Reliance is placed on the judgement of the controller, head of department or manager. The assumption is that he or she understands what the needs are and what the community wants. This is a quick and tidy approach at its design and planning stage. However, participants are denied any involvement in the programme process. The director or manager is unwilling to share and to adapt. Such an approach makes it difficult to adapt to a more community-orientated strategy.

The 'prescriptive' approach [7] and 'perceived need' approach [8] are very similar to the authoritarian approach. They too require a diagnosis of needs. Programming by perceived needs is a tempting approach to adopt because it appears to be based on needs. However, without community involvement, it relies on professional expertise to diagnose other people's needs.

14.4.5 The political/social approach

Edginton *et al.* and Kraus and Curtis both use the term 'socio-political'. In this case pressure from groups, often linked to social causes, is used as a basis for a community programme. Such causes are invariably grist to the political mill – they carry councillor support. Many people, such as members and officers working in local government, are subject to political pressure. For example, crime, poverty, deprivation and social disorder may call for particular kinds of recreation planning and programming. Or in contrast economic problems and rate burdens could invite commercial interest where public provision was formerly available. *Recreation Managers do not operate in a vacuum but have to respond to political and social pressure and to changing conditions.*

14.4.6 Action – investigation – creation plan approach

Tillman [9] suggests that a three-phase plan to programming is the most effective. The *action plan* is in actuality reaction to the demands generated by the community. The *investigation plan* is concerned with fact-finding. The *creation plan* is the interactive relationship between participants and professionals. The professionals use their own expertise and actively seek the views and involvement of participants. Such a three-phase plan, allied to aims and objectives could form a logical basis for programming.

14.4.7 External requirements approach

Here the programme is basically dictated by an authority, an institution or a governing body. It tends to have uniform standards, leadership and resources and there is an external assessment for measuring. A Scout or Girl Guide troop, for example, will satisfy headquarters' requirements. Such organizations normally have vertical management structures, a hierarchical leadership pattern, similar resources, administration and an external reward system. Uniformed groups – para-medical, (British Red Cross, St John Ambulance Brigade), religious (Girls' Life Brigade, Boys' Brigade) and newer groups like the Majorettes – are clear examples.

14.4.8 Cafeteria style approach

James Murphy is reported to have termed this approach the 'cafeteria' style [7]. In this 'smorgasbord' approach a variety of diverse choices are assembled giving many opportunities. People can make their own selection. This is a useful approach in that there is a variety of choice; people may not know what they want and can try things out, 'suck it and see'. It is a safe approach. However, it is not determined by needs or specific interests of the community. While appearing the answer to the manager's dilemma, it is ineffective in the use of resources, in that it can create and provide services which are unused because they have not been chosen. In addition, it is very difficult to set objectives and measure success – some activities will be winners and others losers but the reasons may not be known; for example, poor marketing, rather than the activity, may be the cause. Nevertheless, any comprehensive programming will need to indulge in a cafeteria approach for some of its recreation programmes.

14.4.9   The demand approach: offer what people want

Here programmers rely on consumer input. This is the most usual form of programming in the public sector. Clubs, associations and interest groups make known their demands. Hence, managers are faced with scores of applications requesting specific facilities. However, the most vocal, the most aware and the socially articulate will make their demands known most readily. The approach is not concerned with equitable distribution and may result in narrow segmental programming. Many people and groups will not be aware of the recreation options and benefits. Most comprehensive programmes however, will and should include this approach within the overall plan.

14.4.10   The community-orientation approach

This is a process based on using people's talents and capabilities. Here individuals are involved in the planning process. The approach is only possible by using professionals or capable amateurs to meet people on their own patch, for example, through outreach programmes, associations and community counsellors.

The *'discovery approach'* is an extension and continuation of community orientation. It assumes that people can work together, there being no superior or subordinate relationships. One's knowledge, skills, abilities and interests are used to meet another's needs without necessarily imposing value systems or external expectations. The approach is a people-to-people approach of interactive discovery requiring community face-to-face leadership.

14.4.11   Community leadership approach

Here consumer input is made possible through advisory boards, user committees, tenants' groups and other action groups. They represent concerns of the community. This approach assumes that individual interests are represented by their group. This, of course, is not wholly possible, but it does indicate community interaction and a level of democracy. As Edginton *et al.* emphasize, it opens channels of communication between providers and consumers [7]. It is a valuable tool for the recreation programmer.

In summary, this section has described very briefly twelve specific approaches to community recreation programming. Which approach or method is the most appropriate? Which direction should Recreation Managers take? The review has brought to light several important factors to be borne in mind when programming, it has unveiled many problems and it offers some solutions. The next section considers the problems, the lessons to be learned and suggests a solution to some of the problem areas – a logical approach to community recreation programming.

14.5 THE NEED FOR A COMPREHENSIVE, COORDINATED, OBJECTIVE APPROACH

The Recreation Manager is faced with the twin dilemmas:

1. Which strategic direction should he or she take in programming?
2. Which methods should be adopted to meet objectives?

Yet *the manager* is the key person in finding solutions. This is where the manager should come into his or her own. He or she will be trained and experienced to 'read' the situation. One of the guiding principles will be that *programming must be situationally and culturally specific*. There are different communities, different problems, different aims and, therefore, different objectives. The good manager must be a realist and use whatever approaches and options are open to meet needs and demands effectively and to be efficient in planning and operating the programme. The Recreation Manager must:

1. Understand the lessons to be learned from the various strategies and approaches.
2. Understand the problems within current community recreation programming.
3. Devise a logical and objective approach to his or her own situation, bearing in mind the resources available and the constraints to programming.

14.5.1 The lessons to be learned

As we have seen throughout this book need assessment is extremely difficult and complex. Moreover, even if a manager has a good deal of information – demographic, leisure behaviour, surveys, records – interpreting data is difficult. An activity, for example, is not necessarily of importance; what it *does* for a person is important. Part of the solution is gradually to make it possible for people to interpret their own needs and plan their own programmes. Managers must, therefore, *learn how to involve people in programme planning*.

Important lessons can be learned about the *ways* in which programmes have evolved and the results of the various approaches. From careful observation of over 100 recreation centre programmes [10], several generalizations can be made:

1. Many programmes have become excellent with improved management performance.
2. However, there are serious problems within recreation programming and many ineffective programmes. The accent has been on efficiency and tradition, not on effectiveness and community need.
3. There appear to be two major strategic directions in which programme planning can be undertaken. One relies on using programmers to 'dictate' what the programme shall be (this is the most usual). The other starts with communities – the role of the professional being one of enabling and assisting. A combination of the two is necessary.
4. The strategy balance and the specific approaches employed depend on the organization, department capability, the aims, the community to be served, other providers, staff skills, money, facilities and a whole variety of other factors. Programmers are thus caught in the system of 'having' to proceed along certain lines.
5. Most programmers do not use a single approach. Most use a number of approaches but they are often an untidy mix, a 'hotch-potch' overlapping and uncoordinated.
6. Even where managers have considerable leeway, programmes are often the result of educated guesswork and are built up on hunches. This results in a hit or miss approach and lack of predictability; it is certainly not built on people's needs but rather on managers' ideas.
7. Programming is a continuous and changing process requiring constant monitoring and thorough evaluation. This assumption leads logically towards a programming approach which is geared to systems which are tailor-made to particular settings and situations.

Integral to the lessons to be learned and the problems encountered in recreation programming, is the fact that *many managers in community recreation have little knowledge, limited experience and poor training in the context of recreation programming*.

14.5.2 Specific problems within recreation programmes

In order to get the objectives right, Recreation Managers should consider the problems of many of the programmes currently practised. Working from operational experience, five problems appear to occur constantly within recreation facility programmes:

1. Demands are not assessed.
2. Objectives are rarely measurable.
3. Programmes tend to be too traditional, static and much 'the same old thing' – the same activities, same methods, same people. Programmes lack variety and novelty. Often a 'take it or leave it' approach is adopted, regardless of whether the programme is appropriate to the target groups in the community.
4. Many programmes which are claimed to be comprehensive are imbalanced: clubs, leagues and classes abound in community centres, table tennis and discos in youth centres and there are generally few community-orientated programmes in community facilities. There is a myopic view of a programme.
5. Programme worth is increasingly being judged on numbers allied to financial viability. Qualitative programming gives way under such strain.
6. Risk avoidance leads to a lack-lustre approach, lack of creativity, stifled programmes, lack of adventure and non-appeal for young people.
7. Resources in many areas are under-utilized. Some facilities are used for single purposes which occupy only a proportion of time and a narrow segment. Many resources – schools, church buildings, factory canteens, industrial recreation facilities – remain under-used. Programmes could be coordinated through a department or through an expanded leisure centre programme.
8. Programme monitoring and evaluation is rarely carried out.

14.5.3 The need for objectivity and flexibility

The basic assumption was made at the start of this chapter that programming was a process. It is logical, therefore, to use a programming system which is a systematic process, a system which takes a wide and open view of the variety of possibilities. *First*, the approach must be capable of incorporating both major strategies – social planning and community development. *Second*, the approach must be capable of handling any of the options, from the wholly authoritarian-directed service at one extreme to the participant-controlled programme at the other.

Relating programme to the styles of management and leadership discussed in the last chapter, the direct services approach adopts a more task-orientated stance; the community approach adopts a stance akin to a relationship-orientated style. As we learned from the last chapter, the management style must be appropriate to the situation. Different approaches will suit different situations at different times. The *Programming by objectives* method builds on the principles of Management by Objectives. It is a planning approach to achieve measurable targets, which lead to ultimate aims. It coordinates the network of several specific approaches; it sets targets, plans, implements, controls and monitors. It is a practical, objective approach which gets things done. Of all the approaches, it embraces several styles, yet avoids needless duplication because there is a coordinated network plan. It is businesslike. It is a professional approach.

In the section to follow 'programming by objectives' will be shown to be a planning and operational approach to achieve effective community recreation programming.

14.6 PROGRAMMING BY OBJECTIVES AND LEISURE FACILITY PROGRAMMES

Building on the lessons learned from the directional strategies and the specific programming approaches, this section is concerned with reaching a logical sequence of interrelated actions which go to making up a community recreation programme. The approach adopted is that of *'programming by objectives'*. A logical progression is needed starting from principles through to actions and evaluation and continuing the cycle. *First*, there must be an agreement of philosophy and aims, *second*, an assessment of demand and resources, *third*, the setting of objectives and targets, *fourth*, consideration of ways to achieve objectives, *fifth*, analysis of the activity and user patterns, *sixth*, anticipation of the problems, *seventh*, marketing the programme and *eighth*, evaluating and monitoring progress. This progression is covered in Sections 14.6–14.9.

14.6.1 Establish the aims of the recreation organization

The first step in the process is for Recreation Managers to guide policy-makers in formulating the aims (the long term goals) of the organization and hence the recreation programme. In formulating aims several conceptual ideas arise and centre around terms such as the 'philosophy', 'purposes', 'principles', the 'rationale' and the 'policies' of an organization and its services. Discussion of the ideas emanating from these terms will lead to the establishing of *aims*.

A programme needs to be based on a sound philosophy. It needs principles on which to guide its course and policies on which to plan and establish effective procedures. The *philosophy* can be regarded as the broad conceptual framework of the organization and its purposes and principles. It gives the organization a *rationale* – a justification for its existence. The *purpose* is synonymous with the rationale, the basic reason for an organization, department or programme existing. The purpose of a service might be, for example, 'to enrich lives and improve the quality of life through recreation and leisure opportunity'.

The *principles* are the fundamental beliefs arising from within the philosophy and purposes of an organization. The principles lead to major *policy* guidelines. These guidelines give direction and for local authority services can be summarized into statements which are the consensus of the community. These statements become the *aims* of the organization, the department, the service or the programme.

The aims of a community recreation service could include, for example:

1. To serve and give substantial leisure opportunity to *all* people in the community regardless of race, colour, creed, age, sex, ability or disability.
2. To meet significant *social needs*.
3. To *involve people* in the community in recreation programming.
4. To provide the most appropriate service to serve the *greatest number* of people in the community and also serve those in *greatest need*, recognizing the need for balance between majority and minority interests.
5. To *market* community recreation effectively to discover *need*, to supply appropriate services and to attract participants.
6. To give range, diversity and *balance* to programmes.
7. To provide programmes which are *flexible* enough to cope with changing demands.
8. To make the *fullest use* and most imaginative use of all resources.
9. To give a large measure of *choice* through which variety, novelty and depth of programming is possible.
10. To *stimulate* community initiatives and spontaneous activity.
11. To manage services and facilities with capable and suitably qualified and *trained personnel*.
12. To regularly and systematically *evaluate* progress.

14.6.2 Assess demand

Two fundamental ideas relating to demand assessment are:

1. That assessing demand runs parallel with the formulation of aims.
2. That general management, marketing and programming go hand in hand; they are completely interrelated; they each need the same basic information – assessment of need, evaluation of resources and opportunities, and the establishment of a community 'profile' on which to base programmes.

The Recreation Manager collates all the marketing information and discovers as much as possible about the community and the range of interests. Next the manager evaluates what resources are available – the areas, facilities, organizations, agencies, personnel and finance. (Methods of assessing demand and gathering marketing information are covered in Chapter 17.)

In programming at a recreation facility, such as a sports centre, the manager will need to establish who the customer might be – the prospective participants and the non-participants. This is more specific than a community demand assessment. It arises out of the assessment and helps with the setting of objectives. To what extent will the facilities and activities attract individuals, casual users, recreational groups, clubs, leagues, classes, courses and events? Will schools, industries and other institutions be hiring for their own communities? From the experience at other centres, the manager will know that different people have different needs, for example:

1. *Recreational user* – a pleasant environment to play and meet.
2. *High standard player* – specific sports requirements.
3. *Older user* – active and passive pursuits, warmth; a social setting.
4. *Young adults* – novelty, adventure, noise; play at all levels; social needs, youth culture.
5. *Parent/housewife* – daytime activities; somewhere for children, not just a crèche for infants but play opportunity for young children.
6. *Manager and staff* – functional and attractive centre; facilities grouped to assist management, supervision and communication; designs which make it easy to maintain.
7. *Mayor and councillors* – A centre which the council can be proud of, which meets the needs of all, which does not lose too much money, which has high throughput, and is a showpiece!

By recognizing the different needs of people, managers are able to add another important factor to programme balance.

14.6.3 Set objectives

Objectives are different from aims. Aims are long term, ultimate goals, which reflect the purposes of an organization. Objectives are short range, attainable ends, leading towards the aims. They are shorter term and must be *measurable*. Objectives should be written as statements that are quantifiable with some dimension of *time*. Objectives answer questions such as: what? how? when by? how measured? Objectives describe the way in which action is to be carried out *and* how results are to be measured. Objectives can also be broken down into several shorter term *targets*.

In addition to objectives which are measured quantitatively, some objectives are needed which can be measured by more qualitative criteria.

For example, *performance* objectives (e.g. improving performance) are written in terms of the behaviour to be demonstrated by people as a result of the programme. Here the focus is on the participant behaviour, rather than on the actions of the manager.

Many organizations set 'objectives' which are not amenable to measurement. They are often conceptual or philosophical. Unless there are known objectives as *ends*, a manager will not know that an end has been reached. Objectives such as 'to maximize use', 'to serve as many people as possible', 'to provide activities for the whole community' are meaningless unless they have some yardsticks with which to evaluate the results. They must be measurable. For example, take a hypothetical case at an indoor recreation centre:

Aim number 5

'To attract as many physically active participants as possible in the widest range of activities at all levels'. Having undertaken an assessment of resources, a space capacity analysis of a centre, and gauged the level of demand, the manager can set realistic objectives to meet the aim.

Objective number 5

'Achieve a throughput target of 300 000 *participants* to the centre in the financial year – 150 000 for water sports, 100 000 for fifteen 'dry' sports and 50 000 for social recreation and family activities. The coaching programme to include twenty instructional courses for beginners in ten sports, ten improver courses in eight sports and five advanced courses in five sports.'

In the same way objectives can be set for *general throughput, casual use, income, expenditure, bar and catering, family use, new innovations, events, educational use, club use* etc. In addition, social platitudes could become reality through objective setting. Instead of 'to assist the "young unemployed" and "young offender" through the recreation programme', an operational objective can be defined in terms of targets: 'to create 20 coaching course places during the daytime for young adults to gain preliminary coaching certificates in Association Football, canoeing, climbing and swimming by the end of the financial year.' Or 'to offer three places for the Intermediate Treatment of Offenders to work with the physically handicapped programme during the weekends from May to September'.

The objectives of the Concordia Leisure Centre [11], not only have clearly stated intentions with specific targets for every objective, but also the objectives are clarified and broken down to indicate the ways in which they can be achieved. Included within ten specific centre objectives in 1978/9 were 'to maximize the number of people in membership (target:

13 500)', 'To maximize the takings from bars and catering (target: £175 000)', 'To give casual bookings by individuals and families first priority – squash 70%; sports hall – four half-halls for midweek evenings is the maximum for other than casual use, etc.', 'To develop and maintain club activity so as to allow for the development of competitive sports (target: one club per sport)'.

Objectives make it easier for ideas to come to fruition as they focus everyone's attention on the target – what has to be done to succeed.

The manager is the key person in the setting of objectives. Policy-makers need his or her professional expertise; staff and participants, too, need to be involved in the making up of objectives. The Manager is the link man. Many factors have to be taken into consideration, for example:

1. The known demands and the latent and potential demands.
2. The nature of the activities.
3. The facilities available.
4. The staff resources, helpers and volunteers.
5. The funds allocated.
6. The participants.
7. The times, seasons, and sessions.
8. The linkage to other facilities and service.
9. The opportunity for development.
10. The balance of opportunity.

Two very important elements within community programme objective setting are the need to 'balance' the programme and to achieve appropriate income/expenditure ratios. These matters are discussed in relation to indoor leisure centres in particular.

(a) Setting targets for a balanced programme at a leisure centre

Consideration must be given to the wide spectrum of users and categories of uses, so that there is something for almost everybody in the community-wide recreation programme. Balance, therefore, implies *diversity*, not necessarily within specific programmes but diversity in the community-wide programme. Also because of conflicting claims on facilities it is necessary to establish priorities. Objectives, therefore, need to cover the whole spectrum of the programme at any establishment. At the Huddersfield Sports Centre [12], in order to 'balance community demands against financial profitability', the centre manager identified six main areas for the programme – educational usage, public usage, teaching courses, club usage, major spectator events and social events – and with his management team endeavoured to allocate sufficient time and support to achieve a balance between the six areas.

(b) Achieving income/expenditure ratios at a leisure centre

Continuing with the example of recreation centres in Britain, these have long been regarded by most authorities as a social service and most centres have been heavily subsidized. Since the mid 1970s, however, financial accountability has loomed large in the running of recreation services. Although public centres do not run at a profit, it should be possible to have many of the comprehensive centres, with profitable activities, balancing the normal running costs with income, if not wholly, then at a good income/expenditure ratio. In terms of revenue income and expenditure, income targets can be set to achieve a minimum proportion of the running costs, the proportion taking into account the aims of the organization, the facilities and the programmes. Most comprehensive public recreation centres should achieve (say) 65% to 90% of normal running costs and centres could be designed and managed with a view to aiming in the direction of break-even running targets by offsetting profitable activities against highly subsidized activities. However, the political and social implications are complex. While aspects of a community recreation programme can be 'made to pay', many others need total support in order to meet particular individual and community needs.

(c) Aspects of programme balance at a leisure centre

To balance the programme at a new leisure centre, the programme should develop slowly. The temptation to go for an 'instant centre' should be resisted. Carefully planned development is essential in order to ensure that saturation by extremely popular and well-established activities is avoided. However, the demand for popular activities should be met as far as possible. This can be done initially through a 'casual' user policy and even groups could book facilities on a casual basis. In this way time can be built into the programme for the development of activities for which facilities have not previously been available and for which demand may build up slowly. No regular programme should be instigated until after an initial experimental period when a variety of activities, on a fairly casual basis, have been tried. Casual bookings, 'taster courses', coaching sessions, demonstrations and a number of incentives should be tried out.

To achieve balance in a public sports centre, answers to many questions must be sought, e.g. what must be sacrificed? Where is the line to be drawn between public use, club use, individual member use? What standards should be aimed for? How much depth can be sacrificed for width? How can fair distribution be achieved between schools, youth service, clubs, tournaments, events and non-sporting events?

In a sports centre participants group themselves into four main areas. First, as *individuals*, who want to book a game or who want some spontaneous activity like kicking a ball about; second, as *learners* in a class or group – the demand for coaching in many sports is insatiable; third, as members of a *club* – people want to play in teams and groups: primary group belonging is very important (as shown in earlier chapters); many sports can only be played in groups; without clubs they would die; and, fourth, as *spectators and supporters* – therefore matches, tournaments, events and entertainment should be programmed. To achieve balance in a sports centre the programme must reflect all four categories.

Experience in centres has shown that the more 'community' the programme – mothers, crèche, children, disadvantaged groups – the less the economic viability. In addition, general coaching, training and high level performers require considerable subsidy. Certain facilities also need heavy subsidy in order to function, e.g. theatres, swimming pools and outdoor playing pitches.

Some of the best community work will need subsidy. If the programmes were made to pay, then it would be decidedly different. In order to yield economic returns programmes would have to be centred on the activities which were popular and economic. Programmes might then cater only for those who wanted particular activities and could afford to pay for them.

Charges should be talked of in terms of value for money and value to the customer. The greater part of the centre income will come from charges made for activity. At leisure centres a basic principle of charging is on a per capita activity contribution plus an entry fee or on a space-time hire charge. This is normally fixed for adults and reduced rates applied to special categories, e.g. children and old age pensioners.

There are arguments both for and against the standardization of charges. It makes sense to have a broad framework of 'norms' in the public sector, which can be adapted to given situations. National surveys of charges for recreation facilities, for example by the Chartered Institute of Public Finance and Accountancy [13], can assist managers in looking at the spread of charges. Variable charges should be considered as a marketing tool to optimize participation.

This section has shown how important it is not only to have general aims but also to have measurable objectives in all areas of the recreation programme.

14.7 PROGRAMMING ACTIONS AND OVERCOMING PROBLEMS AT LEISURE CENTRES

In this section ten programming actions within a recreation facility programme are considered, namely, *membership, casual/club use, activities analysis, user patterns, programme patterns, programme problems, administrative problems, flexibility, expanding the programme* and *gaining social acceptance*. Three main aspects are not included – staffing, marketing and major events. These are considered separately in Chapters 15, 16 and 17.

The management actions and problems facing a Recreation Manager are clearly illustrated in examining the workload of a medium sized leisure centre. [14]. The Leatherhead Leisure Centre comprises a swimming pool complex, sports hall, six squash courts, indoor bowls, club rooms and social suite. In its first years of opening (1975/77) the operation of the centre involved the following:

1. Processing 10 000 members annually.
2. Collecting £4000 per week.
3. 10 000 users per week of whom 45% were non-members.
4. Dealing with 700 incoming booking telephone calls per week.
5. 290 incoming business telephone calls per week.
6. 160 units of correspondence per week including 30 applications.
7. 15 business visits per week.
8. Hiring 350 rackets per week.
9. 168 water test readings per week.
10. Dealing with 10 accidents per week.
11. Collecting and recording 50 items of lost property per week.
12. Blowing up 700 arm bands for non-swimmers per week.
13. Bar visited by 2000 per week (3500 glassfulls – serving and washing).
14. Cafeteria visited by 4000 per week (2200 cups coffee/tea, 2000 portions of chips).
15. The Duty Manager walking 20 miles per week.
16. The Technical Assistant walking 10 miles to check plant/machinery.
17. 1.5 tons of rubbish disposed of each week.
18. Liaison with over 100 local and regional bodies during the year.
19. 70 different activities/interests; 219 courses; 25 schools; 40 clubs.
20. 82 opening hours (100 hours staffed) per week.
21. 52 full-time equivalent staff employed.

Comparison with a larger indoor recreation centre, ten years later, shows the same intensity of use and substantial workload encountered [15]. Dacorum Sports Centre comprises a large main hall, ancilliary halls, four squash courts, fitness centre and climbing wall on the 'dry' side and on the 'wet' side a 33 metre pool, separate diving area and learner's pool. The diving pit is separate from the main pool and includes 5 m, 3 m and 1 m boards.

The operation of the Centre in the 1984/85 financial year included a throughput of 811 520 attendances and income of £412 627 and required 50 full-time staff to operate the Centre worth in excess of £4.5 million. In this highly effective centre the operation for a typical week involved:

1. An average weekly cash flow of £8600.
2. 17 000 users per week
3. 800 incoming booking telephone calls per week.
4. 1200 incoming general telephone calls per week.

5. 300 units of correspondence per week.
6. 30 incoming applications for regular or one-off bookings per week.
7. 30 incoming queries and comments per week.
8. Hiring 70 rackets per week.
9. 28 water test readings per week.
10. Watching 5000 people swim safely per week.
11. Attending 15 accidents per week.
12. Collecting and recording 50 articles of lost property per week.
13. The Duty Officers walking 20 miles per week.
14. On the technical side, 10 tons of rubbish disposed of each week.
15. Plant Operators walking 10 miles per week checking plant.
16. 110 gauges checked each week plus other machinery and ongoing repairs to items from doors to drains.
17. 126 000 gallons of water used every week for the pools, showers etc.

In a newsletter to staff the manager wrote:

'These figures are listed to illustrate the scale of operation which all require your time and care to be completed properly – and I am well aware that I have missed off many tasks . . . every member of staff without exception is contributing to the Centre and on behalf of the Council, Director of Leisure and elected members I wish to thank you all for your support and effort in 1984/85. Well done.' [15]

Staff involvement, as we have seen in Chapter 13, is essential to long term effective management.

This brief 'run down' of actual centres illustrates the scale of operation. At many large leisure centres staff cover the buildings 24 hours a day and opening hours can approximate 100 per week and some centres have revenue expenditure of nearly £2 million per annum.

14.7.1 Membership schemes

The *ways* in which people have to use recreation facilities, the procedures and the systems and the formal and informal social filters they have to go through, all affect the use of facilities and programmes. Three highly debatable issues relating to public recreation facilities are:

1. Membership schemes.
2. Total casual use.
3. Semi-exclusive use.

Recreation Managers must consider the advantages and disadvantages of such use, bearing in mind the aims of the organization and the programme objectives. For example, in order to achieve income targets, some methods may have to be adopted such as reserving space for commercial or club bookings at higher charges, or, in order to meet social objectives, methods may have to be used to halve the cost to certain disadvantaged groups. First, what are the assets and problems relating to membership schemes?

(a) The advantages of a membership system
The advantages of a membership system are many. They include:

1. A body of support; a list of people to inform; the spreading of information.
2. Could give a sense of identity and involvement and could encourage regular usage with attached and unattached users.
3. A sense of pride in the facilities could be created thereby reducing the risks of misuse; easier access for members might help prevent bottlenecks at reception.
4. Could facilitate individual and group casual bookings.
5. Could enable the formation of groups based on the centre at various levels of performance.
6. Could help foster the social aspects within the centre.
7. Increases the centre's flexibility concerning licensing agreements.
8. Could help to give users a 'voice' on the management of the centre.
9. May assist financially with meeting income targets (at some centres over £50 000) but if income was the main priority then additional entry charges with no membership fee could yield greater income.

Amongst the benefits to members or registered users could be: free entry to the centre when no special events are being held, no cash deposits on hired equipment (deposit membership card instead), and the right to book facilities in advance in person or by telephone without advance payment.

(b) The disadvantages of a membership system
Despite the many advantages, the benefits for some could act as deterrents to others. The semi-exclusive nature of the system may act as a social filter: the formalities of membership, the form filling and the need to know what to do and how to behave could give the impression of being too formal and structured. Additional staff and time will be required to cope with the membership system. Additional administrative costs would be incurred. But probably most important of all is the fact that given good management most of the membership advantages could be inculcated into a non-membership system, e.g. information, club grouping, identity, social development, users' committees and others.

(c) Possible solutions – keep all options open
At new community recreation centres *all possible options* should be left

open to encourage use by the community *in the ways they want to*. In time a system most appropriate to people and management could evolve. Some suggestions are:

1. Free entry – pay for activity.
2. Nominal entry charge – pay for activity.
3. Registered user or 'friend of the centre' card – free or nominal entry.
4. Free 'membership' for any disadvantaged, with some tangible incentive to visit; nominal cost for most.
5. A membership scheme with member benefits.

The dilemma facing managers is how to achieve commitment by the community *and* produce income *and* still remain socially acceptable. A non-exclusive membership may help, i.e. people can become members *if* they want to. Do not force this or make it compulsory. Create a *quality* image, e.g. laminated membership card, real benefits for members, quality handouts, a bright and professional image. This approach has great benefits with games like badminton and squash and activities such as sauna and special courses.

14.7.2 Casual-use and club-use policies

Along with the issue of membership, leisure centres are faced with the problem of individual, group, club, league, association and event programming. Some take the view that use should be totally casual; others take the view that club and group use is essential. In the comprehensive community recreation programme, it is important that many options are available.

(a) In comprehensive programmes avoid totally exclusive use

Community recreation centres belong to the community. It is difficult to maintain this with totally exclusive use. The call for exclusive use is bound to come at all centres. Accept this only when it suits the centre and on such terms that make it possible to have some measure of control. Alternatively, assist clubs in finding premises; support them administratively and encourage them to help themselves. The key is to develop and programme slowly, working on operational experience but maintaining motivational impetus.

(b) In comprehensive programmes avoid totally casual use

A programme given over entirely to casual use can be as limiting as an exclusive use programme. It is non-adaptive and inflexible. It does not encourage involvement, growth or development. It ignores groups and club needs and many individual preferences. Casual use, however, is a most important ingredient of any comprehensive programme. It is a major priority for many activities such as swimming, squash and many of the individual and small group activities.

Managers may consider that a casual use policy is an easy and effective option to meet needs. But casual use needs a good deal of planning and control. For example, it is difficult to leave space for the casual user to 'pop in' when so inclined. In its normal usage the concept of the 'casual user' is a misnomer. There is nothing less casual than booking a court in advance or organizing a five-a-side team, opponents to play, booking space, paying in advance and ensuring patterns of behaviour acceptable to the organization.

This type of casual use is made easier if individuals or groups can book in advance in person or over the telephone and if payment can be made on the day of play. In order to help people in this way, there needs to be some method of ensuring that those who book do actually play and pay. Some form of registration for those who wish to book in advance or join a coaching group or a nursery group may be necessary. Without such a system casual users must first book, then pay and, a week later, play. Most people will not make the journey if the chances are only slight that they may get a game. In the main, people will come if their activity is guaranteed. Even those coming for junior open sessions, young people's open evenings, holiday programmes, ladies' mornings etc., on a casual basis, *will not come if their expectations are not realized*. Hence the casual user needs:

1. Space and times suitable for him/her.
2. Semi-guaranteed participation.
3. Opportunities to book in advance in person or on the telephone.
4. The opportunity to pay on the day, if advance payment is too difficult.
5. The opportunity to join open sessions for recreation.
6. The opportunity to receive teaching and coaching.
7. The opportunity to join like-minded people in teams, leagues, clubs and groups
8. The opportunity to join the centre as a leisure base.

This flexible approach needs skilful and sensitive management. It also needs a system that enables the individual to use the centre *in the way he or she chooses*. People, therefore, need a variety of choice.

14.7.3 Analyse and choose activities

The Recreation Manager will need to choose activities which collectively are the most likely to meet objectives. By analysing various activities, choosing priorities and analysing user patterns and behaviour, he or she can be in a better position to balance the programme. Analysis of the activities gives a guide to programme content.

What are the requirements for the different activities? Which activities are popular and why? Which are poorly supported and why? Which require control and supervision? Which give the most administrative and organizational headaches? What are their requirements on manpower, equipment, maintenance?

It is useful, for example to:

1. Put activities into groups and *categories*.
2. List the *special* activities.
3. Analyse *space* allocation.
4. Group *compatible* activities of space and time and function.
5. Consider aspects of danger, noise, standards and age *incompatibilities*.

The more the manager can learn about the nature of the activities, the more understanding of the requirements, problems and solutions will be gained.

In Table 14.1 a method of analysing a sports activity is shown. It is simply a means of illustrating that a great deal can be learned by understanding something of the ingredients of each activity. By asking fourteen basic questions of the sports activity and linking the results to the programme objectives, the most appropriate activities could be chosen. For example, if the objective was to accommodate as many different people as possible to sports activities then a successful programme should include as many sports as possible which have the following criteria:

1. Has a low threshold of skill for enjoyment.
2. Uses a small unit of time.
3. Can be played by all.
4. Can be followed over a span of years.
5. Gives steady progress at competitive levels.
6. Gives opportunity to join a club.
7. Gives novelty and fun.

Judged by these criteria such sports as swimming, squash, badminton, roller and ice skating, snooker, darts and keep fit of all kinds rate high in sports programme priorities.

14.7.4 Analyse user patterns

In Table 14.2 an illustration is given as to what people do with their time at a recreation facility. An analysis of user patterns and how time is spent is rarely considered in setting up a programme. That people come to play a sport or attend a class is known, but that is only one use of their time.

Table 14.1 Analysing sports activities

This table is put forward not as a method or system to follow, but simply to illustrate that much can be learned from an analysis of the activities that might be included in recreation programmes

1. *Numbers* How many can play in a given time and space? Swimming, keep fit and gymnastics score high
2. *Space* How much room is needed? Tennis scores low; snooker and pool high
3. *Technical* What specialist equipment is needed? Gymnastics, skiing, fencing score low
4. *Age and sex* Can a sport be played by all? Team games like basketball and netball are single sex and relatively young
5. *Life span* Can a sport be played over a span of years? Golf, sailing, and badminton score high
6. *Competition* Is there steady progress of competitive levels? Judo scores high
7. *Skill* Is there a low threshold of skill for enjoyment? Running, swimming, squash, darts score high; karate, fencing, tennis low
8. *Time* How short a unit of leisure time is needed? Squash scores high, cricket low
9. *Club* Can a club be joined easily? Soccer and team games score high; golf, polo, sailing low
10. *Organization* How easy is the personal organization factor? Swimming, dancing, darts, pool score high; team games, booking systems sports, low
11. *Social* How much fun and social mixing is generated? Ice skating, skiing, score high
12. *Income* Is the sport income producing? Squash, badminton score high; team games, minority sports, low
13. *Expenditure* What is the cost in money, staff and resources? Coaching and advanced training are costly
14. *Image* How does the sport rate as highly attractive? Soccer for boys, horse-riding for girls, bowls for the older, adventure sports for youth, all score high

Research into leisure centres [16] has shown that only a small proportion of customers use ancillary facilities such as catering. Observing what they do and monitoring use will assist in providing the most appropriate services and operational methods. This requires no sophisticated statistical methodology as the simple user pattern in the table illustrates. The common features for all customers are *arriving* and *leaving*. They are all-important yet so many recreation facilities give little attention to reception areas which are light, spacious, easy to use and welcoming. Little attention is paid to information services, cutting down on queues, or analysing how people get from A to B without going through a labyrinth of corridors. The impression of arriving and of leaving is important to ensure that people will want to come again.

Table 14.2 What customers do and what facilities and services they need at a leisure centre

This table illustrates customer behaviour at a centre. Managers should observe systematically and learn from customer behaviour

1. *Arrive* Need car parking, signs, reception, foyer, easy access to information, shops, telephone; need welcoming, interesting; they should know where to go, where to change, eat, watch
2. *Change* Pleasant, functional, easy access to playing areas without backtracking; changing system that is easy and helpful: security system. Much improvement may be needed in changing accommodation
3. *Participate* Recreationally, competitively, coaching, training; all ages and standards; schools; large areas indoors and outdoors adaptable to change – flexibility; special areas for either specific sports or groups of sports; a need for a free unsophisticated area for a 'kick-about' area both indoor and outdoor
4. *Walk and look* Outdoors – landscaping, trees and flowers, walks, lighted paths, signs, pleasing design features; aesthetic and useful considerations. Indoors – circulation improvements; attractive environment; things to see; easy access to viewing hall and specialized areas; display, information
5. *Socialize* Talking, eating, drinking are essential ingredients in any community centre. Pleasing environment for sitting out and socializing; crèche; reading; entertainment; cafe; restaurant, vending; bars; lounges. Outdoor picnic areas, benches, café, kiosks, playgrounds
6. *Watch* Casual, tournaments, special events. Whatever the centre there is a need to watch. A playing area bounded by four walls with no watching facility falls short – it becomes a training hall
7. *Meet* Clubs, associations, groups need rooms, preferably as a home on a shared basis; AGMs, conferences, regular meetings, casual meetings. Otherwise they will meet and eat and drink elsewhere
8. *Leave* Will the experience, the facilities, programme and environment encourage people to come back, to make repeat visits?

14.7.5 Establish programme patterns, seasons, time zones

In comprehensive programmes, in addition to working out how people are going to use the facilities and which activities are to be programmed, priorities of use, seasonal patterns and time zones must be allocated.

Time is the basis on which a programme operates. Managers must for example establish hourly, daily, weekly and seasonal patterns of use, balance between sport, art, social and, for sports, balance between racket games and ball games and between clubs, leagues, casual use and courses.

Different systems will be needed for different groups of activities and different times. For example, the policy should change from off-peak to peak times. Off-peak times could be used, say, 50% for educational uses,

25% casual and 25% for community programme for mothers and toddlers, old age pensioners, disabled, disadvantaged, plus classes and courses. Peak hours – lunchtimes, evenings and weekends – could achieve, say, 50% casual use. But much will depend on the facilities themselves and the objectives of the programme. Good management is vital to establish workable and acceptable systems and patterns of use.

14.7.6   Anticipate the problems

Managers need operational experience to anticipate problems. At centres these are legion: different uses, spaces, time allocations, seasons, incompatibilities, safety, noise, levels of skill, ages, conflicting claims, changeovers, club takeovers, under-programming, over-programming, lack of flexibility, too few staff, inadequate finance, design problems, local authority constraints and price sensitive areas: swimming, bowls and theatre have long been heavily subsidized.

At sports centres managers must cope with space problems; for example some games require a large amount of space for a few people, others require a small amount of space for many; they may also require a large amount of space for a short time and others a small amount of space for a very long time.

Teams and clubs need some semi-exclusive use and some autonomy but such use may invalidate other space. Competition is rarely outside team organization. The programme must, therefore, be flexible to cope with change. For example, take the introduction of volleyball to a centre. A taster course is run; this leads to a beginner's course; a team is formed for friendlies; then matches; a club evolves; management decide that the competitive game can be handed over entirely to the club; the club then needs facilities.

Will the facilities be found at that centre or somewhere else? Or will the club die? Local authority recreation departments can coordinate the facilities from many agencies and take a 'global' view of developing patterns and resource availability. In this way recreation executives can take a helicopter view of the terrain – the higher up the chain of command the broader the view. For such a developing and dynamic programme *flexible* policies are needed in order to cope with changing demands.

14.7.7   Build flexibility into the programme

Flexible programming can achieve wider use and variety. It can maximize utilization, improve public relations, bring more people into the centre, give greater community awareness and enhance prestige.

Flexibility is not just for improvement, however, it is a necessity for daily operation. There always exists a possibility of disruption and a need for a change of course, requiring reserve plans or alternative methods. With new programmes the need is even greater for problems and changes are more likely to occur.

In the first year of a centre it is wise to leave sufficient time for casual booking, for tasters, new ideas, new people and experiments. This needs management enthusiasm and courage for there will be many pressures on space and time. In addition, while flexibility can lead to a wider programme, greater turnover, cross subsidy and a more balanced programme it can also create problems. It is demanding on staff time and initiative and can create difficulties with changeovers, cleaning and maintenance.

The greater the multiple use, the greater the organizational problems. Smaller packages or single-line programming lack flexibility but are easier to handle. While there is a place for both kinds of approach, a multiactivity centre, with a wide range of people and interests, calls for a flexible programming policy – but balance is required. Too much flexibility will not provide the regular base needed by customers.

14.7.8 Avoid administrative problems

Managers must be efficient. They must choose staff and *train them* to handle the administration and organization systems and select carefully those who will take functional responsibility. Some hints to avoid some problems include:

1. Systems must be devised without too many complexities, too many categories and classifications.
2. Neatly written communications and articulate verbal communications assist.
3. Do not rely on forms. Ask: Is the hirer aware of the amenities? Is he or she taking things for granted? Is it clear what the forms mean? Written application only is insufficient. Always talk. Then write confirmation.
4. Booking sheets and calendars are very important documents. Use only one with preferably one person or one group of people completing it. Use easy codings.
5. Avoid management short cuts. Managers create problems by appearing to promise customers what may or may not be available. This can lead to apparent double booking in the customer's mind and managers lose credibility.
6. Have booking sheets checked with someone in higher authority. Avoid making out the sheets in the turmoil of reception: the greatest frustration for staff and customers alike is at the reception desk.
7. Simplify systems. Avoid complications, e.g. devise systems to let users know what courts are available, without having a desk conversa-

tion. Use modern technologies to solve operational problems and to create greater effectiveness.
8. Choose receptionists and train them well – they are the front-line ambassadors of the centre.

14.7.9   Programme development and expansion

It has been shown that programming is not only a process but also that it should be changing and dynamic. Static programmes do not take into account new demands, changing needs and new opportunities for people. Many managers will say that their recreation centres are already full up. However, static programmes lose impetus, they become stagnant and in the long run are the poorer for all. A programme must adapt to changing demands. But how can more be achieved? The manager must be creative, look to suggestions from all sources and learn from the experience of others. Ten ways of expanding a recreation centre programme to optimize the use of the resources can be found in Table 14.3.

14.7.10   Achieving social acceptance

It has been shown that recreation facilities must be both accessible and socially acceptable. Recreation is as much a social experience as a physical experience. Methods of achieving social acceptance, enhancing the programme and creating attractive images are covered in a later chapter. At this stage, the point is being made that one of the programming factors relates to the acceptance by people of what a programme has to offer. By appointing a manager with flair for 'selling' the recreation centre and by spending time on promotion, considerable interest can be generated. The programme and the centre must be made socially acceptable. The activity as such is only one factor in programming. What it *does* for people is important. Leisure behaviour is social behaviour. People will go, in most cases, where it pleases them to go – when there is sufficient choice. When there is limited choice keen participants will go anywhere. Poor management has very often been overlooked because managers possessed the only facilities available, e.g. the only swimming pool in the district or the only hall large enough for basketball.

Staff and customers need to be kept informed and given reasons for certain management actions. Managers should use a variety of communication systems – children; notices; face-to-face selling from reception, bar, sports shop; suggestions box, invite comments; involve people; hand all users occasional written information. Centre notices are often scruffy, ill-prepared, cluttered and unsightly; they look amateur and do little to enhance management credibility. Often they have been prepared hurriedly and by a caretaker or well-meaning member of staff.

Table 14.3   Ten ways of expanding a recreation facility programme

---

1. Leave some *free space* all the time. It allows for flexibility, expansion and change. Uncommitted space can assist in people dropping in, casual use and many programming aspects. If courts always appear fully booked people will not drop in on the off-chance. There will be nobody to take up cancellations and few to circulate cafeterias while waiting. Try some non-bookable space. Use a cancellations board.

2. Build up a range of *substitute activities*, substitute times and alternatives for people to try. Encourage new ideas.

3. *Avoid establishing the instant programme.* It will leave no room to develop. Do not stretch the staff too much or the systems to breaking point.

4. Sell off-peak times: try *package deals*, or two for one, or three for two systems. Provide daytime courses for non-active and active. Sell classroom accommodation. Sell *self-service*.

5. With educational use make sure that the regulations permit *re-letting of space* at half terms, during exam periods.

6. Let people *watch*. Activity breeds activity. Fun and skill will sell itself.

7. Follow each course with a *follow-up*. This may have to be in other premises.

8. Try *time experiments*: cut down time for some; extend playing hours, early and late; avoid changeover gaps.

9. Try *space experiments*: fit new groups into small spaces; set number standards; fit 20% more recreational courts into the same space – competitive space.

10. *Develop the centre into a community hub – a resource base. It will then act as a catalyst or headquarters or coordination centre for facilities and programmes both near and far.*

This table illustrates a few of the ways of expanding a programme. It should be read in conjunction with the guidelines relating to marketing a recreation centre (page 449).

They can be highly damaging to the image.

Managers must create the kind of image that all want to be associated with and to bathe in its reflection. These and other factors in promoting a recreation centre are given in Chapter 16.

14.8 RECREATION PROGRAMME EVALUATION

Section 14.7 was concerned with ten areas for management action in programming. An eleventh is programme evaluation.

In the USA considerable work has been undertaken on recreation programme evaluation [17]. In the UK comparatively little has been achieved in this area, particularly in terms of community recreation. It is crucially important to evaluate the programme. How else can a manager know whether the objectives have been met, the goals reached? Evaluation is often thought of in terms of the end result of a programme only – the 'bums on seats' approach. However, this is only part of the evaluation picture. Evaluation is methodically appraising a programme's worth, taking into consideration:

1. The *input* – how much has gone into the programme, planning and organization.
2. The *process* – what has actually occurred during the programme.
3. The *outcomes* – what were the end results and how did these compare with the target objectives and performance objectives.

The *input* is the planning stage. What were the total costs of the exercise? How many resources were used? How many staff and how much time and effort were put into the operation? What marketing was undertaken? Was it sufficient? What were the total man-hours? In other words, what was involved in putting the programme together?

The *process* is concerned with the running of the operation. What actually went on? This gives clues as to why a programme was successful or unsuccessful. It refreshes one's memory. It lets others know about the running of the programme and what methods were employed, what management style was predominant, what leadership techniques were successful.

The *outcome* is comparing programme objectives with actual performance. Why have objectives if you do not gauge whether they have been achieved? Outcomes are often too heavily weighted on financial performance. While this is paramount in the commercial setting, in community recreation programmes financial yardsticks are but one measure. The question is: *did the programme fulfil its purpose?*

14.8.1 When, how and who should evaluate?

(a) When?
How often should evaluation be undertaken? This depends on the nature of the programme. Events need evaluation on completion; classes could be evaluated yearly or, if considerable monitoring is necessary, then termly. A community programme may need two years to give it a fair 'crack of the whip'. A recreation strategy may need four or five years to develop. In these cases evaluation of the parts will be necessary at more frequent intervals.

(b) How?
Evaluation should be undertaken with objectives and aims in mind. Programmes need *time* to develop; time is needed for adjustment; time is needed for experiment. *Piecemeal* evaluation or evaluation every time things go wrong is foolhardy; it will lead to narrow programmes where

staff are afraid to put a foot wrong. Another weak form of evaluation is the *checklist*. Simply to check off what technical actions had to be undertaken can result in the 'supervisory mind', the 'caretaker attitude' to a programme – the very attitudes one is trying to avoid, in bringing satisfying recreation experiences to people.

(c) Who?

Who should undertake the evaluation? Again much will depend on the nature of the programme and the objectives. *Inside* evaluation can be important in getting a better feel of what has transpired but is more likely to be biased. Outside evaluation is likely to be more objective but can be hampered by staff suspicion of the motives behind the evaluation or worry about the outcomes: it is natural that staff feel that they are being judged. Managers and staff in any walk of life, particularly in an emerging profession like recreation management, appear vulnerable to criticism and judgements, although no apportionment of blame may be made. On the other hand, praise and success is a powerful motivator. Another problem with outside evaluation is that the evaluator's goals may be different from the organization's goals. Even within the same leisure centre one manager may be primarily concerned with the number of users past the turnstile. How many annual reports will crow at the fact that the turnstiles registered a given number during the year, a higher percentage rate than elsewhere?

A combination of inside and outside evaluation makes better sense. If it can be handled, then the possible involvement of *everyone* is better still – the policy-makers, the officers, the staff and the participants. We have seen how employee motivation improves performance when they are involved in the decision-making process. Staff and leaders are closest to people; they and the participants are first-hand observers. Therefore, managers should endeavour to collect information from everyone. What was good? What went wrong? Why? How can the programme be improved? This style of evaluation needs skilful and sensitive handling.

Some guidelines to improved evaluations are as follows:

1. Let all know what is going on. There is fear of the unknown.
2. Managers should be unobtrusive, and often redundant in information gathering.
3. Ask about the programme in as many different ways as possible.
4. Be clear and unambiguous to avoid misunderstandings.
5. Be sensitive to pressures and timing. Consider when people are likely to be most objective, not after emotional discussions.
6. Inculcate a sense of all contributing to positive goals; avoid subjective carping, looking for scapegoats or 'nit-picking'.
7. Be prepared for the unexpected; the unintentional often hides deeper

truths; value *serendipity* (the faculty of making fortunate and unexpected discoveries by accident!)

14.9 COMMUNITY RECREATION PROGRAMMING: SUMMARY

Community recreation programming is a process. The recreation programme is the means to achieve the aims and objectives of the recreation organization. There are many agencies, authorities and organizations whose function it is to provide recreation. The local authority, however, has a special enabling and coordinating function in addition to supplying its own services and facilities.

Programming hinges around five main factors: the policies, the people, the activities, the facilities and the management. There are many ways in which programmes can be classified such as by function, by areas and facilities, by people and social interaction and by the expected outcomes of the recreation programme. The classification into functional activities is the most common.

There are different approaches to programming. Two major directions can be loosely termed 'social planning', where the locus of control is with the authority and professionals, and 'community development', which is a more people-oriented direction. There are a great variety of specific methods of approach such as programming 'by the desires of the participants', 'by perceived needs', 'by cafeteria style' and 'by external requirements'. In practice a mix of approaches is tried but without a sound coordinating network. 'Programming by objectives' is an approach which meets many of the inherent problems in other more subjective methods.

In this approach the Recreation Manager undertakes several actions. He or she works with policy-makers to establish aims. At the same time he or she finds out as much as possible about the prospective participants. Consumer interests become focal points of concern.

Objectives are set and put down in writing. They are arrived at having given consideration to aims, organization, community, resources and staff. Activities are chosen bearing in mind the needs and the constraints, e.g. facilities available, time, costs, staff etc. The programme is then assembled, marketed and presented. This will include sectors of the programme where community initiatives are given full rein, enabled by organization resources. It will also include several approaches – meeting demands, giving choice, trying experiments. The programme will be constantly monitored; it is important to keep in touch with the programme and the people. This is best achieved by grass roots face-to-face work. Finally, the programme is evaluated. The evaluation is concerned with the input (what has gone into the planning), the process (what has occurred) and the actual outcome. It is important to remember, however, that programming is an ongoing, *continuous* process. Hence, while there are steps in the procedure, different sections will be at different stages – the whole programme will be changing and evolving. This is why high quality management is needed to coordinate and control the entire operation. *Recreation programming needs quality recreation managers.*

In the plan below 'Programming by Objective' is illustrated in a seven-stage action plan.

14.10   SEVEN STEPS TO PROGRAMMING

1.   Interpret policy, establish aims and guidelines

(a) Understand the general purpose of the organization, its philosophy and the fundamental beliefs arising from the philosophy.

(b) These deliberations lead first to a statement of principles and policies, second to the aims and goals of the organization and third produce major policy guidelines and the directional strategy weighting.

2.   Assess current and potential demand

(a) Evaluate current resources, facilities, programmes, organizations and opportunities. Collate marketing information.

(b) Establish a community and potential user profile.

(c) Identify market gaps and determine areas of deficiency.

(d) This will give a picture of the prospective consumers and type of services and activities to meet needs and demands.

(e) Train staff.

3.   Set objectives

(a) Set relatively short range attainable targets in each area.

(b) Make each objective measurable and within a time-span. Involve policy makers, staff and community in objective setting.

(c) Policies and market needs and demands are translated into action through setting objectives and implementing the programme.

(d) Set appropriate balance between community-orientated and pro-fessionally-directed approaches.

4.   Plan the programme

(a) Determine programme areas (arts, sports, social etc.).

(b) Determine programme forms (clubs, courses, events etc.).

(c) Choose activities and methods which collectively are most likely to meet objectives.

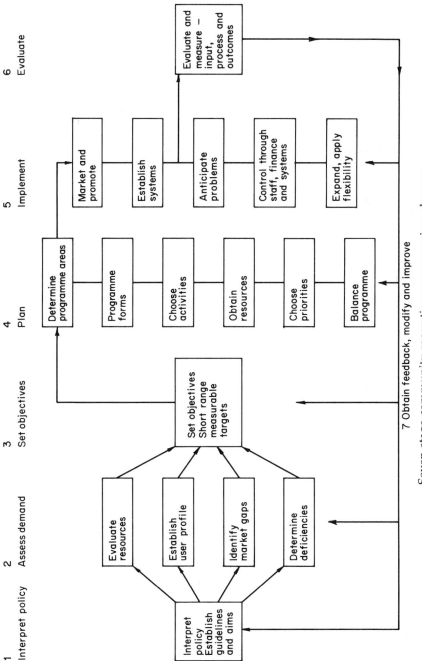

1	2	3	4	5	6
Interpret policy	Assess demand	Set objectives	Plan	Implement	Evaluate

Evaluate and measure – input, process and outcomes

Market and promote

Establish systems

Anticipate problems

Control through staff, finance and systems

Expand, apply flexibility

Determine programme areas

Programme forms

Choose activities

Obtain resources

Choose priorities

Balance programme

Set objectives Short range measurable targets

Evaluate resources

Establish user profile

Identify market gaps

Determine deficiencies

Interpret policy Establish guidelines and aims

7 Obtain feedback, modify and improve

Seven stage community recreation programming planner.

(d) Analyse the activities to provide the appropriate conditions.
(e) Choose priorities to most effectively meet objectives.
(f) Balance the programme providing width and depth.
(g) Establish programme patterns e.g. weekly, seasonal.

5. Implement the programme

(a) Construct, promote and implement the programme.
(b) Implement marketing strategy and techniques.
(c) Anticipate the likely problems; be ready with alternatives.
(d) Establish easily handled systems and methods.
(e) Train staff to undertake responsibilities and gain success.
(f) Control the programme through staff span, financial and systems control.
(g) Expand the programme with new activities, methods and people.
(h) Apply flexibility to meet changing situations.
(i) Establish a community network through community development.

6. Evaluate

(a) To what extent has the programme been successful or unsuccessful?
(b) Determine user profile, catchment areas and cost effectiveness.
(c) Use information from all directions.
(d) Use several criteria to measure profits both quantitative and qualitative.
(e) Evaluate not just end results like turnover but the input, the process and the outcomes – the operation from beginning to end.

7. Obtain feedback and modify programme

(a) As part of evaluation obtain feedback through the community network and community leader resources.
(b) Ask how the programme can be improved. Modify the programme appropriately.

REFERENCES AND NOTES

1. Erikson, E. (1963), *Eight Ages of Man in Childhood and Society* 2nd edn, Norton, New York.
2. Meyer, H.D. (1957), The Adult Cycle, *Annals of the American Academy of Political Science and Society*, **33**, 58–67.
3. Farrell, P. and Lundegren, H.M. (1978), *The Process of Recreation Programming*, John Wiley, New York.
4. Butler, G.D. (1976), *Introduction to Community Recreation*. McGraw-Hill, New York, p. 231.

5. Edginton, C.R., Compton, D.M. and Hanson, C.J. (1980), *Recreation and Leisure Programming: A Guide for the Professional*, Saunders College, Philadelphia, pp. 28–43.
6. Ibid., p. 38.
7. Ibid., Chapter 2.
8. Kraus, R.G. and Curtis, J.E. (1977), *Creative Administration in Recreation and Parks*, C.V. Mosby, Saint Louis.
9. Tillman, A. (1974), *The Program Book for Recreation Professionals*, National Press Books, Palo Alto, California, pp. 57–58.
10. Author's observation from: The Sports Council Sports Centre Management Award 1975–78; Polytechnic of North London DMS (Rec.) Recreation Centre Visits 1971–80; Polytechnic of Central London DALA Arts Centre Visits 1973–77; author's surveys of managers and centres 1973–84.
11. Evidence given to Sports Council Management Award 1977–78.
12. Evidence given to Sports Council Management Award 1977–78.
13. Chartered Institute of Public Finance and Accountancy (1978), *Charges for Leisure Services*, 1983–4 – *A Sample Survey*. CIPFA, London.
14. Information obtained from the manager's programme analysis (1977), Leatherhead Leisure Centre.
15. Information obtained from the manager's newsletter to staff, 1st May 1985, Dacorum Sports Centre.
16. Scottish Sports Council, (1979), *A Study of Sports Centres and Swimming Pools*: Volumes 1 and 2. *Main Report, A Question of Balance*, Scottish Sports Council, Edinburgh.
17. Theobald, W.F. (1979), *Evaluation of Recreation and Park Programs*, John Wiley, New York.

Chapter 15

Staffing

★

"Him? He's only my assistant."

★

15.1   INTRODUCTION

One of the key areas in the management of recreation services departments and facilities is the staffing structure. The way in which staff are organized is a crucial factor in the performance and level of success of management. The structure represents the way in which the work is organized and shared out and the manner in which an organization is managed.

This chapter is written in four brief parts. *First*, the problems of staffing within recreation services are considered and these demonstrate the need for better understanding and more effective organization of staff. *Second*, some legislation relating to staff employment is summarized. *Third*, the principles of management which concern staffing, such as 'chains of command' and 'span of control', are considered. *Fourth*, the formulation of organization and staffing structure is examined. *Finally* as part of the summary, a 12-point staffing guideline for recreation facility managers is put forward for consideration.

15.2   STAFF AND STAFFING STRUCTURES IN RECREATION ORGANIZATIONS

Every recreation service from the smallest to the largest has an organization and staffing structure of some kind; it may not be written, but it exists. Used effectively the structure provides the framework through which the work operations proceed in an orderly manner towards organizational objectives. The staffing structure has an effect on the recreation programme just as the facilities themselves affect the programme. That is not to imply that the more staff one has, the better or more varied the programme. Rather the way staff are organized, deployed and motivated will have decided effects on the results.

Staffing structures, the types of staff and the levels of staffing in recreation services vary considerably from authority to authority, organization to organization and from centre to centre, even where facilities are comparable and where policies appear to run parallel. At some similar large recreation centres in the United Kingdom staff numbers can vary from 50 to 100.

In public recreation, financed in large measure by rates and taxes and subject to large bureaucratic administrative machinery, one might expect to find a considerable level of uniformity. However, in the United Kingdom there are almost as many *different* recreation structures as there are authorities and it is difficullt to find two precisely the same. While different localities have different facilities and different problems and different circumstances, it is understandable that variations exist. However, the variations in structure, methods, approaches and personnel are so wide and so totally different – from a small subsection to a major comprehensive department in towns of the same size and with similar ranges of services – that comparative studies are needed to highlight the benefits and limitations of different systems.

Not only are structures different in recreation organizations, but also the types of staff vary. In addition, staff vary within the same organization from full-time to part-time, temporary, casual and voluntary. There are recreation executives, senior, middle and line managers, recreation officers, wardens, park-keepers, coaches, teachers, community workers, youth workers, play leaders, artists, caterers, technicians, supervisors, administrators and the whole range of technical, clerical and maintenance staff. They have variations in Contracts of Employment, job descriptions, training and benefits. They work different hours and different shifts and many work long unsocial hours. With most comprehensive recreation facilities opening hours are long, as much as 100 hours a week. In these circumstances, even the most dedicated manager is in essence a part-timer.

The allocation of revenue expenditure towards staffing, particularly in public recreation facilities, takes the largest share of operating costs. For example, in recreation centres in the United Kingdom, salaries and wages account generally for 55–70% of the operating expenditure. In times of economic stringency, reduction in staff is one method of increasing profits or reducing deficits. How important it is, therefore, to demonstrate clearly the appropriate levels and duties of staff as a means towards achieving objectives. In many public recreation organizations the staffing structure is inappropriate to the needs. The structure of, say, an arts centre may be unhappily embedded within a local authority departmental structure with a hierarchy, levels and status positions which have little relationship to programming needs, the needs of staff and, possibly least of all, the needs of users. Fitting new types of facility and services into outmoded structures highlights the problem even more clearly.

Many new recreation centres require managers with considerable decision-making powers and senior staff to take full reponsibility in unsocial hours (usually peak hours, in terms of attendances, events and programme variety). They need structures which are flexible enough to respond to changes, in order to meet less predictable community demand.

Despite local government reorganization, the 'new wave' in recreation and the emergence of an embryo profession of recreation management, staff in some cases are having to fit into structures and systems designed in times past to suit the Victorian 'parks – pitches – pools' era. In one London borough, a vast community sports and recreation centre had its director replaced by an administrator so that the centre's organization structure could fit into the borough departmental structure! The bureaucracy could not handle flexibility, not even at one centre, which had demonstrated itself to be unique, something outside the normal run of events.

Many recreation facilities, particularly in the voluntary sector, are managed by a leader and many volunteers. They take responsibility for facilities, plant, programme and personnel. Even in public recreation centres the level of part-time staff can be high. It is not unusual to find a centre at 10.00 p.m. manned by a supervisor and a few part-timers; managers and senior staff have long since gone.

Different forms of community recreation management may be needed to optimize, promote and encourage recreation. Part-time paid staff, coaches, helpers, community workers and volunteers may be needed to help to meet the needs, particularly of those who find it difficult to make use of public recreation facilities.

It is apparent that recreation services call for special, sensitive handling of staff. Staff have a variety of duties and the facilities are open for long hours. The nature of the job – that of creating satisfaction for people in their leisure time – requires that good staff have personal commitment and an understanding of the user requirements. *If staff flexibility is required, then organization and employer flexibility are also required.*

It is important for managers in recreation services to have knowledge, experience and understanding of staff, staff relations and organizational structures. Managers will have to work within structures often not of their choosing, they will have to be negotiators, decision-makers, communicators and understanders of a wide variety of professional and lay staff. Effective structures and good handling of staff are essential for effective management.

15.3   STAFFING AND LEGISLATION

The employment of staff and staff relations are governed to a considerable extent by government legislation. In recent years there have been fundamental changes in the law in the United Kingdom, which have far-reaching consequences for employers and employees. Recent legislation has set new standards in personnel policies and in employer-employee relationships and has provided statutory bodies to enforce the new standards.

There are well over thirty salient Acts of Parliament which have a bearing on staff relations and employment, 50% of which have been introduced or have been changed in the past ten years. Most legislation has put obligations and constraints on employers and extensive rights have been given to unions and to the employees. An exception was the

Industrial Relations Act 1971, which while imposing restrictions on management, had far more effect on unions. This Act, however, was repealed in 1974.

The new Acts have undoubtedly improved the working conditions and job security of employees in general. The effects of the new legislation has been most dramatic on industry. They have been less dramatic in the public sector where many of the new obligations were already being practised, for example, equal pay. For all employers and employees the position is now much clearer than in times past. Employees now have a much clearer idea of their position within their authority or factory; employers have a detailed procedural guide to employment matters. In *theory*, if the procedures are carefully and sensitively followed there will be less conflict.

Problems, however, still arise and statutory bodies have been appointed to ensure that the law is adhered to. For example, Industrial Tribunals were established by the *Industrial Training Act 1964* as a type of court which was suitable for hearing matters of industrial relations legislation. The tribunals cover not only matters arising from that Act but also the *Equal Pay Act*, the *Sex Discrimination Act*, the *Employment Protection Act* and the *Race Relations Act* and several minor Acts. Appeals go before the Employment Appeals Tribunal. Much of the work carried out in the field of recreation and leisure is subject to these Acts. For example, much of the work is undertaken in unsocial hours when there are pressures of urgency relating to, say, mounting a major sporting spectacular, a town festival, a major concert or television programme. Unsocial hours, special duties and overtime hours of full-time staff, have to be handled along with part-time staff, volunteers and temporary staff. The kinds of work and the complex nature of recreation programmes often produce the pressures which cause tensions and can lead to disputes. Managers should be aware of the laws which regulate staff relations. A thumbnail sketch of some of the relevant Acts of Parliament can be found in Table 15.1.

Despite legislation, tribunals and procedural guidelines, the problem of employment and staff relations is one of the primary factors in poor public relations, poor communications, mismanagement and low morale, all leading to less successful business enterprises whether in the private, commercial or public sectors, whether in the context of factory, school, swimming pool or opera house.

15.4 STAFFING AND PRINCIPLES OF MANAGEMENT

Some top level managers and senior personnel are concerned with the formulation of policies and organizational structures. Most managers, however, are appointed to positions in existing organizations, to which

Table 15.1 What do key Acts say about staffing?

Employment liability

Two Acts were passed in 1969. In the *Employers' Liability (Compulsory Insurance) Act* employees must be covered against injury or disease. Certificate must be displayed where all staff can see it. The *Employer's Liability (Defective Equipment) Act* ensures that any injury suffered by an employee through defective equipment is held to be the fault of the employer. The employer can counter-claim against supplier or employee for negligence.

Employment protection

Two Acts in 1975 and 1978 provide machinery for promoting good industrial relations. Short time and lay-offs have certain payment entitlements. Time off can be taken for public duties. Pregnant women are entitled to paid leave and their job back. The 1975 Act formed the Conciliation and Arbitration Service (ACAS).

Health and safety at work

Before this Act was passed in 1974 there were hundreds of regulations. Only two thirds of employees were covered. Health and Safety Commission was established. Employers have to provide workers with safety instructions, training and supervision. This is an 'enabling' Act. It lays down general principles to be followed, carries legal weight, which places obligations on employers including; display of instructions, consultation with unions. The *employee* has to take care for the health and safety of himself and others affected by his actions or omissions.

Employment of children

This Act of 1973 and the *Young Persons Employment Act 1938* specify the minimum age below which a child cannot be employed and the hours older children are allowed to work.

Sex discrimination

The 1975 Act makes it unlawful to discriminate in employment, training and education. The Equal Opportunities Commission enforces legislation.

Race relations

Discrimination is unlawful on grounds of colour, race, nationality or ethnic origin in this 1976 Act. A Commission for Racial Equality assists individuals who believe they have been discriminated against.

Equal payment

The Act of 1970 came into force in 1975. It is obligatory for employers to pay men and women the same rates of pay for undertaking the same work. Its purpose is to eliminate discrimination in pay and other employment matters; holidays, sickness benefits, bonus, overtime etc. The *Equal Pay (Amendment) Regulations, 1983* have since been introduced to assist in the assessment of what constitutes 'the same work'.

Employment

The *Employment Act 1980* made alterations to closed shop agreements. Alterations to unfair dismissal – onus of proof shifted from employer to employee. Small firm, exclusion with regard to maternity rights. This Act reduces the former rights of individual employees and their trade unions. The 1980 Act was amended by the *Employment Act 1982* which further strengthened the position of employers in cases of industrial disputes and provides for the payment by the State of compensation to former workers dismissed for non-membership of a trade union.

Contracts of employment

The 1972 Act requires all employees to be given a contract. Minimum periods of notice must be given. Contracts must give details of dates, rates of pay, hours, holidays, sick leave, pension rights and discipline and grievance procedures. The Act establishes the right of employers and employees to a minimum period of notice.

Trade union and labour relations

This 1974 Act repealed the *Industrial Relations Act 1971* but re-enacted its unfair dismissal provision, restored status of unions and employers organizations, and repealed the worker's right not to belong to a union, leading to 'closed shops'. The maximum compensation in cases of unfair dismissal is currently regulated by the *1982 Unfair Dismissal (Increase of Compensatory Limit – No.2) Order*. The *Trade Union Act, 1984* imposes certain conditions upon Unions wishing to be immune from liability for loss or damage caused to others during individual disputes. The major condition is that union activities must have the support of the membership established by secret ballot.

Disabled Persons

The *Disabled Persons Employment Act, 1944*, as amended by the 1958 Act, established a voluntary register of disabled people. Duties are placed on employers with 20 or more employees. The standard quota is 3% of the total workforce. The Manpower Services Commission has established a Disablement Advisory Service. Its 1984 *Code of Good Practice on the Employment of Disabled People* is the first government document of its kind in Europe.

Redundancy payments

This Act passed in 1965 was a major step forward in job security. It requires an employer to make a lump sum compensation to an employee who is made redundant after at least 104 weeks of reckonable service since the age of 18, unless the employer can prove to a tribunal that the employee was fairly dismissed and not made redundant. The amount of compensation is regulated by the *Employment Protection (Variation of Limits) Order*. The 1983 Order stipulated that from February 1st 1984 the maximum payment for dismissal stood at £4350.

Training

The *Industrial Training Act (1982)* empowers the Secretary of State to establish Training Boards to improve provision for industrial and commercial training. There are approximately 24 Boards in existence.

they have to adapt. It is important that managers at all levels understand the structure, the principles on which it is based and the components which go to make it up.

According to the International City Management Association [1] three basic principles of management must be considered in establishing an organizational structure, namely:

1. Unity of command.
2. Logical assignment.
3. Span of control.

15.4.1 Unity of command

The principle of 'unity of command' states that each individual in an organization should be responsible to *only one* superior. Adherence to this principle establishes a precise *chain of command* within the organization.

Situations exist in recreation organizations which do not follow such a principle. For example, at one recreation centre the head groundsman is answerable to *both* a centre manager and an assistant technical officer at the town hall. At another, a Recreation Manager is responsible to both a centre director *and* a borough recreation officer. At another establishment, while the principle of unity of command exists (in that the centre manager is responsible to only one person), he is answerable not to the borough director of recreation but to the chief executive!

15.4.2 Logical assignment

The principle of 'logical assignment' states that staff doing the same work should be grouped together and that work is planned and scheduled in a logical order.

Situations exist in recreation where structures and departmentalism are put first and the job in hand second. Without logical assignment there will be duplication, overlap, confusion, resentment, power struggles, drawing in of responsibilities to heighten status, keeping things close to the chest, and not sharing, which all lead to poor performance. Here again personalities are blamed but the greater responsibility rests with those responsible for the structure and its logical implementation.

15.4.3 Span of control

The principle of 'span of control' is a misnomer. The principle states that there are limiting factors which must be considered in deciding the number of subordinates a member of staff can effectively handle. Span of control may be more accurately defined as 'span of management' because the limiting factors are many. They include the number of *people* that can be supervised, the *distance* over which control can be exercised, the amount of *time* in which to exercise control, and the number of *activities* that a manager can effectively manage. The span of management is then a statement of those *limitations*.

It is not possible to state the exact number of people a manager should 'control'. Much depends on his or her knowledge, ability, time, energy, personality and the environment and situation in which work must be undertaken. The type of work, in addition to the capacities of the manager, must also be considered. Too few staff under one's control can lead to under-utilization of a manager's talents; efficiency and effectiveness will be limited by too many staff.

In recreation services many managers have responsibility for a large geographical area. Members of staff directed by a specific manager should not be situated too close if this results in over-supervision. However, they should not be located too far away to lead to under-supervision. In some services, recreation personnel have responsibilities 'out-in-the-sticks' or tucked away out of sight. It is only when something goes wrong – the books are 'cooked' or somebody is injured – that supervision comes into question. In some cases little work had been undertaken for weeks; no action may be taken until a complaint is made or a major problem occurs. Depending on the capacities of managers and staff, resources available and systems, the most feasible distance should be established.

Time is a very limiting factor. Every manager has to allocate time to:

1. *Routine work*, which is usually delegated but must be supervised.
2. *Regular work* a manager must do himself.
3. *Special work* and assignments.
4. *Creative work.*

Executives and senior managers often give very little time to the routine supervisory work, the kind of face-to-face work with the workforce. Many pool supervisors, green-keepers, community art workers and play leaders would not be able to recognize the director of leisure services or head of department if he or she walked into their work situation!

It is clear that a manager's ability to manage staff is limited. A narrow span of 'control' makes it possible to supervise work tightly but it does not give assistant staff the opportunity to make decisions or feel a sense of commitment and achievement. Recreation needs highly motivated staff. Recreation also needs many specialists such as coaches, community leaders, park wardens and outdoor activity specialists, who need principle guidelines and support, but also a level of autonomy rather than overt control and supervision.

In addition, staff develop skills peculiar to the job and special expertise. This technical know-how can be harnessed to improve job satisfaction and involvement in decision-making processes, which impinge on their area of work. Drucker states that performance will be improved by decentralization. 'It will make it possible for good men, hitherto stifled, to do a good job effectively. It will make better performers out of many mediocre men by raising their sights and the demands on them. It will identify the poor performers and make possible their replacement' [2].

15.5. ORGANIZATION AND STAFFING STRUCTURES

A good organization and staff structure will assist greatly in the achievement of the goals of any organization. However, it is not a panacea or alternative to good management; *it is a means towards an end*. A 'good' structure, as such, does not exist in isolation. It is only good if it is good for the organization it serves.

Structures will depend on several important factors:

1. The nature of the controlling body (local authority, commercial entrepreneur, private club).
2. The aims and objectives of the organization (profit making, service orientation).
3. The financial targets.
4. The scale and nature of the facilities and resources.
5. The layout and design.
6. The nature of the service to be provided.
7. The levels of performance (top level, casual, formal, informal, beginners or a comprehensive range).
8. The hours of operation.

15.5.1 Formulating a staff structure

In some situations staff structures have been charted even *before* an organization has outlined its policies, objectives and target programmes. In such cases assumptions have been made that it is possible to strike the right balance on paper, bearing in mind the levels of staffing in other authorities or organizations, the hierarchical system within the overall authority and the funds which are likely to be available for staffing. Such mismanagement is born out of the belief that it is the way in which squares and rectangles fit neatly into a comprehensive family tree and which lends support to the status quo, that will find favour. But the first step should *not* be the discussion of a structure, rather an analysis of the organization and its policies which the structure is to serve. Many leisure centres in the United Kingdom have tried to copy or to emulate a structure which has been developed elsewhere. But all the centres are different; each has its own identity; each has its own budget targets; each has its own assets and problems. *Structures must be developed which meet the needs of the situation.*

Organization and staff structures should not be *static*, determined and fixed forever. Structures must be changed to meet changing situations. For example, a manager usually comes into a structure previously determined, and finds ways of improving performance or ways in which the staff will respond to his or her ideas. Programmes will change. Staff will develop and some will move on. Financial forecasts will alter. Therefore, appraisals, say, after one or two years, should be undertaken and changes implemented to meet the new situation. It is said that we can be certain of only one thing – change. Changes in structure, changes in style, changes in objectives are always necessary but seldom implemented in public recreation services. Commercial organizations must of necessity change the way the structure works to be effective financially.

15.5.2 Departmental structures

To be effective managers must divide the workload into manageable parts. The main purpose of dividing the work is to establish methods of determining individual groups, and section responsibilities, the distribution of authority to individuals and the processes of delegation. The most used method of dividing work is *departmentalization*, that is, dividing the workforce into units and departments.

According to Grossman [3] there are four avenues managers can follow in creating departments: by *function, type of clientele, geographic area* or *process*.

Function departments   These are departments in which staff are grouped according to function, for example, sports coaching department, arts and crafts department, maintenance department.

Clientele departments   These departments are grouped according to the clientele they are to serve, for example, junior department, youth department, senior citizen's department.

Geographic departments   Departments where staff are grouped according to the area in which they work, for example, a large borough could have regional recreation departments.

Process departments   These are usually service-giving departments and grouped according to the process used in providing the particular services, for example, an information service or counselling department.

Most recreation executives use a combination of these strategies or adjust elements of specific strategies to create the appropriate departmental structure. However, the structure often evolves haphazardly and lacks planning and coordination. What is important is that the manager knows the possibilities and the alternatives and logically thinks through them, broadening his or her horizons to accommodate the variety of methods and approaches to develop the most appropriate departmental structure.

15.5.3   Formal and informal structures

Once the work is departmentalized, managers must make decisions relating to *levels of authority*. It is these decisions which establish *chains of command* within an organization. Authority levels establish the organization's power structure. Staff appointed to high authority levels normally have more power. They have a greater say in group management decisions.

Inflexible, bureaucratic adherence to chains of command, however, are inappropriate for much of the 'gelling' of an organization. The structure is there as a framework. Within and around the formal structure there is very soon built up an *informal structure*. 'It is the informal structure which provides for cross-communication rather than going through the channels' [4]. Much of the important 'human' work which makes an organization 'tick' is undertaken through cross-communication. A recreation department and youth department often work out joint problems without going through their departmental channels.

An example of good cross-communication is shown at one recreation centre developed by a trust. Daytime integrated sports coaching classes are run for mothers, unemployed youngsters, school and college pupils – all within the same space/time allocation, utilizing the most appropriate coaches from any of the organizations. The possibility of these classes being held would have been remote if procedures and communications had been conducted through the four formal structures of the sports trust, the county council, the technical college and the local schools. The informal structure and communications network enabled those with first hand knowledge to make decisions relating to work, which they are the best to advise upon. This informal process cuts across organizational boundaries, budgets, space and time allocations, staff and administrative red tape. One of the skills of the good manager is to permit, within certain limits, a level of face-to-face work which in essence *bypasses the chain of command*.

Nancy Foy [5] believes that it is time we 'humanized' our systems. We need not scrap them, as long as they remain human in scale. While organizations and the people in them need rituals and regular checkpoints they also need information about their own work groups, their own outputs and so on. 'A lot of information that can't be transmitted formally can flow informally, with complete credibility and confidentiality, once people believe they are hearing the truth and able to tell it as well'.

15.5.4 Line and line and staff organizations

Organizational charts normally depict either *line* or *line and staff* organizations. In *line* organizations authority is passed on from the highest to the lowest levels via a *chain of command*.

In *line and staff* organizations, staff personnel are incorporated in addition to 'line' staff. 'Staff' personnel are frequently specialists who service 'line' personnel, for example, financial, programming and personnel specialists. In many recreation organizations 'staff' sections have line staff under the direction of a sectional head. A director of coaching, for example, may be responsible for four individual coaches who may work with specialist supervisors. The principle of 'logical assignment', however, needs sensitive manipulation (see 15.4.2).

In many recreation organizations, individual 'staff' personnel may function *both* as line managers and as 'staff' managers. For example, at the Leatherhead Leisure Centre, where, in its early days, staffing levels were being kept arbitrarily low for economic reasons, each senior 'staff' – recreation officer, technical officer and administrative officer – had to spend a good proportion of his or her normal working week supervising the day-to-day operations of the centre as duty manager, responsible for plant, staff, public and programme. Their 'staff' functions were carried out in office hours and their 'line' functions were carried out in the evenings and at weekends.

'Line and staff' organizations are more flexible than 'line' organizations. They permit 'line' personnel to carry out the regular work – the use of the resources and the facilities by the public – leaving certain specialist functions to 'staff' personnel. The International City Management Association [6] differentiates the functions of line and staff as follows:

Line functions	*Staff functions*
Line directs or orders	Staff advise
Line has responsibility to carry out activities from beginning to end	Staff studies, reports, recommends, but does not carry out
Line follows chain of command	Staff assists line but is not part of chain
Line decides when and how to use staff	
	Staff always available for line use
Line is the doing part of the organization	Staff is the assisting part of the organization

15.5.5 The organization chart

The organization chart is the most common approach to portraying the organization's structure. It illustrates the hierarchy, functions and chain of command. Strict adherence at all costs to charts and family trees is not advocated but as a general framework it helps staff within an organization to visualize and understand, to see clear lines for effective and efficient accomplishment of its objectives. Where a recreation service such as the Sports Council or Arts Council are geographically spread, or where there is difficulty in perceiving the roles of particular departments, the organization chart has considerable advantage. The organization chart, however, must not be given permanent status, as though it was indestructible. It portrays the organization, acts as a framework for sharing the work and indicates levels of responsibility. It should be used to further the work of the organization.

The structure is not infallible; it has limitations. First, it is *skeletal*, in static form. It is representative only as long as the status quo remains. Second, it has little flesh about the skeleton; it is *not precise* about amounts of authority and responsibility. *Third*, and most important, it does *not portray the essential informal structure* and relationships. Some managers become over-concerned with preserving and enhancing the organization structure itself, rather than with helping to serve its stated principles, its aims and objectives. However, the organizational structure, used wisely, is one of the tools to promote successful management performance.

15.5.6 Designing a structure

The actual structure of an organization will depend on several factors:

1. The nature of the controlling body.
2. The aims and objectives of the organization.
3. The scale and nature of its facilities and resources.
4. The geographical distribution of its facilities.
5. The nature of the service provided.
6. The stability of the environment in which the organization operates.
7. The quality of the management and staff within the organization.

The various organization structures used in the delivery of leisure services fall along a continuum between a *mechanistic model* (which is rigidly structured) at one extreme to an *organic model* (which is flexibly structured) at the other (Fig.15.1). These and other models are discussed below.

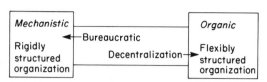

Fig. 15.1 Organizational models.

Organic organization

1. Better suited to operate in an environment where change is a factor – it is adaptable to changing conditions.
2. One's special knowledge and experience are looked at in terms of what they can contribute to the overall task.
3. Problems are not pushed upward, downward or sideways, i.e. 'buck passing' is discouraged.
4. Control, authority and communications move through a wide network rather than a single hierarchical structure.
5. Communication tends to be more lateral than vertical and content consists of information and advice rather than instructions and decisions.

Mechanistic organization

1. Operates more effectively when the environment is stable.
2. Control, authority and communication usually follow hierarchical patterns.
3. The work is broken down into differentiated tasks with precise instructions that become highly standardized.
4. Interaction tends to follow hierarchical lines between superior and subordinate.
5. There is a general assumption that those higher up the hierarchy are better equipped to make the more important decisions.
6. Operational actions tend to be governed by instructions issued by superiors.

Vertical and horizontal structures

In an organization which is highly structured the role expectations of its members are strictly controlled, leaving little room for individual discretion and initiative. In contrast, in a loosely structured organization there are fewer constraints leaving a person with considerable discretion to define his or her own role to achieve the overall objective. The right balance for maximum effectiveness must be achieved.

Bureaucracy

The bureaucratic model is the most widely implemented form of organization. It is a vertical structure. Authority is located at the top of the hierarchy and flows downwards through the organization. The division of labour emphasizes the heirarchical structure and establishes a superior /subordinate relationship. This allows the various activities to be sub-divided into a specific set of tasks with the roles of individuals clearly defined.

15.6 STAFFING: SUMMARY

This chapter has been concerned with staff and staffing structures within recreation organizations. It is clear that the Recreation Manager should understand the way in which staff are employed, trained and deployed in order to maximize efficiency and bring out the best in staff. The manager should understand the law and the principles of management as they relate to staffing, the formulation of organization structures and the specialist responsibilities and staffing functions within recreation services and recreation facility management. To conclude, a 12-point recreation facility staffing guideline is presented.

15.7 TWELVE GUIDELINES TO RECREATION FACILITY STAFFING

1. *Train and deploy.* Recognize that the way staff are trained and deployed affects results.
2. *Study legislation, principles and structures.* Understand 'unity of command', 'logical assignment' and 'span of control'. Recognize the limitations of span of control.
3. *Create formal structures.* Provide for clear lines of authority and chains of command – a formal structure.
4. *Permit informal structures.* Recognize informal structures and their importance to essential cross-communications. In doing so, accept levels of bypassing chains of command.
5. *Present sound proposals.* Sound staffing proposals (essential levels, responsibilities, roles) are needed, not weak proposals which then make it possible for authorities to reduce staff levels in order to increase profits or reduce deficits.
6. *Create team management.* Recognize the value of team management to coordinate long hours and a varied programme – all employees are in essence part-timers.
7. *Use 'line and staff'.* Avoid rigid 'line' structures. Consider appropriate hybrids to meet particular situations. Think through the problem logically. Structures must be tailor-made to suit the services to be given.
8. *Make conditions flexible.* The complexity, hours and patterns of use

call for flexible staff attitudes. Therefore, organizational flexibility is essential. Staff should have titles which give them a broad scope of duties and which do not limit their function.

9. *Construct departments and decentralize.* Divide the work out into departments, units or sections and identify their functions. Identify the tasks and responsibilities attached to each position so that the delegation can be effectively achieved. Encourage decentralization to help many staff undertake a job more effectively, to grow in the job and to attain greater job satisfaction.

10. *Start with essential staff.* When opening new facilities start with essential staff only and then build up as needs dictate. If not staff will tailor-make their work-rate to fit the position, which they will soon handle with consummate ease. The full-time staff positions should be limited to immediate recognizable functions. To cope with initial, additional demands, use part-time staff but recognise the strain on full-time staff. Training and supervision is, however, more difficult with part-timers.

11. *Consider alternative structural elements.* Consider the relative value of different forms of community recreation management. Do not be afraid to encourage, train and support voluntary assistants, particularly where certain community needs are not being met. Consult with Trade Unions so that there is an appreciation of voluntary commitment to serve the community and not in order to replace paid staff.

12. *Use structures as means, not ends.* Remember that a structure chart is a tool to management. It must be used. It must be changed to meet changing situations. Do not be preoccupied with structures and family trees. Structures are means towards ends, not ends in themselves.

REFERENCES AND NOTES

1. International City Management Association (1965), *Basic Concepts of Organization, Bulletin 3: Effective Supervisory Practices.* ICMA, Washington, D.C.
2. Drucker, P.F. (1955), *The Practice of Management*, Pan Books, London.
3. Grossman, A.H. (1980), *Personnel Management in Recreation and Leisure Services*, Groupwork Today, South Plainfield, NJ. p.64.
4. Ibid., p.65.
5. Foy, N. (1981), The Human Side of Information, *Management Review and Digest*, Oct, 1981.
6. International City Management Association (1965), *Basic Concepts of Organization, Bulletin 3: Effective Supervisory Practices*, ICMA, Washington, DC. p.5.
   Additional suggested reading for employers, managers and employees in the United Kingdom.
   Janner, G. (1979), *Janner's Compendium of Employment Law*, Business Books, London.
   Alston, R. (1976), *Industrial Relations and the Law*, Financial Techniques, Woking.

Birtles, B. and Hewitt, P. (1980), *Your Rights at Work*, National Council for Civil Liberties, London.

Arbitration and Conciliatory Advisory Service (ACAS) (1980), *Industrial Relations Handbook*, HMSO, London.

Waud, C. (1985 *Guide to Employment Law 1985*, Hamsworth Publications for Associated Newspapers, London.

Chapter 16

Marketing of recreation

★

If you can't do it excellently, don't do it at all.
Because if it's not excellent it won't be profitable or fun
and if you're not in business for fun or profit,
what the hell are you doing here

Robert Townsend

★

It's an unfortunate fact that marketing – the profession, trade, way of life or what you will – is held in pretty low esteem by the public at large. It's probable, of course, that the public at large doesn't actually understand what marketing's about, but for many, the term has too close an association with the street trader, who would sell his sister if the price were right.

The whole panoply of consumer persuasion, from advertising and PR, through sales promotion, packaging, point-of-sale display and salesman-ship itself, is bundled together in many minds as prima facie *proof that marketing is immoral, in practice if not in theory.*

Marketing 26 April 1984

16.1 INTRODUCTION

We are all influenced by marketing. In Western civilization marketing is part of the fabric by which we go about our daily business. 'It is part of the modern survival kit – because we depend on it' [1].

The marketing of recreation and leisure is undertaken by *all* those involved in providing services, resources and goods for recreation and leisure, whether in the public, private or commercial sectors. Public knowledge, or lack of knowledge, about services and facilities and the image they portray are essential components of marketing. Every organization in the recreation business is, therefore, already 'marketing'. The question is whether they are marketing well or badly.

The marketing of recreation by local authorities has been generally unimaginative, traditional and politically centred, although there are many outstanding exceptions. Marketing in commercial enterprise is a multi-million pound industry. It is an imaginative, mature and sophisticated business with powerful influences for good *and* for bad. The marketing in the private, non-profit-making organizations has been parochial and ingrowing. The composite of public/commercial/private marketing of recreation has fallen short of excellence and its assets and liabilities insufficiently explored by recreation professionals.

This chapter explores the possibilities for improved marketing of recreation services and products, particularly in the public sector. What is marketing and why is it practised? Who does the marketing and to whom? What is to be marketed and what is the marketing approach? What actions, measurements, ideas and strategies can be employed? What hints can be given to the manager of recreation? What are the assets and problems relating to marketing in the public sector?

16.2   MARKETING: WHAT IS IT AND WHO DOES IT?

In the commercial world marketing has proved to be an effective means of making greater profits. It has been a means of greater success. It means business. That is why marketing is important in the commercial sector. For recreation services in the public sector it can mean greater success and can assist in meeting organizational objectives and public recreation demands.

The purpose of marketing is to earn profit by 'adding maximum value at minimum cost' [1]. Put simply, marketing is concerned with satisfying customers profitably! However, in the public sector 'profit' should be measured *not* just in terms of money but also by the numerical turnover, the quality of the services, the range of people, the choice and scope of the programme, the improvements made and other relevant criteria.

Marketing is a process and coordination network that analyses, creates, develops products and services, packages, prices, promotes, distributes and sells. *It is a beginning-to-end-process.* This 'marketing mix' is usually aimed at a segment of the public or a target market.

The marketing process is *coordinating* the activities of the business in the pursuit of maximum added value at minimum cost. It is a *linkage* function for saleable goods or services. *Its point of origin is consumer demand.*

One feature of the concept of marketing is that of *voluntary exchange*. 'It calls for offering something of value to someone in exchange for something else of value' [2]. For example, public recreation is provided for the community in exchange for people's money, time and rates.

'Commercial' marketing and 'service' marketing have much in common but there are conceptual differences. In the commercial field the product is subordinate to the fundamental aim – achievement of sales targets and the making of financial profits. In the services field, the quality of the service is paramount.

16.2.1   The marketing approach

Traditionally many companies are *product-orientated*; they have a predetermined product or service. They find customers and convice them they want the product. The approach is, 'This is what *we* want and what *we've* got – now sell it'. Local government services work in this way. For example, facilities are built, equipment is installed, markings are put on to the floors, programmes are devised, times are decided, charges are determined, systems are established, and the council will proudly announce that the facility is open. Many councillors will then say of the facility, 'It is there for them to use; if they don't use it that is their lookout.

We provide plenty of opportunity in our town'.

The marketing way reverses the process and *starts with the customer*. It says, 'This is what the customer wants – now make it'. It then designs, produces and delivers the *satisfactions* for the customer at a profit. Using the findings of a market research programme, i.e. information received, management organizes its business to ensure that the product is *tailor-made* for the market. When wants have been ascertained sales resistance is apt to evaporate. The Japanese perfection in mass production, efficiency and knowledge of what the public wants in design, looks, performance, and price has reaped harvests in the motor cycle and motor car industries. The question for Recreation Managers is: what does the public want from recreation services?

Local authorities are in the marketing business. They have to compete for a share of the market. The financial profit motive, however, is not normally an issue, although greater stress on viability and commercial approaches are increasingly being employed. Viable services are important but service to the public at large is pre-eminent. Since the mid 1960s local authorities have been giving more attention than before to recreation provision and opportunity for the socially disadvantaged – the less able, the disabled, the unemployed school leaver, ethnic minorities, the mother at home with young children, young people and the ageing. *Social marketing* is a concept currently in vogue. It is seen as one of the new trends, which could be used to enhance social and community programmes. However, recession and tighter budgets have had some profound effects in cutbacks.

16.3 MARKETING IN THE PUBLIC SECTOR

An emerging marketing myth is that local authorities can market public recreation in exactly the same way as one can market breakfast cereals, cameras or holidays. While local authorities have elements within their services which could be commercially orientated, and while marketing techniques can be used to promote recreation programmes, the overall purpose of the authority is not to make financial profit but to meet need. Moreover, the recreation product is extremely difficult to define and quantify, and quality of the service is difficult to measure. The aims and objectives, too, are decidedly different from many commercial undertakings: financial yardsticks are only one measurement and should normally be quite secondary to other criteria. Local councils have political, governmental, traditional and institutional constraints, in addition to social and moral obligations. Marketing is needed but the *way* in which it is processed should be different between the commercial product and the local authority service 'product'.

Public sector marketing is a hybrid of approaches which have evolved historically and are now caught up with commercial approaches, primarily to limit subsidy or to help make the facilities pay for themselves. With the possibility of central government introducing competitive tendering in respect of public services (including recreation services), recreation managers will be under far greater pressure to 'perform'.

16.3.1 The concept of social marketing

Marketing is typically defined in business terms as the planning, pricing, promoting, distribution and servicing of goods and products. It has been concerned with economic exchange of goods. As such it has been associated with business objectives to sell products and to learn about the kinds of products and services that the public would like to purchase.

The concept of marketing, however, can be interpreted as much broader than just economic exchange and could also 'logically encompass exchanges dealing with social issues and ideas' [3]. Most people are familiar with recent attempts to project politicians and political platforms through marketing. 'For example, an individual participating in an election exchanges his vote for the promise of the enactment of a particular political platform if his candidate is elected. Thus, this situation involves exchange' [3]. Marketing, it is argued, includes the facilitating of *social exchanges* as well as goods and services.

Kotler and Zaltman [4] define social marketing as 'The design, implementation and control of programmes calculated to influence the acceptability of social ideas and involving consideration of product planning, pricing, communication, distribution and market research.' Marketing, then, can encompass political campaigns, community programmes and social causes, such as pollution control, family planning, health, stop smoking campaigns, equal rights and peace campaigns. The 1985 UK/ USA 'Live Aid' concerts were testimony of the power of marketing social causes.

Any new trend is likely to have both positive and negative effects. Marketing can improve the chances of useful social and community programmes coming to fruition. However, marketing can also be seen as having potential ethical problems. Those who are economically powerful could use marketing techniques to enhance ideas which may promote causes that are *not* socially beneficial.

Social marketing can be utilized in the recreation field for causes and community projects and assist in recreation planning. A whole range of recreation aims could be brought to public attention, for example, recreation for the disabled, health and fitness, 'Sport for all', 'Art for all' and

'Music for all' campaigns. However, its sensitive application is enormously important to avoid the criticism of indoctrination, for social marketing could be a powerful instrument which can affect the way people think, speak and act. This, of course, is the purpose of some marketing and this is why the causes and issues must be debated and adjudged by society to be beneficial.

16.3.2 Marketing of public authority recreation services and facilities

The marketing of public authority services and facilities has not been studied extensively. The work by Cowell [5] spearheaded inroads into marketing in the public sector. An exploratory study was carried out to discover the extent to which marketing 'was being applied by local authority recreation, leisure and sports centre managers in "selling" the services for which they were responsible' [5].

Forty-nine centres involving 55 management staff were included in the study. The broad conclusion of the study was that there was 'no major evidence of marketing being applied to local authority recreation and sports centre planning and provision. However, the question now raised is whether it is reasonable to expect that marketing could and should be applied to this area'. There were several outstanding exceptions to the general finding. This is not surprising in view of the fact that about 20% of the sample was made up of regional winners for the UK Sports Centre of the Year Award Scheme. Even so the overall picture was one of little evidence of marketing application.

The findings are of interest. Objectives 'frequently' had not been set and a good deal of discretion had been left to the manager. Demand assessments were rarely undertaken. The product was regarded 'as a portfolio of activities, events or facilities'. There were very few price experiments or uses of prices as promotional devices. 'One manager confessed that how prices were set in his centre was "one of life's mysteries".' Siting of the centres had, by and large, been on the availability of land. Promotional budgets were small and even small budgets were sometimes underspent. Success of centres was identified on somewhat negative criteria, i.e. not over-spending budgets, reducing deficits and absence of complaints. Little incentive could be given to staff by managers within the local government system.

Cowell states that the absence of substantial marketing should not necessarily be seen as criticism. Should marketing be practised? Three main possible explanations were put forward for the relative lack of marketing – *general constraints, institutional constraints* and *services restraints*. Marketing has been developed in economic contexts. In addition 'the local authority situation in which marketing might have been applied has changed rapidly from one of expansion to one of restraint' [5]. Is marketing relevant in times of scarcity and restriction? Marketing has only recently been concerned with social and service issues. These general constraints have made it difficult for local authorities to adapt to a marketing approach.

The nature of local authorities themselves can militate against marketing approaches. Most managers have not 'graduated' in business situations. They are untrained in management and marketing. Profit as a measure of success does not dominate decision-making. 'Providing for everybody's needs may make good political sense; it is unlikely to make sound marketing sense where segmentation is in vogue. Organisational structures too are often extended and are rarely designed for speedy response to the market place; political interests cloud issues; the committee system can delay decision making; local authorities interpret their sport, leisure and recreation responsibilities differently [5].' Many authorities see recreation services as 'social' services. Such are the 'institutional' constraints.

The third constraint is the 'service' constraint. The service is being sold, not a product. Theorists themselves argue about the basic differences between products and services. While the difference may not be substantial, some important differences do emerge. 'The nature of what is being sold may thus account for the limited evidence of marketing application in local authority settings' [5].

In the commercial sector financial profits are used as measuring criteria. In local authorities, financial pressures are not concerned primarily with the product and service but with political policy, local government funding and the fixing of the local rates. Panic measures may demand that income be maximized and expenditure minimized. This may mean that expenditure in one vital area is reduced, which could then work against achieving the objectives – a treatment least likely to effect a cure.

The fixing of prices is a complicated and varied business. The report by the Scottish Sports Council, *A Study of Sports Centres and Swimming Pools* [6], looked into the use and management of facilities in Scotland. It reported:

'In most cases, the facility managers had no direct control, although many of them would have influence on policy decisions. The pricing schedules in almost every case were complicated, with differences often amounting only to a few pence. There appeared to be little evidence of an overall rational basis for the fixing of prices, with probably the commonest base being that of comparison with other adjacent and/or similar facilities' [6].

In addition there was no clear evidence of price being used as a regulator of demand and only one example of it being used as a promotional tool. These findings are very similar to those of Cowell. Similarly promotion of the facilities was 'in all cases' unsophisticated and subject to very small budgets.

It is clear that, while marketing may have considerable benefits in local authority provision and management of recreation, *the use of marketing approaches must be adapted to suit the social, political, economic and institutional structure within the local government setting.*

16.4   CONSTRUCTING A MARKETING PLAN

In order to market successfully there needs to be a marketing strategy – *a marketing plan.* In planning a programme a Recreation Manager takes intitial actions to, as it were, construct a 'community profile' and this is used as a basis for programming and marketing the programme. This can be achieved by collecting, collating and analysing relevant information in order to obtain a clearer view of where the most profitable business opportunities lie, i.e. seeking the information needed for decision-making. This involves seeking answers to fundamental questions. What business are we in? What is the market structure? Who are the competitors? Who are the customers? What are the products? Table 16.1 outlines in simple form ten basic questions the marketer should ask. Such an initial approach provides information. *But it is only information.* It will not make decisions. It represents a reconnaissance of the market. It needs to be turned into a plan of action.

Having undertaken the reconnaissance and arrived at a profile of the community or market sector or target group, the manager must then construct a marketing plan. Several basic steps should be taken to arrive at a sound plan.

(a) Define the problem
This could be implementing a community programme, or opening a leisure centre, or producing a series of festivals or keeping the public informed of the services.

(b) Collect and evaluate relevant information
The initial information gathering will have shown up the target 'zones'. More precise information relating to these zones needs collating.

(c) Set objectives
As we have seen in the programming section, this implies setting measurable targets and simplifying and concentrating effort towards the attainment of specific goals.

(d) Decide a course of action, i.e. a marketing plan
This plan should be undertaken with the support and commitment from all concerned – committees, staff and project representatives. The marketing plan is the method by which resources are deployed, so that

Table 16.1 Ten-point guideline: marketing information needed to construct a marketing plan

---

1. *What business are we in?*
   Activities business? Entertainment business? Playing, eating and drinking business?

2. *What is the market structure?*
   Many small facilities or few large facilities? What scope and range?

3. *What are the market trends?*
   Expanding or contracting? What are the limitations? Growth ideas?

4. *What is our share of the market?*
   Do we have the only public theatre? Are 80% of the squash courts at one centre?

5. *What is our business reputation?*
   How does our name go down with customers? Have price increases lowered acceptance?

6. *Who are our potential customers?*
   All the family or the young and active? Who uses which products?

7. *Who are our competitors?*
   How will this affect strategy? Their strengths? Their weaknesses?

8. *What are the products?*
   Which activities sell the fastest and why? Which the slowest and why?

9. *What are the financial factors?*
   Production, marketing costs? Profit/loss margins?

10. *What are the particular circumstances?*
    Of crucial importance to the marketing approach is an understanding of consumers. What are the needs and demands of the community? Where are the marketing gaps? What needs to be done?

---

the attack on the market has the biggest chance of success. This involves various operations known as the *marketing mix*, which consists of *products, prices, distribution, communication, communications* and *selling*.

(e) Put the plan down in writing
When the organization and staff have been committed to marketing the project, the plan should be committed to paper, so that the inputs, processes and outputs can be measured.

(f) Take action, organize and control
The planning organization, controls and measurement are the responsibility of the manager. Marketing a leisure centre, for example, is the prime

responsibility of the centre manager. It is too important to be delegated or left to somebody else. The manager needs authority to control the marketing mix.

(g) Monitor and evaluate

Check progress systematically and evaluate the work that goes into marketing, the actions taken and the results that accrue. Marketing is a continuous cycle, a hand-in-glove, beginning-to-end-process, along with general management and programming.

(h) Modify and improve

16.5   THE RECREATION PRODUCT

The first aspect to consider in the 'marketing mix' is the product. What is the recreation product? This is a more difficult question than it might appear to be. Commercial leisure normally has a finite answer and a measurable target. For example, at a squash club the object could be to enrol 1000 squash members at £100 per head and sell 70% of court space during the 80 hours of opening at £3 an hour. But even in this simple objective of selling memberships and utilizing space there are many service elements – efficiency, attractive facilities, ambience, après-squash – all of which go to make up the product and bring satisfaction to the user.

The recreation product in local authority services is rarely spelled out. The selling of spaces, times and activities is understood. What is not understood is the creating of an environment in which people can *experience recreation* through an activity of their choice. Demand for a recreation product may arise out of choice, out of opportunity, from the facilities themselves or from the policies of management. On the other hand, demand for a recreation product can be stifled by restrictive policies, limited opportunities, highly exclusive clubs, lack of choice, vested interests and other demotivators. For example, a sports facility requiring a playing-in standard, or an enrolling fee, or a proposer and seconder on an application form, may attract better players, more affluent people and those who can handle the whole 'joining' process; others may find the joining process itself intimidating and a major stumbling block to participation. The objectives determine the recreation products and their promotion.

Facilities, opportunities and 'welcome' can stimulate demand and expand a recreation market dramatically. Take the game of squash. Over the span of a few years squash, previously the game for those in private, exclusive clubs and for many who had been to public schools and university, became one of the most popular participation sports in the United Kingdom. The Squash Rackets Association, which has been in existence for over 50 years, claims much credit for spreading their game in the United Kingdom and across the world in recent years. But facts prove that the Association had minimal effect on the recent upsurge of the game in the UK. The game remained a minority interest for a handful of privileged people *until squash facilities became available to the general public.* This came about in large measure through the indoor sports centre movement in general and from public participation at the first two indoor sports centres at Crystal Palace and Harlow in 1964. Almost every other comprehensive indoor sports centre since then has included squash provision. In the nine years prior to 1963 courts were being built at a rate of 1.3% a year. In the nine years prior to 1972 (the growth years of the sports centre movement) courts were increased by 8.4% a year [7]. Added to this initial impetus from public courts becoming available, commercial entrepreneurs were quick to seize the profitable ends of the sports centre movement with squash in the lead. By 1980 there were believed to be some 6000 squash courts in the UK with nearly a fifth of them in sports centres run by local authorities [8]. Since then there has been a levelling out of demand. This is an example of where the facilities themselves, allied to management policy – that of expanding the market to the general public – created demands, new facilities and a dramatic increase in active participation. In other words the *opportunity* to play squash provided by those from outside squash circles (public and commercial providers) made it into a boom sport. Sponsorship and exposure has done the same for other sports such as snooker and darts.

Most recreation programmes, even those designed with major speciality areas, such as drama or cycling, tend to market more than one product. How many products are to be marketed? In the public sector it has been shown, in recent years, not only that a *combination of facilities* attracts greater use and is more economical, but also that the spin-off to other activities expands the market [9]. Local authorities have had a tradition of building single activity facilities like swimming pools. In the new recreation centres where there are swimming pools and 'dry' facilities, the combination of 'wet and dry' has increased numbers; the spin-off *to* and *from* swimming has been considerable at some centres.

Markets rarely remain static. Managers should, therefore, *avoid putting all their eggs in one basket.* In addition, if the aim of a council is to give the public a level of freedom of choice, then it is important to give that choice and variety within the overall service.

Some products will cease to contribute to 'profits' or 'benefits'. New products may be the life-blood of some static leisure services. The answer may be to introduce *new looking* products to create new images. 'New looking products carry advantages to stress new customer benefits [10].' What do potential customers *think* the product is? *Their* notion of what it is and what the benefits are, is what matters.

Products may decline but demand for the type of product may still be rising. We go to the cinema less often but there is a greater demand for more entertainment. The history of mass leisure during this century demonstrates this – music halls, radio, spectator sports, television. In recent times we have seen the craze of skateboarding take rapid growth only to plummet just as rapidly. However, new looking activities such as roller skating, roller surfing, roller disco and roller hockey are activities on *wheels*. Activities like these have captured some of the existing market but have expanded the 'activities on wheels' market considerably. At a sports centre in Batley, roller skating was introduced and proved popular and profitable. However, skating sessions almost emptied the swimming pool of its clients; swimming and skating were attracting the same young people. The manager decided to make alterations to the timing of the two activities to enable young people to skate, then swim. In this way he created more activities for the same people and new activities for new people. The market was expanded. This example shows the integration of programming and marketing. The craze of BMX riding is important to support but must be seen in the overall context of market growth and level.

16.5.1 Pricing the products

The pricing policy is an important factor in financial planning and in the overall strategy. It is a vital part of marketing. Several questions arise and need decision: should we price high and then reduce, price low for a quick penetration of the market, price at one rate for all the customers, offer special rates, discounts, packages? Commercial marketing is profit-orientated, therefore it is price sensitive; products must be gauged at the right price to attract customers and to make a profit. Discussion is often centred on keeping prices low, but in many exclusive establishments pricing high can achieve the type of response aimed to meet objectives.

Local authority pricing is largely based on tradition and what is an 'acceptable' level compared with other authorities. It is largely a matter of guesswork based on a 'feel' for what the market will pay and what other authorities charge. The Chartered Institute of Public Finance and Accountancy (CIPFA) shows great similarity between authorities in terms of pricing levels. Facilities for arts and sports have been kept at relatively low costs based on political and social judgements and intuition. In recent years, however, the running costs of recreation services and centres has called for a more objective financial appraisal. Authorities are asking themselves: is it possible to cover running costs? Is it possible to offset viable against non-viable activities? Should subsidy be given in greater measure to certain sectors of the community?

There is fierce competition in the commercial world. Competitive pricing and good margins are valuable weapons for salesmen. There are special bonuses for stockists. Promotional devices are endless. Discounts apply. Attractions in the form of stamps, wrappers, competitions, free glasses at petrol stations, incentive schemes, holidays for two and a host of other methods are tried. The inventiveness is endless. Commercial marketing is not just concerned with the product (it is quite secondary to other factors) but with the benefits to the customers if *they buy* the product and to the salespeople, *if they sell* it.

Local authorities are not under such fierce competition. Authorities have far greater scope to use recreation resources to enlarge opportunities and help to meet people's needs. But local authorities must first discover needs and wants and then attract people to the services offered. The 'wrong' services could be offered at no charge at all and still people will spend their time and their money on other apparently less worthy products!

Price, therefore, may not be as important after all? Cheapness may be one criterion but not necessarily the only criterion. Rambling, camping, tennis, museums, theatres and athletics, for example, are relatively cheap activities, yet they attract only certain small segments of the population. Marketers, i.e. managers, have the task of changing images in order to draw people to the recreation product.

16.6 THE CUSTOMER

In very few instances do people really know what they want, even when they say they do.

Advertising Age

All customers have many similar needs yet they *vary* greatly and so does their spare cash. In addition, in times of economic recession, the disposable income of many people diminishes, while the costs of goods and services increase. Not only do customers vary one from another; the same customers may vary from one sitution to another, from one mood to another, from one inclination to another. Therefore, in recreation we must market for both the *similarities* and *differences* of customers.

Many factors affect demand as we have seen – social class, age, family, education, looks, personal aspirations, income, government restrictions, hire purchase, fashion, social attitudes, choices, motivations and many more. Customers are under constant pressure, whether as individuals or companies. In the past there were small, concentrated and highly profitable markets. Now there are widespread mass markets with affluence. There is far greater choice.

Customers are not static, unquestioning beings, but dynamic and often highly irrational people. They do not remain the same. Situations can change people. Therefore, there is a need for flexibility in management style. *Managers must vary their responses so that they continue to be appropriate to changing situations.* In recreation services we cannot satisfy all people all the time but we can go a long way towards satisfying most people, as Ted Blake [10] believes, by treating them with *importance, attention* and *understanding.* This underlines the importance of staff training.

In recreation services there is often the tendency to treat managers as important, systems as important, organizational structures as important. Such services are not customer-orientated, and may not meet customer expectations. To satisfy customers, managers must keep promises, be honest and not try to 'con' the customer. Organizations should not be greedy and kill the golden goose. How many authorities are saying 'Put up the price of squash, badminton and sauna; there is demand; they'll pay'. This will work when demand outstrips supply but when supply outstrips demand then one is into a highly competitive market. In addition, the amount of one's disposable income influences decisions. But how much will *they* pay? How many of the young or less well-off will continue to pay? Are there alternatives or substitute activities for them? There are many 'theys'. At recreation centres, for example, the customers are a variety of people. They include the individuals, their friends, their families, the organizations (who buy for others), the supporters, spectators, schools, parents and visitors. *Each link in the chain is a customer* [10]. The network is wider than we at first imagine, the chain is longer.

In order to market recreation successfully we must *sell benefits* to customers. These benefits go to make up the picture of 'success'. Local authorities have special benefits to give, particularly to those who are least able to fend for themselves. Special groups include the old, the young, the handicapped, the unemployed and especially the jobless school-leaver. The problem is compounded in that they have *more* free time, *less* disposable income and *poor* mobility. Young people, for example, need a favourable concept of themselves; they need to realize some of their dreams. The marketing of leisure can assist in this image seeking. Yet the young are susceptible to marketing; commercial enterprise has been quick to seize the opportunity to provide what they are looking for. Pop culture, fashion, music and drink take a massive share of leisure spending. The pub, for example, is the youth centre for many young people.

Suffice it to say that, in terms of marketing, the customer is the key. In leisure management we must, therefore, be *customer orientated.*

16.6.1 Depth approach to marketing

All of us can be influenced and manipulated, far more than we realize, through marketing. Efforts are constantly being made to channel our *unthinking* habits, our buying decisions and our thought processes through the use of psychiatry and the social sciences. 'Typically these efforts take place beneath our levels of awareness, so that appeals which move us are often, in a sense, "hidden" ' [11]. Some 'manipulating' has been amusing; some disquieting. The 'depth' approach, as Packard calls it, is being used in a variety of fields and on a variety of unsuspecting people. 'The use of mass psychoanalysis to guide campaigns of persuasion has become the basis of a multi-million dollar industry. Professional persuaders have seized upon it in their groping for more effective ways to sell us their wares – whether products, ideas, attitudes, candidates, goals or states of mind [11].'

The 'persuaders' are looking for the whys of our behaviour – why wives are drawn into illogical purchases or fill shopping baskets in a supermarket as though under hypnosis, why men buy certain drinks or cars. Packard believes that the 'persuaders' see us typically as 'bundles of day-dreams, misty hidden yearnings, guilt complexes, irrational emotion blockages. We are image lovers given to impulse and compulsive acts' [12]. It seems that our subconscious can be 'pretty wild and unruly'. The persuaders stop at nothing. Nothing is immune or sacred. Agencies seek to discover the psychological concomitants of the housewife's menstrual cycle for its effects on selling certain food products, psychiatry probing techniques have been used on young girls and public relations experts are even advising churchmen on improving communications and messages to their congregation. Cheskin [13] adds support to Packard:

'Motivation research is the type of research that seeks to learn what motivates people in making choices. It employs techniques designed to reach the unconscious or subconscious mind because preferences generally are determined by factors of which the individual is not conscious . . . Actually in the buying situation the consumer generally acts emotionally and compulsively, unconsciously reacting to the images and decisions which in the subconscious are associated with the product.'

Marketing is, then, potentially powerful and equally potentially dangerous. What people tell interviewers at a surface, conscious level, could have little bearing on how they will actually behave in a buying situation. The manipulators are working *beneath* the surface of conscious life. Most recreation research concerned with public sector provision has been based on surface level surveys and questionnaires and on quantitative analysis. Research which is more qualitative and looks beneath the surface is required to help to understand people's motivations in making recreation choices.

16.6.2   The myths of marketing

The term marketing conjures up pictures of exciting bold adventures into the selling of products and services. It has an appeal and an aura, particularly for young aspiring managers (including managers of recreation) who are going to hit the success trail and put their facilities and programmes on the map through marketing. Marketing has developed a 'reputation'. However, along with the reputation a number of myths have been developed. Wilson [14] exposes six myths of marketing. These are expanded or adjusted to the recreation setting in (a) to (f) below:

(a) The first myth is that marketing departments ensure marketing orientation

Wilson believes that such action 'is an immediate signal to all other parts of the company that they can forget the subject' [14]. It ignores the important contribution that other departments make. The case is put in forthright terms by Townsend [15] in *Up the Organisation*:

'Marketing departments – like planning departments, personnel departments, management development departments, advertising departments and public relations departments – are usually camouflage designed to cover up for lazy or worn out chief executives. Marketing in the fullest sense of the word, is the name of the game. So it had better be handled by the boss and his line, not by staff hecklers. Once or twice a year for three or four days the boss takes ten, twenty or thirty of his key people, including some from the ad. agency and controller's office, away to some secluded spot. On average they spend twelve hours a day asking unaskable questions, rethinking the business (What are we selling? To whom? At what prices? How do we get to him? In what form?), four hours a day relaxing and exercising and eight hours a day sleeping. It's hard work. But more good marketing changes will come out of such meetings than out of any year-round staff department of 'experts' with 'marketing' signs on the door.'

(b) The second myth is that 'creative copying' is the best method of 'adding' products

'Who were the first to ascend Everest? Now who were the second'? The first product to find a niche in the customer's mind is difficult to dislodge. In the world of sport and recreation, we all know who ran the first mile in under four minutes; many still call any new synthetic track 'Tartan'; and Kodak instant cameras are still called 'Polaroids'. It will be a long time before Sir Clive Sinclair's electric car is lost to our memories. Firsts are highly influential – both failures and successes. It is important, therefore, to have *successful firsts*.

To market successfully, not only is it important to have firsts, but also it is important to *innovate continuously*. The story of the Dassler brothers is one of firsts and continuous innovation [16]. The brothers were born in Herzogenaurach, a Bavarian mill town. They were in a family sports shoe business. In 1948 Adolf Dassler and Rudolf Dassler had an argument, split up and never spoke to each other again. Adolf (called himself Adi) formed Adidas, Rudolf formed Puma. Between them they captured 80% of the German market and 55% of world sales.

Adidas became the front runner. In 1952 they introduced the now famous Adidas trefoil at the Helsinki Olympic Games. In 1954, at the final of the World Cup between West Germany and Hungary, the German team were able to change their studs in their boots to cope with difficult ground conditions, leaving Hungary to slide around the turf and lose. The innovation of the screw-in stud had made an immediate and lasting impression. For the 1978 World Cup an ultra-lightweight boot with a humidity footbed to cope with the Argentinian climate, was used by almost every team. The ultra-lightweight boot was introduced when it was realized that footballers spent 90% of their time running, not kicking. The four-spiked nylon track shoe, the injected spiked shoes with 30 varieties, and many other firsts can be credited to the firm. Ninety-five per cent of the gold medal winners at the Montreal Olympic Games wore some item of Adidas clothing. At the Moscow Olympic Games 32 000 officials were kitted out under the Adidas contract. Firsts are important.

(c) The third myth is that all price pressures come from customers
Pressure is just as likely to come from salesmen to obtain the friendship of the buyers and to capture a string of orders.

(d) The fourth myth is that services are just intangible products
While the tools of marketing need not vary greatly between products and services, the method of application and message conveyed should be very different. 'Few services are marketed well (they may be *advertised* well but advertising is only one tool)' [14]. Services are a mix of concrete things such as shop, hotel room, aircraft, sports centre and intangible service elements, for example, speed, accuracy, efficiency, ambience. People are not machines and the 'quality' of people varies; the 'quality' of the same person will vary too. Receptionists will react differently to different customers; they will also act differently to the same customer in situations of stress. In the marketing of services *people* are being marketed. Therefore, the bulk of the effort should take place in the pre-sale

period. *One of the problems in recreation management is that staff are not trained or adequately briefed for the most important job which has to be done – communicating with the public.* Training, motivating and encouraging is needed 'at the sharp end'. 'The service, in fact, has to be marketed as hard to its practitioners as to its customers' [14].

(e) Myth number five is that marketing research can solve all marketing problems

It cannot. It is dangerous to suppose that the answer lies in more information. Market research does not replace the need for judgement. It is an aid to judgement.

(f) Myth six suggests that the market share is a measure of market success

It does not necessarily mean effective marketing effort and does not mean higher profits. Many companies with greater market share operate on very low profit levels; some take no profit at times, and others make losses to keep the market share. The recent cut price wars in airline flights is one example.

Hence it would appear that a number of claims have been made for marketing which are not substantiated. Marketing should be seen, not as infallible strategies for success, but as different strategies in different situations and as one of the means towards success.

16.7   THE MOTIVATOR AND THE SELLER

Motivation is not a one-way process. People need to be motivated to buy; sellers need to be motivated to sell. The motivation to achieve in the commercial sector is clear; it means business. The profit element provides the justification, the reason for doing it and the measure of how effective expenditures have been. Marketing in the public sector hinges to a considerable extent on the motivations of the mangers and staff. *Local authorities have been slow in recognizing staff motivational needs in order to achieve.* Targets, incentives and commitment are important.

Selling is often thought of synonymously with marketing. It is not. It is, however, a vital component of the 'marketing mix'. Selling means persuading potential customers to buy. In order to buy, potential customers might change their current preferences and substitute what they had to what is now on offer. (This illustrates the concept of voluntary exchange mentioned in Section 16.2). Customers need a satisfactory *choice*. The greater variety of choice, the greater the possibility that more people will find a recreative activity which will be satisfying to them and which they will want to buy again.

16.7.1   What motivates people to 'buy' recreation

What motivates people to make choices? Vance Packard's *Hidden Persuaders* makes us aware that there are factors of which the individual is unconscious and people do different things from what they say they will. *Impressions* could decide the customer's response. Recreation facilities must, therefore, create the 'right' impression. Marketing slogans preach: 'it is not the product but the *promise*'. There is a need in recreation to be selling both the product *and* the promise. First impressions count. The selling of 'pop music' singles is often marketed on what are sometimes termed 'hookers' – those lines, rhythms or jingles which you catch onto and cannot get out of your head, however hard you try. A Eurovision Song Contest No. 1 is an example. One of the best-selling Top Twenty Hits of 1973, *Tie a Yellow Ribbon*, was revived in 1981 to welcome home to the USA the Iranian hostages and again in 1985 for the hostages from Beirut. The jingle had not been forgotten; the message had not been forgotten. The ribbon symbolism has since been used as a mark of peace on the 40th anniversary of the dropping of the first atomic bomb on Hiroshima.

Marketing slogans can become part of the product itself and hence a great deal of marketing can be undertaken at very little cost. Leisure equipment, clothing and fashion can carry slogans, messages and communications which become embedded in the minds of consumers. To return from shopping in London's West End carrying a Harrod's carrier bag confers a kind of status on the carrier. The trefoil or the laurel wreath seen on a sports shirt carries the name and markets the goods: 'carrying an Adidas sports bag and wearing an Adidas sports shirt confer status beyond what might be expected from association with the names of professional sportsmen' [17].

Cooperative marketing spreads the burden of promotional expenditure. Kelloggs, for example, has supported over 30 promotions involving toys, video recorders, sports bags, tennis rackets and bathroom scales. The television and radio media are flooded with advertising jingles. The jingles remain in the head and promote products for a very long time to come. Wilson and West [17] recall that in 1971 Coca-Cola commissioned a jingle for a new advertising campaign. This was heard repeatedly on television and in cinemas throughout the world. The copyright was assigned to a musical company and a new lyric was written. The former commercial jingle entered the singles record charts as *'I'd like to Teach the World to Sing'*. But the pop song never lost its association with the Coca-Cola advertisement. 'So the company not only recovered much (if not all) of the original investment; it also continued to enjoy a promotional benefit.'

Recreation professionals must ask themselves the question: what is the message we want to convey? What is the image we want to portray? The top newspaper in terms of sales in 1985 was the *News of the World* with nearly 5 million. *The Sun* newspaper had a daily circulation of over 4 million, i.e. nine times that of *The Guardian*. *The Guardian* markets news, information and current affairs. *The Sun* markets entertainment, titillation and curiosity, as much as news and current affairs. It is no use, therefore, giving the same sales message to *Sun* and *Guardian* readers. The message must fit the readership. The sales message of the *Financial Times* is apposite 'No FT – no comment!'

However, depending on circumstances, mood or inclination people's tastes will vary in reading habits, musical appreciation, or sporting activities. At a recreation centre, for example, the same player will at one time behave aggressively, competitively and with single-minded ruthlessness and later in the bar with bonhomie. *Hence we must have different messages and different images to suit varying circumstances.* The marketing approach must be flexible to be appropriate to changing customer demands.

Recreation services and recreation centres must find the *psychological hooks* that people can latch on to. A favourable *attitude* must be developed. Recreation centres must be socially acceptable – leisure behaviour is in large measure social behaviour. The product or service must be moved quickly to the user or the user must be moved to the product quickly and conveniently. How important it is, therefore, to *site* facilities where people can see them and can gain easy access to them. How important also to improve transport systems for those without cars. Recreation facilities must be *accessible* and *acceptable*.

Commercial marketing has shown that in order to retain one's share of the market there must be adequate before- and after-sales service. Recreation organizations rarely carry out either pre-sales consumer tests or after-sales feedbacks. Beginner badminton and squash courses are held and when they are over many pupils are left to their own devices to find the courts, the clubs and the progressions to improve their game. The follow-up to a young people's climbing course indicated that none of the climbers had been climbing since the introductory course – the nearest mountains were 100 miles away and no attempts had been made to help organize trips! As with the commercial product, the customer must be kept informed of the product and kept continuously aware of its benefits.

16.7.2 Recreational personnel need training in marketing

Who should do the selling? The British Productivity Council estimate that in 95% of cases there must be *face-to-face* selling. Commercial organizations spend considerable effort in training and briefing staff, teaching staff how to talk with, meet with, and communicate with customers. *Training of staff in public facilities is extremely poor*. Many who are in the greatest need of training are those who manage facilities and are not released by their authorities for training, or those who work at a face-to-face level with customers. It is these staff at the 'sharp end' – the receptionists, the caretakers, groundsmen, park keepers, supervisors of all kinds – who have the job of meeting and motivating the public. With some notable exceptions (like many reception staff) face-to-face employees are so often the least capable of communicating with and handling customers. They have not been trained, encouraged, motivated, made to feel important or supported. Yet it is they who are called upon to undertake the most important job – that of communicating with people. People market recreation. Staff in recreation services need understanding and help in carrying out this important function; they need *training*. Regrettably many recreation services, far from motivating people, sometimes serve to demotivate them, achieving the complete opposite of that which was intended.

16.7.3. The recreation demotivators

Marketers – i.e. Recreation Managers – must, therefore, not only have concern with what motivates people to recreation, but also with what *demotivates*. Nothing demotivates more than poor handling of the public: rudeness, 'take it or leave it', ruined expectations, dissatisfactions, broken promises. The package holiday scandals of holidaymakers being sent to the wrong place or double-bookings demotivate. Dirty changing rooms and no hot water demotivate.

Recreation, as we have seen, is marketed largely through people. Recreation Managers and recreation personnel have important roles to play. Since the reorganization of local government there has been a very considerable increase in the number of recreation personnel, services and facilities. Much attention has been given to the emerging 'profession' of recreation management. Time, effort and initiatives have been expended on gaining 'professional status', on the guarding of professional jealousies, on the rights of staff, the pay scales and conditions outlined in the 'purple book' [18] and on manoeuvring into positions of importance. Managers' over-concern with their own positions and preoccupations with all the administrative technicalities and systems, can take the time, the capacity and the heart out of marketing recreation for people and militate against customer orientation. If managers become greedy, judging success by their personal goals, then an aura can be engendered which could demotivate potential customers.

Recreation service is primarily concerned with the consumers, and about *their* needs. Things get done because of men and women with conviction. [15] In recreation the 'light of conviction' is often seen in the eyes of junior staff, who may not have the necessary experience but can, with enthusiasm, 'reach the parts others cannot reach'. They should be encouraged, for recreation can be best marketed by people who are involved, committed and who undertake their work with conviction and enthusiasm.

Satisfying customers brings benefits. Success in selling recreation lies, not in leisure departments, centre management, committees or even in the facilities themselves but out in the market, in the minds and pockets of the customers.

16.8 COMMUNICATION

So far we have looked briefly at the customer, the products, pricing, buying, motivating and selling. Another ingredient of the 'marketing mix' is communications. It is a process of familiarizing, reminding and creating favourable attitudes and a willingness to buy. The process is one of pulling customers to the product using words, music, pictures and symbols to present an image of the product that is attractive, if not compelling.

Communication makes known through *advertising*, converts through *propaganda* and secures public notice through *publicity*. Much of this work is cemented together in a network of *public relations*.

The media are a major vehicle by which managers can communicate their products and services. The more direct forms include television, radio, press, advertisements and the cinema. The less direct include literature and information, direct mail, public relations, exhibitions, packaging, sales gimmicks, incentives and sponsorship.

Coverage of a recreation programme or event or issue could fix an image in the minds of the public. Such an image is difficult to eradicate, particularly if the image is a poor one. The press can give a negative image in minutes. The press is often seen as challenging, questioning and embarrassing the local authority. Therefore, the only effective approach is to influence the control of the image-making and take a hand in managing the coverage. This can be achieved (provided the product or service is as good as it can be) by turning opportunity to advantage as Roger Quinton was able to show at the Leatherhead Leisure Centre in its early days: make friends with reporters; be on first name terms; talk their language; inform them and keep them up to date with the news [19]. Write out weekly columns; prepare press handouts. Invite the media personnel to functions. Let them have stories which bring you free advertising. However, guard against giving exclusive interviews – one friend could mean a dozen enemies. Good press coverage will help the public to say that their money on a recreation facility is well spent. (With the development of the first community multisport centre in Harlow in 1960, the author wrote a half-page column in the *Harlow Citizen* to communicate with the public about the new centre and its benefits. The two-year column had a significant effect on public awareness.)

Television advertisements are extremely expensive and so are paid advertisements in the press. A 30 second spot on just one commercial television station can cost several thousand pounds. A page of advertising in *The Guardian* cost £14 000 and in *The Sun* up to £27 000 in 1985. Even in local papers a page of advertising can cost up to £3000. Display advertising had risen faster than the rate of inflation in 1985. In contrast the local cinema can be a relatively cheap form of advertising. As cinema-going audiences are largely young people, then products, activities and services that appeal to young people could be effectively advertised in local cinemas. The medium is clearly most successful in reaching 15 to 24 year olds. Local radio advertising can vary in cost but to get across to young people local radio could pay dividends. Poster advertising can be very indifferent compared with face-to-face communication – human communication – which makes greater impact. The message to Recreation Managers appears to be to look at the whole variety of ways of communicating, to try out various forms, 'shop around', then act positively and measure results.

16.9 ACTIONS, ORGANIZATION AND MEASUREMENT

Marketing needs *organization*. It is through organization that control and results are achieved. The marketer is a blend of administrator and entrepreneur. Getting action involves organizing people and what they do.

The final steps in the marketing plan are to take action, control the action and measure the results. Measurement is essential, yet in many local authority programmes, measurement is undertaken without any objective criteria. In the market-orientated business, in the commercial sector, there are two distinguishing features:

1. The coordination of the marketing activities is undertaken by the *boss*.
2. *Financial yardsticks* are used to measure performance [20].

The commercial field is concerned primarily with making financial profits. Therefore, financial planning is the key. The marketer must know where he or she is going, has been and is now. He or she charts a course, making adjustments, works on known routes, tries to better these, and experiments with new ways. He or she keeps an eye open for competitors and plans meticulously. Therefore, the marketer must be fed with the most up-to-date information. (How often have we been given invaluable information – after the event! In the author's early days of inexperienced management two senior heads of department with much experience came up with crucial late information which might have made the disasters into success.)

'Service' marketing differs conceptually in that performance is measured by the quality of the service, people's response to the service and many other criteria. Both 'service' and 'commercial' marketing, however, are concerned with 'profit' making, though profits are defined differently. In the 'service' organization profit can be interpreted in terms of numbers, quality, performance, people's response and other criteria. The dilemma for the manager in the public sector experienced by leisure centre mangers in particular and pointed out by Quinton [19] is how to achieve support and commitment by the community and achieve an acceptable level of income, yet still remain a service which is socially acceptable.

16.10   MARKETING CONCLUSIONS

Marketing approaches to recreation products and services, using a marketing plan, will increase the probability of success in both public and private sectors. The marketing approach ensures that when a product or service is made available to the consumer it has been planned, designed, packaged, promoted and delivered in such a manner that the customer is not only persuaded to buy but also to repeat the experience as often as possible. While impulse buying, like attending an event or 'having a go' are important, repeat visits and repeat buying of the recreational experience are even more important. People get 'hooked' on products. Once caught with the bug of playing golf, squash, snooker, sauna bathing or yoga, we are anxious to participate even more. Impulse buying may attract people but this needs to be capitalized, for new-found satisfying experiences want to be bought again, and again. They become habit forming.

Marketing involves all the aspects and circumstances surrounding a particular product, activity, event or ongoing programme. A trip to a sports event, an outing to the theatre, a game of badminton or a drive to a country park all take organization and planning. A theatre outing could involve booking in advance, a drive into the city, baby-sitters, a meal after the event, saving up to afford it and a new outfit for the occasion. This is not an impulse purchase. The theatre has had to compete with all the other competitors to achieve a sale. Not only does marketing need organizing, but also *people need skills to organize themselves or be assisted in that organization.*

Marketing objectives need quantifying to measure success or failure. If all the staff accept these and feel part of the decision-making process, the objectives become self-motivating. Therefore, managers should ensure that staff are given all the background and resources which they need to meet targets. The communications network must be comprehensive and function at *all* levels. The right information is needed at the right time.

Marketing needs a budget. The crumbs that local authorities spend, usually under the heading 'Advertising' are short sighted. Many seaside resorts, theatres and festivals are well publicized and some are marketed well. However, the general picture is poor. For example, many authorities have a revenue expenditure at leisure centres in the region of £1 million and more yet spend less than 0.5% on marketing and promotion.

The marketing process and approaches will need to be adjusted to meet the conceptual differences to be found in local authority services. Local authorities have great opportunities to market their services to meet their aims and objectives. Their services on the whole fail to attract the majority of the underprivileged and lower socio-economic groups. Indeed, one might argue that the higher up the social scale you go the more of your entertainment, such as opera, ballet and music, is paid out of public money. Great opportunities exist to meet community need but very sensitive, humane handling of the marketing process must be achieved.

At the start of this chapter it was stated that marketing is concerned with voluntary exchange and that community recreation services are provided in exchange for people's money, time and rates and taxes. If the public does not want what is provided and is not prepared to pay the costs and give up the time, then local authority support could well be reduced. Therefore, recreation managers must be concerned with the question: are the customers satisfied with the service. It is not just how many participated but whether the market target groups were reached with satisfying results and whether objectives were met. Community recreation marketing is concerned with identifying and responding to what the community needs and wants and is prepared to support.

In summary, marketing needs *objectives*, a *plan, action* and *measurement*. Marketing need not be a highly sophisticated and learned process. A marketing plan is a statement about what actions are to be undertaken to meet objectives. Marketing affects people's attitudes. It affects the way they speak, look, think and behave. Managers of recreation should encourage people to look more favourably towards the products and services being offered by their organizations. What is of greater importance is that managers should ascertain first what is likely to be most satisfying to customers and try to provide what is needed. This can be undertaken more successfully through marketing approaches adapted to meet the demands of the situation.

16.11 RECREATION FACILITY MARKETING HINTS

1. Know your company, your organization, your authority. Marketing is your business. Identify your market segments and targets.
2. Know what business you are in and the goals of the enterprise. Make a reconnaissance then create a master plan and budget.
3. Know your consumer, your customers in their variety. Talk to local groups; visit establishments; encourage suggestions.
4. Know your competitors, their facilities, activities and programmes.
5. Keep in touch with the trade, the recreation business. Use PR network. Make friends with the press.
6. Plan meticulously: undertake qualitative fact finding; identify market gaps; check facts; test preliminary ideas. Think through the process.
7. Measure profits by activities, choices, ages, ranges, improvements, scope, financial targets; increase turnover – those who attend may spend.
8. Create your image – put one in or people will make their own; maintain a good public image of the facility; efficient reception – no queues; staff are smart; support local causes; help local groups to use the facility as a resource centre.
9. Innovate: accept originality, risk, boldness, flexibility, exploration; accentuate the positive.
10. Originate: firsts are remembered; copying comes second at best. Changing circumstances mean new opportunities.
11. Motivate: make staff part of the team – committed; inculcate identity. Create an organic type of organization to encourage staff initiative in order to change and adapt to changing circumstances.
12. Customer orientate: understand the character of consumers; tastes are fickle; remember the customer loves himself – mention his/her interest; sell benefits, provoke curiosity; let user feel positively identified; keep promises; provide choice; keep abreast with factors that influence/inhibit participation.
13. Give something away for nothing: free 'have-a-go's'; inducements.
14. Make the rules fair, easily understood and easily operated. In programmes where all expect to be treated alike ensure no exclusivity for some, perks for others.
15. Make the facilities attractive: clean, maintained, colourful; cluttered, scribbled notices give slovenly appearance, poor images. Create a quality image.
16. Make the facilities accessible: influence the journey with signs, maps,

parking, lighting, attractive welcoming entrance. Reinforce the general awareness of facilities with attractive signs, exhibitions/displays in local libraries and other public places.

17. Inform as many as possible: information well distributed; circulate across the community in homes, school, work and shops; collate all that is going on and let people know; others will reciprocate.

18. Communicate at all levels of the organization; make it two-way communication; make the message clear to staff and users. To help ensure good communication with users establish an *animateur* approach, liaison officers, users committees, suggestions boxes.

19. Promote in tangible ways: balloons, badges, plastic bags for swimming gear, cards, wrappings, diaries, logos, souvenirs, flags, promotions, exhibitions, events; press, cinema, radio, television; talks; visits to; visits from; promote through children, parents. For specific promotion use brochures, posters, newsletters, newspapers, media etc. plus house to house delivery by paper boys, Boy Scouts and centre participants.

20. Involve well-known names – some can market 'magic'. Find sponsors. Grant wherever possible certificates and awards especially to young participants.

21. Sell success: make people into better players, better coaches, better administrators, better supporters; make people healthier, slimmer, fitter; sell glamour; sell risk, excitement and adventure particularly to young people.

22. Make people feel happy; sell fun; make the social point the focal point, the facilities socially acceptable.

23. Experiment: try out new ideas; try packages not just single lines; extend leisure self-service – early swims, late squash, self-bookings. Experiment with prices.

24. Expand the market with new products, new looking products, new activities for the same customers and for new customers. Encourage staff and customers to share ideas; prolong the 'product life cycle' of popular activities.

25. Beware the perils of helter-skelter growth; don't put all your eggs in one basket.

26. Vary the attack: if everybody knows you are going to shout when you stand up, they will turn off their receivers. Create different messages for different 'publics'; vary the prices – use differential pricing policies as a marketing tool. Handle the 'marketing mix' yourself.

27. Train your staff: inculcate right attitudes; involve them; select carefully; brief them on how to meet, talk and handle people.

28. Study the market continuously; never be satisfied; study dissatisfactions; avoid complacency; watch competitors; is there a better way – a

more effective way; analyse assets and liabilities.

29. Manage with flair and charisma allied to objectivity and administrative skill; think through the consequences of your actions. Develop management flexibility to be a man or woman for all situations.

30. Carry on thinking.

REFERENCES AND NOTES

1. McIver, C. (1968), *Marketing*, 3rd edn (revised and edited G.C. Wilson) Business Publications, London.

2. Kotler, P. (1975), *Marketing for Non-Profit Organisations*, Prentice-Hall, Englewood Cliffs, New Jersey, p.5.

3. Laczniak, G.R. *et al.* (1979), *J. Marketing*, **43**, 29–36.

4. Kotler, P. and Zaltman, G. (1971) *J. Marketing*, **35**, 3–12.

5. Cowell, D. (1978), Paper presented at the Marketing Education Group (MEG) Conference, Hull College of Higher Education, *Marketing's Application to Public Authority Sport, Recreation and Leisure Centres.*

6. Scottish Sports Council (1979), *A Study of Sports Centres and Swimming Pools: A Question of Balance*, Volumes 1 and 2, Chapter 10: Marketing. SSC, Edinburgh.

7. Jenkins, A. (1974), *The Case for Squash*, A and C. Jenkins in conjunction with the Squash Rackets Association.

8. Martin, W.H. and Mason, S. (1980), *The UK Sports Market*, Leisure Consultants, Sudbury, Suffolk.

9. This is the general finding coming out of a number of surveys and undertaken by the Sports Council and agencies such as the Built Environment Research Group.

10. Quoted by Ted Blake in several presentations on Marketing Sport and Recreation during the 1970s.

11. Packard, V. (1965), *The Hidden Persuaders*, Pelican Books, Harmondsworth, p.11.

12. Ibid., p.14

13. Cheskin, L. Quoted in Ibid., pp. 14–15.

14. Wilson, A. (1979), Six myths of marketing, *Management Today*, August, pp. 63–64.

15. Townsend, R. (1970), *Up the Organisation*, Coronet Books, London, p. 96.

16. Willatt, N. (1979), How Adidas ran faster, *Management Today*, December, pp. 58–61.

17. Wilson, A. and West, C. (1982), Effective marketing at minimum cost, *Management Today*, January, pp. 72–78.

18. National Joint Council for Local Authorities, *Administrative, Professional, Technical and Clerical Services Handbook*, scheme of conditions of service, NJCLA, London.

19. Information obtained from Roger Quinton, first manager of the Leatherhead Leisure Centre.

20. Read: McIver, C. (1968), *Marketing*, 3rd edn. (revised and edited by G.C. Wilson), Business Publications, London; Townsend, R. (1970), *Up the Organisation*, Coronet Books, London; Diggle, K. (1976), *Marketing the Arts*, City University, London, p.8; The Marketing of Local Authority Leisure Services (1984), *European Journal of Marketing*, **18**, No. 2; Henry, I. (1983), Marketing Objectives in Public Sector Marketing, *Leisure Management*, November and December; Blois, K.J. and Octon, C.M. (Loughborough University) (1983), Marketing Planning of Local Authority Leisure Centres, *Leisure Management*, August.

Chapter 17

Event management

If you can't do it excellently, don't do it at all
Robert Townsend

★

17.1 MAJOR EVENTS IN THE RECREATION PROGRAMME

Events are an important part of any comprehensive community recreation programme. They capture the imagination. Events can involve the community; they can increase awareness; they can help put an organization or an activity on the map. Events can bring top class performers, entertainment, novelty, adventure, surprise and fun to add height, width, depth and glamour to a programme. Events have appeal. Well organized they can be a boon to any community and recreation organization. Badly organized they can detract. The public has become far more sophisticated in its taste when it comes to the organization and running of events. Recreation Managers must be capable of controlling the planning and running of major events.

This chapter is written for Recreation Managers who have to present major events throughout the course of the year as part of the total recreation programme. The principles and many of the methods will apply to all event organizers but it is recognized from the outset that some organizations are set up as specialized event producers. The most well known in Great Britain is the Wembley Stadium Ltd. with its outdoor stadium, indoor arena, conference centre and squash centre. In local authorities too there are specialized event departments and committees to stage the county show, the town annual show or festival. In national sports administration, committees and staff exist to administer international events. While all event organizers can learn something from this brief chapter on events, it is the Recreation Manager, whose special events are *superimposed* on all his or her other tasks, that this is primarily intended to serve.

This chapter is written in the following sequence. *First*, the question is raised: what is a major event and what makes it special? *Second*, the formulation of policies and event organization strategies are noted. *Third*, organization structures are discussed. *Fourth*, budgets are shown to be integral to all major events. *Fifth*, the special staffing requirements are considered. *Sixth*, the need for detailed and meticulous planning is shown. *Seventh*, all events are subject to problems and learning from these is an important clue to better future events. *Finally*, as part of the chapter summary an event planning guideline, an event checklist and an event planning process model are put forward for consideration.

17.2 SPECIAL CHARACTERISTICS AND FUNCTIONS OF MAJOR EVENTS

What is a major event? It can be an event, project or attraction of any kind that is outside the 'run of the mill' activities. It usually has some significance. It usually attracts a crowd or draws the attention of the media. It can be international, national, regional or local. It can include sport, art, music, drama, festival or tournament. It can be competitive, fund raising, social or just plain good fun. It can be the town annual show or the village fête, the athletics championships or the Boy Scouts' sports. It can be an exhibition, a meeting, a rally or a talk. The scope of major events is as wide as the scope of the leisure and recreation spectrum.

17.2.1 The special characteristics of events

There are four main features which characterize a major event:

1. Events have distinctive characteristics.
2. Events have considerable advantages for improving the programme and management performance.
3. Events present acute and often immediate problems to all organizers.
4. Events lend themselves to certain styles of management.

The distinctive characteristics readily identified are that first, they have a *starting and finishing point*. Second, they have *fixed deadlines* and third, the event organization is usually *superimposed on other work*.

Events carry advantages to improve programming and management. First, they capture the imagination of 'sellers' and 'buyers'. Second, they are a means of promoting the organization and creating favourable images. Third, their organization crosses administrative and departmental boundaries; *they unify the organization*. Fourth, they encapsulate the resources of an organization and test them to reveal its strengths and weaknesses. Fifth, they may break new ground and could present the organization as pioneers.

However, events pose many problems to all organizers. Most problems can be anticipated but many will be unforeseen. The event is like the normal programme speeded up and delivered within a given space of time; this concentrates all the advanced planning and actions into specific hours and moments. Problems can thus be dramatic and could prove devastating. One problem is that managers and event organizers cannot depend on established routines. Another, is that there are dangers in dates slipping by in preparation, targets not being met and budgets being overspent. In addition, there are dangers in lack of coordination bringing inadequate linkages, mis-communications, omissions, duplications, wasted effort and inadequate controls.

Events lend themselves to certain management styles and methods. First, events need a coordinator; his or her role is paramount. Second, they need precision, deadlines and fast decisions and this differs from most normal programming issues. Third, tight administration, using flow chart organization and checklists can help to meet deadlines and objectives. Fourth, entrepreneurial skills, allied to good administration, can be put to best effect. Fifth, because events are task-orientated, a more authoritarian style of leadership or 'benevolent dictatorship' may be required, particularly in the late stages of detailed preparation and on the day itself.

17.3   EVENT PLANNING STAGES AND ORGANIZATION

All events need good planning and organization. Regrettably, all events are not well planned and organized, even many events of considerable significance, particularly in the public sector. Recreation Managers must guide event organizers in the basic principles of planning and organization.

The organization approach for an event will depend on the particular circumstances but it is usually worth recognizing ten interrelated planning stages in the life cycle of a major event:

1. Policy formation.
2. Feasibility study and decision-making.
3. Appointment of organizing committee and coordination.
4. Objective setting.
5. Budgeting.
6. Organization structure.
7. Staffing personnel.
8. Detailed planning.
9. Event presentation, including preparation, closure and clearing.
10. Evaluation, feedback and modification for future events.

17.3.1   Policy formation

First, formulate the idea. Debate, reason out and answer fundamental questions: *why* is the event proposed? *What* is it for? *How* will the event be run? *Where* will it be held? *Who* will be responsible for its planning and operation? *When* will it be held? If the idea is a good one planners can take the idea to the next stage of considering its feasibility.

17.3.2   Feasibility study and decision-making

In considering the feasibility of an event it is important to explore in greater depths the questions already raised. What are the assets? What are the costs, not just in terms of money but in terms of manpower, time, effort? Will the effort result in meeting the aims of the event? Can the problems be overcome?

If the event is not feasible, planners should have the courage to say 'no'. Regrettably, many events have taken place without considering their feasibility and they should never have been held. If the event is feasible *and* there is positive commitment to the project, then it is important to *make a firm decision*, allowing ample time for forward planning and detailed planning. Coinciding with the decision to go ahead four crucial tasks should be undertaken, namely:

1. Announce the decision to hold the event.
2. State clearly the nature of the event and the aims of the event; commit these to writing.
3. Appoint an events main committee – a *working* committee.
4. Appoint the key figure in the planning and control of the event – *the coordinator*.

17.3.3   Set objectives

Be clear and unequivocal in stating the precise objectives as measurable targets. Make them unambiguous. Include all main areas and units of the programme. In particular be precise about the financial estimates and budgeting. In formulating the objectives the coordinater should consult with the policy-makers and the key personnel involved in it whether as representatives or organizations or as unit or team leaders. Set the dates, times, specific deadlines and critical dates in the planning stages.

17.4   EVENT ORGANIZATION STRUCTURES

Organization is concerned with planning, establishing an organization structure and developing working relationships and methods to achieve objectives. Organizational structures cover the chains of command, the spans of control and the discrete units or teams or working parties dealing with the various areas of work. The structure must cover the broad spectrum of the event. An event such as a leisure festival involving community groups might have several units, for example:

1. *Programme and content*: activities, organizations etc.
2. *Budget*: accounting, income and expenditure in *all* areas.
3. *Marketing*: awareness, publicity, media etc.
4. *Personnel and staffing*: contracts, duties etc.
5. *Administration*: programmes, printing, box office, legal etc.
6. *Technical*: resources, equipment, preparation etc.
7. *Services*: parking, cloaks, information, first aid etc.
8. *Catering and social*: routine, special entertaining etc.

There should be a working group for each area and a section leader who accepts the responsibility and links with the main coordinator. It is important to *agree the precise roles, responsibilities, tasks and dates.*

17.4.1 Roles and responsibilities

Everyone involved in an event should know who they are responsible to, who is responsible to them, who they are working with and what exactly is their function in the organization. Areas of responsibility and tasks to be done should be handled in discrete units, linked together through a coordinated network.

Key factors in the make up of the organization are:

1. The people carrying out the planning.
2. The task units.
3. The heads of the units.
4. Their span of control.

There must first be sufficient keen and knowledgeable people prepared to give time and effort to the tasks. But there must also be an efficient organization to make the best use of such people.

People need an optimum amount of responsibility. We learned in an earlier chapter on staffing that span of control depended on many factors, and that there were dangers in either too wide or too narrow a span. We also learned that although formal structures were important, the informal structures were also critical to the harmony and efficiency of an organization. Unfortunately, with many event organizations the structures are poor and without coordination. The result is that informal dealings flourish without coordination, misunderstandings and miscommunications abound, leaving many parts of the planning falling between two stools. *'It will be all right on the night' is a totally inadequate substitution for good organization* [1]. On the day, organizers have found that there is no staging, no public address or it does not work, lights will not come on, the changing rooms are in the nearest school a mile away, the VIPs are standing in the rain trying to convince the doorman that they have been invited, the performers cannot get into the ground because the entrance is blocked and the grand piano has been delivered to another venue! The lack of coordination and task responsibilities is evident in such situations.

17.4.2 Organization and work flow charts

Planning and organization are important. Once principles have been agreed and objectives set then the structure for organizing the event can be put together. The use of an *organization chart is helpful*. It helps to clarify any ambiguities and provides an overall picture indicating the various responsibility areas. As indicated earlier, its main disadvantage is that it shows the formal relationships only. However, this is not too limiting for events. *Events are finite, fixed occasions requiring task operations that need to be controlled and, particularly in the latter stages, handled autocratically to meet deadlines.* For major international events such as an international tourna-ment, an organization handbook will be necessary in addition to an organization chart. The Scottish Sports Council organization manual for such major events is relevant in such cases [2].

In addition to the structure a *work flow chart* indicating critical paths will be valuable for programming and timetabling the work of commmittees, task units and sections. It indicates the flow pattern, the critical dates, the deadlines, the merging of two sections at appropriate times and the interrelationships between sections.

17.5 BUDGETS

All major events need a budget. The extent to which they do depends on the nature of the event and on the objectives. Is the event designed to give a free service to the public: an open day in the park, free band concerts, children's festival or a sports centre open day? Is the event designed as a crowd puller on a break-even financial exercise: an entertainment talent contest or a sports tournament? Is the event a sponsored event to draw in the crowds and capture the eye of the media: a national basketball tournament or a one-day county cricket match? Is the event totally sponsored such as a firm's exhibition or a television 'Super Stars' or 'It's a Knockout'? Is the event primarily designed to raise funds for the orga-nization or another charitable cause?

Most local authority sponsored events are heavily subsidized – by the rates. Town shows, orchestral concerts, free pop festivals in the park, old-time music halls, painting competitions, exhibitions and many thousands of events are run because they enhance the quality of a town's life and are part of our heritage and traditions.

17.5.1 Evaluate the true costs

As far as the Recreation Manager is concerned, all events, even those totally subsidized, in reality cost a great deal of money. *They must all have budgets* and must all achieve the income/expenditure balance or ratio set in the objectives. Equally important is that the event must be run excellent-ly. The principle for the Recreation Manager to work to is that of being *professional*. Regardless of whether the event is free, the facilities are free or the staff are already paid for, the Recreation Manager should *always evaluate the true costs.*

It will normally cost money to use, hire or acquire facilities and make them functional and attractive for the event. There will be costs for electricity, water and technical and maintenance aspects. There will be costs of transport. Equipment may need to be hired, purchased, borrowed and transported. Additional staffing, stewards, voluntary helpers and personnel connected with the event will be required. Administration costs will include not only the promotion, printing, tickets, posters, financial costing and preparations, but also the whole office backup administrative services such as telephone, stationery and man-hours. There will normally be costs for mounting the event itself, the programme costs, the cost of artists, hospitality, the additional insurances and legal costs. The hidden costs of most events are enormous. The good manager should know what they are. They may not be of great importance to one event but they will be of great importance to many others.

Most events will accrue some income. Even events which are 'free' to the consumer may be raising income from some sources such as grant aid from the local authority. Income can be derived from direct methods and indirect methods. The direct methods include gate receipts, programmes, bar and catering, car parking, cloakrooms and costs of other services. The indirect methods include advertising, donations, sponsorships, sales, raffles and fund raising of a variety of sorts. Sometimes the amount of effort put into running the annual dinner raffle is more than that put into the whole event itself!

17.5.2   Budget targets

Events, then, need a budget and all events need expenditure limits. A large proportion of events also need income targets. If budget targets are known from the outset and are included in the objectives of the event, and are known to all, then everyone is working to the agreed targets for the event. Many events lend themselves to a break-even figure, for example an entertainment festival may cost in cash terms £2000 and is to run for one week; the objective could then be to attract a minimum of say 4000 customers at an average spend of 50p; or 2000 customers at an average spend of £1. Numbers over this become a bonus, but normally not a profit. Extra income that might accrue will normally help to meet hidden costs, or help the organization, or boost the funds for the charity.

The risk element with most events is very high, particulary when they are at the mercy of the weather, or the call of the television on Cup Final Day, or when new ideas are being tried or when dealing with an unknown quantity. *There are risks enough without taking even greater financial ones such as overspending budgets or minimizing income.* Events need not only the budget, therefore, but also a coordinator to ensure that financial targets are worked to.

17.6 STAFF AND PERSONNEL

17.6.1 The coordinator and unit heads

All events need personnel. The number and type will depend on the nature of the event. All events need a *coordinator*. The coordinator does not organize directly. He or she is the leader, the link person, the informer, the one person who knows generally what is going on in each unit, section or team. The coordinator does not have to know every detail but needs to know who has the knowledge and whose responsibility it is. The coordinator must control and monitor progress using the most efficient methods – meetings, sectional heads reporting, work flow charts. He or she needs to be an encourager, yet firm in handling situations. Towards the later stages of the planning, in particular, the coordinator will have to exert pressure and make authoritative decisions in order to meet the deadlines. He or she is the key figure in any event organization – the link and the controller.

The coordinator will normally work with a team of sectional heads of departments. Each team head and each discrete unit will have its clear responsibilities, duties, times, deadlines and calendars, but all within the overall organizational design. Without linkages it is possible for one unit to function independently, making its own contribution unilaterally without thought to the overall success of the project.

17.6.2 Other staff and helpers

Events are usually run with many different types of staff and helpers. Large scale events will have full-time staff, part-time paid staff, paid casual staff and volunteers and will also delegate certain functions to organizations or concession others. Information to all concerned throughout the planning is essential to keep people motivated, involved and committed, in addition to keeping abreast of information. *So often those in the firing line are ill-informed.*

Paid staff will need to know well in advance their pay, the times and the conditions; Trade Unions may well be involved; there will be irregular hours, different rates of pay and insurance aspects. Volunteers will also need to know exactly where they stand, what their responsibilities are and how far these extend. Legal problems are always to be borne in mind with special events; contractual problems, insurance details and promotional aspects will call for professional legal advice.

Staff and helpers need to know what their job is, what is expected of them, who they are responsible to, who is responsible to them and what they have to do to be successful. They must be highly committed and involved. This is the job of the coordinator and the teams heads. The answer is never to be complacent nor take people for granted. *Motivation, acknowledgement, praise and thanks are important.*

17.7 DETAILED PLANNING: THE EVENT AND THE EVALUATION

The event itself should be preceded by detailed planning, it should be excellently presented with a memorable start and finish and it should be closed efficiently. A careful evaluation and follow-up should also be part of the whole process.

The *detailed planning* can be assisted by the use of work flow charts, critical paths, signposts, targets and dates. Five steps must be taken in the final stages for many major events. *First*, the detailed final plan must be produced. *Second*, checklists must be carefully followed. *Third*, contingency plans must be formulated. *Fourth*, the event should be practised or even components rehearsed, including staff duties and *fifth*, all possible elements should be double checked.

The event itself, having been thoroughly planned, should normally go well. However, there will invariably be problems. *The coordinator must be totally free* to make objective decisions should these be required. Section leaders also need to be relatively free to control their own sections.

The *closure* is an important component of the whole event. Closing ceremonies, hospitality, the thanks to all, cashing up, stock checking, clearing up and motivating workers to carry things through to the end all make for ultimate success. After the event the accounting, reports, lessons to be learned, making good damage and writing 'thank yous' must be undertaken. A social event to thank the workers should be considered, in addition to thanking them on the day itself.

In the cold light of day, a full *evaluation* is needed which assesses the preparation, the organization structure, the event, the results, the feedback from spectators, participants and staff and the lessons for future events. A report should be prepared both for record purposes (sometimes queries continue for several years!) and to assist in the future planning of events (see Section 14.8).

Having considered the theoretical base from which to stage minor events it is salutary to consider the range of problems that can occur leading up to events and at the events themselves. Some of these problems are raised before summarizing conclusions.

17.8 MAIN PROBLEM AREAS IN STAGING MAJOR EVENTS

In order to run efficient, memorable events it is wise to consider the problems of previous events. Some main and some minor faults are listed below. Seven areas have been identified. The first mentioned is possibly the most critical yet the most frequently violated.

1. *Insufficient consideration of the organization structure, aims and objectives at the outset.* This invariably leads to poor communication, duplication of effort but, even more serious, lack of direction, authority and controls.
2. *No appointment of a coordinator.* This is the key figure. There is usually a chairman and sectional heads of committees but rarely a coordinator with the authority and responsibility for operational control.
3. *Failure to maintain accurate written records of all that transpires during the planning stages.* If good records are kept they act as reminders and checks for work to be carried out. Rarely are there flow charts with deadlines plotted. Much is kept in one's head. This leads to misunderstandings and recriminations on the day.
4. *Organizations give themselves insufficient planning time.* Even when they do have sufficient time so much effort is put in at the last moment. This can lead to overloading and frustration through poor planning.
5. *Committee and unit structures are in many cases too narrow or too unwieldy.* Many are far too large. Others leave matters to the one person. These individuals invariably take on far too much. They see the event as *their* event. They are so keen to do the job that they will not share responsibility or delegate duties. Others are very busy people, take on events as social obligations and over commit themselves. These problems are typical of the amateur approach but *must not* be part of the professional Recreation Manager's repertoire.
6. *At recreation centre events there are often problems with governing bodies.* This usually stems from lack of agreement on *principles* and organization in the first place. There are problems with looking after guests. Relationships with staff (who have heavy additional duties in addition to their normal work) are often strained. The technical problems are considerable, for example, noise from other parts of the centre, keeping the audience informed, the import of a whole range of additional equipment, the extra floor markings or take-up of markings, the additional stage lighting, decor, the need for additional seating and many others.
7. *No matter what the organization or event, some problems should not be tolerated and must be ironed out for the next event.* They include weak coordinator and sectional heads, faulty public address, keen but ineffective announcers, insufficient staff, insufficient food and drink, failure to inform the police, no first aid, no plans for inclement weather, no press coverage, no litter containers, embarrassing pauses between activities, programmes overrunning, no hospitality for visitors, untidy and careless presentations, no colour, no glamour, no heightened emotion – no umph!

Some problems can be put right immediately for the next event, others need time and consideration and planning. This is the role of the

Recreation Manager. Well-run events will have the following features:

1. Clear and agreed *objectives* to which all are committed.
2. Discrete *units* to undertake specific tasks yet work as a whole.
3. A *coordinator* of calibre and authority.
4. *Unity* of effort.
5. Efficient lines of *communication*.
6. No *duplication* of effort or waste of time.
7. 'Professional' presentation with some glamour, novelty, surprise, tension or heightened awareness or emotion – an *experience* people will want to buy again.

17.9   EVENT MANAGEMENT: SUMMARY

Experience of running events shows that although all events differ one from another, in terms of management approaches, *the similarities are greater than the differences*. While policies, programme and content will differ considerably, a planning sequence similar to the one proposed in this chapter, serves the requirements for many events.

No one method of organizing a major event is best and all others second best. The method will depend on the event and the circumstances surrounding it. However, some ways are more effective than others; they are more objective, they are better planned, costed and controlled.

What experience has shown is that there has very often been insufficient thought given to the planning and organization of the event *before* committees are set, jobs allocated and decisions made to go ahead. Forward planning, organization structure, objective setting and communications are integral main issues to successful event management.

Events are important strings of the Recreation Manager's bow. Their organization is important to his or her repertoire of skills. Events lend themselves to certain styles of managment such as management by objectives. They need a sound logical framework, with a starting and finishing point. Events need thorough planning, imaginative marketing and excellent presentation.

A seven step simple guideline for improved event planning

1. *Formulate the idea or receive a proposal*: Ask why, what, how, where and when? Is proposal from reputable body with financial/administrative credibility? Does event fulfil purposes of the organization? If it is a good idea go on to Step 2.
2. (a) *Consider the feasibility or evaluate proposal*: What are assets, problems, support, cost in terms of money, effort, time? What is possible disrup-

tion to normal programme/organization? If it is feasible go on to Step 2(b).

(b) *Announce decision, the event and its aims or sign contract:* If 'outside' organizers, establish terms, areas of responsibility *re* staffing, equipment, accommodation etc. and appoint representative to their committee. In-house organizers go on to Step 3.

3. (a) *Appoint event committee:* Must include people with commitment, authority and energy.

(b) *Appoint the coordinator:* Give resources, authority and support.

(c) *Set objectives, targets, budgets:* Must be measurable, timed, dated; draw up draft planning flow chart.

4. *Establish organization structure:* Fix discrete units/teams with unit leader: give roles, targets, responsibilities.

5. (a) *Plan dates backwards from event day:* Agree planning flow chart with dates and use it.

(b) *Each key unit leader should have own calendar:* Within agreed overall plan.

(c) *Fix key meetings long in advance.*

(d) *Circulate information very regularly:* Communicate often.

(e) *Monitor progress:* Check meticulously.

(f) *Check budgets systematically.*

(g) *Follow detailed plan:* Use checklists; anticipate problems, make contingency plans and emergency procedures, practice and rehearse; double check.

(h) *Resist afterthoughts.*

6. (a) *Present event with class, flair and imagination.*

(b) *Keep coordinator totally free:* Effective decisions under crisis.

(c) *Close event with crescendo:* Good impression to start and finish. Clear with precision and tidily.

(d) *Give thanks on the day.*

7. *Evaluate and account:* Thank officially; collect feedback from promoters, participants, staff, spectators; report and record. Has the event fulfilled its purposes, met objectives? What lessons are there for future events?

Events lend themselves to organization structures, work flow charts and to methods of checking action. A checklist is one of the additional methods. However, events vary so much that detailed checklists to cover all events would be inappropriate, could waste time and effort, and could run into thousands of items. It is important never to use the one checklist for all events. No two events are the same. Even twin events programmed at different periods or at different locations will differ in some respects. A checklist summary, however, could be of value to check up on the various areas. A detailed list or amendments could be undertaken for each event.

EVENTS CHECKLIST

1. Facilities for events

Accommodation
Alternative areas, e.g. wet weather
Car park
Changing rooms
Cloakrooms
Crèche/childminding
Exhibition areas
First aid and medical rooms
Lavatories
Lost property room
Offices
Officials' rooms
Performers' rooms
Playing areas
Poster sites
Reception areas
Rehearsal
Sales points
Security rooms
Social, bar and catering areas
Storage
VIP rooms
Warm-up/practice areas

2. Staff/ personnel
(full time, part time,
    casual, voluntary)

Attendants
Barmen
Cashiers
Caterers
Cleaners
Cloakroom attendants
Doctor/medical staff
Electricians
Maintenance personnel
Officials
Patrols

Receptionists
Safety – lifeguards
Secretaries
Security guards
Stewards
Technicians
Telephonists
Traders/exhibitors

3. Administration, documentation and finance

Admission
Appeals/fund raising, grants,
    lotteries
Arrival/departure
Budget
Cash flow/security/change
Contracts
Copyright
Documentation
Franchise
Identification/passes
Insurance – accident, third party,
    weather
Invitations
Legal aspects
Licencing – extension, spectators,
    entertainment
Organization structure
Printing
Programmes
Sales
Seating arrangements
Stationery
Stock checking
Tickets

4. Equipment

Chairs and tables

Communications – bleep system,
  two-way radio
Decoration/decor/floral
Directional signs
Display boards
Fencing/barriers
Flags
Heating
Lighting – stage, TV, generator,
  emergency
Marquees
Projection equipment – film
  overhead projection, slide
Public address – records, tapes,
  national anthems
Scoreboards
Signs – No Smoking
Spectator stands
Staging
Uniforms for staff; protective
  clothing

5. Presentation and media

Advertising
Ceremonies
Commentators/announcers
Dress rehearsal
Entertainment
Films/photography
Interpreters
Interviews
Marketing
Music
Presentation – programme,
  timetable of events

Press
Prizes/medals
Protocol
Publicity
Radio
Souvenirs
Sponsorship/patronage
Theme/logo/image
TV
VIPS

6. Support services

AA/RAC

Bar
Catering } Public,
  performers,
  guests

Car parking
Changing
Cloakrooms
Emergency procedures
Exhibition
Hotels
Information
Lost property
Maintenance
Medical
Police
Red Cross/St John
Secretarial
Security
Shops
Telephone/telex
Transport
Travel agency

REFERENCES AND NOTES

1. Read: *What Every Exhibitor Ought to Know*, the companion booklet to the films *It'll be OK On The Day* and *How not to Exhibit Yourself*, Video Arts Ltd, 1975.
2. The Scottish Sports Council (1980), *Major Events: An Organisation Manual*, SSC, Edinburgh.

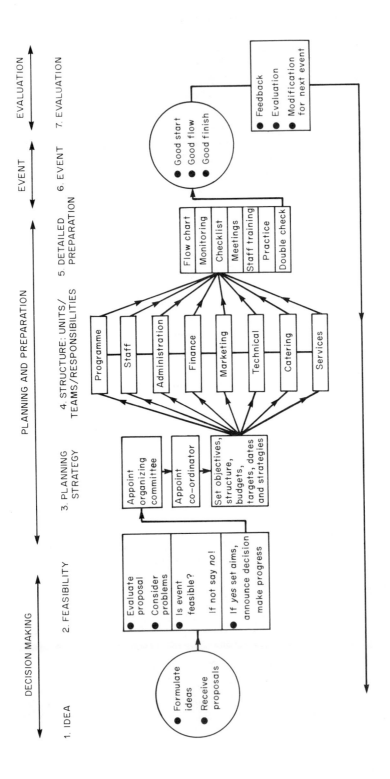

DECISION MAKING

PLANNING AND PREPARATION

EVENT

EVALUATION

1. IDEA

2. FEASIBILITY

3. PLANNING STRATEGY

4. STRUCTURE: UNITS/ TEAMS/RESPONSIBILITIES

5. DETAILED PREPARATION

6. EVENT

7. EVALUATION

- Formulate ideas
- Receive proposals

- Evaluate proposal
- Consider problems
- Is event feasible?
  If not say *no*!
- If yes set aims, announce decision make progress

Appoint organizing committee

Appoint co-ordinator

Set objectives, structure, budgets, targets, dates and strategies

Programme
Staff
Administration
Finance
Marketing
Technical
Catering
Services

Flow chart
Monitoring
Checklist
Meetings
Staff training
Practice
Double check

- Good start
- Good flow
- Good finish

- Feedback
- Evaluation
- Modification for next event

Seven stage event planner.

Event organization information can be obtained from the Sports Councils, Arts Councils, and many other agencies, e.g. read *Community Arts Festival Handbook*, Greater London Arts Association, *Planning Your Course or Conference, Municipal Entertainment* supplement and Spencer, P.J. (1982), *OK On The Day*, National Association of Youth Clubs, Leicester.

Chapter 18

Training for recreation management

Leisure is the growth industry of the national economy, employing 1.8 million people, over 8% of the nation's workforce. Employment on this scale raises substantial questions about training and career development in this emerging profession.

★

18.1   INTRODUCTION

Although until comparatively recently almost all the recreation management training initiatives were instigated from within the recreation management movement, recent government actions in relation to cuts in local government expenditure levels, the establishment of the Audit Commission and the publication of the Department of the Environment's consultative document *Competition in the Provision of Local Authority Services* [1] have emphasized the need for a highly efficient and effective recreation service. This in turn necessitates a comprehensive training programme for the industry.

This chapter examines the recreation management training situation in the UK and is divided into distinct sections. The *first* section covers the historical perspective of recreation management training in the UK and looks at the 'professional' bodies in their separate and diverse forms; the advantages of amalgamation are discussed together with the associated problems. *Second*, the different views on 'training', 'development' and 'education' are presented. *Third*, fundamental questions are asked relating to training for recreation management, namely: Why train? What to train? How to train? Training for whom? *Fourth*, the current situation relating to courses is examined. *Finally*, to put matters into the 'professional' perspective the question is asked: Is recreation management a profession?

18.2   THE HISTORICAL PERSPECTIVE OF RECREATION MANAGEMENT TRAINING IN THE UK

The concept of recreation management, as we know it today in the United Kingdom, has only emerged since the mid 1960s as a direct result of the development of the sport and recreation centre movement. Prior to that time various 'professional' bodies had been running training courses and awarding institution qualifications for many years, with some institutions going back to the 1920s.

The need for professional management of sports centres prompted the Sports Council to set up a working party which reported its findings, *Professional Training for Recreation Management*, in 1969 [2].

In the decade to follow, sport and leisure centres grew towards the 600 mark. The reorganization of local government brought about new leisure departments and a greater awareness was created as to the benefits of improved management of recreation. There was also the growing realization that recreation management applied to a much broader field than was once appreciated. Not only were there thousands of local authority posts across a broad spectrum of recreation including the arts, country-side and water recreation, but also many thousands of posts held in the commercial, private, voluntary and institutional sectors.

Historically events have moved rapidly on the 'training' scene with a plethora of courses, certificates, diplomas and degrees in a disparate variety of guises. However, there has been *little coordination, few controls, overlapping, imbalance and lack of any standardization.* The growth of the recreation centre movement, the creation of hundreds of new jobs and the new awakening towards management of recreation facilities led to the instigation of a government working party in 1977 [3].

Training for recreation management is thus in its infancy, although specialist sections of the recreation market are experienced, matured and successful operations.

18.2.1 The recreation management training committee – 'The Yates Committee'

The Recreation Management Training Committee, under the Chairmanship of Mrs Anne Yates, was appointed in 1977 by the Secretaries of State for Education and Science and for the Environment to 'review and make recommendations on the training of staff in the management of resources and facilities for sport and for all forms of outdoor recreation' [3]. The Committee was the first to acknowledge its narrow terms of reference, particularly when local authorities had already, in many cases, set up comprehensive departments which included management within the arts, entertainment and other leisure fields, left out of the Yates terms of reference.

The report [4] is the most comprehensive of its kind yet produced. As a background to the study the report looks at the *ad hoc* development of recreation provision in the UK and examines the role of the different providers. It then examines the organizations in the public, private, commercial and voluntary sectors, interprets the differing management levels and attempts to estimate the number of managers employed in the leisure industry. With the results of the different surveys the committee had commissioned, the report attempts to determine the skills, techniques and areas of knowledge that managers of different levels require and attempts to equate these with the present network of recreation management courses available.

The main recommendations of the report are claimed to be 'evolutionary' as opposed to 'revolutionary' and include:
The formation of Regional Training Committees   The report states that

'the existing informal network of links are not satisfactory. They are failing to meet the needs of practising managers . . . There is much duplication in effort and resources. They are often competing and often incompatible . . . It is time for them to be replaced by a consistent pattern of arrangements . . . to give those working in this field a common, co-ordinated base at local, regional and national levels for assessing present and future need and for meeting that need.'

With a membership comprising employers, trade unions, professional bodies, educational institutions, users (represented through the Regional Councils for Sport and Recreation) and appropriate advisory and consultative bodies, it was considered that the proposed committee would be best located in the existing Regional Management Centres.

A National Council for Leisure Because of the fragmented nature of responsibility for recreation and leisure at central government level and with the range of national agencies available, the Yates Committee considered the need for a national forum and coordinating body. Such a Council 'would give formal recognition and embodiment to the concept of leisure straddling the functions of the existing agencies' and 'would not diminish the roles or the work of the existing agencies but would enhance them through its collective approach to the problems of leisure in a changing society.' [4]

The establishment of a single professional institute for leisure managers The publication of the report took the Yates Committee some seven years to produce and its actual publication was further delayed by the deliberations of the Department of the Environment. Such a delay reduced the expected impact of the report upon the industry and to some extent its credibility also suffered. Further, one of the recommendations in the report – to create a single professional institute – has been overtaken by events with the formation of the Institute of Leisure and Amenity Management (ILAM), although the industry is still some way from establishing a single all-embracing institute for leisure management. The reaction of the existing professional bodies such as ILAM [5] and the Institute of Baths and Recreation Management (IBRM) [6] to the report has largely been complimentary and both bodies have pledged their support to the proposed Regional Training Committee. The recommendation for the creation of a National Council for Leisure has been rejected by the Minister of Sport. This action was supported by the Sports Council on the grounds that it would 'have overlapped in its functions with existing bodies' [7].

Although not all the Regional Management Centres have remained in being, progress has been made in the London and North Western regions to create a Regional Training Committee with the assistance of the Manpower Services Commission by means of a local collaboration scheme; whilst in the Yorkshire and Humberside, South Western and East Midlands regions the Sports Council has taken the initiative and

Table 18.1   The main professional bodies of recreation management

Date founded	Name	Areas of interest/ sources of members	Approximate membership
1921	Institute of Baths and Recreation Management	Pools and indoor sports centres	1400 (excluding associates and affiliates)
1956	Recreation Managers' Association	Company sports and social clubs	1000 approx.
1958	Association of Playing Fields Officers	Playing fields (mainly in education authorities)	200 approx.
1983	Institute of Leisure and Amenity Management	Generally all aspects of the leisure/recreation service – especially the public sector	3700 approx.

significant progress has been made in creating Regional Training Committees in these regions.

18.3   THE 'PROFESSIONAL' BODIES REPRESENTING RECREATION MANAGERS

There are a large number of associations and institutes connected to the field of recreation management with many overlapping interests. The major bodies, together with their founding dates, main areas of interest, sources of members and membership numbers in 1985 are given in Table 18.1.

As well as these bodies there are:

1. Countryside Recreation Management Association.
2. Chief Leisure Officers Association.
3. Tourism Society.
4. Society of Professional Arts Administrators.
5. Library Association.
6. Museums Association.
7. Leisure Studies Association.
8. Entertainments and Arts Management.
9. The Physical Education Association.

In addition, the 1981 *Recreation Management Handbook* [8] lists eighty-one other associations connected in some way with leisure provision.

The structures and organization of the main bodies concerned are described below.

18.3.1 Institute of Baths and Recreation Management (IBRM)

The IBRM was founded in 1921 as the Association of Baths Superintendents. It is a limited company and a registered charity, supported by the fees of its members. There are five regional branches.

Although its stated aims are to foster the study of the technique, design and operation of swimming pools, public laundries, sports centres and allied amenities, and to train management personnel for these services, the Institute would claim that its current training programme which 'managers have to successfully complete to be eligible for full membership, equips managers with the necessary knowledge, skills and techniques to competently manage all indoor recreation facilities' [6].

Currently the Institute is reassessing its role in line with its members' career expectations and the changing demands imposed by local government upon its membership, and is anxious that its training programme reflects the needs of both its members and the segments of the leisure service it is intended to serve.

The Institute has six types of membership (student, member, fellow, associate, corporate affiliate and trade affiliate) with qualification for membership essentially revolving around the passing of the intermediate and final examinations. The day release courses offered in preparation for these examinations are available at selected colleges in London, the East and West Midlands, the North East, the North West and Wales, whilst a correspondence course is administered by the National Association of Local Government Officers (NALGO). Correspondence courses are available for those who find the formal courses inaccessible. It is the Institute's belief that there is a need for a degree of specialist technical training for the lower and middle management levels and this is reflected in their intermediate examination syllabus.

As part of its continuing management training programme the Institute also organizes branch meetings with lectures, regional seminars, a four-day annual conference, short courses and publishes a bi-monthly journal named *Baths Service and Recreation Management*.

18.3.2 Recreation Managers' Association (RMA)

The RMA was founded in 1956 and until 1970 was known as the Industrial Sports Clubs Secretaries Association. Its original name indicates its main areas of recruitment, although the association is now open to the secretaries of any form of non profit-making recreation concern. The RMA has no formal branches.

The RMA runs a correspondence course dealing with the practical aspects of recreation management such as the organization of sporting events, catering and bar control, finance and office management and which can finally lead to the award of a diploma.

There are five types of membership (full, association, student, regional associate and commercial associate). Qualification for membership is by virtue of position held. There is an annual four-day conference each autumn and an association journal published each month.

18.3.3 Association of Playing Fields Officers (APFO)

The APFO, founded in 1958, is mainly comprised of playing fields officers employed by education authorities and responsible for the provision and maintenance of playing fields and recreation facilities for schools and young people. Its objectives are to promote the science and techniques of design, construction and management of sports grounds, landscape and associated facilities, and to improve the professional abilities of people employed in such work.

There are five types of membership (fellow, member, licentiate member, junior member and honorary member). Qualifications for membership are essentially based on post held and length of experience. The APFO has five branches and runs an annual conference. It produces no publications and organizes no courses.

18.3.4 Institute of Leisure and Amenity Management (ILAM)

The ILAM was created on 1st January 1983, and was the result of the amalgamation of

(a) Institute of Parks and Recreation Administration (IPRA)
(b) Institute of Municipal Entertainment (IME)
(c) Association of Recreation Managers (ARM)
(d) Institute of Recreation Management (IRM)

(a) Institute of Parks and Recreation Administration (IPRA)

IPRA was founded in 1926 with the primary aim of ensuring that the personnel responsible for the operation and organization of parks departments were properly trained and qualified. The IPRA had ten regional branches, and ran a one-year full-time residential course in park and recreation administration at its staff college near Reading. Day release and correspondence courses were also available.

There were five types of membership (registered, studentship, fellow, associate, licentiate and affiliateship). Membership revolved around the possession of the Diploma of Park and Recreation Administration, although associate and licentiate membership was available to those with other approved qualifications. IPRA held an annual conference and issued a monthly publication, *The Journal of Park and Recreation Administration*.

(b)   Institute of Municipal Entertainment (IME)

Founded in 1947 and originally known as the Institute of Entertainment Managers, the IME merged with the Civic Entertainments Officers Association in 1975 to create the Institute and was divided into seven areas. Its aim was to develop the professional skills needed to manage the entertainment and leisure services offered to the community by local authorities and grant-aided bodies. An entrance examination was held annually and a correspondence course was also available.

There were three types of membership (affiliate, associate, and fellow) of which only associate membership required a relevant qualification. The journal *Entertainment and Arts Management* was published monthly and its publication has continued since the amalgamation. The IME's amalgamation with other institutes to form ILAM, however, was not welcomed by all members and some formed a breakaway group called the Association of Entertainment and Arts Management.

(c)   Association of Recreation Managers (ARM)

The formation of ARM stemmed from three sources – the growth of community sports and leisure centres, the first National Recreation Management Conference and a series of informal seminars organized by practising centre directors and managers during the late 1960s. Formed in 1969, ARM attracted a large proportion of these managers into its ranks and broadened and expanded its sphere of influence, catering for chief officers, recreation officers within local authorities, managers of swimming pools, trainee managers and students. Its expansion was rapid and the association had eleven regional branches.

Membership was of three types (full, associate and student) and was dependent upon the position of responsibility held. The growth in its membership was staggering and reflected the growth of recreation facilities and services.

The ARM published a quarterly magazine, *ARM News*, and sent other information including job advertisements to its members on a weekly basis.

(d)   Institute of Recreation Management (IRM)

The IRM was established in 1970 at the instigation of the IBRM as a body for senior Recreation Managers, particularly (but not exclusively) those in local authority leisure service departments. Membership of the IRM was intended to be a second qualification rather than a substitute for existing ones, and a condition of membership was that membership of any other professional body held when joining the IRM had to be retained. One of its objectives was, in fact, 'to promote effective cooperation between related bodies in recreation management'. There were four branches.

There was an institute diploma obtainable through a combination of home course work and residential modules at Loughborough University. Membership of IRM was of four types (fellow, member, association member and registered student), dependent upon qualifications held and length of experience.

ILAM aims 'to set professional standards for the whole of the Leisure and Amenity Management Industry including Public, Private and Voluntary Sectors' [5], and emphasizes that 'We are an Institute of *Management*, different from the Institutes which amalgamated, which although they were increasingly alive to modern management, were either basically technically orientated or operated on informal qualifications' [5].

In the first two years of the Institute's inception the qualifications of the IME, IPRA and IRM continued until the Autumn of 1985, when the new ILAM examination structure came into operation. The new examination structure is divided into two major divisions, with Part I (Associate Member) and Part II (Member) levels. The content of the course is divided into three parts:

1. Philosophy of Leisure and Recreation
2. Administration and Management
3. Specialisms
   Parkland and Environment
   Sports and Recreation
   Entertainment and Tourism
   Arts and Culture

The weighting for the different elements are shown in Fig. 18.1 and it is interesting that all students will have to fulfil a two-year period of professional practice under supervision. The normal time-span for the completion of the examinations for full membership will be five years, although exemptions will be given to those students with appropriate academic qualifications which can substantially reduce the study time period. To assist students in their study for the examinations it is proposed to have an array of teaching modes including day release courses, short courses, correspondence courses, etc.

As part of its continuing training programme ILAM organizes an annual conference, an annual seminar (which has involved case studies and management games) regional seminars, field visits, and a monthly

	Weighting part I	Examinations part I	Weighting part II		Examinations part II
Common core and specialism A, B, C or D	40%	3 exams			
Philosophy of leisure and recreation	25%	1 exam			
Planning and provision			25%		Exam
Management	35%				
Finance				Finance	Exam
Marketing		1 exam	40%	Marketing	Exam
Human resources				Human resources	Exam
Economics		1 exam		Economics	Exam
Business law					
Stats/OR/comp and res method				Stats/OR/comp and res method	Exam
Public administration and office practice					
Managerial studies applied to leisure and recreation			15%		Exam
Specialist management study			20%		Exam

5 years relevant work experience with at least two years management experience

Professional practice examination

Fig. 18.1 Examination structure for ILAM syllabus.

journal recently renamed *The Leisure Manager*. To assist it in its educational and training programme ILAM has recently appointed an Education and Training Officer, whose salary is jointly paid for by the Manpower Services Commission and the Sports Council.

Additionally, the Institute publishes the proceedings of its major conferences and seminars and for its members offers The Direct Mail Advertising and Appointments Service.

18.3.5 Other bodies

(a) Countryside Recreation Management Association (CRMA)

CRMA's main purpose is to provide a forum for those with an interest in countryside recreation.

(b) Chief Leisure Officers Association (CLOA)

CLOA was formed in 1976 because some officers were dissatisfied with the performance of IRM. CLOA is a body for chief officers in comprehensive leisure service departments in local government, and membership is by virtue of the post held.

(c) Tourism Society

This was originally the Institute of Tourism. Its general object is 'to improve and maintain the standards of professional competence of persons involved or engaged in tourism and in the provision of tourism services and to enhance the standing of such persons'.

(d) Society of Professional Arts Administrators (SPAA)

The society's aims seem to be concerned with the welfare of its members (giving support over conditions of service, salaries and promotion prospects) rather than with the unification and professionalization of arts administration. At present there is no body specifically concerned with these functions although the dividing line between 'arts' and 'entertainment' is by no means distinct and there appear to be areas of overlap with other arts associations.

(e) Library Association (LA)

The LA is much older than most of the professional bodies within the sphere of leisure provision, being founded in 1877. It does not officially see itself as a leisure or recreation profession and opposes the inclusion of libraries within leisure service departments. The LA maintains a register of Chartered Librarians, entry being by diploma or degree.

(f) Museums Association

This is a body for museum staff. Membership is by diploma.

(g) Leisure Studies Association (LSA)

The LSA was formed in 1975 and although its membership includes many practising recreation managers the Association is largely a forum for academics. It organizes about four conferences per annum and the proceedings are normally published and available to purchase at minimal cost. These form an invaluable source of reference for those interested in leisure studies, especially students. Additionally the Association circulates a periodical newsletter to its members and in conjunction with the publishers E. & F.N. Spon Ltd., publish a monthly *Leisure Studies Journal*. Currently the Association has some 350 members.

(h) Association of Entertainment and Arts Management (AEAM)

AEAM was formed just prior to the creation of ILAM. Its aims are 'broadly to provide members with a means of meeting with colleagues in the entertainment and arts management field for discussion, training and activity on both a social and professional basis [9]. The current membership is in the region of 200.

'Neither A.E.A.M. nor S.P.A.A. seem to be interested in a listed professional qualification. As most of their members work within a public service which demands a professional qualification for appointment to many posts, or to progress beyond basic salary levels, this reduces them to a level of a social club rather than that of a professional association.' [9]

(i) Physical Education Association (PEA)

The PEA, founded in 1899, currently has approximately 5000 members. Members are required to possess an approved professional qualification in physical education and allied areas or have a general physical education background deemed appropriate by the membership committee. There are eight membership categories (fellow, member, licentiate, overseas, student, husband and wife, retired and corporate).

While the PEA is primarily concerned with the teaching of physical education, many of its members are deeply involved in the management of recreation, directly as managers or indirectly as teachers involved in community work or with joint or dual use facilities.

The association produces a bi-monthly publication – *The British Journal of Physical Education*. It runs courses, conferences and international symposia and provides library and information services.

18.4 AMALGAMATION OF INSTITUTES AND ASSOCIATIONS?

Despite the creation of the ILAM the range and variety of associations, overlapping areas of interest and the relatively recent inclusion of the term 'recreation' in the titles of the former IPRA and the IBRM and RMA indicates that first, many associations see the need to expand their role beyond their particular specialisms; and second, that there are more associations vying for the same members.

In a survey of managers and assistant managers in recreation centres in England and Wales undertaken for the Recreation Management Training Committee [10] it was found that the vast majority of managers belonged to an association or institution and over two thirds of assistant managers did so. A further survey of ARM members [11] showed that approximately 50% of members belonged to more than one association and that 40% of these (20% of the total sample) were members of the IBRM. In addition, 8% of the sample were members of the British Institute of Management, and the then IRM and RMA had approximately 7.5% each. This could reflect the situation that existed at the time – that no existing association or institution was able to cater for the diverse needs of the Recreation Manager.

With the creation of ILAM the situation has improved with a reduction in the number of associations and institutions involved in recreation management, but there is clear evidence that many IBRM members and AEAM members are also members of ILAM.

Evidence of further overlap exists in the examination syllabuses of the IBRM and the ILAM courses. The ILAM's common core part of the course has considerable similarity to sections of the IBRM course. The IBRM have acknowledged this and hope to liaise with ILAM to jointly offer courses containing these common elements.

Within the recreation management field itself the manager is dealing more and more with areas which come under the auspices of a range of associations. This is true not only with the heads of comprehensive leisure service departments, but also with the managers of leisure centres who may be responsible for both wet and dry sports facilities, may promote entertainment events as well as sports activities and may have responsibility for the programming and maintenance of outdoor facilities.

There are common areas of interest, therefore, covering a range of recreation associations, and amalgamation of these associations may provide a necessary rationalization of the present fragmented and confused situation. The Yates Committee [4] acknowledged the need for a form of amalgamation; 'We therefore recommend that all existing professional bodies should direct their efforts towards the establishment of a single professional institute for leisure managers'. Amalgamation is, however, a contentious issue between the various bodies involved and there are arguments both for and against it.

18.4.1 The problems of creating an amalgamated body

Arguments in favour. The arguments in favour of amalgamation generally revolve around the undeniable benefits to be gained from such action. A single association would end the confusion and frustration felt by employers, people already within the recreation management field and people trying to enter it. It would have the weight, authority and financial resources to place recreation management on a more professional footing, to rationalize, control and monitor the quality and content of the numerous education and training courses, to implement a career situation which at present does not exist, and to view constantly the recreation management field, reacting to changes that occur faster than can an association which is primarily concerned with one specialist area.

Contrary arguments. Arguments against amalgamation tend to revolve around either the mechanics of it (how will we amalgamate our administration, membership grading, journals etc.) or the basic concern about loss of status and identity that may be felt to occur when a small association is swallowed up by a larger conglomerate. The IBRM in particular is proud of its training record and examination system and is reluctant to place itself on an equal footing with other associations whose membership requirements they believe to be less stringent. There is also fear that particular specialisms will be lost if incorporated within one global recreation management association, although there is also danger that specialist associations, particularly facility-based ones, may lose sight of the fact that their specialism is only a means to an end – that of satisfying people's recreational needs – and is not the end itself. As Kraus [12] stated '. . . we must ask if the individual is taking a major part in creating his own occupation or whether the occupation or profession is bearing on him to the point where he is made over in the image of the occupation'.

Action. Action was taken in an attempt to resolve the problem. The major associations of recreation management were aware of the issues involved, and the establishment of a National Advisory Committee of the Leisure Profession (NACOLP) in 1975 indicated a move toward collective action. Then, in 1978, the ARM, IME, IPRA and IRM, formed a steering committee of two elected members from each association in order 'to positively pursue amalgamation as an achievable objective and to consider the form that the new organization might take'.

The problems associated with amalgamation negotiation were extremely complex. The RMA withdrew from the early discussion as their membership was not local authority based, in contrast to the other organizations. IBRM also discontinued at an early stage, then rejoined in 1979, but withdrew apparently due to their charitable status and certain financial tax considerations relating to the IPRA.

Proposals for the amalgamation of ARM, IME, IPRA and IRM into the Institute of Leisure and Amenity Management were published in October 1981 and the new body came into being on 1 January 1983. It was however, a considerable misfortune to start the new institute without the IBRM. Not only is it the oldest institute but is the acknowledged authority on one of the major components of leisure and recreation. The history of recreation in Britain owes it much and the amalgamated body is not comprehensive without it. An amalgamation without IBRM was, in Colbeck's words to be 'regarded with dismay' [13].

Early in 1985 IBRM members were sent a questionnaire which included a question on whether their interests were best served by having one 'Professional' institution. The responses indicated that the majority of members were in favour of having one such body – perhaps a Federation – but not necessarily an amalgamated institute such as ILAM. [14]

With regard to the Arts a similar situation exists. A Working Party called 'Towards an Institute for Administrators in the Arts and Entertainements' was set up in 1980 with encouragement from the Arts Council, City University and others and, after four years deliberation, came to the conclusion not to progress with the formation of a 'professional' organization. This is rather surprising since they saw 'no merit in their potential members joining ILAM' [9].

18.5 TRAINING, DEVELOPMENT OR EDUCATION

There appears to exist some confusion and conflict of use over the three terms management 'training', management 'development', and management 'education'. At times these terms appear to be interchangeable, and sometimes one term may be all-embracing, encompassing three meanings in one.

James [15] states that a common view is that

'education is a process which helps to equip the manager with key knowledge and skills (such as handling concepts and techniques) that enable him to take his place in "management" – not in a specific management job. Training is the means whereby specific job-related skills and knowledge are acquired for the "here and now". Development is seen as embracing both education and training, and also personal as well as job needs for the future'.

Blake [16] provides perhaps a more concrete distinction between management education and training by comparing education with the role of the coach, and training with the role of the trainer. He states that:

'Conventional training produces conventional responses, habits, skills for specific situations or roles, whereas education encourages reflective thinking on general principles that can be effective in many varied situations. Further, the success of training has depended more on what the learner has done for him rather than what he is allowed to do for himself. With training and lecturing the mind grows by the acquisition of facts. With education and real project work the mind develops in form with increased power to acquire and use knowledge'

However, Blake finally favours the use of the term 'training' to encompass both training and education specifically appropriate to management development.

The Sports Centre Management Discussion Group [17] also use the word 'training' in an embracive sense, including within it both 'training' and 'development'. Their definition of management development as consisting of 'providing opportunities for managers to develop themselves' may, however, leave something to be desired, and again Blake's definition may be more enlightening. In discussing why the term 'development' is used instead of 'growth', he says.

'If a tadpole just grew, it would be just a bigger tadpole, still restricted to just those things that a tadpole can do. But a tadpole does not just grow into being more of the same things, it develops into a frog with a much greater choice and range of behaviour with not only a greater flexibility of response options to situations, but more important, the ability to change its situation. Development does the same for managers' [16].

The Recreation Management Training Committee refers to training as including 'any formal programme of instruction in management skills' [3]. Drucker [18] views *management* development (organizational need, acquisition of new skills and knowledge etc.) as entirely different from *manager* development (appraising your own performance, self-development).

Parker [19] introduces a further dimension when looking at the 'professional' and 'academic' content of Leisure Studies Courses. Figure 18.2 illustrates Parker's perception that professional training, professional education and academic education fall along a continuum. He sees professional training as being 'specialised rather than general' with the emphasis on training people for specific types of job in the sport, recreation or leisure industries. In the middle range of Parker's continuum is professional education where courses are 'designed for people who intend to start a career in sport, recreation or leisure but who have not made up their mind about which specialisation to aim for.' (Such courses strive to achieve a balance between professional and academic

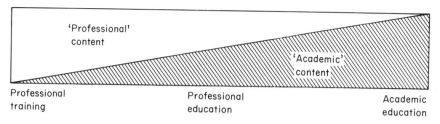

Fig. 18.2 Parker's Training–education continuum.

content.) Thirdly, there is academic education, where the 'course is unconcerned with what profession or job the student will subsequently enter or seek to enter'. Consequently, academic education is pursued for its own sake and for the personal development of the individual concerned.

Management *education* may therefore be seen as a process of active learning and enquiry (including learning from one's peers) with learner input a necessary part of this process. Management *training* may be seen as an input process from teacher to learner, whereby the learner is equipped with the specific job related knowledge and skills needed to carry out his or her job successfully. Finally, management *development* may be seen as encompassing both management education and training, increasing the manager's adaptability and flexibility, maximizing his or her strengths and overcoming weaknesses.

Although all three terms are defined here, for the sake of simplicity when discussing the broad issues related to recreation management training, education and development, the term 'training' will be used to embrace all three, although it is recognized that it is a far from satisfactory description.

18.6 WHY TRAIN?

The specialist needs of recreation management have been recognized for some time now as apparent from the long history of the IBRM and the former IPRA training schemes. The expanding requirement of the Recreation Manager in terms of both knowledge and skills has been reflected by the attempts to broaden the IRBM and IPRA syllabuses beyond their technical specialisms, the establishment of DMS and MSc courses specializing in recreation management, and the setting up of integrated leisure service departments. The recent report entitled *Leisure Policy for the Future* [20] stresses the need to turn attention towards management training in all fields of leisure provision 'in order to secure more efficient uses of resources and more effective connections with people's needs'.

Recreation management can therefore be viewed as an area of knowledge in its own right, and it is unlikely that an outsider with no prior knowledge or experience of it could enter the recreation management field and operate effectively within it. The question then is not whether there is anything to learn but whether experience on its own is the best teacher, or whether training (be it before, during or after) is a necessary and useful adjunct to it. As James stated [15]:

'Practical and proven experience is often quoted as the essential ingredient for effective management performance. Theory and theorists are often held up as being "woolly and out of touch". Yet it has been rightly said that there is nothing so practical as a good theory and all practical action begins and ends with it. However, experience alone is not enough. A "practical man" calls upon his experience to solve a problem. He is using that acquired knowledge as a body of theory to enable him to take the appropriate action. But theory acquired by direct experience alone, by trial and error, or as a result of sitting next to "Nellie" can be of low quality and exceptionally time consuming. Ten years of experience can be one year's experience ten times over. We need to supplement practical experience with appropriate theory'.

Training, therefore, is necessary not only for those entering the field, but also for those already in it in order that:

1. They can utilize the accumulated experience and knowledge of others, as well as more effectively harnessing their own experience.
2. Their skills can be amended and supplemented as the changing demands on the Recreation Manager require new and different insights and abilities.

However, many managers and potential managers appear to undertake 'training' solely to gain qualifications.

For example, in the Yates recreation centre survey [10] it appeared that answers to questions on qualifications pointed to their desirability for status, structure and promotion but staff did not find such qualifications essential to the job as such. Indeed, the relative merits of education and formal qualifications rated extremely low compared with other aspects of training.

In the ARM survey [11] 84% of respondents felt that they had a need to extend their training and/or qualifications. Yet only one third of the sample were currently engaged in obtaining such qualifications. This indicates that there is a felt need and a known demand which needs to be met, but whether the need is for training or qualification is not known.

18.7 INCORPORATING THE THREE APPROACHES INTO TRAINING

In looking at the three basic philosophies behind 'what to train?' there appear to be strengths and weaknesses in each. The reality may be that there are elements of truth in each and that there are some management skills that are applicable in any management situation (perhaps human relations, or budgeting). There are some management skills particularly relevant to recreation management as a whole (notably planning the recreation programming) and there are some management skills which are specifically linked to a particular recreation management subdivision (perhaps the skills needed to balance countryside recreation and conservation).

If this is accepted it will be necessary to determine exactly which skills are of a general nature and can be taught to all Recreation Managers and exactly which skills are specialist and can be taught to those wishing to enter a particular recreation subdivision.

A compromise approach such as that currently used on the DMS course at the Polytechnic of North London and to some extent incorporated in the proposed ILAM course is that recreation management courses – especially those for middle management – can be divided into three distinct phases: (i) Theoretical and conceptual; (ii) Applied perspective in a recreation management environment and (iii) Problem solving.

With regard to the actual content of the courses, the Yates Committee identified the management functions and activities, together with appropriate areas of knowledge and skills in relation to three distinct management levels, – first line or junior management, middle management and senior management. These are illustrated in Table 18.2.

The Local Government Training Board held a series of Recreation/ Leisure Management Consultative Seminars to determine the training needs of managers. As a result of these seminars they identified the following training needs [21]:

1. Management development skills for Chief Leisure Officers.
2. Marketing and public relations skills.
3. Skills and knowledge to establish departmental policy or strategy around which to base performance objectives.
4. Management knowledge and skill to undertake a user-orientated approach as opposed to the traditional and outdated facility-orientated approach.
5. Coordinating and influencing skills to make more effective use of the voluntary sector to maximize services to the general public.

Table 18.2 Recommended Recreation Management Training Structure

Function	Activity	Knowledge	Skills
First line or junior management			
Planning	Scheduling Objective setting	Theory of recreation Management by objectives and target setting Scheduling techniques Basic financial and cost statements	
Organizing	Attending meetings Staff recruiting Staff development Industrial relations	Committee procedures Job descriptions Interviewing techniques Employment law Health and Safety at work	Decision-making Leadership Motivation Written communication Counselling
Implementing	Leading groups Coaching staff Relating to users	Training techniques	
Controlling	Maintaining records Counselling and appraisal	Appraisal techniques	
Middle management (as above but also)			
Planning	Interpreting policy Short term planning Programming Budgeting User surveys	Planning techniques Use of statistics Financial records Cost statements Survey techniques	
Organizing	Controlling meetings	Organization procedure	

Table 18.2 continued

Function	Activity	Knowledge	Skills
	Obtaining material resources Marketing and PR Designing administrative systems	Purchasing Staff selection Marketing methods Systems design techniques	Delegating Understanding of group working Working with staff
Implementing	Coordinating	Organization development	Problems analysis Report writing
Controlling	Assembling summaries of information Preparing reports and financial statements Reviewing performance	Information systems Counselling Techniques of analysis	

Senior management (as above but also)

Function	Activity	Knowledge	Skills
Planning	Forecasting Deciding policy Manpower planning Reconciling conflicting interests	Economics Managerial financial ratios Provision of capital Network planning Research techniques	
Organizing	Structuring the organization	Understanding of organizational structures Organizational change and development	Considering alternative solutions
Implementing	Representing the organization Policy direction	Organizational politics	
Controlling	Reviewing performances against the organization's targets		

Source: *The Recreation Managers Training Committe Final Report* (1984) [4] p. 64.

18.8 HOW TO TRAIN?

There is a wide range and variety of options available for the implementation of training schemes – full-time courses, part-time courses, sandwich courses, day release courses, in-service training – as well as considerations as to the balance between theoretical and practical input. To a large extent the type of training (in terms of part-time, full-time courses etc.) will depend on the needs of the individuals for whom the training is designed, their availability for study, their finances, and extent of training they require. However, as far as methods of training are concerned there seems to be considerable consensus of opinion on the need for theoretical input to be tempered by practical experience, either before or during the course. For this very reason many courses, including degree and diploma, have a student placement requirement as part of the course. Also, the proposed ILAM course includes a two-year period of supervised professional practice that all students have to undertake for acceptance as full members.

In the Yates Recreation Centre Survey of managers and assistant managers [10], practical experience was seen as pre-eminent to be appropriate for the jobs and the call was for more short courses, modular courses, day release and in-service training. This implies the need for colleges and polytechnics to be far more flexible in the mode of courses offered.

Nancy Foy [22] considers that classroom instruction provides little opportunity to practice what is taught and sees the need to improve the 'credibility and relevance in management education' with 'more project-orientated work, exchanges and other joint activities that might help bridge the real or perceived gaps between management education and managers'. Many courses view field visits as an integral part of the course and extensively use case studies and management games.

Pick [23], in looking at training for arts administration, states that an academic institution may be 'a convenient place to locate the administration of training and research but it is important that at every stage practising and professional administrators are at the centre of developments', and Gage [24] emphasizes the benefits to be gained through the students attempting implementation of course teaching in a practical environment.

Hitchin [25] comes out strongly in favour of practical experience being gained *before* any formal management training is undertaken, believing that 'good managers cannot be created irrespective of the length and sophistication of training methods used unless they have innate abilities', and consequently 'if young men are allowed to opt to take management degrees straight from College many, perhaps the majority, will be doing so without any knowledge as to whether they possess the necessary 'innate qualities'. He concludes from this that where 'resources are centred on potential failures those resources are being wasted'. Hitchin, therefore, believes that it is necessary to 'select people from within the profession and who have been in it for at least three years and preferably longer' in order that there will be time for their potential to be evaluated and the possible value of management training to them to be assessed.

The problem here is that the opportunity to display management potential depends greatly on the degree of responsibility delegated by those higher up the management tree. A bad manager of human resources can stifle potential management ability and consequently progress for the potential manager may be slow and frustrating. Similar problems may also arise for those having studied another discipline at college but wishing to enter recreation management. The possession of the innate ability that Hitchin sees as a prerequisite for good management is not less likely to exist among a body of graduates than among any other group, but there is a danger that those graduates who possess such abilities may find, owing to the lack of a management qualification (or the opportunity to study for one) that they have to enter the field at a level which is too low both in terms of responsibility and challenge, and consequently become frustrated and leave. The difficulty, therefore, for both those already within the field and those wishing to enter it is to achieve a balance between the practicality of *objectively* assessing management potential and the possibility of losing good potential managers who have a positive contribution to make towards recreation management.

18.9   WHAT TO TRAIN?

In looking at 'who to train?' a wide range of training needs have been identified. These included both the needs of the organization and the individual concerned. However, it is at present questionable whether the actual content of the training needs to be as wide ranging as the people it is intended to serve. In the ARM survey members were asked in which direction they would wish to extend their training. 36% called for business management, 19% recreation management, 8% recreation and leisure studies, 5.5% local government studies and 4% general administration, i.e. over 70% called for subject areas applicable to the wide range of recreation management. Less than 20% called for specialist training.

The basis of most arguments on what to train, essentially revolves around how specialist or how general such training should be, with these arguments tending to fall into one of three categories:

1. That recreation management is composed of two separate elements – recreation and management – and that the management element is applicable to any management situation (this seems to be the present basis of most courses).

2. That recreation management is an area of knowledge in its own right with a set of specific skills that are applicable across the recreation sphere.
3. That recreation management is composed of specialist management subdivisions (e.g. baths management, countryside management, arts management) with particular skills unique to that subdivision.

18.9.1　Recreation management is composed of two separate elements

The arguments in favour of this tend to see the recreation element as comprising an essentially technical body of knowledge. Good management is seen to require something more than this, and to be applicable in varying degrees to all management decisions. Drucker [26] states that 'Businesses are different, but business is much the same, regardless of size and structure of products, technology and markets, of culture and managerial competence. There is a common business reality'.

The principle appears to find support in the Yates recreation centre survey [10].

Despite the wide range of skills required for good recreation management five main skills were predominant: *managing people, diplomacy and public relations, organizing and planning, administrative and personal character qualities*. The major problem for managers was staffing and for assistant managers staff relations. Recreation centre management opinion pointed in the direction of courses primarily concerned with the management of people and the administration of programmes and services with technical specialities only as a subsidiary input, perhaps on an optional or choice basis.

This seems to be the view taken (either through belief or expediency) by a large number of the existing training courses at the academic institutions. Harrison [27], in reference to the MSc course at Loughborough University of Technology makes the position clear.

'A suggestion often made in connection with the course has been that Recreation Management students should be taught separately throughout their programme, and that the contextual framework for all their teaching, including management studies, should be recreation. The view that has prevailed at Loughborough, however, has been that management is management, whatever its context and that a reasonable expectation of higher degree students is that they should be capable of carrying economic principles, concepts and skills of financial management, marketing etc. into their own spheres of management application'.

This belief is reinforced by the subjects taught not only on the MSc at Loughborough, but also on the DMS at the Polytechnic of North London, and other academic institutions. Subjects such as economics, finance, quantitative analysis and techniques, marketing and human aspects are taught in a broad management context, usually by management studies staff.

A Dartington Amenity Research Trust (DART) paper [28] which compares DART research into the non-public sector with that of the Local Government Training Board (LGTB) into recreation management in local authorities, also comes to the conclusion that a large part of management training is of a general nature.

'In both sectors, the main emphasis is on matters which might be seen as not specific to recreation itself or (put another way) as relevant to any business or department. Thus in the DART report, the main emphasis is on organizing ability, business sense, financial or accountancy skill, marketing, law, personnel management and handling of the public. In the LGTB report [21] the main emphasis was on a broad approach to management development: particular skills included "influencing skills", man management, forecasting, delegation, control, review and evaluation'

In a joint paper issued by DART and the Institute of Local Government studies *The Management Challenge for Local Government* [29] no distinction is made for the management of their recreation services. The emphasis is on the need for a flexible management approach which is needed to cope with a changing political, social and demographic environment.

Knowledge of the technical aspects of recreation is, therefore, seen as an adjunct to the necessary management skills, which are relevant in most management situations, not just that of recreation management.

18.9.2   Recreation management is an area of knowledge in its own right

This viewpoint holds that management skills are not necessarily applicable to any situation but are specific to the context in which they are being used, depending on whether *recreation* management is viewed as a *general* or a *specific* situation.

Rosemary Stewart [30] states that

'. . . the job of the manager is varied; the differences may be as much, if not more than, the similarities. These lists of management functions ignore the diversity of management; the job of the top manager bears little resemblance to that of the junior manager, or that of being a coke manager in a steel mill is hardly comparable with being an advertising manager to a popular shoe manufacturer. These jobs differ because they have different functions, but even more because the situation of the firm is so dissimilar'.

This view was endorsed by the then IPRA [31], who considered that 'the theory that a person trained as a manager can manage anything is now very suspect'. Further weight is added to this argument by the Sports Centre Management Discussion Group [32], which analysed management training in view of its relevance to sports centre management and concluded that:

1. 'Management training in this country tends to be based on the needs of production industry despite the claims that it is generalist training.
2. The functioning of a centre is different from a production industry so the training for the management of a centre should not be so closely related to industry'.

A possible explanation for the different interpretation of the functions of management as perceived by Drucker and Stewart is that the former is basically concerned with efficiency, i.e. the optimum use of the resources that are at the disposal of the organization, whilst in a service industry the emphasis is on effectiveness, which can be seen as providing a service that meets the needs of the community it is to serve, i.e. providing the right service in the right place at the right time. It is possible to manage a recreation service efficiently whilst failing to meet the needs of a community. In this sense, *effectiveness* is the more important goal for recreation managers.

If the argument that management training needs to be specialist in nature is accepted, then the degree to which specialization is necessary has to be determined. Some see general recreation management skills as being applicable to a wide range of recreation subdivisions. Pick [33] does not believe that the old distinctions between heritage arts, leisure activities, community arts, sports and games apply to what is actually happening in any part of Britain.

'In a conversation last week between myself and two theatre administrators we listed the various events we had helped to promote in the last five years. Answers included sky diving, bingo, beagling, flower show, go-go dancing, rush weaving course, basketball tournament, kinetic sculpture, fancy dress parades, cookery demonstrations and pop concerts. Is there, I wonder, any substantial organization now which does not offer food and drink, a spread of activities, but which exists *solely* for one form of entertainment?'

Viewed in this way there would appear to be considerable overlap between the recreation sub-divisions, particularly with regard to programming and promotional skills. Further areas of common interest may be identified by looking at an analysis [34] of the topics most requested by arts administrators for inclusion in training schemes. These were bookkeeping, fund raising/grant applications, contract characteristics (performers), law affecting venue and performance, publicity, catering management, event/festival planning, box office systems analysis, print buying, inter personal skills, wage and salary administration, and communities and facilities. Nearly all these topics could be as equally relevant to a syllabus for the training of leisure centre managers, community centre wardens and organizers of outdoor events in parks and the countryside and consequently would seem to indicate that the training requirements of a number of the recreation management subdivisions are similar in a number of ways.

18.9.3 Recreation management is composed of specialist subdivisions

This argument takes the viewpoint that management skills are specific to the management situation further than that discussed in the previous section. It states that the various subdivisions of recreation management are the specialist management situations, rather than recreation management as a whole. It sees the management training requirements of a baths manager to be different from those of a countryside manager, or those of a sports hall manager to be different from those of an entertainments manager. This would appear to be true to a limited extent since the lack of specialist technical knowledge about swimming pools, horticulture, countryside maintenance etc. could have a noticeably adverse effect on the efficient and effective functioning of a manager involved with any of these recreation subdivisions. Other management skills needed, however, may not be *so* specialist, being relevant to either recreation or management in general.

One of the major problems in interpreting recreation management as a series of specialisms, is that training may become supervisory or technically-orientated instead of *management*-orientated. This would support the theory of Katz [35] who claims that as one ascends the managerial ladder the amount of technical skills and knowledge required decreases whilst the conceptual skills and knowledge requirement increases. Another problem is that specialist approaches tend to be facility-orientated. Such an approach may fail to ask the fundamental question of whether the facility is needed and what its function is. Without 'people' insights the *facility* may become more important than the people it serves.

18.10 TRAINING FOR WHOM?

Any coherent system of training, education and development must be structured around the needs of the people it is intended to serve. If training is to be effective we need to ask, '*who* is it for?' before we can ask, '*what* should it be?'

Who *is* it for? A crude breakdown of the recreation management field might come up with the following three divisions:

1. People already within recreation management.
2. People belonging to an occupation or profession that has connections with, or requires knowledge of, recreation management.
3. Those trying to enter the field.

18.10.1   People already within recreation management

There are a large number of managers involved in an occupational capacity with recreation: there are managers in the public, commercial, voluntary and institutional sectors. There are indeed a very considerable number of paid managers within the voluntary sector. There are different types of managers – top, senior, middle, first-line, trainees, voluntary and even part-time managers. Any training system will have to take into account that these managers belong to a wide variety of recreational backgrounds. The type of organization they belong to may be privately or commercially orientated; it may be a voluntary organization, or it may be a local authority. How far, therefore, should any systematic scheme of training cast its net? Are the management training requirements for the different types of organization essentially similar or utterly different? Is the type of training that would benefit the manager of a local authority sports centre the type of training that would benefit the manager of a commercially run health studio? Are the skills required by a local authority entertainment's officer the same skills as those required by the manager of a commercially owned theatre?

Are there certain specialisms within recreation management where the skills are valid and effective no matter what type of organization is involved, and are there specialisms where such a carry-over of skills from one type of organization to another is not successful?

The 'specialisms' themselves pose similar problems. Traditionally, the management of recreation has been divided into different areas – the management of sport, of parks, of the countryside, of entertainments, arts, libraries and museums. Are there common elements of management between these specialisms, and how specialized would any specialist training have to be? What sort of training would be required for the Recreation Manager who is involved with, or responsible for, a number of these areas – the head of a leisure services department, the manager of a leisure centre, or the warden of a community centre? Are, in fact, the traditional divisions of recreation management still valid, or does the Recreation Manager of today have to possess a knowledge and understanding of recreation that goes beyond the scope of any one specialism?

The recent trend amongst labour controlled councils in the London area is to manage their recreation services with a more 'decentralized' approach (i.e. where the organizational structure is divided on a geographical basis as opposed to a functional division). The system implies that the area managers must have a good conceptual grasp of the skills, techniques and knowledge required to manage the different services under his or her control.

Any recommendations on training will also have to take into consideration that within any organization or specialism there are different levels of authority and that the training requirements of the people occupying the posts at these various levels are likely to be different. The report of the Yates Committee identifies four levels of management hierarchy: top management/senior management/middle management and first-line or supervisory grades, and claims that 'General management education and training (to meet the needs of first and middle levels of management,) may be met through

- the NEBSS Certificate in Supervisory Studies;
- the BTEC Certificate in Management Studies;
- the CNAA Diploma in Management Studies;
- MSc Courses'

The Yates Committee believe that provision for senior and top levels of management should be met through short intensive programmes and in some cases through post graduate study in universities and colleges of higher education. Unfortunately, this training hierarchy is not nationally accepted and the courses are not readily accessible in all the regions of the UK.

The problem is exacerbated by the lack of any rationalization of job titles and conditions of service within local authorities. The post of 'supervisor' within a recreation centre can at present involve as much as duty manager responsibility or as little as being liable for the setting up of equipment.

There are a number of other issues that have to be examined when considering training for those already within the recreation management field. From the surveys quoted earlier it is clear that a high proportion of the managers see a qualification such as the DMS as a means of career advancement. Yet the requirements for entry on to a DMS course are restrictively academically orientated, ideally requiring a first degree, with admission for non-academically qualified candidates (who must be aged 27 or over with at least four years' experience in a position of responsibility) being allowed only exceptionally. It should be noted, however, that in practice many of the successful candidates for entry fall within this category. A more positive approach needs to be taken towards meeting the requirements of the experienced manager who wishes to learn, develop and progress within the field and who may only be able to do the latter by gaining a prestigious qualification.

Financial support for Recreation Managers wishing to undertake training is another area of concern. For full-time courses, such as the MSc and DMS, grants are unlikely to be forthcoming, for they fall within the discretionary award category, whilst secondments at present are few and far between. The practising manager may have family and mortgage commitments, being unable to afford either time off or loss of income to pursue a full-time course, and if he or she undertakes a part-time course the shift work which is an integral part of a large number of Recreation Managers' jobs may prove a hindrance to regular course attendance. The ILAM course with its different training modes – college based courses with exceptions, distant learning modules, correspondence course (in conjunction with NALGO) appears to be an alternative that will meet the requirement of many in the field, although it will, by its very nature, be rather time consuming.

18.10.2   Connected occupations or professions

There is a range of occupations and professions that have links with recreation management and may often influence or be involved with the provision or management of recreation. Where there is an absence of the necessary planning expertise within a local authority leisure department or its constituent parts, town planners have been responsible for the production of recreation strategy plans despite a limited knowledge of the field. Architects with a restricted understanding of user and management requirements have designed leisure facilities. Tourist officials, youth workers, social workers, those working with the elderly or the disabled, and headmasters or physical education teachers responsible for the running of dual use schemes, are all concerned in some way and to some extent with the management of recreation. Yet few have ever received any formal management training.

Should courses, therefore, be established to cater for these groups? Are their training requirements similar or will they differ from profession to profession? Can recreation management be divided up into modules, any number or combination of which can be taught according to the needs of the profession it is serving? Or will each profession or occupation need a course specifically designed to meet its requirements?

These questions should be considered since the professions such as social workers, youth workers and even headmasters involved with dual use schemes can have a profound, if intangible, influence on the quality of life of the individuals and groups with whom they are involved, while town planners and architects can be responsible for more quantifiable effects by influencing (perhaps wrongly) expenditure on capital projects and the consequent level of recurrent costs that usually accompanies such expenditure. Courses such as the part-time postgraduate course, Diploma in Leisure Planning at the Polytechnic of North London, help to fill the current vacuum and attracts students from far outside the London region.

Concern has recently been expressed by the Local Government Training Board [21] regarding the training of elected members especially 'to raise members awareness of the issues and problems most prevalent in the industry today'. The Chairman of Leisure Services of a London Borough was awarded the Certificate in Management Studies (Recreation) in 1985 and this may well be the start of a trend!

Most important of all, however, all people involved in some way with the recreation needs of the community and the people within it should be able to both identify these needs and contribute *effectively* towards meeting them.

18.10.3 Those trying to enter recreation management

One of the most significant findings in the Yates recreation centre survey was that Recreation Managers look for colleagues who are *experienced*, have pleasing personalities and who are enthusiastic and reliable.

If given the choice, when making appointments of management colleagues, respondents would choose applicants with experience, in preference to those who were trained or highly qualified but not experienced. This raises the fundamental issue: how then do potential management staff gain the necessary experience to be welcomed into the fold? In contradiction to this finding (and perhaps of even greater significance) is the fact that 43% of the managers questioned in the same survey had no previous recreation centre experience! The situation that existed in the late 1960s and early 1970s was that many managers went straight to the top management post from outside the industry and entry into recreation management was a haphazard mixture of luck and opportunity. Today the situation has significantly changed with the majority of the middle and senior management posts being filled from within the industry.

A clear and defined career structure is needed with an identification of the various entry points into the field and the training requirements for each. This the Yates Committee has attempted to do, but that recommendation has not met with universal approval (Fig.18.3).

In looking at 'training for whom?' therefore, it would appear that any training system has to take into account that an individual could work for any one of a number of different types of organization (public, private, commercial, voluntary etc.), could be involved in any number of specialisms (arts, sports, countryside etc.), or could belong to another profession with some recreation management responsibility. The system will have to take into account the different levels of responsibility within an organization, the requirements of the practising manager and the needs of those trying to enter the field. It will have to be decided whether this training system will be all-embracing or will be geared towards a particular type of organization (e.g. public sector only) and particular specialisms (e.g. the Recreation Management Training Committee makes a distinction

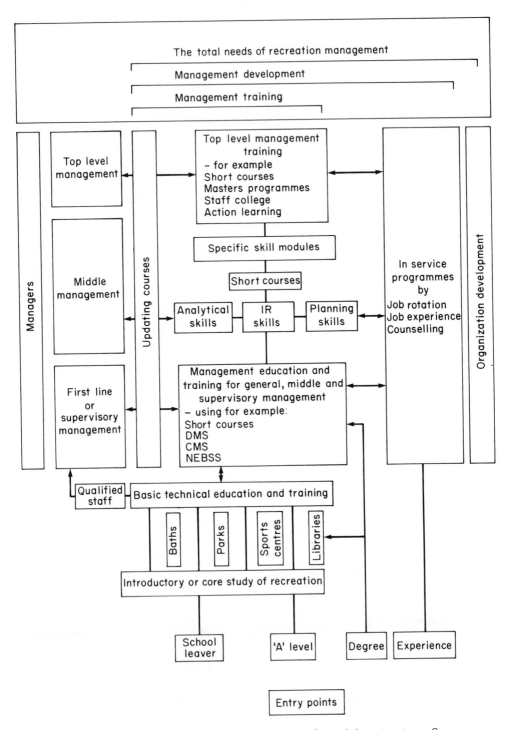

Fig. 18.3 Yates Committee's recommendation of a training structure. Source: *Recreation Management Training Committee: Final Report* [40].

between 'recreation' and 'cultural' activities). Essentially, it will have to identify the training needs of those involved with, or wishing to become involved with recreation management, be wary of 'artificial' divisions within recreation, identify common needs where they exist, and cater for specialisms when it is necessary to do so.

18.11 COURSES IN RECREATION MANAGEMENT

The Sports Council's 1969 report [2] recommended that a broader and more management-orientated course than those offered at that time by the various professional bodies of recreation be established. The working party suggested that this course should take the form of a Diploma in Management Studies (DMS) in Recreation Management. This suggestion was implemented in 1971 with the setting up of a one-year full-time DMS (Recreation Management) course at the Polytechnic of North London. Prior to the report's publications Loughborough University had already started a full-time course in recreation management leading to the qualification of MSc.

Since this time a proliferation of full-time, part-time and sandwich, short and day release courses, all connected in some way to recreation management have sprung up. They are either full recreation management courses, courses with a recreation management option or courses closely allied to recreation management. They can lead to certificates, diplomas, first or second degrees.

Unfortunately, however, many of these courses have received considerable criticisms. Harrison [36] claims that

'Polytechnics and Colleges of Higher Education have too often developed their new courses for reasons of convenience rather than fresh vocational adequacy. Degrees in Sport and Recreation, Recreation Studies, etc. have arisen often from the historical pre-dispositions of institutions toward physical education when more teacher-education was needed than at present.'

This is supported by the Yates Committee who claimed that:

'The most frequent criticism of existing provision was that many courses were staffed by people who lacked specific knowledge and practical experience in recreation and, it was tartly observed, who lacked any awareness of their own lack of experience . . . The most dismissive comment we heard was that many courses had been created by colleges jumping on the band wagon of recreation; many of the syllabuses had been designed by people with no experience of the actual requirements of the job, were pretentious and inadequate, promised more than they could give and contained only what the colleges could provide for and not what was needed' [4].

More recently the Local Government Training Board [21] found, arising from their seminars, that 'not a little dissatisfaction was expressed about current education and training provision, in particular its irrelevance to modern recreation issues and its lack of a practical approach'. Although such criticisms are of a general nature and do not apply to all courses, they are nevertheless a terrible indictment on the overall quality of the recreation management courses in the UK.

The scale of the recreation management training provision can be seen from the list of courses compiled by ILAM in July 1985 [37]. This lists the following courses which are primarily concerned with recreation management training or have a strong recreation bias:

24 National Examinations Board in Supervisory Studies (NEBSS) Courses.
14 Business and Technician Education Council Courses (BTEC) – National Diplomas/Certificates.
 8 Institute of Baths and Recreation Management (IBRM) courses – Intermediate and Diploma.
36 College Diplomas and Certificates in Recreation and Sports Studies.
25 First degree courses in recreation management studies, sports studies, sports science and related subjects.
16 Postgraduate courses at universities, polytechnics and colleges of higher education – eg. DMS (Recreation).

These courses, which are run at colleges, polytechnics and universities throughout the country are a mere tip of this rapidly expanding field. The greatest expansion has been at pre-career level. In 1985, 101 City and Guilds of London Institute Courses for the certificate in Recreation and Leisure Studies (no. 778/481) were offered. These courses are divided into four parts: Part 1 – A general introduction to working in recreation and leisure environments: Part 2 – Working in recreation and leisure environments; Part 3 – Organizing recreation and leisure environments; Part 4 – Managing recreation and leisure environments. The mode of study can be by day release, block release, evening courses or full-time courses and each stage of the course will cover between 200 and 300 hours.

The Business and Technician Education Council since its formation in 1983 has made a considerable impact on the range of courses offered involved with recreation management. In the 1983/84 academic year in their 'Distribution, Hotel and Catering and Leisure Services' category there were just over 6500 registered students for their National Diploma and Certificate courses and in travel and tourism alone they offer 205 courses throughout the UK. BTEC is primarily a validating body. For its major pre-career awards BTEC is in the process of issuing course specifications for National Certificate and Diploma Courses for Leisure Management modules to be offered by colleges as from October 1986 and has issued guidelines on course content for its Higher National Certificate and Diploma Courses.

Such is the success of some HND Leisure Management Courses that each year the number of applications received exceeds the places available by some 500%. Although this illustrates that there is adequate demand for courses one wonders whether there are adequate job opportunities available for all those that successfully complete the numerous recreation management courses. Additionally BTEC propose to introduce from September 1986 a further course, 'The Certificate of Pre-vocational Education', which will have one option category of study devoted to 'Recreation Services'. With regard to the post-experience category of courses, BTEC offers a Certificate in Management Studies with a recreation management specialization.

At first degree level most courses fall within the Leisure/Recreation Studies or Sports Studies category with the recreation management input being comparatively small. This is largely due to the attitude of the CNAA who perceive the study of 'management' to be largely an inappropriate area of study at first degree level. The university sector, however, is free from such constraints.

Because of the difficulty students encounter in obtaining grants and other forms of financial support for postgraduate courses, the expansion of courses at this level has largely been for part-time courses at masters level. The Polytechnic of North London offers an MA in Leisure and Recreation Studies and an M Phil under a Recreation Management Group Scheme Course; Ulster University offers a MA in Leisure Studies; Sheffield University an MA in Leisure Management; City University of London offers a part-time MA course in Museum and Gallery Administration and full-time courses in Arts Administration, Arts Management in Education and Museums and Gallery Administration. Loughborough University offers a range of postgraduate courses including a full-time MSc in Recreation Management.

The DMS (Recreation Management) Course was perceived in the survey of Sports Centre Management as being the most appropriate qualification for recreation managers. It is therefore surprising that in recent years there has been an actual decline in the number of DMS (Recreation Management) courses offered. Of the three courses currently offered only one has an integrated approach.

The other courses have 'recreation management' as an option or an extra. In such circumstances it is questionable whether the courses have adequate time to cover all the essential material. Further, the DMS is essentially a post-experience course and one doubts how appropriate such courses are to students straight from university with no previous working experience. Additionally, a range of short courses leading to various qualifications in arts administration, tourism, play leadership, community and youth work and the various librarian courses are available.

A comprehensive *Handbook of Careers in Tourism and Leisure* was published by the English Tourist Board in 1985. This publication covers the opportunities for jobs in the industry from such diverse occupations as snack bar staff to airport managers and is complemented by a separate *Directory of Courses in Tourism and Leisure*. The *Directory* lists a complete range of over 2000 courses available in the industry from day release City and Guilds to three-year full-time degree courses and includes many highly specialized qualifications.

In the light of the Yates Committee and other criticisms relating to current recreation management courses, the proposed expansion of further courses is a cause of some concern. With most colleges and polytechnics currently experiencing a reduction in the level of resources available there is a possibility that the quality of the courses may deteriorate further!

18.12   WHO DO RECREATION MANAGERS REPRESENT?

The leisure 'industry' is a vast one. The number of people employed in leisure and recreation both as managers and subordinates has increased substantially over the last 15 years. Many of the managers and leaders in this field may not even be aware that they are in the recreation management business!

Although it is difficult to determine the precise number of people employed in the leisure industry, in 1984 it was estimated that this was in the region of 1.37 million, of which approximately one million were in what one may loosely term tourism [38]. The breakdown of the employees is shown below.

Hotels and guesthouses	254 000
Pubs, bars	243 900
Restaurants, cafes, snack bars	190 000
Clubs	149 700
Contract catering	117 800
Other tourist accommodation	51 900
Tourism and other services	39 300
Libraries, museums, art galleries	63 500
Sport and other recreation	263 900
Total	1 374 800

The total represents a 12% increase since 1980 [39], but this may partly be due to differences in the occupational categories included in the surveys, although recent forecasting indicates the likely continued growth in the number of peole employed in the leisure industry.

The Morrell Report on employment in tourism, published in 1985 by the British Tourist Authority suggested 250 000 more jobs by 1990 assuming an average 2% growth in output [40], or 400 000 more jobs should the growth in spending be increased to 4% per annum in real terms. The Hotel and Catering Industry Training Board produced a forecast for their training needs of 183 000 extra jobs by 1987. A special report for Mecca Leisure Limited by the Henley Centre for Forecasting looked at employment in 'away from home leisure'. They forecast the creation by 1994 of something between 175 000 and 350 000 jobs, including part-time jobs, and an overall forecast increase of 109 000 – 191 000 in the full-time job equivalent figures, depending on economic growth and productivity within the leisure industry. The most recent forecast is that the continued growth of employment in tourism will be at the rate of some 50 000 jobs per annum [41].

Preliminary research undertaken by the Dartington Amenity Research Trust for the Recreation Management Training Committee revealed that there was a need for training in the non-public sector far greater than had previously been anticipated. DART estimated that the non-public sector contains a minimum of 750 000 people involved in the management of sport and outdoor recreation alone. Ninety-five per cent of these people are voluntary officials. The remaining 40 000 are paid officials, 17 500 of whom work in commercial or private organizations, 20 000 in voluntary organizations and 2000 in institutional bodies.

In terms of the public sector as we saw in Chapter 1, public authorities employ 130 000 personnel in recreation, parks, baths, libraries and museums. Despite the economic situation the indications are that this is likely to increase rather than decrease in the future, especially if the Sports Council's target of building over 3000 sports halls by 1991 is achieved.

Estimates for top, senior, middle and first line managers in local authority departments vary, but conservatively well over 4000 exist. In countryside recreation, taking into account country parks, water recreation, the National Trust, the national parks and countryside recreation estimates put the figure at nearly 6000 paid posts.

DART findings confirm the size, diversity and complexity of the non-public sector. While numbers are significant and there are even more paid recreation managers than in the public sector, there is little history of pre-career training, and training courses and qualifications appear to apply more to those recruited to the public sector. In-house training such as in hotels and catering and in the sorts of organization like the large multinational companies described in Chapter 3, indicates that considerable training is going on but there is little evidence of learning from each other and little cross recruitment from the two sectors. Greater linkages should be forged between the two in order to embrace many ideas which may at present go unheeded.

18.13 RECREATION MANAGEMENT: AN EMERGING PROFESSION IN THE UNITED KINGDOM?

Whether the managers in the Leisure Industry consider themselves to be professionals is dependent upon their perception of the nature of their work and its value to society, and their capability and standing within the community. From the journals published by the different recreation management associations and institutions it is apparent that the managers within the Industry clearly perceive themselves as professionals. It is, however, questionable whether the rest of society view recreation managers in the same light as the high status occupations such as the Church, the Law and Medicine who are generally regarded as being at the pinnacle of the professional hierarchy.

Although there is no generally accepted definition of the word 'profession' there appears to be an acceptable criterion for evaluating whether an occupation is of a professional status.

Sessoms [42], writing about the evolution of recreation professionalism in America, has described a profession as implying 'a defined and distinctive body of knowledge attained through a disciplined, formal education process prior to sanction for practice. It bridges technique and immediate application with theory, sets standards and serves social needs'. Murphy [43] in 1980 claimed that whilst accepting the concept that recreation management encompasses a relevant body of knowledge, it is not adequately defined and lacks 'a formal education process for entry into the occupation'. Although both 'recreation' and 'management' can only be regarded as secondary disciplines, they do, however, draw on primary disciplines such as sociology, psychology, etc. Entrance to the major recreation management institutes is by means of a formal examination, and in the case of ILAM proof of practical competence is also required. It would thus appear that the recreation management occupation has significantly advanced along the professionalization continuum.

Greenwood [44] states that the continuum of professionalization runs from 'well recognized and undisputed professions to the least skilled and attractive occupations'. Blumer [45] has defined 'professionalization' as representing:

'. . . an indigenous effort to introduce order into areas of vocational life which are prey to the free-playing and disorganizing tendencies of a vast, mobile and differential society undergoing continuous change. Professionalization seeks to clothe a given area with standards of excellence, to establish rules of conduct, to develop a sense of responsibility, to set criteria for recruitment and training, to ensure a measure of protection for members, to establish collective control over the area and to elevate it to a position of dignity and social standing in society'.

Despite the production of the Yates Committee Report and the formation of ILAM there is still a multiplicity of overlapping organizations connected with recreation management in the UK. Further, with the numerous recreation management courses now available being largely decentralized and being part of an uncoordinated training network, the recreation management occuption is some way from achieving a professional status.

To conclude in the words of Murphy:

'. . . it is possible to discern a consensus of opinion in the literature related to acceptable criteria for determining professional status. Application of these criteria to recreation management serve to negate any possible claim to professional status at the present time. There is evidence, however, of a discrete occupational group evolving, albeit at present in a fragmented form. It is an extremely young occupation which requires additional organization and systemization, so that a unified and cohesive occupational structure may be developed' [43].

In this book we have shown that provision for recreation is made by three main sectors: public, voluntary and commercial. The recreation managers represented by the institutions and associations discussed in this chapter and the managers that emerge from the courses and training schemes represent only a small part of the world of leisure and recreation and its management, primarily those areas in the hands of public or semi-public bodies. The range and scope of recreation requiring management, however, is very wide. The non-public sector made up of voluntary organizations and commercial bodies is barely touched by current levels of recreation management. Even in the public sector many areas of leisure and recreation are not encompassed, for example in the education-related leisure field.

Whether working in the public or non-public sector recreation managers are concerned with creating opportunities for people's recreational experience. They must attract the public or fail. Recreation is a 'people-orientated' business. Training, therefore, must concern itself primarily as a people-orientated service. Training is a means of acquiring new skills and new knowledge because things are always changing. Managers and organizations must evolve as needs change, rather than simply becoming more efficient, consolidating the status quo and thus becoming less effective. Yet no amount of training and management education will guarantee making a successful manager. According to James [15], the best managers are seen to be 'dynamic in action and positive in outlook'.

REFERENCES AND NOTES

1. Department of the Environment (1985) *Competition in the Provision of Local Authority Services* DOE, London.
2. Sports Council (1969) *Professional Training for Recreation Management*: report of a working party (Chairman D.D. Molyneux), Sports Council, London.
3. Department of the Environment (1978), *Recreation Management Training Committee: Interim Report* (A discussion paper) (Chairman Anne Yates) HMSO, London.
4. Department of the Environment (1984), *Recreation Management Training Committee: Final Report*, HMSO, London.
5. ILAM (1984), *Report of the Yates Committee on Recreation Management Training. Response to the Minister of Sport*, Lower Basildon, Reading.
6. IBRM (1985), 'Response to the Minister for Sport on the Recreation Management Training Committee's Report (Yates)' *Baths Service and Recreation Management*, May/June.
7. Sports Council (1984), Sports Council response to Yates' In McKinney, G. (ed.) 'Yates and After: The Management of Recreation Management Training'. *Leisure Studies Association Newsletter Supplement*, November.
8. The Institute of Recreation Management (ed.) (1981), *The Recreation Management Handbook* 3rd Edn, E. and F. N. Spon, Ltd. London.
9. Easton, D. (1984), 'Professional Training: thoughts about the future' *Entertainments and Arts Management*, May.
10. Torkildsen, G. (1978), Report to the London Regional Management Centre for the Recreation Management Training Committee (Yates Committee) on Sport and Recreation Centre Management Staff, in collaboration with N. Stang and the Polytechnic of North London, unpublished.
11. Torkildsen, G. (1978), Report of a Survey of ARM members for the Association of Recreation Managers, unpublished.
12. Kraus, E.A. (1971), *Sociology of Organisations*, Little, Brown, Boston, p.2.
13. Colbeck, D. (1981) *Leisure Management*, **1**, (3) October/November, p.57.
14. Torkildsen G. and Street A. (1985) *IBRM. An Appraisal and Strategies for the Future*, unpublished.
15. James, R.D. (1980), Occasional paper: *Wisdom Lost in Knowledge: Notes on the Diploma in Management Studies (R) Course*, unpublished.
16. Blake, T.M. (1970) Occasional paper: *Management Training and Development (MTD)*, unpublished work.
17. Sports Centre Management Discusssion Group (1976), *Report of the Working Party on Training for Recreation within Sports Centre Complexes*, coordinated by the Sports Council (Northern Region), p.4
18. Drucker, P.F. (1977), Training Programme: The Manager and the Organisation, BNA Communications Europe promotion material.
19. Parker, S. (1984), 'The Core of Leisure Studies' in McKinney G. (ed) 'Yates and After: The Management of Recreation Management Training' *Leisure Studies Association Newsletter Supplement*, November.
20. Chairman's Policy Group (1983), *Leisure Policy for the Future* Sports Council, London.

21. Local Government Training Board (1985), *Recreation and Leisure Management: A report in Education and Training Needs* LGTB, Luton.
22. Foy, N. (1978), *The Missing Links: British Management Education in the Eighties*, Oxford Centre for Management Studies
23. Pick, J. (1978), Training: the future. *Municipal Entertainment*, **5**, No. 10, June, p.12
24. Gage, W.L. (1978), Training Arts Administration, *Municipal Entertainment*, **5**, No. 7, March.
25. Hitchin, H.T. (1977), Recreation Management Training, *Baths Service*, May/June pp.53–58
26. Drucker, P.F. (1969), *Managing for Results*, Pan Piper Books, London.
27. Harrison, F. (1980), Occasional Paper: *MSc in Recreation – Ten Years On*, unpublished.
28. Dartington Amenity Research Trust (DART) (1980), Discussion Document: *Links between the Public and Non-Public Sectors*, for Recreation Training Committee, unpublished.
29. Local Government Training Board, Institute of Local Government Studies (1985), *The Management Challenge for Local Government*, a joint paper. LGTB, Luton.
30. Stewart, R. (1970), *Managers and Their Jobs*, Pan Piper Books, London.
31. Institute of Parks and Recreation Administration (1970) Evidence to Yates Committee reported in *Parks and Recreation*, April 1979, p.23.
32. Sports Centre Management Discussion Group (1976), *Report of the Working Party on Training for Recreation with Sports Centre Complexes*, coordinated by the Sports Council (Northern Region) p.2.
33. Pick, J. (1978), Training: the future, *Municipal Entertainment*, **5**, No. 10, June, p.11.
34. Gage, W.L. (1978), Training arts administration, *Municipal Entertainment*, **5**, No. 7, March, p.11.
35. Kahn, D. and Katz, R.L. (1966), *The Social Psychology of Organisations*, Wiley, New York.
36. Harrison, F. (1984), 'A New Degree in Recreation Management: A Discussion Paper' in McKinney, G. (ed) 'Yates and after: The Management of Recreation Management Training', *Leisure Studies Association Newsletter Supplement*, Nov.
37. ILAM (1985), 'Education and Training: A Guide to courses in leisure management' *The Leisure Manager*, Sept.
38. Banks, R. (1985), *New Jobs from Pleasure. A Strategy for Creating New Jobs in the Tourist Industry*. Conservative Association Central Office.
39. Corley, J. (1982), Office of Population Censuses and Surveys, London. Employment in the leisure industries in Britain 1960–80 *Leisure Studies*, **1**, January, pp.109–11.
40. British Tourist Authority (1985), *Employment in Tourism*, BTA, London.
41. Lord Young (1985), *Pleasure, Leisure and Jobs: The Business of Tourism*, HMSO, London.
42. Sessoms, H.D. (1975), Our body of knowledge: myth or reality? *Parks and Recreation* (USA) Nov. p.30.
43. Murphy, W. (1980) Occasional Paper: *Professionalism and Recreation Management*, unpublished.

44. Greenwood, E. (1966) Elements of professionalisation – social work, in Voller, H.M. and Mills, D.L. (eds) (1966), *Professionalisation*, Prentice Hall, Englewood Cliffs, New Jersey.
45. Blumer, H. (1966), in Preface of Voller, H.M. and Mills D.L. (eds) (1966) *Professionalisation*, Prentice Hall, Englewood Cliffs, New Jersey.

Chapter 19

Conclusions

Many people suffer from a lingering feeling that leisure is something of a luxury. As an escape from the commendable pursuits of earning a living and making a contribution to the national economy, leisure seems tainted. When carried to excess it is called idleness. But the Committee believe that it is time for the puritan view of leisure to be jettisoned. Leisure is as much a part of life as work and it plays an equally important part in man's development and the quality of his life . . . In its own way it is almost as important to the well-being of the community as good housing, hospitals and schools

House of Lords Report

★

SUMMARY

This book set out with the objective of furthering an understanding and improving the management of recreation. It has been written in five parts. Part One described the function and scope of the main providers – public, voluntary and commercial – and that of the national agencies. Part Two asked the deceptively simple question – what is recreation? It proved to be complex and a far from easy question to answer. Play, recreation and leisure were found to be separate entities, yet overlapping and often used interchangeably. Part Three was concerned with the people who were to benefit from recreation planning, provision and management. What were the needs of people and what influences condition leisure and recreation choice? Part Four moved into the planning process, explored strategies and approaches and the Recreation Manager's role in the process. The value of the manager in coordinating the planning, design and management of facilities was evident. Part Five looked into the principles of management and how these relate to recreation. General management techniques were described and specialist recreation management skills were analysed. Several management guidelines were put forward for improved management of recreation based on an 'aims – objectives – actions – evaluation' approach. Finally, the question of training for recreation management was debated.

DISCUSSION

Leisure and recreation are means and ways in which people spend their free time. Within their umbrella are a vast range of activities: sport, art, entertainment, going to the cinema or live entertainment, holidays and eating out. Leisure is one of the few growth areas in the current economic climate in the United Kingdom. Well into the foreseeable future there will be an increasing demand for centres of interest to satisfy the rising expectations of people in all walks of life and all sections of the community. Well researched patterns of social change show that the trend will continue well into the 21st century. Therefore new facilities specially selected for their social and economic value should be developed. In addition, existing services, facilities and operations should be improved to take full advantage of a positive leisure climate and to meet rising expectations.

Leisure and recreation are personal. What is pleasure to one person (say, gardening) is drudgery to someone else. Also what is pleasure for some people is employment to someone else. The leisure industry, providing services in parks and pools, sports complexes, theatres, restaurants, hotels, theme parks and places of historic interest, is a growing one.

In the past two decades, 1000 new public indoor sport and recreation facilities and many diverse commercial attractions, from snooker halls and health clubs to theme parks have been built.

Tastes and expectations are changing. Customers are increasingly knowledgeable. Furthermore, there is an insistent demand evident for value for money. Facility planners must be opportunity planners. Free choice is a key element in leisure time pursuits. This is reflected in the very large number of existing leisure activities and those which must be considered in the planning stages of any major development.

The benefits of providing for these trends will include a healthier and more relaxed population, a more effective use of leisure time, job creation, and above all, greater personal fulfilment. The case for leisure and recreation investment and support is well made.

In terms of public provision, central government is shown to have immense power and can direct, constrain and control local government and national agencies. Also apparent are the overlaps between government departments, tiers of local government and between different areas of recreation such as conservation and recreation.

In terms of community recreation management, the local authority is the key institution. It has considerable problems, however. Recreation is not regarded as a main priority in structure plans. Services are fragmented, concurrent powers lead to overlap and duplication, and permissive powers result in wide variation of provision. In addition, the aims and objectives of local authority services are unclear. They have considerable permissive powers. They have relative freedom to provide their own local services. They can act independently or in partnership. They can enable and support. However, they need a rationale – a reason for providing. Local authorities provide recreation services, perhaps because they have always done so, but why they do and what the major purpose of such provision is, is not clear. Recreation lacks visionary leaders; it lacks sufficient trained personnel; it lacks a comprehensive, representative body to state its case. Strong recreation management can help local authorities to coordinate the resources of the main providers and coordinate the functions of different tiers of local government. For example, education authorities have a statutory duty to provide for people's spiritual, physical and mental development. Its resources can be more fully harnessed.

The voluntary provider has an important role also to play in community recreation. The range and diversity of voluntary leisure groupings, group belonging and self-help are significant factors in the management of leisure and recreation. Voluntary organizations may well hold one of the keys to individual self-fulfilment. Thus, Recreation Managers must understand and enable voluntary groups to flourish.

The magnitude of the commercial sector and its influence on leisure consumption is immense. Well over one-third of the 'leisure pound' is spent on alcoholic drink; one-third is spent on leisure in and around the home and one-fifth goes on holidays, gambling and entertainment. Only 3% is spent on sport and recreation. Hence, commercial leisure provision is different from local authority provision: it chooses profitable activities. Despite overlaps with other sectors, the commercial world is different. All efforts go in producing financial profits. The Recreation Manager should be aware of the different approaches and learn which techniques are best applied to specific situations.

The word 'recreation' is used so widely and frequently that its precise meaning is unclear. Recreation thinkers more frequently look at recreation and leisure, not so much in terms of activities, but in terms of satisfying or life enhancing experiences – activities being a means towards re-creation. Thus, recreation can be viewed as individual experience (what it does for a person), as activities, or as an institution – the structure in which recreation is made available to the public. I believe that leisure opportunity is the vehicle through which people can play and find recreation and in so doing meet some of their human needs. As we move into a period of fewer jobs and where the importance of paid work as a means of organizing one's life is declining, there is a need to rethink what leisure is and means to people.

The correlation between recreation participation and variables such as social class, education and income is high. The extent to which participation is influenced or conditioned by such factors is not clear and the question is raised whether recreation policies and management can overcome many of the apparent constraints to wider participation. I believe that good management can remove many of the artificial barriers and that planning, location, perception, accessibility, choice, social acceptance, the atttitude of managers and the quality of management have very important effects. Resourceful people are those who can overcome obstacles and find preoccupying activities and interests. Leisure and recreation management has much to offer in the way of enabling people to develop skills, to discover themselves and reach beyond their grasp.

Recreation Managers must, above all else, be good managers. They need an understanding of general management principles, processes, practices and the ability to handle people. They must have skills of leadership, decision-making, communications and administration. They have to choose, train and deploy staff wisely. They need objectivity, financial acumen and marketing ability. But as well as general management, specialist management is necessary. Management must be appropriate to different situations and the manager must adapt his or her style of management to be appropriate to changing situations. Operational practice, specific techniques and programming often require specialist knowledge. The marketing process, for example, will need to be adjusted to meet the conceptual difference to be found in local government services.

In essence Recreation Managers are no different from other managers.

Whether they operate in the public, voluntary or commercial sector, a part of their job is to provide people with opportunities to experience recreation. Managers must understand the nature of the recreation experience and what motivates people to recreation. They must create environments in which recreation is more likely to occur. Then, they can define managerial objectives, develop skills for the job and utilize the resources at their disposal. Managers need multi-skill qualities for both general and specialist management. All providers and managers must attract the public or fail. Recreation is a people-orientated business.

A Recreation Manager is not someone who comes out of college with a certificate. Nor is he or she someone who, through experience, can operate a facility but fails to appreciate what it means to achieve an effective service. A grasp of theory accelerates the learning through job experience. However, the opposite is not necessarily true. Job experience may or may not accelerate a grasp of theory. In this book a theory–practice orientation is advocated to produce the most effective Recreation Managers. Yet no amount of training will make the manager. He or she is a mixture of someone with objectivity, craft and humanity. There is much to be said for practical, simple, commonsense approaches to management. We have somehow managed to make management something terribly academic and difficult. While knowledge, logic and technical ability are important, there is an important place also for enthusiasm, charisma and empathy. There is room for belief and conviction.

Recreation is a tangible means of improving the lot of individuals in society. The message to policy-makers is clear: make savings on capital if you must, but never on good management. A great deal can be done without major capital expenditure. There exists a gulf between well-meaning public providers and the actual public themselves. There is inarticulation and miscommunication at the interface between people and providers. Recreation Managers can help to mesh together the resources that already exist, help to make the connections, and the linkages. Enabling, encouraging and supporting can be achieved in a thousand and one small ways. 'Small things make a big difference', particularly when it is personal satisfactions with which recreation management is ultimately concerned.

Today there are more facilities and greater opportunities than ever before. There is much to be done. While there is a plethora of educational courses and institutional training, the whole training scene needs rationalizing. A career structure or system of career opportunity needs to be formulated. Facility design mistakes must be eliminated; technical improvements should be constantly sought. Local government bureaucracy can be reduced by involving people in planning, by investing in recreation personnel in the community, by taking on a coordinating function and an enabling role. Recreation Managers should help to develop more people-serving concepts with an emphasis on concern for the user. They should challenge the assumptions of traditional leisure services by asking the right questions and re-examining the justification for provision and services. Recreation providers and managers should be concerned, not just with the quantity of facilities, but also with the quality of the experience. Hence, the cornerstone of recreation and its management must be concerned first, foremost and always with people.

Recreation Managers must develop a 'helicopter' view of their leisure services: the higher they go, the greater the vision. They need to view, not just the array of facilities, but the interconnections, the junctions of the various pathways, the fuels that make the processes effective, and the blockages that cause the hold-ups.

Here, then, is the conflict, the dilemma: recreation is concerned with human experience. It defies management. But management is the instrument by which environments can be shaped, opportunities can be given and people can be taught to cope. The challenge, therefore, is not just in facilities, programmes, costs, income or even in numbers, but whether recreation services can provide opportunities for recreation to occur and where individuals can choose, learn, and control the content of their leisure behaviour.

In this book the need for a re-orientation of philosophy is suggested towards a better people and process management orientation. In addition, it is suggested that an investment in managers, in the emerging profession of recreation management and in recreation management education and training will enhance leisure and recreation services to the benefit of all concerned and in particular to the people who they are intended to serve.

Leisure and recreation management is concerned with policies, politics, planning, provision, programmes and people. But at its core it is concerned with individual and collective behaviour. Julian Huxley, in the *Bulletin of Atomic Scientists* states: 'The leisure problem is fundamental. Having to decide what we shall do with our leisure is inevitably forcing us to re-examine the purpose of human existence, and to ask what human fulfilment really means.' I believe that recreation management should be concerned with such fulfilment, with a love for life, for people and for the human expression of recreation that leisure opportunity affords. At the end of the day recreation is about one person and his or her experience. But personal self-fulfilment carries a bonus: what is fulfilling for the individual can also be good for society. 'When life becomes meaningful for the individual then the whole community is also enriched'.

Index

★